Dictionary of British Portraiture

IN FOUR VOLUMES

EDITED BY RICHARD ORMOND AND MALCOLM ROGERS

WITH A FOREWORD BY JOHN HAYES
DIRECTOR OF THE NATIONAL PORTRAIT GALLERY

VOLUME

4

The Twentieth Century · Historical figures born before 1900

COMPILED BY DR ADRIANA DAVIES

B.T.BATSFORD LTD · *LONDON*
IN ASSOCIATION WITH
THE NATIONAL PORTRAIT GALLERY · *LONDON*

ISBN 0 7134 1474X

Filmset in 'Monophoto' Bembo by
Servis Filmsetting Ltd, Manchester
and printed in Great Britain by
Robert Maclehose Ltd
Glasgow
for the publishers
B.T.Batsford Ltd
4 Fitzhardinge Street
London W1H 0AH

DICTIONARY OF
BRITISH PORTRAITURE

Volume 4

Foreword

This four-volume *Dictionary of British Portraiture* was the idea of Sam Carr, Director of Batsford. He was correct in his view that there exists no comprehensive handbook to the portraits of famous British men and women. Specialized surveys and studies there are, but no compact work to which the researcher or layman can turn easily for information about the likeness of this or that individual. The present dictionary cannot claim to be a complete or exhaustive study; inevitably there has to be a degree of selection in the people represented, and the portraits that have been listed. This is explained in the introduction. But within these limitations it does offer a reliable guide to the portraiture of a wide range of eminent British men and women from the Medieval period to the present day.

The dictionary relates directly to the purposes for which the National Portrait Gallery was founded in 1856: the collection, preservation and study of historical portraits. It has been compiled mainly from the Gallery's own immense archive, and I am delighted that its resources should be made available in this way. The information in the archive has been gathered slowly over the course of the last century or so by many devoted scholars and members of staff, and I think it is only right that I should first record our debt to them. Without their labours such a dictionary could never have been compiled. I would also like to pay a special tribute to the staff of the Guthrie Room, who maintain the archive, add to its holdings, and answer so many questions so patiently and efficiently. The work of editorial supervision has been handled most competently by my colleagues, Richard Ormond and Malcolm Rogers, who originally discussed the project with Sam Carr, and have guided all four volumes through the press. To Sam Carr himself we are grateful for his continuing enthusiasm and support, without which the project would never have materialised. Mrs Underwood and Vanessa Ferguson undertook the task of typing the entries with unusual thoroughness and accuracy. Finally, I must thank our two hard-working and dedicated compilers, who took on the daunting job of recording and researching the thousands of portraits listed here. It is a tribute both to their enthusiasm and to their composure in the face of sometimes inadequate, sometimes confusing records, that the work has been completed so expeditiously. We are deeply grateful to them for the skill and accuracy with which they have carried out their task.

JOHN HAYES

Introduction

The aim of the present dictionary is to provide a listing of the portraits of famous figures in British history that are either in galleries, institutions and public companies, or in collections accessible to the public. It is intended for the general researcher and student who needs a reliable guide to portraits on public view of which illustrations can be obtained relatively easily. It is not concerned with the intricacies of iconography, though decisions have had to be taken about the likely authenticity of particular images, nor is it comprehensive. The decision to exclude portraits in private collections was dictated by the need to limit the scope of the work, by the difficulty of obtaining permission from owners to use their names, and by the impossibility of directing readers to the specific location of privately-owned works. In a few entries it has been indicated that a privately-owned portrait is the only known likeness, or the most significant likeness, of a particular person.

Each volume of this dictionary covers a different historical period. Though there were arguments in favour of dividing the dictionary alphabetically, it was decided on balance that it would be more useful to make each volume self-contained. The chronological dividing-lines are inevitably arbitrary, and will mean that certain figures, whose contemporaries appear in one volume, are by accident of birth in another. If the reader knows the birth date of his or her chosen subject, there should be no problem in turning to the correct volume, and at the end of this volume there is a complete index to the whole work.

The question of selection was a thorny one. We have relied heavily, though not exclusively, on the *Dictionary of National Biography*, and, for those sitters who died after 1960, on *Times Obituaries*, 3 vols (1951–75). Readers will no doubt be disappointed by some omissions, but it is important to remember that the non-appearance of a particular figure may simply reflect the fact that no authentic portrait of him or her is known.

The Gallery's archive is, in general, weak in the field of twentieth century portraiture, and there are no catalogues for a number of important collections. It proved impossible to follow up the large photographic libraries, both public and commercial, and reliance has been placed on the Gallery's own holdings. The National Photographic Record was established by the National Portrait Gallery in 1917, to document well-known contemporary figures, and its work continued until 1970.

The entries themselves are cast in a condensed form, but we hope they will be comprehensible once the format has been mastered.

The arrangement of the entries is as follows:

Surname of the sitter, with Christian names (peers are listed under their titles)
Birth and death dates, where known

Profession or occupation
Known portraits, recorded under:

P	Paintings	SC	Sculpture
D	Drawings	T	Tapestry
M	Miniatures	W	Stained-glass windows
MS	Manuscripts	PR	Prints
SL	Silhouettes	C	Caricatures
G	Groups	PH	Photographs

Within each category portraits are listed chronologically, and then alphabetically by name of artist where known.

Information on individual portraits is arranged as follows:

name of artist
date of portrait where known
size (ie half length, whole length, etc)
other distinguishing features (with Garter, in a landscape, etc)
medium, in the case of drawings, groups, prints and caricatures
location, with accession number in the case of national galleries and museums

For further details see abbreviations opposite.

The absence of illustrations will be a cause of complaint. But the only possible solution would have been to illustrate everything (a selection would have satisfied few), and that would have made the series prohibitively large and expensive. In any case the dictionary has been conceived as a reference work and not a picture book, and it is as such that it must stand or fall.

RICHARD ORMOND

MALCOLM ROGERS

Abbreviations

A

ABERCONWAY, Henry Duncan McLaren, 2nd baron (1879-1953) industrialist.
P SIR OSWALD BIRLEY, c1948, hl, seated in Bodnant Gardens, Royal Horticultural Society, London.

ABERCORN, James Albert Edward Hamilton, 3rd Duke of (1869-1953) governor of Northern Ireland.
P FRANK MCKELVEY, DoE, London.
C 'HODGE', wl in uniform, lith, for *Vanity Fair*, 16 Feb 1899, NPG.
PH ALEXANDER BASSANO, 1894, hl, neg, NPG X7117.

ABERCROMBIE, Lascelles (1881-1938) poet and critic.
PH WALTER STONEMAN, 1937, hl, NPG (NPR).

ABERCROMBIE, Sir (Leslie) Patrick (1879-1957) architect and professor of town planning.
PH HOWARD COSTER, various sizes and negs, NPG X2400-01 and X2481-82.

ABERDARE, Clarence Napier Bruce, 3rd Baron (1885-1957) athlete.
P FLORA LION, 1947, tql seated, National Museum of Wales 703, Cardiff.

ABRAHAM, James Johnston (1876-1963) surgeon and author.
PH HOWARD COSTER, 1938, various sizes and negs, NPG X2402-03, X2490-95, and X3528.

ABRAHAMS, Bertram Louis (1870-1908) physician.
P SOLOMON J. SOLOMON, 1908, hs, Royal College of Physicians, London.

ACKERLEY, Joe Randolph (1896-1967) author and literary editor of *Listener*.
PH HOWARD COSTER, c1939, various sizes and negs, NPG X2405-06 and X2496-99.

ACTON, Sir Edward (1865-1945) judge.
P JOHN ST HELIER LANDER, Wadham College, Oxford.

ACTON, Richard Maximilian Dalberg-Acton, 2nd Baron (1870-1924) diplomat.
PH J.C.SCHAARWÄCHTER, hs, print, NPG X8.

ADAMI, John George (1862-1926) pathologist.
P F.T.COPNALL, hl?, Liverpool University.
PH WALTER STONEMAN, 1917, hs in uniform, NPG (NPR).

ADAMS, Bernard (d 1965) portrait painter.
PH GABOR DENES, 1953, group with Adams' portrait by Simon Elwes, print, NPG X4993.

ADAMSON, William (1863-1936) chairman of Parliamentary Labour Party.
P TOM CURR, Dover House, DoE.
D DAVID FOGGIE, 1934, pencil, SNPG 1798.
C SIR DAVID LOW, head, pencil, NPG 4529(1).

ADCOCK, Arthur St John (1864-1930) critic and writer.
PH JOHN RUSSELL & SONS, before c1915, hs, print, for *National Photographic Record*, vol I, NPG.

ADDISON, Christopher Addison, 1st Viscount (1869-1951) statesman and anatomist.
PH HOWARD COSTER, hs, 4 negs, NPG X2413, X2516-17 and X2614.

WALTER STONEMAN, 1937, hs, for NPR, NPG X6958.

ADDIS, Sir Charles Stewart (1861-1945) banker.
PH VANDYK?, 1922, hs, print, NPG X9.

ADRIAN, Edgar Douglas, Lord (1889-1977) physiologist and chancellor of Cambridge University.
P RUSKIN SPEAR, 1953, hs in robes, Trinity College, Cambridge. A.R.MIDDLETON TODD, 1955, tql seated in robes, Royal Society, London.
D EDWARD HALLIDAY, Royal Society of Medicine, London. RODRIGO MOYNIHAN, 1950, pencil, Trinity College. ROLAND H.RUSHTON, w/c, Royal Society of Medicine. ROBERT TOLLAST, c1964, hs, Churchill College, Cambridge.
SC F.E.McWILLIAM, bronze bust, Trinity College.
PH GODFREY ARGENT, 1969, hs, for NPR, NPG X16. UNKNOWN, hs in robes, print, NPG X269.

'AE', see George William Russell.

AGATE, James Evershed (1877-1947) dramatic critic and author.
PH HOWARD COSTER, c1933, various sizes and negs, NPG X1711, X2520-29 and X10296. FELIX MAN, 1939, hl seated, print, NPG X1148. UNKNOWN, hs, print, NPG X17.

AGNEW, Sir William Gladstone (1898-1960) vice-admiral.
PH WALTER STONEMAN, 1946, hl in uniform, NPG (NPR).

AINLEY, Henry Hinchliffe (1879-1945) actor.
D EDMOND KAPP, 1932, hs?, Barber Institute, Birmingham University.
SL H.L.OAKLEY, 1920, hs, profile, NPG.
C HARRY FURNISS, wl seated, profile, pen and ink, NPG 3414.
PH FOULSHAM AND BANFIELD, c1908?, tql, postcard, NPG X5150. HOWARD COSTER, 1929, various sizes, prints and negs, NPG X2282, X3426 and X10297-99.

AINSWORTH, Harrison (1888-1965) editor of *The People*.
PH HOWARD COSTER, various sizes and negs, NPG X2416 and X2537-42.

AIRLIE, David Lyulph Gore Wolseley Ogilvy, 12th earl of (1893-1968) soldier and statesman.
P ERNEST BOARD, 1923, tql, Airlie Castle, Tayside region, Scotland. SIR OSWALD BIRLEY, tql seated, Airlie. SIR W.O.HUTCHISON, 1956, tql in Thistle robes, Airlie.
D WILLIAM STRANG, 1918, hs in uniform, pencil and chalk, Airlie.
PH UNKNOWN, c1956, tql seated in uniform, print, NPG X21.

AITCHISON, Craigie Mason Aitchison, Lord (1882-1941) lord justice-clerk of Scotland.
P STANLEY CURSITER, 1937, tql seated in robes, Parliament Hall, Edinburgh.

AITKEN, Charles (1869-1936) director of the Tate Gallery.
P STEPHEN BONE, c1932, tql, TATE 4618.
PR FRANCIS DODD, 1914, tql seated, etch, NPG.
PH LAFAYETTE, hs, profile, print, NPG X26.

AITKEN, William Maxwell, see 1st Baron Beaverbrook.

AKERS, Sir Wallace Alan (1888-1954) chemist.
PH WALTER STONEMAN, 1947, hs, NPG (NPR).

AKERS-DOUGLAS, Aretas, see 2nd Viscount Chilston.

ALANBROOKE, Alan Brooke, 1st Viscount (1883-1963) field-marshal.
P R.G.EVES, 1940, hs in uniform, Staff College, Camberley, Surrey. SIR JAMES GUNN, 1957, hl seated in robes, Royal Artillery Mess, Woolwich. PATRICK PHILLIPS, 1957, tql seated in robes, Queen's University, Belfast.
D JULIET PANNETT, head, chalk, NPG 4346.
PH HOWARD COSTER, various sizes and negs, NPG X2417–18 and X2552. WALTER STONEMAN, 1941, hs in uniform, for NPR, NPG X1436 and X4152.

ALBERT Victor Christian Edward, Prince, see Duke of Clarence.

ALBERY, Sir Bronson James (1881-1971) theatre director.
PH HOWARD COSTER, 1930s, various sizes and negs, NPG X2419–26 and X10300–04.

ALCOCK, Sir John William (1892-1919) aviator.
P AMBROSE MCEVOY, 1919, tql, NPG 1894. SIR JOHN LAVERY, hl in flying kit, Royal Aero Club on loan to RAF Museum, Hendon.
PH Various photographs, Royal Aeronautical Society, London.

ALDENHAM, Walter Durant Gibbs, 4th Baron (1886-1969) banker.
P ANTHONY DEVAS, c1953, tql seated, National Westminster Bank, London.
G JOHN WARD, 'Directors of Westminster Bank, 1968', line and wash, National Westminster Bank.
PH DESMOND O'NEILL, 1968, hl, print, NPG.

ALDINGTON, Richard (1892-1962) poet, critic and novelist.
PH HOWARD COSTER, 1931, various sizes, prints and negs, NPG X2427–28, X3431 and X10305–08.

ALDRICH-BLAKE, Dame Louisa Brandreth (1865-1925) surgeon.
P SIR WILLIAM ORPEN, 1923, tql, Royal Free Hospital School of Medicine (formerly London School of Medicine for Women). HERMANN SALOMON, 1926, tql, Wellcome Institute, London. UNKNOWN, tql, Elizabeth Garrett Anderson Hospital, London.
PH Various photographs, Royal Free Hospital.

ALEXANDER of Hillsborough, Albert Victor Alexander, 1st Earl (1885-1965) first lord of the Admiralty.
PH HOWARD COSTER, 1940s, various sizes, print and negs, NPG X2553–58 and X2432. WALTER STONEMAN, 4 hs portraits, 1929, 1940 and 1942, NPG X533 and NPG (NPR).

ALEXANDER of Teck, Alexander Augustus Frederick, Prince, see 1st Earl of Athlone.

ALEXANDER of Tunis, Harold Rupert Leofric George Alexander, 1st Earl (1891-1969) field-marshal.
P R.G.EVES, 1940, hs in uniform, IWM. SIR OSWALD BIRLEY, 1944, tql in uniform, Harrow School, Middx. HENRY CARR, 1947, tql, IWM; version, Cavalry and Guards Club, London. JOHN GILROY, c1957, tql in Garter robes, McGill University, Montreal, Canada; oil study, head, NPG 4689.
D SYDNEY MORSE-BROWN, 1943, hs, crayon, IWM.
SC DONALD GILBERT, 1946, bronze bust, Harrow School.
PH HOWARD COSTER, hs, various negs, NPG X2559–62.

ALEXANDER-SINCLAIR, Sir Edwyn Sinclair (1865-1945) admiral.
D FRANCIS DODD, 1917, charcoal and w/c, IWM.
G A.S.COPE, 'Naval Officers of World War I, 1914–18', oil, 1921, NPG 1913.
PH UNKNOWN, 1939, hl seated, profile, print, NPG X37.

ALEXANDRA Victoria Alberta Edwina Louise Duff, see Princess Arthur of CONNAUGHT.

ALLEN, Sir Hugh Percy (1869-1946) musician.
P LEONARD CAMPBELL TAYLOR, 1937, hs, Royal College of Music, London.
D J.S.SARGENT, 1925, head, New College, Oxford.
SC UNKNOWN, plaster bust, Royal College of Music.

ALLEN, Percy Stafford (1869-1933) president of Corpus Christi College, Oxford, and Erasmian scholar.
P H.A.OLIVIER, 1929, hl, Corpus Christi College.

ALLEN, Walter Godfrey (b1891) architect.
PH HOWARD COSTER, various sizes and negs, NPG X2429–32.

ALLEN of Hurtwood, Reginald Clifford Allen, Baron (1889-1939) Labour politician.
PH WALTER STONEMAN, 1932, hl, NPG (NPR).

ALLENBY of Megiddo, Edmund Henry Hynman Allenby, 1st Viscount (1861-1936) field-marshal.
P JAMES MCBEY, 1918, hl in uniform, IWM. P.TENNYSON COLE, 1920, hl, Cavalry and Guards Club, London. J.S.SARGENT, c1922, profile head, Leicester Art Museum, oil sketch for 'General Officers', NPG 1954. J.S.SARGENT, c1922, hs in uniform, South African National Gallery, Cape Town. P.T.COLE, c1924, tql in uniform, IWM.
D FRANCIS DODD, 1917, tql seated, charcoal and w/c, IWM. J.MCBEY, 1917, Generals Allenby and Bailleul, ink and w/c, IWM. J.MCBEY, 1918, various heads, pencil, IWM. S.J.DOUGLAS, 1919, hs, pencil, IWM. E.H.KENNINGTON, head, chalk, NPG 2906.
G J.MCBEY, 'Entry of Allies into Jerusalem', oil, c1917–19, IWM. J.S.SARGENT, 'General Officers of World War I, 1914–18', oil, 1922, NPG 1954. MRS ALBERT BROOM, wl in uniform with Earl of Granard and H.V.Cowan?, ph, 1920s, NPG X1143. LEOPOLD PILICHOWSKI, military group, oil, c1927, Jerusalem University.
SC H.A.PEGRAM, 1929, bronze bust, War Office, London; plaster cast, IWM.
C SIR BERNARD PARTRIDGE, wl treading on serpent with Lord Curzon, ink, for *Punch*, 8 Feb 1922, NPG.
PH REV H.H.WILLIAMS, 1917, tql on horseback riding into Jerusalem, IWM. WALTER STONEMAN, 1919, hs in uniform, 2 prints, NPG (NPR). BASSANO, 1922, profile bust in uniform, print, Staff College, Camberley, Surrey. W.STONEMAN, 1931, hs, NPG (NPR).

ALNESS, Robert Munro, 1st Baron (1868-1955) lord justice-clerk.
P J.B.SOUTER, 1932, tql seated in privy council uniform, Parliament Hall, Edinburgh.
PH WALTER STONEMAN, 2 hs portraits, 1931 and 1943, NPG (NPR).

ALTRINCHAM, Edward William Macleay Grigg, 1st Baron (1879-1955) politician and administrator.
PH WALTER STONEMAN, 3 hs portraits, 1921, 1931 and 1941, NPG X386 and NPG (NPR).

AMERY, Leopold Charles Maurice Stennett (1873-1955) statesman and journalist.
P SIR JAMES GUNN, 1942, hl, NPG 4300; version, Rhodes House, Oxford. SIMON ELWES, c1954, hl in robes, Rhodes House.
PH HOWARD COSTER, various sizes, prints and negs, NPG X2444–45 and X2571. SIR CECIL BEATON, 1944, hl seated, NPG. SIR C.BEATON, 1944, hl with Lady Amery, print, NPG.

AMOS, Sir Maurice (Percy) Sheldon (1872-1940) jurist and judge in Egypt.
PH WALTER STONEMAN, 1930, hs, NPG (NPR).

AMPTHILL, Arthur Oliver Villiers Russell, 2nd Baron (1869-1935) governor of Madras and grand master of English freemasonry.

P SIR A.S.COPE, c1925, wl in robes of Order of the Star of India, Freemasons' Hall, London.

SL HUBERT LESLIE, 1926, hs, profile, NPG.

PH WALTER STONEMAN, 1921, hs, NPG (NPR). UNKNOWN, 1930, tql in Grand Master's robes, print, NPG x7957.

AMULREE, William Warrender Mackenzie, 1st Baron (1860-1942) lawyer and industrial arbitrator.

PH WALTER STONEMAN, 1936, hl, NPG (NPR).

ANDERSON, Dame Adelaide Mary (1863-1936) first woman inspector of factories.

PH OLIVE EDIS, 1930s, tql seated, print, NPG x316. WALTER STONEMAN, 1930, hl, NPG (NPR).

ANDERSON, Sir Alan Garrett (1877-1952) shipowner and public servant.

PH OLIVE EDIS, 1902, hs, print, NPG x60. WALTER STONEMAN, 1918, hs, NPG (NPR). OLIVE EDIS, c1920?, hs, profile, print, NPG x59.

ANDERSON, Sir Hugh Kerr (1865-1928) physiologist and university administrator.

P SIR WILLIAM ORPEN, 1922, Gonville and Caius College, Cambridge.

SC HAROLD C.W.SOPER, mural monument, Gonville and Caius College Chapel.

ANDERSON, Sir John, see Viscount Waverley.

ANDERSON, Sir Kenneth Arthur Noel (1891-1959) general and governor of Gibraltar.

D SYDNEY MORSE-BROWN, 1954, conté pencil, IWM.

PH WALTER STONEMAN, 1943, hs, NPG (NPR).

ANDERSON, Mrs Stella, see Benson.

ANDERSON, Sir Warren Hastings (1872-1930) lieutenant-general.

P By or after SIR OSWALD BIRLEY, hs in uniform, Staff College, Camberley, Surrey.

D OLIVE SNELL, hs in uniform, w/c, Staff College.

PH WALTER STONEMAN, 1928, hs in uniform, NPG (NPR).

ANDREWS, Sir James, Bart (1877-1951) lord chief-justice of Northern Ireland.

PH UNKNOWN, wl? in robes, Royal Courts of Justice, Belfast.

ANGELL, Sir Norman (1874-1967) writer.

D EDMOND KAPP, 1914, head, profile, ink, NPG 5129.

PH HOWARD COSTER, 1938, various sizes, print and negs, NPG x2580-81, x2453 and x86. WALTER STONEMAN, 1954, hl, NPG (NPR).

ANGWIN, Sir (Arthur) Stanley (1883-1959) engineer.

PH WALTER STONEMAN, 1943, hs, NPG (NPR).

ANREP, Boris (1883-1969) mosaic artist.

G HENRY LAMB, family group, oil, 1920, Museum of Fine Arts, Boston, USA.

SC Self-portrait, 1952, bust, 'The Modern Virtues', one of several mosaics, National Gallery, London.

ANSON, Peter F. (1879-1975) writer and artist.

PH HOWARD COSTER, c1933, various sizes and negs, NPG x2455-57 and x10320-25.

APPLETON, Sir Edward Victor (1892-1965) physicist.

P SIR W.O.HUTCHISON, c1959, tql seated in robes, Edinburgh University.

PH WALTER STONEMAN, 1930, hs, NPG (NPR). HOWARD COSTER, 1940s, various sizes and negs, NPG x2458-60 and x2589-90.

ARBUTHNOT, Sir Robert Keith, 4th Bart (1864-1916)

rear-admiral.

G SIR A.S.COPE, 'Naval Officers of World War I, 1914-18', oil, 1921, NPG 1913.

ARDEN-CLOSE, Sir Charles Frederick (1865-1952) geographer.

PH WALTER STONEMAN, 3 hs portraits the 1st in uniform, 1917, 1928 and 1939, NPG (NPR).

ARDIZZONE, Edward Jeffrey Irving (1900-1979) artist.

P H.M.CARR, 1944, hs, IWM.

PH HOWARD COSTER, 1954, various sizes and negs, NPG x1713-14.

ARKWRIGHT, Sir Joseph Arthur (1864-1944) bacteriologist.

PH WALTER STONEMAN, 2 hs portraits, 1930 and 1943, NPG (NPR).

ARLEN, Michael (1895-1956) writer.

D EDMOND KAPP, 1921, pencil, Barber Institute, Birmingham University. EDMUND DULAC, 1925, hs, profile, w/c, University of Texas, Austin, USA.

C SIR BERNARD PARTRIDGE, 1928, with five others, drawing for *Punch*, 21 May, 1928, V & A.

PH HOWARD COSTER, various sizes, prints and negs, NPG x2464-70, x2596 and x10326.

ARLISS, George (1868-1946) actor.

P V.U.NOYES, hs as Shylock, Garrick Club, London.

D ANDERS RANDOLPH, hs as Disraeli, pastel?, Garrick Club.

ARMSTRONG, William (1882-1952) actor and theatrical producer.

P WILHELM KAUFMANN, 1929, hl seated, Walker Art Gallery, Liverpool.

ARNAUD, Yvonne (1893-1958) actress.

PH PAUL TANQUERAY, 1931, tql, print, NPG x7244. SIR CECIL BEATON, 1944, hl, profile, print, NPG.

ARNOLD, Tom (1897?-1969) theatrical producer and manager.

PH LENARE, 1949, various sizes and negs, with wife and/or son, NPG x4001-07.

ARTHUR, Frederick Patrick Albert, Prince, see Prince of CONNAUGHT.

ASCHE, (Thomas Stange Heiss) Oscar (1871-1936) actor, theatre manager and writer.

PR HOWARD VAN DUSEN AND HASSALL, hs and wl in character, lith, NPG.

C ALICK P.F.RITCHIE, wl in character, lith, for *Vanity Fair*, 29 Nov 1911, NPG.

PH JOHNSTON & HOFFMANN, c1906, tql in character, postcard, NPG x332.

ASHBEE, Charles Robert (1863-1942) architect.

D WILLIAM STRANG, 1903, hs, profile, King's College, Cambridge. W.STRANG, c1903, hs, Art Workers Guild, London.

SC A.G.WYON, 1929, bust, Art Workers Guild.

ASHBRIDGE, Sir Noel (1889-1975) electrical engineer.

P F.O.SALISBURY, 1953, Institution of Electrical Engineers, London.

PH WALTER STONEMAN, 1947, hs, NPG (NPR).

ASHBY, Arthur Wilfred (1886-1953) agricultural economist.

P PERCY HORTON, 1953, Institute for Research in Agricultural Economics, Oxford.

ASHBY, Dame Margery Corbett-, see Corbett-Ashby.

ASHBY, Thomas (1874-1931) archaeologist.

D SIR GEORGE CLAUSEN, 1925, hs, profile, pencil, NPG 3169.

SC DAVID EVANS, 1925, bronze head, NPG 4281.

ASHFIELD, Albert Henry Stanley, Baron (1874-1948) chairman of the London Passenger Transport Board.

P SIR WILLIAM ORPEN, 1930, tql, London Transport headquarters.

PH WALTER STONEMAN, 1917, hs, when Rt Hon A.H.Stanley, NPG (NPR). HOWARD COSTER, 1930s, various sizes and negs, NPG X2476 and X2597–99.

ASHLEY, Wilfrid William, see Baron Mount Temple.

ASHTON, Winifred, see Clemence Dane.

ASHWELL, Lena Margaret (1872-1957) actress, theatrical producer and writer.

PH MRS ALBERT BROOM, tql, print, NPG X121. UNKNOWN, c1904, hs in character, Rotary postcard, NPG X337.

ASKWITH, George Ranken Askwith, Baron (1861-1942) barrister and government arbitrator.

C WALLACE HESTER ('WH'), wl, mechanical repro, for 'Men of the Day', *Vanity Fair*, 25 Oct 1911, NPG.

PH JOHN RUSSELL & SONS, c1915, hs, print, for *National Photographic Record*, vol 2, NPG.

ASLIN, Charles Herbert (1893-1959) architect.

P ALLAN GWYNNE-JONES, tql seated, RIBA.

ASQUITH, Cynthia Mary Evelyn, née Charteris, Lady (1887-1960) writer and secretary to Sir J.M.Barrie.

D J.S.SARGENT, 1909, head, charcoal, University of Texas, Austin, USA.

PH SIR CECIL BEATON, hl, print, NPG.

ASQUITH, Emma Alice Margaret (Margot), see Countess of Oxford and Asquith.

ASQUITH of Bishopstone, Cyril Asquith, Baron (1890-1954) judge.

PH WALTER STONEMAN, 1946, hs in robes, NPG (NPR). LENARE, 1954, several death-bed negs, NPG X6817–19.

ASQUITH of Yarnborough, Helen Violet Bonham-Carter, Baroness (1887-1969) patron of the arts, writer and woman of affairs.

SC OSCAR NEMON, 1960–69, bronze bust, NPG 4963.

PH SIR CECIL BEATON, hs with bust of Sir Winston Churchill, print, NPG. G.C.BERESFORD, 1907, hs, neg, NPG X6442. HOWARD COSTER, various sizes and negs, NPG X3017–25. SEFTON SAMUELS, 1951, tql with Sir Winston Churchill, print, NPG.

ASTBURY, Sir John Meir (1860-1939) judge.

P A.J.DE KAPPAY, 1914, Trinity College, Oxford.

PH WALTER STONEMAN, 1936, hs, NPG (NPR).

ASTON, Francis William (1877-1945) experimental physicist.

PH WALTER STONEMAN, 2 hs portraits, 1932 and 1943, NPG (NPR).

ASTOR, Nancy Witcher Astor, née Langhorne, Viscountess (1880-1964) first woman MP.

P J.S.SARGENT, 1908, tql, Cliveden (NT), Bucks.

D J.S.SARGENT, 1923, hs, chalk, NPG 4885.

G CHARLES SIMS, 'The Introduction of Lady Astor to the House of Commons', oil, 1923, Palace of Westminster, London, on loan to the Virginia Historical Society, Richmond, USA.

C BERT THOMAS, hl, ink, NPG 4542.

PH OLIVE EDIS, 1920, tql, profile, print, NPG X339. WALTER STONEMAN, 1921, hs, NPG (NPR). G.C.BERESFORD, 1920s, hs, print, NPG X125. DOROTHY WILDING, c1937?, wl in peer's robes, print, NPG X4360. HUGH CECIL, c1928–37, hl in academic robes, profile, print, NPG. MADAME YEVONDE, 1942, hl, NPG X126. SIR CECIL BEATON, 1949, tql seated, print, NPG.

ASTOR, Waldorf Astor, 2nd Viscount (1879?-1952) newspaper proprietor and public servant.

P P.A.DE LÁSZLÓ, 1931?, hl, Cliveden (NT), Bucks. SIR JAMES GUNN, c1944, tql seated in lord mayor's robes, Guildhall, Plymouth.

PH WALTER STONEMAN, 1921, hs, NPG (NPR).

ASTOR of Hever, John Jacob Astor, 1st Baron (1886-1971) newspaper proprietor and public servant.

P CUTHBERT ORDE, 1950, tql seated, Times Newspapers Ltd, London.

D Probably C.ORDE, 1951, hs, chalk sketch, Times Newspapers.

G SIR OSWALD BIRLEY, wl with Geoffrey Dawson, and W.Lints Smith, oil, 1937, Times Newspapers.

PH WALTER STONEMAN, 1924, hs, NPG (NPR).

ATHLONE, Alexander Augustus Frederick Cambridge, 1st Earl of (1874-1957) soldier and governor-general of South Africa and Canada.

P FRANCIS HODGE, 1937, tql in robes, Athlone House, Middlesex Hospital, London. AUGUSTUS JOHN, 1941, tql in lord chancellor's robes, University of London. HENRY CARR, 1948, tql, Government House, Ottawa, Canada. SIR JAMES GUNN, 1955, tql seated in robes, Vintners' Hall, London.

G LAURITS TUXEN, 'Marriage of King George V and Queen Mary', oil, 1893, Royal Coll. L.TUXEN, 'Marriage of Princess Maud and Prince Charles of Denmark', oil, 1896, Royal Coll. F.O.SALISBURY, wedding group of Princess Mary, oil, 1922, Harewood House, W Yorks, and Royal Coll.

C SIR LESLIE WARD ('Spy'), wl, lith, for *Vanity Fair*, 9 Dec 1908, NPG.

PH MRS ALBERT BROOM, c1911–12, equestrian military group, neg, NPG X275. MRS A.BROOM, c1911–12, tql in uniform, neg, NPG X122. MRS A.BROOM, c1914, wl with Marquess of Cambridge and Major E.P.Brassey, print, NPG X1144. WALTER STONEMAN, 3 hs portraits, the 1st in uniform, 1919, 1931 and 1946, NPG (NPR). Various photographs, Royal Coll.

ATHLONE, Alice Mary Victoria, Countess of (1833-1981) sister-in-law of Queen Mary.

G LAURITS TUXEN, 'The Royal Family at the Time of the Jubilee', oil, 1887, Royal Coll. L.TUXEN, 'Marriage of King George V and Queen Mary', oil, 1893, Royal Coll.

PH HILLS & SAUNDERS, c1883–84, with father Duke of Albany, cabinet, NPG AX5552. SNOWDON, 1978, print, NPG X7801. MADAME YEVONDE, tql seated and wl, prints, NPG X11628–30. Several royal groups, NPG. Various photographs, Royal Coll.

ATHOLL, Katharine Marjory Stewart-Murray, Duchess of (1874-1960) public servant.

P GEORGE HENRY, 1903, wl, Blair Castle, Tayside region, Scotland. SIR JAMES GUTHRIE, 1924, Blair Castle.

SC PRINCE SERGE YOURIEVITCH, bronze bust, Blair Castle.

PH WALTER STONEMAN, 1925, hs, semi-profile, NPG (NPR). HOWARD COSTER, 1930s, hs, NPG X2478.

ATKIN, James Richard Atkin, Baron (1867-1944) judge.

P SIR OSWALD BIRLEY, tql seated in robes, Gray's Inn, London.

ATKINS, Sir Ivor Algernon (1869-1953) organist and choirmaster.

PH WALTER STONEMAN, 2 hs portraits, 1925 and 1936, NPG (NPR).

ATKINSON, Sir Edward Hale Tindal (1878-1957) lawyer.

PH WALTER STONEMAN, 1947, hs, NPG (NPR).

ATTLEE, Clement Attlee, 1st Earl (1883-1967) prime minister.

P GEORGE HARCOURT, 1946, hl, NPG 4593. SIR OSWALD BIRLEY, 1948, hl in robes, University College, Oxford. RODRIGO

MOYNIHAN, 1948, hl, Oxford and Cambridge University Club, London. DEREK FOWLER, 1955, hl in robes, Haileybury and Imperial Service College, Herts. L.B.GOWING, 1962, hl seated, Inner Temple, London.
SL H.L.OAKLEY, hs, profile, NPG.
G UNKNOWN, 'General Election, 1945', ph, NPG (*Daily Herald*).
SC DAVID MCFALL, 1965, bronze head, NPG 4601.
PH HOWARD COSTER, various sizes and negs, NPG X2605–10 and X2615–16. J.S.LEWINSKI, 1967?, hs, print, NPG. FELIX MAN, 1939, hl with Arthur Greenwood, print, NPG P16. WALTER STONEMAN, 3 hs portraits, 1930, 1940 and 1941, NPG (NPR).

AUBREY, Melbourn Evans (1885-1957) Baptist minister.
P F.O.SALISBURY, hl seated in robes, Baptist Church House, London.

AUCKINLECK, Sir Claude (1884-1981) field-marshal.
P R.G.EVES, 1940, hs, NPG 4639.
SC BIANCA LOWENSTEIN, bronze bust, National Army Museum, Sandhurst.
PH WALTER STONEMAN, 3 hs portraits, 2 in uniform, 1936 and 1945, NPG (NPR) and NPG X344.

AUMONIER, Stacy (1887-1928) writer.
D E.H.HORWITZ, 1926, hs, chalk, NPG 2777.
PH HOWARD COSTER, 1926, various sizes and negs, NPG X2611–13 and X2617–21.

AUSTIN, Herbert Austin, Baron (1866-1941) motor manufacturer.
PH WALTER STONEMAN, 1937, hs, for NPR, NPG X347.

AVON, (Robert) Anthony Eden, 1st Earl of (1897-1977) prime minister.
P SIR WILLIAM COLDSTREAM, tql seated in robes, Christ Church, Oxford.
D EDMOND KAPP, 1935, hl, profile, lithographic chalk, NPG 4907.
C SIR DAVID LOW, 3 pencil sketches, NPG 4529 (120–22). DAVID LEVINE, wl, ink, NPG.
PH SIR CECIL BEATON, hl, print, NPG. WALTER STONEMAN, 1942, 2 hl portraits, for NPR, NPG X139 and X352. W.STONEMAN, 1950, hs, NPG (NPR), MADAME YEVONDE, print, NPG X11652.

AVONDALE, Albert Victor Christian Edward, Duke of, see Duke of Clarence.

AYLMER, Sir Felix (1899-1979) actor.
P JOHN GILROY, tql, British Actors Equity Association, London. SIR JAMES GUNN, c1962, hl seated, Garrick Club, London.
PR ROBERT LUTYENS, c1962, hl seated, one of group of 'Old Burgundians', type of lith, NPG.
PH GODFREY ARGENT, 1968, hs, NPG (NPR).

AYLMER-JONES, Sir Felix E., see Aylmer.

AYRES, Ruby Mildred, Mrs Reginald William Pocock (1883-1955) romantic novelist.
PH HOWARD COSTER, c1935, various sizes and negs, NPG X10331–35.

B

BABINGTON, Sir John Tremayne, see Tremayne.

BABINGTON, Sir Philip (1894-1965) air marshal.
PH HOWARD COSTER, various sizes and negs, NPG X2635-40.
WALTER STONEMAN, 1941, hs in uniform, NPG (NPR).

BACKHOUSE, Sir Roger Roland Charles (1878-1939) admiral.
PH WALTER STONEMAN, 1932, hl in uniform, NPG (NPR).

BACON, Sir Reginald Hugh Spencer (1863-1947) admiral.
D FRANCIS DODD, 1917, hs, charcoal and w/c, IWM.

BADELEY, Henry John Fanshawe Badeley, Baron (1874-1951) clerk of the Parliaments and engraver.
PH WALTER STONEMAN, 1937, hs, NPG (NPR).

BAHR, Sir Philip Manson-, see Manson-Bahr.

BAILEY, Sir Abe, 1st Bart (1864-1940) South African financier and statesman.
P P.A.DE LÁSZLÓ, 1916, hs, Royal Institute of International Affairs, Chatham House, London. SIR OSWALD BIRLEY, 1932, tql seated, Royal Institute of International Affairs.
D FRED MAY, 1933, hs, profile, gouache, NPG.
C SIR LESLIE WARD ('Spy'), wl, Hentschel-Colourtype, for *Vanity Fair*, 9 Sept 1908, NPG.
PH WALTER STONEMAN, 1921, hs, NPG (NPR).

BAILEY, Cyril (1871-1957) classical scholar.
D SIR WILLIAM ROTHENSTEIN, chalk, Balliol College, Oxford.
PR ANDREW FREETH, etch, Balliol College.
PH WALTER STONEMAN, 2 hs portraits, 1933 and 1945, NPG (NPR).

BAILEY, Henry Christopher (1878-1961) crime writer.
PH HOWARD COSTER, various sizes and negs, NPG X2650-57.

BAILLIE, Charles Wallace Alexander Cochrane, see 2nd Baron Lamington.

BAILLIE, Sir James Black (1872-1940) vice-chancellor of Leeds University.
P GEORGE FIDDES WATT, c1924-38, hs in robes, University of Leeds.
PH WALTER STONEMAN, 1931, hl, NPG (NPR).

BAIN, Sir Frederick William (1889-1950) chemical industrialist.
D SIR JAMES GUNN, c1947-49, hs, Confederation of British Industry, London.
PH WALTER STONEMAN, 1947, hs, NPG (NPR).

BAIRD, Dorothea (1873-1933) actress.
PH LONDON STEREOSCOPIC CO, c1894, wl as Rosalind, cabinet, NPG X152. ALFRED ELLIS, 1895, hs as Trilby, print, NPG X362. T.C.TURNER, 1896, wl as Trilby, photogravure, NPG X6403.

BAIRD, John Logie (1888-1946) television pioneer.
P JAMES KERR-LAWSON, hl seated, Glasgow University.
D J.KERR-LAWSON, c1943, hs, pencil, SNPG 1437.
SC DONALD GILBERT, 1943, bronze bust, NPG 4125.
PH LONDON NEWS AGENCY, 1924, tql with Mayor of Hastings, print, NPG X11616. A.SPENCER, 1927, wl seated with R.F.Tiltman, print, NPG X11613. UNKNOWN, c1927, hs, print, NPG X11612. UNKNOWN, c1927, tql with Sir Oliver Lodge, print,

NPG X11615. UNKNOWN, 1932, wl with R.F.Tiltman, print, NPG X11614. HOWARD COSTER, c1936, various sizes and negs, NPG X2658-67.

BAIRSTOW, Sir Leonard (1880-1963) expert on aerodynamics.
PH WALTER STONEMAN, 1921, hs, NPG (NPR).

BAKER, Charles Henry Collins (1880-1959) art historian.
D FRANCIS DODD, 1932, hs, chalk, NPG 4355.
PH UNKNOWN, 1928, hs, print, NPG X363. UNKNOWN, hs, print, NPG X264. UNKNOWN, wl, print, NPG X265.

BAKER, Sir Herbert (1862-1946) architect.
P A.K.LAWRENCE, c1936, wl, Bank of England, London.
D SIR WILLIAM ROTHENSTEIN, 1925, hs, chalk, NPG 4763.
SC SIR CHARLES WHEELER, c1932-37, bronze head, South Africa House, London. SIR C.WHEELER, 1944, marble bust, Bank of England.

BAKER, Herbert Brereton (1862-1935) chemist.
PH WALTER STONEMAN, 1917, hs, NPG (NPR).

BAKER, James Franklin Bethune-, see Bethune-Baker.

BAKER, Philip John Noel-, see Baron Noel-Baker.

BAKER, Richard St Barbe (b1889) forestry adviser and silviculturist.
PH HOWARD COSTER, c1932, various sizes and negs, NPG X2668-76.

BALCON, Sir Michael (1896-1977) film producer.
PH HOWARD COSTER, various sizes and negs, c1936, NPG X1719-20 and X2682-93; 1954, hs, profile, NPG X163. WALTER STONEMAN, 1948, hs, NPG (NPR). WALTER BIRD, 1961, hs, NPG (NPR). GODFREY ARGENT, 1970, hs, for NPR, NPG X164.

BALDWIN of Bewdley, Stanley Baldwin, 1st Earl (1867-1947) statesman.
P GLYN PHILPOT, 1926, tql in robes, Carlton Club, London. SIR OSWALD BIRLEY, 1928, tql, Goldsmiths' Hall, London. R.G.EVES, c1933, hl, NPG 3551. W.T.MONNINGTON, 1933, hl, Trinity College, Cambridge. SIR O.BIRLEY, 1938, tql in robes, Carlton Club, London. FRANCIS DODD, 1943, tql seated, Rhodes House, Oxford; study sketch, chalk, 1942, NPG 4425.
D SIR WILLIAM ROTHENSTEIN, 1928, hs, profile, chalk, NPG 3866.
M W.C.DONGWORTH, c1930, hs, oval, NPG 5030.
SC LADY KATHLEEN KENNET, c1925, bust, Bewdley Town Hall, Worcs. NEWBERRY TRENT, 1927, bronze bust, Harrow School, Middx.
C SIR MAX BEERBOHM, 1924, 'The Old and Young Self', chalk, Athenaeum Club, London. SIR BERNARD PARTRIDGE, various cartoons, ink, for *Punch*, 7 Nov 1923, 19 Nov 1924 and 1 Nov 1926, NPG.
PH SIR BENJAMIN STONE, 1909, wl, print, NPG. WALTER STONEMAN, 1920, hs, NPG (NPR). VANDYK, 1927, 2 hs portraits, prints, NPG X372 and X373. W.STONEMAN, 1938, hs, NPG X1434. HOWARD COSTER, 1930s, hs, various negs, NPG X2694-98.

BALFOUR, Sir Andrew (1873-1931) expert in tropical medicine and public health and novelist.
SC ALAN HOWES, 1932, relief portrait on bronze tablet, London School of Hygiene and Tropical Medicine, London.

PH WALTER STONEMAN, 2 hs portraits, the 1st in uniform, 1919 and 1930, NPG (NPR).

BALFOUR, Henry (1863-1939) anthropologist.
PH WALTER STONEMAN, 2 hs portraits, 1926 and 1937, NPG (NPR).

BALL, Albert (1896-1917) fighter-pilot.
P DENHOLM DAVIS, tql in uniform with aircraft, probably based on photograph, Castle Museum, Nottingham. EDWARD NEWLING, 1919, tql in uniform, Castle Museum; version, IWM.
SC HENRY POOLE, 1921, statue on monument, Castle Museum grounds; bronze cast of statuette, NPG 2277.
PH UNKNOWN, c1916–17, various photographs, IWM.

BALL, John (1861-1940) golfer.
P R.E.MORRISON, tql with club, Royal Liverpool Golf Club, Hoylake, Cheshire.
PH ELLIOTT & FRY, wl with club, photogravure, NPG.

BANKS, Leslie James (1890-1952) actor.
P W.R.SICKERT, 1937, tql as Petruchio with Edith Evans as Katharine, Bradford City Art Gallery.

BANTOCK, Sir Granville Ransome (1868-1946) composer.
P J.B.MUNNS, 1920, tql seated, Barber Institute, University of Birmingham. G.H.B.HOLLAND, 1933, hs, NPG 4457.
PH HERBERT LAMBERT, c1922, hl, photogravure, NPG AX7743. WALTER STONEMAN, hs, for NPR, NPG X379.

BARBIROLLI, Sir John (1899-1970) conductor.
SC BYRON HOWARD, head, Royal Philharmonic Society on loan to Royal Festival Hall, London.
PH WALTER STONEMAN, 1952, hl seated, NPG (NPR).

BARCROFT, Sir Joseph (1872-1947) physiologist.
P R.G.EVES, 1937, hl in robes, Department of Physiology, Cambridge University.

BARGER, George (1878-1939) chemist.
PH WALTER STONEMAN, 1921, hs, NPG (NPR).

BARING, Maurice (1874-1945) man of letters.
SL HUBERT LESLIE, 1925, 2 profile heads, NPG.
G SIR JAMES GUNN, wl with G.K.Chesterton and Hilaire Belloc, oil, 1932, NPG 3654.
PH CLAUDE HARRIS, 1929, hs, print, NPG X11895. WALTER STONEMAN, 1931, 2 hs portraits, NPG (NPR). HOWARD COSTER, 1934, hs, print and neg, NPG X2699 and AX3516.

BARING, Rowland Thomas, see 2nd Earl of Cromer.

BARKER, Sir Ernest (1874-1960) scholar.
PH WALTER STONEMAN, 2 hs portraits, 1944 and 1954, NPG (NPR).

BARKER, Sir Herbert Atkinson (1869-1950) manipulative surgeon.
P AUGUSTUS JOHN, c1917, hl seated, NPG 4189.
C 'ELF', wl seated, Hentschel-Colourtype, for *Vanity Fair*, 8 Dec 1909, NPG.

BARKLA, Charles Glover (1877-1944) Nobel prize winning physicist.
D DAVID FOGGIE, 1934, head, pencil, Edinburgh University.
PH WALTER STONEMAN, 1926, hs, NPG (NPR).

BARMAN, Christian (b1898) architect and industrial designer.
PH HOWARD COSTER, various sizes and negs, NPG X2700–03.

BARNES, Ernest William (1874-1953) bishop of Birmingham.
D EDMOND KAPP, 1930, hs, profile, charcoal, Barber Institute, Birmingham University.
SC DAVID WYNNE, 1954, bronze relief portrait, hl, profile, Birmingham Cathedral.

PH WALTER STONEMAN, 1918, hs, NPG (NPR). UNKNOWN, c1924, tql in robes, print, NPG (Anglican Bishops).

BARNES, Sir Kenneth Ralph (1878-1957) principal of the Royal Academy of Dramatic Arts.
SC CLEMENCE DANE, 1956, bronze bust, Royal Academy of Dramatic Art, London.
PH WALTER STONEMAN, 2 hs portraits, 1943 and 1954, NPG (NPR).

BARNES, Ronald Gorell, see 3rd Baron Gorell.

BARNES, Sidney Francis (1876-1967) cricketer.
PH UNKNOWN, 1953, hs, print, NPG X557.

BARNETT, Lionel David (1871-1960) orientalist.
PH WALTER STONEMAN, 1937, hs, NPG (NPR).

BARRATT, Sir Arthur Sheridan (1891-1966) air marshal.
P T.C.DUGDALE, IWM.
PH HOWARD COSTER, various sizes and negs, NPG X2704–10. WALTER STONEMAN, 1943, hs in uniform, NPG (NPR).

BARRIE, Sir James Matthew (1860-1937) writer.
P SIR WILLIAM NICHOLSON, 1904, hl, profile, SNPG 1438. SIR JOHN LAVERY, 1930s, wl seated, SNPG 1309.
D HARRY FURNISS, c1900–10, tql, profile, pen and ink, NPG 3420. W.T.MONNINGTON, 1932, hs, pencil, NPG 3539.
C SIR MAX BEERBOHM, 1912, wl, Ashmolean Museum, Oxford. SIR DAVID LOW, 1927, wl, chalk, NPG 4557. ALFRED LOWE, hs, Garrick Club, London.
PH BARRAUD, 1880s, tql seated, print, NPG X5161. G.C.BERESFORD, 4 hs portraits, prints, NPG X228–30 and X635. A.L.COBURN, 1909, hs, photogravure, NPG AX7791. FREDERICK HOLLYER, hs, print, V & A. WALTER STONEMAN, 1922, 2 hs portraits, NPG (NPR). Various photographs, SNPG.

BARTHOLOMEW, John George (1860-1920) cartographer.
P E.A.WALTON, tql with globe, SNPG 1994.

BARTON, Sir Sidney (1876-1946) diplomat.
PH WALTER STONEMAN, 1939, hl in uniform, NPG (NPR).

BATEMAN, Henry Mayo (1887-1970) cartoonist.
SL H.L.OAKLEY, 1929, hs, profile, NPG.
C Self-portrait, 1933, wl seated with Howard Coster, ink, NPG. Self-portrait, 1964, wl sketching, ink, NPG.
PH HOWARD COSTER, 1933, various sizes and negs, NPG X2731–39.

BATES, Sir Percy Elly, 4th Bart (1879-1946) merchant and ship-owner.
P SIR GERALD KELLY, 1947, Midland Bank, Liverpool.
PH G.C.BERESFORD, 1913, hs, neg, NPG X6435. WALTER STONEMAN, 1921, hs, NPG (NPR).

BATESON, William (1861-1926) biologist.
D WILLIAM STRANG, 1910, hs, chalk, Zoology Department, Cambridge University. E.WELLS, 1914, hs, chalks, John Innes Institute, Norwich. SIR WILLIAM ROTHENSTEIN, 1917, hs, chalk, NPG 4379. W.A.FORSTER, 1923, profile head, chalk, NPG 2147.
C D.G.LILLIE, 1909?, wl with two birds, w/c, NPG.
PH V.H.MOTTRAM, 1909, hs, semi-profile, print, NPG X259. OSTERSTOCK, 1910?, hl, print, NPG X5163.

BATHURST, Charles, see Viscount Bledisloe.

BATSFORD, Harry (1880-1951) publisher, bookseller and author.
P JOHN BERRY, c1951, hl seated, B.T.Batsford Ltd, London.
PH UNKNOWN, various photographs, Batsford.

BAX, Sir Arnold (Edward Trevor) (1883-1953) composer.
P VERA BAX, hl seated, Royal Academy of Music, London.
D POWYS EVANS, late 1920s, head, pen and ink, NPG 4400.

sc UNKNOWN, 1953, death mask, University College, Cork, Eire.
PH HERBERT LAMBERT, *c*1922, hs, profile, photogravure, NPG AX7753. HOWARD COSTER, 1930s, various sizes and negs, NPG X2772–76. WALTER STONEMAN, 1947, hs, NPG (NPR).

BAX, Clifford (1886-1962) dramatist.
PH A.L.COBURN, 1916, hs, photogravure, NPG AX7833. HOWARD COSTER, various sizes and negs, NPG X2777–85.

BAYLIS, Lilian Mary (1874-1937) theatrical manager.
P CHARLES E.BUTLER, 1926, wl in doctoral robes, Old Vic Theatre on loan to Camperdown House, London. ANN DALSTON, *c*1930, hl seated in stage box, Old Vic Theatre. ETHEL GABAIN, hl seated, Sadler's Wells Theatre, London. CECIL LESLIE, 1931, hl, NPG 5309; version, Vic-Wells Association on loan to Old Vic Theatre.
D SIR WILLIAM ROTHENSTEIN, 1916, hs, chalk, Old Vic Theatre.
PH Various photographs, Old Vic Theatre.

BAYLISS, Sir William Maddock (1860-1924) physiologist.
G UNKNOWN, garden party, ph, Physiology Department, University College, London.
PH WALTER STONEMAN, 1917, hs, NPG (NPR). Various photographs, Physiology Department, University College.

BEARDSLEY, Aubrey Vincent (1872-1898) illustrator.
P W.R.SICKERT, 1894, wl, profile, TATE 4655. J.E.BLANCHE, 1895, tql, NPG 1991.
D Self-portrait, hs, pen and ink, BM. W.R.SICKERT, hs, profile, NPG 1967.
PR SIR WILLIAM ROTHENSTEIN, *c*1898, tql seated, profile, lith, NPG.
C ALFRED BRICE ('Grip'), wl, indian ink and wash, for *The Sketch*, 13 May 1896, V & A. SIR MAX BEERBOHM, *c*1895, wl, drg, Ashmolean museum, Oxford.
PH JOHN RUSSELL & SONS, *c*1890, hs, print, NPG P43. FREDERICK H.EVANS, 1895, 2 hs portraits, profile, prints, NPG X1005–06. FREDERICK HOLLYER, hl seated, print, V & A. UNKNOWN, wl seated, print, NPG X4608.

BEATTY, David Beatty, 1st Earl (1871-1936) admiral.
P SIR JOHN LAVERY, *c*1918–19, hl in uniform, IWM; study for 'The End', IWM. SIR WILLIAM ORPEN, *c*1926, hs in uniform, SNPG 1036. COWAN DOBSON, 1936, formerly United Services Club (c/o Crown Commissioners), London.
D FRANCIS DODD, 1914?, wl seated, charcoal and w/c, IWM. SIR A.S.COPE, *c*1921, hs in uniform, NMM, Greenwich, sketch for 'naval Officers', NPG 1913.
G SIR A.S.COPE, 'Naval Officers of World War I, 1914–18', oil, 1921, NPG 1913. SIR J.LAVERY, 'The End' (Admiral Beatty reading surrender terms to German Navy), oil, 1924, IWM.
sc WILLIAM MCMILLAN, 1948, bust, Trafalgar Square, London.
PR HENRIK LUND, lith, IWM.
C R.S.SHERRIFFS, wl on Nelson's column, ink and charcoal?, NPG.
PH WALTER STONEMAN, 1919, hs in uniform, NPG (NPR).

BEAUCHAMP, William Lygon, 7th Earl (1872-1938) politician.
D CHARLES GERE, hs, oval, w/c, NPG.
C LESLIE WARD ('Spy'), wl, lith, for *Vanity Fair*, 20 July, 1899, NPG.
PH G.C.BERESFORD, 1910, hs, neg, NPG X6436. WALTER STONEMAN, 2 hs portraits, *c*1917 and 1930, NPG (NPR).

BEAVER, Sir Hugh (1890-1967) businessman and public servant.
D SIR JAMES GUNN, *c*1959, hs, Confederation of British Industry, London.
PH WALTER STONEMAN, 1947, hs, NPG (NPR).

BEAVERBROOK, William Maxwell Aitken, 1st Baron (1879-1964) statesman and newspaper proprietor.
P W.R.SICKERT, 1935, tql, NPG 5173. GRAHAM SUTHERLAND, 1951,

tql seated, Beaverbrook Art Gallery, Fredericton, New Brunswick, Canada; study head, 1950, Beaverbrook Art Gallery. G.SUTHERLAND, 1952, head, NPG 5195.
PH HOWARD COSTER, *c*1930, various sizes and negs, NPG X2803–08. UNKNOWN, *c*1930, hs, print, NPG X678. FELIX MAN, *c*1951, hl, print, NPG X1149.

BEDFORD, Liza, see Lehmann.

BEDFORD, Mary du Caurroy Russell, Duchess of (1865-1937) amateur nurse and aviator.
P MISS SMITH, wl in robes, Woburn Abbey, Beds.
D 'C.A.T.', 1906, hs, w/c, Woburn Abbey.
PH Various photographs, Woburn Abbey.

BEECHAM, Sir Thomas, 2nd Bart (1879-1961) conductor.
P W.R.SICKERT, 1930, hl, Museum of Modern Art, New York. G.T.STUART, 1953–54, head, NPG L106.
D EDMOND KAPP, 1919–58, various sketches, ink, chalk or charcoal, Barber Institute, Birmingham University. ERNEST PROCTER, 1929, tql, profile, pencil, NPG 4975(10 and 11). HILDA B.WIENER, 1935, tql, pencil, V & A.
sc IVAN MESTROVIC, 1915, bronze bust, Manchester City Art Gallery. DAVID WYNNE, 1957, bronze head and hands, NPG 4221. D.WYNNE, *c*1957, 2 bronze statuettes, St Helen's Museum and Art Gallery. D.WYNNE, bronze head, Royal Philharmonic Society on loan to Royal Festival Hall, London. MURIEL LIDDLE, *c*1961, bust, Royal Philharmonic Orchestra, London.
C EDMUND DULAC, *c*1925, wood and wax statuette in evening dress with baton, Museum of London.
PH H.WALTER BARNETT, 2 hl portraits, prints, V & A. FELIX MAN, 1936, tql conducting orchestra, print, NPG X1150.

BEERBOHM, Sir Henry Maximilian ('Max') (1872-1956) writer and caricaturist.
P J.E.BLANCHE, 1903, Ashmolean Museum, Oxford, on loan to Merton College, Oxford. SIR WILLIAM NICHOLSON, 1905, wl, profile, NPG 3850. ALBERT RUTHERSTON, 1909, University of Texas, Austin, USA. R.G.EVES, 1936, hs, TATE 4895.
D SIR WILLIAM ROTHENSTEIN, 1915, pencil, Manchester City Art Gallery. EDMOND KAPP, 1923, ink, charcoal or wash, Barber Institute, Birmingham University. SIR W.ROTHENSTEIN, 1928, head, profile, pencil, NPG 4141. R.G.EVES, 1936, hs, pencil, NPG 4000.
sc LADY KATHLEEN KENNET, statuette, Merton College.
PR SIR W.ROTHENSTEIN, 1898, tql, profile, lith, NPG.
C Self-portrait, *c*1893, wl, drg, Merton College. Self-portrait, *c*1900, wl, profile, drg, Ashmolean Museum, Oxford. Self-portrait, 1923, wl reclining, w/c, NPG 5107. Self-portrait, pen and wash, University of Texas.
PH A.L.COBURN, 1908, wl, photogravure, NPG AX7783. FILSON YOUNG, 1916, wl seated, profile, print, NPG X3767. SIR CECIL BEATON, tql, print, NPG.

BEIT, Sir Otto John, 1st Bart (1865-1930) financier and philanthropist.
P SIR WILLIAM ORPEN, 1914, wl seated, Johannesburg Art Gallery, South Africa.
sc OMAR RAMSDEN, 1932, relief portrait on bronze plaque, Imperial College of Science and Technology, London.

BEITH, John Hay ('Ian Hay') (1876-1952) soldier, novelist and playwright.
P T.C.DUGDALE, *c*1940, tql in uniform, Garrick Club, London.
SL H.L.OAKLEY, hs, profile, NPG.
PH WALTER STONEMAN, 1939, hs, for NPR, NPG X380. HOWARD COSTER, 1930s, various sizes and negs, NPG.

BELISHA, (Isaac) Leslie Hore-, see Hore-Belisha.

BELL, Clive (1881-1964) writer on art.
P ROGER FRY, *c*1924, hl seated, NPG 4967.
G VANESSA BELL, family group, oil, 1924, City Art Gallery, Leicester.
SC BORIS ANREP, 1933, as Bacchus in 'The Awakening of the Muses', mosaic, National Gallery, London.
PH Various photographs, NPG (Strachey Coll).

BELL, Enid Moberly (1881-1967) headmistress and biographer.
P LASENBY, 1949, hl, Lady Margaret School, Parsons Green, London. D.S.SWAN, hs, Lady Margaret School.
D T.BINNEY GIBBS, 1922, hs, sanguine, Lady Margaret School.
SC EDMUND WARE, 1934, bronze bust, Lady Margaret School.

BELL, George Kennedy Allen (1883-1958) bishop of Chichester.
P SIR WILLIAM COLDSTREAM, 1954, hl seated in robes, TATE T74. A.R.MIDDLETON TODD, 1955, hl in robes, Bishop's Palace, Chichester. ERIC KENNINGTON, *c*1958, hs, The Deanery, Canterbury.
PH HOWARD COSTER, *c*1936, various sizes and negs, NPG X2397-98, X2825-29 and X10345-52. H.COSTER, 1954, hs, NPG X2360-1. UNKNOWN, hs, print, NPG (Anglican Bishops).

BELL, Gertrude Margaret (1868-1926) traveller and archaeologist.
D FLORA RUSSELL, 1887, hs, w/c, NPG 4385.
SC ANNE ACHESON, after J.S.Sargent (1923), posthumous, bronze bust, Royal Geographical Society, London.
PH J.WESTON AND SONS, hs, print, Royal Geographical Society. UNKNOWN, 1918, hs, print, Royal Geographical Society. Various photographs, Gertrude Bell Archive, Library, University of Newcastle upon Tyne.

BELL, Vanessa, née Stephen (1879-1961) painter.
P DUNCAN GRANT, *c*1918, tql seated, NPG 4331. D.GRANT, 1942, wl seated, TATE 5405.
SC MARCEL GIMOND, *c*1922-26, lead cast of bust, NPG 4349.
PH Various photographs, NPG (Strachey Coll).

BELLOC, (Joseph) Hilaire (Pierre René) (1870-1953) poet and author.
P SIR JAMES GUNN, 1950, tql seated, the Oxford University Union.
D DAPHNE POLLEN, 1932, hs, semi-profile, chalk, NPG 4008. FRANK BRANGWYN, *c*1950, hs, sanguine, Museum and Art Gallery, Dundee.
G SIR J.GUNN, wl with G.K.Chesterton and Maurice Baring, oil, 1932, NPG 3654.
C SIR MAX BEERBOHM, *c*1906, wl sitting on floor, drg, Yale University Library, New Haven, USA. SIR BERNARD PARTRIDGE, tql, pencil, for *Punch*, 17 August 1927, NPG 3664
PH A.L.COBURN, 1908, hs, photogravure, NPG AX7784. T.R.ANNAN AND SONS, 1910, hs, profile, print, NPG P21. G.C.BERESFORD, *c*1913, 2 hs portraits, prints, NPG X707-08. E.O.HOPPÉ, 1915, hs, print, NPG X7930. JOHN GAY, 1948, tql seated, print, NPG (*Daily Herald*).

BENN, Sir Ernest John Pickstone, 2nd Bart (1875-1954) publisher and economist.
P SIR WILLIAM ORPEN, Benn Brothers Ltd, London.

BENN, William Wedgwood, see 1st Viscount Stansgate.

BENNETT, (Enoch) Arnold (1867-1931) novelist.
D M.DU MAYNE, 1891, w/c, City Museum and Art Gallery, Stoke-on-Trent. SIR WILLIAM ROTHENSTEIN, 1920, head, chalk, Stoke-on-Trent Art Gallery. W.E.TITTLE, 1923, hs, pencil, NPG 2664. KATHERINE SHACKLETON, *c*1925, chalk, Stoke-on-Trent Art Gallery. EMOND KAPP, 1929, chalk, Barber Institute, Birming-

ham University.
SC THEODORE SPICER-SIMSON, profile head, plasticene medallion, NPG 2043.
C HARRY FURNISS, *c*1910, 3 portraits, pen and ink, NPG 3422-24. 'OWL', wl, mechanical repro, for *Vanity Fair*, 2 April 1913, NPG. SIR MAX BEERBOHM, 1922, tql with H.G.Wells, drg, Ashmolean Museum, Oxford. SIR DAVID LOW, 1926, wl, profile, chalk, NPG 4561. SIR BERNARD PARTRIDGE, tql, profile, pencil, for *Punch*, 21 May 1928, NPG 4075. SIR B.PARTRIDGE, wl as news-vendor, ink and w/c, for *Punch*, 21 May 1928, NPG. SIR WILLIAM NICHOLSON, with St Bernard dog, ink, Stoke-on-Trent Art Gallery.
PH A.L.COBURN, 1913, hs, photogravure, NPG AX7797. G.C.BERESFORD, 1927, 2 hs portraits, prints, NPG X731 and X733. HOWARD COSTER, 1929, 2 hl portraits, one a profile, prints, NPG AX2299 and X2850.

BENNETT, George Macdonald (1892-1959) chemist.
PH UNKNOWN, hs, print, Chemistry Department, King's College, London.

BENNETT of Edgbaston, Peter Frederick Blaker Bennett, Baron (1880-1957) industrialist.
P SIR JAMES GUNN, *c*1956, hs, Joseph Lucas Industries Ltd, Birmingham.
D SIR J.GUNN, *c*1940, hs, Confederation of British Industry, London.
PH WALTER STONEMAN, 1948, hs, NPG (NPR).

BENSON, Arthur Christopher (1862-1925) man of letters.
P R.E.FULLER MAITLAND, Magdalene College, Cambridge. SIR WILLIAM NICHOLSON, 1924, tql seated in robes, Fitzwilliam Museum, Cambridge.
G H.ABBOTT, wl with brothers Edward Frederic and Robert Hugh, ph, NPG X4610.
C SIR LESLIE WARD ('Spy'), wl in robes, lith, for *Vanity Fair*, 4 June 1903, NPG.
PH VANDYK, *c*1911, tql seated, print, NPG X4609.

BENSON, Edward Frederic (1867-1940) author.
G H.ABBOTT, wl with brothers Arthur Christopher and Robert Hugh, ph, NPG X4610.
PH HOWARD COSTER, *c*1936, various sizes and negs, NPG X2851-56.

BENSON, Godfrey Rathbone, see 1st Baron Charnwood.

BENSON, Robert Hugh (1871-1914) Catholic writer and apologist.
G H.ABBOTT, wl with brothers Arthur Christopher and Edward Frederic, ph, NPG X4610.

BENSON, Stella, Mrs Anderson (1892-1933) novelist.
D CUTHBERT ORDE, 1934, hl, w/c, NPG 3321.

BENTLEY, Edmund Clerihew (1875-1956) writer.
D HUGH RIVIERE, 1915, hs, charcoal, NPG 4931.
PH HOWARD COSTER, *c*1936, various sizes and negs, NPG X2857-62.

BERESFORD, George Charles (1864-1938) photographer.
PH Self-portrait, *c*1935-36, hs, neg, NPG X6439.

BERESFORD, John Davys (1873-1947) writer.
PH HOWARD COSTER, 1934, various sizes, prints and negs, NPG X757, X1723, AX3511 and X2867-70.

BERKELEY, Randal Mowbray Berkeley, 8th Earl of (1865-1942) scientist.
P SIR WILLIAM ORPEN, 1925, tql seated in hunt dress, Berkeley Castle, Glos.
PH WALTER STONEMAN, 1939, hs, profile, for NPR, NPG X5905.

BERNARD, John Henry (1860-1927) archbishop of Dublin and provost of Trinity College, Dublin.

PH UNKNOWN, c1911, hs in robes, print, NPG (Anglican Bishops).

BERNERS, Gerald Hugh Tyrwhitt-Wilson, 14th Baron (1883-1950) musician, artist and author.
P REX WHISTLER, 1929, tql seated at easel, NPG 5050.
D SIR WILLIAM ROTHENSTEIN, 1923, hs, chalk, NPG 4380.
PH HERBERT LAMBERT, c1922, tql, photogravure, NPG AX7752. WALTER STONEMAN, 1923, hs, NPG (NPR). SIR CECIL BEATON, 1943, wl seated, profile, print, NPG.

BERNSTEIN of Leigh, Sidney Lewis Bernstein, 1st Baron (b1899) film producer.
PH HOWARD COSTER, 1934, various sizes and negs, NPG x2911–21.

BERRY, James Gomer, see 1st Viscount Kemsley.

BERRY, William Ewert, see 1st Viscount Camrose.

BESSBOROUGH, Vere Brabazon Ponsonby, 9th Earl (1880-1956) governor-general of Canada.
PH UNKNOWN, 1925, hs, print, NPG x922. WALTER STONEMAN, 2 hs portraits, 1930 and 1948, NPG (NPR).

BETHUNE-BAKER, James Franklin (1861-1951) professor of divinity.
D RANDOLPH SCHWABE, 1935, hs, pencil, Divinity School, Cambridge University.

BETTERTON, Henry Bucknall, see Baron Rushcliffe.

BEVAN, Aneurin (1897-1960) statesman.
SC PETER LAMBDA, 1945, bronze bust, NPG 4993.
C SIR DAVID LOW, 1935, profile head, pencil, NPG 4529(23).
PH SIR CECIL BEATON, 1940, hs, print, NPG x5168. WALTER STONEMAN, 1945, hs, NPG (NPR). HOWARD COSTER, various sizes and negs, NPG x1728–29 and x2930–31. Various photographs, NPG (*Daily Herald*).

BEVAN, Robert Polhill (1865-1925) painter.
P Self-portrait, c1913–14, hs, NPG 5201.

BEVERIDGE, William Henry Beveridge, 1st Baron (1879-1963) economist and 'father' of British Welfare State.
P SIR WILLIAM NICHOLSON, tql seated in robes, London School of Economics.
C SIR BERNARD PARTRIDGE, wl dressed as woman with foundling, pen and ink, for *Punch*, 22 Nov 1944, NPG.
PH SIR CECIL BEATON, hs, print, NPG x7758. G.C.BERESFORD, 1917, hs, neg, NPG x6440. HOWARD COSTER, various sizes and negs, NPG x2932–36. FELIX MAN, 1939, hs, print, NPG P11. RAMSEY AND MUSPRATT, hs, print, NPG x933. WALTER STONEMAN, 2 hs portraits, 1919 and 1953, NPG (NPR).

BEVIN, Ernest (1881-1951) statesman.
P T.C.DUGDALE, 1945, tql seated, NPG 3921.
SC EDWIN WHITNEY-SMITH, 1929, bronze bust, Foreign Office (DoE), London. SIR JACOB EPSTEIN, 1943, bronze bust, TATE 5689.
C SIR DAVID LOW, 1933, tql, chalk, NPG 4558. GEOFFREY DAVIEN, 1946, wl oil?, NPG.
PH FELIX MAN, c1939–40, hs, print, NPG P12. SIR CECIL BEATON, 1940, hl seated, print, NPG. WALTER STONEMAN, 2 hs portraits, 1940 and 1941, NPG (NPR) and NPG x381. HOWARD COSTER, 1940s, various sizes and negs, NPG x1730–38 and x2936–46.

BICESTER, Vivian Hugh Smith, Baron (1867-1956) banker.
P SIR WILLIAM ORPEN, 1919, hl seated, Guardian Royal Exchange Assurance, London. SIR JAMES GUNN, c1950, hl, Morgan Grenfell & Co, London.
G SIMON ELWES, group of partners, oil, 1955, Morgan Grenfell.
PH WALTER STONEMAN, 2 hs portraits, 1938 and 1947, NPG (NPR).

BIDDER, George Parker (1863-1953) marine biologist.
P R.G.EVES, c1934, hs, Marine Biological Association, Plymouth.

BIFFEN, Sir Rowland Harry (1874-1949) geneticist and professor of agricultural botany.
P KENNETH GREEN, 1926, tql seated, Department of Agriculture, University of Cambridge.

BIKANER, Sir Ganga Singh Bahadur, Maharaja of (1880-1943) statesman and general.
P SIR WILLIAM ORPEN, 1919, hs in uniform, NPG 4188. SIR JAMES GUTHRIE, c1919–21, tql in uniform, SNPG 1130, study sketch for 'Statesmen', NPG 2463.
G SIR W.ORPEN, 'The Signing of Peace in the Hall of Mirrors, Versailles, 1919', oil, IWM. SIR J.GUTHRIE, 'Statesmen of World War I, 1914–18', oil, c1924–30, NPG 2463.
PH WALTER STONEMAN, 1930, hl in uniform, NPG (NPR).

BINNIE, William James Eames (1867-1949) civil engineer.
P JOHN ST HELIER LANDER, 1939, hl, Institution of Civil Engineers, London.

BINYON, (Robert) Laurence (1869-1943) poet and art historian.
D WILLIAM STRANG, 1901, hs, pencil, NPG 3185. SIR WILLIAM ROTHENSTEIN, 1916, hs, City Art Gallery, Manchester. FRANCIS DODD, 1920, hs?, charcoal, The Athenaeum Club, London. EDMOND KAPP, 1921, ink, charcoal or wash, Barber Institute, Birmingham University.
PR SIR W.ROTHENSTEIN, 1898, hl seated, lith, NPG, and Bradford Art Gallery. W.STRANG, 1898, hl, etch, NPG. W.STRANG, 1918, head, etch, NPG.
PH HECTOR MURCHISON, c1913, tql seated, profile, print, NPG x964. HOWARD COSTER, c1934, various sizes and negs, NPG x1739 and x2965–68. G.C.BERESFORD, before 1938, hs, neg, NPG x6441.

BIRCH, Sir (James Frederick) Noel (1865-1939) general.
D FRANCIS DODD, 1917, hs, charcoal and w/c, IWM.
PH WALTER STONEMAN, 2 hs portraits, the 1st in uniform, 1919 and 1931, NPG (NPR).

BIRCH, Lamorna (1869-1955) artist.
D J.A.GRANT, 1946, hs, pastel, NPG 5084.

BIRD, Cyril Kenneth ('Fougasse') (1887-1965) caricaturist.
C SIR DAVID LOW, 4 sketches, pencil, NPG 4529(24–27).
PH HOWARD COSTER, c1934, various sizes, prints and negs, NPG x966–68, x1740, AX3521 and x2969–79.

BIRD, Sir James (1883-1946) naval and aircraft constructor.
PH WALTER STONEMAN, 1946, 2 hs portraits, NPG (NPR).

BIRDWOOD, William Riddell Birdwood, 1st Baron (1865-1951) field-marshal.
P ALFRED HAYWARD, 1919, hl seated in uniform, IWM. WALTER URWICK, 1920, tql, Cavalry and Guards Club, London. UNKNOWN, Peterhouse College, Cambridge.
D J.S.SARGENT, 1916, hs in uniform, chalk, NPG 4186. FRANCIS DODD, 1917, tql in uniform, charcoal and w/c, IWM. SIR WILLIAM ORPEN, 1917, wl on horseback, pencil and w/c, IWM.
G J.S.SARGENT, 'General Officers of World war I, 1914–18', oil, 1922, NPG 1954.
SC SIGISMUND DE STROBL, 1936, terracotta bust, IWM.
PH WALTER STONEMAN, 2 hs portraits in uniform, 1919 and 1931, NPG (NPR). W.STONEMAN, hs, print, NPG x382.

BIRKENHEAD, Frederick Edwin Smith, 1st Earl of (1872-1930) lord chancellor.
P SIR OSWALD BIRLEY, copy, tql seated, NPG 2552. SIR JOHN LAVERY, hl, profile, Gray's Inn, London. HARRINGTON MANN, c1921, tql in robes, Wadham College, Oxford. GLYN PHILPOT,

tql seated in robes, Gray's Inn.

D EDMOND KAPP, 1914, hs and wl, Barber Institute, Birmingham University.

SC CLARE SHERIDAN, 1924, bronze bust, Gray's Inn.

C SIR LESLIE WARD ('Spy'), wl, lith, for *Vanity Fair*, 16 Jan 1907, NPG. 'NIBS', wl, profile, lith, 9 Aug 1911, NPG. SIR BERNARD PARTRIDGE, wl seated as snake charmer, ink and w/c, for *Punch*, 7 Nov 1927, NPG. SIR B.PARTRIDGE, tql, ink and w/c, for *Punch*, 21 May 1928, NPG. R.S.SHERRIFFS, 1929, hs, profile, ink, NPG 5224(4).

PH WALTER STONEMAN, 1919, hs in robes, NPG (NPR).

BIRKETT, William Norman Birkett, 1st Baron (1883-1962) judge.

C SIR DAVID LOW, 4 heads, profile, pencil, NPG 4529(28–31).

BIRLEY, Sir Oswald Hornby Joseph (1880-1952) painter.

P Self-portrait, 1915, Musée de Luxembourg, Paris.

PH SIR CECIL BEATON, wl with wife and daughter, print, NPG.

BLACKETT, Sir Basil Phillott (1882-1935) financial administrator.

C SIR DAVID LOW, head, profile, pencil, NPG 4529(33).

PH WALTER STONEMAN, 2 hs portraits, 1921 and 1931, NPG (NPR).

BLACKETT, Patrick Maynard Stuart Blackett, 1st Baron (1897-1974) physicist.

P WILLIAM EVANS, tql seated, Royal Society, London. EMANUEL LEVY, 1956, hs, NPG 5010. CLAUDE ROGERS, 1965, tql seated, profile, Imperial College of Science and Technology, London.

C SIR DAVID LOW, 1949, wl seated, chalk, NPG 4565. SIR D.LOW, various sketches, pencil, NPG 4529(34–39).

PH WALTER BIRD, 1966, hs, NPG (NPR). HOWARD COSTER, various sizes and negs, NPG x2986–89. ROGER MAYNE, hs, semi-profile, print, NPG x4069. LUCIA MOHOLY, 1936, hs, print (1978), NPG P127. WALTER STONEMAN, 1942, 4 hl portraits, for NPR, NPG x2986–89.

BLACKMAN, Frederick Frost (1866-1947) plant physiologist.

P HENRY LAMB, 1937, hl, Department of Botany, Cambridge University.

C D.G.LILLIE, wl with Sir Arthur Tansley, w/c, NPG.

BLACKMAN, Vernon Herbert (1872-1967) professor of botany.

SC AUDREY BLACKMAN, c1953, bronze bust, Imperial College of Science and Technology, London.

PH WALTER STONEMAN, 1944, hs, NPG (NPR).

BLACKWELL, Sir Basil Henry (b1889) bookseller.

P VESLA STRANG, 1969, tql seated, Blackwell Scientific Publications, Oxford. JOHN WARD, 1979, hl seated, Basil Blackwell Publishers, Oxford.

PH Various photographers, Blackwell Group Ltd, Oxford.

BLACKWOOD, Algernon Henry (1869-1951) writer.

PR WALTER TITTLE, 1922, head, lith, NPG.

PH HOWARD COSTER, 1929, various sizes, prints and negs, NPG x2265 and x2990–94.

BLAKE, Dame Louisa Brandreth Aldrich-, see Aldrich-Blake.

BLAKISTON, Herbert Edward Douglas (1862-1942) president of Trinity College, Oxford.

P ALLAN GWYNNE-JONES, posthumous, Trinity College.

PH WALTER STONEMAN, 1933, hs, NPG (NPR).

BLAND, Sir (George) Neville (1886-1972) diplomat.

PH WALTER STONEMAN, 2 hs portraits, 1937 and 1957, for NPR, NPG x1093–94.

BLANESBURGH, Robert Younger, Baron (1861-1946) judge.

P H.G.RIVIERE, c1933, Balliol College, Oxford.

BLEDISLOE, Charles Bathurst, Viscount (1867-1958) agriculturist and public servant.

P UNKNOWN, c1919–25?, wl in hunting dress, Royal Agricultural College, Cirencester, Glos.

BLISS, Sir Arthur (1891-1975) composer.

P MARK GERTLER, 1932, hs, NPG 5305.

D RICHARD STONE, 1969–70, head, chalk, NPG 5055.

SC LUCY LYONS, 1965, bronze bust, Royal College of Music, London.

PH HERBERT LAMBERT, c1922, hs, photogravure, NPG x7755. WALTER STONEMAN, 1952, hl, NPG (NPR). WALTER BIRD, 1963, tql seated, NPG (NPR). MARK GERSON, 1966, hs, print, NPG x1083.

BLOGG, Henry George (1876-1954) coxswain of Cromer lifeboat.

P T.C.DUGDALE, 1942, tql, Royal National Lifeboat Institution, London.

D WILLIAM DRING, 1942, pastel, IWM.

SC JAMES WOODFORD, bronze bust, Cromer, Norfolk.

PH OLIVE EDIS, c1942?, hs, print, NPG x5211.

BLOW, Hilda, Mrs Sydney Blow, see Trevelyan.

BLUMENFELD, Ralph David (1864-1948) newspaper editor.

P PATRICK LARKIN, Daily Express, London. NEVILLE LEWIS, 1927, hl seated, Stationers' and Newspaper Makers' Company, London. FAITH K.SAGE, tql, Stationers' Company.

PH HOWARD COSTER, 1929, various sizes and negs, NPG x2158 and x3005–09.

BLUNDEN, Edmund (1896-1974) poet, writer and teacher.

P DOUGLAS BLAND, 1957, tql seated, University of Hong Kong.

D RALPH HODGSON, 1921, hl seated, profile, pencil, NPG 4976. SIR WILLIAM ROTHENSTEIN, 1922, hs, profile, NPG 4977. JOYCE FINZI, 3 heads, 1952, 1953 and early 1960s, Reading University Library.

BODKIN, Sir Archibald Henry (1862-1957) lawyer.

PH WALTER STONEMAN, 1931, hs in robes, NPG (NPR).

BODKIN, Thomas (1887-1961) teacher and writer on art.

P BERNARD FLEETWOOD-WALKER, 1955, Birmingham City Art Gallery. JAMES SLEATOR, hl seated, NGI.

D SEÁN O'SULLIVAN, NGI.

SC SIR CHARLES WHEELER, 1955, terracotta bust, NPG 5015.

PH HOWARD COSTER, various sizes and negs, NPG x3010–14. CHARLES W.HEATH, 1961, various deathbed portraits, prints, NPG x1127–30.

BOLDERO, Sir Harold Esmond Arnison (1889-1960) physician and medical administrator.

P HAROLD KNIGHT, 1957, hl in robes, Middlesex Hospital, London.

PH WALTER STONEMAN, c1950, hs, NPG (NPR).

BOLITHO, Sir Edward Hoblyn Warren (d1969) lieutenant-colonel.

PH OLIVE EDIS, 1931, tql seated, print, NPG x1133.

BOLITHO, (Henry) Hector (1898-1974) biographer.

PH HOWARD COSTER, various sizes and negs, NPG x3015–16 and x10388–95.

BOLS, Sir Louis Jean (1867-1930) lieutenant-general.

PH WALTER STONEMAN, 1919, hs in uniform, NPG (NPR).

BOMBERG, David Garshen (1890-1957) painter.

P Self-portrait, 1937, hl, Slade School of Art, University of London. Self-portrait, 1937, Birmingham City Art Gallery.

D Self-portrait, c1913–14, head, chalk, NPG 4522. Self-portrait, 1931, hs, charcoal and wash, NPG 4821.

BOND, Sir (Charles) Hubert (1870-1945) psychiatrist and administrator.
PH WALTER STONEMAN, 1932, hs in uniform, NPG (NPR).

BONDFIELD, Margaret Grace (1873-1953) politician and first woman cabinet minister.
M W.M.KNIGHT, 1937, head, oval, NPG 3966.
PH WALTER STONEMAN, 1930, hs, NPG (NPR).

BONE, Sir Muirhead (1876-1953) draughtsman, etcher and painter.
P STEPHEN BONE, wl, Dundee City Art Gallery.
D FRANCIS DODD, 1907, tql, ink, SNPG 2057. F.DODD, 1931, tql seated, chalk, NPG 4428. STANLEY SPENCER, head, pencil, NPG 4453.
SC JACOB EPSTEIN, bronze head, Dundee City Art Gallery.
PR F.DODD, tql seated, etch, 1st and 2nd state, NPG 3079 and 3079a.

BONHAM-CARTER, Sir Edgar (1870-1956) jurist and administrator.
PH WALTER STONEMAN, 1931, hs, NPG (NPR).

BONHAM-CARTER, Helen Violet, see Baroness Asquith.

BONNEY (William Francis) Victor (1872-1953) gynaecologist.
P SIR OSWALD BIRLEY, 1926, tql seated, Royal College of Surgeons, London.
G MOUSSA AYOUB, 'Council of College of Surgeons, 1926–27', oil, c1927–29, Royal College of Surgeons.

BORDEN, Mary, Lady Spears (1886-1968) writer.
PH HOWARD COSTER, 1931, various sizes, print and negs, NPG X10441–44 and X2284.

BOSANQUET, Robert Carr (1871-1935) archaeologist.
PH UNKNOWN, hs, semi-profile, print, School of Archaeology and Oriental Studies, Liverpool University.

BOSWELL, Percy George Hamnall (1886-1960) geologist.
PH LAFAYETTE LTD, 1935, hs, print, NPG X1174. WALTER STONEMAN, 1945, 2 hs portraits, NPG X1173 and NPG (NPR).

BOTHA, Louis (1862-1919) South African soldier and statesman.
P SIR JAMES GUTHRIE, c1919–21, hs in uniform, SNPG 1139, study sketch for 'Statesmen', NPG 2463. J.BLAIR LEIGHTON, 1924, tql in uniform, Palace of Westminster, London.
D J.S.SARGENT, c1921, wl, pencil, NPG 2908(8), study sketch for 'Generals of WWI', NPG 1954.
G J.S.SARGENT, 'General Officers of World War I, 1914–18', oil, 1922, NPG 1954. SIR J.GUTHRIE, 'Statesmen of World War I, 1914–18', oil, c1924–30, NPG 2463.
C 'RYG', wl, lith, Vanity Fair, 29 May 1907, NPG.

BOTTOMLEY, Gordon (1874-1948) poet and dramatist.
P SIR JAMES GUTHRIE, 1923, hs, Carlisle City Art Gallery. A.K.HENDERSON, c1939?, hs, Carlisle Gallery.
D PAUL NASH, 1912, hs, ink, Carlisle Gallery. SIR WILLIAM ROTHENSTEIN, 1916, hs, pencil, Carlisle Gallery. BEN J.FLETCHER, 1918, charcoal and chalk, Carlisle Gallery. P.NASH, 1922, head, pencil and chalk, Carlisle Gallery. SIR W.ROTHENSTEIN, 1922, head, chalk, Carlisle Gallery. C.H.SHANNON, 1924, head, profile, chalk, NPG 4150.
PH T.R.ANNAN & SONS, 1930s, hs, profile, print, NPG X3772. HOWARD COSTER, 1939, various sizes and negs, NPG X2206 and X3041–51.

BOTTOMLEY, Horatio William (1860-1933) journalist and politician.
D EDMOND KAPP, 1928, head, Barber Institute, Birmingham University.
PH SIR BENJAMIN STONE, 1911, wl, print, NPG.

BOTTOMLEY, Sir Norman Howard (1891-1970) air chief marshal.
P T.C.DUGDALE, IWM.
PH HOWARD COSTER, early 1940s, various sizes and negs in uniform, NPG X3037–40.

BOUGHTON, Rutland (1870-1960) composer.
D CHRISTINA WASHE, 1911, hs, pencil, NPG 4932.
PH HERBERT LAMBERT, c1921, hs, profile, print, NPG P111.

BOULT, Sir Adrian (b1889) conductor.
P KAZUNORI ISHIBASHI, 1923, tql seated, Royal College of Music, London.
D EDMOND KAPP, 1932, chalk, Barber Institute, Birmingham University. RICHARD STONE, 1972, head, profile, chalk, NPG 4906. HILDA WIENER, pencil, Royal College of Music.
SC WILLIAM REDGRAVE, bronze head, Royal Festival Hall, London.
PR E.KAPP, c1932, tql, lith, NPG 5130.
PH HOWARD COSTER, 1933, various sizes, prints and negs, NPG X1747, AX3472, X3051–53 and X10445–51. WALTER STONEMAN, 2 hl portraits, 1942 and 1953, NPG (NPR). KARL POLLAK, 1948, 2 hl portraits, prints, NPG. CRISPIAN WOODGATE, 1950s, various sizes and prints, NPG X1180–83. WALTER BIRD, 1963, hs, NPG (NPR). J.S.LEWINSKI, 1967, hl, profile, print, NPG. SEFTON SAMUELS, 1969, 2 tql portraits, prints, NPG. LAELIA GOEHR, before 1977, various sizes and prints, NPG X5589–96.

BOURCHIER, Arthur (1863-1927) actor-manager.
P CHARLES BUCHEL, 1906, as Shylock, Royal Shakespeare Theatre, Stratford-upon-Avon. C.BUCHEL, 1910, wl as Henry VIII, Strand Theatre, London. SIR GERALD KELLY, 1923, wl as Long John Silver, Garrick Club, London.
D C.BUCHEL, 1905, as Shylock, w/c, Strand Theatre.
C SIR LESLIE WARD ('Spy'), tql, lith, Vanity Fair, 5 March 1896, NPG.
PH ELLIS & WALERY, tql as Shylock, postcard, NPG X1189. HISTED, hs, photogravure, NPG X6414. LANGFIER, tql, postcard, NPG X1188.

BOURDILLON, Sir Bernard Henry (1883-1948) colonial governor.
PH WALTER STONEMAN, hs, for NPR, NPG X4666.

BOURNE, Sir Alan George Barwys (1882-1967) general.
PH WALTER STONEMAN, 1945, hs in uniform, NPG (NPR).

BOURNE, Francis Alphonsus (1861-1935) archbishop of Westminster and cardinal.
P SIR JOHN LAVERY, 1921, tql seated in robes, Allen Hall, Westminster Diocesan Seminary, London. A.CHEVALLIER TAYLER, 1934, tql in robes, profile, Archbishop's House, Westminster, London.
C SIR LESLIE WARD, 1910?, wl in robes, w/c, NPG 4592.
PH G.C.BERESFORD, 3 portraits in robes, 1905, 1912 and 1922, negs, NPG X6443–45.

BOURNE, Robert Croft (1888-1938) politician and oarsman.
C 'APE JUNIOR', wl profile, mechanical repro, Vanity Fair, 29 March 1911, NPG.

BOWATER, Sir Eric Vansittart (1895-1962) industrialist.
P ANNA ZINKEISEN, Bowaters United Kingdom Paper Company, London.

BOWEN, Elizabeth (1899-1973) novelist.

P ANDRE DURAND, 1969, tql seated, NPG 5134.

PH SIR CECIL BEATON, 1943, hl, print, NPG. HOWARD COSTER, various sizes and negs, NPG x3054–57.

BOWEN, Marjorie, see Gabrielle Margaret Vere LONG.

BOWHILL, Sir Frederick William (1880-1960) air chief marshal.

P TOM GILFILLAN, hl in uniform, Royal Aero Club on loan to RAF Museum, Hendon. J.HUGHES-HALLETT, copy, hl in uniform, on loan to RAF Museum.

PH HOWARD COSTER, various sizes and negs in uniform, NPG x3073–80.

BOWLEY, Sir Arthur Lyon (1869-1957) statistician.

P STELLA BOWEN, 1936, hs, London School of Economics.

PH WALTER STONEMAN, 2 hs portraits, 1922 and 1945, NPG (NPR).

BOWMAN, Sir James (b1898) trade unionist and public servant.

C SIR DAVID LOW, several heads, profile, pencil, NPG 4529(52–55).

BOWRA, Sir Maurice (1898-1971) classical scholar and writer.

P HENRY LAMB, 1952, tql seated, Wadham College, Oxford; study sketch, chalk, NPG 4667.

BOYCE, Sir Rubert William (1863-1911) pathologist and hygienist.

P R.E.MORRISON, University of Liverpool.

BOYCOTT, Arthur Edwin (1877-1938) pathologist and naturalist.

PH WALTER STONEMAN, 1921, hs, NPG (NPR).

BOYD-ORR, John Boyd Orr, 1st Baron (1880-1971) nutritionist and first director of UN Food and Agriculture Organization.

SC BENNO SCHOTZ, 1950, bronze head, Hunterian Art Gallery, Glasgow University.

PH WALTER STONEMAN, 1953, hs, NPG (NPR).

BOYLE, Sir William Henry Dudley, see 12th Earl of Cork and Orrery.

BRABAZON of Tara, John Theodore Moore-Brabazon, 1st Baron (1884-1964) statesman and sportsman.

P FRANK EASTMAN, 1951, hs, Royal Aero Club on loan to RAF Museum, Hendon. A.E.COOPER, 1958, RAF Museum.

D A.E.COOPER, 1958, hs, pastel, NPG 4442.

SC DAVID McFALL, 1964, bronze bust, Royal Institution of Great Britain, London.

PH SIR CECIL BEATON, 1940, hl, print, NPG. WALTER STONEMAN, 1944, hs, NPG (NPR). WALTER BIRD, 1962, hs, NPG (NPR).

BRADBURY, John Swanwick Bradbury, 1st Baron (1872-1950) civil servant.

C POWYS EVANS ('Quiz'), hl, lith, for *The Saturday Review*, 3 Oct 1925, NPG.

BRADFORD, Sir John Rose, Bart (1863-1935) physician and physiologist.

P RANDOLPH SCHWABE, posthumous, University College Hospital, London.

BRAGG, Sir William Henry (1862-1942) physicist and crystallographer.

P SIR WILLIAM NICHOLSON, 1932, Royal Institution of Great Britain, London. C.E.S.PHILLIPS, 1939, Royal Institution. HAROLD KNIGHT, 1941, tql seated in robes, Royal Society, London.

D ERIC KENNINGTON, 1927, pencil, Trinity College, Cambridge. RANDOLPH SCHWABE, 1932, hs, pencil, NPG 3255. SIR WILLIAM

ROTHENSTEIN, 1934, head, sanguine, Carlisle City Art Gallery. TOM PURVIS, pen and ink, Royal Institution.

PH WALTER STONEMAN, 3 hs portraits, 1920, 1931 and 1938, NPG (NPR).

BRAGG, Sir (William) Lawrence (1890-1971) physicist and crystallographer.

D R.J.BURN, 1950, chalk, Trinity College, Cambridge.

G TERENCE CUNEO, lecturing to children, oil, 1962, Royal Institution of Great Britain, London.

SC JOHN MILLS, c1966, bronze bust, Royal Institution. J.MILLS, 1967, bronze relief portrait, Royal Institution.

PH GODFREY ARGENT, 1970, hs, for NPR, NPG x1356–57. ELLIOT & FRY, 3 portraits, prints, NPG x1359–61. WALTER STONEMAN, 1943, hl, NPG (NPR). UNKNOWN, c1937–38, hl, print, NPG x1355.

BRAID, James (1870-1950) golfer.

P SIR JAMES GUNN, hl, Walton Heath Golf Club, Tadworth, Surrey.

C SIR LESLIE WARD ('Spy'), wl with club, lith, for *Vanity Fair*, 26 June 1907, NPG. SIR BERNARD PARTRIDGE, with 5 others for *Punch's Almanack*, 1922, pen, pencil and w/c, V & A.

PH UNKNOWN, hs, print, Walton Heath Golf Club.

BRAIN of Eynsham, Walter Russell Brain, 1st Baron (1895-1966) physician and neurologist.

SC SIR JACOB EPSTEIN, 1959, bronze bust, Royal College of Physicians, London.

PH WALTER STONEMAN, 1952, hs, NPG (NPR). WALTER BIRD, 1962, hs, NPG (NPR).

BRAITHWAITE, Dame (Florence) Lilian (1873-1948) actress.

PR HOWARD VAN DUSEN AND HASSALL, hs and wl in character, lith, NPG.

C R.S.SHERRIFFS, 1937, head, ink and grey wash, NPG.

PH MRS ALBERT BROOM, various sizes and negs, NPG x768, x925 and x1364–66. UNKNOWN, hs, postcard, NPG x1367.

BRAITHWAITE, Sir Walter Pipon (1865-1945) general.

PH WALTER STONEMAN, 3 hs portraits, the 1st in uniform, 1919, 1931 and 1943, NPG (NPR).

BRAITHWAITE, Warwick (1896-1971) conductor.

PH HOWARD COSTER, various sizes and negs, NPG x3104–07.

BRANCKER, Sir William Sefton (1877-1930) major-general and air vice-marshal.

D FRANCIS DODD, 1918, hs?, charcoal and w/c, IWM. SIR BERNARD PARTRIDGE, 1929, wl seated, pencil, NPG 3665.

SC L.F.ROSLYN, 1919, bronze bust, IWM.

PH HOWARD COSTER, c1926, various sizes, prints and negs, NPG x2245, x3118–25 and x3538–40.

BRANGWYN, Sir Frank (1867-1956) artist.

P Self-portrait, 1920, hs, Uffizi, Florence. JAMES KERR-LAWSON, c1936, tql seated, Ferens Art Gallery, Hull.

D WALTER HODGSON, 1892, hs, profile, pencil and w/c, NPG 4041(5). PHIL MAY, c1904, hs, chalk, NPG 4057. ALBERT DE BELLEROCHE, 1922, hs with palette, chalk, Brangwyn Museum, Bruges, Belgium. LOUIS GINNETT, 1936, head, chalk, NPG 5194. A.H.KNIGHTON-HAMMOND, 1937, hl, sanguine, NPG 4374. JOSEPH SIMPSON, 1930s, hs, charcoal, Carlisle City Art Gallery; and tql, pencil and w/c, William Morris Gallery, Walthamstow, London. AUGUSTUS JOHN, 1947, hs, profile, chalk, Morris Gallery. Several self-portraits, Morris Gallery, Dundee City Art Gallery and Ferens Gallery.

SC ALFRED DRURY, 1918, bronze bust, Herbert Art Gallery, Coventry. ANASTAS BOTZARITCH SAVA, c1925–30?, sculpture, Ferens

Gallery. ALBERT TOFT, 1938, bronze statuette, Morris Gallery; bust, National Museum of Wales, Cardiff.

PR ERNEST LUMSDEN, 1921, tql seated, etch, Morris Gallery. A.H.KNIGHTON-HAMMOND, 1939, hl seated, etch, NPG 4373. J.SIMPSON, 1930s, tql seated, etch, NPG. J.SIMPSON, hs, woodcut with w/c wash, Morris Gallery.

C POWYS EVANS, 1922, ink, National Museum of Wales.

PH A.L.COBURN, 1904, hs, photogravure, NPG AX7771. LOCKETT THOMSON, 1926, 2 hl portraits, prints, NPG X4272–73. UNKNOWN, hs, print, NPG X4271.

BRAYTON, Lily (1876-1953) actress.

M WINIFRED C.DONGWORTH, 1921, head in character for *Chu Chin Chow*, oval, NPG 5032. W.C.DONGWORTH, 1920s, hs, profile, oval, NPG 5033.

PH ELLIS & WALERY, hl, profile, photogravure, NPG X6416. HISTED, 1901, hs, photogravure, NPG X6417. UNKNOWN, hs, profile, postcard, NPG X4282.

BRENAN, (Edward Fitz-) Gerald (b1894) writer.

P DORA CARRINGTON, c1921, hs, NPG 5197.

PH JOHN HOPE-JOHNSTONE, c1922, 2 tql seated portraits, prints, NPG P134(20–21).

BRENTFORD, William Joynson-Hicks, 1st Viscount (1865-1932) statesman.

P SIR A.S.COPE, c1930, hl, Scotland Yard, London.

C SIR BERNARD PARTRIDGE, with 5 others, drg, for *Punch*, 21 May 1928, V & A.

PH WALTER STONEMAN, 1925, hs, NPG (NPR).

BRESSEY, Sir Charles Herbert (1874-1951) civil engineer.

PH WALTER STONEMAN, 1940, hs, for NPR, NPG X4161.

BRETT, Oliver Sylvain Balliol, see 3rd Viscount Esher.

BRIAN, Havergal (1876-1972) composer.

PH JOHN GOLDBLATT, c1970–71, 3 portraits, prints, NPG X1465–67.

BRIDGE, Frank (1879-1941) composer.

D MARJORIE FORSS, several wl sketches, pencil, Royal College of Music, London.

SC UNKNOWN, 1941, plaster death mask, Royal College of Music.

PH HERBERT LAMBERT, c1922, hs, photogravure, NPG AX7749. Various photographs, Royal College of Music.

BRIDGES, Edward Ettingdene Bridges, 1st Baron (1892-1969) public servant.

P ALLAN GWYNNE-JONES, 1962, hl in robes, University of Reading.

PH WALTER STONEMAN, 1940, hs, NPG (NPR).

BRIDGES, Sir (George) Tom (Molesworth) (1871-1939) lieutenant-general.

D FRANCIS DODD, 1918, hs?, charcoal and w/c, IWM.

PH WALTER STONEMAN, 1918, hs in uniform, NPG (NPR).

BRIDIE, James, see Osborne Henry MAVOR.

BRITTAIN, Vera Mary (1894-1970) author and journalist.

PH HOWARD COSTER, 1936, various sizes, prints and negs, NPG X1754 and X3142–47. MARK GERSON, 1954, hs, print, NPG X4305.

BROAD, Charlie Dunbar (1887-1971) professor of moral philosophy.

D RUSKIN SPEAR, 1948, hs?, chalk, Trinity College, Cambridge.

PH WALTER STONEMAN, 1930, hl, NPG (NPR).

BROCK, Sir Osmond de Beauvoir (1869-1947) admiral.

D FRANCIS DODD, 1917, hs?, charcoal and w/c, IWM.

G SIR A.S.COPE, 'Naval Officers of World War I, 1914–18', oil, 1921, NPG 1913.

PH WALTER STONEMAN, 2 hs portraits in uniform, 1919 and 1934, NPG (NPR).

BROCKHURST, Gerald Leslie (b1890) painter and etcher.

PH HOWARD COSTER, c1938, various sizes, prints and negs, NPG X1755–56 and X3151–70. UNKNOWN, 1947, tql with wife, print, NPG X725.

BRODZKY, Horace (1885-1969) painter, draughtsman and etcher.

P NINA HAMNETT, c1915, tql seated, Southampton Art Gallery.

D HENRI GAUDIER-BRZESKA, c1913, hs, chalk, Princeton University Art Museum, New Jersey, USA.

SC H.GAUDIER-BRZESKA, 1913, bronze bust, TATE T129.

PR Self-portrait, 1919, lino-cut, V & A.

BROGAN, Sir Denis William (1900-1974) political scientist and writer.

PH HOWARD COSTER, various sizes and negs, NPG X3171–74. WALTER STONEMAN, 1955, hl, NPG (NPR).

BROOK, Clive (1887-1974) actor.

PH SIR CECIL BEATON, 1930, tql seated, profile, print, NPG.

BROOKE, Alan England (1863-1939) Biblical scholar.

P HENRY LAMB, King's College, Cambridge.

PH WALTER STONEMAN, 1934, hs, NPG (NPR).

BROOKE, Basil Stanlake, see 1st Viscount Brookeborough.

BROOKE, Rupert Chawner (1887-1915) poet.

P CLARA EWALD, 1911, hs, NPG 4911; version, King's College, Cambridge.

D J.H.THOMAS, posthumous, head, profile, oval, pencil, NPG 2448.

PH SPEIGHT, 1903, hs, oval, carte, NPG X4696. GEORGE A.DEAN, 1905, hl, carte, NPG X4697. SCOTT & WILKINSON, 1906, wl in classical dress, print, NPG X4698. V.H.MOTTRAM, c1907, hs, profile, print, NPG X4700. EMERY WALKER, after Sherrill Schell, 1913, various sizes, glass positive, NPG P101 (a–g). UNKNOWN, 1913, wl seated with D.C.Scott, print, NPG X4699. UNKNOWN, hs, print, NPG X4701.

BROOKEBOROUGH, Basil Stanlake Brooke, 1st Viscount (1888-1973) statesman.

PH HOWARD COSTER, various sizes and negs, NPG X3183–86. WALTER STONEMAN, 1948, hl, NPG (NPR). WALTER BIRD, 1962, hl, NPG (NPR).

BROOKE-POPHAM, Sir (Henry) Robert (Moore) (1878-1953) air chief marshal.

P T.C.DUGDALE, IWM.

PH WALTER STONEMAN, 1943, hs in uniform, NPG (NPR).

BROOKS, Sir (Reginald Alexander) Dallas (1896-1966) commandant-general Royal Marines.

PH WALTER STONEMAN, 1944, hs in uniform, NPG (NPR). LENARE, 1948, several sizes and negs, one with wife, NPG X3319–21.

BROOKS, (William) Collin (1887-1959) writer.

PH HOWARD COSTER, 1935, various sizes, prints and negs, NPG AX3514, X3187–91 and X10480–81.

BROPHY, John (1899-1965) writer.

PH HOWARD COSTER, head, neg, NPG X3192.

BROUGH, Robert (1872-1905) artist.

D JAMES CADENHEAD, pencil, SNPG 1228.

SC FRANCIS DERWENT WOOD, bronze head, SNPG 1477.

BROWN, Sir Arthur Whitten (1886-1948) air navigator and engineer.

P SIR JOHN LAVERY, hl, Royal Aero Club on loan to RAF Museum, Hendon.

PH Various photographs, Royal Aeronautical Society, London.

BROWN, Douglas Clifton, see 1st Viscount Ruffside.

BROWN, Ernest (1881-1962) statesman and free churchman.
C SIR DAVID LOW, hs, profile, pencil, NPG 4529(67).
PH HOWARD COSTER, various sizes, prints and negs, NPG X1759 and X3203–09. WALTER STONEMAN, 1941, hl, NPG (NPR).

BROWN, F.Gregory (1887-1941) artist.
PH HOWARD COSTER, c1927, various sizes, print and negs, NPG AX3434 and X3210–25.

BROWN, Ivor John Carnegie (1891-1974) drama critic and author.
PH ANGUS MCBEAN, c1950, hs, print, NPG P57. HOWARD COSTER, various sizes and negs, NPG X3226–31.

BROWN, Sir John (1880-1958) lieutenant-general Territorial Army.
PH WALTER STONEMAN, 1934, hs, NPG (NPR).

BROWN, Sir Walter Langdon-, see Langdon-Brown.

BROWN, William Francis (1862-1951) Roman Catholic Bishop.
PH HOWARD COSTER, various sizes and negs, NPG X3232–39.

BROWN, William John (1894-1960) union leader, politician and writer.
PH HOWARD COSTER, 1930s, various sizes, prints and negs, NPG X1760, AX3452, AX3518 and X3242–59. WALTER STONEMAN, 1948, hl, NPG (NPR).

BROWNE, Edward Granville (1862-1926) Persian scholar and orientalist.
P CHARLES SHANNON, Pembroke College, Cambridge.

BROWNE, Valentine Edward Charles, see 6th Earl of Kenmare.

BROWNING, Sir Frederick (Arthur Montague) (1896-1965) lieutenant-general.
PH WALTER STONEMAN, 2 hl portraits, the 1st in uniform, 1944 and 1955, NPG (NPR).

BROWNING, Sir Montague Edward (1863-1947) admiral.
G SIR A.S.COPE, 'Naval Officers of World War I, 1914–18', oil, 1921, NPG 1913.
PH WALTER STONEMAN, 1919, hs in uniform, NPG (NPR).

BRUCE, Sir Henry Harvey (1862-1948) admiral.
D FRANCIS DODD, 1917, charcoal and w/c, IWM.

BRUCE, Clarence Napier, see 3rd Baron Aberdare.

BRUNDRETT, Sir Frederick (1894-1974) scientific adviser to Ministry of Defence.
PH WALTER STONEMAN, 1954, hl, NPG (NPR). WALTER BIRD, 1965, hs, NPG (NPR).

BRYANT, Sir Arthur (Wynne Morgan) (b1899) historian.
PH PAUL TANQUERAY, 1931, hl, print, NPG X7255. HOWARD COSTER, c1934, various sizes, print and negs, NPG AX3502 and X3277–87.

BRZESKA, Henri Gaudier-, see Gaudier-Brzeska.

BUCHAN, Charles Murray (1891-1960) footballer and journalist.
PH UNKNOWN, hs, print, NPG X4852.

BUCHAN, John, see 1st Baron Tweedsmuir.

BUCHANAN, George (1890-1955) politician.
PH WALTER STONEMAN, 1946, hs, NPG (NPR).

BUCHANAN, Sir George Cunningham (1865-1940) civil engineer.
PH WALTER STONEMAN, 1932, hs, NPG (NPR).

BUCHMAN, Frank Nathan Daniel (1878-1961) founder of 'Moral Re-Armament' Association.

D EDMOND KAPP, 1935, Barber Institute, Birmingham University.
PH HOWARD COSTER, c1937, various sizes and negs, NPG X3315–27.

BUCKMASTER, Stanley Owen Buckmaster, 1st Viscount (1861-1934) lord chancellor and statesman.
P G.FIDDES WATT, c1920, hl in robes, Lincoln's Inn, London. R.G.EVES, posthumous, hs in robes, Christ Church, Oxford.
D EDMOND KAPP, 1929, Barber Institute, Birmingham University.
C 'OWL', nearly wl in robes, mechanical repro, for Vanity Fair, 19 Nov 1913, NPG. HARRY FURNISS, 2 wl, ink, NPG 3426–27.
PH JOHN RUSSELL & SONS, 1915, hs in robes, NPG (NPR).

BUCKNILL, Sir Alfred (Townsend) (1880-1963) judge.
PH WALTER STONEMAN, 1936, hs, NPG (NPR).

BULFIN, Sir Edward Stanislaus (1862-1939) general.
P JAMES MCEVOY, 1918, IWM.
PH WALTER STONEMAN, 1920, hs in uniform, NPG (NPR).

BULLETT, Gerald William (1893-1958) writer.
PH HOWARD COSTER, 1926 and 1954, various sizes, prints and negs, NPG AX2244, X2293–96 and X3328–36.

BULLOCH, William (1868-1941) bacteriologist, pathologist and medical historian.
P SIR LUKE FILDES, 1913, hs, University of Aberdeen.
PH WALTER STONEMAN, 1917, hs, NPG (NPR).

BULLOUGH, Elsie (1886-1962) actress 'Lily Elsie'.
P SIR J.J.SHANNON, c1916, hl, NPG 4322.
PR HOWARD VAN DUSEN AND HASSALL, hs and wl, lith, NPG.
PH SIR CECIL BEATON, hl, print. MRS ALBERT BROOM, wl, neg, NPG X1092. ROTARY PHOTO, hs, postcard, NPG.

BULWER-LYTTON, Victor Alexander George, see 2nd Earl of Lytton.

BURGE, Hubert Murray (1862-1925) bishop of Southwark and Oxford.
P GEORGE HARCOURT, 1921, tql seated, Winchester College, Hants. M.I.COHEN, 1920s, tql seated in robes, Diocese of Oxford.
C SIR LESLIE WARD ('Spy'), wl in academic robes, lith, for Vanity Fair, 2 July 1903, NPG.
PH UNKNOWN, tql, print, NPG (Anglican Bishops).

BURKITT, Francis Crawford (1864-1935) professor of divinity.
PH WALTER STONEMAN, 1921, hs, NPG (NPR).

BURNET, John (1863-1928) classical scholar.
PH WALTER STONEMAN, 1917, hs, NPG (NPR).

BURNETT, Dame Ivy Compton-, see Compton-Burnett.

BURNETT, Sir Robert Lindsay (1887-1959) admiral.
P EDWARD ROWORTH, 1950, hl seated in uniform, NMM, Greenwich.
D WILLIAM DRING, 1942, pastel, IWM.
PH WALTER STONEMAN, 2 hl portraits in uniform, 1942 and 1953, NPG (NPR).

BURNETT-STUART, Sir John Theodosius (1875-1958) general.
PH WALTER STONEMAN, 1920, hs, NPG (NPR).

BURNHAM, Sir Harry Lawson Webster Levy-Lawson, 1st Viscount (1862-1933) newspaper proprietor and public servant.
PH JOHN RUSSELL & SONS, c1915, hs, print, for National Photographic Record, vol 1, NPG. WALTER STONEMAN, 1932, hs, NPG (NPR).

BURRELL, Sir William (1861-1958) art collector.
PH Various photographs, Burrell Coll, Glasgow Art Gallery.

BURROWS, Christine Mary Elizabeth (1872-1959) prin-

cipal of St Hilda's and St Anne's Colleges, Oxford.
P CATHERINE OULESS, c1927, St Hilda's College.
D L.LESLIE BROOKE, 1919, hs, chalk, St Hilda's College. JANE DE GLEHN, 1929, chalk, St Anne's College.

BURROWS, Sir Frederick (1887-1973) last governor of Bengal.
PH WALTER STONEMAN, 1946, hs, NPG (NPR).

BURT, Sir Cyril (1883-1971) professor of psychology.
PH WALTER STONEMAN, 1947, hs, NPG (NPR).

BURTON, Sir Montague Maurice (1885-1952) multiple tailor.
P R.G.LEWIS, hs, Burton Group Ltd, Leeds.
PH Various photographs, Burton Group.

BURY, John Bagnell (1861-1927) classical scholar and historian.
PH WALTER STONEMAN, 1919, 2 hs portraits, NPG (NPR).

BUTLER, Sir Harold Beresford (1883-1951) public servant.
P FRANK EASTMAN, Nuffield College, Oxford.
PH WALTER STONEMAN, 1948, hs, NPG (NPR).

BUTLER, Sir James (Ramsay Montague) (1889-1975) historian and educationist.
D HENRY LAMB, 1949, pencil, Trinity College, Cambridge.
PH WALTER BIRD, 1962, hs, NPG (NPR).

BUTLER, Sir Montagu Sherard Dawes (1873-1952) Indian administrator and master of Pembroke College, Cambridge.
PH WALTER STONEMAN, 1932, hs, NPG (NPR).

BUTLER, Sir Neville Montagu (1893-1973) statesman and diplomat.
PH WALTER STONEMAN, 1947, hs, NPG (NPR). LENARE, 1949, various sizes and negs, some with family, NPG X4014-20.

BUTLER, Sir (Spencer) Harcourt (1869-1938) Indian administrator.

SC G.H.THOMAS, c1925, equestrian statue, Lucknow, India. G.H.THOMAS, c1931, statue, Rangoon, Burma.
PH WALTER STONEMAN, 1930, hs, NPG (NPR).

BUTLIN, Sir William Edmund (1899-1977) founder of Butlin's Holiday Camps.
C SIR DAVID LOW, several heads, pencil, NPG 4529(69–70).

BUTT, Sir Alfred, 1st Bart (1878-1962) bloodstock breeder, politician and theatre manager.
C 'H.C.O.', wl, Hentschel-Colourtype, for *Vanity Fair*, 21 Dec 1910, NPG.
PH LENARE, 1946, various sizes and negs, NPG X1300–04.

BUTT, Dame Clara Ellen (1872-1936) singer.
PH DINHAM, c1900, tql with her husband, Kennerley Rumford, postcard, NPG X4935. DOVER STREET STUDIOS, 1911, wl in character, print, NPG X1449. OLIVE EDIS, 1920s, wl, print, NPG X4934.

BUTTERWORTH, George Sainton Kaye (1885-1916) composer.
PH ROSSMONT, hs, print, Royal College of Music, London.

BUXTON, Noel Edward Noel-, see 1st Baron Noel-Buxton.

BUXTON, Patrick Alfred (1892-1955) medical entomologist.
PH WALTER STONEMAN, 1955, hs, NPG (NPR).

BYNG of Vimy, Julian Hedworth George Byng, 1st Viscount (1862-1935) field-marshal.
P P.A.DE LÁSZLÓ, 1933, tql seated in uniform, NPG 3786. F.O.SALISBURY, hs in uniform, semi-profile, IWM.
D FRANCIS DODD, 1917, charcoal and w/c, IWM. J.S.SARGENT, wl, sketch for 'General Officers', NPG 2908(5).
G J.S.SARGENT, 'General Officers of World War I, 1914–18', oil, 1922, NPG 1954.
C SIR BERNARD PARTRIDGE, 1926, wl, ink, NPG 3666.
PH WALTER STONEMAN, 1918-19, hs, NPG (NPR).

C

CABLE, (Alice) Mildred (1878-1952) missionary.
P E.O.FEARNLEY-WHITTINGSTALL, 1953, hs, British and Foreign Bible Society, London.
PH Various photographs, Bible Society, London.

CADE, Sir Stanford (1895-1973) surgeon and specialist in radium treatment of cancer.
PH WALTER STONEMAN, 1946, hs in uniform, NPG (NPR). WALTER BIRD, 1959, hs, NPG (NPR).

CADMAN, John Cadman, 1st Baron (1877-1941) scientist and public servant.
P J.A.A.BERRIE, tql seated, British Petroleum Co Ltd, London.
PH WALTER STONEMAN, 1933, hs, NPG (NPR).

CADOGAN, Sir Alexander George Montagu (1884-1968) public servant.
PH WALTER STONEMAN, 3 hs portraits, 1934, 1941 and 1953, NPG (NPR).

CAIRD, Sir James, 1st Bart (1864-1954) shipowner and founder of the National Maritime Museum, Greenwich.
SC SIR W.R.DICK, c1936, marble bust, NMM, Greenwich.
PH Several photographs, NMM.

CAIRNS, David Smith (1862-1946) Scottish theologian.
P GORDON SHIELDS, Christ's College, Aberdeen.

CAIRNS, Sir Hugh William Bell (1896-1952) neurosurgeon.
PH WALTER STONEMAN, 1947, hs, NPG (NPR).

CALDECOTE, Thomas Walker Hobart Inskip, 1st Viscount (1876-1947) lawyer and statesman.
P AUGUSTUS JOHN, 1942, hl, Inner Temple, London.

CALLENDER, Sir Geoffrey Arthur Romaine (1875-1946) naval historian and first director of the National Maritime Museum, Greenwich.
P D.S.EWART, 1945, hl in robes, NMM, Greenwich.
PH WALTER STONEMAN, 1944, hl, NPG (NPR).

CALMAN, William Thomas (1871-1952) zoologist.
PR W.T.MORNINGTON, 1936, lith, BM (Natural History).

CALTHORPE, Sir Somerset Arthur Gough- (1864-1937) admiral.
P PHILIP CONNARD, 1918, IWM.
PH WALTER STONEMAN, 1925, hs and hl in uniform, NPG (NPR).

CAMBRIDGE, Alexander Augustus Frederick William, see 1st Earl of Athlone.

CAMERON, Sir David Young (1865-1945) painter and etcher.
P A.K.LAWRENCE, hs, SNPG 2193.
PH UNKNOWN, hl, profile, print, NPG X5017.

CAMERON, Sir Donald Charles (1872-1948) colonial governor.
PH WALTER STONEMAN, 1932, hs, NPG (NPR).

CAMERON, (George) Basil (1884-1975) conductor.
D EDMOND KAPP, 1943, Barber Institute, Birmingham University.
PH UNKNOWN, c1966, hs, print, NPG X5016.

CAMM, Sir Sydney (1893-1966) aviation pioneer.
P FRANK EASTMAN, c1954-55, hs, Royal Aeronautical Society, London.

CAMPBELL, Sir Gerald (1879-1964) diplomat.
PH HOWARD COSTER, various sizes and negs, NPG X3548-53. WALTER STONEMAN, 2 hs portraits, the 1st in uniform, 1934 and 1953, NPG (NPR).

CAMPBELL, Gordon (1886-1953) vice-admiral.
D FRANCIS DODD, 1917, charcoal and w/c, IWM.

CAMPBELL, Henry Colville Montgomery (1887-1970) bishop of London.
P A.R.THOMSON, 1961, wl in robes, Fulham Palace, London.

CAMPBELL, Sir Malcolm (1885-1948) racing motorist.
SC H.A.STERMANN, c1935, bronze mask, NPG 4195.

CAMPBELL, Mrs Patrick, née Beatrice Stella Tanner (1865-1940) actress.
P CHARLES SHANNON, 1907, tql seated, TATE 2995. J.S.ELAND, hs, Garrick Club, London.
PR VIOLET, DUCHESS OF RUTLAND, hs, lith, NPG.
PH SIR CECIL BEATON, 1938, hl, print, NPG. G.C.BERESFORD, 1902, 3 hs portraits, negs, NPG X6459-60, and print, X5039. BIOGRAPH, c1901, wl, print, NPG X4611. UNKNOWN, hl, profile, print, NPG X5040. UNKNOWN, tql, oval, print, NPG X5041.

CAMPBELL, Sir Ronald Hugh (1883-1953) diplomat.
PH WALTER STONEMAN, 1938, hl, NPG (NPR).

CAMPION, Gilbert Francis Montriou Campion, 1st Baron (1882-1958) clerk of the House of Commons.
PH VANDYK, hl seated in robes, print, NPG X5022.

CAMROSE, William Ewert Berry, 1st Viscount (1879-1954) newspaper proprietor.
P SIR OSWALD BIRLEY, tql seated, Daily Telegraph, London.
PH HOWARD COSTER, c1939, various sizes and negs, NPG X10258-65.

CAPE, (Herbert) Jonathan (1879-1960) publisher.
P COLIN COLAHAN, hl seated, Jonathan Cape Ltd, London.
PH Various photographs, Jonathan Cape.

CAREY, (Francis) Clive (Savill) (1883-1968) professor of music.
P CLARA EWALD, c1910, hs, Royal College of Music, London.
C UNKNOWN, pencil, Royal College of Music.

CARLING, Sir Ernest Rock (1877-1960) surgeon and pioneer in radiotherapy.
P A.C.DAVIDSON-HOUSTON, Westminster Hospital, London.
PH WALTER STONEMAN, 1949, hs, NPG (NPR).

CARNARVON, George Edward Stanhope Molyneux Herbert, 5th Earl of (1866-1923) Egyptologist.
PH HARRY BURTON, various photographs, Griffiths Institute, Ashmolean Museum, Oxford.

CARPENTER, Alfred Francis Blakeney (1881-1955) vice-admiral.
P SIR A.S.COPE, 1918, hs, NPG 3971.
PH WALTER STONEMAN, 1918, hs in uniform, NPG (NPR). OLIVE EDIS, 1920s, hs in uniform, print, NPG X5697.

CARPENTER, Sir (Henry Cort) Harold (1875-1940) metallurgist.
PH WALTER STONEMAN, 1936, 2 hs portraits, NPG (NPR).

CARTER, Sir Edgar Bonham-, see Bonham-Carter.

CARRINGTON, Dora (1893-1932) artist.
D ELSIE MCNAUGHT, c1911, hl, pastel, Slade School of Art, London University.
PH Various photographs, NPG (Strachey Coll).

CARR-SAUNDERS, Sir Alexander Morris (1886-1966) director of the London School of Economics.
PH WALTER STONEMAN, 1946, hs, NPG (NPR).

CARRUTHERS, Douglas (1882-1962) explorer and naturalist.
SC MARY CARRUTHERS, 1936, bronze bust, Royal Geographical Society, London.

CARTER, Howard (1874-1939) Egyptologist.
P WILLIAM CARTER, 1924, tql seated, profile, Griffiths Institute, Ashmolean Museum, Oxford.
PH Various photographs, Griffiths Institute.

CARY, (Arthur) Joyce (Lunel) (1888-1957) novelist and poet.
D KATERINA WILCZYNSKI, 1954, hl, pen and ink, NPG 4822.
PR Self-portrait, 1956, head, lith, NPG 4113.
PH MARK GERSON, 1953, hs, profile, print, NPG x5696.

CARY-ELWES, Gervase Henry, see Elwes.

CASEMENT, Sir Roger David (1864-1916) Irish patriot.
P SARAH PURSER, 1927, hl, NGI 938; study sketch from life, NGI 1376.
D SIR WILLIAM ROTHENSTEIN, 1911, 2 hs portraits, chalk, NPG 3867. LEONHARD FANTO, 1916, hs, chalk, BM.
G SIR JOHN LAVERY, 'Trial of Roger Casement, 1915', oil, on loan to the Society of King's Inn, Dublin.
SC AUGUST WECKBECKER, plaster/bronze bust?, NGI 8032.

CASEY, William Francis (1884-1957) editor of *The Times*.
D CUTHBERT ORDE, 1951, hs, semi-profile, chalk, Times Newspapers Ltd, London.

CASSELS, Sir James Dale (1877-1972) judge.
PH WALTER STONEMAN, 1939, hs in robes, NPG (NPR).

CASSELS, Sir Robert Archibald (1876-1959) general.
PH WALTER STONEMAN, 1935, hs in uniform, NPG (NPR).

CASSON, Sir Lewis (1875-1969) actor, producer and manager.
D E.MEAR, w/c, Garrick Club, London.
PH T.P.ANDREW, hs, print, NPG x5708. GODFREY ARGENT, c1968, tql seated with Sybil Thorndike, print, NPG x5707. WALTER STONEMAN, 1946, hs, NPG (NPR).

CASSON, Dame Sybil, see Thorndike.

CASTLEROSSE, Valentine Charles Browne, Viscount, see 6th Earl of Kenmare.

CATHCART, Edward Provan (1877-1954) physiologist.
PH WALTER STONEMAN, 1932, hs, NPG (NPR).

CATTO, Thomas Sivewright Catto, 1st Baron (1879-1959) governor of the Bank of England.
P DAVID ALISON, c1948, hl seated, Bank of England, London. SIR JAMES GUNN, 1952, Morgan Grenfell & Co Ltd, London.
PH WALTER STONEMAN, 1943, hs, NPG (NPR).

CAVAN, Frederick Rudolph Lambart, 10th Earl of (1865-1946) field-marshal.
P SIR WILLIAM ORPEN, tql seated in uniform, Cavalry and Guards Club, London.

D FRANCIS DODD, 1917, charcoal and w/c, IWM.
G J.S.SARGENT, 'General Officers of World War I, 1914-18', oil, 1922, NPG 1954.
PH S.A.CHANDLER, c1917, hl in uniform, print, NPG x5715. WALTER STONEMAN, 2 hs portraits in uniform, 1923 and 1932, NPG (NPR).

CAVELL, Edith (1865-1915) nurse.
SC SIR GEORGE FRAMPTON, 1920, marble statue, St Martin's Place, London; bust, IWM.
PH Various photographs, IWM. UNKNOWN, hs, oval, photogravure postcard, NPG x4185.

CAVENDISH, Victor Christian William, see 9th Duke of Devonshire.

CAYZER, Herbert Robin, see 1st Baron Rotherwick.

CECIL, Edward Herbert Gascoyne-Cecil, Lord (1867-1918) soldier and civil servant.
C SIR LESLIE WARD ('Spy'), wl, profile, lith, for *Vanity Fair*, 9 Nov 1899, NPG.

CECIL, Hugh Richard Heathcote Gascoyne-Cecil, Lord, see Baron Quickswood.

CECIL, James Edward Hubert Gascoyne-, see 4th Marquess of Salisbury.

CECIL, Robert Arthur James Gascoyne-, see 5th Marquess of Salisbury.

CECIL of Chelwood, (Edgar Algernon) Robert Gascoyne-Cecil, 1st Viscount (1864-1958) statesman and president of the League of Nations.
P AUGUSTUS JOHN, 1919, hs, Hatfield House, Herts. SIR WILLIAM ORPEN, c1917-19, hl seated, NPG 4184. JOHN MANSBRIDGE, 1931, tql seated, NPG 4112. P.A.DE LÁSZLÓ, 1932, hs, Hatfield House. P.A.DE LÁSZLÓ, 1932, tql seated in robes, University of Birmingham.
D SIR WILLIAM ROTHENSTEIN, 1922, head, chalk, NPG 4769. SIR W.ROTHENSTEIN, 1922, sanguine, Manchester City Art Gallery.
G F.H.SHEPHERD, family group, oil, 1928, University College, Oxford; version, Hatfield House.
SC SIEGFRIED CHAROUX, 1945, bronze head, Royal institute of International Affairs, Chatham House, London.
PR EDMOND KAPP, hl, lith, NPG.
C SIR FRANCIS CARRUTHERS GOULD, 2 wl, ink, NPG 2827 and 2865. SIR LESLIE WARD ('Spy'), wl in robes, profile, lith, for *Vanity Fair*, 22 Feb 1906, NPG. SIR MAX BEERBOHM,, 1913, 'Cecils in Conclave', wash, Hatfield House. SIR M.BEERBOHM, 1921, wl with Lord Hugh Cecil, pencil and wash, Ashmolean Museum, Oxford.
PH WALTER STONEMAN, 2 hs portraits, 1931 and 1943, NPG (NPR). KARL POLLAK, 1947, 3 hl portraits, prints, NPG.

CHADWICK, Sir James (1891-1974) physicist.
PH Possibly by HOWARD COSTER, hs, copy neg, NPG x10633.

CHADWICK, Roy (1893-1947) aeronautical engineer.
PH Various photographs, Royal Aeronautical Society, London.

CHAMBERLAIN, (Arthur) Neville (1869-1940) prime minister.
P SIR OSWALD BIRLEY, c1933, tql, Birmingham City Art Gallery. SIR JAMES GUNN, c1939, tql, Carlton Club, London. HENRY LAMB, c1939, tql, NPG 4279.
SC MURIEL HILEY, bronze medallion, National Museum of Wales 1362, Cardiff. LADY KATHLEEN KENNET, 1936, bronze bust, Birmingham City Art Gallery. VICTOR DEMANET, 1938, head, profile, bronze medal, NPG 4268.
PR ANDREW MACLAREN, 1940, hs, lith, NPG 4413.

C SIR BERNARD PARTRIDGE, various cartoons, ink and w/c, for *Punch*, 1 Nov 1926, and 22 June 1932, NPG. SIR DAVID LOW, hs, profile, pencil, NPG 4529(73).

PH WALTER STONEMAN, 2 hs portraits, 1921 and 1937, NPG (NPR).

CHAMBERLAIN, Sir (Joseph) Austen (1863-1937) statesman.

P I.M.COHEN, wl in Garter robes, Cordwainers' Company, London. SIR JOHN LAVERY, hs, Municipal Gallery of Modern Art, Dublin. SIR WILLIAM ROTHENSTEIN, 1936, tql seated in chancellor's robes, University of Reading.

SC SIGISMUND DE STROBL, 1935, bronze bust, NPG 5059

C SIR LESLIE WARD ('Spy'), wl, lith, for *Vanity Fair*, 3 Aug 1899, NPG. SIR DAVID LOW, 1926, tql, chalk, NPG 4562. SIR BERNARD PARTRIDGE, wl with 1st Viscount Bridgeman, ink and w/c, for *Punch's Almanack*, 7 Nov 1927, NPG.

PH BASSANO, hs, print, for *Our Conservative and Unionist Statesmen*, vol 2, NPG. OLIVE EDIS, hs, print, NPG X5756. JOHN RUSSELL & SONS, hs, print, NPG X5755. SIR BENJAMIN STONE, 1897, wl, print, NPG. WALTER STONEMAN, 2 hs portraits, 1920 and 1931, NPG (NPR).

CHAMBERS, Sir Edmund Kerchever (1866-1954) English scholar.

D SIR WILLIAM ROTHENSTEIN, 1924, hl, chalk, NPG 4139.

PH WALTER STONEMAN, 1926, hs, NPG (NPR).

CHAMBERS, Raymond Wilson (1874-1942) scholar and writer on English language and literature.

PH WALTER STONEMAN, 1933, hl, NPG (NPR).

CHANCELLOR, Sir John Robert (1870-1952) soldier and administrator.

PH WALTER STONEMAN, 1919, hs, NPG (NPR). HUGH CECIL, 1920s, hs, 2 prints, NPG X5757-58.

CHANDOS, Oliver Lyttelton, 1st Viscount (1893-1972) politician and industrialist.

PR FELIKS TOPOLSKI, hl, lith, for *Topolski's Chronicle*, vol VIII, 1960, NPG.

C SIR DAVID LOW, 2 profile heads, pencil, NPG 4529(78-79).

PH WALTER BIRD, 1962, hs, NPG (NPR).

CHANNON, Sir Henry ('Chips') (1897-1958) politician and writer.

PH HOWARD COSTER, *c*1930, various sizes and negs, NPG X10711-14. SIR CECIL BEATON, 1943, tql, print, NPG.

CHAPLIN, Sir Charles (1889-1977) comedian.

SC JO DAVIDSON, 1925, bronze head, National Portrait Gallery, Smithsonian Institution, Washington, USA.

C R.S.SHERRIFFS, hs, profile, ink, NPG 5224(9).

CHAPMAN, David Leonard (1869-1958) chemist.

D RANDOLPH SCHWABE, 1946, hs, pencil, Jesus College, Oxford.

CHAPMAN, Robert William (1881-1960) scholar and university publisher.

G UNKNOWN, Oxford University Press staff, print, Oxford University Press, london.

PH WALTER STONEMAN, 1949, hs, NPG (NPR).

CHAPMAN, Sydney (1888-1970) scientist.

PH UNKNOWN, *c*1913-19, tql seated, print, Trinity College Library, Cambridge.

CHAPMAN, Sir Sydney John (1871-1951) economist and civil servant.

PH WALTER STONEMAN, 2 hs portraits, 1920 and 1931, NPG (NPR).

CHARLES, Sir John Alexander (1893-1971) chief medical officer for Ministry of Health.

PH UNKNOWN, *c*1958, hs, print, NPG X5765.

CHARLESWORTH, Martin Percival (1895-1950) classical scholar.

PH WALTER STONEMAN, 1945, hl, NPG (NPR).

CHARNWOOD, Godfrey Rathbone Benson, 1st Baron (1864-1945) Liberal politician and man of letters.

PH WALTER STONEMAN, 1920, hs, NPG (NPR).

CHATFIELD, Alfred Ernle Montacute Chatfield, 1st Baron (1873-1967) admiral.

P R.G.EVES, 1937, hs in uniform, NPG 4602.

PH WALTER STONEMAN, 1919, hs in uniform, NPG (NPR).

CHAVASSE, Christopher Maude (1884-1962) bishop of Rochester.

P SIR OSWALD BIRLEY, 1938, tql seated in robes, St Peter's College, Oxford. MURRAY URQUART, 1957, hs, Bishop's Palace, Rochester.

P WALTER STONEMAN, 1945, hl in robes, NPG (NPR). WALTER BIRD, 1961, hs in robes, NPG (NPR).

CHEESMAN, Robert Ernest (1878-1962) colonel and explorer.

PH UNKNOWN, 2 photographs, Royal Geographical Society, London.

CHELMSFORD, Frederic John Napier Thesiger, 1st Viscount (1868-1933) viceroy of India.

P SIR GERALD KELLY, *c*1923, wl, All Souls' College, Oxford.

PH WALTER STONEMAN, 1921, hs, NPG (NPR). UNKNOWN, *c*1921, wl in robes, print, NPG X6013.

CHERRY-GARRARD, Apsley George Benet (1886-1959) polar explorer.

SC IVOR ROBERT-JONES, 1962, bronze statuette, St Helen's Church, Wheathampstead, Herts.

PH FRANK DEBENHAM, *c*1911-12, various photographs, Scott Polar Research Institute, University of Cambridge. H.G.PONTING, *c*1911-12, various photographs, Scott Institute.

CHERWELL, Frederick Alexander Lindemann, 1st Viscount (1886-1957) scientist and politician.

P HENRY CARR, 1946, IWM.

CHESSER, Elizabeth Sloan (*d*1940) physician and writer on hygiene.

PH HOWARD COSTER, *c*1930, hs, various negs, NPG X10746-50.

CHESTERTON, Gilbert Keith (1874-1936) poet, novelist and critic.

D ALFRED PRIEST, 1909, hs, profile, charcoal, St Paul's School, London. FLORENCE HOLMS, 1920s, hl, profile, pencil, NPG. SIR WILLIAM ROTHENSTEIN, 1922, hl, seated, sanguine, Manchester City Art Gallery. ALFRED WOLMARK, 1928, head, ink, Aberdeen Art Gallery, and University of Texas, Austin, USA. EDMOND KAPP, 1932, chalk, Barber Institute, Birmingham University. SIR JAMES GUNN, 1932, 2 hl studies for NPG 3654, chalk and pencil, NPG 3984-85. STRICKLAND BROWN, w/c and pastel, University of Texas.

SL H.L.OAKLEY, hs, profile, NPG.

G SIR J.GUNN, wl seated with Maurice Baring and Hilaire Belloc, oil, 1932, NPG 3654.

SC THEODORE SPICER-SIMSON, 1922, relief portrait on medallion, plasticine, NPG 2045. MARIA PETRIE, 1929, bronze bust, NPG 3240.

PR WALTER TITTLE, 1922, head, lith, NPG.

C SIR MAX BEERBOHM, 1904, 'giving the world a kiss', drg, Yale University Library, New Haven, USA. STRICKLAND, wl, lith, for *Vanity Fair*, 21 Feb 1912, NPG. SIR M.BEERBOHM, 1912, tql, making an after dinner speech, pencil and w/c, Ashmolean

Museum, Oxford. SIR M.BEERBOHM, 1925, wl, 'The Old and Young Self', w/c, Ashmolean Museum. SIR DAVID LOW, c1926–27, various sketches, pencil, NPG 4529(80–83).

PH J.C.ANNAN, tql seated, 2 prints, NPG X6021–22. A.L.COBURN, 1904, hs, photogravure, NPG AX7769. HOWARD COSTER, 1926 and c1934, various sizes, prints and negs, NPG X1787–91, AX2260 and X10512–15. HECTOR MURCHISON, hl, print, NPG X12600. WALTER STONEMAN, 1931, hs, NPG (NPR).

CHETWODE, Sir Philip Walhouse Chetwode, 1st Baron (1869-1950) field-marshal.

P SIR OSWALD BIRLEY, c1936, tql, Cavalry and Guards Club, London.

C 'WHO', wl in uniform, mechanical repro, for *Vanity Fair*, 14 Dec 1910, NPG.

PH WALTER STONEMAN, 2 hs portraits in uniform, 1925 and 1945, NPG (NPR).

CHEYNEY, Peter, see Southouse-Cheyney.

CHILDE, Vere Gordon (1892-1957) archaeologist and prehistorian.

PH WALTER STONEMAN, 1945, hs, NPG (NPR).

CHILDERS, (Robert) Erskine (1870-1922) author and politician.

D JOHN KEATING, NGI.

CHILDS, William Macbride (1869-1939) educationist and founder of University of Reading.

P ERIC KENNINGTON, 1939, tql seated in robes, profile, University of Reading.

CHILSTON, Aretas Akers-Douglas, 2nd Viscount (1876-1947) diplomat.

PH WALTER STONEMAN, 1933, hs, NPG (NPR).

CHISHOLM, Hugh (1866-1924) journalist and editor of the *Encyclopaedia Britannica.*

PH UNKNOWN, hl seated, print, Encyclopaedia Britannica Inter-National, London.

CHRISTIE, Dame Agatha, Lady Mallowan (1890-1976) writer.

SC LYN KRAMER, 1972, wl, life-size wax figure, Madame Tussaud's, London.

PH BASSANO & VANDYK, 1932, 3 hs portraits, negs, NPG. GODFREY ARGENT, 1969, 2 hs portraits, for NPR, NPG X6027.

CHRISTIE, John (1882-1962) founder of the Glyndebourne Festival.

PH SIR CECIL BEATON, 1956, hs, print, NPG. GUY GRAVETT, various photographs, Glyndebourne Festival Opera, Lewes, E Sussex.

CHURCH, Richard (1893-1972) poet, critic and novelist.

D A.O.SPARE, 1953, pastel, University of Texas, Austin, USA.

PH HOWARD COSTER, 1939, various sizes, prints and negs, NPG X1792 and X10805–13. WALTER BIRD, 1958, hs, NPG (NPR).

CHURCHILL, Sir Winston Leonard Spencer (1874-1965) statesman.

P ERNEST TOWNSEND, c1915, National Liberal Club, London. SIR JOHN LAVERY, 1915, hl in uniform, Chartwell (NT), Kent. SIR J.LAVERY, hl, Municipal Gallery of Modern Art, Dublin. SIR JAMES GUTHRIE, c1919–21, hl, SNPG 1131, study for 'Statesmen', NPG 2463. W.R.SICKERT, 1927, head, NPG 4438. F.O.SALISBURY, 1942, hl in 'siren suit', Chartwell. F.O.SALISBURY, 1943, tql in chancellor's robes, Bristol University. ARTHUR PAN, 1943–44, tql seated, American Embassy, London; version, Sheffield University. A.E.COOPER, 1943, hl, profile, Carlton Club, London. DOUGLAS CHANDOR, 1946, tql seated in Air Force uniform,

National Portrait Gallery, Washington DC, USA. SIR OSWALD BIRLEY, 1946, tql seated, Palace of Westminster, London. ARTHUR HAYWARD, 1946, tql, University of Canterbury. A.E.COOPER, 1950, tql seated, Junior Carlton Club, London. SIR O.BIRLEY, 1951, tql in uniform, Trinity House, London. GRAHAM SUTHERLAND, 1954–55, tql in Garter robes, study, Beaverbrook Art Gallery, Fredericton, Canada. MAX NAUTA, c1955, tql seated, Lower House of the Dutch Parliament, The Hague, Netherlands. RUSKIN SPEAR, Beaverbrook Art Gallery.

D JOHN TENNIEL, 1890, pencil, Chartwell. J.S.SARGENT, 1925, hs in robes of Chancellor of Exchequer, charcoal, Chartwell. EDMOND KAPP, 1929, chalk, Barber Institute, Birmingham University. G.SUTHERLAND, 1954, various sketches for destroyed portrait, ink, chalk, pencil and/or gouache, Beaverbrook Art Gallery. BERNARD HAILSTONE, 1956, head, chalk and pencil, NPG 4458. JULIET PANNETT, 1964, tql seated, pencil, NPG 4474.

G SIR J.GUTHRIE, 'Statesmen of World War I, 1914–18', oil, c1924–30, NPG 2463.

SC CLARE SHERIDAN, 1942, bronze head, Chartwell. SIR JACOB EPSTEIN, 1946, bronze head, IWM. BORIS ANREP, 1952, wl with demon, Mosaic, National Gallery, London. OSCAR NEMON, 1953, bronze bust, Royal Coll. O.NEMON, 1959, bronze statue, Guildhall, London.

PR HENRIK LUND, lith, IWM.

C SIR LESLIE WARD ('Spy'), wl, mechanical repro, for *Vanity Fair*, 27 Sept 1900, NPG. SIR BERNARD PARTRIDGE, 'The Cabinet Cherubs', ink, for *Punch*, 22 April 1908, NPG. 'NIBS', wl, profile, lith, for *Vanity Fair*, 8 March 1911, NPG. SIR B.PARTRIDGE, various cartoons, pen, ink, and/or w/c, for *Punch*, 8 Feb 1911, 1 Oct 1924 and 7 Nov 1927, NPG. SIR DAVID LOW, hs and hl, pencil, NPG 4529(84–85).

PH JOHN RUSSELL & SONS, 1920, hs, print, NPG X5912. EDWARD STEICHEN, 1932, tql, print, Museum of Modern Art, New York. UNKNOWN, c1939?, wl, postcard, NPG X1620. VIVIENNE, c1935–40, hs, print, NPG X6039. WALTER STONEMAN, 1941, various sizes, prints and negs, NPG X403 and X6138–40. YOUSUF KARSH, 1941, tql, print, Sheldon Memorial Art Gallery, University of Nebraska, USA. HOWARD COSTER, 1940s, hs, profile, print, NPG X1772. A.C.COOPER, 1942, various sizes and prints, NPG X6123–32. SEFTON SAMUELS, 1951, tql with Lady Violet Bonham-Carter, print, NPG. W.STONEMAN, 1953, various sizes, prints and negs, NPG X6133–37.

CHUTER-EDE, James Chuter Ede, Baron (1882-1965) politician.

PH WALTER STONEMAN, 1941, hs, NPG (NPR). HOWARD COSTER, various sizes and negs, NPG X11552–57.

CITRINE, Walter McLennan Citrine, 1st Baron (b1887) trade union official and public servant.

PH HOWARD COSTER, 1930s, various sizes and negs, NPG X10814–25. WALTER STONEMAN, 2 hs portraits, 1935 and 1948, NPG X5890 and NPG (NPR). WALTER BIRD, 1959, hs, NPG (NPR).

CLAPHAM, Sir Alfred William (1883-1950) archaeologist.

PH WALTER STONEMAN, 1944, hs, NPG (NPR).

CLAPHAM, Sir John Harold (1873-1946) historian.

P SIR JAMES GUNN, King's College, Cambridge.

PH WALTER STONEMAN, 2 hs portraits, 1930 and 1940, NPG (NPR).

CLARENCE and Avondale, Albert Victor Christian Edward, Duke of (1864-1892) eldest son of King Edward VII.

P JAMES SANT, 1874, head, oval, Royal Coll, study for 'Victoria and grandchildren'. HEINRICH VON ANGELI, 1875, head, Royal Coll. CARL JOHN, jun, 1882, hl with brother George in midshipman's uniform, Royal Coll. FRANKLIN TUTTLE, 1885, tql, Trinity College, Cambridge. SIR LUKE FILDES, 1895?, hs in uniform, oval, Royal Coll.

D SIR HUBERT VON HERKOMER, 1892, hs, w/c, Royal Coll. Various w/c and other drgs, Royal Coll.

G K. W.F.BAUERLE, wl with brother George and sister Louise, oil, c1871, Royal Coll. J.SANT, 'Victoria with 3 of her grandchildren', oil, c1872, Royal Coll. NICHOLAS CHEVALIER, 'The Marriage of the Duke of Edinburgh', oil, 1874, Royal Coll. H.VON ANGELI, 'Prince and Princess of Wales with Albert Victor and Maud', oil, 1876, Royal Coll. LAURITS TUXEN, 'Prince and Princess of Wales and Albert Victor', oil, 1884, Det National historiske Museum Paa Frederiksborg, Hillerod, Denmark. L.TUXEN, 'The Royal Family at the Time of the Jubilee', oil, 1887, Royal Coll.

SC F.J.WILLIAMSON, 1877, marble statue and bust, Royal Coll. COUNT VICTOR GLEICHEN, 1878, bronze statuette with brother George V, Royal Coll. W.J.S.WEBBER, 1890, marble bust, Royal College of Music, London. SIR ALFRED GILBERT, 1892–99, marble and bronze tomb effigy, Albert Memorial Chapel, Windsor.

PR Various popular prints, NPG.

PH W. & D.DOWNEY, c1877, wl seated in sea cadet uniform, carte, NPG X1509. CHANCELLOR, hs as young man, postcard, NPG. W. & D.DOWNEY, c1890, tql in uniform, postcard, NPG. LAFAYETTE, c1890s, 3 postcards, 2 in uniform, NPG. G.COOPER, c1890s, tql seated, postcard, NPG. HILL & SAUNDERS, 1891, hs, oval, and 1865 as infant with parents, oval, postcard, NPG. GUNN & STEWART, 1891, tql with fiancée (later Queen Mary), postcard, NPG. F.THURSTON, 1891, wl with fiancée, print, NPG X4103. JOHN RUSSELL, 1891, tql in uniform, photogravure, NPG X4097. Various family groups as infant, NPG. Various photographs, Royal Coll.

CLARENDON, George Herbert Hyde Villiers, 6th Earl of (1877-1955) public servant.

P ROY DE MAISTRE, 1949, tql seated in Garter robes, Royal Commonwealth Society, London.

PH UNKNOWN, c1899, hs, print, NPG X6079. WALTER STONEMAN, 3 hs portraits, 1917, 1930 and 1943, NPG (NPR).

CLARK, George Sidney Roberts Kitson, see Kitson Clark.

CLARK, Sir Wilfred Edward Le Gros (1895-1971) professor of anatomy.

P ANNA ZINKEISEN, c1962, hl, Salters' Company, London.

PH WALTER STONEMAN, 1949, hs, NPG (NPR). GODFREY ARGENT, 1969, 2 hs portraits, NPG X6097 and NPG (NPR).

CLARK, Sir William Henry (1876-1952) civil servant.

PH WALTER STONEMAN, 3 hs portraits, 1918, 1932 and 1948, NPG (NPR). UNKNOWN, tql in uniform, print, NPG X6098.

CLARKE, Sir Fred (1880-1952) educationist.

P RAYMOND COXON, 1950, wl seated, Institute of Education, London.

CLARKE, Louis Colville Gray (1881-1960) connoisseur, collector and museum director.

P SIR JAMES GUNN, 1959, hl with glass, Fitzwilliam Museum, Cambridge. SIR J.GUNN, c1954–59, head, study for Society of Dilettanti Group, Althorp, Northants. AUGUSTUS JOHN, Trinity Hall, Cambridge.

D A.JOHN, 1915, hs, pencil, Fitzwilliam Museum. M.GABOR, 1933, hs, pencil, Fitzwilliam Museum.

G SIR J.GUNN, 'Society of Dilettanti Conversation Piece', oil, c1954–59, Society of Dilettanti, Brooks's Club, London.

SC SIR JACOB EPSTEIN, 1951, bronze bust, Fitzwilliam Museum.

CLARKE, Maude Violet (1892-1935) historian.

G UNKNOWN, 1934, wl with Senior Common Room, ph, Somerville College, Oxford.

CLARKE, Sir Travers (Edwards) (1871-1962) lieutenant-general.

P SIR WILLIAM ORPEN, 1917, IWM.

PH OLIVE EDIS, hs in uniform, print, NPG X6081. WALTER STONEMAN, 1919, hs in uniform, NPG (NPR).

CLARKE HALL, Lady Edna, see HALL.

CLAUSON, Albert Charles Clauson, Baron (1870-1946) judge.

P L.CAMPBELL TAYLOR, 1939, tql, Merchant Taylors' Company, London.

CLAY, Sir Henry (1883-1954) economist.

D KENNETH KNOWLES, Nuffield College, Oxford.

PH WALTER STONEMAN, 1949, hl, NPG (NPR).

CLAYTON, Sir Gilbert Falkingham (1875-1929) soldier and administrator.

PH WALTER STONEMAN, 1919, hs in uniform, NPG (NPR).

CLAYTON, Philip Thomas Byard (1885-1972) founder padre of Toc H.

P ARNOLD MASON, c1947, hl seated with dog, Toc H, Talbot House, London.

D SIR WILLIAM ROTHENSTEIN, 1920, head, sanguine, Toc H Headquarters, Aylesbury, Bucks.

PH WALTER STONEMAN, 2 hs portraits, the 1st in uniform, 1933 and 1953, NPG (NPR). HOWARD COSTER, c1937, hs, various negs, NPG X10837–47.

CLEMENTI, Sir Cecil (1875-1947) colonial administrator and traveller.

P A.SCHUSTER, University of Hong Kong.

PH WALTER STONEMAN, 1931, 2 hs portraits, NPG (NPR).

CLERK, Sir George Russell (1874-1951) diplomat.

SC CLARE SHERIDAN, bronze head, British Embassy (DoE), Ankara, Turkey.

PH WALTER STONEMAN, 2 hs portraits, 1931 and 1947, NPG (NPR).

CLIFFORD, Sir Eric (George Anderson) (1900-1964) vice-admiral.

PH WALTER STONEMAN, 1951, hs in uniform, NPG (NPR).

CLIVE, Sir Robert Henry (1887-1948) diplomat.

PH WALTER STONEMAN, 1933, hs, NPG (NPR).

CLOSE, Sir Charles Frederick Arden-, see Arden-Close.

CLUTTON-BROCK, Arthur (1868-1924) essayist, critic and journalist.

D SIR WILLIAM ROTHENSTEIN, 1916, hs, pencil, NPG 4770. SIR W.ROTHENSTEIN, 1919, hs, chalk, TATE 3887.

CLYDE, James Avon Clyde, Lord (1863-1944) lord justice-general of Scotland.

D R.S.FORREST, hl seated in robes, w/c, Parliament Hall, Edinburgh.

PH W.CROOKE, c1920, tql, print, NPG X6182. WALTER STONEMAN, 2 hs portraits, 1924 and 1938, NPG (NPR).

CLYDESMUIR, David John Colville, 1st Baron (1894-1954) public servant.

PH WALTER STONEMAN, 2 hs portraits, 1931 and 1943, NPG (NPR).

CLYNES, John Robert (1869-1949) trade unionist.

P MARGARETTA HICKS, National Union of General and Municipal Workers, Woodstock College, Surbiton, Surrey.

PH WALTER STONEMAN, 1924, hs, NPG (NPR). UNKNOWN, wl with Will Thorne, print, NPG (Daily Herald).

COATES, Eric (1886-1957) composer.
PH K.N.COLLINS, c1935, hs, print, Royal College of Music, London. WALTER STONEMAN, 1947, hs, NPG (NPR).

COATES, Wells Wintemute (1895-1958) architect and industrial designer.
PH HOWARD COSTER, 1930s and 1954, various sizes, prints and negs, NPG X2334 and X3542-49.

COBHAM, Sir Alan (1894-1973) pioneer aviator.
P F.O.SALISBURY, 1926, tql in flying kit, NPG 5018. HOWARD BARRON, hl, Royal Aero Club on loan to RAF Museum, Hendon.
G FRED ROE, hs with civic dignitaries, pencil, 1926, NPG. UNKNOWN, 'Banbury on Aviation Day', ph, 1932, NPG X3774.
C FRED MAY, pen and ink, RAF Museum, Hendon.
PH HOWARD COSTER, 1927, hs, various prints and negs, NPG X1793, AX2277 and X3390-94. WALTER STONEMAN, 1952, hs, NPG (NPR).

COBURN, Alvin Langdon (1882-1966) photographer.
PH Self-portrait, 1922, hs with book, photogravure, NPG AX7841.

COCHRAN, Sir Charles Blake (1872-1951) theatrical manager.
D POWYS EVANS, head, pencil, NPG 4460.
SC PETER LAMBDA, bronze head, Adelphi Theatre, London.
C R.S.SHERRIFFS, 1934, hs, profile, ink and pencil, NPG 5224(5).
PH HOWARD COSTER, 1928, hs, print and neg, NPG X1794 and X10522; and 1929, hs with Beverley Nichols, print, NPG AX2314. BASSANO, 1932, various sizes, 4 prints, NPG X12168-71.

COCHRANE-BAILLIE, Charles Wallace Alexander, see 2nd Baron Lamington.

COCKCROFT, Sir John Douglas (1897-1967) nuclear physicist.
D H.A.FREETH, 1957, hs, profile, chalk, NPG 4812. ROBERT TOLLAST, c1964, hs, Churchill College, Cambridge.
PH WALTER STONEMAN, 1946, hs, NPG (NPR).

COCKERELL, Douglas Bennett (1870-1945) bookbinder and printer.
PH UNKNOWN, 1938, hs, print, NPG X6291.

COCKERELL, Sir Sydney Carlyle (1867-1962) director of the Fitzwilliam Museum, Cambridge.
D FRANCIS DODD, 1937, hs, chalk, Fitzwilliam Museum. DOROTHY HAWKSLEY, 1952, head, pencil, NPG 4325. D.HAWKSLEY, 1960, hs, w/c, NPG 4324.
PH UNKNOWN, 1891, wl seated with Mr Rooke, print, NPG X3737. WALTER STONEMAN, 1917, hs, NPG (NPR).

COCKIN, Frederick Arthur (1888-1969) bishop of Bristol.
PH WALTER STONEMAN, 1955, hl seated in robes, NPG (NPR).

COCKS, Arthur Herbert Tennyson Somers-, see 6th Baron Somers.

COHEN, Harriet (d1967) pianist.
D EDMOND KAPP, 1930 and 1938, studies at the piano, Barber Institute, Birmingham University.
PH UNKNOWN, wl with G.B.Shaw, print, NPG X1464.

COHEN, Sir Lionel Leonard Cohen, Lord (1888-1973) judge.
D SIR DAVID LOW, 3 heads, pencil, NPG 4529(87-89).
PH WALTER STONEMAN, 1944, hl in robes, NPG (NPR). LENARE, 1953, various sizes and negs in peer's robes, some with wife, NPG X5342-49.

COHEN, Sir Robert Waley (1877-1952) industrialist.
PH WALTER STONEMAN, 1927, hs, NPG (NPR).

COKAYNE, Brien Ibracan, see 1st Baron Cullen of Ashbourne.

COKER, Ernest George (1869-1946) engineer.
PH WALTER STONEMAN, 1917, hs, profile, NPG (NPR).

COLE, George Douglas Howard (1889-1959) university teacher, writer and socialist.
D SIR WILLIAM ROTHENSTEIN, c1940, head, profile, chalk, Nuffield College, Oxford.
PH HOWARD COSTER, wl with wife, various negs, NPG X10859-64.

COLE, Dame Margaret Isabel (1893-1980) author and lecturer.
PH HOWARD COSTER, wl with husband, various negs, NPG X10859-64.

COLERIDGE-TAYLOR, Samuel (1875-1912) musical composer.
PH UNKNOWN, c1888, wl with violin, carte, Royal College of Music, London. UNKNOWN, c1896, hs and tql seated, prints, Royal College of Music. DEBENHAM & GOULD, c1900, hs, print, Royal College of Music. JASPER REDFERN, c1902, hs, print, Royal College of Music. BREITKOPF & HÄRTEL, early 1900s, hs, postcard, Royal College of Music.

COLLES, Henry Cope (1879-1943) musical historian and critic.
PH UNKNOWN, hl with music score, print, Royal College of Music, London.

COLLINGWOOD, Robin George (1889-1943) philosopher and historian.
PH WALTER STONEMAN, 1934, hl, NPG (NPR). UNKNOWN, print, Pembroke College, Oxford. UNKNOWN, print, Magdalen College, Oxford.

COLLINS, Josephine ('José') (1887-1958) actress and singer.
PR HOWARD VAN DUSEN AND HASSALL, wl and hs, lith, NPG.

COLLINS, Michael (1890-1922) Irish revolutionary leader.
P SIR JOHN LAVERY, 1922, wl lying in state, Municipal Gallery of Modern Art, Dublin. LEO WHELAN, (posthumous), Dail Eireann, Dublin.
SC F.W.DOYLE-JONES, 1923, bronze bust, NGI 8001. SEAMUS MURPHY, marble bust?, Municipal Gallery of Modern Art. ALBERT POWER, 1936, bronze bust?, NGI 8070. THEODORE SPICER-SIMSON, 1922, plasticine medallion, NGI 8139, and bronze cast, NGI 8216.
C SIR BERNARD PARTRIDGE, wl with Viscount Craigavon and bull labelled 'IRA', pen and ink, for *Punch*, 15 Feb 1922, NPG.

COLUM, Padraic (1881-1972) Irish poet and man of letters.
D ROBERT GREGORY, black crayon, NGI. LILY WILLIAMS, pastel, Abbey Theatre, Dublin. J.B.YEATS, hl, pencil, Abbey Theatre.
SC E.T.QUINN, bronze bust, Municipal Gallery of modern Art, Dublin. THEODORE SPICER-SIMSON, 1923, bronze medallion, NGI 8221.

COLVILLE, David John, see 1st Baron Clydesmuir.

COLVILLE, Sir Stanley Cecil James (1961-1939) admiral.
D FRANCIS DODD, 1917, charcoal and w/c.
PH WALTER STONEMAN, 2 hs portraits in uniform, 1917 and 1938, NPG (NPR).

COMPER, Sir (John) Ninian (1864-1960) church architect.
P BEATRICE BRIGHT, 1930s, hs, NPG 4808.
PH WALTER STONEMAN, 1950, hl seated and hs, NPG (NPR).

COMPTON-BURNETT, Dame Ivy (1892-1969) writer.
PH WALTER BIRD, hl, print, for NPR, NPG X6344. BILL BRANDT, 1949, hs, print, NPG. HOWARD COSTER, hs, print and negs, NPG X1774

and X3348–50.

CONDER, Charles (1868-1909) painter.
P SIR WILLIAM ROTHENSTEIN, 1892, wl, Toledo Museum of Art, Ohio, USA. Self-portrait, c1895–1900, hs, Manchester City Art Gallery. Self-portrait, before 1899, tql seated, Carlisle City Art Gallery. J.E.BLANCHE, 1904, tql seated, TATE 5754.
D SIR W.ROTHENSTEIN, 1893, wl, charcoal and chalk, TATE 4010. SIR W.ROTHENSTEIN, 1896, hl reclining, pencil, NPG 2558. SIR W.ROTHENSTEIN, 1897, head, profile, pastel, Ashmolean Museum, Oxford. SIR WILLIAM ORPEN, c1900, seated with female nude, chalk, V & A. Self-portrait, 1905, hs, chalk, NPG 4556.
G CHARLES RICKETTS, 'A Fancy Dress Party', oil, c1903, Carlisle City Art Gallery.
PR HENRI TOULOUSE-LAUTREC, 1893, hl, lith, Aberdeen Art Gallery.
C SIR MAX BEERBOHM, 1905, indian ink, w/c and red chalk, Ashmolean Museum.
PH Attrib F.H.Evans, c1895–96, 2 hs portraits, prints, NPG X1146–47.

CONGREVE, Sir Walter Norris (1862-1927) general.
D FRANCIS DODD, 1917, charcoal and w/c, IWM.
M UNKNOWN, hs in uniform, oval, Royal Green Jackets Museum, Peninsula Barracks, Winchester.

CONINGHAM, Sir Arthur (1895-1948) air marshal.
PH WALTER STONEMAN, 1946, hl in uniform, NPG (NPR).

CONNARD, Philip (1875-1958) painter.
P Self-portrait, hs, NPG 4702.
PH WALTER STONEMAN, 1930, hs, NPG (NPR).

CONNAUGHT, Alexandra Victoria Alberta Edwina Louise Duff, Duchess of Fife and Princess Arthur of (1891-1959) grand-daughter of King Edward VII.
PH W. & D.DOWNEY, c1891, wl with parents Duke and Duchess of Fife, postcard, NPG. W. & D.DOWNEY, c1892, wl with grandmother, Queen Alexandra, print NPG X6856. A.CORBETT, c1910, tql with mother and sister Maud, postcard, NPG. LALLIE CHARLES, c1911, 2 portraits with mother and sister, tql, postcards, NPG. Various photographs, Royal Coll.

CONNAUGHT, Arthur Frederick Patrick Albert, Prince of (1883-1938) soldier and governor-general of South Africa.
G LAURITS TUXEN, 'Marriage of princess Maud and Prince Charles of Denmark', oil, 1896, Royal Coll.
C 'OWL', wl, lith, for 'Men of the Day', *Vanity Fair*, 15 Oct 1913, NPG.
PH P.L.POCOCK (W. & D.DOWNEY), 1907, family group at Windsor, print, NPG X1585. UNKNOWN, 1909, the Paddock at Epsom on Derby Day, print, NPG X7802. MRS ALBERT BROOM, equestrian group in Hyde Park, neg, NPG X709. W. & D.DOWNEY, pre 1913, hs in uniform, postcard, NPG X6349. W. & D.DOWNEY, pre 1913, tql in uniform, profile, print, NPG X6350.

CONNAUGHT, Princess Patricia of, see Ramsay.

CONNELL, Mrs A.B., see de Valois.

CONSTABLE, William George (1887-1976) art critic and historian.
P ELIZABETH POLUNIN, c1936, hl seated, profile, NPG 5090.

CONWAY, Robert Seymour (1864-1933) classical scholar and comparative philologist.
PH WALTER STONEMAN, 1921, hs, NPG (NPR).

CONYNGHAM, Sir Gerald Ponsonby Lenox-, see Lenox-Conyngham.

COOK, Arthur Bernard (1868-1952) classical scholar and archaeologist.

P TREVOR HADDON, 1933, Queen's College, Cambridge.

COOK, Arthur James (1883-1931) miners' leader.
C POWYS EVANS ('Quiz'), 'Mr Cook, the miners' leader, begging not to be made a Hero', mechanical repro, for *Saturday Review*, 29 Aug 1925, NPG.
PH Various photographs, Trades Union Congress, London.

COOK, Sir Basil Alfred Kemball-, see Kemball-Cook.

COOK, Sir James Wilfred (1900-1975) scientist and university administrator.
PH WALTER STONEMAN, 1938, hl, NPG (NPR). WALTER BIRD, 1962, hs, NPG (NPR).

COOK, Sir Joseph (1860-1947) prime minister of Australia.
P SIR JAMES GUTHRIE, c1919–21, hs, SNPG 1136, study sketch for 'Statesmen', NPG 2463.
G SIR J.GUTHRIE, 'Statesmen of World war I, 1914–18', oil, c1924–30, NPG 2463.

COOK, Stanley Arthur (1873-1949) biblical scholar, archaeologist and student of religion.
PH WALTER STONEMAN, 1934, hs, NPG (NPR).

COOKE, George Albert (1865-1939) regius professor of Hebrew and canon of Christ Church, Oxford.
P HUGH RIVIERE, 1935, Christ Church.

COOPER, Alfred Duff, see 1st Viscount Norwich.

COOPER, Lady Diana, see 1st Viscountess Norwich.

COOPER, Sir (Francis) D'Arcy, Bart (1882-1941) industrialist.
P GEORGE HARCOURT, 1936, tql seated, Unilever House, London.

COOPER, Dame Gladys (1888-1971) actress.
P JOHN COLLIER, 1915, wl, Garrick Club, London.
G MRS ALBERT BROOM, theatrical group, ph neg, NPG X1141.
PR CHARLES BUCHEL & HASSALL, hs and wl, lith, NPG.
C R.S.SHERRIFFS, 1938, hs, ink and wash, NPG.
PH GODFREY ARGENT, 1970, 2 portraits, NPG (NPR). DOROTHY WILDING, various sizes, prints and postcards, NPG X6374–89.

COOPER, Sir (Thomas) Edwin (1874-1942) architect.
PH WALTER STONEMAN, 1937, hs, NPG (NPR).

COOPER of Culross, Thomas Mackay Cooper, Baron (1892-1955) lord justice-general of Scotland.
P SIR W.O.HUTCHISON, 1956, tql seated in robes, Parliament Hall, Edinburgh.
PH WALTER STONEMAN, 1937, hs, NPG (NPR).

COPE, Sir Vincent Zachary (1881-1974) surgeon.
PH WALTER STONEMAN, 1956, hs, NPG (NPR).

COPPARD, Alfred Edgar (1878-1957) short story writer and poet.
PR R.J.GIBBINGS, 1928, woodcut, V & A.
PH HOWARD COSTER, 1931, various sizes, prints and negs, NPG X1797, AX3430 and X10532–38.

COPPOCK, Sir Richard (1885-1971) trade unionist.
PH HOWARD COSTER, various sizes and negs, NPG X11012–19.

CORBETT-ASHBY, Dame Margery (b1882) honorary president of the International Alliance of Women.
D EDMOND KAPP, 1934, Barber Institute, University of Birmingham.
PR E.KAPP, hs profile, lith, NPG.
PH WALTER BIRD, 1967, hl, NPG (NPR).

CORK and ORRERY, Sir William Henry Dudley Boyle, 12th Earl of (1873-1967) admiral.

PH WALTER STONEMAN, 2 hs portraits, the 1st in uniform, 1930 and 1942, NPG (NPR).

CORNFORD, Francis Macdonald (1874-1943) classical scholar.
D ERIC GILL, 1929, head, pencil, Trinity College, Cambridge.
PH WALTER STONEMAN, 1938, hs, NPG (NPR).

CORNWALLIS, Sir Kinahan (1883-1959) administrator and diplomat.
PH WALTER STONEMAN, 2 hs portraits, 1933 and 1947, NPG (NPR).

CORNWALLIS-WEST, Mrs George, see Mrs Patrick Campbell.

COSTER, Howard (Sydney Musgrave) (1885-1959) photographer.
D ERIC GILL, 1931, hs, profile, pencil, NPG 5196.
C H.M.BATEMAN, 1933, wl photographing Bateman, ink, NPG.
PH Self-portrait?, tql seated, print, NPG X1799.

COTTESLOE, John Walgrave Halford Fremantle, 4th baron (b 1900) a chairman of the Arts Council of Great Britain.
G JOHN WARD, 'A meeting of the Society of Dilettanti at the St James's Club in 1973', oil, 1973–76, Society of Dilettanti, Brooks's Club, London.
SC FRANTA BELSKY, 1976, bronze head, National Theatre, London.
PH WALTER BIRD, 1959, hs, NPG (NPR).

COTTESLOE, Sir Thomas Francis Fremantle, 3rd Baron (1862-1956) authority on firearms and marksman.
PH WALTER STONEMAN, 1932, hs, profile, NPG (NPR).

COUCH, Sir Arthur Thomas Quiller-, see Quiller-Couch.

COUPLAND, Sir Reginald (1884-1952) historian of the British Empire and Commonwealth.
D F.A.DE BIDEN FOOTNER, Community Centre, Wootton, Berks.
PH WALTER STONEMAN, 1949, tql seated, profile, NPG (NPR).

COURTAULD, Samuel (1876-1947) industrialist and art patron.
P ROY DE MAISTRE, 1947, hs, Courtaulds Ltd, London. A.PANN, hs, Courtaulds Ltd.
SC BENNO ELKAN, bronze head, Courtauld Institute Art Galleries, London.

COURTNEY, Dame Kathleen (1878-1974) suffragette and chairman of United Nations Association.
PH GODFREY ARGENT, 1970, hs, for NPR, NPG X6907. UNKNOWN, several photographs, Fawcett Library, City of London Polytechnic.

COWAN, Sir Walter Henry, Bart (1871-1956) admiral.
P RODRIGO MOYNIHAN, IWM. L.CAMPBELL TAYLOR, 1920, IWM.
G SIR A.S.COPE, 'Naval Officers of World War I, 1914–18', oil, 1921, NPG 1913.
PH WALTER STONEMAN, 2 hs portraits in uniform, 1919 and 1931, NPG (NPR).

COWANS, Sir John Steven (1862-1921) general.
D FRANCIS DODD, 1917, charcoal and w/c, IWM.
G J.S.SARGENT, 'General Officers of World War I, 1914–18', oil, 1922, NPG 1954.
PH WALTER STONEMAN, 1919, hs in uniform, NPG (NPR).

COWARD, Sir Noel (1899-1973) actor and playwright.
P CLEMENCE DANE, c1945, hs, profile, NPG 4950. EDWARD SEAGO, hs, Garrick Club, London.
D EDMOND KAPP, 1930, chalk, Barber Institute, Birmingham University.
SC C.DANE, after 1945, bronze bust, NPG 4951.
PH GODFREY ARGENT, 1968, tql seated, for NPR, NPG X6949. SIR CECIL

BEATON, 1942, hl, print, NPG. HOWARD COSTER, 1939, various sizes, print and negs, NPG X1800 and X11064–73. PAUL TANQUERAY, 1952, hl, print, NPG X7259. DOROTHY WILDING, various sizes and prints, NPG X6916–48.

COWLEY, Sir Arthur Ernest (1861-1931) orientalist and librarian of Bodleian Library, Oxford.
P HARRY COLLISON, 1925, hl seated in doctoral robes, Bodleian Library.

COWPER, Frank Cadogan (1877-1958) painter.
PH ELLIOTT & FRY, hs as young man, cabinet, NPG X6911. JOHN RUSSELL & SONS, c1915–17, hs, profile, print, for *National Photographic record*, vol I, NPG. WALTER STONEMAN, 1934, hs, NPG (NPR).

COX, Alfred (1866-1954) general practitioner and medical secretary of the British Medical Association.
P SIR A.S.COPE, c1932, hl, BMA House, London.

COX, E.Albert (1876-1955) artist and decorator.
PH HOWARD COSTER, 1927, hl, print, NPG AX2355.

COX, Sir Percy Zachariah (1864-1937) soldier, administrator and diplomat.
SC UNKNOWN, bronze-painted plaster bust, Royal Geographical Society, London.
PH WALTER STONEMAN, 1924, hs, NPG (NPR).

CRADDOCK, Sir Reginald Henry (1864-1937) Indian civil servant and MP.
PH WALTER STONEMAN, 1930, hs, NPG (NPR).

CRADOCK, Sir Christopher George Francis (1862-1914) admiral.
G SIR A.S.COPE, 'Naval Officers of World War I, 1914–18', oil, 1921, NPG 1913.

CRAIG, (Edward) Gordon (1872-1966) theatrical producer and designer.
D SIR WILLIAM ROTHENSTEIN, 1922, sanguine, Manchester City Art Gallery.
C Self-portrait, 1919, wl in cloak, woodcut, University of Hull. R.S.SHERRIFFS, hs, ink, NPG 5224(6). SIR MAX BEERBOHM, 1924, wl with Martin Hardie and Hardie's son, w/c, V & A.
PH BILL BRANDT, 1956, hl, print, NPG. SIR CECIL BEATON, 1962, hs, print, NPG.

CRAIG, James, see 1st Viscount Craigavon.

CRAIG, Sir John (1874-1957) steelmaster.
PH WALTER STONEMAN, 1946, hs, NPG (NPR).

CRAIGAVON, Sir James Craig, 1st Viscount (1871-1940) statesman.
P SIR JOHN LAVERY, 1923, Ulster Museum, Belfast.
SC L.S.MERRIFIELD, statue, Northern Ireland Houses of Parliament, Stormont.
C 'WHO', wl, Hentschel-Colourtype, for *Vanity Fair*, 19 July 1911, NPG. SIR BERNARD PARTRIDGE, wl with Michael Collins and bull labelled 'IRA', pen and ink, for *Punch*, 15 Feb 1922, NPG.
PH WALTER STONEMAN, 1917, hs, NPG (NPR). OLIVE EDIS, 2 hs portraits, prints, NPG X5207 and X6994.

CRAIGIE, Pearl Mary Teresa (1867-1906) novelist and dramatist 'John Oliver Hobbes'.
SC UNKNOWN, bronze portrait plaque, University College, London.
PH G.C.BERESFORD, c1903, hs, neg, NPG X6997. LONDON STEREOSCOPIC CO, hs, postcard, NPG X6998.

CRAIGIE, Sir William Alexander (1867-1957) lexicographer and philologist.

P HAROLD SPEED, c1949, hl in robes, Oriel College, Oxford.
PH WALTER STONEMAN, 1932, hs, NPG (NPR).

CRASTER, Sir (Herbert Henry) Edmund (1879-1959) librarian of Bodleian Library, Oxford.
P AUGUSTUS JOHN, 1944, Bodleian Library.
PH WALTER STONEMAN, 1946, hs, NPG (NPR). UNKNOWN, neg, Bodleian Library.

CRAWFORD and BALCARRES, David Alexander Edward Lindsay, 27th Earl of (1871-1940) politician and art connoisseur.
P SIR JAMES GUNN, 1939, wl seated, profile, NPG 3088.
D SIR WILLIAM ROTHENSTEIN, c1938, head, chalk, NPG 4771.
C FRED MAY, 1935, hs, profile, gouache, NPG.
PH G.C.BERESFORD, 1903, 3 hs portraits, print and 2 negs, NPG X7009 and X6477-78. JOHN RUSSELL & SONS, 1921, 2 hs portraits, prints, NPG X7010-11.

CRAWFORD and BALCARRES, David Robert Alexander Lindsay, 28th Earl of (1900-1975) art connoisseur and public servant.
PH WALTER STONEMAN, 1950, hs, NPG (NPR). UNKNOWN, tql seated, print, NPG X7012.

CRAXTON, Harold (1885-1971) pianist.
PH GODFREY ARGENT, 1970, tql seated at piano, for NPR, NPG X7018.

CREASY, Sir George Elvey (1895-1972) admiral.
PH WALTER STONEMAN, 1945, hl in uniform, NPG (NPR).

CREED, John Martin (1889-1940) theologian.
PH WALTER STONEMAN, 1940, hs, NPG (NPR).

CREED, Sir Thomas Percival (1897-1969) judge and public servant.
PH GODFREY ARGENT, 1968, hs, for NPR, NPG X7021.

CREEDY, Sir Herbert James (1878-1973) civil servant.
PH WALTER STONEMAN, 2 hs portraits, 1919 and 1933, the 2nd in uniform, NPG (NPR).

CRIPPS, Sir (Richard) Stafford (1889-1952) statesman and lawyer.
P I.M.COHEN, c1931, hs, NPG 4672. SYDNEY WHITE, c1950, hs, DoE (The Treasury, London).
D WYNDHAM LEWIS, hs, pen and ink and w/c, Cecil Higgins Art Gallery, Bedford.
SC SIR JACOB EPSTEIN, bronze bust, St Paul's Cathedral, London.
PH FELIX MAN, 1939, wl seated, print, NPG X1151. WALTER STONEMAN, 3 hs portraits, 1931, 1942 and 1949, NPG (NPR) and NPG X409. HOWARD COSTER, 1940s, hs, various negs, NPG X11109-12.

CROCKER, Sir John Tredinnick (1896-1963) general.
PH WALTER STONEMAN, 2 hs portraits in uniform, 1944 and 1955, NPG (NPR).

CROFT, Henry Page Croft, 1st Baron (1881-1947) politician.
PH HOWARD COSTER, various sizes and negs, NPG X11116-11120. WALTER STONEMAN, 1942, hs, for NPR, NPG X4652.

CROMER, Rowland Thomas Baring, 2nd Earl of (1877-1953) lord chamberlain of the household.
C POWYS EVANS ('Quiz'), hs, mechanical repro, for *The Saturday Review*, 6 March 1926, NPG.
PH WALTER STONEMAN, 2 hs portraits, 1917 and 1952, the 1st in uniform, NPG (NPR). DOROTHY WILDING, 1940s, hl, NPG X7038.

CROOKSHANK, Harry Frederick Comfort Crookshank, 1st Viscount (1893-1961) statesman.
PH WELDMAN?, hs, print, NPG X7045.

CROSS, Sir Ronald Hibbert, 1st Bart (1890-1968) governor

of Tasmania.
PH WALTER STONEMAN, 2 hs portraits, 1940 and 1947, NPG X412 and NPG (NPR).

CROW, Sir Alwyn Douglas (1894-1965) pioneer in design of rocket weapons.
PH WALTER STONEMAN, 1944, hs, NPG (NPR).

CROWDY, Dame Rachel Eleanor, Mrs C.Thornhill (1884-1964) public servant.
D A.O.SPARE, 1914-18, pastel and w/c, IWM.
PH OLIVE EDIS, 1914, hl at desk, print, NPG X7055. G.C.BERESFORD, 1923, hl seated, profile, neg, NPG X6481.

CROWE, Sir Edward Thomas Frederick (1877-1960) public servant.
PH WALTER STONEMAN, 2 hs portraits, 1930 and 1945, NPG (NPR).

CRUIKSHANK, Robert (1899-1974) bacteriologist.
PH UNKNOWN, hs, print, Bacteriology Dept, University of Edinburgh Medical School.

CRUIKSHANK, Robert James (1898-1956) journalist.
PH HOWARD COSTER, 1936, various sizes and negs, NPG X11138-45.

CRUM, Walter Ewing (1865-1944) Coptic scholar.
PH WALTER STONEMAN, 1932, hs, NPG (NPR).

CRUTTWELL, Charles Robert Mowbray Fraser (1887-1941) historian.
P GRACE CRUTTWELL, c1937, tql seated in robes, Hertford College, Oxford.
PH WALTER STONEMAN, 1931, hs, NPG (NPR).

CULLEN of Ashbourne, Brien Ibracan Cokayne, 1st Baron (1864-1932) governor of the Bank of England.
P SIR WILLIAM ROTHENSTEIN, c1926, hs, Bank of England; study head, chalk, NPG 4773. A.K.LAWRENCE, 1929?, head, profile, Bank of England, London.
PH WALTER STONEMAN, 1932, hs, NPG (NPR).

CULLIS, Winifred Clara (1875-1956) physiologist.
P ALICE BURTON, Crosby Hall, London. PHYLLIS DODD, Royal Free Hospital School of Medicine (formerly London School of Medicine for Women).
PH MADAME YEVONDE, 1944, print, NPG X11645. Various photographs, Royal Free Hospital.

CUNDALL, Charles (1890-1971) artist.
D JAMES GRANT, c1945, pastel, Manchester City Art Gallery.

CUNDELL, Edric (1893-1961) composer and conductor.
D EDMOND KAPP, 1938, Barber Institute, Birmingham University.
PH OLIVE EDIS, tql, profile, print, NPG X5206.

CUNLIFFE-LISTER, Sir Philip, see 1st Earl of Swinton.

CUNNINGHAM, Sir John Henry Dacres (1885-1962) admiral.
P JOHN WORSLEY, 1945, IWM. SIR OSWALD BIRLEY, c1945-48, hs in uniform, Royal Naval College, Greenwich.
PH WALTER STONEMAN, 2 hs portraits in uniform, 1941 and 1946, NPG (NPR). WAYLAND, tql in uniform, print, NPG X7078.

CUNNINGHAM of Hyndhope, Andrew Browne Cunningham, 1st Viscount (1883-1963) admiral.
P ROWLAND LANGMAID, 1942, hl in uniform, NMM, Greenwich. HENRY CARR, 1943, IWM. D.S.EWART, c1944, tql in uniform, DoE (Ministry of Defence, London). SIR OSWALD BIRLEY, c1945-48, hs in uniform, Royal Naval College, Greenwich.
G SIR MUIRHEAD BONE, presenting White Ensign to Dean at St Giles' Cathedral, Edinburgh, chalk, 1945, IWM.
SC FRANTA BELSKY, bust, Trafalgar Square, London.
PH WALTER STONEMAN, 2 hs portraits, 1932 and 1945, NPG (NPR).

CURRIE, Sir Arthur William (1875-1933) Canadian general.
p SIR WILLIAM ORPEN, c1918, hl, Canadian War Memorials Coll, National Gallery of Canada, Ottawa, Canada.
g J.S.SARGENT, 'General Officers of World War I, 1914–18', oil, 1922, NPG 1954.

CURRIE, Sir James (1868-1937) educationist.
sc SIR WILLIAM GOSCOMB JOHN, c1918, bust, Gordon Memorial College, Khartoum, Sudan.

CURRIE, Sir William Crawford (1884-1961) shipping magnate.
p R.J.SWAN, after E.I.Halliday, c1960, hs, P & O, London.
PH WALTER STONEMAN, 1942, hs, NPG (NPR). Various photographs P & O.

CURTIS, Lionel George (1872-1955) public servant.
p SIR OSWALD BIRLEY, 1932, wl? seated, Royal Institute of International Affairs, Chatham House, London.
sc KOSTEK WOJNAROWSKI, 1953, bronze bust, Royal Institute of International Affairs.
PH RAMSEY & MUSPRATT, hs, print, NPG x7086.

CURTIS, Dame Myra (1886-1971) civil servant and principal of Newnham College, Oxford.
PH WALTER STONEMAN, 1957, hs, NPG (NPR).

CURZON, Charles Edward (1878-1954) bishop of Exeter.
PH WALTER STONEMAN, 1945, hs, NPG (NPR). UNKNOWN, hl in robes, print, NPG (Anglican Bishops).

CURZON, Francis Richard Henry Penn, see 5th Earl Howe.

CUSHNY, Arthur Robertson (1866-1926) pharmacologist.
PH UNKNOWN, c1925–26, hs, print, Pharmacology Department, Edinburgh University.

CUST, Henry John Cockayne (1861-1917) politician and journalist.
PR UNKNOWN, 1892, hs, lith, NPG.
PH LONDON STEREOSCOPIC CO, tql seated, postcard, NPG x7092.

CUTLER, Kate (1870-1955) actress.
PH BASSANO, 1895, various sizes and negs, NPG x413–17. JOHNSTON & HOFFMANN, c1905?, tql seated, postcard, NPG x7096.

D

DAIN, Sir (Harry) Guy (1870-1966) chairman of the British Medical Association.
P DAVID JAGGER, c1952, BMA House, London.
PH WALTER BIRD, 1961, hs, NPG (NPR).

DALBERG-ACTON, Richard Maximilian, see 2nd Baron Acton.

DALE, Sir Henry Hallett (1875-1968) medical researcher.
P FRANCIS DODD, c1944, tql seated, National Institute for Medical Research, London. SIR JAMES GUNN, 1945, hl seated, Royal Society, London. A.R.MIDDLETON TODD, 1952, tql seated in robes, Salters' Company, London.
PH HOWARD COSTER, c1930, various sizes and negs, NPG X11180-87. WALTER STONEMAN, 3 hs portraits, 1931, 1943 and 1953, NPG (NPR).

DALRYMPLE-HAMILTON, Sir Frederick Hew George (1890-1974) admiral.
PH WALTER STONEMAN, 1942, hs in uniform, NPG (NPR).

DALTON, Edward Hugh John Neale Dalton, 1st Baron (1887-1962) politician and economist.
C GEOFFREY DAVIEN, 1947, bust, plaster, NPG.
PH WALTER STONEMAN, 1945, hs, for NPR, NPG X1443.

DALTON, Ormonde Maddock (1866-1945) classical scholar and medieval archaeologist.
PH WALTER STONEMAN, 1925, hs, NPG (NPR).

DAMPIER, Sir William Cecil, formerly Wetham (1867-1952) scientist and agriculturist.
PH WALTER STONEMAN, 1943, hs, NPG (NPR).

DANE, Clemence, pseudonym of Winifred Ashton (1888-1965) novelist and playwright.
D FRED YATES, 1917, head, pastel, NPG 4490. S.H.GILL, 1942, hs, profile, pencil, NPG.
PH HOWARD COSTER, 1934, various sizes, print and negs, NPG X7975 and X11203-07. MARK GERSON, 1953, tql, print, NPG X7976.

DARBISHIRE, Dame Helen (1881-1961) principal of Somerville College, Oxford.
P SIR WILLIAM COLDSTREAM, 1938-39, hl seated, Somerville College.
PH WALTER STONEMAN, 1947, hl, NPG (NPR).

D'ARCY, Martin Cyril (1888-1976) philosopher and Jesuit.
P AUGUSTUS JOHN, 1939, hs, Campion Hall, Oxford.
SC FREDERICK SHRADY, bronze bust, Campion Hall.
PH HOWARD COSTER, c1938, various sizes and negs, NPG X11220-28. GODFREY ARGENT, 1968, tql seated, for NPR, NPG X7983. UNKNOWN, 1968, hl, print, NPG X7984.

DARE, Phyllis (1890-1975) actress.
PR CHARLES BUCHEL and HASSALL, hs and wl, lith, NPG..
C J.ROSS, wl with two men in evening dress, wash, NPG.
PH ROTARY PHOTO, c1905?, hs, profile, postcard, NPG X7986.

DARE, Zena, the Hon Mrs Brett (1887-1975) actress.
PH ROTARY PHOTO, c1904, hs, postcard, NPG X7988. UNKNOWN, c1908, hs, tinted postcard, NPG X7989.

DARWIN, Bernard (1876-1961) writer and golfer.
D POWYS EVANS, c1930, hs, pen and ink, NPG 4462.
PH G.C.BERESFORD, 2 hs portraits, 1921 and 1927, negs, NPG X6483-84. HOWARD COSTER, c1936, various sizes and negs, NPG X10558-61 and X11246.

DARWIN, Sir Charles Galton (1887-1962) theoretical physicist.
P ROBIN DARWIN, hl seated, National Physical Laboratory, Teddington, Middx.
PH WALTER STONEMAN, 3 hs portraits, 1926, 1943 and 1953, NPG (NPR). Various photographs, National Physical Laboratory.

DASHWOOD, Edmée Elizabeth Monica (1890-1943) writer 'E.M.Delafield'.
PH HOWARD COSTER, various sizes and negs, NPG X10435-40.

DAVID, Albert Augustus (1867-1950) headmaster and bishop of Liverpool.
P SIR WALTER RUSSELL, Rugby School, Warwicks.
SC LADY KATHLEEN KENNET, c1939, bronze bust, Diocesan House, Liverpool.
PH HOWARD COSTER, various sizes and negs, NPG X11258-64. WALTER STONEMAN, 1939, hs in robes, NPG (NPR). UNKNOWN, hl, print, NPG (Anglican Bishops).

DAVIDSON, John Colin Davidson, 1st Viscount (1889-1970) politician.
PH WALTER STONEMAN, 2 hs portraits, 1936 and 1949, NPG (NPR).

DAVIDSON, Sir John Humphrey (1876-1954) major-general.
PH WALTER STONEMAN, 1936, hs, NPG (NPR).

DAVIE, Thomas Benjamin (1895-1955) pathologist and teacher.
SC I.MITFORD-BARBERTON, bronze head, University of Cape Town, South Africa.

DAVIES, Clement (1884-1962) politician.
PH WALTER STONEMAN, 1948, hs, NPG (NPR). WALTER BIRD, 1962, NPG (NPR).

DAVIES, David Davies, 1st Baron (1880-1944) public benefactor.
P SYDNEY MORSE-BROWN, 1939, hs, National Museum of Wales 479, Cardiff. MURRAY URQUHART, 1950, National Library of Wales, Aberystwyth.
SC SIR WILLIAM GOSCOMBE JOHN, c1937, bust, National Library of Wales.
PH WALTER STONEMAN, 1921, hs, NPG (NPR). Various photographs, National Library of Wales.

DAVIES, Gwen Ffrangcon-, see Ffrangcon-Davies.

DAVIES, Sir (Henry) Walford (1869-1941) musician.
D EVAN WALTERS, charcoal, National Museum of Wales, Cardiff.
PH WALTER STONEMAN, 1936, hs, for NPR, NPG X423.

DAVIES, Randall Robert Henry (1866-1946) critic, author and collector.
D RANDOLPH SCHWABE, 1939, head, chalk, NPG 3621.

DAVIES, William Henry (1871-1940) poet.
P AUGUSTUS JOHN, c1921, hl, National Museum of Wales 542, Cardiff. HAROLD KNIGHT, hl, National Museum of Wales 236. SIR WILLIAM NICHOLSON, 1927–28, hl seated, NPG 4194.
D A.JOHN, 1918, hs, pencil, NPG 3149. JOHN WHEATLEY, 1919, wl seated, pen and ink, and wash, BM. POWYS EVANS, c1922, head, pen and ink, NPG 4396.
SC SIR JACOB EPSTEIN, 1916, bronze cast of head, NPG 3885, and Newport Art Gallery. THEODORE SPICER-SIMSON, c1922, plasticine medallion, NPG 2046.
PH A.L.COBURN, 1913, hl, photogravure, NPG AX7812 and AX7848. HECTOR MURCHISON, hs, print, NPG.

DAVIES, Sir William (Llewelyn) (1887-1952) librarian of National Library of Wales.
D DAVID BELL, 1943, pencil, National Library of Wales, Aberystwyth.
PH WALTER STONEMAN, 1944, hs, NPG (NPR). Various photographs, National Library of Wales.

DAVIS, Sir Herbert (1891-1972) vice-chairman of Unilever.
D UNKNOWN, 1930s, tql, w/c, Unilever House, London.

DAVISON, Sir Ronald Conway (1884-1958) authority on unemployment and social insurance.
PH WALTER STONEMAN, 1940, hs, NPG (NPR).

DAWBER, Sir (Edward) Guy (1861-1938) architect.
P FRED ROE, 1926, head, NPG 4168. SIR WILLIAM ORPEN, 1930, tql seated, RIBA.
C SIR DAVID LOW, profile head, with another of Sir Arbuthnot Lane, pencil, NPG 4529(109).
PH WALTER STONEMAN, 1934, hs, NPG (NPR).

DAWKINS, Richard McGillivray (1871-1955) Byzantine and modern Greek scholar.
P WILLIAM ROBERTS, c1939–40, hs, Emmanuel College, Cambridge.
D HENRY LAMB, pencil, Exeter College, Oxford.
PH WALTER STONEMAN, 2 hs portraits, 1933 and 1945, NPG (NPR).

DAWSON, (George) Geoffrey, real name Robinson (1874-1944) editor of *The Times*.
P FRANCIS DODD, 1943, tql seated, Rhodes House, Oxford.
D SIR WILLIAM ROTHENSTEIN, 1923, hs, chalk, NPG L168(8).
G SIR OSWALD BIRLEY, wl with Lord Astor of Hever and W.Lints Smith, oil, 1937, Times Newspapers Ltd, London.

DAWSON of Penn, Bertrand Edward Dawson, 1st Viscount (1864-1945) physician.
P P.A.DE LÁSZLÓ, 1937, tql seated in robes, Royal College of Physicians, London.
PH WALTER STONEMAN, 1921, hs, NPG (NPR). DOROTHY WILDING, hs, print, NPG.

DEAKIN, Arthur (1890-1955) trade union leader.
C SIR DAVID LOW, several heads, pencil, NPG 4529(110–115).
PH WALTER STONEMAN, 1949, hs, NPG (NPR).

DEAN, Basil (1888?-1978) stage and film producer.
PH HOWARD COSTER, various sizes and negs, NPG X11272–79.

DE BEER, Sir Gavin Rylands (1899-1972) scientist and director of the British Museum of Natural History.
PH WALTER STONEMAN, 1955, hs, NPG (NPR).

DEBENHAM, Frank (1883-1965) founder director of Scott Polar Research Institute, Cambridge.
D H.A.FREETH, 1961, hl seated, w/c, Scott Polar Research Institute. H.A.FREETH, 1961, hs, semi-profile, chalk and charcoal, Scott Institute.

PH H.G.PONTING, 1911, various photographs, Scott Institute. Various photographs, Scott Institute.

DEBURGH, William George (1866-1943) philosopher.
PH WALTER STONEMAN, 1939, hs, NPG (NPR). VICTOR WHITE & CO, tql seated, Archives Department, University of Reading Library.

DE CASALIS, Jeanne (1898-1966) actress and comedienne.
SC FRANK DOBSON, 1934, bronze bust, TATE 4796.

DE CHAIR, Sir Dudley Rawson Stratford (1864-1958) admiral.
D FRANCIS DODD, 1917, charcoal and w/c, IWM.
PH WALTER STONEMAN, 2 hs portraits in uniform, 1919 and 1933, NPG (NPR).

DEEPING, (George) Warwick (1877-1950) novelist.
D KATHLEEN SHACKLETON, 1936, head, chalk, NPG 5142.
PH HOWARD COSTER, various sizes and negs, NPG X11280–87.

DE FRECE, Matilda Alice, Lady, see Vesta Tilley.

D'EGVILLE, Sir Howard (d1965) secretary-general of the Commonwealth Parliamentary Association.
PH WALTER STONEMAN, 1929, hs, NPG (NPR).

DE HAVILLAND, Sir Geoffrey (1882-1965) aircraft engineer and designer.
P SIR OSWALD BIRLEY, 1940, tql seated in flying dress, British Aerospace Aircraft Group, Hatfield, Herts.
PH HOWARD COSTER, c1937–38, various sizes and negs, NPG X11288–91. WALTER STONEMAN, 1944, hl, NPG (NPR). YOUSUF KARSH, c1950s, 3 hs portraits, prints, British Aerospace. HAY WRIGHTSON, hs, print, NPG.

DELAFIELD, E.M., see Dashwood.

DE LA MARE, Walter John (1873-1956) poet and novelist.
D SIR WILLIAM ROTHENSTEIN, 1921, Lockwood Memorial Library, Buffalo, USA. SIR W.ROTHENSTEIN, c1929, head, chalk, NPG 4142. AUGUSTUS JOHN, 1950, head, chalk, NPG 4473.
SC THEODORE SPICER-SIMSON, plasticine medallion, NPG 2047.
PR WALTER TITTLE, 1922, hs, lith, NPG.
C SIR DAVID LOW, head, pencil, NPG 4529(231). R.S.SHERRIFFS, wl with 'red-riding hood', ink and charcoal?, NPG.
PH HOWARD COSTER, c1928, 2 hs portraits, negs, NPG X11305–06. HECTOR MURCHISON, c1930s, hs, print, NPG. HERBERT LAMBERT, 1937, hs, print, NPG X1503. WALTER STONEMAN, 1939, hs, NPG (NPR). MARK GERSON, 1953, hl, print, NPG.

DE LÁSZLÓ, Philip Alexius, see László.

DELEVINGNE, Sir Malcolm (1868-1950) civil servant and reformer.
PH WALTER STONEMAN, 1919, hs, NPG (NPR).

DE LISLE, Sir (Henry de) Beauvoir (1864-1955) general.
PH ELLIOTT & FRY, 1890s, wl on horseback with polo mallet, photogravure, NPG. WALTER STONEMAN, 1918, hs in uniform, NPG (NPR).

DELIUS, Frederick (Fritz Theodor Albert) (1862-1934) composer.
P JELKA DELIUS, 1912, hl seated, Percy Grainger Museum, University of Melbourne, Australia. ERNEST PROCTER, 1929, tql seated in wheelchair, Albert Hall, London; study head, NPG 3861. JACOB KRAMER, 1932, hs, profile, Leeds City Art Gallery. SIR JAMES GUNN, 1932, wl seated in wheelchair, Bradford City Art Gallery.
D EDVARD MUNCH, c1890, hs, Munch Museum, Oslo. E.PROCTER, 1929, various sketches made at Queen's Hall, London, during Delius Festival, NPG 4975(1–36). AUGUSTUS JOHN, 1929, head, pencil, Birmingham City Art Gallery. EDMOND KAPP, 1932, tql

seated, crayon, BM. E.KAPP, 1932, hs, Barber Institute, Birmingham University.

SC ELEUTARIO RICCARDI, c1920, bronze bust, Royal College of Music, London.

PR E.MUNCH, 1920, hs, lith, Munch Museum. E.MUNCH, 1922, hs, profile, in concert hall, lith, Toledo Museum of Art, USA.

PH Various photographs, Frederick Delius Trust, London. Various photographs, Percy Grainger Museum.

DELLER, Sir Edwin (1883-1936) principal of the University of London.

D HELEN M.CAMPBELL, hs, pencil, University of London.

DEMPSEY, Sir Miles Christopher (1896-1969) general.

P BERNARD HAILSTONE, 1946, IWM.

PH WALTER STONEMAN, 1944, hl in uniform, NPG (NPR).

DENMAN, Gertrude Mary, Lady (1884-1954) public servant.

P ANTHONY DEVAS, c1951, tql seated, Denman College, Marcham Park, Berks.

PH UNKNOWN, hs, print, National Federation of Women's Institutes, London.

DENMAN, Sir Thomas Denman, 3rd Baron (1874-1954) soldier and governor-general of Australia.

PH BASSANO, 1894, 4 portraits in uniform, negs, NPG X7139–42. WALTER STONEMAN, 5 hs portraits, 1917, 1928, 1940 and 1953, NPG (NPR).

DENNING, Alfred Thompson Denning, Baron (b1899) master of the rolls.

P EDWARD HALLIDAY, 1974, tql seated in robes, Lincoln's Inn, London. JOHN WARD, 1978, tql in robes, Birkbeck College, London.

G NORMAN HEPPLE, 'A Short Adjournment', oil, 1958, Lincoln's Inn.

PH WALTER STONEMAN, 1945, hs in robes, NPG (NPR). WALTER BIRD, 1964, hs in robes, NPG (NPR). ARNOLD NEWMAN, 1978, tql in robes, print, NPG.

DENNIS, Geoffrey Pomeroy (1892-1963) writer.

PH HOWARD COSTER, various sizes and negs, NPG X11307–15.

DENNISTON, John Dewar (1887-1949) classical scholar.

PH WALTER STONEMAN, 1938, hl, NPG (NPR).

DENNY, Sir Maurice Edward, 2nd Bart (1886-1955) engineer and shipbuilder.

P D.S.EWART, 1953, tql seated, NMM, Greenwich.

PH WALTER STONEMAN, 1947, hl, NPG (NPR).

DENT, Edward Joseph (1876-1957) musical scholar.

P LAWRENCE GOWING, 1948, King's College, Cambridge.

D SYDNEY WATERLOW, 1900, wl seated, pencil, Fitzwilliam Museum, Cambridge. EDMOND KAPP, 1941, hs, lampblack and stump, Fitzwilliam Museum.

C A.P.THOMPSON, c1901, wl, drg, King's College.

DENVILLE, Alfred Arthur Hinchcliffe (1876-1955) theatrical producer and MP.

PH WALTER STONEMAN, 1938, hs, NPG (NPR).

DERBY, Edward George Villiers Stanley, 17th Earl of (1865-1948) secretary of state for war.

P F.T.COPNALL, Constitutional Club, Liverpool. SIR JAMES GUNN, hs, profile, Wellington College, Crowthorne, Berks. EDWARD HALLIDAY, c1935; University of Liverpool. SIR WILLIAM LLEWELLYN, c1934, (copy), tql seated, Chamber of Commerce, Liverpool. SIR WILLIAM ORPEN, 1919, hs, NPG 4185. SIR W.ORPEN, Masonic Temple, Liverpool.

D INGLIS SHELDON-WILLIAMS, 1900, tql seated in uniform, pencil

and w/c, NPG 4039(2).

PH JOHN RUSSELL & SONS, before 1917, hl, NPG (NPR). WATER STONEMAN, 1921, 2 hs portraits, NPG (NPR) and NPG X426. UNKNOWN, 1937, 3 portraits in robes for coronation of George VI, NPG (Daily Herald).

DE ROBECK, Sir John Michael (1862-1928) admiral.

D FRANCIS DODD, 1917, charcoal and w/c, IWM.

G SIR A.S.COPE, 'Naval Officers of World War I, 1914–18', Oil, 1921, NPG 1913.

DERRICK, Thomas (1885-1954) mural painter and illustrator.

PH HOWARD COSTER, 1932, hs, various sizes, print and negs, NPG AX3449 and X11327–32.

DE SELINCOURT, Ernest, see Selincourt.

DETMOLD, (Charles) Maurice (1883-1908) painter, etcher and illustrator.

D E.J.DETMOLD, 1899, hs, pencil, NPG 3036.

DETMOLD, Edward Julius (1883-1957) painter, etcher and illustrator.

D C.MAURICE DETMOLD, 1899, hs, profile, pencil, NPG 3037.

DE VALERA, Eamon (1882-1975) Irish nationalist leader and president.

P C.C.BRADSHAW, 1916, hs, NGI. SIR JOHN LAVERY, 1921, hl, Municipal Gallery of Modern Art, Dublin. LEO WHELAN, 1955, Commissioners of Public works, Dublin.

D SEAN O'SULLIVAN, 1931, NGI.

SC JEROME CONNOR, 1968, bronze bust, NGI 8053.

C SIR BERNARD PARTRIDGE, wl as bullfighter, pen and ink and w/c, for Punch Almanack, 1922, NPG. SIR B.PARTRIDGE, wl seated on chair on railway track, pen and ink, for Punch, 4 Feb 1942, NPG.

PH HOWARD COSTER, 1939, various sizes, print and negs, NPG AX2208 and X11334–42.

DE VALOIS, Dame Ninette, Mrs A.B.Connell (b1898) director of the Royal Ballet.

SC F.E.McWILLIAM, 1964, bronze cast of head, NPG 4679, and Royal Opera House, Covent Garden. KARIN JONZEN, c1974, clay bust, Theatre Museum, V & A; bronze cast, Sadler's Wells, London.

PH SIR CECIL BEATON, hl, print, NPG. Various photographs, Royal Opera House.

DEVERELL, Sir Cyril John (1874-1947) field-marshal.

PH WALTER STONEMAN, 2 hs portraits in uniform, 1920 and 1936, NPG (NPR).

DEVLIN, Joseph (1871-1934) Irish politician.

P SIR JOHN LAVERY, 1928, Ulster Museum, Belfast.

SC FRANCIS DOYLE-JONES, c1934, bronze bust, Municipal Gallery of Modern Art, Dublin.

DEVONSHIRE, Victor Christian William Cavendish, 9th Duke of (1868-1938) governor-general of Canada.

P P.A.DE LÁSZLÓ, 1928, tql seated in robes, Chatsworth, Derbys.

D SIR WILLIAM ROTHENSTEIN, 1916, head, semi-profile, pencil, NPG 4775.

C HARRY FURNISS, wl in cream pot, ink, NPG 3562. R.S.SHERRIFFS, wl, ink, NPG.

PH WALTER STONEMAN, 1923, hs and hl, NPG (NPR).

DE WIART, Sir Adrian Carton (1880-1963) general.

P SIR WILLIAM ORPEN, 1919, hl in uniform, NPG 4651.

D'EYNCOURT, Sir Eustace Henry William Tennyson-, see Tennyson-d'Eyncourt.

DICK, Sir William Reid (1879-1961) sculptor.

P PHILIPPE LEDOUX, 1934, tql in studio, NPG 4809.

PH WALTER STONEMAN, 2 hs portraits, 1930 and 1947, NPG (NPR). HOWARD COSTER, various sizes, print and negs, NPG X1810 and others.

DICKINSON, Goldsworthy Lownes (1862-1932) philosopher.
P L.C.DICKINSON, c1868, hs, NPG 4293. ROGER FRY, 1925, hl, King's College, Cambridge.
D R.FRY, 1893, hs, chalk, NPG 3151.
PH A.BOUGHTON, c1916, hl, print, NPG. WALTER STONEMAN, 1931, hs, NPG (NPR). UNKNOWN, c1932, 2 hl portraits, prints, NPG.

DICKSON-POYNDER, Sir John, see 1st Baron Islington.

DILL, Sir John Greer (1881-1944) field-marshal.
SC HERBERT HASELTINE, equestrian statue, Arlington Cemetery, Virginia, USA; quarter-size bronze statuette, Staff college, Camberley, Surrey.
PH WALTER STONEMAN, 3 hs portraits in uniform, 1920, 1932 and 1941, NPG (NPR).

DIXON, Sir Arthur Lewis (1881-1969) civil servant.
P SIR WILLIAM ROTHENSTEIN, 1941, hl, Manchester City Art Gallery.

DIXON, Henry Horatio (1869-1953) professor of botany.
PH WALTER STONEMAN, 1922, hs, NPG (NPR).

DOBBIE, Sir William George Shedden (1879-1964) lieutenant-general and governor of Malta.
P HENRY LAMB, 1943, hs in uniform, IWM. SIR JAMES GUNN, tql, Royal Engineers Headquarters Mess, Chatham.
SC DONALD GILBERT, 1943, plaster bust, IWM.
PH WALTER STONEMAN, 2 hl portraits in uniform, 1933 and 1942, NPG (NPR) and NPG X5907.

DOBBS, Sir Henry Robert Conway (1871-1934) Indian civil servant and administrator of Iraq.
PH WALTER STONEMAN, 1930, hs, NPG (NPR).

DOBELL, Sir Charles Macpherson (1869-1954) general.
D J.S.SARGENT, 2 wl sketches, studies for NPG 1954, NPG 2908(6–7).
G J.S.SARGENT, 'General Officers of World War I, 1914–18', oil, 1922, NPG 1954.
PH WALTER STONEMAN, 1920, hs in uniform, NPG (NPR).

DOBRÉE, Bonamy (1891-1974) English literary critic and scholar.
P MAURICE DE SAUSMAREZ, University of Leeds.
PH HOWARD COSTER, 3 hs portraits, negs, NPG X11362–64.

DOBSON, Frank (1888-1963) sculptor.
PH HOWARD COSTER, 1929, various sizes, print and negs, NPG AX2338 and X11028–36.

DOBSON, Sir Roy Hardy (1891-1968) aircraft designer.
PH WALTER STONEMAN, 1949, hs, NPG (NPR).

DODD, Charles Harold (1884-1973) New Testament scholar.
P EDMUND H.NELSON, Jesus College, Cambridge.
PH WALTER STONEMAN, 1946, hs, NPG (NPR). WALTER BIRD, 1962, hs, NPG (NPR).

DODD, Francis (1874-1949) painter and etcher.
P STEPHEN BONE, c1936, wl with books, Manchester City Art Gallery. Self-portrait, tql seated, Fitzwilliam Museum, Cambridge.
D D.S.MACCOLL, 1939, head, pencil, the Athenaeum, London.
PR RANDOLPH SCHWABE, 1916, tql seated, etch, NPG.
PH A.C.COOPER, c1936, hl at easel, print, NPG. WALTER STONEMAN, 1935, hs, NPG (NPR).

DODGSON, Campbell (1867-1948) critic and art historian.

D WOLFGANG BORN, 1936, hs, pencil, Fitzwilliam Museum, Cambridge. FRANCIS DODD, tql seated, chalk, BM. CATHARINE DODGSON, 1934, hs, chalk, BM.
PR F.DODD, 1908, tql seated, etch, NPG. WILLIAM STRANG, hs as young man, etch, NPG. H.A.FREETH, 1938, tql seated, etch, NPG, V & A.
PH WALTER STONEMAN, 1939, hl, semi-profile, NPG (NPR).

DODDS, Sir (Edward) Charles (1899-1973) biochemist.
P RAYMOND PIPER, 1967, hl seated, Royal College of Physicians, London.
PH WALTER STONEMAN, 1943, hl, NPG (NPR). GODFREY ARGENT, 1970, hs, NPG (NPR).

DOHERTY, Hugh Lawrence (1875-1919) lawn tennis player.
C SIR LESLIE WARD ('Spy'), wl with racquet, lith, for *Vanity Fair*, 1 Sept 1904, NPG.
PH ELLIOTT & FRY, wl with brother 'R.F.', photogravure, NPG.

DON, Alan Campbell (1885-1966) dean of Westminster.
D FRANCIS DODD, hs, chalk, NPG 4539.
PH WALTER STONEMAN, 1948, hs, NPG (NPR). KARL POLLAK, hs, print, NPG.

DONALD, Sir Robert (1860-1933) journalist.
PH WALTER STONEMAN, 1924, hs, NPG (NPR).

DONALDSON, St Clair George Alfred (1863-1935) bishop of Salisbury.
P SIR OSWALD BIRLEY, 1932, tql seated in robes, Bishop's Palace, Salisbury.
PH WALTER STONEMAN, 1933, hs, NPG (NPR). UNKNOWN, hl, print, NPG (Anglican Bishops).

DONNAN, Frederick George (1870-1956) physical chemist.
PH WALTER STONEMAN, 1922, hs, profile, NPG (NPR).

DONOGHUE, Stephen (1884-1945) jockey and trainer.
P SIR A.J.MUNNINGS, 1921, wl on horseback, The Stewards of the Jockey Club, Newmarket. LYNWOOD PALMER, 1922, (copy), wl on Captain Cuttle, Stewards of Jockey Club. SIR JOHN LAVERY, 1923, wearing the King's colours, Royal Scottish Academy, Edinburgh.

DONOUGHMORE, Richard Walter John Hely-Hutchinson, 6th Earl of (1875-1948) chairman of committees of House of Lords.
C SIR LESLIE WARD ('Spy'), wl, profile, lith, for *Vanity Fair*, 9 Feb 1905, NPG.
PH WALTER STONEMAN, 1931, 2 hs portraits, NPG (NPR).

DOUGLAS, Lord Alfred Bruce (1870-1945) poet.
PH UNKNOWN, 1893, wl seated with Oscar Wilde, print, William Andrews Clark Library, University of California, Los Angeles, USA. O.WILDE, 1897, hl at table, print, W.A.Clark Library. G.C.BERESFORD, 1902, hs, neg, NPG X6487. Various photographs, W.A.Clark Library. HOWARD COSTER, 1930s, various sizes and negs, NPG X11377–92.

DOUGLAS, Edgar, see Lord Adrian.

DOUGLAS, (George) Norman (1868-1952) novelist.
P DESMOND HARMSWORTH, 1933, University of Texas, Austin, USA. MICHAEL AYRTON, 1948, hl seated on beach, Sheffield City Art Gallery.
D M.AYRTON, 1948, hl, ink and wash, NPG 4146.
PH SIR CECIL BEATON, tql, print, NPG. BILL BRANDT, 1946, wl seated, print, NPG. HOWARD COSTER, various sizes and negs, NPG X11408–10. UNKNOWN, 1949, hl seated with bust of himself when a boy, print, NPG X7766.

DOUGLAS, Sir (Henry) Percy (1876-1939) hydrographer and vice-admiral.
PH WALTER STONEMAN, 2 hs portraits in uniform, 1919 and 1933, NPG (NPR).

DOUGLAS, James (1867-1940) journalist and writer.
PH HOWARD COSTER, 1929, various sizes, print and negs, NPG AX2312 and X11393-11407.

DOUGLAS, Sir William Scott (1890-1953) civil servant.
PH WALTER STONEMAN, 1942, hs, NPG (NPR).

DOUGLAS-PENNANT, Sir Cyril Eustace (1894-1961) admiral.
P BERNARD HAILSTONE, IWM.
PH WALTER STONEMAN, 1946, hs in uniform, NPG (NPR).

DOUGLAS-SCOTT-MONTAGU, John Walter Edward, see 2nd Baron Montagu of Beaulieu.

DOUGLAS of Kirtleside, William Sholto Douglas, 1st Baron (1893-1969) air marshal.
P SIR JAMES GUNN, IWM.
D ERIC KENNINGTON, 1941, pastel, IWM.
PH WALTER STONEMAN, 2 hs portraits in uniform, 1938 and 1945, NPG (NPR) and NPG X434. HOWARD COSTER, 1940s, various sizes and negs, NPG X11411-19. WALTER BIRD, 1961, hs, NPG (NPR).

DOWDING, Hugh Caswall Tremenheere Dowding, 1st Baron (1882-1970) air chief marshal.
P ANTONY BATES, c1969, RAF Museum, Hendon. SIR WALTER RUSSELL, IWM.
D SIR WILLIAM ROTHENSTEIN, 1939, sanguine, IWM.
PH VANDYK, c1931, hs in uniform, print, NPG.

DOWNEY, Richard Joseph (1881-1953) Roman Catholic archbishop of Liverpool.
P STANLEY REED, c1949-50, hl in robes, NPG 5023; wl, St Joseph's College, Upholland, Archdiocese of Liverpool.
PH HOWARD COSTER, various sizes and negs, NPG X11420-25.

DOWSON, Ernest (1867-1900) poet.
D CHARLES CONDER, head, profile, pencil, NPG 2209.
PH UNKNOWN, tql seated, print, Lessing F.Rosenwald Coll, Library of Congress, Washington DC, USA.

DREYER, Sir Frederic Charles (1878-1956) admiral.
PH WALTER STONEMAN, 1936, 2 hs portraits in uniform, NPG (NPR).

DREYER, Georges (1873-1934) pathologist.
PH WALTER STONEMAN, 1933, hs, NPG (NPR).

DRINKWATER, John (1882-1937) poet and playwright.
P SIR WILLIAM ROTHENSTEIN, c1918, hl, NPG L168(9).
D SIR W.ROTHENSTEIN, 1917, hs, pencil, Minneapolis Institute of Arts, Minnesota, USA. JOYCE W.THOMPSON, 1935, head, chalk, NPG 4094.
SC ANASTAS BOTZARITCH SAVA, bronze head, Royal Society, London.
PH HOWARD COSTER, 1930s, various sizes and negs, NPG X11430 and others. WALTER STONEMAN, 1931, hs, NPG (NPR).

DRIVER, Sir Godfrey Rolles (1892-1972) Hebrew and Semitic scholar.
P WILLIAM DRING, 1961, hs, Magdalen College, Oxford.
PH WALTER STONEMAN, 1944, hs, NPG (NPR).

DROGHEDA, Henry Charles Ponsonby Moore, 10th Earl of (1884-1957) public servant.
PH WALTER STONEMAN, 1942, hs, NPG (NPR).

DRUMMOND, Flora (1879-1949) suffragette.
P FLORA LION, 1936, tql, SNPG 2229.

DRUMMOND, Sir Jack Cecil (1891-1952) nutritional biochemist.
PH WALTER STONEMAN, 1944, hs, NPG (NPR).

DRUMMOND, James Eric, see 16th Earl of Perth.

DRUMMOND, Sir Peter Roy Maxwell (1894-1945) air marshal.
D ERIC KENNINGTON, 1942, pastel, IWM. H.A.FREETH, 1943, pencil, IWM.
PH WALTER STONEMAN, 1943, hs in uniform, NPG (NPR).

DUCKWORTH, Wynfrid Laurence Henry (1870-1956) anatomist.
P JAMES WOOD, Jesus College, Oxford.

DU CROS, Sir Arthur Philip, 1st Bart (1871-1955) pioneer of pneumatic tyre industry.
C 'H.C.O.', wl, Hentschel-Colourtype, for *Vanity Fair*, 6 Jan 1910, NPG.

DUDLEY, William Humble Ward, 2nd Earl of (1867-1932) lord-lieutenant of Ireland and governor-general of Australia.
P SIR JOHN LONGSTAFF, Parliament House, Canberra, Australia.
PH GRAPHIC PHOTO UNION, c1924, tql with wife-to-be Gertie Millar, print, NPG. GRAPHIC PHOTO UNION, c1924, wl with best man Major Dudley Gilroy, print, NPG.

DUFF, Sir Alexander (Ludovic) (1862-1933) admiral.
P J.A.M.HAY, 1925, hs in uniform, NMM, Greenwich.
PH WALTER STONEMAN, 2 hs portraits, the 1st in uniform, 1917 and 1931, NPG (NPR).

DUFF, Sir James Fitzjames (1898-1970) vice-chairman of BBC.
PH WALTER STONEMAN, 1950, hs, NPG (NPR). WALTER BIRD, 1960, hs, NPG (NPR).

DUGDALE, Thomas Cantrell (1880-1952) portrait painter.
P Self-portrait, hl, NPG 3919.
PH KARL POLLAK, print, NPG. WALTER STONEMAN, 1950, hs, NPG (NPR).

DUKES, Ashley (1885-1959) dramatist, critic and theatre manager.
PH HOWARD COSTER, various sizes and negs, NPG X11455-58 and X11475.

DUKES, Sir Paul (1889-1967) diplomat and journalist.
PH KARL POLLAK, hs, print, NPG. WALTER STONEMAN, 1947, hs, NPG (NPR).

DULAC, Edmund (1882-1953) artist.
SL H.L.OAKLEY, hs, profile, NPG.
C R.S.SHERRIFFS, head, pencil, NPG.
PH A.L.COBURN, 1914, tql seated, profile, photogravure, NPG X7825. HOWARD COSTER, 1930s, various sizes and negs, NPG X11459-68.

DU MAURIER, Sir Gerald Hubert Edward Busson (1873-1934) actor-manager.
P C.A.BUCHEL, tql as the Admirable Crichton, Garrick Club, London. JOHN COLLIER, 1922, wl in theatre, Town Hall, Haverstock Hill, Hampstead, London.
D EDMOND KAPP, 1928, Barber Institute, Birmingham University.
PR C.A.BUCHEL and HASSALL, hs and wl as Captain Hook, lith, NPG.
C HARRY FURNISS, wl, profile, pen and ink, NPG 4095(3). SIR LESLIE WARD ('Spy'), wl, Hentschel-Colourtype, for *Vanity Fair*, 25 Dec 1907, NPG.
PH HOWARD COSTER, various sizes, print and negs, NPG X1815 and X11475-89. FOULSHAM & BANFIELD, hs as 'Arsène Lupin', postcard, NPG. CLAUDE HARRIS, hs, print, NPG X5599.

DUNBAR-NASMITH, Sir Martin (Eric), see Nasmith.

DUNCAN, Sir Andrew Rae (1884-1952) public servant.
P FRANK EASTMAN, after photograph, 1954, British Steel Corporation, London.
PH WALTER STONEMAN, 1938, hs, for NPR, NPG X6956. HOWARD COSTER, various sizes and negs, NPG X11511–16.

DUNCAN, Sir Patrick (1870-1943) South African statesman and governor-general.
SC M.KOTTLER, bust, Queen's Hall, Houses of Parliament, Cape Town, South Africa.
PH WALTER STONEMAN, 1937, 2 hs portraits, NPG (NPR) and NPG X6957.

DUNDAS, Lawrence John Lumley, see 2nd Marquess of Zetland.

DUNHILL, Thomas Frederick (1877-1946) composer.
PH UNKNOWN, hs as young man, print, Royal College of Music, London.

DUNHILL, Sir Thomas Peel (1876-1957) surgeon.
P SIR JAMES GUNN, tql seated, St Bartholomew's Hospital, london. SIR J.GUNN, Royal Australasian College of Surgeons, Melbourne, Australia.
PH WALTER STONEMAN, 2 hs portraits, 1934 and 1952, NPG (NPR).

DUNLOP, Ronald Ossory (1894-1973) painter.
P Self-portrait, 1950, TATE T171. Self-portrait, Bradford City Art Gallery.

DUNROSSIL, William Shepherd Morrison, 1st Viscount (1893-1961) speaker of the House of Commons.
P E.O.FEARNLEY-WHITTINGSTALL, posthumous, Palace of Westminster, London.
PH HOWARD COSTER, various sizes and negs, NPG. WALTER STONEMAN, 2 hs portraits, 1936 and 1945, NPG (NPR).

DUNSANY, Edward John Moreton Drax Plunkett, 18th Baron of (1878-1957) writer.
SC THEODORE SPICER-SIMSON, 1922, plasticine medallion, NPG 2048; bronze cast, NGI 8223.

PH WALTER STONEMAN, 1930, hs, NPG (NPR).

DUNSTAN, Sir Wyndham Rowland (1861-1949) chemist and director of the Imperial Institute.
P COLIN FORBES, 1906, Chemical Society, Burlington House, London.
PH WALTER STONEMAN, 1933, hs, NPG (NPR).

DUNSTERVILLE, Lionel Charles (1865-1946) soldier and writer.
PH G.C.BERESFORD, 1923, hs, neg, NPG X6489. HOWARD COSTER, various sizes, print and negs, NPG X1817 and X11517–29. WALTER STONEMAN, 1937, hs, NPG (NPR).

DU PARCQ, Herbert Du Parcq, Baron (1880-1949) judge.
PH WALTER STONEMAN, 2 hs portraits, the 2nd in robes, 1932 and 1943, NPG (NPR).

DUVEEN, Sir Joseph Duveen, Baron (1869-1939) art dealer and benefactor.
P WALTER TITTLE, tql seated, Guildhall, Hull.
D W.TITTLE, hs, pencil, NPG 2484.
G SIR JOHN LAVERY, 'Lord Duveen of Millbank at Home', oil, c1937, Ferens Art Gallery, Hull.
SC W.R.DICK, stone bust, NPG 3062.
PH G.C.BERESFORD, 1930, hs, neg, NPG X6492. DOROTHY WILDING, tql, print, NPG.

DYSON, Sir Frank (Watson) (1868-1939) astronomer.
PH WALTER STONEMAN, 1919, hs, NPG (NPR).

DYSON, Sir George (1883-1964) director of the Royal College of Music.
P ANTHONY DEVAS, 1952, hl seated, Royal College of Music, London.
SC ELIZABETH MARKS, 1948, plaster bust, Royal College of Music.
PH WALTER STONEMAN, 2 hs portraits, 1943 and 1953, NPG (NPR).

DYSON-SMITH, Charles William (d1961) sculptor.
D ALAN STERN, 1959, wl, w/c, Chelsea Arts Club, London.
G T.C.DUGDALE, 'Lunch at the Chelsea Arts Club', oil, 1935, Chelsea Arts Club.

E

EARLE, Sir Lionel (1866-1948) civil servant.
D SIR WILLIAM ROTHENSTEIN, 1933, chalk, DoE (Southbridge House, London).
SC UNKNOWN, bronze head, DoE (Lambeth Bridge House Library, London).
PH WALTER STONEMAN, 1917, hs, NPG (NPR). UNKNOWN, hl seated, print, NPG.

EARP, Thomas Wade (1892-1958) art critic.
D WYNDHAM LEWIS, 1932, head, pencil and w/c, Wakefield City Art Gallery, W Yorks.

EAST, Sir (William) Norwood (1872-1953) criminal psychologist.
PH WALTER STONEMAN, 1947, hl, NPG (NPR).

ECCLES, Sir John Arthur Symons (1898-1966) admiral.
PH WALTER STONEMAN, 1949, hs in uniform, NPG (NPR).

ECKERSLEY, Peter Pendleton (1892-1963) chief engineer British Broadcasting Corporation.
PH OLIVE EDIS, tql seated as young man, print, NPG X5196.

ECKERSLEY, Thomas Lydwell (1886-1959) theoretical physicist and engineer.
PH WALTER STONEMAN, 1938, hs, NPG (NPR).

EDDINGTON, Sir Arthur Stanley (1882-1944) astronomer.
D SIR WILLIAM ROTHENSTEIN, c1928-29, hs, profile, chalk, NPG 4656. AUGUSTUS JOHN, 1933, chalk, Trinity College, Cambridge.
PH WALTER STONEMAN, 2 hs portraits, 1925 and 1938, NPG (NPR) and NPG X1437. HOWARD COSTER, 1936, various sizes, print and negs, NPG AX3522 and X11538-51.

EDE, James Chuter, see Baron Chuter-Ede.

EDEN, Sir Anthony, see 1st Earl of Avon.

EDGE, Selwyn Francis (1868-1940) pioneer motorist.
PH LONDON STEREOSCOPIC CO, c1907-09, hs, print, NPG.

EDIS, Olive, Mrs Galsworthy (1872?-1955) photographer.
PH Self-portrait, 1918, 2 hs portraits, one with camera, prints, NPG X7959-60.

EDMONDS, Sir James Edward (1861-1956) military historian.
PH WALTER STONEMAN, 1919, hs in uniform, NPG (NPR).

EDRIDGE-GREEN, Frederick William (1863-1953) authority on colour perception.
P FREDERICK WALENN, 1895, hl, Royal College of Surgeons, London.
C GEORGE BELCHER, wl, charcoal, Royal College of Surgeons.

EDWARD VIII, see Duke of Windsor.

EDWARDS, Alfred (1888-1958) politician.
PH WALTER STONEMAN, 1948, hs, NPG (NPR).

EDWARDS, Ness (1897-1968) politician.
PH WALTER STONEMAN, 1949, hs, NPG (NPR).

EDWARDS, Walter James (1900-1964) civil lord of the Admiralty.
PH WALTER STONEMAN, 1946, hs, NPG (NPR).

EGERTON, Sir Alfred Charles Glyn (1886-1959) scientist.

PH HOWARD COSTER, various sizes and negs, NPG X11558-62. WALTER STONEMAN, 2 hs portraits, 1932 and 1954, NPG (NPR).

EGLINTON, John, see William Kirkpatrick Magee.

ELIAS, Julius Salter, see Viscount Southwood.

ELIOT, Sir Charles Norton Edgecumbe (1862-1931) diplomat and orientalist.
PH WALTER STONEMAN, 1920, hs, NPG (NPR).

ELIOT, Thomas Stearns (1888-1965) poet.
P WYNDHAM LEWIS, 1938, tql seated, Durban Municipal Art Gallery, South Africa; study, Eliot House, Harvard University, Cambridge, Mass, USA. W.LEWIS, 1949, tql seated, Magdalene College, Cambridge. PATRICK HERON, 1949, hs, NPG 4467. SIR GERALD KELLY, 1965, tql seated, University of Texas, Austin, USA.
D W.LEWIS, hs, pen and w/c, National Gallery of Victoria, Melbourne, Australia. W.LEWIS, 1925, head, pencil, University of Texas.
SC SIR JACOB EPSTEIN, 1951, plaster cast of bust, NPG 4440, and bronze cast, University of Texas. BORIS ANREP, 1952, wl seated as 'Leisure' in 'The Modern Virtues', mosaic, National Gallery, London.
PR EDGAR A.HOLLOWAY, hs, etch, NPG.
PH SIR CECIL BEATON, 3 heads, print, NPG. WALTER STONEMAN, 1948, hs and hl seated, NPR and NPG X11136. FELIX MAN, 1949, hl seated, print, NPG X11152. MARK GERSON, 1960, with wife and W.H.AUDEN, print, NPG X4599. Various photographs, Horton Coll, Harvard University.

ELIZABETH, The Queen Mother (b1900) Queen of George VI.
P R.G.EVES, 1924, hs, NPG 4145. P.A.DE LÁSZLÓ, 1925, hl seated, Royal Coll. MARGARET LINDSAY WILLIAMS, 1920s, hs, Royal Coll. SIR OSWALD BIRLEY, 1937, hl, Queen's Own Yorkshire Light Infantry, Pontefract, Yorks. T.M.RONALDSON, 1937, tql seated, Royal Coll. SIR GERALD KELLY, c1938-45, wl, Coronation portrait, Royal Coll; various studies, tql and wl, NPG 4962, NPG 5287 and DoE (Palace of Westminster). SIR JAMES GUNN, c1945-46, tql seated, Middle Temple, London. PIETRO ANNIGONI, 1963, hs in academic robes, University of London. MAURICE CODNER, 1964?, tql seated, Royal Coll. LEONARD BODEN, 1971, wl seated, Royal College of Music, London. SUSAN CRAWFORD, 1972, hl, Royal Highland Regiment (Black Watch), Edinburgh. RICHARD STONE, c1974, tql seated, 1st Battalion of the Royal Anglian Regiment, Tidworth, Hants.
D J.S.SARGENT, 1923, hs, profile, charcoal, Royal Coll.
G F.O.SALISBURY, 'Jubilee Service for George V', oil, 1935, Royal Coll; related 'Thanksgiving Service', oil, Guildhall, London. SIR J.GUNN, 'Conversation Piece at the Royal Lodge, Windsor, 1950', oil, NPG 3778.
SC UNKNOWN, 1937, coronation medal, NPG.
PH RITA MARTIN, 1907, hs with muff, neg, NPG. VANDYK, 1922, hl, neg, NPG. BASSANO, 1923, various wedding portraits, NPG. Various photographs, singly, and family groups, mid 1920s on, by MARCUS ADAMS, SIR CECIL BEATON, BERTRAM PARK, DOROTHY WILDING and LISA SHERIDAN, NPG and Royal Coll.

ELLERMAN, Sir John Reeves (1862-1933) financier and shipowner.
P SIR LUKE FILDES, 1922, tql, Ellerman Lines Ltd Group, London.

ELLES, Sir Hugh Jamieson (1880-1945) general.
P SIR WILLIAM ORPEN, 1918, IWM.
PH WALTER STONEMAN, 2 hs portraits, the 2nd in uniform, 1919 and 1920, NPG (NPR).

ELLIS, Sir (Bertram) Clough Williams-, see Williams-Ellis.

ELLIS, Thomas Evelyn Scott-, see 8th Baron Howard de Walden.

ELLIS, Sir William Henry (1860-1945) civil engineer and steel maker.
P ERNEST MOORE, tql seated, NPG 4927.

ELMHIRST, Leonard Knight (1893-1974) chairman of the Dartington Hall Trust and educational reformer.
PH Various photographs, Dartington Hall Trust, Totnes, Devon.

ELPHINSTONE, Sir (George) Keith (Buller) (1865-1941) engineer.
PH WALTER STONEMAN, 1930, hs, NPG (NPR).

ELSIE, Lily, see Mrs Bullough.

ELTON, Oliver (1861-1945) scholar and critic.
P HENRY CARR, University of Liverpool. AUGUSTUS JOHN, c1925, hs, University of Liverpool.
G ALBERT LIPCZINSKI, staff group, oil, 1915, Faculty of Arts, University of Liverpool.
PH WALTER STONEMAN, 1930, hs, NPG (NPR).

ELTON of Headington, Godfrey Elton, 1st Baron (1892-1973) general secretary of the Rhodes Trust and writer.
PH WALTER STONEMAN, 1934, hs, NPG (NPR).

ELVEY, Maurice (1887-1967) film-maker.
PH HOWARD COSTER, c1936, various sizes and negs, NPG X11577-81.

ELVIN, Sir (James) Arthur (1899-1957) founder of Wembley Stadium.
SC A.J.BANKS, bronze bust, Wembley Stadium, London.

ELWES, Gervase Henry (Cary-) (1866-1921) singer.
PH FRIEDRICH MÜLLER, 1889, hs, print, NPG. JOHN RUSSELL & SONS, before 1917, hs, semi-profile, print, for *National Photographic Record*, vol 2, NPG.

EMERSON, Sir Herbert William (1881-1962) civil servant.
PH WALTER STONEMAN, 3 hs portraits, 1933 and 1944, NPG (NPR).

ENTWISTLE, William James (1895-1952) scholar.
PH WALTER STONEMAN, 1950, hs, NPG (NPR).

EPSTEIN, Sir Jacob (1880-1959) sculptor.
D AUGUSTUS JOHN, c1900, head, chalk, NPG 4119. Self-portrait, 1901, hs, chalk, Walsall Museum and Art Gallery. POWYS EVANS, c1925, head, pen and ink, NPG 4397. Self-portrait, 1920, bronze head, University of Hull.
SC Self-portrait, c1912, bronze head, NPG 4126. Self-portrait, bronze, Castle Museum, Nottingham.
PR FRANCIS DODD, 1909, tql, etch, University of Hull. AUGUSTUS JOHN, etch, City Art Gallery, Auckland, New Zealand.
PH E.O.HOPPÉ, c1911-12, hl, print, Department of English, University of Reading. A.L.COBURN, 1914, hs, profile, photogravure, NPG X7820. G.C.BERESFORD, various sizes and negs, 1917, 1923 and 1924, NPG X6395-96 and X6493-96. HOWARD COSTER, 1930s, various sizes, print and negs, NPG X11043-47 and X2381. GEOFFREY IRELAND, 1950s, various sizes and prints, NPG X8495-96 and others.

ERVINE, St John Greer (1883-1971) playwright and author.
SC THEODORE SPICER-SIMSON, c1920s, plasticine medallion, NPG 1049.
C SIR DAVID LOW, hl, pencil, NPG 4529(123).
PH HOWARD COSTER, c1939, various sizes and negs, NPG X11758-68.

ESHER, Oliver Sylvain Balliol Brett, 3rd Viscount (1881-1963) public servant.
PR WALTER TITTLE, 1922, hs, lith, NPG.
PH WALTER STONEMAN, 2 hs portraits, 1930 and 1955, NPG (NPR).

ESMOND, Henry Vernon (1869-1922) actor and dramatist.
C WALLACE HESTER, wl, mechanical repro, for *Vanity Fair*, 14 May 1913, NPG.
PH T.C.TURNER, c1895, 2 tql portraits, photogravure, NPG.

EUMORFOPOULOS, George (1863-1939) art collector and patron.
SC DORA GORDINE, 1938, bronze head, V & A. IVAN MESTROVIC, bust, BM.
PR GERH FRANKL, c1938, drypoint, V & A.

EVAN-THOMAS, Sir Hugh (1962-1928) admiral.
D FRANCIS DODD, 1917, charcoal and w/c, IWM.
PH WALTER STONEMAN, 1921, hs in uniform, NPG (NPR).

EVANS, B. Ifor (b1899) literary scholar.
P SIR WILLIAM COLDSTREAM, tql, University College, London.
PH HOWARD COSTER, various sizes and negs, NPG. WALTER STONEMAN, 1946, hs, NPG (NPR).

EVANS, Dame Edith (1888-1976) actress.
P ETHEL GABAIN, c1935, tql in costume, City of Stoke-on-Trent Art Gallery. W.R.SICKERT, c1935, hl with Peggy Ashcroft in *Romeo and Juliet*, Leeds City Art Gallery. W.R.SICKERT, 1937, tql with Leslie Banks in *The Taming of the Shrew*, Bradford City Art Gallery. ROBERT BUHLER, 1959, wl as 'Volumnia', Royal Shakespeare Theatre, Stratford-upon-Avon.
D WYNDHAM LEWIS, 1932, hl, pencil and wash, Ashmolean Museum, Oxford.
PH GODFREY ARGENT, 1970, hl, NPG (NPR). SIR CECIL BEATON, hl, print, NPG. HOWARD COSTER, 2 portraits, negs, NPG. ANGUS McBEAN, 1959, hs, profile, print, NPG P64. A.McBEAN, 1959, hl in costume, print, NPG X5839. MADAME YEVONDE, 1937, wl in costume, print, NPG.

EVANS, Edwin (1874-1945) music critic.
P WYNDHAM LEWIS, c1922, wl seated, Scottish National Gallery of Modern Art, Edinburgh.

EVANS, Edward Ratcliffe Garth Russell, see 1st Baron Mountevans.

EVANS, Sir Guildhaume Myrddin-, see Myrddin-Evans.

EVANS, Sir (Worthington) Laming Worthington-, see Worthington-Evans.

EVERSHED, Francis Raymond Evershed, 1st Baron (1899-1966) judge and master of the rolls.
P NORMAN HEPPLE, 1958, wl, profile, NPG 4678.
G N.HEPPLE, 'A Short Adjournment', oil, 1958, Lincoln's Inn, London.
PH HOWARD COSTER, c1940, various sizes and negs, NPG X11790-93. WALTER STONEMAN, 1944, hs, NPG (NPR). WALTER BIRD, 1962, hs, NPG (NPR).

EVES, Reginald Grenville (1876-1941) painter.
P Self-portrait, 1908, hs, NPG 3826.

EWINS, Arthur James (1882-1957) pharmacologist.
PH WALTER STONEMAN, 1954, hl, NPG (NPR).

F

FABER, Sir Geoffrey Cust (1889-1961) publisher.
PH WALTER STONEMAN, 1954, hl seated, NPG (NPR).

FABER, Oscar (1886-1956) consulting engineer.
SC SIR CHARLES WHEELER, bronze bust, Bank of England, London.
PH UNKNOWN, print, Oscar Faber & Partners, St Albans.

FAIRBAIRN, Stephen (1862-1938) oarsman.
P JAMES QUINN, c1926, hs, Jesus College, Cambridge.

FAIRBRIDGE, Kingsley Ogilvie (1885-1924) founder of farm schools overseas.
P A.K.LAWRENCE, posthumous, wl, profile, Rhodes House, Oxford.

FAIREY, Sir (Charles) Richard (1887-1956) aircraft manufacturer.
P CUTHBERT ORDE, c1930-34, wl seated, Royal Aeronautical Society, London. FRANK EASTMAN, 1962, hs, Royal Aero Club on loan to RAF Museum, Hendon.

FAIRFIELD, (Frederick) Arthur Greer, 1st Baron (1863-1945) judge.
P LULU GREER, hl seated in robes, Gray's Inn, London.

FAIRLEY, Sir Neil Hamilton (1891-1966) professor at the London School of Hygiene and Tropical Medicine.
PH WALTER STONEMAN, 1946, hl seated, NPG (NPR).

FAITHFULL, Lilian Mary (1865-1952) principal of Cheltenham Ladies' College and pioneer of higher education for women.
P GERALD KELLY, c1923, Cheltenham Ladies' College.
PH LAFAYETTE, 1907, print, Cheltenham Ladies' College.

FALKNER, Sir (Donald) Keith (b1900) singer and former director of the Royal College of Music.
P SONIA MERVYN, 1960, hl seated, Royal College of Music. LEONARD BODEN, 1974, Royal College of Music.
PH GODFREY ARGENT, 1970, hs, NPG (NPR).

FALLS, Cyril (Bentham) (1888-1971) scholar, author and soldier.
PH HOWARD COSTER, 1940s, various sizes and negs, NPG X12087-90.

FARMER, Sir John Bretland (1865-1944) botanist.
D F.A.DE BIDEN FOOTNER, 1929, chalk, Imperial College of Science and Technology, London.
PH WALTER STONEMAN, 1933, hs, NPG (NPR).

FAUSSET, Hugh I'Anson (1895-1965) author and literary critic.
PH HOWARD COSTER, various sizes and negs, NPG X12211-14 and X12222.

FAWCETT, Sir Luke (1881-1960) trade unionist.
D SIR DAVID LOW, head, profile, pencil, NPG 4529(124).
PH WALTER STONEMAN, 1949, hs, NPG (NPR).

FAY, Frank (1870-1931) actor and producer.
P J.B.YEATS, 1904, hs, The Abbey Theatre, Dublin.

FAY, William George (1872-1947) actor and producer.
P J.B.YEATS, c1904, hl, The Abbey Theatre, Dublin. J.B.YEATS, Municipal Gallery of Modern Art, Dublin.
D J.B.YEATS, 1904, pencil, NGI.

FEGAN, Ethel Sophia (1877-1975) librarian.
G BASSANO, staff group, ph, 1919, Girton College, Cambridge. HILL AND SAUNDERS, 'Farewell Party for H.M.R.Murray', ph, 1936, Girton College.
PH UNKNOWN, 2 portraits, prints, Girton College.

FELLOWES, Edmund Horace (1870-1951) clergyman and musical scholar.
PH WALTER STONEMAN, 1944, hs, NPG (NPR).

FELLOWES, Sir Edward (Abdy) (1895-1970) clerk of House of Commons and chairman of the British Broadcasting Corporation.
PH WALTER STONEMAN, 1955, hs, NPG (NPR). WALTER BIRD, 1962, hs, NPG (NPR).

FERGUSON, Ronald Crauford Munro-, see 1st Viscount Novar.

FERGUSSON, Sir Charles, 7th Bart (1865-1951) soldier and administrator.
D FRANCIS DODD, 1917, charcoal and w/c, IWM.
PH WALTER STONEMAN, 1919, hs in uniform, NPG (NPR).

FERGUSSON, John Duncan (1874-1961) painter.
PH A.L.COBURN, 1919, hs, photogravure, NPG AX7838.

FERMOR, Sir Lewis Leigh (1880-1954) geologist.
PH WALTER STONEMAN, 1937, hs, for NPR, NPG X435.

FERRANTI, Sebastian Ziani de (1864-1930) electrical engineer and inventor.
P DAVID JAGGER, 1931, tql seated in academic robes, Institution of Electrical Engineers, London.

FFOULKES, Charles John (1868-1947) first curator of the Imperial War Museum and master of the armouries of the Tower of London.
P MAURICE CODNER, 1937, tql in uniform, IWM.

FFRANGCON-DAVIES, Gwen (b1896) actress.
P HAROLD KNIGHT, tql, National Museum of Wales 279, Cardiff. W.R.SICKERT, 1932, wl as Isabella of France, TATE 4673.
G ANGUS MCBEAN, 'King Lear, Royal Shakespeare Theatre', ph, 1950, print, NPG X5842.

FIELD, Sir Frederick Laurence (1871-1945) admiral.
D FRANCIS DODD, 1917, charcoal and w/c, IWM.
PH WALTER STONEMAN, 2 portraits in uniform, hs and hl, 1919 and 1930, NPG (NPR).

FIFE, Alexandra Victoria Alberta Edwina Louise, Duchess of, see Princess Arthur of CONNAUGHT.

FIFE, Louise Victoria Alexandra Dagmar, Duchess of, see LOUISE VICTORIA Alexandra Dagmar.

FIGGIS, John Neville (1866-1919) historian and divine.
M KATHLEEN FIGGIS, Community of the Resurrection, Mirfield, Yorks.

FILDES, Sir Paul (1882-1971) pathologist.
P SIR LUKE FILDES, 1919, hs in uniform, NPG 4843.
PH WALTER STONEMAN, 1934, hl, NPG (NPR).

FILON, Louis Napoleon George (1875-1937) mathematician.

mathematician.

P BARBARA PRICE HUGHES, c1930, University of London.

PH WALTER STONEMAN, 1918, hs in uniform, NPG (NPR).

FINCH, George Ingle (1888-1970) chemist.

PH WALTER STONEMAN, 2 hs portraits, 1938 and 1947, NPG (NPR).

FINLAY, William Finlay, 2nd Viscount (1875-1945) judge.

D CHARLOTTE BLAKENEY WARD, tql in robes, pastel, Middle Temple, London.

PH WALTER STONEMAN, 2 hs portraits, 1920 and 1944, NPG (NPR).

FIRBANK, Ronald (1886-1925) novelist.

D AUGUSTUS JOHN, c1914, pencil, University of Texas, Austin, USA. A.JOHN, c1915, head, pencil, NPG 4600.

FIRTH, John Rupert (1890-1960) professor of general linguistics.

PH UNKNOWN, hs, semi-profile, print, Department of Phonetic Linguistics, School of Oriental and African Studies, University of London.

FISHER, Herbert Albert Laurens (1865-1940) historian, statesman and warden of New College, Oxford.

P SIR WILLIAM NICHOLSON, c1932. New College, Oxford.

D FRANCES CATHERINE DODGSON, New College. SIR WILLIAM ROTHENSTEIN, 1915, hs, pencil, Sheffield University. SIR W.ROTHENSTEIN, 1917, hs, pencil, Mappin Art Gallery, Sheffield.

SC BEN ZWI, c1937-38, bronze bust, New College. SIR JACOB EPSTEIN, bust, New College.

PH WALTER STONEMAN, 3 hs portraits, 1919 and 1931, NPG (NPR). OLIVE EDIS, 1930s, 3 hs and tql portraits, prints, NPG x5191-94. HOWARD COSTER, 1930s, various sizes and negs, NPG x12238-41.

FISHER, Sir (Norman Fenwick) Warren (1879-1948) civil servant.

PH WALTER STONEMAN, 1923, hs, NPG (NPR).

FISHER, Sir Ronald Aylmer (1890-1962) biologist.

PH WALTER STONEMAN, 4 hs portraits, 1931, 1943 and 1953, NPG (NPR).

FISHER, Sir William Wordsworth (1875-1937) admiral.

PH WALTER STONEMAN, 1930, hs, NPG (NPR).

FISHER of Lambeth, Geoffrey Francis Fisher, Baron (1887-1972) archbishop of Canterbury.

P R.G.EVES, c1934, tql seated in robes, Repton School, Derbys. ALEX CHRISTIE, 1945, tql seated in robes, Fulham Palace, London. A.R.MIDDLETON TODD, 1953, tql seated in robes, Lambeth Palace, London.

SC SIR JACOB EPSTEIN, 1959, bronze bust, the Church Commissioners, London.

PH SIR CECIL BEATON, tql in robes, with priest, print, NPG. HOWARD COSTER, 1953, various sizes, prints and negs, NPG x1824-26 and x12225-37. ROGER MAYNE, 1956, tql with wife at garden party, print, NPG x4068. WALTER STONEMAN, 2 hs portraits, 1938 and 1945, NPG (NPR). MADAME YEVONDE, wl, print, NPG x11657. UNKNOWN, tql, print, NPG (Anglican Bishops).

FITZMAURICE, Sir Maurice (1861-1924) chief engineer to the London County Council.

P GEORGE HARCOURT, c1924, tql, NPG 4928.

FITZROY, Edward Algernon (1869-1943) speaker of the House of Commons.

P SIR OSWALD BIRLEY, 1943, wl in robes, Palace of Westminster, London.

PH MRS ALBERT BROOM, wl in uniform, neg, NPG x171. WALTER STONEMAN, 1928, hs, NPG (NPR).

FLECK, Alexander Fleck, 1st Baron (1889-1968) chemist.

P LAWRENCE GOWING, 1957, tql seated, NPG 4662.

PH HOWARD COSTER, 1944 and 1956, various sizes and prints, NPG x1829-32. WALTER BIRD, 1964, hs, NPG (NPR).

FLEMING, Sir Alexander (1881-1955) discoverer of penicillin.

P T.C.DUGDALE, c1949, hl in robes, Wright-Fleming Institute, St Mary's Hospital, Paddington, London. ETHEL GABAIN, IWM. ANNA ZINKEISEN, posthumous, tql seated in robes, St Mary's Hospital.

D HELEN M.CAMPBELL, 1944, head, pencil, NPG 3988.

SC E.R.BEVAN, 1948, bronze head, Wright-Fleming Institute, and SNPG 1835. E.J.CLARK, c1946, bronze bust, Wright-Fleming Institute. FRANK KOVAKS, c1955, bronze bust, Royal College of Physicians, London. F.KOVAKS, 1955, bronze medallion, NPG 4238.

PR J.A.GRANT, 1944, hl, lith, NPG 5085.

PH WALTER STONEMAN, 1943, hs, NPG (NPR). HOWARD COSTER, 1954, various sizes, prints and negs, NPG x1833-38. DR P.N.CARDEW, 1954, 3 hl portraits in laboratory, prints, Department of Audio Visual Communication, St Mary's Hospital.

FLEMING, Sir Arthur Percy Morris (1881-1960) engineer.

PH WALTER STONEMAN, 1948, hs, NPG (NPR).

FLEMING, Dorothy Leigh, Mrs O.A.Fleming, see Sayers.

FLETCHER, Sir Banister Flight (1866-1953) architect and architectural historian.

P SEYMOUR LUCAS, 1917, hl in robes, RIBA. G.HILLYARD SWINSTEAD, c1920, tql in robes, RIBA. GLYN PHILPOT, 1931, hl, profile, RIBA.

PH WALTER STONEMAN, 1940, various sizes, for NPR x1423-26.

FLETCHER, Sir Frank (1870-1954) headmaster.

P GEORGE HARCOURT, c1915, Marlborough College, Wilts.

SC SIR JACOB EPSTEIN, bronze bust, Charterhouse School, Godalming, Surrey.

FLETCHER, Hanslip (1874-1955) artist.

PH KARL POLLAK, hl, print, NPG.

FLETCHER, Reginald Thomas Herbert, see Baron Winster.

FLETCHER, Sir Walter Morley (1873-1933) physiologist and administrator.

SC DORA CLARKE, posthumous, bust, National Institute for Medical Research, London.

PH ELLIOTT & FRY, hs, print, NPG. WALTER STONEMAN, 1917, hs, NPG (NPR).

FLETT, Sir John Smith (1869-1947) geologist.

PH WALTER STONEMAN, 1917, hs, NPG (NPR).

FLINT, Sir William Russell (1880-1969) artist.

PH WALTER STONEMAN, 1947, hs, NPG (NPR).

FLOREY, Howard Walter Florey, Baron (1898-1968) pathologist.

P HENRY CARR, 1965, tql seated in robes, The Royal Society, London. H.CARR, Queen's College, Oxford.

PH WALTER STONEMAN, 1943, hs, NPG (NPR). WALTER BIRD, 1960, hs, NPG (NPR).

FLOWER, Sir Cyril Thomas (1879-1961) Deputy Keeper of the Records and antiquarian.

PH WALTER STONEMAN, 1946, hs, NPG (NPR).

FLOWER, Robin Ernest William (1881-1946) scholar and poet.

PH WALTER STONEMAN, 1934, hs, NPG (NPR).

FOGERTY, Elsie (1865-1945) teacher of speech and drama.

P R.G.EVES, c1937, Central School of Speech and Drama, London.

FOOT, Isaac (1880-1960) politician.
PH WALTER STONEMAN, 1931, hl, NPG (NPR).

FORBES, Sir Charles Morton (1880-1960) admiral.
P SIR OSWALD BIRLEY, c1945-48, hs in uniform, Royal Naval College, Greenwich.
PH WALTER STONEMAN, 2 hs portraits in uniform, 1932 and 1943, NPG (NPR).

FORBES, (Joan) Rosita (1893-1967) traveller, lecturer and author.
PH HOWARD COSTER, various sizes and negs, NPG.

FORD, Ford Madox (formerly Ford Hermann Hueffer) (1873-1939) author and critic.
P JANICE BIALA, Olivet College, Michigan, USA. G.T.HARTMANN, 1927, University of Texas, Austin, USA.
D ALFRED WOLMARK, 1927, head, pen and ink, NPG 4454. Self-portrait, crayon, Manchester City Art Gallery.

FORESTER, Cecil Scott (1899-1966) novelist.
PH HOWARD COSTER, various sizes and negs, NPG.

FORSTER, Edward Morgan (1879-1970) novelist.
P DORA CARRINGTON, c1924-32, hs, profile, NPG 4698. FELIKS TOPOLSKI, 1961, University of Texas, Austin, USA.
D SIR WILLIAM ROTHENSTEIN, 1923, hl seated, chalk, King's College, Cambridge. EDMOND KAPP, 1930, hs, profile, King's College. E.KAPP, 1930, Barber Institute, Birmingham University.
C SIR MAX BEERBOHM, 1940, wl, drg, King's College.
PH SIR CECIL BEATON, hl, print, NPG. BILL BRANDT, 1947, hl seated, print, NPG. HOWARD COSTER, 1930s, various sizes and negs, NPG x10403-18. Various photographs, King's College.

FOSS, Hubert James (1899-1953) musician, writer and musical editor of the Oxford University Press.
PH UNKNOWN, hs, neg, Oxford University Press, London.

FOSTER, Sir (Thomas) Gregory, 1st Bart (1866-1931) educationist.
P SIR WILLIAM ORPEN, c1930, University College, London.
PH JOHN RUSSELL & SONS, c1917, hs, print, for *National Photographic Record*, vol 2, NPG.

FOTHERGILL, John Rowland (1876-1957) archaeologist and innkeeper.
PH HOWARD COSTER, various sizes and negs, NPG.

FOTHERINGHAM, John Knight (1874-1936) historian and authority on ancient astronomy.
PH WALTER STONEMAN, 1933, hl, NPG (NPR).

FOWLER, Alfred (1868-1940) astrophysicist.
PH WALTER STONEMAN, 1926, hs, NPG (NPR).

FOWLER, Sir Ralph Howard (1889-1944) mathematician and mathematical physicist.
PH WALTER STONEMAN, 1943, hs, NPG (NPR).

FOX, Sir Cyril Fred (1882-1967) archaeologist and director of National Museum of Wales.
D EVAN WALTERS, 1937, hs, charcoal, National Museum of Wales, Cardiff.
SL UNKNOWN, 1933, profile, National Museum of Wales.
PH ELLIOTT & FRY, 1931, hs, print, National Museum of Wales, and NPG. WALTER STONEMAN, 2 hs portraits, 1945 and 1958, NPG (NPR).

FOX, Dame Evelyn Emily Marian (1874-1955) pioneer worker in the field of mental health.
D JAMES GRANT, posthumous, pastel, National Association for Mental Health, London.

FOX-STRANGWAYS, Giles Stephen Holland, see 6th Earl of Ilchester.

FOYLE, Gilbert Samuel (1886-1971) bookseller.
PH REGINALD HAINES, 1940s, hs, print, Foyles Educational Ltd, Burgess Hill, Sussex.

FOYLE, William Alfred (1885-1963) bookseller.
PH UNKNOWN, 3 portraits, prints, NPG x8345-47. Various photographs, W. & G.Foyle Ltd, London.

FRAMPTON, Sir George James (1860-1928) sculptor.
D Self-portrait, 1894, hs, pencil, NPG 3043. WILLIAM STRANG, hl seated with bust, The Art Workers' Guild, London.
C SIR MAX BEERBOHM, 1908, hl, pencil, University of Texas, Austin, USA. SIR BERNARD PARTRIDGE, 1927, tql, pencil, NPG 3669.
PH G.C.BERESFORD, 1902, profile head, neg, NPG x6502. G.C.BERESFORD, 1902, hs, print, NPG. UNKNOWN, 1914, tql, print, NPG. WALTER STONEMAN, 1924, hs, NPG (NPR).

FRANKAU, Gilbert (1884-1952) novelist.
PH HOWARD COSTER, various sizes and negs, NPG.

FRANZISKA JOSEPHA Louise Augusta, Princess, see Marie Louise.

FRASER, Sir (Arthur) Ronald (1888-1974) diplomat and author.
PH CLAUDE HARRIS, 1926, hs, print, NPG. WALTER STONEMAN, 1949, hs, NPG (NPR).

FRASER, Claud Lovat (1890-1921) artist and designer.
D PAUL NASH, hs, profile, pencil, Ashmolean Museum, Oxford.
PH G.C.BERESFORD, 1911, hs, semi-profile, neg, NPG x6503. G.C.BERESFORD, 1911, hs, profile, print, NPG.

FRASER, (William) Lionel (1895-1965) businessman.
PH UNKNOWN, hs, print, Banque de Paris et des Pays-Bas, London.

FRASER of Lonsdale, (William Jocelyn) Ian Fraser, 1st Baron (1897-1974) public servant.
PH WALTER BIRD, 1963, hs, NPG (NPR). REX COLEMAN, hs, profile, print, St Dunstan's, London. ELLIOTT & FRY, c1947, hs, profile, print, NPG. FAYER, hs, profile, print, St Dunstan's.

FRASER of North Cape, Bruce Austin Fraser, 1st Baron (b1888) admiral.
P SIR OSWALD BIRLEY, c1945-48, hs in uniform, Royal Naval College, Greenwich.
PH WALTER STONEMAN, c1940s, hl in uniform, for NPR, NPG x436.

FREEMAN, John (1880-1929) poet.
D LAURA KNIGHT, c1928?, hs, charcoal, NPG 4040.

FREEMAN, Sir Wilfrid Rhodes, 1st Bart (1888-1953) air chief marshal.
PH HOWARD COSTER, various sizes and negs, NPG. WALTER STONEMAN, 1941, hs in uniform, NPG (NPR).

FREEMAN-THOMAS, Freeman, see 1st Marquess of Willingdon.

FREMANTLE, John Walgrave Halford, see 4th baron Cottesloe.

FREMANTLE, Sir Thomas Francis, see 3rd Baron Cottesloe.

FREETH, Francis Arthur (1884-1970) chemist.
PH WALTER STONEMAN, 1945, hs, NPG (NPR). THE KYNOCH PRESS, c1955, hl, print, NPG.

FRENCH, Evangeline Frances (1869-1960) missionary.

G HAY WRIGHTSON, wl seated with sister Francesca, Mildred Cable and Chinese girl, ph, British and Foreign Bible Society, London.
PH H.WRIGHTSON, tql seated, semi-profile, print, Bible Society.

FRENCH, Francesca Law (1871-1960) missionary.
G HAY WRIGHTSON, wl seated with sister Evangeline, Mildred Cable and Chinese girl, ph, British and Foreign Bible Society, London.
PH HOWARD COSTER, hs and tql seated, prints, Bible Society. H.WRIGHTSON, hl seated, print, Bible Society.

FRENCH, Sir Henry (Leon) (1883-1966) civil servant and president of the British Film Producers Association.
PH WALTER STONEMAN, 2 hs portraits, 1938 and 1957, NPG (NPR).

FRERE, Walter Howard (1863-1938) bishop of Truro, historian and liturgiologist.
P HAROLD KNIGHT, c1933, Bishop's Palace, Truro; copy, Community of the Resurrection, Mirfield, Yorks.
PH OPIE LTD, 1933, wl seated in robes, print, NPG. WALTER STONEMAN, 1941, 4 hs portraits, for NPR, NPG x441-4.

FREYBERG, Bernard Freyberg, 1st Baron (1889-1963) governor-general of New Zealand and general.
P AMBROSE McEVOY, 1918, IWM.
PH LENARE, 1939, various sizes and negs, NPG x787-97.

FRITSCH, Felix Eugen (1879-1954) algologist.
P F.M.HAINES, Botany Department, Queen Mary College, London.
PH WALTER STONEMAN, 1932, 2 hs portraits, NPG (NPR).

FRY, (Anna) Ruth (1878-1962) relief worker and Quaker.
P T.C.DUGDALE, c1935, hl, Religious Society of Friends, London.
PH LUCIA MOHOLY, 1935, hs, print (1978), NPG P129.

FRY, Charles Burgess (1872-1956) sportsman.
PH HOWARD COSTER, various sizes and negs, NPG. ROTARY PHOTO, hs, postcard, NPG.

FRY, Roger Eliot (1866-1934) critic and painter.
P Self-portrait, 1918, tql seated, King's College, Cambridge. Self-portrait, c1930-34, hs with palette, NPG 3833. VANESSA BELL, c1933, tql seated with Julian Bell, King's College. Self-portrait, 1934, hs, King's College.
D JEAN MARCHAND, 1913, hl, chalk, NPG 4570.

C W.R.SICKERT, c1911, hl, 'Vision, Volume and Recession', pen and ink, Islington Public Libraries, London. SIR MAX BEERBOHM, 1913, pen, pencil and w/c, King's College. SIR M.BEERBOHM, 1931, wl, profile, chalk, NPG 3858.
PH UNKNOWN, c1900, hs, print, NPG. A.L.COBURN, 1913, hs, photogravure, NPG AX7798. A.C.COOPER, 1918, tql seated, print, NPG x4294. LENARE, c1930-34, hs, profile, print and neg, NPG x4516. UNKNOWN, c1930-34, head, print, NPG. Various photographs, NPG (Strachey Coll).

FRY, (Sara) Margery (1874-1958) penal reformer.
P ROGER FRY, Somerville College, Oxford. CLAUDE ROGERS, 1939, hs, NPG 5240.
PH UNKNOWN, c1950s?, hs, print, NPG.

FRY, Sheila Penrose, see Kaye-Smith.

FULLER, Sir Cyril Thomas Moulden (1874-1942) admiral.
D MUIRHEAD BONE, chalk and w/c, IWM.
PH WALTER STONEMAN, 1930, 2 hs portraits in uniform, NPG (NPR).

FURNISS, Henry Sanderson, see 1st Baron Sanderson.

FURSE, Charles Wellington (1868-1904) painter.
PH UNKNOWN, 1903, wl painting Mr and Mrs Oliver, photogravure, for D.S.MacColl, *Illust Memoir of C.W.Furse*, 1908, NPG.

FURSE, Dame Katharine (1875-1952) pioneer service woman.
P C.W.FURSE, c1903-4, wl as 'Diana of the Uplands', TATE 2059. MARCELLE MORLEY, in WRNS uniform, WRNS Headquarters, Furse House, London. GLYN PHILPOT, 1920, IWM.
PH G.C.BERESFORD, 1918, hs in uniform, neg and postcard, NPG x6505.

FURSE, Michael Bolton (1870-1955) bishop of St Albans.
PH UNKNOWN, hs, print, NPG (Anglican Bishops).

FURSE, Sir Ralph Dolignon (1887-1973) colonial administrator.
PH G.C.BERESFORD, 1913, hs, profile, neg, NPG x6504. STACEY WARD STUDIO, c1950, hs, print, NPG.

FYFE, David Patrick Maxwell, see 1st Earl of Kilmuir.

FYLEMAN, Rose Amy (1877-1957) writer for children.
PH HOWARD COSTER, various sizes and negs, NPG.

G

GAINFORD, Joseph Albert Pease, 1st Baron (1860-1943) politician and businessman.
PH JOHN RUSSELL & SONS, *c*1915, tql seated, print, for *National Photographic Record*, vol I, NPG. WALTER STONEMAN, 2 hs portraits, 1917 and 1938, NPG (NPR).

GAITSKELL, Sir Arthur (*b*1900) public servant.
PH HOWARD COSTER, 1950s, hs, print, NPG X1841.

GALE, Sir Humfrey Myddleton (1890-1971) lieutenant-general.
P HENRY CARR, 1943, IWM.
PH WALTER STONEMAN, 1946, hs in uniform, NPG (NPR). WALTER BIRD, 1959, hs, NPG (NPR).

GALLACHER, William (1881-1965) Communist MP.
PH HOWARD COSTER, various sizes and negs, NPG.

GALSWORTHY, John (1867-1933) novelist.
P GEORG SAUTER, *c*1905-6, hs, The Library, Birmingham University. R.H.SAUTER, 1923, hl seated, profile, Birmingham University Library. R.H.SAUTER, *c*1932-33, Birmingham University Library.
D R.H.SAUTER, 1927, hs, charcoal, Birmingham University Library. E.J.SULLIVAN, 1930, tql seated, pencil, BM. R.H.SAUTER, 1932, hs, profile, charcoal, Birmingham University Library.
SC LADY KATHLEEN KENNET, *c*1910, bronze mask, Temple Newsam House, Leeds; Manchester City Art Gallery; Birmingham University Library. THEODORE SPICER-SIMSON, 1921, profile head, bronze plaque, NPG 3649. DAVID EVANS, 1929, bronze bust, NPG 4208.
PR WILLIAM STRANG, 1920, hs, profile, etch, NPG.
C SIR MAX BEERBOHM, 1909, wl with satyr, drg, Birmingham University Library. SIR M.BEERBOHM, 1924, 'Breezy Jack of Biarritz', drg, The Lilly Library, Indiana University, USA. SIR DAVID LOW, 1927, various sketches, pencil study and finished drg, NPG 4529(132-40). R.S.SHERRIFFS, *c*1930, wl on ass, ink and pencil, NPG.
PH A.L.COBURN, 1909, hs, photogravure, NPG AX7790. E.O.HOPPÉ, 1911, hs, profile, print, Enthoven Coll, V & A. JOHN RUSSELL & SONS, before 1917, print, for *National Photographic Record*, vol I, NPG. OLIVE EDIS, 1922, tql seated, print, NPG X5100, and autochrome, X7178.
PH WALTER STONEMAN, 1924, hs, NPG (NPR). HOWARD COSTER, 1929, various sizes, prints and negs, NPG X1843 and others. Various photographs, Birmingham University Library.

GALSWORTHY, Olive, see Edis.

GALVIN, George (1860-1904) comedian 'Dan Leno'.
D Self-portrait, hs, pen and ink, NPG 2750.
PH ROTARY PHOTO, 1903, tql family group, postcard, NPG. UNKNOWN, hs, postcard, NPG.

GAMAGE, Sir Leslie (1887-1972) businessman.
PH GODFREY ARGENT, 1970, wl, NPG (NPR).

GAME, Sir Philip Woolcott (1876-1961) air vice-marshal.
PH HOWARD COSTER, various sizes and negs, NPG. WALTER STONEMAN, 2 hs portraits, the 2nd in uniform, 1935 and 1942, NPG (NPR).

GANN, Thomas William Francis (1867-1938) archaeologist.
PH Several photographs, Museum of Mankind, London.

GARBETT, Cyril Forster (1875-1955) archbishop of York.
P DAVID JAGGER, 1951, tql seated in robes, Bishopthorpe Palace, York.
PH HOWARD COSTER, various sizes, print and negs, NPG X1846 and others. WALTER STONEMAN, 2 hs portraits, 1919 and 1945, NPG (NPR). UNKNOWN, hl, print, NPG (Anglican Bishops).

GARDINER, Sir Alan Henderson (1879-1963) Egyptologist.
PH WALTER STONEMAN, 2 hs portraits, 1930 and 1945, NPG (NPR). LAFAYETTE, 1938, hs, print, NPG.

GARDINER, (Alfred) Clive (1891-1960) painter and art teacher.
SC IVOR ROBERTS JONES, 1953, bronze bust?, Goldsmiths College, University of London.

GARDINER, Alfred George (1865-1946) author and journalist.
C R.S.SHERRIFFS, hs, ink, NPG.
PH JOHN RUSSELL & SONS, tql seated, print, NPG.

GARDNER, Ernest Arthur (1862-1939) classical scholar and archaeologist.
P SIDNEY CARLINE, wl in vice-chancellor's robes, Senate House, University of London.

GARNER, William Edward (1889-1960) chemist.
D SIR W.T.MONNINGTON, chalk, University of Bristol.
PH WALTER STONEMAN, 1948, hs, NPG (NPR).

GARNETT, David (*b*1892) author.
PH MARK GERSON, 1953, hs, print, NPG.

GARNETT, Edward (1868-1937) author and publisher.
D FRANCIS DODD, *c*1926, charcoal, TATE 4227.
PH LUCIA MOHOLY, 1936, head, profile, print (*c*1978), NPG P132.

GARNETT, (James Clerk) Maxwell (1880-1958) educationist and Secretary of the League of Nations Union.
PH KARL POLLAK, hs, print, NPG.

GARRARD, Apsley George Benet Cherry-, see Cherry-Garrard.

GARROD, Heathcote William (1878-1960) scholar.
P RODRIGO MOYNIHAN, 1947, Merton College, Oxford.
PH WALTER STONEMAN, 1932, hs, NPG (NPR).

GARSTANG, John (1876-1956) archaeologist.
P G.H.NEALE, 1906, Blackburn Grammar School, Lancs.

GARVIE, Alfred Ernest (1861-1945) theologian and church leader.
P G.E.BUTLER, tql seated in robes, profile, New College, London, on loan to Dr Williams's Library, London.

GARVIN, James Louis (1868-1947) journalist.
C ALICK P.F.RITCHIE, wl, Hentschel-Colourtype, for *Vanity Fair*, 13 Sept 1911, NPG. SIR BERNARD PARTRIDGE, tql, pencil, for *Punch*, 25 April 1928, NPG 3670.
PH A.L.COBURN, 1913, hs, photogravure, NPG AX7814. WALTER STONEMAN, 1942, various sizes, for NPR, NPG X6983-87.

GASCOYNE-CECIL, see Cecil.

GASELEE, Sir Stephen (1882-1943) librarian and scholar.

P JOHN INNES, *c*1944, after a photograph, Magdalene College, Cambridge.

PH WALTER STONEMAN, 1936, hs, NPG (NPR).

GASK, George Ernest (1875-1951) surgeon.

G MOUSSA AYOUB, 'Royal College of Surgeons Council, 1926–27', oil, *c*1927–29, Royal College of Surgeons, London.

GATENBY, James Brontë (1892-1960) zoologist.

P H.W.ADDISON, Trinity College, Dublin.

GATER, Sir George Henry (1886-1963) educationist.

PH WALTER STONEMAN, 1941, hs, NPG (NPR).

GAUDIER-BRZESKA, Henri (1891-1915) sculptor and draughtsman.

P ALFRED WOLMARK, *c*1913, Musée de Beaux-Arts d'Orléans, France.

D Self-portrait, 1912, hs, chalk, NPG 4814. Self-portrait, 1913, hs, pastel, Southampton City Art Gallery. Various self-portrait drgs, pen and ink, pencil and/or crayon, Kettle Yard, University of Cambridge.

SC Self-portrait, bronze head, 'The Idiot', Auckland City Art Gallery, New Zealand.

GAULT, (Andrew) Hamilton (1882-1958) brigadier.

PH WALTER STONEMAN, 1932, hs, NPG (NPR).

GAUVAIN, Sir Henry John (1878-1945) surgeon and specialist in tuberculosis.

P F.O.SALISBURY, tql seated in robes, Lord Mayor Treloar Orthopaedic Hospital, Alton, Hants.

PH Various photographs, Lord Mayor Treloar Hospital.

GAY, (Reginald Moxon Armitage) Noel (1898-1954) composer of light music.

PH HOWARD COSTER, various sizes and negs, NPG.

GEDDES, Auckland Campbell Geddes, 1st Baron (1879-1954) public servant.

PH OLIVE EDIS, 1916, 3 portraits, prints, NPG. WALTER STONEMAN, 1917, 2 hs portraits, NPG (NPR). O.EDIS, 1920, tql seated in uniform, print, NPG; hs, autochrome, NPG x7179.

GEDDES, Sir Eric Campbell (1875-1937) politician, administrator and businessman.

P HERBERT OLIVIER, 1919, DoE. SIR JAMES GUTHRIE, *c*1919–21, SNPG 1129, study for 'Statesmen', NPG 2463. R.G.EVES, *c*1922, Dunlop Group of Companies, London.

G SIR JAMES GUTHRIE, 'Statesmen of World War I, 1914–18', oil, *c*1924–30, NPG 2463.

C SIR BERNARD PARTRIDGE, wl as 'Mrs Partington', w/c and pen and ink, for *Punch Almanack*, 1922, NPG. FRED MAY, 1935, hs, profile, gouache, NPG.

PH WALTER STONEMAN, 1917, hs in uniform, NPG (NPR). OLIVE EDIS, *c*1920s, hs, autochrome, NPG x7180.

GELLIBRAND, Sir John (1872-1945) major-general.

P JAMES QUINN, Australian War Memorial, Canberra.

PH WALTER STONEMAN, 1919, hs in uniform, NPG (NPR).

GEMMELL, Sir Arthur (Alexander) (1892-1960) obstetrician and gynaecologist.

P STANLEY REED, 1956, Royal College of Obstetricians and Gynaecologists, London.

GENÉE-ISITT, Dame Adeline (1878-1970) dancer.

PH Various photographs, Royal Academy of Dancing, London.

GEORGE V (1865-1936) reigned 1910–36.

P JAMES SANT, 1872, head, oval, Royal Coll, study for 'Victoria

and grandchildren'. CARL SOHN, jun, 1882, hl with Duke of Clarence in midshipman's uniform, Royal Coll. HEINRICH VON ANGELI, 1893, head, oval, Royal Coll. SIR LUKE FILDES, 1893, hs in uniform, Royal Coll. SIR JOHN COLLIER, 1900, wl in uniform, Trinity House, London. HUGH DE T.GLAZEBROOK, *c*1901–08, Royal Marines Museum, Southsea. SIR LUKE FILDES, 1912, wl in naval uniform and parliamentary robes, Royal Coll; version, Palace of Westminster, London. SIR JOHN LAVERY, 1913, head, Royal Coll, study for NPG 1745. SIR A.S.COPE, *c*1912–13, wl in naval uniform, formerly United Service Club (c/o Crown Commissioners), London. LANCE CALKIN, *c*1914, hs, oval, NPG 4604. A.T.NOWELL, 1920, tql seated, Leys School, Cambridge. RICHARD JACK, 1926, wl in robes, one of pair, Royal Coll. SIR A.S.COPE, 1926, tql, seated, Royal College of Music, London. SIR A.S.COPE, 1928, wl in uniform, Royal Academy, London. SIR OSWALD BIRLEY, various portraits, 1928–1934, National Museum of Wales 595, Cardiff; Lincoln's Inn; Royal Coll; and NPG 4013. JOHN ST HELIER LANDER, 1935, wl in robes, Victoria College, Jersey; version, Canada House, London. F.O.SALISBURY, *c*1935, tql in robes, profile, National Gallery, Washington DC, USA. A.J.MUNNINGS, *c*1936, wl on his pony 'Jock', Ipswich Corporation. FREDERIC WHITING, 1930s, wl on horseback, NPG 5094. CHARLES SIMS, SNPG 974.

D SIR W.Q.ORCHARDSON, *c*1897, head, pencil, Royal Coll, Study for 'Four Generations'.

G K.W.F.BAUERLE, wl with brother Albert Victor and sister Louise, oil, *c*1871, Royal Coll. J.SANT, 'Victoria with 3 of her grandchildren', oil, *c*1872, Royal Coll. LAURITS TUXEN, 'The Royal Family at the Time of the Jubilee', oil, 1887, Royal Coll. L.TUXEN, marriage group, oil, 1893, Royal Coll. L.TUXEN, 'Marriage of Princess Maud and Prince Charles of Denmark', oil, 1896, Royal Coll. SIR W.Q.ORCHARDSON, 'Four Generations', oil, *c*1897–99, Royal Agricultural Society, London; study, NPG 4536. E.A.ABBEY, 'The Coronation of King Edward VII', 1902', oil, 1904, Royal Coll. SIR J.LAVERY, 'The Royal Family at Buckingham Palace, 1913', oil, NPG 1745. J.H.F.BACON, Coronation portrait, oil, 1912, Royal Coll. F.O.SALISBURY, 'Burial of the Unknown Warrior', oil, 1920, Palace of Westminster. A.J.MUNNINGS, 'Their Majesties Return from Ascot', oil, 1925, TATE 4956. F.O.SALISBURY, 'Thanksgiving Service of the King's Silver Jubilee', oil, 1935, Guildhall, London. F.O.SALISBURY, 'Jubilee Service', oil, 1935, Royal Coll.

SC F.J.WILLIAMSON, 1877, marble statue and bust, Royal Coll. COUNT VICTOR GLEICHEN, 1878, bronze statuette with brother, Duke of Clarence, Royal Coll. ALFRED DRURY, 1906, marble bust, Bradford City Art Gallery. SIR W.H.THORNYCROFT, 1907, bronze bust, National Gallery of Canada, Ottawa. SIR GEORGE FRAMPTON, 1913, marble bust, Guildhall, London. SIR W.R.DICK, 1933, marble bust, Royal Coll. LADY KATHLEEN KENNET, *c*1935, head, Royal Coll. FELIX WEISS, 1935, bronze bust, NPG 2796. SIR W.R.DICK, 1937, marble tomb effigy with Queen Mary, St George's Chapel, Windsor.

PR UNKNOWN, tql with brother, Duke of Clarence, lith, for *The Whitehall Review*, 16 Aug 1879, NPG.

C SIR LESLIE WARD ('Spy'), wl in sailor uniform, lith, for *Vanity Fair*, 24 May 1890, NPG. SIR MAX BEERBOHM, 1899, in naval costume, drg, Ashmolean Museum, Oxford. 'APE JUNIOR', wl, mechanical repro, for *Vanity Fair*, 21 June 1911, NPG.

PH Various photographs and postcards, singly and in groups, by BASSANO, HOWARD COSTER, W. & D.DOWNEY, E.O.HOPPÉ, LAFAYETTE, REMBRANDT, JOHN RUSSELL & SONS, VANDYK and others, NPG and Royal Coll.

GEORGE VI (1895-1952) reigned 1936–52.

P R.G.EVES, 1924, hs, NPG 4144. SIMON ELWES, 1936?, wl, Cavalry and Guards Club, London. FRANCIS HODGE, c1938, tql in uniform, Royal College of Surgeons, London. SIR OSWALD BIRLEY, 1939, tql, Royal Agricultural Society, London. SIR GERALD KELLY, c1939–45, wl, Coronation portrait, Royal Coll. SIR G.KELLY, c1939–45, hl in Garter robes, Trinity College, Cambridge, and NPG 5286. SIR O.BIRLEY, c1945, Royal Naval College, Greenwich. DENIS FILDES, 1948, tql in uniform, Staff College, Camberley, Surrey. EDWARD SEAGO, 1948, tql seated in uniform, RAF College, Cranwell, Lincs. D.FILDES, 1949, tql in Admiral's uniform, Inner Temple, London, and DoE (Royal College of Defence Studies). MAURICE CODNER, c1951, wl in field marshal's uniform and Garter robes, Honourable Artillery Company, Armoury House, London.

G F.O.SALISBURY, 'Burial of Unknown Warrior', oil, 1920, Palace of Westminster, London. F.O.SALISBURY, 'Jubilee Service for George V', oil, 1935, Royal Coll; related 'Thanksgiving Service', oil, Guildhall, London. F.O.SALISBURY, Coronation group, oil, 1938, Royal Coll. SIR JAMES GUNN, 'Conversation Piece at the Royal Lodge, Windsor, 1950', oil, NPG 3778.

SC SIR W.R.DICK, bronze head, Royal Coll, and NPG 4114. LADY KATHLEEN KENNET, c1935–37, bronze head, Royal Coll. WILLIAM MACMILLAN, bronze statue, The Mall, London.

PR H.RAYNER, 1939, hs, drypoint etch, NPG and V & A.

PH Various photographs, singly and in groups, by BASSANO, SIR CECIL BEATON, MRS ALBERT BROOM, W. & D.DOWNEY, OLIVE EDIS, BERTRAM PARK, WALTER STONEMAN, DOROTHY WILDING, VANDYK and others, NPG and Royal Coll.

GEORGE, David Lloyd-, see 1st Earl Lloyd-George.

GEORGE, Gwilym Lloyd, see 1st Viscount Tenby.

GEORGE, (Mary) Dorothy (1878-1971) social and economic historian.
PH HOWARD COSTER, hs, print, NPG X1850.

GERE, Charles March (1869-1957) artist.
P Self-portrait, c1939, hl with brushes, Cheltenham Art Gallery.
PR FRANCIS DODD, 1927?, tql seated, drypoint etch, NPG.
PH LAFAYETTE, hs, print, NPG.

GERMAN, Sir Edward (1862-1936) composer.
SL H.L.OAKLEY, hs, profile, NPG.
PR FLORA LION, hs, lith, NPG 3951.
PH BAILEY, 1922, group at 'Bournemouth Music Festival', postcard, NPG. BAILEY, c1922, wl, print, NPG. VANDYK, tql with SIR A.C.MacKENZIE, print, NPG.

GERTLER, Mark (1891-1939) painter.
P Self-portrait, 1920, hs, Arts Council of Great Britain, London.

GIBB, Sir Alexander (1872-1958) engineer.
P KATHARINE LLOYD, tql seated in Archer's uniform, SIR A.Gibb and Partners, London. LEONARD CAMPBELL TAYLOR?, wl in academic dress, SIR A.Gibb and Partners, Reading. UNKNOWN, hl seated, SIR A.Gibb and Partners, Reading.
D SIR WILLIAM ROTHENSTEIN, c1937, Institution of Civil Engineers, London. 'G.S.', hl seated, charcoal, SIR A.Gibb and Partners, London.
PH WALTER STONEMAN, 2 hs portraits, the 1st in uniform, 1920 and 1943, NPG (NPR).

GIBB, Sir Claude Dixon (1898-1959) engineer.
PH WALTER STONEMAN, 2 hs portraits, 1945 and 1957, NPG (NPR).

GIBBINGS, Robert John (1889-1958) wood-engraver, author and book designer.
PH HOWARD COSTER, 1938, various sizes, print and negs, NPG X2336 and others. MARK GERSON, 1954, hl, print, NPG.

GIBBS, (Cecil) Armstrong (1889-1960) composer.

PH HERBERT LAMBERT, c1922, hl seated, profile, photogravure, NPG AX7754.

GIBBS, Sir Philip (Armand Hamilton) (1877-1962) journalist and author.
PH HOWARD COSTER, various sizes, print and negs, NPG X1851 and others. WALTER STONEMAN, 3 hs portraits, 1920, 1931 and 1945, NPG (NPR).

GIBBS, Walter Durant, see 4th Baron Aldenham.

GIFFARD, Sir George James (1886-1964) general.
PH WALTER STONEMAN, 2 hs portraits, 1936 and 1945, NPG (NPR) and NPG X445.

GILES, Peter (1860-1935) philologist.
P ALFRED HAYWARD, 1934, Emmanuel College, Cambridge.

GILL, (Arthur) Eric (Rowton) (1882-1940) sculptor and typographer.
D SIR WILLIAM ROTHENSTEIN, 1921?, head, chalk, NPG 4647. Self-portrait, 1927, head, profile, pencil, NPG 4661. DESMOND CHUTE, c1938, head, profile, pencil, NPG 3957.
SC UNKNOWN, medal, NPG.
PR Self-portrait, 1908 and 1927, several wood engr, V & A.
PH HOWARD COSTER, 1927 and 1935, various sizes, prints and negs, NPG AX2305, X1862–73 and others.

GILLIAT, Sir William (1884-1956) obstetrician.
P DAVID ALISON, c1952, Royal College of Obstetricians and Gynaecologists, London. E.I.HALLIDAY, posthumous, Royal Society of Medicine, London.

GILLIES, Sir Harold Delf (1882-1960) plastic surgeon.
P BERNARD ADAMS, 1939?, Queen Mary's Hospital, Roehampton, London. HOWARD BARRON, hs, Royal College of Surgeons, London.
G HENRY TONKS, 'Operating Theatre Scene', pen and ink, Royal College of Surgeons.
PH WALTER STONEMAN, 1940, hs, for NPR, NPG X446.

GILMOUR, Sir John, 2nd Bart (1876-1940) politician.
P SIR JAMES GUTHRIE, 1934, wl in uniform, DoE (Scottish Office, Dover House, London).
PH WALTER STONEMAN, 1922, hs, NPG (NPR).

GINNER, (Isaac) Charles (1878-1952) artist.
P MALCOLM DRUMMOND, c1911, hl, Southampton Art Gallery.
D Self-portrait, 1940s, tql seated, pen, ink and w/c, NPG 4992.

GINSBERG, Morris (1889-1970) sociologist.
PH WALTER STONEMAN, 1957, hs, NPG (NPR).

GIRDLESTONE, Gathorne Robert (1881-1950) orthopaedic surgeon.
P FRANK EASTMAN, Nuffield Orthopaedic Centre, Headington, Oxford.
D SIR WILLIAM ROTHENSTEIN, head, chalk, NPG 4801.

GLENNY, Alexander Thomas (1882-1965) immunologist.
PH WALTER STONEMAN, 1944, hs, NPG (NPR). Various photographs, Wellcome Foundation, London.

GLOUCESTER, Henry William Frederick Albert, Prince and Duke of (1900-1974) 3rd son of King George V and governor-general of Australia.
P A.M.BARTON, 1954, tql in uniform, Cavalry and Guards Club, London.
G F.O.SALISBURY, 'Jubilee Service for George V', oil, 1935, Royal Coll; related 'Thanksgiving Service', oil, Guildhall, London.
PH SIR CECIL BEATON, tql seated singly and with Duchess, prints, NPG. W. & D.DOWNEY, hs in sailor suit as boy, oval, postcard, NPG. OLIVE EDIS, c1920, hs, autochrome, NPG X7183. WALTER

STONEMAN, 4 hs portraits, 1921, 1938 and 1941, NPG (NPR) and NPG X447. DOROTHY WILDING, 4 portraits in uniform, prints, NPG. HAY WRIGHTSON, 1935, wedding group, print, NPG X4194. Various photographs, Royal Coll.

GLOVER, Terrot Reaveley (1869-1943) classical scholar and historian.
D W.FISK-MOORE, c1940s, hs, charcoal, St John's College, Cambridge.
C GERALD OWST, 1920, in classical dress, for *Old Cambridge Magazine*, pen, St John's College.
PH Various photographs, St John's College.

GLUCK, Helen (1896-1978) artist.
P ROMAINE BROOKS, 1923–24, 'Peter (A Young English Girl)', hl seated, National Collection of Fine Arts, Washington DC, USA. Self-portrait, 1942, head, NPG CP4.

GLYN, Elinor (1864-1943) novelist.
P ARNOLD MASON, 1942, hl seated, NPG 4283.
PH SZEKELY, hs, print, NPG X4074. PAUL TANQUERAY, c1932, hs with two cats, print, NPG.

GODDARD, Rayner Goddard, 1st Baron (1877-1971) lord chief justice.
P SIR JAMES GUNN, c1949, tql seated in robes, Inner Temple, London.
PH WALTER STONEMAN, 4 hs portraits, 1932, 1946 and 1956, NPG (NPR). MADAME YEVONDE, in robes, colour print, NPG.

GODFREY, John Henry (1888-1971) admiral.
PH WALTER STONEMAN, 1945, 2 hs portraits in uniform, NPG (NPR).

GODFREY, Peter (1899-1970) stage and film director.
PH HOWARD COSTER, various sizes and negs, NPG.

GODFREY, William (1889-1963) cardinal.
P A.R.THOMSON, c1960, wl in robes, St Edmund's College, Ware, Herts. UNKNOWN, English College, Rome.
PH HOWARD COSTER, various sizes and negs, NPG.

GODLEY, Sir Alexander John (1867-1957) general.
P SIR WALTER RUSSELL, 1919, IWM.
D FRANCIS DODD, 1917, charcoal and w/c, IWM.
PH WALTER STONEMAN, 1918, hs in uniform, NPG (NPR). UNKNOWN, hs in uniform, print, NPG X3768.

GOGARTY, Oliver Joseph St John (1878-1957) surgeon and writer.
SC THEODORE SPICER-SIMSON, bronze medallion, NGI 8222.

GOLD, Sir Harcourt Gilbey (1876-1952) oarsman.
C SIR LESLIE WARD ('Spy'), wl, lith, for *Vanity Fair*, 23 March 1899, NPG.
PH WALTER STONEMAN, 1949, tql seated, NPG (NPR).

GOLDING, Louis (1895-1958) novelist.
D EDMOND KAPP, 1930, Barber Institute, Birmingham University.
PH HOWARD COSTER, various sizes and negs, NPG.

GOLLANCZ, Sir Israel (1863-1930) scholar and man of letters.
PH WALTER STONEMAN, 1918, hl, NPG (NPR).

GOLLANCZ, Sir Victor (1893-1967) publisher and writer.
PH Various photographs, Victor Gollancz Ltd, London.

GONNE, Maud, Mrs John MacBride (1866-1953) Irish patriot.
P SARAH PURSER, tql with monkey, Municipal Gallery of Modern Art, Dublin.
D S.PURSER, hs, pastel, NGI. S.PURSER, hs, pastel, Municipal Gallery of Modern Art.
SC LAWRENCE CAMPBELL, 1932, bronzed plaster bust, Municipal

Gallery of Modern Art.

GOOCH, George Peabody (1873-1968) historian.
PH WALTER STONEMAN, 2 hs portraits, 1930 and 1943, NPG (NPR).

GOODE, Sir William Athelstane Meredith (1875-1944) journalist and financial adviser.
PH WALTER STONEMAN, 2 hs portraits, 1918 and 1941, NPG (NPR).

GOODENOUGH, Frederick Craufurd (1866-1934) banker.
P J.P.B.BARNES, hs, Barclays Bank Ltd, London.
PH G.C.BERESFORD, tql, neg, NPG X6507. OLIVE EDIS, 1931, hs, print, NPG.

GOODENOUGH, Sir William Edmund (1867-1945) admiral.
D FRANCIS DODD, 1917, charcoal and w/c, IWM.
G SIR A.S.COPE, 'Naval Officers of World War I, 1914–18', oil, 1921, NPG 1913.
PH WALTER STONEMAN, 2 hs portraits, the 1st in uniform, 1919 and 1931, NPG (NPR).

GOODENOUGH, Sir William Macnamara, 1st Bart (1899-1951) banker.
P SIR JAMES GUNN, c1948, tql seated, Barclays Bank International Ltd, London.
PH OLIVE EDIS, 1931, tql seated, print, NPG.

GOODEY, Tom (1885-1953) nematologist.
PH WALTER STONEMAN, 1953, hs, NPG (NPR).

GOODHART-RENDEL, Harry Stuart (1887-1959) architect.
P AUGUSTUS JOHN, c1940, hs, RIBA.
SC DORA GORDINE, c1938, bronze head, RIBA.

GOODRICH, Edwin Stephen (1868-1946) zoologist.
PH WALTER STONEMAN, 1931, hs, NPG (NPR). UNKNOWN, print, Merton College, Oxford.

GOOSSENS, Sir Eugene (1893-1962) conductor.
PH HERBERT LAMBERT, c1923, hs, photogravure, NPG AX7757.

GOOSSENS, Leon Jean (b1897) oboist.
PH HOWARD COSTER, 1935, various sizes, print and negs, NPG. GODFREY ARGENT, 1968, 2 hs portraits, NPG (NPR).

GORDON, George Stuart (1881-1942) president of Magdalen College, Oxford, and professor of poetry.
P SIR WILLIAM COLDSTREAM, 1938, Magdalen College.
PH WALTER STONEMAN, 1931, hs, NPG (NPR).

GORDON, Mervyn Henry (1872-1953) medical bacteriologist.
PH WALTER STONEMAN, 1936, hs, NPG (NPR).

GORDON-TAYLOR, Sir Gordon (1878-1960) surgeon.
P SIR JAMES GUNN, Royal Australasian College of Surgeons, Melbourne, Australia; oil study, Royal College of Surgeons, London. ANNA ZINKEISEN, 1958, tql seated in robes, Middlesex Hospital, London.
PH HOWARD COSTER, various sizes and negs, NPG. WALTER STONEMAN, 1947, hl in uniform, NPG (NPR).

GORE, Spencer Frederick (1878-1914) painter.
P ALBERT RUTHERSTON, 1902, hl, profile, NPG 3320. HAROLD GILMAN, c1906–07, hs, Leeds City Art Gallery. Self-portrait, 1914, hs, NPG 4981.

GORE, Wiliam George Arthur Ormsby-, see 4th Baron Harlech.

GORELL, Ronald Gorell Barnes, 3rd Baron (1884-1963) author and editor.
PH WALTER STONEMAN, 3 hs portraits, the 1st in uniform, 1919, 1931

and 1946, NPG (NPR).

GORST, Sir (John) Eldon (1861-1911) consul-general in Egypt.
P CECIL JAMESON, c1907, hs, DoE (British Embassy, Cairo).

GORT, John Standish Surtees Prendergast Vereker, Viscount (1886-1946) field-marshal.
P HENRY CARR, c1940, tql in uniform, Cavalry and Guards Club, London. R.G.EVES, 1940, 2 hs portraits in uniform, IWM. E.B.SEAGO, 1940, hl in uniform, IWM.
C JAN ROSCIWESKI ('Tom Tit'), pen and ink, IWM.
PH WALTER STONEMAN, 1939, 2 hs portraits in uniform, NPG (NPR).

GOSLING, Harry (1861-1930) trade union leader.
PH WALTER STONEMAN, 1924, hs, NPG (NPR).

GOSSAGE, Sir (Ernest) Leslie (1891-1949) air marshal.
D HENRY LAMB, 1942, chalk, IWM.
PH HOWARD COSTER, various sizes and negs, NPG. WALTER STONEMAN, 1937, hs in uniform, NPG (NPR).

GOTT, William Henry Ewart (1897-1942) lieutenant-general.
P PATRICK PHILLIPS, posthumous, hl in uniform, semi-profile, Royal Green Jackets Museum, Peninsula Barracks, Winchester.

GOUGE, Sir Arthur (1890-1962) marine aircraft designer.
PH WALTER STONEMAN, 1948, hl, NPG (NPR).

GOUGH, Herbert John (1890-1965) engineer.
PH WALTER STONEMAN, 2 hs portraits, 1933 and 1947, NPG (NPR). UNKNOWN, c1950-55, hs, print, Unilever Ltd, London.

GOUGH, Sir Hubert (de la Poer) (1870-1963) general.
D FRANCIS DODD, 1917, charcoal and w/c, IWM. SIR WILLIAM ROTHENSTEIN, 1918, hs, sanguine, Birmingham City Art Gallery. SIR W.ROTHENSTEIN, 1932, head, chalk, NPG 4776.
SC PATRICIA KAHN, 1961, ciment fondu head, NPG 4477.

GOUGH-CALTHORPE, Sir Somerset Arthur, see Calthorpe.

GOWER, George Granville Sutherland-Leveson-, see 5th Duke of Sutherland.

GOWERS, Sir Ernest Arthur (1880-1966) public servant.
PH WALTER STONEMAN, 2 hs portraits, 1930 and 1953, NPG (NPR).

GOWRIE, Alexander Gore Arkwright Hore-Ruthven, 1st Earl of (1872-1955) soldier and governor-general of Australia.
P SIR CHARLES WHEELER, Parliament House, Canberra. PAUL FITZGERALD, Cavalry and Guards Club, London.
PH WALTER STONEMAN, 1922, hs in uniform, NPG (NPR). JOHN RUSSELL & SONS, c1945, tql in uniform, print, NPG.

GRACEY, Sir Douglas David (1894-1964) general.
PH WALTER STONEMAN, 1949, hs in uniform, NPG (NPR).

GRAHAM, John Anderson (1861-1942) missionary.
P JOHN DOBBIE, 1930s, tql seated in doctoral robes, Church of Scotland Offices, Overseas Council, Edinburgh.

GRAHAM, Sir Ronald William (1870-1949) diplomat.
PH WALTER STONEMAN, 1933, hs, NPG (NPR).

GRAHAM-HARRISON, Sir William Montagu (1871-1949) parliamentary draftsman.
PH WALTER STONEMAN, 1930, hs, NPG (NPR).

GRAHAM-HODGSON, Sir Harold Kingston, see Hodgson.

GRAHAM-LITTLE, Sir Ernest Gordon Graham (1867-1950) physician.

PH UNKNOWN, hs, print, NPG.

GRAHAME-WHITE, Claude (1879-1959) pioneer aviator and aircraft manufacturer.
P ARTHUR PAN, 1951, hs, Royal Aero Club on loan to RAF Museum, Hendon.
SC UNKNOWN, bronze head, RAF Museum.
C 'TEC', wl in flying gear, Hentschel-Colourtype, for *Vanity Fair*, 10 May 1911, NPG.
PH UNKNOWN, hs, photogravure, for *Reign of George V*, vol 1, 1913, NPG.

GRAINGER, Percy Aldridge (1882-1961) pianist and composer.
D J.S.SARGENT, c1907, head, profile, chalk, Grainger Museum, University of Melbourne, Australia. G.W.LAMBERT, head, profile, with Henry Tonks, pencil, NPG 3137A.
PH Various photographs, Grainger Museum. Various photographs, Percy Grainger Library Society, White Plains, New York, USA.

GRANET, Sir (William) Guy (1867-1943) barrister, railway administrator and chairman.
C SIR LESLIE WARD ('Spy'), wl, Hentschel-Colourtype, for *Vanity Fair*, 11 Nov 1908, NPG.
PH WALTER STONEMAN, 2 hs portraits, 1917 and 1927, NPG (NPR).

GRANT, Sir (Alfred) Hamilton, 12th Bart (1872-1937) Indian civil servant.
P UNKNOWN, Government House, Peshawar, India.
PH WALTER STONEMAN, 1930, hs, NPG (NPR).

GRANT, Duncan James Corrowr (1885-1978) painter.
P Self-portrait, c1909, hs, NPG 5131. VANESSA BELL, 1934, wl seated, Williamson Art Gallery, Birkenhead.
PH GODFREY ARGENT, 1968, various sizes, NPG (NPR). SIR CECIL BEATON, hl, print, NPG. Various photographs, NPG (Strachey Coll).

GRANVILLE-BARKER, Harley (1877-1946) actor, producer and dramatist.
P J.E.BLANCHE, 1930, tql seated, NPG 3842.
D J.S.SARGENT, 1900, hs, chalk, NPG 4178. EDMOND KAPP, 1913, hs?, Barber Institute, Birmingham University.
SC LADY KATHLEEN KENNET, bronze bust, Royal Shakespeare Theatre, Stratford-upon-Avon.
PR WILLIAM STRANG, head, etch, for *W.Strang: Catalogue of his etched work 1882-1912*, NPG.
C SIR MAX BEERBOHM, 1923, tql, pencil and w/c, Garrick Club, London. SIR M.BEERBOHM, 1923, 'The British Drama', drg, William Andrews Clark Memorial Library, UCLA, California.
PH A.L.COBURN, 1906, hs, photogravure, NPG AX7775. G.C.BERESFORD, 1918, hs in uniform, neg, NPG X6431. WALTER STONEMAN, 1931, hs, NPG (NPR).

GRAVES, George Windsor (1873?-1949) comedian.
D EDMOND KAPP, 1919, Barber Institute, Birmingham University.
PR CHARLES BUCHEL and HASSALL, hs and wl in character, lith, NPG.

GRAVES, Robert (b1895) poet.
P JOHN ULBRICHT, 1966, head, Lockwood Memorial Library, State University of New York, Buffalo, USA. JOHN ALDRIDGE, 1968, hs, NPG 4683.
D ERIC KENNINGTON, 1918, head, pastel, National Museum of Wales, Cardiff.
SC MARJORIE FITZGIBBON, bronze bust, Library, Royal Dublin Society. DOROTHY SIMMONS, c1941-42?, head, Lockwood Memorial Library.
PH BILL BRANDT, 1941, hl, print, NPG. MEL STERN, 1972, 3 portraits, prints, NPG X1590-2. PETER STARK, 1970s, 4 portraits, prints, NPG X1534-37.

GRAY, Sir James (1891-1975) zoologist.
P ROBERT LUTYENS, King's College, Cambridge.
SC SIR JACOB EPSTEIN, 1956, bronze bust, Department of Zoology, University of Cambridge.
PH WALTER STONEMAN, 2 hs portraits, 1931 and 1939?, NPG (NPR).

GRAY, John (1866-1934) Roman Catholic priest and writer.
PR RAYMOND SAVAGE, tql seated, lith, NPG 3844. C.H.SHANNON, 1896, lith, Carlisle City Art Gallery.

GREEN, Charles Alfred Howell (1864-1944) archbishop of Wales.
PH UNKNOWN, tql seated, print, NPG (Anglican Bishops).

GREEN, Frederick William Edridge-, see Edridge-Green.

GREEN, (William) Curtis (1875-1960) architect.
PH WALTER STONEMAN, 1933, 4 portraits, for NPR, NPG X4632-35.

GREENE, Harry Plunket (1865-1936) singer.
PH BACON, hl, postcard, Royal College of Music, London. ELLIOTT & FRY, tql, postcard, Royal College of Music. ELLIS & WALERY, hl, postcard, Royal College of Music. ERIC MILLAR, 1935, wl, neg, NPG. UNKNOWN, hs, postcard, Royal College of Music. UNKNOWN, wl in garden, print, Royal College of Music.

GREENE, Wilfrid Arthur Greene, Baron (1883-1952) judge.
P (HELEN) GLUCK, 1940, hs in robes, Inner Temple, London.

GREENWOOD, Arthur (1880-1954) politician.
PH WALTER STONEMAN, 3 hs portraits, 1924, 1930 and 1941, NPG (NPR). HOWARD COSTER, 1930s, various sizes and negs, NPG. FELIX MAN, 1939, hs with 1st Earl Attlee, print, NPG P16. LENARE, 1939, 3 portraits, negs, NPG X784-86. KARL POLLAK, 1948, hs, print, NPG.

GREENWOOD, Hamar Greenwood, 1st Viscount (1870-1948) politician.
PH WALTER STONEMAN, 1918, hs in uniform, NPG (NPR).

GREER, (Frederick) Arthur, see 1st Baron Fairfield.

GREG, Sir Walter Wilson (1875-1959) scholar and bibliographer.
PH WALTER STONEMAN, 1930, hs, NPG (NPR).

GREGORY, Frederick Gugenheim (1893-1961) plant physiologist.
PH WALTER STONEMAN, 1940, hs, NPG (NPR).

GREGORY, John Walter (1864-1932) geologist and explorer.
PH WALTER STONEMAN, 1920, hs, NPG (NPR).

GREGORY, Sir Richard Arman, Bart (1864-1952) scientific writer and journalist.
P H.R.DOBSON, 1929, hl, NPG 5117.
PH WALTER STONEMAN, 1936, hs, NPG (NPR).

GREIFFENHAGEN, Maurice William (1862-1931) painter.
P Self-portrait, hl, Marylebone Public Library, London.

GRENFELL, Bernard Pyne (1869-1926) papyrologist.
PH WALTER STONEMAN, 1917, hs, NPG (NPR).

GRENFELL, David Rhys (1881-1968) politician.
PH WALTER STONEMAN, 2 hs portraits, 1941 and 1954, NPG (NPR).

GRENFELL, Edward Charles, see 1st Baron St Just.

GRENFELL, Sir Wilfred Thomason (1865-1940) medical missionary.
PH WALTER STONEMAN, 1928, hs, NPG (NPR).

GREVILLE, Frances Evelyn, see Countess of Warwick.

GREY, Charles Grey (1875-1953) writer on aviation.
P FRANK EASTMAN, 1957, hl seated, Royal Aero Club on loan to RAF Museum, Hendon.

GREY of Fallodon, Edward Grey, 1st Viscount (1862-1933) foreign secretary and president of League of Nations.
P G.FIDDES WATT, c1915-17, wl in garter robes, DoE (Foreign Office, London). SIR JAMES GUTHRIE, c1919-21, hs, profile, SNPG 1133, study for 'Statesmen', NPG 2463. SIR J.GUTHRIE, c1919-21, hs, NPG 3545. SIR WILLIAM ORPEN, 1925, National Liberal Club, London. HAROLD SPEED, c1927, in academic robes, Oxford and Cambridge Club, London. SIR J.GUTHRIE, 1928, tql seated, Balliol College, Oxford. H.SPEED, c1927-33, tql seated in academic robes, semi-profile, NPG 3120.
D SIR WILLIAM ROTHENSTEIN, 1920, head, chalk, NPG 3869.
G SIR J.GUTHRIE, 'Statesmen of World War I, 1914-18', oil, c1924-30, NPG 2463.
C HARRY FURNISS, c1900, hl and tql, profile, pen and ink, NPG 3388 and 3578. SIR LESLIE WARD ('Spy'), wl, lith, for *Vanity Fair*, 5 Feb 1903, NPG. SIR BERNARD PARTRIDGE, wl with President Roosevelt, pen and ink, for *Punch*, 29 march 1911, NPG. 'OWL', wl as 'Secretary Bird' taking olive branch to Turkey and the Balkans, mechanical repro, for *Vanity Fair*, 2 March 1913, NPG.
PH H.WALTER BARNETT, hl, print, NPG X8019. WALTER STONEMAN, 2 hs portraits, 1918 and 1931, NPG (NPR).

GRIERSON, Sir Herbert John Clifford (1866-1960) scholar.
P KENNETH GREEN, 1935, tql seated, University of Edinburgh.
D DAVID FOGGIE, 1932, hs, pencil, University of Edinburgh.
PH WALTER STONEMAN, 1929, hs, NPG (NPR).

GRIERSON, John (1898-1972) film producer.
D EDMOND KAPP, 1946, hs, ink, Barber Institute, Birmingham University.

GRIEVE, Christopher Murray (1892-1978) poet, author and journalist 'Hugh Macdiarmid'.
P WILLIAM CROSBIE, 1943, hl seated, Glasgow City Art Gallery. F.TRISTRAM RAINEY, 1946, Lockwood Memorial Library, State University of New York, Buffalo, USA.
SC BENNO SCHOTZ, 1958, bronze bust, BBC Scotland. ALAN THORNHILL, 1974, bronze head, NPG 5230.

GRIFFIN, Bernard William (1899-1956) cardinal.
P ALLAN GWYNNE-JONES, hl seated in cardinal's robes, Archbishop's House, Westminster Cathedral.
SC FIORE DE HENRIQUES, c1956, bronze bust, Archbishop's House.
PH HOWARD COSTER, various sizes and negs, NPG.

GRIFFITH, Alan Arnold (1893-1963) aeronautical engineer and chief scientist of Rolls-Royce Ltd.
PH UNKNOWN, hs, print, Rolls-Royce Ltd, Aero Division, Derby. UNKNOWN, hs, print and neg, Royal Aircraft Establishment, Farnborough, Hants.

GRIFFITH, Arthur (1872-1922) Irish political leader.
P SIR JOHN LAVERY, Municipal Gallery of Modern Art, Dublin. LEO WHELAN, tql, Dail Eireann, Dublin. LILY WILLIAMS, Municipal Gallery of Modern Art.
SC ALBERT POWER, 1922, bronze bust?, NGI 8100.

GRIFFITH, Francis Llewellyn (1862-1934) Egyptologist.
P KENNETH GREEN, 1932, hs in academic robes, Griffith Institute, Ashmolean Museum, Oxford.
PH WALTER STONEMAN, 1932, hs, NPG (NPR).

GRIFFITHS, James (1890-1975) politician.
PH WALTER STONEMAN, 1945, hs, NPG (NPR). WALTER BIRD, 1965, hs, NPG (NPR).

GRIFFITHS, Sir John Norton-, see Norton-Griffiths.

GRIGG, Edward William Macleay, see 1st Baron Altrincham.

GRIGG, Sir (Percy) James (1890-1964) secretary of state for war.
PH WALTER STONEMAN, 2 hs portraits, 1934 and 1942, NPG (NPR) and NPG X4640.

GROSSMITH, George (1874-1935) actor-manager and playwright.
D EDMOND KAPP, 1919, Barber Institute, Birmingham University.
C SIR MAX BEERBOHM, 1910, with the Gaiety Chorus, ink and w/c, V & A. R.S.SHERRIFFS, hs, ink, NPG 5224(7).
PH HOWARD COSTER, 1933, various sizes, print and negs, NPG AX3469 and others. ELLIS & WALERY, tql and wl in character, postcards, NPG. LOCK & WHITFIELD, hs, print, NPG. JOHN RUSSELL & SONS, c1917, hl in naval uniform, print, for *National Photographic Record*, vol 1, NPG.

GUEDALLA, Philip (1889-1944) historian and essayist.
D SIR WILLIAM ROTHENSTEIN, hl, chalk, NPG 4802.
C SIR MAX BEERBOHM, 1929, wl, drg, National Gallery of Victoria, Melbourne, Australia.
PH HOWARD COSTER, 1930, various sizes, print and negs, NPG X1889 and others.

GUEST, Frederick Edward (1875-1937) politician and promoter of aviation.
PH WALTER STONEMAN, 1921, hs, NPG (NPR).

GUEST, Ivor Churchill, see 1st Viscount Wimborne.

GUILLEBAUD, Claude William (1890-1971) economist and arbitrator.
D JOHN HOOKHAM, early 1940s, hs, pencil, St John's College, Cambridge.
PH Several photographs, St John's College.

GUINNESS, Rupert Edward Cecil Lee, see 2nd Earl of Iveagh.

GUINNESS, Walter Edward, see 1st Baron Moyne.

GUNN, Sir (Herbert) James (1893-1964) artist.
P SIR W.O.HUTCHISON, 1911, tql seated in lamplight, SNPG 2378.
PH WALTER BIRD, 1963, hs, NPG (NPR).

GUNTHER, Robert William Theodore (1869-1940) zool-ogist and antiquary.
PH ELLIOTT & FRY, c1925, hs, print, NPG.

GURNEY, Sir Henry Lovell Goldsworthy (1898-1951) colonial civil servant.
P HAROLD SPEED, tql in uniform, Legislative Council Chamber, Kuala Lumpur, Malaya.

GUTHRIE, Sir (William) Tyrone (1900-1971) actor-manager.
PH SIR CECIL BEATON, hs, print, NPG. HOWARD COSTER, 1930s, various sizes and negs, NPG. WALTER BIRD, 1962, hs, NPG (NPR). Various photographs, The Theatre Museum, V & A.

GUTTERIDGE, Harold Cooke (1876-1953) barrister and professor.
PH UNKNOWN, hs as elderly man, print, Trinity Hall, Cambridge.

GUY, Sir Henry Lewis (1887-1956) chartered mechanical engineer.
PH WALTER STONEMAN, 2 hs portraits, 1936 and 1953, NPG (NPR).

GWYER, Barbara Elizabeth (1881-1974) principal of St Hugh's College, Oxford.
D H.A.FREETH, 1948, head, pencil, St Hugh's College.
G HENRY LAMB, conversation piece, oil, 1936, St Hugh's College.
SC MIRIAM COATMAN, bust, St Hugh's College.

GWYER, Sir Maurice Linford (1878-1952) lawyer and civil servant.
PH WALTER STONEMAN, 1931, hs, NPG (NPR).

GWYNN, Stephen Lucius (1864-1950) writer and Irish nationalist.
D SIR WILLIAM ROTHENSTEIN, 1915, hs, chalk, NPG 4777. SIR W.ROTHENSTEIN, 1916, hs, chalk, Municipal Gallery of Modern Art, Dublin.

GWYNNE, Howell Arthur (1865-1950) journalist.
PH WALTER STONEMAN, 1938, hs, NPG (NPR).

GWYNNE-JONES, Allan (b1892) painter and etcher.
P Self-portrait, c1922, hl, TATE T2077.

GWYNNE-VAUGHAN, Dame Helen Charlotte Isabella (1879-1967) botanist and organizer of Women's Army Auxiliary Forces.
P P.A.DE LÁSZLÓ, c1907, wl in Academic robes, Birkbeck College, University of London. SIR WILLIAM ORPEN, 1918, IWM.
PH LAFAYETTE, hs, print, NPG.

H

HADOW, Grace Eleanor (1875-1940) pioneer in social work and principal of Society of Oxford Home-Students (now St Anne's College).
PH BASSANO, hs in academic robes, profile, print, National Federation of Women's Institutes, London.

HAHN, Kurt (1886-1974) educationist and headmaster of Gordonstoun.
PH HOWARD COSTER, various sizes and negs, NPG.

HAIG, Douglas Haig, 1st Earl (1861-1928) field-marshal.
P SIR WILLIAM ORPEN, 1917, hs in uniform, Brasenose College, Oxford, and IWM. HERBERT OLIVIER, 1919, DoE (Paris Chancery). SIR JAMES GUTHRIE, 1921, tql seated in uniform, Royal and Ancient Golf Club of St Andrews. SOLOMON J.SOLOMON, 1922, hs in uniform, IWM. J.S.SARGENT, c1922, hs in uniform, SNPG 1010, study for 'General Officers', NPG 1954.
D MRS GRAHAM SMITH, 1894, hs, chalk, NPG 1801A. SIR MUIRHEAD BONE, 1916, hl seated, black chalk, IWM. FRANCIS DODD, 1917, charcoal and w/c, IWM.
G J.S.SARGENT, 'General Officers of World War I, 1914–18', oil, 1922, NPG 1954.
SC A.F.HARDIMAN, 1937, bronze equestrian statue, Whitehall, London. WILLIAM MCMILLAN, statue, Clifton College, Bristol. G.E.WADE, 1922, bronze equestrian statue, Castle Esplanade, Edinburgh.
PR HENRIK LUND, lith, IWM.
PH WALTER STONEMAN, 1914, tql in uniform, NPG X449. JOHN RUSSELL & SONS, c1915, hs in uniform, for *National Photographic Record*, vol 1, NPG. BASSANO, c1919, hs in uniform, print, NPG. W.STONEMAN, 1925, 2 hs portraits in uniform, NPG (NPR).

HAIGH, Mervyn George (1887-1962) bishop of Coventry and Winchester.
P PETER GREENHAM, c1953, wl in robes of Garter prelate, Bishop's Palace, Winchester.
SC UNKNOWN, head, Bishop's Palace, Coventry.
PH WALTER STONEMAN, 2 hs portraits, 1939 and 1945, NPG (NPR). UNKNOWN, hl, print, NPG (Anglican Bishops).

HAILEY, William Malcolm Hailey, 1st Baron (1872-1969) civil servant and colonial administrator.
P SIR JAMES GUNN, 1954, tql seated, Royal Institute of International Affairs, Chatham House, London, and Rhodes House, Oxford. GLYN PHILPOT, tql in uniform, Lawrence Memorial Hall, Lahore, India.
C SIR DAVID LOW, 2 heads, pencil, NPG 4529(161–62).
PH WALTER STONEMAN, 2 hs portraits, 1930 and 1945, NPG (NPR).

HAILSHAM, Douglas McGarel Hogg, 1st Viscount (1872-1950) statesman and lord chancellor.
P SIR WILLIAM NICHOLSON, 1930, tql seated in robes, Lincoln's Inn, London. J.A.BERRIE, late 1940s, hs, Abbey National Building Society, Head Office, London. UNKNOWN, Polytechnic of Central London.
PH WALTER STONEMAN, 2 hs portraits, 1922 and 1933, NPG (NPR). UNKNOWN, hs, print, NPG.

HAINING, Sir Robert Hadden (1882-1959) general.
PH WALTER STONEMAN, 1941, 2 hs portraits in uniform, NPG X562

and NPG (NPR).

HAIRE, Norman (1892-1952) birth control and sex education pioneer.
D EDMOND KAPP, 1929, Barber Institute, Birmingham University.

HAKING, Sir Richard Cyril Byrne (1862-1945) general.
D FRANCIS DODD, 1917, charcoal and w/c, IWM.

HALCROW, Sir William Thomson (1883-1958) civil engineer.
P SIR JAMES GUNN, c1946–47, Institution of Civil Engineers, London.
PH WALTER STONEMAN, 2 hs portraits, 1944 and 1954, NPG (NPR).

HALDANE, Elizabeth Sanderson (1862-1937) public servant and writer.
PH WALTER STONEMAN, 1921, hs, NPG (NPR).

HALDANE, John Burdon Sanderson (1892-1964) theoretical biologist.
P CLAUDE ROGERS, 1957, hl, University College, London; study sketch, hl seated, pencil, BM.
PH OLIVE EDIS, 1925, hs, profile, print, NPG. UNKNOWN, United Front meeting in Trafalgar Square in January 1937, NPG (*Daily Herald*). HOWARD COSTER, 1938, various sizes, print and negs, NPG X1948 and X12252–63. WALTER STONEMAN, 1943, hs, NPG (NPR).

HALDANE, John Scott (1860-1936) physiologist and philosopher.
P P.A.DE LÁSZLÓ, 1933, on loan to SNPG L269.
PH SIR BENJAMIN STONE, 1902, wl, print, NPG. WALTER STONEMAN, 1931, hs, NPG (NPR).

HALFORD, Frank Bernard (1894-1955) aircraft engine designer.
P FRANK EASTMAN, 1957, tql seated, Royal Aero Club on loan to RAF Museum, Hendon.
PH UNKNOWN, hs, print, British Aerospace Aircraft Group, Hatfield, Herts.

HALIFAX, Edward Frederick Lindley Wood, 1st Earl of (1881-1959) statesman.
P SIR OSWALD BIRLEY, 1932, wl in Garter robes, Viceroy's House, New Delhi. SIR O.BIRLEY, c1947, tql seated in chancellor's robes, All Souls College, Oxford. LAWRENCE GOWING, c1952, tql seated, Christ Church, Oxford.
D STANLEY ANDERSON, 1932, hs, chalk, NPG 4214. JACOB KRAMER, 1931, head, pastel, Harrogate Corporation Art Gallery. ERIC KENNINGTON, 1940, pastel, IWM.
PH SIR CECIL BEATON, hl, print, NPG. HOWARD COSTER, various sizes and negs, NPG. WALTER STONEMAN, various portraits, 1923, 1934 and 1948, NPG (NPR). UNKNOWN, 1931, wl in vice-regal robes, print, NPG.

HALL, Sir (Alfred) Daniel (1864-1942) educationist, administrator and scientific research worker.
P CHRISTOPHER HALL, Lord Wandsworth College, Long Sutton, Hants.
D SIR RICHARD PAGET, chalk sketch, The Athenaeum, London.
PH WALTER STONEMAN, 2 hs portraits, 1921 and 1940, NPG (NPR).

HALL, Arthur Henry (1876-1949) engineer.
PH UNKNOWN, hs, print and neg, Royal Aircraft Establishment, Farnborough, Hants.

HALL, Sir Arthur John (1866-1951) physician.
P ERNEST MOORE, University of Sheffield.
PH ELLIOTT & FRY, tql seated, print, NPG.

HALL, Edna Clarke, Lady (1879-1979) artist.
D AUGUSTUS JOHN, hs, pencil, Carlisle City Art Gallery. A.JOHN, hs, sanguine, Carlisle City Art Gallery. Self-portrait, 1899, tql seated, w/c, Manchester City Art Gallery.

HALL, George Henry Hall, 1st Viscount (1881-1965) first lord of the Admiralty.
PH WALTER STONEMAN, 1946, hs, NPG (NPR).

HALL, (Marguerite) Radclyffe (1886?-1943) novelist.
P CHARLES BUCHEL, 1918, tql seated, NPG 4347.
PH HOWARD COSTER, 1930s, various sizes and negs, NPG X10419-24.

HALL, Sir (William) Reginald (1870-1943) admiral.
D FRANCIS DODD, 1917, charcoal and w/c, IWM.
SC LADY KATHLEEN KENNET, c1926, bust, Royal Naval College, Dartmouth.
PH WALTER STONEMAN, 1917, 2 hs portraits in uniform, NPG (NPR).

HALL, (William) Stephen Richard King-, see Baron King-Hall.

HALL-PATCH, Sir Edmund ('Leo') (1896-1975) civil servant.
PH WALTER STONEMAN, 1952, hs, NPG (NPR).

HALLETT, Sir Theodore John (1878-1957) vice-admiral.
PH WALTER STONEMAN, 1945, hl in uniform, NPG (NPR).

HALLIBURTON, William Dobinson (1860-1931) physiologist and biochemist.
PH JOHN RUSSELL & SONS, c1915-17, hs, print, for *National Photographic Record*, vol 1, NPG.

HALLIDAY, Sir William Reginald (1886-1966) classical scholar and principal of King's College, London.
PH WALTER STONEMAN, 1947, hs, NPG (NPR).

HALSEY, Sir Lionel (1872-1949) admiral.
P SIR OSWALD BIRLEY, tql in masonic robes, Halsey Masonic Hall, Watford.
D FRANCIS DODD, 2 portraits, charcoal and w/c, IWM.
PH WALTER STONEMAN, 1917, hs in uniform, NPG (NPR).

HAMBLEDEN, William Frederick Danvers Smith, 2nd Viscount (1868-1928) philanthropist.
SC Probably by ARTHUR G.WALKER, c1930, bronze bust, Lincoln's Inn Fields, London.
C SIR LESLIE WARD ('Spy'), wl, lith, for *Vanity Fair*, 8 Dec 1904, NPG.
PH JOHN RUSSELL & SONS, c1917, hs, print, for *National Photographic Record*, vol 1, NPG. WALTER STONEMAN, 1920, hs, NPG (NPR).

HAMBOURG, Mark (1879-1960) pianist.
SC ALBERT TOFT, 1904, bronze bust, Royal College of Music, London.
C SIR LESLIE WARD ('Spy'), wl, lith, for *Vanity Fair*, 29 April 1908, NPG.
PH JOHN RUSSELL & SONS, c1917, hl, print, for *National Photographic Record*, vol 1, NPG. UNKNOWN, hs, postcard, NPG. UNKNOWN, hs, profile, print, NPG.

HAMILTON, Cicely (Mary), real name Hammill (1872-1952) author, playwright and journalist.
P THOMAS LOWINSKY, Graves Art Gallery, Sheffield.
D EDMOND KAPP, 1931, Barber Institute, Birmingham University.

PH LENA CONNELL, hs, print, NPG.

HAMILTON, James Albert Edward, see 3rd Duke of Abercorn.

HAMMOND, John Lawrence Le Breton (1872-1949) journalist and historian.
D SIR WILLIAM ROTHENSTEIN, 1923, head, chalk, NPG 4778.
PH WALTER STONEMAN, 1945, hs, NPG (NPR). HOWARD COSTER, 1930s, various sizes and negs, NPG.

HAMMOND, Sir John (1889-1964) animal scientist.
PH WALTER STONEMAN, 2 hs portraits, 1933 and 1945, NPG (NPR).

HAMNETT, Nina (1890-1956) sculptor, painter and author.
P ROGER FRY, 1917, tql seated, Roger Fry Coll, Courtauld Institute of Art, London. R.FRY, wl seated, University of Leeds. W.R.SICKERT, c1915-16, wl seated with Roald Kristian, TATE 5288.

HANBURY-WILLIAMS, Sir John Coldbrook (1892-1965) chairman of Courtaulds Ltd and banker.
P DAVID JAGGER, Courtaulds Ltd, London.
PH WALTER STONEMAN, 1950, hs, NPG (NPR). HOWARD COSTER, 1953, various sizes and prints, NPG X1899, X2181-82 and X2201-02.

HANCOCK, Dame Florence (1893-1974) trade unionist.
PH Various photographs, Trades Union Congress, London.

HANCOCK, Sir Henry (Drummond) (1895-1965) civil servant.
PH WALTER STONEMAN, 1950, hs, NPG (NPR).

HANDLEY, Thomas Reginald ('Tommy') (1892-1949) radio comedian.
SL H.L.OAKLEY, hs, profile, NPG.

HANKEY, Sir Maurice Pascal Alers Hankey, 1st Baron (1877-1963) statesman.
P HERBERT OLIVIER, 1919, DoE (Paris Chancery). SIR WILLIAM ORPEN, 1919, hs in uniform, NPG 4650.
PH WALTER STONEMAN, 3 hs portraits, 1917, 1939 and 1947, NPG (NPR) and NPG X453.

HANNEN, Nicholas James (1881-1972) actor.
P FLORENCE GREY-EDWARDS, Garrick Club, London. EDWARD SEAGO, hs, Garrick Club.
PH HOWARD COSTER, c1926, various sizes, print and negs, NPG X2180 and others.

HANNON, Sir Patrick Joseph Henry (1874-1963) politician.
PH HOWARD COSTER, 1930s, various sizes and negs, NPG. WALTER STONEMAN, 2 hs portraits, 1937 and 1948, NPG (NPR).

HANWORTH, Ernest Murray Pollock, 1st Viscount (1861-1936) judge.
P J.M.CREALOCK, Inner Temple, London.
PH WALTER STONEMAN, 1917, hs, NPG (NPR). UNKNOWN, hs, print, Grocers' Hall, London.

HARCOURT, Sir Cecil Halliday Jepson (1892-1959) vice-admiral.
PH WALTER STONEMAN, 1942, hs in uniform, NPG (NPR).

HARCOURT, George (1868-1947) painter.
P SIR HUBERT VON HERKOMER, 1901, Watford Museum, Herts.
D Self-portrait, 1896, hs, profile, pencil, NPG 3045.
PH WALTER STONEMAN, 1930, hs, NPG (NPR).

HARCOURT, Lewis Harcourt, 1st Viscount (1863-1922) politician.
P SOLOMON J.SOLOMON, c1922-23, hs, profile, London Museum.
C SIR BERNARD PARTRIDGE, 'The Cabinet Cherubs', ink, for *Punch*,

22 April 1908, NPG.
PH WALTER STONEMAN, *c*1917, 3 hs portraits, prints, NPG (NPR).

HARDIE, Martin (1875-1952) artist and museum official.
P JAMES MCBEY, hl seated, Aberdeen Art Gallery.
PR J.MCBEY, 1915–19, hl seated, etch, NPG.
C SIR MAX BEERBOHM, 1924, wl with his son and Gordon Craig, w/c, V & A.

HARDIMAN, Alfred Frank (1891-1949) sculptor.
PH WALTER STONEMAN, 1946, hs, NPG (NPR).

HARDINGE of Penshurst, Alexander Henry Louis Hardinge, 2nd Baron (1894-1960) private secretary to King Edward VIII and King George VI.
PH WALTER STONEMAN, 1937, hs, NPG (NPR).

HARDWICKE, Albert Edward Philip Henry Yorke, 6th Earl of (1867-1904) under-secretary of state for war.
C SIR LESLIE WARD ('Spy'), tql, profile, lith, for *Vanity Fair*, 4 April 1901, NPG.

HARDWICKE, Sir Cedric (Webster) (1893-1964) actor.
SL HUBERT LESLIE, 1925, hs, NPG.
PH WALTER STONEMAN, 1945, hs, NPG (NPR). Various photographs, The Theatre Museum, V & A.

HARDY, Sir William Bate (1864-1934) biologist.
D FRANCIS DODD, 1941, crayon, Gonville and Caius College, Cambridge.
PH WALTER STONEMAN, 1917, hs, NPG (NPR).

HAREWOOD, Henry George Charles Lascelles, 6th Earl of (1882-1947) art patron and son-in-law of King George V.
P SOLOMON J.SOLOMON, 1922, hl, Harewood House, W Yorks. SIR A.J.MUNNINGS, 1930, wl on horseback with the Princess Royal, Harewood House. SIR WILLIAM NICHOLSON, 1936, wl in Garter robes, Harewood House; version, Freemasons' Hall, London.
D J.S.SARGENT, 1923, hs, charcoal, Harewood House.
G F.O.SALISBURY, wedding portrait, oil, 1922, Harewood House.
PH WALTER STONEMAN, 1927, hs, NPG (NPR).

HAREWOOD, Mary Victoria Alexandra Alice, Countess of, see MARY, princess royal.

HARINGTON, Sir Charles ('Tim') (1872-1940) general.
PH WALTER STONEMAN, 1918, hs in uniform, NPG (NPR).

HARLAND, Henry (1861-1905) novelist.
PH UNKNOWN, 1900, hl seated, print, NPG x4617.

HARLECH, William George Arthur Ormsby-Gore, 4th Baron (1885-1964) public servant.
P DAVID BELL, 1950, tql, National Museum of Wales 726, Cardiff. R.BROADLEY, 1952, tql seated in robes, Midland Bank Ltd, Poultry, London. SIR JAMES GUNN, *c*1954–59, seated with wine glass, Althorp, Northants, study for Society of Dilettanti group.
G SIR J.GUNN, 'Society of Dilettanti Conversation Piece', oil, 1954–59, Society of Dilettanti, Brooks's Club, London.

HARMSWORTH, Alfred Charles William, see 1st Viscount Northcliffe.

HARMSWORTH, Harold Sidney, see 1st Viscount Rothermere.

HARPER, Sir George Montague (1865-1922) lieutenant-general.
SC UNKNOWN, bronze relief portrait, Salisbury Cathedral.
PH WALTER STONEMAN, 1918, hs in uniform, NPG (NPR).

HARRADEN, Beatrice (1864-1936) novelist.
PR After photo by MIDGLEY ASQUITH, hs, woodcut, for *Illust London News*, 20 March 1897, NPG.

HARRIS, Sir Arthur Travers, 1st Bart (*b*1892) air chief marshal.
P H.A.OLIVIER, RAF Museum, Hendon, London.
SC PAMELA TAYLOR, bronze head, RAF Museum.
PH WALTER STONEMAN, 1940, hl in uniform, for NPR, NPG x4128. UNKNOWN, *c*1945, hl seated, print, NPG.

HARRIS, Frederick Leverton (1864-1926) politician and art collector.
C SIR LESLIE WARD ('Spy'), wl, Hentschel-Colourtype, for *Vanity Fair*, 30 Dec 1909, NPG.
PH WALTER STONEMAN, 1923, hs, NPG (NPR).

HARRISON, Henry (1867-1954) Irish nationalist and writer.
P S.C.HARRISON, 1932, NGI 1281.

HARRISON, Sir William Montagu Graham-, see Graham-Harrison.

HART, Sir Basil (Henry) Liddell, see Liddell Hart.

HART, Sir Raymund George (1899-1960) air marshal.
PH WALTER STONEMAN, 2 hs portraits in uniform, 1945 and 1958, NPG (NPR).

HARTLEY, Arthur Clifford (1889-1960) engineer and inventor.
P JOHN CODNER, RIBA.

HARTLEY, Sir Harold (1878-1972) brigadier-general and scientist.
P SIR CYRIL HINSHELWOOD, after a photograph?, Royal Society, London.
PH WALTER STONEMAN, 1946, hs, NPG (NPR). UNKNOWN, *c*1967, 2 hs portraits, prints, NPG.

HARTOG Sir Philip(pe) Joseph (1864-1947) educationist.
P HELENA DARMESTETER, hs, School of Oriental and African Studies, University of London.
PH WALTER STONEMAN, 1931, hs, NPG (NPR).

HARTREE, Douglas Rayner (1897-1958) scientist.
PH WALTER STONEMAN, 1944, hs, NPG (NPR).

HARTRICK, Archibald Standish (1864-1950) painter and lithographer.
P Self-portrait, *c*1912, hs, NPG 4193. Self-portrait, chalk, SNPG 1200.
PR VINCENT LINES, 1932, hs, chromo-lith, V & A.

HARTY, Sir (Herbert) Hamilton (1879-1941) musician.
D HAROLD SPEED, 1905, crayon, NGI.
C WILLIAM WEATHERBY, 1926, wl, indian ink and wash, Manchester City Art Gallery.

HARVEY, Sir Ernest Musgrave (1867-1955) banker.
P SIR OSWALD BIRLEY, 1936, tql seated, Bank of England, London.

HARVEY, Sir John Martin Martin-, see Martin-Harvey.

HARVEY of Tasburgh, Oliver Charles Harvey, 1st Baron (1893-1968) diplomat.
PH WALTER STONEMAN, 1947, hs, NPG (NPR). WALTER BIRD, 1958, hs, NPG (NPR).

HARWOOD, Sir Henry Harwood (1888-1950) admiral.
P SIR OSWALD BIRLEY, *c*1945–48, hs in uniform, Royal Naval College, Greenwich. DOUGLAS WALES-SMITH, after a photograph, NMM, Greenwich.
PH WALTER STONEMAN, hs in uniform, for NPR, NPG x4158.

HASLETT, Dame Caroline Harriet (1895-1957) electrical engineer.
P SIR GERALD KELLY, *c*1948, Royal Society of Arts, London. DOROTHY VICAJI, Electrical Association for Women, London.
PR ETHEL GABAIN, *c*1947, lith, IWM.

PH HOWARD COSTER, various sizes and negs, NPG.

HASSALL, John (1868-1948) poster artist.
P SIR JAMES GUNN, c1936, The Savage Club, London.
C STRICKLAND, hl profile, mechanical repro, for *Vanity Fair*, 21 Aug 1912, NPG.

HASTINGS, Sir Patrick Gardiner (1880-1952) barrister and author.
C N.C.BENTLEY, 1948, hl in robes, ink and pencil, NPG 4339.

HATHAWAY, Dame Sybil (1884-1974) Dame of Sark.
PH WALTER BIRD, 1965, hs, NPG (NPR).

HATTON, Sir Ronald George (1886-1965) horticulturist and director of the East Malling Research Station.
PH WALTER STONEMAN, 1945, hs, NPG (NPR).

HAWKE, Sir (John) Anthony (1869-1941) judge.
P R.G.EVES, c1910, hl in robes, Middle Temple, London.
PH WALTER STONEMAN, 1934, hs in robes, NPG (NPR).

HAWKE of Towton, Martin Bladen Hawke, 7th Baron (1860-1938) cricketer.
PR W.ALLINGHAM, after photograph by Dickinson & Foster, 1894, tql, stipple and line, NPG.
PH WALTER STONEMAN, 1920, hs, NPG (NPR).

HAWKINS, Sir Anthony Hope (1863-1933) novelist 'Anthony Hope'.
P HUGH DE T.GLAZEBROOK, c1904, Garrick Club, London. A.A.WOLMARK, 1908, hl, NPG 3974.
C HARRY FURNISS, c1910, wl seated, pen and ink, NPG 3465. SIR DAVID LOW, face, profile, pencil, NPG 4529(172).
PH G.C.BERESFORD, 1903, 3 hs portraits, print and negs, NPG x6519-20. JOHN RUSSELL & SONS, c1915, hs, print, for *National Photographic Record*, vol I, NPG. WALTER STONEMAN, 1924, hs, NPG (NPR).

HAWORTH, Sir (Walter) Norman (1883-1950) chemist.
PH WALTER STONEMAN, 1943, hs, NPG (NPR).

HAWTREY, Sir Ralph George (1879-1971) economist.
PH WALTER STONEMAN, 3 hs portraits, 1939, 1948 and 1958, NPG (NPR).

HAY, Ian, see John Hay BEITH.

HEAD, Sir Henry (1861-1940) neurologist.
D FRANCIS DODD, 1927, pencil, Trinity College, Cambridge.
PH WALTER STONEMAN, 1917, hs, NPG (NPR).

HEADLAM, Arthur Cayley (1862-1947) bishop of Gloucester.
P GEORGE HALL NEALE, c1935, tql seated in robes, Bishop's Palace, Gloucester.
PH WALTER STONEMAN, 2 hs portraits, 1921 and 1938, NPG (NPR). UNKNOWN, tql, print, NPG (Anglican Bishops).

HEADLAM-MORLEY, Sir James Wycliffe (1863-1929) political historian.
PH SIR EMERY WALKER, photogravure, Royal Institute of International Affairs, Chatham House, London.

HEAL, Sir Ambrose (1872-1959) furniture designer and dealer.
P EDWARD HALLIDAY, 1933, hl, Heal and Son Ltd, London.

HEARD, William Theodore (1884-1973) cardinal.
P DEREK HILL, tql seated in robes, Balliol College, Oxford. UNKNOWN, English College, Rome.

HEARLE, Francis Trounson (1886-1965) aeronautical engineer.
PH YOUSUF KARSH, 1950s, 2 hs portraits, prints, British Aerospace

Aircraft Group, Hatfield, Herts. UNKNOWN, 2 tql seated portraits, prints, British Aerospace.

HEATH, Ambrose (1891-1969) culinary journalist, author and broadcaster.
PH HOWARD COSTER, c1939, various sizes, prints and negs, NPG x3359-62 and others.

HEATH, Sir (Henry) Frank (1863-1946) academic and scientific administrator.
PH WALTER STONEMAN, 1917, hs, NPG (NPR).

HEATH, Sir Thomas Little (1861-1940) civil servant and authority on ancient mathematics.
D T.MARTINE RONALDSON, 1927, charcoal, Trinity College, Cambridge.
PH WALTER STONEMAN, 1931, hs, NPG (NPR).

HEATH ROBINSON, William, see Robinson.

HEELIS, Mrs Beatrix, see Potter.

HEILBRON, Sir Ian Morris (1886-1959) chemist.
PH HOWARD COSTER, various sizes and negs, NPG. WALTER STONEMAN, 2 hs portraits, 1931 and 1953, NPG (NPR).

HEINEMANN, William (1863-1920) publisher.
PH Various photographs, William Heinemann Ltd, London.

HELY-HUTCHINSON, Richard Walter John, see 6th Earl of Donoughmore.

HENDERSON, Arthur (1863-1935) Labour leader and statesman.
D EDMOND KAPP, 1935, wl, profile, Barber Institute, Birmingham University.
M LILIAN M.MAYER, c1924, hs, oval, NPG 2067.
PR E.KAPP, 1930s, hl seated, lith, NPG.
PH JOHN RUSSELL & SONS, c1915, hs, print, for *National Photographic Record*, vol I, NPG.

HENDERSON, Arthur (1893-1968), see Baron Rowley.

HENDERSON, Sir David (1862-1921) lieutenant-general.
D FRANCIS DODD, 1917, tql seated in uniform, charcoal and w/c, IWM.
PH WALTER STONEMAN, 1918, hs in uniform, NPG (NPR).

HENDERSON, Sir Hubert Douglas (1890-1952) economist.
PH WALTER STONEMAN, 1947, hs, NPG (NPR).

HENDERSON, Sir Nevile Meyrick (1882-1942) diplomat.
PH WALTER STONEMAN, 1935, hs, NPG (NPR).

HENRIQUES, Sir Basil Lucas Quixano (1890-1961) youth worker.
PH WALTER STONEMAN, 1955, hl, NPG (NPR). HOWARD COSTER, 1956, hs, print, NPG x1912. UNKNOWN, hs, print, Bernhard Baron and St George's Jewish Settlement, London.

HENRY William Frederick Albert, Prince, see Duke of GLOUCESTER.

HENSON, Herbert Hensley (1863-1947) bishop of Hereford and Durham.
P HAROLD SPEED, Auckland Castle, Durham.
C WALLACE HESTER ('W.H.'), wl, profile, mechanical repro, for *Vanity Fair*, 24 April 1912, NPG.
PH WALTER STONEMAN, 1918, hs, NPG (NPR). UNKNOWN, print, College of St Hild and St Bede, University of Durham.

HENSON, Leslie Lincoln (1891-1957) actor-manager.
D EDMOND KAPP, 1930, Barber Institute, Birmingham University.
C UNKNOWN, Garrick Club, London.
PH LENARE, 1942, various sizes and negs, NPG x904-08.

HERBERT, Sir Alan Patrick (1890-1971) humorist and politician.
P RUSKIN SPEAR, tql seated, NPG 4894.
SL H.L.OAKLEY, hs, profile, NPG.
PH HOWARD COSTER, c1930, various sizes, print and negs, NPG AX2309 and others. MARK GERSON, 1965, hs, print, NPG. N.VOGEL, c1969, 3 portraits, prints, NPG. GODFREY ARGENT, 1970, tql seated, NPG (NPR).

HERBERT, George Edward Stanhope Molyneux, see 5th Earl of Carnarvon.

HERTZ, Joseph Herman (1872-1946) chief rabbi of the United Hebrew Congregations of the British Empire.
P JOSEPH OPPENHEIMER, 1938, wl seated, Jews' College, London.
P WALTER STONEMAN, 1943, hs, NPG (NPR).

HESELTINE, Philip Arnold (1894-1930) composer and writer 'Peter Warlock'.
D ERNEST PROCTER, 1929, hs, profile, with Delius, pencil, NPG 4975(8).

HESS, Dame Myra (1890-1965) concert pianist.
D EDMOND KAPP, 1931, tql, Barber Institute, Birmingham University.
SC SIR JACOB EPSTEIN, plaster bust, North Carolina Museum of Art, Raleigh, USA.
PH HOWARD COSTER, 1930s, various sizes and negs, NPG. WALTER STONEMAN, 1957, tql seated at piano, NPG (NPR).

HETHERINGTON, Sir Hector (James Wright) (1888-1965) principal and vice-chancellor of Glasgow University.
P SIR W.O.HUTCHISON, University of Liverpool.
PH WALTER STONEMAN, 3 hs portraits, 1931, 1948 and 1958, NPG (NPR).

HEWART, Gordon Hewart, 1st Viscount (1870-1943) lord chief justice of England.
P JOHN ST HELIER LANDER, c1925, University College, Oxford. SIR OSWALD BIRLEY, 1935, hl seated in robes, Inner Temple, London.
D G.C.JENNIS, portrait sketch, V & A.
C SIR DAVID LOW, various heads, pencil, NPG 4529(171).

HEWITT, Sir Edgar Rainey Ludlow-, see Ludlow-Hewitt.

HEWLETT, Maurice Henry (1861-1923) novelist.
P J.K.LAWSON, 1904, wl seated, NPG 2800; pencil study, NPG 3263.
D SIR WILLIAM ROTHENSTEIN, 1898, head, chalk, NPG 2213.
G J.K.LAWSON, c1904, wl seated with his wife and artist's wife, pencil, NPG 3264.
PR WALTER TITTLE, 1922, hs, lith, NPG.
C SIR MAX BEERBOHM, 1908, wl, drg, Ashmolean Museum, Oxford. W.HESTER, hs, mechanical repro, for *Vanity Fair*, 5 March 1913, NPG.
PH G.C.BERESFORD, 1903, hs, prints and neg, NPG x6517 and others. A.L.COBURN, 1914, hs, photogravure, NPG x7822.

HEYWORTH, Geoffrey Heyworth, 1st Baron (1894-1974) industrialist.
PH WALTER STONEMAN, 1955, hs, NPG (NPR).

HICHENS, Robert Smythe (1864-1950) novelist.
C SIR MAX BEERBOHM, 1898, wl, drg, V & A.
PH JOHN RUSSELL & SONS, c1915, hs, print, for *National Photographic Record*, vol 1, NPG.

HICHENS, (William) Lionel (1874-1940) businessman.
PH G.C.BERESFORD, 1915, hs, neg, NPG x6518.

HICKS, Sir (Edward) Seymour (George) (1871-1949) actor-manager and author.
P MAURICE CODNER, c1931, wl as 'The Man in Dress Clothes',

Garrick Club, London.
C SIR MAX BEERBOHM, 1900, drg, University of Texas, Austin, USA.
PH ALFRED ELLIS, 1894, hs in character, print, NPG. ELLIS & WALERY, 1890s, tql in character, postcard, NPG. J.BEAGLES & CO, 1890s, hs, postcard, NPG. HOWARD COSTER, 1930s, various sizes and negs, NPG.

HICKS, Ellaline, Lady, see Terriss.

HICKS, George Ernest (1879-1954) trade unionist.
PH WALTER STONEMAN, 1945, hs, NPG (NPR). Various photographs, Trades Union Congress, London.

HICKS, William Joynson-, see 1st Viscount Brentford.

HIGGINS, Edward John (1864-1947) 3rd general of the Salvation Army.
D F.O.SALISBURY, 1934, Salvation Army, London.

HIGGINS, Sir John Frederick Andrews (1875-1948) air marshal.
PH WALTER STONEMAN, 1930, hs, NPG (NPR).

HILL, Archibald Vivian (1886-1977) physiologist.
D H.A.FREETH, 1957, tql seated, profile, w/c, NPG 4813. H.A.FREETH, 1957, hs, w/c, King's College, Cambridge.
PH WALTER STONEMAN, 2 hs portraits, 1933 and 1942, NPG (NPR).

HILL, Sir Arthur William (1875-1941) botanist.
PH WALTER STONEMAN, 1931, 2 hs portraits, NPG (NPR).

HILL, Sir George Francis (1867-1948) numismatist.
P SIR JAMES GUNN, 1937, hl seated, BM. H.G.RIVIERE, 1938, Merton College, Oxford.
D F.C.DODGSON, BM.
SC ARTHUR LOWENTHAL, 1935?, bronze medallion, profile, BM.
PH WALTER STONEMAN, 1925, hs, NPG (NPR).

HILL, Sir Leonard Erskine (1866-1952) physiologist.
PH WALTER STONEMAN, 1933, hs, NPG (NPR).

HILL, Leonard Raven-, see Raven-Hill.

HILL, Sir Roderic Maxwell (1894-1954) air chief marshal.
P RODRIGO MOYNIHAN, IWM. J.R.SWAN, after a photograph, 1955, hl seated in uniform, Imperial College of Science and Technology, London.

HILTON YOUNG, (Edith Agnes) Kathleen, see Lady Kennet.

HILTON YOUNG, Edward, see 1st Baron Kennet.

HIND, Arthur Mayger (1880-1957) historian of engraving.
D FRANCIS DODD, c1953, hl seated, charcoal, BM.

HINDLE, Edward (1886-1973) biologist.
SC PETER LAMBDA, 1949, bronze bust, Institute of Biology, London.
PH WALTER STONEMAN, 1946, hs, NPG (NPR).

HINDLEY, Sir Clement Daniel Maggs (1874-1944) railway engineer and public servant.
P ANTHONY DEVAS, 1940, Institution of Civil Engineers, London.
PH WALTER STONEMAN, 1931, hs, NPG (NPR).

HINKS, Arthur Robert (1873-1945) astronomer and geographer.
PH HUGH RUTTLEDGE, 1939, 2 hl portraits, prints, Royal Geographical Society, London.

HINKSON, Katharine, née Tynan (1861-1931) poet and novelist.
P J.B.YEATS, 1896, Municipal Gallery of Modern Art, Dublin.

HINSHELWOOD, Sir Cyril (Norman) (1897-1967) scientist and Nobel Prize winner for chemistry.

P DOUGLAS H.ANDERSON, 1958, hl seated in robes, Physical Chemistry Laboratory, Oxford. E.I.HALLIDAY, c1965, hs, Exeter College, Oxford.
PH WALTER STONEMAN, 2 hs portraits, 1931 and 1947, NPG (NPR).

HINSLEY, Arthur (1865-1943) cardinal.
P SIMON ELWES, 1940, tql seated in robes, Archbishop's House, Westminster, London. NEVILLE LYTTON, 1942, tql seated in robes, St Edmund's College, Ware, Herts. UNKNOWN, several portraits, English College, Rome.
PH HOWARD COSTER, various sizes and negs, NPG.

HIRST, Francis Wrigley (1873-1953) economist and Liberal writer.
PH G.C.BERESFORD, hs, print, NPG.

HIRST, George Herbert (1871-1954) cricketer.
C SIR LESLIE WARD ('Spy'), wl, lith, for *Vanity Fair*, 20 Aug 1903, NPG.

HITCHCOCK, Sir Alfred Joseph (1899-1980) film producer-director.
SC JEAN FRASER, 1967, wax head, Madame Tussaud's Ltd, London.
PH HOWARD COSTER, c1936, various sizes, prints and negs, NPG X3563-69 and others. BOB WILLOUGHBY, 1964, hl seated, print, NPG P138.

HITCHENS, Ivon (1893-1979) landscape painter.
PH J.S.MURRAY, 1933, wl in studio, print, NPG P135. J.S.LEWINSKI, 1964, hl, print, NPG.

HOARE, Sir Reginald Hervey (1882-1954) diplomat.
PH WALTER STONEMAN, 1933, hs, NPG (NPR).

HOARE, Sir Samuel John Gurney, see Viscount Templewood.

HOBART, Sir Percy Cleghorn Stanley (1885-1957) major-general.
D ERIC KENNINGTON, c1944, 2 hs portraits, pastel, The Tank Museum, Bovington Camp, Wareham, Dorset.
PH WALTER STONEMAN, 1952, hs in uniform, NPG (NPR).

HOBBES, John Oliver, see Pearl M.T.Craigie.

HOBBS, Sir John Berry ('Jack') (1882-1963) cricketer.
SL H.L.OAKLEY, hs, profile, NPG.
C R.S.SHERRIFFS, 1936, wl, ink, NPG 5224(8).
PH WALTER STONEMAN, 1953, hs, NPG (NPR).

HOBDAY, Sir Frederick Thomas George (1869-1939) veterinary surgeon.
P JOHN HASSALL, 1936, wl in uniform, Royal Veterinary College, London.

HODGKINS, Frances Mary (1869-1947) painter.
P SIR CEDRIC MORRIS, City Art Gallery, Auckland, New Zealand.

HODGSON, Sir Harold Kingston Graham- (1890-1960) radiologist.
PH WALTER STONEMAN, 1950, hs, NPG (NPR).

HODGSON, Ralph (1871-1962) poet.
SC THEODORE SPICER-SIMSON, 1922, plaster mould for medallion, NPG 4704; bronze cast, 1970, NPG 4704A.

HODGSON, Sir Robert MacLeod (1874-1956) diplomat.
PH WALTER STONEMAN, 1931, hs, NPG (NPR).

HODSOLL, Sir (Eric) John (1894-1971) wing commander.
PH WALTER STONEMAN, 1948, hs, NPG (NPR).

HODSON, James Lansdale (1891-1956) novelist and playwright.
PH HOWARD COSTER, various sizes and negs, NPG.

HOGARTH, David George (1862-1927) archaeologist and traveller.
PH WALTER STONEMAN, 1917, hs, NPG (NPR).

HOGBEN, Lancelot (1895-1975) scientist.
PH WALTER STONEMAN, 1936, hs, NPG (NPR). UNKNOWN, 1952, tql, NPG (*Daily Herald*).

HOGG, Douglas McGarel, see 1st Viscount Hailsham.

HOLBROOKE, Josef (1878-1958) composer.
PH HERBERT LAMBERT, c1922, hs, photogravure, NPG AX7748.

HOLDEN, Charles Henry (1875-1960) architect.
P FRANCIS DODD, c1912, tql, Art Workers' Guild, London.
D F.DODD, 1915, tql, chalk, NPG 4427; related etch, NPG 4173.
SC PAUL VINCZE, c1951, portrait medallion, Bristol Public Library. ONSLOW WHITING, c1960, bronze head, RIBA.
PH UNKNOWN, tql seated, print, RIBA.

HOLDSWORTH, Gladys Bertha, Mrs G.L.Holdsworth, see Stern.

HOLDSWORTH, Sir William Searle (1871-1944) lawyer.
P NESTOR CAMBIER, hl seated in doctoral robes, All Souls College, Oxford.
PH WALTER STONEMAN, 1930, hl, NPG (NPR).

HOLLAND, Sir Thomas Henry (1868-1947) geologist and educational administrator.
P JOHN COLLIER, 1911, tql in uniform, University of Edinburgh. STANLEY CURSITER, 1944, tql in vice-chancellor's robes, University of Edinburgh.
PH WALTER STONEMAN, 1928, hs, NPG (NPR).

HOLLIS, Sir Leslie Chasemore (1897-1963) general.
PH WALTER STONEMAN, 1946, hs in uniform, NPG (NPR).

HOLLOND, Henry Arthur (1884-1974) lawyer.
D R.J.BURN, 1933, crayon, Trinity College, Cambridge.

HOLMES, Sir Charles John (1868-1936) painter and critic.
P G.H.B.HOLLAND, 1934, hs with palette, NPG 3549.
C POWYS EVANS, hs, ink, NPG 3307.
PH ELLIOTT & FRY, hl, print, NPG.

HOLMES, Sir Maurice Gerald (1885-1964) educationist.
PH WALTER STONEMAN, 2 hs portraits, 1938 and 1948, NPG (NPR).

HOLMYARD, Eric John (1891-1959) teacher and historian.
PH UNKNOWN, print, Clifton College, Bristol.

HOLROYD, Sir Charles (1861-1917) painter-etcher and director of the National Gallery, London.
D ALPHONSE LEGROS, hs, Art Workers' Guild, London.
PR WILLIAM STRANG, 1909, hs, drypoint etch, NPG. A.LEGROS, hs, etch, NPG.
PH G.C.BERESFORD, c1907, hs, neg, NPG.

HOLST, Gustav Theodore (1874-1934) composer.
P MILLICENT WOODFORDE, c1910-11, wl seated at desk, NPG 4273. BERNARD MUNNS, tql seated, Cheltenham Art Gallery and Museum.
D SIR WILLIAM ROTHENSTEIN, 1920, hs, pencil, Morley College, London. EDMOND KAPP, 1931, chalk, Manchester City Art Gallery. E.KAPP, 1932, Barber Institute, Birmingham University. UNKNOWN, hs, pen and ink, Cheltenham Art Gallery.
G M.ROBERTS, 1925, Holst and St Paul's School orchestra, drg, The Holst Birthplace Museum, Cheltenham, Glos.
PH HERBERT LAMBERT, 1921, hs, profile, print, NPG P109. H.LAMBERT, c1922, hs, photogravure, NPG AX7745. MARTHA STERN, c1920-30, 3 hs portraits, prints, NPG.

HOLTBY, Winifred (1898-1935) writer.

P F.HOWARD LEWIS, after a photograph, 1939, hs, Somerville College, Oxford.

HONE, Evie (1894-1955) artist.
SC OISIN KELLY, bronze bust, Jesuit Novitiate, St Mary's, Emo, Eire.

HONE, Joseph Maunsell (1882-1959) Irish biographer and critic.
P AUGUSTUS JOHN, 1932, hs, TATE 5645.
D A.JOHN, pencil, Municipal Gallery of Modern Art, Dublin.

HOOD, Sir Horace Lambert Alexander (1870-1916) admiral.
G SIR A.S.COPE, 'Naval Officers of World War I, 1914–18', oil, 1921, NPG 1913.

HOOPER, Sir Frederic Collins, 1st Bart (1892-1963) company director.
PH WALTER BIRD, 1962, hs, NPG (NPR).

HOOPER, John Stirling Morley (1882-1974) Methodist missionary.
PH UNKNOWN, hs, print, The Methodist Church, Overseas Division, London.

HOPE, Anthony, see Hawkins.

HOPE, James Fitzalan, see 1st Baron Rankeillour.

HOPE, John Adrian Louis, see 1st Marquess of Linlithgow.

HOPE, Victor Alexander John, see 2nd Marquess of Linlithgow.

HOPETOUN, John Adrian Louis Hope, 7th Earl of, see 1st Marquess of Linlithgow.

HOPKINS, Sir Frederick Gowland (1861-1947) biochemist.
P GEORGE HENRY, 1926, tql in academic robes, Department of Biochemistry, University of Cambridge. MEREDITH FRAMPTON, 1938, hl seated, Royal Society, London.
D ERIC KENNINGTON, 1926, pencil, Trinity College, Cambridge. EDMOND KAPP, 1943, hs, charcoal, Fitzwilliam Museum, Cambridge. E.KAPP, 1943, Barber Institute, Birmingham University.
PH WALTER STONEMAN, 1932, hs, NPG (NPR).

HOPKINS, Sir Richard Valentine Nind (1880-1955) civil servant.
PH WALTER STONEMAN, 1941, hs, NPG (NPR).

HOPKINSON, Bertram (1874-1918) engineer and physicist.
P A.T.NOWELL, 1911, tql in academic robes, Engineering Department, University of Cambridge.

HOPPÉ, Emil Otto (1878-1972) photographer and author.
PH SIR CECIL BEATON, hl seated, print, NPG.

HOPWOOD, Francis John Stephens, see 1st Baron Southborough.

HORDER, Percy (Richard) Morley (1870-1944) architect.
P CLIVE GARDINER, National Institute of Agricultural Botany, Cambridge.

HORDER, Thomas Jeeves Horder, 1st Baron (1871-1955) physician.
P SIR WILLIAM NICHOLSON, wl seated, St Bartholomew's Hospital, London.
SC OLAFF DE WET, c1954–55, bronze head, Royal College of Physicians, London.
PH WALTER STONEMAN, 1933, hs, NPG (NPR).

HORE-BELISHA, (Isaac) Leslie Hore-Belisha, Baron (1893-1957) politician.
P CLARENCE WHITE, 1936, hl seated, NPG 4860.

PH HOWARD COSTER, 1 neg, NPG. WALTER STONEMAN, 2 hs portraits, 1930 and 1949, NPG (NPR).

HORE-RUTHVEN, Alexander Gore Arkwright, see 1st Earl of Gowrie.

HORNBY, Charles Harry St John (1867-1946) printer and connoisseur.
D SIR WILLIAM ROTHENSTEIN, 1923, hl seated, chalk, NPG 3872.
PH UNKNOWN, tql seated in kitchen, print, NPG X3738.

HORNE, Henry Sinclair Horne, Baron (1861-1929) general.
P J.S.SARGENT, c1922, hs in uniform, SNPG 1011, study for 'General Officers', NPG 1954. SIR OSWALD BIRLEY, 1933, tql in uniform, Harrow Scholl, Middx.
D FRANCIS DODD, 1917, charcoal and w/c, IWM.
G J.S.SARGENT, 'General Officers of World War I, 1914–18', oil, 1922, NPG 1954.
PH WALTER STONEMAN, 1917, hs in uniform, NPG (NPR).

HORNE, Robert Stevenson Horne, Viscount (1871-1940) statesman.
P SIR JAMES GUNN, SNPG 1548.
C SIR BERNARD PARTRIDGE, wl as gardener, pen and ink drg, for *Punch*, 10 May 1922, NPG.
PH WALTER STONEMAN, 4 hs portraits, 1918, 1928 and 1939, NPG (NPR).

HORNER, Arthur (1894-1968) trade unionist.
PH Various photographs, Trades Union Congress, London.

HORNIMAN, Annie Elizabeth Fredericka (1860-1937) pioneer of repertory theatre.
P J.B.YEATS, 1904, Abbey Theatre, Dublin.
D L.A.BELL, c1910?, pastel, TATE 4563. FLORA LION, c1912, hs, chalk, NPG 3973.
PH UNKNOWN, c1912–13, 2 tql seated portraits, postcards, NPG.

HORSBRUGH, Florence Horsbrugh, Baroness (1889-1969) politician.
PH WALTER STONEMAN, 1945, hs NPG (NPR).

HORTON, Sir Max Kennedy (1883-1951) admiral.
P SIR OSWALD BIRLEY, c1945–48, hs in uniform, Royal Naval College, Greenwich. DOUGLAS WALES-SMITH, tql in uniform, NMM, Greenwich. JOHN WORSLEY, hl seated in uniform, HMS *Dolphin*, Fort Blockhouse, Gosport, Hants.
PH WALTER STONEMAN, 1933, hs in uniform, NPG (NPR).

HOULDSWORTH, Sir Hubert Stanley, 1st Bart (1889-1956) chairman of the National Coal Board.
P SIR GERALD KELLY, c1953, University of Leeds.
PH WALTER STONEMAN, 1945, hl, NPG (NPR).

HOUSMAN, Laurence (1865-1959) writer.
SC ALEC MILLER, c1924, wooden bust, NPG 4816.
PR SIR WILLIAM ROTHENSTEIN, 1898, hs, lith, NPG, and Bradford City Art Gallery and Museums.
PH HOWARD COSTER, 1936 and 1950, various sizes, prints and negs, NPG X1926–30, AX3512 and others. PAUL TANQUERAY, c1930s, hs, print, NPG.

HOWARD, Leslie (1893-1943) actor.
P R.G.EVES, c1937, hs, NPG 3827. R.G.EVES, hl seated, Huddersfield Art Gallery. R.G.EVES, Garrick Club, London.
PH Various photographs and postcards, The Theatre Museum, V & A.

HOWARD-VYSE, Sir Richard Granville Hylton (1883-1962) major-general.
PH WALTER STONEMAN, 2 hs portraits, the 1st in uniform, 1934 and 1958, NPG (NPR).

HOWARD DE WALDEN, Thomas Evelyn Scott-Ellis, 4th Baron Seaford and 8th Baron (1880-1946) theatre patron and playwright.

SC RODIN, 1905-6, bronze bust, TATE 5034.

C SIR MAX BEERBOHM, wl, drg, University of Texas, Austin, USA. SIR LESLIE WARD ('Spy'), wl, lith, for *Vanity Fair*, 17 May 1906, NPG.

PH WALTER STONEMAN, 1930, hs, NPG (NPR). LENARE, 1940, hs, neg, NPG X803.

HOWARD of Penrith, Esme William Howard, 1st Baron (1863-1939) diplomat.

PH WALTER STONEMAN, 2 hs portraits, 1918 and 1931, NPG (NPR).

HOWE, Francis Richard Henry Penn Curzon, 5th Earl (1884-1964) politician.

PH WALTER STONEMAN, 1919, hs in uniform, NPG (NPR).

HOWELLS, Herbert Norman (b 1892) composer.

P RICHARD WALKER, 1972, hl seated, Royal College of Music, London. LEONARD BODEN, 1974, Royal College of Music. HOWARD MORGAN, 1978, tql seated, NPG 5209.

D SIR WILLIAM ROTHENSTEIN, 1919, hs, sanguine, Royal College of Music. BRENDA MOORE, 1972, pencil, Royal College of Music.

PH HERBERT LAMBERT, c1922, hs, profile, photogravure, NPG AX7756.

HOWORTH, Sir Rupert Beswicke (1880-1964) civil servant.

PH WALTER STONEMAN, 3 hs portraits, the 1st in uniform, 1933 and 1941, NPG (NPR).

HUDSON, Sir Robert Arundell (1864-1927) political organizer.

PH ELLIOTT & FRY, tql seated, print, NPG. WALTER STONEMAN, 1919, hs, NPG (NPR).

HUDSON, Robert Spear Hudson, 1st Viscount (1886-1957) politician.

PH WALTER STONEMAN, 1935, hs, NPG (NPR). HOWARD COSTER, 1930s, various sizes and negs, NPG.

HUEFFER, Ford Hermann, see Ford.

HUGESSEN, Sir Hughe Montgomery Knatchbull-, see Knatchbull-Hugessen.

HUGHES, Richard (1900-1976) writer.

P SYDNEY MORSE-BROWN, 1938, tql, National Museum of Wales 477, Cardiff.

D RUPERT SHEPPARD, 1974, hs, chalk?, National Museum of Wales, Cardiff.

HUGHES, William Morris (1862-1952) Australian prime minister.

P SIR JAMES GUTHRIE, c1919-21, hs, profile, SNPG 1137, study for 'Statesmen' group, NPG 2463. GEORGE LAMBERT, c1929, King's Hall, Parliament House, Canberra, Australia.

G SIR J.GUTHRIE, 'Statesmen of World War I, 1914-18', oil, c1924-30, NPG 2463.

SC F.D.WOOD, 1919, plaster head, IWM, London; version?, terracotta, Art Gallery of New South Wales, Sydney, Australia; bronze cast, Parliament House, Canberra.

HUMPHREY, Herbert Alfred (1868-1951) engineer.

C WALLACE HESTER, wl, mechanical repro, for *Vanity Fair*, 9 April 1913, NPG.

HUMPHREYS, Sir (Richard Somers) Travers (Christmas) (1867-1956) judge.

PH WALTER STONEMAN, 3 hs portraits, the 1st in robes, 1931 and 1946, NPG (NPR).

HUNT, Arthur Surridge (1871-1934) papyrologist.

PH WALTER STONEMAN, 1917, hs in uniform, NPG (NPR).

HUNTER, Sir Ellis (1892-1961) industrialist.

PH WALTER BIRD, 1961, hl, NPG (NPR).

HUNTER, Philip Vassar (1883-1956) electrical engineer.

PH UNKNOWN, c1933-34, hs, print, Institution of Electrical Engineers, London.

HUNTER-WESTON, Sir Aylmer Gould (1864-1940) lieutenant-general.

P E.PATRY, after P.A.de László, 1916, hl in uniform, Royal Engineers Headquarters Mess, Chatham, Kent.

D FRANCIS DODD, 1917, charcoal and w/c, IWM, London.

PH WALTER STONEMAN, 1918, hs in uniform, NPG (NPR). SWAINE, c1917-19, hs in uniform, print, NPG.

HUNTING, Sir Percy Llewellyn (1885-1973) businessman.

P FRANK EASTMAN, after a photograph, hl, Hunting Group of Companies, London.

HURCOMB, Sir Cyril William Hurcomb, 1st Baron (1883-1975) civil servant.

PH WALTER STONEMAN, 3 hs portraits, 1930, 1940 and 1947, NPG (NPR).

HURST, Sir Arthur Frederick (1866-1944) physician.

PH VANDYK, hs, print, Guy's Hospital Medical School, London.

HURST, Sir Cecil (James Barrington) (1870-1963) jurist.

PH WALTER STONEMAN, 1935, hs in robes, NPG (NPR).

HUTCHINSON, Arthur (1866-1937) mineralogist.

P SIR WILLIAM ROTHENSTEIN, Pembroke College, Cambridge.

PH WALTER STONEMAN, 1926, hs, NPG (NPR).

HUTCHINSON, Arthur Stuart Menteth (1879-1971) novelist.

PR WALTER TITTLE, 1922, hs, lith, NPG.

C SIR MAX BEERBOHM, 1923, drg, Savage Club, London.

HUTCHINSON, Francis Ernest (1871-1947) scholar and canon of Worcester.

PH WALTER STONEMAN, 1945, hs, NPG (NPR).

HUTCHINSON, Richard Walter John Hely-, see 6th Earl of Donoughmore.

HUTCHISON, Sir Robert, 1st Bart (1871-1960) physician and paediatrician.

P SIR JAMES GUNN, 1938, tql seated in robes, Royal College of Physicians, London.

HUTCHISON, Sir William Oliphant (1889-1970) portrait painter.

P SIR JAMES GUNN, 1911, wl seated, SNPG 2379.

PH EDINBURGH EVENING NEWS, 1952, wl with Queen at Royal Scottish Academy, print, NPG. MADAME YEVONDE, print, NPG.

HUXLEY, Aldous (Leonard) (1894-1963) novelist.

P FELIKS TOPOLSKI, 1961, University of Texas, Austin, USA.

D SIR WILLIAM ROTHENSTEIN, 1922, hl, profile, chalk, Manchester City Art Gallery. EDMOND KAPP, 1924, Barber Institute, Birmingham University. ALFRED WOLMARK, 1928, head, profile, ink and wash, NPG 4485. A.WOLMARK, 1928, head, ink, Ashmolean Museum, Oxford. GEORGES SCHRIEBER, 1937, hs, pencil, University of Texas.

SC JO DAVIDSON, 1930, terracotta head, National Portrait Gallery Library, Smithsonian Institution, Washington, USA. MARIA PETRIE, c1960, bronze cast of head, NPG 5282.

C SIR DAVID LOW, 1933, 4 sketches, pencil, NPG 4529(173-76). SIR D.LOW, 1938, with Dick Sheppard, pencil, chalk and ink, TATE 5464.

PH SIR CECIL BEATON, tql, print, NPG. HOWARD COSTER, 1934, various sizes, prints and negs, NPG AX3486, X10664–65, X1933 and X10889–97. DOROTHY WILDING, 1930s, tql seated, print, NPG. W.SUSCHITZKY, 1958, 2 hs portraits, prints, NPG. W.SUSCHITZKY, 1958, tql seated with brother Sir Julian, print, NPG.

HUXLEY, Sir Julian Sorell (1887–1975) biologist and writer.
D EDMOND KAPP, 1947, hs and wl, Barber Institute, Birmingham University. RUPERT SHEPHARD, 1960, hs, chalk, NPG 5041.
C SIR DAVID LOW, 1945, tql, pencil, University of Hull.
PH HOWARD COSTER, 1939, various sizes, print and negs, NPG X2162 and others. WALTER STONEMAN, 1956, hs, NPG (NPR). W.SUSCHITZKY, 1958, tql seated with brother Aldous, print, NPG. W.SUSCHITZKY, 1961, 3 portraits, prints, NPG. MARK GERSON, 1965, hl seated, print, NPG. GODFREY ARGENT, 1968, hs, print, NPG (NPR). SIR CECIL BEATON, 1970, tql seated, print, NPG.

HYDE, Douglas (1860–1949) Gaelic revivalist, poet and first president of Eire.
P WILLIAM CONOR, c1937–45, University College, Dublin. SEAN O'SULLIVAN, c1938, tql seated, profile, NGI 1011. SARAH PURSER, NGI 1181. LEO WHELAN, President's Residence, Dublin. J.B.YEATS, 1906, NGI 874. J.B.YEATS, Municipal Gallery of Modern Art, Dublin.
D J.B.YEATS, 1895, pencil, NGI. S.O'SULLIVAN, 1936, NGI. GAETANO DE GENNARO, 1943, hs, pastel, President's Residence, Dublin.
SC SEUMAS MURPHY, bust, President's Residence. THEODORE SPICER-SIMSON, 1922, plasticine medallion, NGI 8141; bronze cast, NGI 8217.

HYDE, Sir Robert (Robertson) (1878–1967) founder and director of the Industrial Welfare Society.
P SIR JAMES GUNN, c1952, tql seated, Industrial Society, London.

HYLTON, Jack (1892–1965) impressario.
C SIR DAVID LOW, various sketches, pencil, NPG 4529(177–80).

HYNDLEY, Sir John Scott Hyndley, 1st Viscount (1883–1963) first chairman of the National Coal Board.
PH WALTER STONEMAN, 1942, 2 hs portraits, NPG (NPR).

I

ILCHESTER, Giles Stephen Holland Fox-Strangways, 6th Earl of (1874-1959) landowner and historian.
P SIR JAMES GUNN, *c*1954–59, seated, semi-profile, Althorp, Northants, study for Society of Dilettanti group.
G SIR J.GUNN, 'Society of Dilettanti Conversation Piece', oil, *c*1954–59, Society of Dilettanti, Brooks's Club, London.
PH WALTER STONEMAN, 1922, hs, NPG (NPR).

ILIFFE, Edward Mauger Iliffe, 1st Baron (1877-1960) newspaper and periodical proprietor.
PH WALTER STONEMAN, 2 hs portraits, 1937 and 1945, NPG (NPR).

IMMS, Augustus Daniel (1880-1949) entomologist.
D PAUL DRURY, 1945, hs, pencil, Zoology Department, University of Cambridge.

INCE, Sir Godfrey Herbert (1891-1960) civil servant.
PH WALTER STONEMAN, 2 hs portraits, 1943 and 1954, NPG (NPR).

INGE, William Ralph (1860-1954) dean of St Paul's.
P P.A.DE LÁSZLÓ, 1934, tql seated, NPG 4856. ARTHUR NORRIS, *c*1934, tql seated, NPG 3920.
D SIR WILLIAM ROTHENSTEIN, 1920, head, chalk, King's College, Cambridge. CATHARINE DODGSON, 1923, King's College. EDMOND KAPP, 1930, Barber Institute, Birmingham University. C.DODGSON, 1934, hs, chalk, King's College.
C WALLACE HESTER ('W.H.'), wl, profile, mechanical repro, for *Vanity Fair*, 31 Jan 1912, NPG. SIR DAVID LOW, *c*1927, head, profile, pencil, NPG 4529(181). SIR BERNARD PARTRIDGE, wl, pen and ink and w/c, for *Punch*, summer number, 21 May 1928, NPG. R.S.SHERRIFFS, wl, titled 'Fantastic Studies', ink and charcoal?, NPG.
PH JOHN RUSSELL & SONS, *c*1915, hs, print, for *National Photographic Record*, vol 1, NPG. WALTER STONEMAN, 1925, hs, NPG (NPR). HOWARD COSTER, 1930s, various sizes and negs, NPG.

INGLIS, Sir Charles Edward (1875-1952) professor of engineering.
P HENRY LAMB, Institution of Civil Engineers, London. H.LAMB, King's College, Cambridge.
D D.GORDON SHIELDS, 1926, tql seated, Department of Engineering, University of Cambridge.

INGLIS, Elsie Maud (1864-1917) physician and surgeon.
SC IVAN MESTROVIC, bronze bust, IWM; version?, SNPG 1825.

INGRAMS, William Harold (1897-1973) colonial administrator and expert on Arabian affairs.
PH UNKNOWN, *c*1935, 2 wl portraits in Arab dress, prints, Royal Geographical Society, London.

INNES, James Dickson (1887-1914) landscape painter.
P AUGUSTUS JOHN, *c*1910–12, tql reclining, National Museum of Wales, Cardiff. IAN STRANG, 1913, hl, National Museum of Wales 694.

D ALBERT RUTHERSTON, 1908, head, profile, pencil, NPG 3054. I.STRANG, 1913, hs, pencil, NPG 4382.

INNES of Learney, Sir Thomas (1893-1971) Lord Lyon King of Arms.
P DON POTTINGER, 1949, tql in robes, Court of the Lord Lyon, Edinburgh.

INSKIP, Thomas Walker Hobart, see 1st Viscount Caldecote.

INVERFORTH, Andrew Weir, 1st Baron (1865-1955) shipowner.
P F.O.SALISBURY, Glasgow City Art Gallery.
PH WALTER STONEMAN, 1919, hs, NPG (NPR).

IRELAND, John Nicholson (1879-1962) composer.
P G.L.RODDON, 1960, hl, NPG 4290.
PH HERBERT LAMBERT, *c*1920, hs, print, NPG P105. H.LAMBERT, *c*1920, hs, photogravure, NPG AX7751.

IRONSIDE, William Edmund Ironside, 1st Baron (1880-1959) field-marshal.
P COLIN CORFIELD, tql seated in uniform, Royal Artillery Mess, Woolwich. KENNETH HAUFF, *c*1941, Tonbridge School, Kent.
D ERIC KENNINGTON, 1940, pastel, IWM.
PH WALTER STONEMAN, 1920, hs in uniform, NPG (NPR).

IRVINE, Sir James Colquhoun (1877-1952) chemist and educationist.
P SIR OSWALD BIRLEY, *c*1934, University of St Andrews, Fife, Scotland. KEITH HENDERSON, University of St Andrews.
PH WALTER STONEMAN, 1925, hs, NPG (NPR).

IRWIN, Noel Mackintosh Stuart (1892-1972) lieutenant-general.
PH WALTER STONEMAN, 1947, hs in uniform, NPG (NPR).

ISAACS, Gerald Rufus, see 2nd Marquess of Reading.

ISAACS, Rufus Daniel, see 1st Marquess of Reading.

ISITT, Dame Adeline, see Genée.

ISLINGTON, Sir John Poynder Dickson-Poynder, 1st Baron (1866-1936) politician and administrator.
PH JOHN RUSSELL & SONS, *c*1915, hs, profile, NPG (NPR). WALTER STONEMAN, 1932, hs, NPG (NPR).

ISMAY of Wormington, Hastings Lionel Ismay, 1st Baron (1887-1965) general.
P ALLAN GWYNNE-JONES, 1959, hs in uniform, NPG 4537.
PH WALTER STONEMAN, 1940, hs in uniform, for NPR, NPG X1019.

IVEAGH, Rupert Edward Cecil Lee Guinness, 2nd Earl of (1874-1967) businessman and public servant.
PH WALTER STONEMAN, 2 hs portraits, 1921 and 1948, NPG (NPR). HOWARD COSTER, 1931, various sizes, print and negs, NPG AX3435 and others.

J

JACKS, Lawrence Pearsall (1860-1955) Unitarian divine.
P GEORGE HARCOURT, c1925, Manchester College, Oxford.

JACKSON, Sir Barry Vincent (1879-1961) founder of the Birmingham Repertory Theatre and Malvern Festival.
P SIR ALFRED MUNNINGS, wl seated in Malvern Hills, The Birmingham Repertory Theatre.
SC WILLIAM BLOYE, c1958, bronze head, Birmingham Rep.
PH HOWARD COSTER, 1930s, various sizes and negs, NPG. WALTER STONEMAN, 2 hs portraits, 1940 and 1948, NPG (NPR).

JACKSON, Sir Cyril (1863-1924) educationist.
PH WALTER STONEMAN, 1917, hs, NPG (NPR).

JACKSON, Sir (Francis) Stanley (1870-1947) cricketer and administrator.
P GERALD REYNELL, Lord's Cricket Ground, London.
C SIR LESLIE WARD ('Spy'), wl, lith, for *Vanity Fair*, 28 Aug 1902, NPG.

JACKSON, Frederick George (1860-1938) explorer and soldier.
P UNKNOWN, hs, Scott Polar Research Institute, Cambridge University.
D H.DIXON, 1893, w/c, Scott Institute.
C SIR LESLIE WARD ('Spy'), tql, w/c, for *Vanity Fair*, NPG 4611.
PH Various photographs, Scott Institute.

JACKSON, Sir Herbert (1863-1936) chemist.
PH WALTER STONEMAN, 1927, hs, NPG (NPR).

JACKSON, Holbrook (1874-1948) author.
PH A.L.COBURN, 1913, hs, photogravure, NPG AX7810. HOWARD COSTER, 1930s, various sizes and negs, NPG.

JACKSON, John (1887-1958) astronomer.
PH UNKNOWN, c1953-55, hs, print, Royal Astronomical Society, London.

JACOB, Sir Claud William (1863-1948) field-marshal.
D FRANCIS DODD, 1917, charcoal and w/c, IWM.
PH WALTER STONEMAN, 2 hs portraits in uniform, 1917 and 1938, NPG (NPR).

JACOB, Sir (Edward) Ian (Claud) (b1899) director-general of the British Broadcasting Corporation.
P NORMAN HEPPLE, c1965, Army and Navy Club, London.
PH HOWARD COSTER, 1953, various sizes, prints, NPG X2159 and X1935-37. WALTER STONEMAN, 2 hs portraits, 1947 and 1958, NPG (NPR).

JACOB, Ernest Fraser (1894-1971) historian and librarian of All Souls College, Oxford.
D H.A.FREETH, 1970, hl, w/c, All Souls College, Oxford.
PH WALTER STONEMAN, 1949, hs, NPG (NPR).

JACOBS, William Wymark (1863-1943) novelist.
P CARTON MOORE-PARK, 1910, hl seated, NPG 3178.
PR WALTER TITTLE, 1922, hs, lith, NPG.
C HARRY FURNISS, wl seated, profile, pen and ink, NPG 3472. SIR DAVID LOW, 2 heads, pencil, NPG 4529(309).
PH JOHN RUSSELL & SONS, c1915, hs, print, for *National Photographic Record*, vol 1, NPG.

JAGGER, Charles Sargeant (1885-1934) sculptor.
P DAVID JAGGER, 1917, hs in uniform, 'Portrait of a British Officer: C.S.Jagger', Graves Art Gallery, Sheffield.

JAMES, Arthur Lloyd, see Lloyd James.

JAMES, Montague Rhodes (1862-1936) biblical scholar, antiquary and palaeographer.
P MARION SAUMAREZ, c1910, tql seated in academic robes, Eton College, Berks. GLYN PHILPOT, 1923, tql seated in robes, King's College, Cambridge. SIR GERALD KELLY, 1935, tql in robes, Eton College. SIR G.KELLY, c1936, hs, NPG 5285.
D WILLIAM STRANG, 1909, hs, semi-profile, chalk, Fitzwilliam Museum, Cambridge. SIR WILLIAM ROTHENSTEIN, 1915, King's College.
PH HOWARD COSTER, 193?, hs, various sizes, print and negs, NPG. WALTER STONEMAN, 1930, hs, NPG (NPR). OLIVE EDIS, c1912, tql seated, print, NPG X6034.

JAMESON, (Margaret) Storm (b1897) novelist.
PH HOWARD COSTER, 1930s, various sizes, prints and negs, NPG X3443-44, X1938 and X1999. GODFREY ARGENT, 1970, hs, NPG (NPR).

JAMESON, Sir (William) Wilson (1885-1962) chief medical officer of Ministry of Health.
PH WALTER STONEMAN, 1941, hs, NPG (NPR).

JARDINE, Douglas Robert (1900-1958) cricketer.
P H.A.OLIVIER, c1934, hl, Lord's Cricket Ground, London.

JARVIE, (John) Gibson (1883-1964) chairman of the United Dominions Trust.
P MAURICE CODNER, 1950, hl seated, United Dominions Trust Ltd, London.
PH Various photographs, United Dominions Trust.

JEANS, Sir James Hopwood (1877-1946) mathematician, theoretical physicist and astronomer.
PH WALTER STONEMAN, 1922, hs, NPG (NPR). HOWARD COSTER, 1930s, various sizes and negs, NPG.

JEBB, Eglantyne (1876-1928) philanthropist and a founder of the Save the Children Fund.
PH Various photographs, Save the Children Fund, London.

JEFFERY, George Barker (1891-1957) mathematician and educationist.
PH WALTER STONEMAN, 1944, hs, NPG (NPR).

JELLICOE, (John) Basil (Lee) (1899-1935) housing reformer.
P HENRY CARR, after photographs, hs, St Pancras Housing Association in Camden, London.
PH Various photographs, St Pancras Housing Association.

JENKINS, Claude (1877-1959) ecclesiastical historian.
PH H.ROLAND WHITE, 2 hs portraits as a young man, prints, Christ Church, Oxford. UNKNOWN, hl seated with two other young men, print, Christ Church. UNKNOWN, 1957, wl in robes with Dr E.Hammerschmidt outside his lodgings in College, print, Christ Church.

JENKINS, Sir David Llewelyn Jenkins, Baron (1899-1969) lord of appeal.

G NORMAN HEPPLE, 'Court of Appeal in 1958', oil, Lincoln's Inn, London.

JENKINSON, Sir (Charles) Hilary (1882-1961) deputy keeper of the Records.
PH WALTER STONEMAN, 1944, tql seated, NPG (NPR).

JENKS, Edward (1861-1939) writer on law and history.
P FRANK BENNETT, 1925, hs in robes, College of Law, London.

JERROLD, Douglas (1893-1964) author and publisher.
PH HOWARD COSTER, 1930s, various sizes and negs, NPG.

JESSE, Fryn Tennyson (1889-1958) novelist and playwright.
PH LENARE, nearly wl, print, W.Heineman Ltd, Windmill Press, Tadworth, Surrey.

JESSOP, Gilbert Laird (1874-1955) cricketer.
C SIR LESLIE WARD ('Spy'), wl, lith, for *Vanity Fair*, 25 July 1901, NPG, and Christ's College, Cambridge.

JOACHIM, Harold Henry (1868-1938) philosopher.
PH WALTER STONEMAN, 2 hs portraits, 1922 and 1932, NPG (NPR).

JOAD, Cyril Edwin Mitchinson (1891-1953) writer and teacher.
PH HOWARD COSTER, 1935, various sizes, print and negs, NPG AX3478 and X10113-25. KARL POLLAK, hl, print, NPG.

JOEL, Solomon Barnato (1865-1931) financier and sportsman.
C 'H.C.O.', wl, Hentschel-Colourtype, for *Vanity Fair*, 20 Jan 1910, NPG.

JOHN, Augustus Edwin (1878-1961) painter.
P SIR WILLIAM ROTHENSTEIN, 1899, hl, Walker Art Gallery, Liverpool. SIR W.ROTHENSTEIN, 1899, wl with wife, 'The Doll's House', TATE 3189. SIR WILLIAM ORPEN, 1900, wl seated, NPG 4252. D.S.MACCOLL, 1907, hs, Manchester City Art Gallery. A.M.DAINTREY, before c1928, hl seated, Manchester City Art Gallery. Self-portrait, c1935-45?, hl with palette, Metropolitan Museum of Fine Art, New York. Self-portrait, c1940, hs, National Gallery of Canada, Ottawa, Ontario. T.C.DUGDALE, 1943, tql seated, National Museum of Wales 725, Cardiff. SIR MATTHEW SMITH, 1944, hs, Montreal Museum of Fine Arts, Canada.
D SIR W.ROTHENSTEIN, c1896-97, hs, chalk, BM. Self-portrait, c1901, hs, chalk, NPG 4577. SIR W.ROTHENSTEIN, 1903, head, chalk, Bradford City Art Gallery. EDMOND KAPP, 1920, Barber Institute, Birmingham University. SIR W.ROTHENSTEIN, 1924, head, chalk, NPG 4246. IVOR ROBERTS-JONES, hl seated in middle age, profile, National Museum of Wales.
G SIR W.ORPEN, group in the Café Royal, oil, 1911-12, Musée d'Art Moderne, Paris; copy, Café Royal, London.
SC SIR JACOB EPSTEIN, 1916, bronze head, NPG 4295, and National Museum of Wales. F.D.WOOD, 1916, bronze bust, Royal Academy, London. BARNEY SEALE, c1937, bronze head, National Museum of Wales.
PR Self-portrait, c1899-1900, head, 'Tête farouche', etch, Fitzwilliam Museum, Cambridge. Self-portrait, 1920, hs, etch, BM. E.S.LUMSDEN, hl seated in middle age, etch, National Museum of Wales. HENRY RAYNER, 1943, head, drypoint etch, NPG.
C SIR MAX BEERBOHM, 1909, wl with models and art critic, drg, National Gallery of Victoria, Melbourne, Australia. SIR BERNARD PARTRIDGE, wl, w/c and pen and ink, for *Punch Almanack*, 1922, NPG. SIR M.BEERBOHM, 1924, pencil and w/c, Ashmolean Museum, Oxford. SIR DAVID LOW, c1926, 2 heads, pencil, NPG 4529(185). A.R.THOMSON, 'A story of 3 Academicians', pen and ink, The Athenaeum, London.

PH G.C.BERESFORD, 1902, various prints and negs, NPG X6524-25 and others. A.L.COBURN, 1914, hs, photogravure, NPG AX7819. JOHN HOPE-JOHNSTONE, c1922, 3 portraits, prints, NPG P134(10, 18 and 35). HOWARD COSTER, 1937, various sizes, print and negs, NPG X10970-85, X1939-41 and X2376.

JOHN, Gwendolen Mary (1876-1939) painter.
P Self-portrait, c1899-1900, hs, TATE 5366. Self-portrait, c1900, hl, NPG 4439.
D AUGUSTUS JOHN, c1900, hl, chalk, Manchester City Art Gallery. A.JOHN, pencil, Manchester City Art Gallery.

JOHN, Sir William Goscombe (1860-1952) sculptor and medallist.
P A.G.WALKER, c1885-86, hs, National Museum of Wales 531, Cardiff. S.H.VEDDER, 1901, hl, National Museum of Wales 410. GEORGE ROILOS, 1903, wl, National Museum of Wales 535. SIR S.L.FILDES, 1924, hs, National Museum of Wales 856. ERICH WOLFSFELD, c1951, hs in studio, NPG 5102.
SC Self-portrait, 1942, bronze head, National Museum of Wales 1401.
PR E.WOLFSFELD, 1944, head, lith, National Museum of Wales.
PH ELLIOTT & FRY, 1912, hs, print, NPG. JOHN RUSSELL & SONS, c1915, hs, print, for *National Photographic Record*, vol 2, NPG. WALTER STONEMAN, 1937, hs, NPG (NPR).

JOHNSON, Alfred Edward Webb-, see Webb-Johnson.

JOHNSON, (Ernest) Borough (1867-1949) painter and lithographer.
PR Self-portrait, 1937, hs, drypoint etch, NPG.

JOHNSON, Hewlett (1874-1966) dean of Canterbury.
P NOWELL JOHNSON, c1932, hl seated in doctoral robes, The Deanery, Canterbury.
SC VERA MUKHINA, 1945, metal bust, NPG 4585.
PH FELIX MAN, c1940, wl with Sir Jacob Epstein in sculptor's studio, print, NPG P15. HOWARD COSTER, 1944, 2 hs portraits, prints, NPG X1945-46.

JOHNSON, John de Monins (1882-1956) printer and scholar.
D E.PLACHTE, 1938, Bodleian Library, Oxford. SIR WILLIAM ROTHENSTEIN, 1940, Oxford University Press. H.A.FREETH, 1956, tql, w/c, Bodleian Library.
PH HOWARD COSTER, 1930, various sizes, print and negs, NPG AX2304 and others.

JOHNSON, Sir Nelson King (1892-1954) meteorologist.
PH WALTER STONEMAN, 1943, hs, NPG (NPR).

JOHNSTON, Edward (1872-1944) calligrapher.
P A.H.KNIGHTON-HAMMOND, 1937, hl seated, NPG 4375.
D EDMOND KAPP, 1940, head, pencil, NPG 3330.

JOHNSTON, George Lawson, see 1st Baron Luke.

JOHNSTON, Thomas (1881-1965) politician.
P SIR JAMES GUNN, SNPG 2056.
PH WALTER STONEMAN, 1941, hs, NPG (NPR).

JOLOWICZ, Herbert Felix (1890-1954) academic lawyer.
PH ILSA BING, 1953, hs, print, Institute of Advanced Legal Studies, University of London.

JONES, (Alfred) Ernest (1879-1958) physician and psycho-analyst.
P RODRIGO MOYNIHAN, c1946, hl seated, British Psycho-Analytical Society, London.
PH Various photographs, British Psycho-Analytical Society.

JONES, Arthur Creech (1891-1964) politician.
PH WALTER STONEMAN, 1945, hs, NPG (NPR).

JONES, Sir (Bennett) Melvill (1887-1975) aeronautical engineer.
PH WALTER STONEMAN, 1944, hs, NPG (NPR).

JONES, Bernard Mouat (1882-1953) chemist.
P HENRY CARR, 1945, University of Leeds.

JONES, Daniel (1881-1967) professor of phonetics.
PH UNKNOWN, hl, print, Department of Phonetic Linguistics, School of Oriental and African Studies, University of London.

JONES, David (1895-1974) artist and writer.
D JOYCE FINZI, head, pencil, Reading University Library. R.H.JONES, 1974, head, National Museum of Wales, Cardiff.
PH NICHOLAS ELDER, 1973, 2 hs portraits, prints, NPG X4047 and X4111.

JONES, (Frederic) Wood (1879-1954) anatomist.
P A.EGERTON COOPER, posthumous, Royal College of Surgeons, London. W.S.MCINNES, Australian College of Surgeons, Melbourne.

JONES, Sir (George) Roderick (1877-1962) chairman and managing director of Reuters.
PH WALTER STONEMAN, 1920, hs, NPG (NPR).

JONES, Sir Harold Spencer (1890-1960) astronomer.
PH WALTER STONEMAN, 1943, hs, NPG (NPR).

JONES, Sir Henry Stuart-, see Stuart-Jones.

JONES, (James) Ira (1896-1960) fighter pilot.
D CUTHBERT ORDE, chalk, RAF Museum, Hendon.
SC KOSTER, 1957, bronze head, RAF Museum.
PH Various photographs, RAF Museum.

JONES, John Daniel (1865-1942) Congregational minister.
P ERNEST MOORE, hs in robes, Congregational Memorial Hall, London.
PH WALTER STONEMAN, 1930, hs, NPG (NPR).

JONES, Sir John Edward Lennard-, see Lennard-Jones.

JONES, Sir John Morris-, see Morris-Jones.

JONES, Owen (Thomas) (1878-1967) geologist.
PH LAFAYETTE, hs, print, Geological Society, London. UNKNOWN, hs, print, Royal Society, London.

JONES, Parry (William John) (1891-1963) singer and teacher.
PH UNKNOWN, tql as Parsifal, profile, print, Royal College of Music, London.

JONES, Thomas (1870-1955) public administrator and writer.
P IVOR WILLIAMS, 1939, National Museum of Wales 893, Cardiff. ERNEST PERRY, 1951, The University College of Wales, Aberystwyth.
D PAUL ARTOT, 1914, National Museum of Wales. SIR WILLIAM ROTHENSTEIN, 1924, head, chalk, NPG 4780. SYDNEY MORSE-BROWN, 1938, National Museum of Wales.
SC L.S.MERRIFIELD, c1928, bust, National Library of Wales, Aberystwyth. SIEGFRIED CHAROUX, 1939, bronze bust, Newport

Museum and Art Gallery.
·PH WALTER STONEMAN, 1930, hs, NPG (NPR).

JOPSON, Norman Brooke (1890-1969) philologist.
D M.W.PORTER, after a photograph, 1969, head, pencil, St John's College, Cambridge.
PH ELLIOTT & FRY, 1936, hs, print, St John's College.

JORDAN, (Heinrich Ernst) Karl (1861-1959) entomologist.
PH UNKNOWN, 2 portraits, Royal Society, London. WALTER STONEMAN, 1933, hs, NPG (NPR).

JORDAN LLOYD, Dorothy, see Lloyd.

JOSEPH, Horace William Brindley (1867-1943) philosopher.
D KENNETH KNOWLES, New College, Oxford.
PH WALTER STONEMAN, 1932, hs profile, NPG (NPR).

JOSEPH, Michael (1897-1958) publisher.
PH HOWARD COSTER, 1938, various sizes, prints and negs, NPG X1943-44 and others.

JOUBERT DE LA FERTE, Sir Philip (Bennet) (1887-1965) air chief marshal.
P SIR JAMES GUNN, IWM. J.HUGHES-HALLETT, copy, hl in uniform, on loan to RAF Museum, Hendon.
PH HOWARD COSTER, 1930s, various sizes and negs, NPG. WALTER STONEMAN, 4 hs portraits, the 1st three in uniform, 1934, 1946 and 1956, NPG (NPR).

JOWITT, William Allen Jowitt, 1st Earl (1885-1957) lord chancellor.
P AMBROSE MCEVOY, 1912, tql, TATE 2999. SIR GERALD KELLY, c1957, tql seated in robes, Middle Temple, London.
D BORIS ANREP, c1952, hs, gouache, cartoon for mosaic, V & A.
SC B.ANREP, 1952, hs in robes, for 'The Modern Virtues', mosaic, National Gallery, London.
PH G.C.BERESFORD, 1914, hs, neg, NPG X6526. WALTER STONEMAN, 2 hs portraits, 1923 and 1942, NPG (NPR). HOWARD COSTER, 1930s, various sizes, print and negs, NPG X1947 and others.

JOYCE, James Augustine (1882-1941) poet, novelist and playwright.
P FRANK BUDGEN, 1919, University of Texas, Austin, USA. F.BUDGEN, Lockwood Memorial Library, State University of New York, Buffalo, USA. PAVEL TCHELITCHEW, c1928-30, head, NGI. J.E.BLANCHE, 1934, hl seated, NGI 1051. J.E.BLANCHE, 1935, tql, NPG 3883. TULLIO SILVESTRI, Lockwood Memorial Library.
D WYNDHAM LEWIS, 1921, head, pen and ink, NGI 3043. AUGUSTUS JOHN, c1930, hs, pencil, University of Texas. DESMOND HARMSWORTH, 2 drgs, 1932 and undated, pen and ink, University of Texas. HARRY KERNOFF, 1935, hs, pastel, University of Texas. SEAN O'SULLIVAN, 1935, hs, profile, chalk, NGI 3037.
SC JO DAVIDSON, 1929, bronze head, University of Texas.
PH BERENICE ABBOTT, 1928, tql seated, print, The Museum of Modern Art, New York.

JOYNSON-HICKS, William, see 1st Viscount Brentford.

K

KAUFFER, Edward McKnight (d1954) artist and designer.
P MAXWELL ARMFIELD, 1915, hs, profile, NPG 4947; study, pencil, NPG 4947A.
PH HOWARD COSTER, 1927?, various sizes, print and negs, NPG AX2279 and others.

KAYE-SMITH, Sheila, Mrs Theodore Penrose Fry (1887-1956) novelist.
PH HOWARD COSTER, various sizes and negs, NPG.

KEEBLE, Sir Frederick William (1870-1952) botanist, civil servant and industrial adviser.
SC FRANK DOBSON, bronze bust, Imperial Chemical Industries Ltd, London.
PH WALTER STONEMAN, 2 hs portraits, 1917 and 1931, NPG (NPR).

KEEBLE, Lady Lillah, see McCarthy.

KEILIN, David (1888-1963) biologist.
D H.A.FREETH, 1952, wl, ink and wash, NPG 4811.

KEIR, Sir David Lindsay (1895-1973) master of Balliol College, Oxford.
PH WALTER STONEMAN, 2 hs portraits, 1946 and 1958, NPG (NPR).

KEITH, Sir Arthur (1866-1955) anatomist and anthropologist.
P W.W.OULESS, c1928, hs in robes, Royal College of Surgeons, London.
D SIR WILLIAM ROTHENSTEIN, 1928, head, pencil, NPG 4140. JULIET PANNETT, 1954, head, chalk, NPG 3986.
SC MALVINA HOFFMAN, 1930, plaster bust, Royal College of Surgeons. R.T.MACKENZIE, 1930, bronze medallion, Department of Anatomy, University of Aberdeen; plaster cast, Royal College of Surgeons. KATHLEEN PARBURY, 1935, bronze bust, Royal College of Surgeons.
PH WALTER STONEMAN, 1921, hs, NPG (NPR).

KEITH, Arthur Berriedale (1879-1944) Sanskrit scholar and constitutional lawyer.
PH WALTER STONEMAN, 1935, hs, NPG (NPR).

KEITH, Sir William John (1873-1937) administrator in Burma.
PH WALTER STONEMAN, 1930, hs in uniform, NPG (NPR).

KELLAWAY, Charles Halliley (1889-1952) scientist.
PH WALTER STONEMAN, 1945, hs, NPG (NPR).

KELLY, Sir David Victor (1891-1959) diplomat.
PH WALTER STONEMAN, 1949, hl, NPG (NPR).

KELLY, Sir Gerald (Festus) (1879-1972) portrait painter.
C SIR DAVID LOW, several heads, pencil, NPG 4529(186–88).

KELLY, Sir John Donald (1871-1936) admiral.
PH UNKNOWN, wl on board ship with another officer, print, NPG.

KELLY, Sir (William Archibald) Howard (1873-1952) admiral.
PH WALTER STONEMAN, 1945, hs in uniform, NPG (NPR).

KEMBALL-COOK, Sir Basil Alfred (1876-1949) civil servant.
PH WALTER STONEMAN, 1919, hs, NPG (NPR).

KEMP, Stanley Wells (1882-1945) zoologist and oceanographer.
PH WALTER STONEMAN, 1933, hs, NPG (NPR).

KEMSLEY, James Gomer Berry, 1st Viscount (1883-1968) newspaper proprietor.
P SIR OSWALD BIRLEY, tql seated, Times Newspapers Ltd, London.
PH WALTER STONEMAN, 1936, hs, NPG (NPR).

KENMARE, Valentine Edward Charles Browne, Viscount Castlerosse and 6th Earl of (1891-1943) press magnate.
P W.R.SICKERT, 1935, wl, Beaverbrook Art Gallery, Fredericton, New Brunswick, Canada.
C SIR DAVID LOW, head, pencil, NPG 4529(72).
PH HOWARD COSTER, 1929–30, various sizes, prints and negs, NPG X2360, AX3482 and X3531–41.

KENNARD, Sir Howard William (1878-1955) diplomat.
PH WALTER STONEMAN, 1933, hs, NPG (NPR).

KENNAWAY, Sir Ernest Laurence (1881-1958) experimental and chemical pathologist.
PH WALTER STONEMAN, 1947, hs, profile, NPG (NPR).

KENNEDY, Sir John Noble (1893-1970) soldier and colonial administrator.
P HENRY LAMB, 1943, IWM.
PH WALTER STONEMAN, 2 hs portraits in uniform, 1941 and 1947, NPG (NPR) and NPG X4156.

KENNEDY, Margaret (1896-1967) novelist.
PH HOWARD COSTER, 1931, various sizes, prints and negs, NPG X1950–51 and others.

KENNET, (Edith Agnes) Kathleen Hilton Young, née Bruce, Lady (1878-1947) sculptor.
P C.H.SHANNON, 1908, hl seated, profile, Johannesburg Art Gallery, South Africa.

KENNET, Edward Hilton Young, 1st Baron (1879-1960) politician and writer.
D SIR WILLIAM ROTHENSTEIN, 1924, hs, chalk, NPG 4800.
C SIR DAVID LOW, head and hl, pencil, NPG 4529(398).
PH WALTER STONEMAN, 3 hs portraits, the 1st in uniform, 1919, 1931 and 1943, NPG (NPR).

KENNEY, Annie (1879-1953) suffragette.
PH Various photographs, Fawcett Library, City of London Polytechnic.

KENNINGTON, Eric Henri (1880-1960) artist.
D SIR WILLIAM ROTHENSTEIN, crayon, Manchester City Art Gallery.
PH HOWARD COSTER, various sizes, prints and negs, NPG X1952–53 and others.

KENYON, Sir Frederic George (1863-1952) scholar and administrator.
D AUGUSTUS JOHN, pencil, British Academy, London.
SC J.A.STEVENSON, c1928, bronze bust, BM.
PH JOHN RUSSELL & SONS, c1915, hs in uniform, print, for *National Photographic Record*, vol 1, NPG. WALTER STONEMAN, 1919, hs, NPG (NPR).

KERR, Sir John Graham (1869-1957) zoologist.
P UNKNOWN, Department of Zoology, University of Glasgow.
PH WALTER STONEMAN, 1917, hs, NPG (NPR).

KERR, (John Martin) Munro (1868-1960) obstetrician and gynaecologist.
P SIMON ELWES, c1954, Royal Society of Obstetricians and Gynaecologists, London.

KERR, Philip Henry, see 11th Marquess of Lothian.

KETTLE, Edgar Hartley (1882-1936) pathologist.
PH WALTER STONEMAN, 1936, hl, NPG (NPR).

KEYES, Sir Roger John Brownlow Keyes, 1st Baron (1872-1945) admiral.
P GLYN PHILPOT, 1918, hs in uniform, IWM. P.A.DE LÁSZLÓ, Royal Marines, Portsmouth. TOM VAN OSS, c1935, hl in uniform, NMM, Greenwich.
D FRANCIS DODD, 1917, charcoal and w/c, IWM.
G SIR A.S.COPE, 'Naval Officers of World War I, 1914–18', oil, 1921, NPG 1913.
PH ELLIOTT & FRY, 1905, tql in uniform, print, NPG. WALTER STONEMAN, 1918, hs in uniform, NPG (NPR). UNKNOWN, c1918, hs in uniform, print, NPG. WALTER STONEMAN, 1940s, tql seated in uniform, for NPR, NPG X1438.

KEYNES, Florence Ada (1861-1958) pioneer of women's rights and social services.
PH OLIVE EDIS, tql seated, print, NPG.

KEYNES, Sir Geoffrey (Langdon) (b1887) surgeon and scholar.
D JOHN WARD, wl seated, pencil and w/c wash, Pembroke College, Cambridge.
SC NIGEL BOONHAM, 1976, bronze head, Royal College of Surgeons, London, and NPG 5182.
PH HILLS & SAUNDERS, 1915, hs in uniform, profile, print, NPG. RAMSEY & MUSPRATT, c1953, hs, print, NPG X1091.

KEYNES, John Maynard Keynes, Baron (1883-1946) economist.
P DUNCAN GRANT, 1908, wl seated, King's College, Cambridge.
D ROGER FRY, charcoal, King's College. GINSBERG, charcoal, King's College. GWEN RAVERAT, hl seated, w/c, NPG 4553. SIR WILLIAM ROTHENSTEIN, head, pencil and chalk, King's College.
SC BENNO ELKAN, posthumous, bronze bust, King's College. B.ELKAN, bronze head, King's College.
C SIR DAVID LOW, 1933, several heads, pencil, NPG 4529(189–91A).
PH WALTER STONEMAN, 3 hs portraits, 1930 and 1940, NPG (NPR). RAMSEY & MUSPRATT, 3 hs portraits, prints, NPG. UNKNOWN, 1933, hl seated with Jan Smuts, print, NPG.

KIGGELL, Sir Launcelot Edward (1862-1954) lieutenant-general.
PH WALTER STONEMAN, 1918, hs in uniform, NPG (NPR).

KILLEARN, Sir Miles Wedderburn Lampson, 1st Baron (1880-1964) diplomat.
PH SIR CECIL BEATON, hl, print, NPG. WALTER STONEMAN, 1946, hs, NPG (NPR).

KILMUIR, David Patrick Maxwell Fyfe, Earl of (1900-1967) lord chancellor.
PH WALTER STONEMAN, 1946, hs, NPG (NPR). WALTER BIRD, 1962, tql seated in robes, NPG (NPR).

KIMMINS, Dame Grace Thyrza (1870-1954) pioneer in work for crippled children.
P HELEN GLUCK, 1944, hs, Chailey Heritage Hospital and School, Chailey, Sussex.
PH Various photographs, Chailey Heritage hospital.

KINDERSLEY, Robert Molesworth Kindersley, 1st Baron (1871-1954) banker and president of the National Savings Committee.
P SIR WILLIAM ORPEN, 1919, hl, National Savings Committee (DoE), London.
PH ELLIOTT & FRY, c1912, hs, profile, print, NPG. WALTER STONEMAN, 2 hs portraits, 1918 and 1945, NPG (NPR).

KING, Harold (1887-1956) organic chemist.
PH Various photographs, National Institute for Medical Research, London.

KING-HALL, (William) Stephen Richard King-Hall, Baron (1893-1966) sailor, writer and commentator.
C SIR DAVID LOW, head, profile, pencil, NPG 4529(196).
PH HOWARD COSTER, 1932, various sizes, print and negs, NPG. WALTER STONEMAN, 1944, hs, NPG (NPR).

KINGDON-WARD, Francis ('Frank') (1885-1958) plant collector, explorer and author.
P E.M.GREGSON, 1952, hs, Royal Geographical Society, London.
PH UNKNOWN, wl and snapshot, prints, Royal Geographical Society.

KINGSFORD, Charles Lethbridge (1862-1926) historian and topographer.
PH BASSANO, c1924, hs, print, British Academy, London. ELLIOTT & FRY, hs, print, NPG.

KINGSLEY, Mary Henrietta (1862-1900) traveller and writer.
PH UNKNOWN, c1896, hs, photogravure, NPG. UNKNOWN, wl, print, Liverpool Library.

KINNEAR, Sir Norman Boyd (1882-1957) ornithologist.
PH WALTER STONEMAN, 1950, hs, NPG (NPR).

KIPLING, (Joseph) Rudyard (1865-1936) writer and poet.
P SIR PHILIP BURNE-JONES, 1899, tql seated, NPG 1863; copy?, Johannesburg Art Gallery, South Africa. WILLIAM STRANG, 1913, hs, profile, Magdalene College, Cambridge.
D W.STRANG, c1898, hl seated, profile, pencil, NPG 2919, engr DAVID STRANG, 1898, etch, NPG. W.CUSHING LORING, 1901, pencil, the Athenaeum, London. EDMOND KAPP, 1914, chalk, Barber Institute, Birmingham University. FRANCIS DODD, 1929, 2 hs portraits, chalk and charcoal, respectively, Fitzwilliam Museum, Cambridge. SIR WILLIAM ROTHENSTEIN, c1932, head, chalk, NPG 3874; related drg, hs, Fitzwilliam Museum.
SC GINETTE BINGGUELY-LEJEUNE, c1936–37, bronze cast of bust, NPG 2955.
PR VIOLET DUCHESS OF RUTLAND, 1891, hs, profile, lith, NPG. SIR WILLIAM NICHOLSON, 1899, hl, profile, coloured woodcut, NPG.
C SIR MAX BEERBOHM, various drgs, Bancroft Library, University of California, Berkeley, USA; Harvard College Library, Cambridge, Mass, USA; Berg Coll, New York Public Library, USA; and Ashmolean Museum, Oxford. SIR M.BEERBOHM, 'Edwardian Parade', oil, University of Texas, Austin, USA. HARRY FURNISS, head and wl, pen and ink, NPG 3478 and NPG 3588. SIR LESLIE WARD ('Spy'), wl, lith, for Vanity Fair, 7 June 1894, NPG.
PH UNKNOWN, c1890s, hs, print, NPG. HENRI MANUEL, c1915, hs, postcard, NPG. WALTER STONEMAN, 2 hs portraits, 1924 and 1934?, NPG (NPR).

KIPPING, Frederic Stanley (1863-1949) chemist.
PH WALTER STONEMAN, 1917, hs, NPG (NPR).

KIRK, Kenneth Escott (1886-1954) bishop of Oxford.
P HAROLD KNIGHT, Diocesan Church House, North Hinksey, Oxon.

PH HOWARD COSTER, 1930s, various sizes and negs, NPG. WALTER STONEMAN, 1945, hs, NPG (NPR).

KIRKPATRICK, Sir Ivone (Augustine) (1897-1964) diplomat.
PH WALTER STONEMAN, 1948, hs, NPG (NPR).

KIRKWOOD, David Kirkwood, 1st Baron (1872-1955) socialist leader.
C SIR DAVID LOW, tql seated, pencil, NPG 4529(197).

KITSON CLARK, George Sidney Roberts (1900-1975) historian.
D DUNCAN GRANT, 1951, charcoal, Trinity College, Cambridge.

KLEIN, Melanie (1882-1960) psycho-analyst and writer.
D ISHBEL McWHIRTER, hs, pencil, NPG 5108.
SC UNKNOWN, bronze bust, British Psycho-Analytical Society, London.
PH Various photographs, British Psycho-Analytical Society.

KNATCHBULL-HUGESSEN, Sir Hughe Montgomery (1886-1971) diplomat.
PH REMBRANDT, c1934-36, wl seated in uniform, print, NPG x7963. WALTER STONEMAN, 1936, hs, for NPR, NPG x5915.

KNIGHT, Harold (1874-1961) artist.
P Self-portrait, c1923, hl with brushes, NPG 4831.

KNIGHT, Dame Laura (1877-1970) artist.
P Self-portrait, 1913, tql with nude model, NPG 4839.
D SIR ALFRED MUNNINGS, c1911, wl seated on beach with the artist's wife, 2 w/c sketches, Sir Alfred Munnings Art Museum, Castle House, Dedham, Essex.
PH WALTER STONEMAN, 1930, hs, NPG (NPR). WALTER BIRD, 1964, hs, NPG (NPR). J.S.LEWINSKI, 1967, hl, print, NPG. N.VOGEL, 1969, 2 hs portraits, prints, NPG. MADAME YEVONDE, 4 prints, NPG.

KNOLLYS, Edward George William Tyrwhitt Knollys, 2nd Viscount (1895-1966) businessman.
D ROBERT TOLLAST, hs, Churchill College, Cambridge.
PH WALTER STONEMAN, 1949, hs, NPG (NPR).

KNOWLES, Michael Clive (in religion David) (1896-1974) divine and historian.

PH WALTER BIRD, 1965, hs, NPG (NPR).

KNOX, Edmund (George) Valpy (1881-1971) editor of *Punch*.
PH HOWARD COSTER, 1933, various sizes, print and negs, NPG AX2300 and x3360-67.

KNOX, Sir Harry Hugh Sidney (1873-1971) general.
PH WALTER STONEMAN, 1928, hs in uniform, NPG (NPR).

KNOX, Sir Robert Uchtred Eyre (1889-1965) secretary of the Political Honours Scrutiny Committee.
PH WALTER STONEMAN, 1941, hs, NPG (NPR).

KNOX, Ronald Arbuthnott (1888-1957) Roman Catholic churchman, scholar and writer.
P SIMON ELWES, c1952, Catholic Chaplaincy, Oxford University.
D POWYS EVANS, c1926, head, pen and ink, NPG 4403.
SC A.J.POLLEN, c1950, bronze cast of head, Trinity College, Oxford.
PH HOWARD COSTER, 1938, various sizes, print and negs, NPG x1954 and others.

KOKOSCHKA, Oskar (1886-1980) artist and writer.
P Self-portrait, 1913, hs, Museum of Modern Art, New York. Self-portrait, 1917, hl, Von der Heydt Museum der Stadt, Wuppertal, W Germany.
D Self-portrait, hs, pencil, St Louis City Art Museum, USA.
SC Self-portrait, hs, polychromed clay plaque, Boston Museum of Fine Arts, USA. DAVID WYNNE, 1965, bronze head, TATE T791.
PR Self-portrait, c1935, hl, lith, Kunstsammlungen der Veste, Coburg, W Germany. Self-portrait, 1965, hs lith, NPG 5156.

KORDA, Sir Alexander (1893-1956) film producer.
PH HOWARD COSTER, tql in studio with technicians, print and neg, NPG x3600 and x10140.

KORDA, Vincent (1897-1979) set-designer and artist.
PH HOWARD COSTER, 1936, various sizes and negs, NPG x10101-11.

KRAMER, Jacob (1892-1962) artist.
SC SIR JACOB EPSTEIN, 1921, bronze bust, TATE 3849, and Leeds City Art Gallery.
PR Self-portrait, 1930, hs, lith, NPG 4871.

L

LAIDLAW, Sir Patrick Playfair (1881-1940) physician.
PH WALTER STONEMAN, 1936, hs, NPG (NPR). Several photographs, National Institute for Medical Research, London.

LAIRD, John (1887-1946) professor of moral philosophy.
PH WALTER STONEMAN, 1933, hs, NPG (NPR).

LAKE, Kirsopp (1872-1946) biblical scholar.
D J.S.SARGENT, hs, Lincoln College, Oxford.

LAMB, Henry Taylor (1883-1960) painter.
P FRANCIS DODD, 1905, hl seated, Manchester City Art Gallery. Self-portrait, 1914, hs, NPG 4432.
D Self-portrait, *c*1906, 2 hs portraits, Ashmolean Museum, Oxford. POWYS EVANS, *c*1928, hs, pen and ink, NPG 4401. Self-portrait, 1950-51, 2 hs portraits, pencil and chalk, NPG 4256-57.

LAMB, Sir Walter Rangeley Maitland (1882-1961) secretary of the Royal Academy of Arts.
P SIR WALTER W.RUSSELL, seated in Secretary's room with John Coy, Royal Academy of Arts, London.
PH WALTER STONEMAN, 2 hs portraits, 1943 and 1947, NPG (NPR).

LAMBART, Frederick Rudolph, see 10th Earl of Cavan.

LAMBE, Sir Charles Edward (1900-1960) admiral.
P E.I.HALLIDAY, HMS *Vernon*, Portsmouth.
PH WALTER STONEMAN, 1951, hs in uniform, NPG (NPR).

LAMBERT, George Lambert, 1st Viscount (1866-1958) yeoman farmer and MP.
P R.G.EVES, 1934, Seale-Hayne Agricultural College, Newton Abbot, Devon.

LAMBERT, George Washington (1873-1930) artist.
P Self-portrait, *c*1900, hs, NPG 3115.

LAMBERT, Herbert (1881-1936) photographer.
PH H.B.GOODWIN, 1929, wl at piano, print, NPG x7595. Self-portrait, wl with camera and hs, prints, NPG x7593-94.

LAMINGTON, Charles Wallace Alexander Cochrane-Baillie, 2nd Baron (1860-1940) governor of Queensland and Bombay.
PH WALTER STONEMAN, 2 hs portraits, the 1st in uniform, 1917 and 1928, NPG (NPR).

LAMPSON, Sir Miles Wedderburn, see 1st Baron Killearn.

LANCHESTER, Frederick William (1868-1946) engineer.
P REGINALD MAIN, hs, Institution of Mechanical Engineers, London.
PH Various photographs, Institution of Mechanical Engineers.

LANE, Sir Hugh Percy (1875-1915) art collector and critic.
P S.C.HARRISON, NGI 1280. JOHN KEATING, Municipal Gallery of Modern Art, Dublin. SIR GERALD KELLY, 1914, tql seated, Crawford Art Gallery, Cork. ANTONIO MANCINI, 1902, wl seated, Municipal Gallery of Modern Art. J.S.SARGENT, 1906, hs, Municipal Gallery of Modern Art.
D J.B.YEATS, 1905, hl, pencil, NGI 2866.
G SIR WILLIAM ORPEN, 'Homage to Manet', oil, 1909, Manchester City Art Gallery.
SC ALBERT POWER, marble bust?, Municipal Gallery of Modern Art.
C SIR MAX BEERBOHM, 2 drgs, Municipal Gallery of Modern Art.

SIR W.ORPEN, 1907, wl with J.M.Synge, W.B.Yeats and Lady Gregory, pen and ink, NPG 4676. SIR W.ORPEN, ink, NGI 7548.
PH G.C.BERESFORD, 1909, hs, print, NPG x6528.

LANG, (Alexander) Matheson (1877-1948) actor-manager and dramatist.
P SOMERLED MACDONALD, as Hamlet, University of Bristol.
PH RITA MARTIN, hl, postcard, NPG.

LANG of Lambeth, (William) Cosmo Gordon Lang, Baron (1864-1945) archbishop of Canterbury.
P G.FIDDES WATT, 1913, tql seated, All Souls College, Oxford. SIR WILLIAM ORPEN, 1924, tql seated, Bishopthorpe Palace, York. P.A.DE LÁSZLÓ, 1932, nearly wl seated, Church House, Westminster, London. SIR WILLIAM LLEWELLYN, *c*1936, tql, Lambeth Palace, London. P.A.DE LÁSZLÓ, 1937, tql seated in robes, Lambeth Palace.
D FRANCIS DODD, pencil, The Athenaeum, London.
C SIR LESLIE WARD ('Spy'), wl, lith, for *Vanity Fair*, 19 April 1906, NPG. R.S.SHERRIFFS, 1930s?, 'Fantastic Studies', pen and ink, NPG.
PH ROTARY PHOTO, *c*1901-08, 2 hs portraits, postcards, NPG. ALBERT HESTER, *c*1909, hs, cabinet, NPG. E.M.SUTCLIFFE, *c*1909, tql seated, print, NPG. JOHN RUSSELL & SONS, *c*1915, hs, print, for *National Photographic Record*, vol 1, NPG. WALTER STONEMAN, 3 hs portraits, 1923 and 1941, NPG (NPR) and NPG x469-70.

LANGDON, Stephen Herbert, (1876-1937) Assyriologist.
PH WALTER STONEMAN, 1932, hs, NPG (NPR).

LANGDON-BROWN, Sir Walter Langdon (1870-1946) physician and professor of physic.
PH WALTER STONEMAN, 1940, hs, NPG (NPR).

LANGTON, Sir George Philip (1881-1942) judge.
PH WALTER STONEMAN, 1931, hs in robes, NPG (NPR).

LARKE, Sir William James (1875-1959) first director of the British Iron and Steel Federation.
PH WALTER STONEMAN, 1947, hl, NPG (NPR).

LASCELLES, Henry George Charles, see 6th Earl of Harewood.

LASKI, Harold Joseph (1893-1950) political theorist.
D JACOB KRAMER, *c*1944, hs, chalk and indian ink, London School of Economics.
PR JACOB KRAMER, 1944, hs, lith, NPG.
C SIR DAVID LOW, 3 heads, pencil, NPG 4529(205-06).

LÁSZLÓ de Lombos, Philip Alexius (1869-1937) portrait painter.
P Self-portrait, 1911, tql with palette, The Uffizi, Florence.
C SIR DAVID LOW, head, profile, pencil, NPG 4529(207).

LATHAM, Charles Latham, 1st Baron (1888-1970) leader of the London County Council.
PH HOWARD COSTER, various sizes and negs, NPG. WALTER STONEMAN, 1943, hs, NPG (NPR).

LAUDER, Sir Harry (1870-1950) comedian.
P JAMES LOCKHART, 1916, hs, Dundee City Art Gallery. JAMES McBEY, *c*1922, tql, Glasgow City Art Gallery. THEODORA ROSCOE, SNPG 1552.
C H.M.BATEMAN, 1915, wl in kilt, pen and wash, SNPG 2202.

LAUGHTON, Charles (1899-1962) actor.
P BRYAN KNEALE, c1959, hl, Castle Museum, Nottingham.
PH HOWARD COSTER, wl, neg, NPG X12265. J.W.DEBENHAM, 1934, wl with Elsa Lanchester, print, the Theatre Museum, V & A.

LAVER, James (1899-1975) art historian and writer.
PH HOWARD COSTER, 1933 and 1936, various sizes, print and negs, NPG AX3450, X1957 and others. KARL POLLAK, hs, print, NPG.

LAWRENCE, (Arabella) Susan (1871-1947) politician.
PH WALTER STONEMAN, 1930, hs, NPG (NPR).

LAWRENCE, David Herbert (1885-1930) novelist.
P JAN JUTA, 1920, head, NPG 4036; charcoal study, 1920, University of Texas, Austin, USA. KAI GÓTZSCHE, c1922, tql seated, University of Texas. DOROTHY BRETT, 1925, hs, NPG 4015. D.BRETT, 1925, University of Texas. KNUD MERRILD, posthumous?, hs, profile, Philadelphia Museum of Art, USA.
D MARIA HUBRECHT, c1920-21, hs, profile, chalk, NPG 5098. EDMOND KAPP, 1923, hs, chalk, NPG 4035. E.KAPP, 1923, Barber Institute, Birmingham University. E.KAPP, 1923, University of Nottingham.
SC JO DAVIDSON, 1930, bronze bust, University of Texas.
PH PETER JULEY & SON, 1929, 2 hs portraits, prints, NPG.

LAWRENCE, Emmeline Pethick-, see Lady Pethick-Lawrence.

LAWRENCE, Frederick William Pethick-, see 1st Baron Pethick-Lawrence.

LAWRENCE, Geoffrey, see 1st Baron Oaksey.

LAWRENCE, Gertrude (1898-1952) actress.
D BEN ALI HAGGIN, 1931, tql, pastel, Museum of the City of new York, USA.
C R.S.SHERRIFFS, hs, profile, ink and wash, NPG.
PH SIR CECIL BEATON, 1930s?, tql, print, NPG MADAME YEVONDE, 1930s, 3 prints, NPG. PAUL TANQUERAY, 1932, tql, print, NPG. DOROTHY WILDING, 1940s, various sizes, prints and negs, NPG.

LAWRENCE, Sir Herbert Alexander (1861-1943) soldier and banker.
P SIR OSWALD BIRLEY, 1942, tql seated, Williams and Glyn's Bank Ltd, London.
PH WALTER STONEMAN, 1918, hs in uniform, NPG (NPR).

LAWRENCE, Sir Paul Ogden (1861-1952) judge.
P HUGH RIVIERE, Roedean School, Sussex.

LAWRENCE, Thomas Edward (1888-1935) 'Lawrence of Arabia'.
P HENRY SCOTT TUKE, wl on beach when a cadet, Clouds Hill (NT), Dorset. JAMES McBEY, 1918, hs in Arab dress, IWM. AUGUSTUS JOHN, 1919, hl in Arab dress, TATE 3566. SIR WILLIAM ROTHENSTEIN, 1919, wl in Arab dress, National Museum, Belgrade, Yugoslavia. A.JOHN, 1935, hs as 'Aircraftman Shaw', cut down 1941, National Gallery of Canada, Ottawa. HERBERT GURSCHNER, posthumous?, hl in symbolic desert landscape, NGI 1184.
D A.JOHN, c1919, head in Arab headdress, profile, pencil, NPG 3187. A.JOHN, 1919, hs and hl in Arab dress, All Souls College, Oxford. ERIC KENNINGTON, c1926, head, All Souls College. E.KENNINGTON, c1926, pastel, University of Texas, Austin, USA. A.JOHN, c1929, hs, chalk, NPG 2910. A.JOHN, c1929, head, pencil, NPG 3188. A.JOHN, 1935, tql as 'Aircraftman Shaw', chalk, Ashmolean Museum, Oxford.
SC F.D.WOOD, 1919, plaster head, IWM; bronze cast, TATE 3602. E.KENNINGTON, 1926, bronze head, NPG 4298, and Clouds Hill. SIR CHARLES WHEELER, 1929, marble head, NPG 5016. E.KENNINGTON, 1939, stone reclining effigy, St Martin's Church,

Wareham, Dorset.
PH UNKNOWN, c1917-18, hl in Arab dress, neg, NPG (*Daily Herald*). UNKNOWN, c1926-28, 3 wl snapshots probably when in India, prints, NPG. UNKNOWN, wl in front of barracks in India, Emery Walker copy neg, NPG. UNKNOWN, 1929, wl at Schneider Trophy race trials, neg, NPG (*Daily Herald*). HOWARD COSTER, 1931, various sizes, prints and negs, NPG AX3424-25, X2380, X1966-71 and X3551-56.

LAWSON, Sir Harry Lawson Webster Levy-, see 1st Viscount Burnham.

LAYTON, Sir Geoffrey (1884-1964) admiral.
P SIR MUIRHEAD BONE, 1945, IWM.
PH WALTER STONEMAN, 2 hl portraits in uniform, 1936 and 1945, NPG (NPR).

LAYTON, Walter Thomas Layton, 1st Baron (1884-1966) economist and newspaper proprietor.
PH WALTER STONEMAN, 3 hs portraits, 1935, 1943 and 1953, NPG (NPR).

LEACH, Bernard (Howell) (1887-1979) potter.
P RYŪSEI KISHIDA, 1913, hl, National Museum of Modern Art, Tokyo.
PH J.S.LEWINSKI, 1970, hl, print, NPG. Various photographs, The Leach Pottery, St Ives, Cornwall.

LEADBITTER, Sir Eric Cyril Egerton (1891-1971) clerk of the Privy Council.
PH WALTER STONEMAN, 1946, hs, NPG (NPR).

LEARMONTH, Sir James (Rögnvald) (1895-1967) surgeon.
PH WALTER STONEMAN, 1949, hl, NPG (NPR).

LEATHERS, Frederick James Leathers, 1st Viscount (1883-1965) minister of war transport.
PH WALTER STONEMAN, 1952, hs, NPG (NPR).

LEAVIS, Frank Raymond (1895-1978) literary critic and scholar.
P PETER GREENHAM, c1962, hl, Downing College, Cambridge.

LEDINGHAM, Sir John Charles Grant (1875-1944) bacteriologist and director of the Lister Institute.
P ALEXANDER CHRISTIE, hs, Lister Institute, Elstree, Herts.
PH WALTER STONEMAN, 1926, hs, NPG (NPR).

LEDWIDGE, Francis (1891-1917) poet.
PH UNKNOWN, hs in uniform, photogravure, NPG.

LEE, Robert Warden (1868-1958) lawyer.
PH WALTER STONEMAN, 1938, hs, NPG (NPR).

LEE of Fareham, Arthur Hamilton Lee, Viscount (1868-1947) statesman, benefactor and patron of the arts.
P P.A.DE LÁSZLÓ, c1921, wl with Lady Lee, Courtauld Institute Galleries, London. SIR JAMES GUNN, c1934, Cheltenham College.
PH G.C.BERESFORD, 2 hs portraits, prints, NPG. OLIVE EDIS, 1917, hs, profile, and tql seated, prints, NPG.

LEEPER, Sir Reginald Wildig Allen (1888-1968) diplomat.
PH WALTER STONEMAN, 1948, hl seated, NPG (NPR).

LEES, George Martin (1898-1955) geologist.
PH SAYER, hs, print, Geological Society, London.

LEESON, Spencer Stottesbery Gwatkin (1892-1956) schoolmaster and bishop.
P SIR OSWALD BIRLEY, Merchant Taylor's School, Northwood, Middx. RODRIGO MOYNIHAN, 1948, hl, Winchester College, Hants.

LE GALLIENE, Richard Thomas (1866-1947) poet and

essayist.

c Sir Max Beerbohm, 1900, wl on a pile of books, drg, Clark Memorial Library, University of California, Los Angeles, USA. Sir M. Beerbohm, pen and indian ink, v & a.

ph W. & D. Downey, 1894, hl seated, profile, NPG.

LEHMANN, Liza, Mrs Herbert Bedford (1862-1918) singer and composer.

pr Flora Lion, 1915, hs, lith, NPG 4118.

LEIGH-MALLORY, Sir Trafford Leigh (1892-1944) air chief marshal.

p Yvonne Jenson, RAF Museum, Hendon.

d Eric Kennington, 1942, pastel, IWM.

LEISHMAN, Sir William Boog (1865-1926) bacteriologist.

p John Hassall, c1926, tql seated, RAMC Mess, London.

ph Various photographs, RAMC.

LEJEUNE, Caroline Alice (1897-1973) film critic and writer.

ph Sir Cecil Beaton, 1942, tql, print, NPG.

LENNARD-JONES, Sir John Edward (1894-1954) scientist and administrator.

ph Walter Stoneman, 2 hs portraits, 1934 and 1945, NPG (NPR).

LENO, Dan, see George Galvin.

LENOX-CONYNGHAM, Sir Gerald Ponsonby (1866-1956) geodesist.

d Henry Lamb, 1947, charcoal and chalk, Trinity College, Cambridge.

ph Walter Stoneman, 2 hs portraits, 1921 and 1932, NPG (NPR).

LESLIE, Sir John Randolph ('Shane') (1885-1971) author and poet.

p Sir John Lavery, Municipal Gallery of Modern Art, Dublin.

ph Howard Coster, tql seated in kilt, print, NPG x1976.

LESTER, Sean (John Ernest) (1888-1959) secretary-general of the League of Nations.

p James Sleator, Palais des Nations, Geneva.

LETHBRIDGE, John Sydney (1897-1961) major-general.

ph Walter Stoneman, 1948, hs in uniform, NPG (NPR).

LEVESON, Sir Arthur Cavenagh (1868-1929) admiral.

d Francis Dodd, 1917, charcoal and w/c, IWM.

g Sir A. S. Cope, 'Naval Officers of World War I, 1914–18', oil, 1921, NPG 1913.

LEVESON-GOWER, George Granville Sutherland-, see 5th Duke of Sutherland.

LEVY, Benn Wolfe (1900-1973) director, playwright and MP.

ph Walter Stoneman, 1947, hs, NPG (NPR).

LEVY, Reuben (1891-1966) Persian scholar.

ph Ramsey & Muspratt, 2 hs portraits, prints, Christ's College, Cambridge.

LEVY-LAWSON, Harry Lawson Webster, see 1st Viscount Burnham.

LEWIS, Sir Aubrey Julian (1900-1975) psychiatrist.

ph Godfrey Argent, 1969, 2 hs portraits, NPG (NPR).

LEWIS, Clive Staples (1898-1963) literary scholar and writer.

g Alan Sorrell, 'Group in Senior Common Room', oil, 1954, Magdalen College, Oxford.

ph Walter Stoneman, 1955, hl seated, NPG (NPR).

LEWIS, (Dominic Bevan) Wyndham (1891-1969) writer and journalist.

ph Howard Coster, various sizes and negs, NPG.

LEWIS, (Howell) Elvet (1860-1953) Welsh poet and preacher.

ph Walter Stoneman, 1949, hs, NPG (NPR).

LEWIS, (Percy) Wyndham (1882-1957) painter and novelist.

p Self-portrait, 1921, hs, Manchester City Art Gallery. Self-portrait, c1920-21, hs as a 'Tyro', Ferens Art Gallery, Hull.

d Self-portrait, 1920, drg?, Lockwood Memorial Library, State University of New York, Buffalo, USA. Self-portrait, 1932, hs, ink and wash, NPG 4528. Self-portrait, 1938, pencil, State University of New York.

g William Roberts, 'Vorticists at the Restaurant de la Tour Eiffel: Spring, 1915', oil, 1961-62, TATE, T528.

pr Augustus John, c1903, (wrongly dated 1893), etch, NPG and BM.

ph G. C. Beresford, 1913, hs, neg, NPG x6535. A. L. Coburn, 1916, tql seated, photogravure, NPG AX7830. G. C. Beresford, 1917, hs in uniform, neg, NPG x6534. Unknown, c1917, wl in uniform, neg, NPG. G. C. Beresford, 1929, wl with pillar, neg, NPG x6536.

LEWIS, Sir Thomas (1881-1945) physician.

p E. J. Walters, 1937, hs, National Museum of Wales 473, Cardiff.

LEWIS, Sir Wilfrid Hubert Poyer (1881-1950) judge.

ph Walter Stoneman, 1935, 2 hs portraits, the 2nd in robes, NPG (NPR).

LEWIS, William Cudmore McCullagh (1885-1956) physical chemist.

ph Cyril Pollard, hs, print, Royal Society, London.

LIDDELL HART, Sir Basil (Henry) (1895-1970) military writer.

sc Marjorie Fitzgibbon, bronze bust, IWM.

ph Howard Coster, 1930s, various sizes and negs, NPG. Walter Bird, 1966, hs, NPG (NPR).

LILLICRAP, Sir Charles Swift (1887-1966) naval architect.

ph Walter Stoneman, 1948, hl, NPG (NPR).

LILLIE, Beatrice, Lady Peel (b1898) actress.

ph Sir Cecil Beaton, 6 heads, print, NPG.

LINDEMANN, Frederick Alexander, see 1st Viscount Cherwell.

LINDGREN, George Samuel Lindgren, Baron (1900-1971) trade unionist and politician.

ph Walter Stoneman, 1946, hs, NPG (NPR). Walter Bird, 1965, tql seated, NPG (NPR).

LINDLEY, Sir Francis Oswald (1872-1950) diplomat.

ph Unknown, hs as a young man, print, NPG. Walter Stoneman, 1943, hs, NPG (NPR).

LINDSAY, David Alexander Edward, see 27th Earl of Crawford and Balcarres.

LINDSAY, David Robert Alexander, see 28th Earl of Crawford and Balcarres.

LINDSAY, Sir Ronald Charles (1877-1945) diplomat.

ph Walter Stoneman, 2 hs portraits, 1925 and 1936, NPG (NPR).

LINDSAY of Birker, Alexander Dunlop Lindsay, 1st Baron (1879-1952) educationist.

p Lawrence Gowing, Balliol College, Oxford.

sc Sir Jacob Epstein, bronze bust, Balliol College.

LINKLATER, Eric (Robert) (1899-1974) author and playwright.

g Stanley Cursiter, 'Authors in Session', oil, 1950, Glasgow Art Gallery and Museum.

ph Howard Coster, 1954, various sizes, prints and negs, NPG x1977-80, x2378 and others.

LINLITHGOW, John Adrian Louis Hope, 7th Earl of Hopetoun and 1st Marquess of (1860-1908) first governor-general of Australia.

P ROBERT BROUGH, 1904, wl in Thistle robes, Hopetoun House, South Queensferry, Scotland.

SC DAVID WATSON STEVENSON, c1891, plaster bust, SNPG 614. SIR GEORGE FRAMPTON, statue, Linlithgow, Scotland. BERNIE RHIND, 1911, statue, Melbourne, Australia.

C SIR LESLIE WARD ('Spy'), wl in lord chamberlain's robes, lith, for *Vanity Fair*, 17 May 1900, NPG.

PH ELLIOTT & FRY, hs, print, for *Our Conservative and Unionist Statesmen*, vol 2, NPG (Album 24).

LINLITHGOW, Victor Alexander John Hope, 2nd Marquess of (1887-1952) Viceroy of India.

P SIR OSWALD BIRLEY, 1945, wl in Thistle robes, Hopetoun House, Queensferry, Scotland. SIR O.BIRLEY, 1950, tql seated in Thistle robes, Midland Bank, Poultry, London.

LISTER, Sir Philip Cunliffe-, see 1st Earl of Swinton.

LITHGOW, Sir James, 1st Bart (1883-1952) shipbuilder and industrialist.

PH WALTER STONEMAN, hs, for NPR, NPG X472.

LITTLE, Andrew George (1863-1945) historian.

PH WALTER STONEMAN, 1923, hs, NPG (NPR).

LITTLE, Sir Charles James Colebrooke (1882-1973) admiral.

PH WALTER STONEMAN, 1935, hl in uniform, for NPR, NPG X6979.

LITTLE, Sir Ernest Gordon Graham Graham-, see Graham-Little.

LITTLEWOOD, John Edensor (1885-1977) mathematician.

D REGINALD BRILL, 1933, pen and ink and sepia, Trinity College, Cambridge.

SC GABRIELLE BOLLOBAS, bust, Institution of Mathematics and its Applications, Southend on Sea, Essex.

PH WALTER STONEMAN, 1932, hs, NPG (NPR).

LITTLEWOOD, Sir Sydney (Charles Thomas) (1895-1967) solicitor.

PH WALTER BIRD, 1962, hs, NPG (NPR).

LIVINGSTONE, Sir Richard Winn (1880-1960) educationist.

P ERIC KENNINGTON, Corpus Christi College, Oxford.

SC KATE PARBURY, c1959, plaster bust, Denman College, Women's Institute, Marcham Park, Berks.

PH WALTER STONEMAN, 1946, hs, NPG (NPR).

LLEWELLIN, John Jestyn Llewellin, 1st Baron (1893-1957) politician and first governor-general of the Federation of Rhodesia and Nyasaland.

P C.J.McCALL, Federal Assembly, Salisbury, Zimbabwe-Rhodesia.

PH WALTER STONEMAN, 1945, hs, NPG (NPR).

LLOYD, Dorothy Jordan (1889-1946) biochemist.

PH UNKNOWN, hs, print, British Leather Manufacturers' Research Association, Northampton.

LLOYD, George Ambrose Lloyd, 1st Baron (1879-1941) statesman.

D SYDNEY MORSE-BROWN, c1938, hs, chalk, National Museum of Wales, Cardiff.

LLOYD, Sir John Edward (1861-1947) Welsh historian.

P E.J.WALTERS, 1937, National Museum of Wales 471, Cardiff.

PH WALTER STONEMAN, 1932, hs, NPG (NPR).

LLOYD, Marie, real name Matilda Alice Victoria Wood

(1870-1922) music-hall comedian.

PH SCHLOSS, c1890s, wl reclining, print, NPG X12456. ROTARY PHOTO, c1905, wl seated, postcard, NPG X12455.

LLOYD, Sir Thomas Ingram Kynaston (1896-1968) civil servant.

PH WALTER STONEMAN, 1948, hl seated, NPG (NPR).

LLOYD-GEORGE, David Lloyd George, 1st Earl (1863-1945) prime minister.

P SIR LUKE FILDES, 1909, tql seated in robes, The Law Society, London. AUGUSTUS JOHN, 1916, hl seated, Aberdeen Art Gallery. C.D.WILLIAMS, 1917, tql, National Museum of Wales 228, Cardiff. H.A.OLIVIER, 1919, DoE (Paris Chancery). SIR JAMES GUTHRIE, c1919-21, hs, SNPG 1126, study for 'Statesmen', NPG 2463. SIR WILLIAM ORPEN, 1927, hl seated, NPG 3244. P.A.DE LÁSZLÓ, 1931, tql, on loan to DoE (Treasury). SIR JOHN LAVERY, 1934?, Municipal Gallery of Art, Dublin. SIR J.LAVERY, 1935, hl seated, National Museum of Wales 516. UNKNOWN, hl seated, NPG 4340.

D ROBIN GUTHRIE, hs, chalk, NPG 3261.

SL H.L.OAKLEY, hs, profile, NPG.

G SIR W.ORPEN, 'A Peace Conference at the Quai d'Orsay', oil, c1919, IWM. SIR W.ORPEN, 'The Signing of Peace in Versailles, 28th June, 1919', oil, IWM. SIR J.GUTHRIE, 'Statesmen of World War I, 1914-18', oil, c1924-30, NPG 2463.

SC E.R.PINCHES, 1919, bronze plaque, National Museum of Wales. SIR WILLIAM GOSCOMBE JOHN, 1921, bronze head, National Museum of Wales 1360. LADY KATHLEEN KENNET, c1923, bronze bust, IWM, and National Museum of Wales 1436. MARGUERITE MILWARD, bronze head, National Museum of Wales 1445. SIR JACOB EPSTEIN, posthumous, plaster head, National Museum of Wales 1484.

PR HENRIK LUND, lith, IWM.

C SIR MAX BEERBOHM, 1908, wl, pencil and wash, NPG 3252. SIR F.C.GOULD, tql and hl with Archbishop of Canterbury, ink, for *Pall Mall Gazette*, NPG 2837 and 2863. HARRY FURNISS, 1890s, hl and tql, NPG 3397-98. SIR DAVID LOW, drg, National Liberal Club, London. SIR BERNARD PARTRIDGE, various cartoons for *Punch*, 1908-45, pen, ink and/or w/c, NPG. SIR LESLIE WARD ('Spy'), wl, Hentschel-Colourtype, for *Vanity Fair*, 13 Nov 1907, NPG.

PH SIR BENJAMIN STONE, 1902, wl, singly and with John Burns, prints, NPG. G.C.BERESFORD, 1902, hs, print and neg, NPG. SIR B.STONE, 1909, wl, print, NPG. G.C.BERESFORD, 1912, hs, neg, NPG X6537. OLIVE EDIS, 1917, 2 hs portraits, prints, NPG. A.L.COBURN, 1918, hs, photogravure, NPG AX7835. WALTER STONEMAN, 1921, hs, print, for NPR, NPG X473. HOWARD COSTER, 1934, various sizes, prints and negs, NPG. FELIX MAN, c1940, hs, print, NPG P10.

LLOYD GEORGE, Gwilym, see 1st Viscount Tenby.

LLOYD JAMES, Arthur (1884-1943) phonetician.

PH UNKNOWN, hs, postcard, Department of Phonetics and Linguistics, University College, London.

LOATES, Thomas (1867-1910) jockey.

C SIR LESLIE WARD ('Spy'), wl, lith, for *Vanity Fair*, 4 Oct 1890, NPG.

LOCKE, William John (1863-1930) novelist.

D J.M.FLAGG, 1909, hs, NPG 3262. GORDON STEVENSON, hl, w/c, Garrick Club, London.

C HARRY FURNISS, c1910, 2 hl portraits, pen and ink, NPG 3485-86.

PH E.O.HOPPÉ, hs, print, NPG. UNKNOWN, hs, print, NPG.

LOCKHART, Sir Robert (Hamilton) Bruce (1887-1970) diplomat, author and journalist.

PH HOWARD COSTER, various sizes and negs, NPG. WALTER STONEMAN, 1943, hs, NPG (NPR).

LODGE, Eleanor Constance (1869-1936) historian and principal of Westfield College, London.
P J.B.SOUTER, 1931, Lady Margaret Hall, Oxford. SIR GERALD KELLY, c1933, Westfield College.
D L.LESLIE BROOKE, 1916, hs, chalk, Lady Margaret Hall.

LOHMANN, George Alfred (1865-1901) Surrey cricketer.
PR UNKNOWN, hs, stipple, NPG.

LONDONDERRY, Charles Stewart Henry Vane-Tempest-Stewart, 7th Marquess of (1878-1949) politician.
P SIR JOHN LAVERY, 1924, hl in chancellor's robes, Ulster Museum, Belfast. WILLIAM CONNOR, 1926, tql in chancellor's robes, Queen's University, Belfast. CUTHBERT ORDE, 1936, hl in uniform, Royal Aero Club on loan to RAF Museum, Hendon.
C SIR DAVID LOW, head, profile, pencil, NPG 4529(210).
PH UNKNOWN, c1910-15, hl, print, NPG. JOHN RUSSELL & SONS, c1915, hs in uniform, print, for *National Photographic Record*, vol 1, NPG. BASSANO, c1915, hs, print, NPG. OLIVE EDIS, c1920-30, 3 hs portraits, 1 autochrome (NPG x7195) and 2 prints, NPG. WALTER STONEMAN, 2 hs portraits, 1927 and 1943, the 2nd in uniform, NPG (NPR). CENTRAL PRESS PHOTOS LTD, c1932-34, wl with James Ramsay MacDonald, print, NPG.

LONDONDERRY, Edith Helen, née Chaplin, 7th Marchioness of (1879-1959) founder of the Women's Legion and political hostess.
P P.A.DE LÁSZLÓ, 1920, hl in uniform, IWM.
PR F.JENKINS, after Ellis Roberts, 1900?, hs, lith, for Mrs F.Harcourt Williamson, *The Book of Beauty*, 1902, NPG.
PH OLIVE EDIS, c1920-30, hs, print, NPG.

LONG, Gabrielle Margaret Vere, née Campbell (1886-1952) novelist, 'Marjorie Bowen' and 'George Preedy'.
PH HOWARD COSTER, 1930s, various sizes, print and negs, NPG x3058-63, x3428 and x10452.

LONGMORE, Sir Arthur Murray (1885-1970) air chief marshal.
P J.HUGHES-HALLETT, copy, hl in uniform, on loan to RAF Museum, Hendon.
PH WALTER STONEMAN, 2 hs portraits, the 1st in uniform, 1931 and 1953, NPG (NPR).

LONGSTAFF, Sir John (1862-1941) painter.
D PHILIP MAY, 1901, tql seated, pencil, NPG 4392.

LORAINE, Sir Percy (Lyham) (1880-1961) diplomat.
PH HISTED, hs, print, NPG.

LORAINE, Violet (Mary) (1886-1956) actress.
PR CHARLES BUCHEL and HASSALL, hs and tql, lith, NPG.

LORIMER, Sir Robert Stodart (1864-1929) architect.
P J.H.LORIMER, 1875, when a boy, TATE 4540. J.H.LORIMER, 1886, tql at drawing board, SNPG 1353.

LOTHIAN, Philip Henry Kerr, 11th Marquess of (1882-1940) journalist and statesman.
P SIR JAMES GUNN, 1943, tql, Rhodes House, Oxford.
D FRANCES DE BIDEN FOOTNER, w/c?, Blickling Hall (NT), Norfolk.
SC UNKNOWN, 1940, plaster cast of death mask, NPG 3245.
PH WALTER STONEMAN, 1921, hs, for NPR, NPG x474.

LOUISE Victoria Alexandra Dagmar, Princess Royal and Duchess of Fife (1867-1931) eldest daughter of Edward VII.
P K.W.F.BAUERLE, 1871, wl with sister Victoria, Royal Coll. JAMES SANT, c1873-74, head, oval, Royal Coll, study for 'Victoria and grandchildren'. HEINRICH VON ANGELI, 1878, head,

oval, Royal Coll.
G K.W.F.BAUERLE, wl with brothers Albert Victor and George, oil, 1871, Royal Coll. J.SANT, 'Victoria with 3 of her grandchildren', oil, c1872, Royal Coll. S.P.HALL, hs with sisters Victoria and Maud, oil, 1883, NPG 4471. LAURITS TUXEN, 'The Royal Family at the Time of the Jubilee', oil, 1887, Royal Coll. L.TUXEN, 'Marriage of King George and Queen Mary', oil, 1893, Royal Coll. L.TUXEN, 'Marriage of Princess Maud and Prince Charles of Denmark', oil, 1896, Royal Coll.
SC MARY THORNYCROFT, 1877, marble statuette with dog, Royal Coll.
PR RIDDLE & COUCHMAN, after photograph by R.Faulkner, hs, oval, lith, for *Illust London News*, 16 Feb 1884, NPG.
PH Various photographs as infant in Royal groups, NPG. W. & D.DOWNEY, 1889, wl with Duke of Fife, wedding postcard, NPG x3805. W. & D.DOWNEY, c1891, tql with Duke and daughter Alexandra, postcard, NPG. A.CORBETT, c1910, tql with Duke, postcard, NPG. A.CORBETT, c1910, tql with daughters Alexandra and Maud Duff, postcard, NPG. LALLIE CHARLES, c1911, 2 portraits with daughters, tql, postcards, NPG. GRAPHIC PHOTO UNION, 1923, wl with daughter Maud on wedding day, print, NPG. Various photographs, Royal Coll.

LOVE, Augustus Edward Hough (1863-1940) mathematician and geophysicist.
PH UNKNOWN, hs, print, Royal Society, London.

LOVETT, (Ernest) Neville (1869-1951) bishop of Salisbury.
PH WALTER STONEMAN, 1937, hs, NPG (NPR). UNKNOWN, hs, print, NPG (Anglican Bishops).

LOW, Sir David (Alexander Cecil) (1891-1963) cartoonist.
P Self-portrait, c1924-25, hs, NPG 4512.
D WYNDHAM LEWIS, 1932, hs, pencil, Education Committee, Wakefield, W Yorks.
PH HOWARD COSTER, 1935, various sizes, print and negs, NPG x1993, x2378 and others.

LOW, Sir Francis (1893-1972) journalist.
PH WALTER STONEMAN, 1950, hs, NPG (NPR).

LOWE, Eveline Mary, née Farren (1869-1956) first woman chairman of the London County Council.
P A.K.LAWRENCE, c1941, County Hall, London.

LOWRY, Laurence Stephen (1887-1976) painter.
P Self-portrait, 1925, hs, City of Salford Museum and Art Gallery.
SC SAMUEL TONKISS, 1971, bronze head, NPG 5091.
PH J.S.LEWINSKI, 1965, tql, print, NPG. SEFTON SAMUELS, 1968, hs, tql and wl, reclining, prints, NPG. PHIL THOMPSON, 1973, hs, print, NPG. S.SAMUELS, 1975, hl with S.Tonkiss and bronze head, colour print, NPG x1457. ROGER BIRCH, 1975, tql, print, NPG x7943.

LOWRY, Thomas Martin (1874-1936) chemist.
PH WALTER STONEMAN, 1931, hs, NPG (NPR).

LOYD, Sir Henry Charles ('Budget') (1891-1973) general.
PH WALTER BIRD, 1965, tql in uniform, NPG (NPR).

LUCAS, Edward Verrall (1868-1938) journalist, essayist and critic.
D ROBIN GUTHRIE, 1937, hs, pen and ink, NPG 3934.
SL HUBERT LESLIE, 1925, hs, profile, NPG.
PH HOWARD COSTER, c1931, various sizes, print and negs, NPG x1995 and others.

LUDLOW-HEWITT, Sir Edgar Rainey (1886-1973) air chief marshal.
P T.C.DUGDALE, IWM. KENNETH GREEN, 1929, RAF Staff College, Bracknell.
PH WALTER STONEMAN, 1946, hl, NPG (NPR).

LUKE, George Lawson Johnston, 1st Baron (1873-1943) businessman and philanthropist.
P WILLIAM BREALEY, Shire Hall, Bedford.

LUKE, Sir Harry Charles (1884-1969) traveller and author.
H WALTER STONEMAN, 1934, hl, for NPR, NPG X4665.

LUKIN, Sir Henry Timson (1860-1925) major-general.
G J.S.SARGENT, 'General Officers of World War I, 1914–18', oil, 1922, NPG 1954.
H WALTER STONEMAN, 1918, hs in uniform, NPG (NPR).

LUMLEY, Sir (Lawrence) Roger, see 11th Earl of Scarbrough.

LUTYENS, Sir Edwin Landseer (1869-1944) architect.
P AUGUSTUS JOHN, c1928, hl seated, Castle Drogo, Devon. MEREDITH FRAMPTON, 1935, hl seated, The Art Workers' Guild, London. ROBERT LUTYENS, 1959, hs, NPG 4481.
D SIR WILLIAM ROTHENSTEIN, 1922, hs, chalk, NPG 3876.
C SIR W.R.DICK, 1932, bronze bust, Government House, New Delhi, India; copy, RIBA. UNKNOWN, 1944, bronze cast of death mask, NPG 3192.
C SIR BERNARD PARTRIDGE, 1927, hs, profile, pen and ink, NPG 3672.
H UNKNOWN, c1920, hs, print, NPG. WALTER STONEMAN, 2 hs portraits, 1924 and 1934, NPG (NPR). HOWARD COSTER, 1930s, various sizes and negs, NPG.

LUXMOORE, Sir (Arthur) Fairfax (Charles Coryndon) (1876-1944) judge.
P JAMES BATEMAN, posthumous, King's School, Canterbury.
H WALTER STONEMAN, 1935, hs in robes, NPG (NPR).

LYGON, William, see 7th Earl Beauchamp.

LYLE of Westbourne, Charles Ernest Leonard Lyle, 1st Baron (1882-1954) industrialist and politician.
P BERNARD DUNSTAN, posthumous, Tate and Lyle Ltd, London.

LYND, Robert Wilson (1879-1949) journalist.

D HENRY LAMB, c1950, hs, chalk, NPG 4666.
SC LADY KATHLEEN KENNET, bronze bust, Queen's University, Belfast.
C SIR DAVID LOW, c1926, head, pencil, NPG 4529(221).
PH UNKNOWN, c1913–14, tql seated with wife and children, print, NPG X1600. HOWARD COSTER, 1933, various sizes, print and negs, NPG AX3467 and others.

LYONS, Sir Henry George (1864-1944) geographer and scientist.
PH WALTER STONEMAN, 1917, hs in uniform, NPG (NPR).

LYTTELTON, Oliver, see 1st Viscount Chandos.

LYTTON, Sir Henry Alfred (1865-1936) actor.
SL H.L.OAKLEY, hs, profile, NPG.
PH F.W.BURFORD, hl in costume uniform, postcard, NPG. HOWARD COSTER, 1930, various sizes, print and negs, NPG X1998 and others.

LYTTON, Neville Stephen Lytton, 3rd Earl of (1879-1951) painter and journalist.
P Self-portrait, 1938, tql, Russell-Cotes Museum, Bournemouth. Self-portrait, hs, oval, Knebworth House, Herts.
D SIR WILLIAM ROTHENSTEIN, 1906, head, profile, sanguine, NPG 4784.

LYTTON, Victor Alexander George Bulwer-Lytton, 2nd Earl of (1876-1947) public servant.
P NEVILLE LYTTON, c1934, wl in Garter robes, Knebworth House, Herts.
SC ONSLOW WHITING, c1937, bronze head, Knebworth. PAUL VINCZE, c1947, relief portrait on bronze medallion, Knebworth.
C SIR LESLIE WARD ('Spy'), wl, lith, for *Vanity Fair*, 19 Sept 1906, NPG.
PH E.MILLS, c1911, hs, print, NPG. WALTER STONEMAN, 2 hs portraits, 1920 and 1943, NPG (NPR). UNKNOWN, c1925, wl in viceregal robes, print, NPG.

M

MACADAM, Sir Ivison (Stevenson) (1894-1974) director-general of the Royal Institute of International Affairs.
PH Various photographs, Royal Institute of International Affairs, Chatham House, London.

MacALISTER, Sir (George) Ian (1878-1957) author.
P HAROLD KNIGHT, c1936, hl, RIBA.

MACAULAY, Dame (Emilie) Rose (1881-1958) author.
PH SIR CECIL BEATON, hs, print, NPG.

McBEY, James (1883-1959) etcher and painter.
P G.L.BROCKHURST, c1931, hl, Boston Public Library, USA.
D Self-portrait, 1914, wl, ink and w/c, Aberdeen Art Gallery and Museum. Self-portrait, 1918, chalk and w/c, IWM. MARTIN HARDIE, 1919, hs, NPG 4463. M.HARDIE, w/c, Aberdeen Art Gallery and Museum.
SC BENNO SCHOTZ, 1924, bronze head, Aberdeen Art Gallery and Museum.

MacBRIDE, Maud, see Gonne.

McCALLUM, Ronald Buchanan (1898-1973) master of Pembroke College, Oxford.
P SIR JAMES GUNN, Pembroke College.
PH WALTER STONEMAN, 1955, hl, NPG (NPR).

McCALMONT, Harry Leslie Blundell (1861-1902) sportsman.
C SIR LESLIE WARD ('Spy'), wl, lith, for *Vanity Fair*, 5 Oct 1889, NPG. SIR LESLIE WARD ('Spy'), wl, lith, for *Vanity Fair*, 9 Jan 1896, NPG.

McCARDIE, Sir Henry Alfred (1869-1933) judge.
SC MARGUERITE MILWOOD, bronze head, Middle Temple, London.

McCARRISON, Sir Robert (1878-1960) medical scientist.
PH WALTER STONEMAN, 1935, hs, NPG (NPR).

MacCARTHY, Sir (Charles Otto) Desmond (1877-1952) author and critic.
P HENRY LAMB, 1940, hl seated, National Museum of Wales 612, Cardiff. DUNCAN GRANT, c1942, hs, NPG 5024. D.GRANT, 1944, almost wl seated, NPG 4842.
D ROBIN GUTHRIE, 1938, hl seated, pencil, NPG 3936. D.GRANT, c1938, head, pencil, NPG 4468.

McCARTHY, Lillah, Lady Keeble (1875-1960) actress.
P CHARLES SHANNON, 1907, wl as Dona Ana in *Man and Superman*, Cheltenham Art Gallery, Glos. C.SHANNON, c1917-18, tql seated in the character of 'The Dumb Wife', Cheltenham Art Gallery.
PR AMBROSE McEVOY, 1919, tql, chromo-lith, poster advertising the season of plays produced at the Kingsway Theatre, London, 1919, V & A.
PH W. & D.DOWNEY, c1906, hs, postcard, NPG. DAILY MIRROR STUDIOS, 1913, wl in costume, print, NPG.

McCORMICK, William Patrick Glyn (1877-1940) vicar of St Martin-in-the-Fields, London.
PH HOWARD COSTER, 2 negs, NPG.

McCREERY, Sir Richard Loudon (1898-1967) general.
PH WALTER STONEMAN, 1946, hs in uniform, NPG (NPR).

McCUDDEN, James Thomas Byford (1895-1918) airman.

P SIR WILLIAM ORPEN, c1917-19, hl seated in uniform, IWM. EDWARD NEWLING, 1919, IWM.
PH Various photographs, IWM.

MacCUNN, Hamish (James) (1868-1916) musical composer
SC D.W.STEVENSON, c1889, plaster bust, SNPG 874.
PR JOHN PETTIE, 1886, hs, lith, NPG.

MacDIARMID, Hugh, see Christopher Murray GRIEVE.

MACDONALD, Sir George (1862-1940) numismatist and archaeologist.
P MAURICE GREIFFENHAGEN, 1929, hl, SNPG 1484. M.GREIFFENHAGEN, 1929, SNPG L171.
PH WALTER STONEMAN, 1917, hs, NPG (NPR).

MACDONALD, Hector Munro (1865-1935) mathematical physicist.
P R.G.EVES, 1933, hs, SNPG 1421. R.G.EVES, 1933, tql seated Aberdeen University.
PH WALTER STONEMAN, 1931, hl, NPG (NPR).

MacDONALD, James Ramsay (1866-1937) prime minister
P SOLOMON J.SOLOMON, c1912, hl seated, NPG 3890. AMBROSE McEVOY, c1926, hl, SNPG 1351. E.J.WALTERS, 1929, hs, National Museum of Wales 834, Cardiff. SIR JOHN LAVERY, 1931, tql, NPG 2959.
D WILLIAM SMALL, 1889, 2 pencil drgs, SNPG 1778. SIR WILLIAM ROTHENSTEIN, 1923, sanguine, Manchester City Art Gallery.
M WINIFRED C.DONGWORTH, c1920-30, hs, oval, NPG 5029. LILIAN M.MAYER, hs, oval, NPG 2066.
G SIR J.LAVERY, 'House of Commons, 1924', oil, Glasgow City Art Gallery.
SC SIR JACOB EPSTEIN, 1934, bronze bust, NPG 2934. SIR J.EPSTEIN bronze bust, SNPG 1352.
C SIR MAX BEERBOHM, 1924, drg, Manchester City Art Gallery. SIR DAVID LOW, c1926, head, pencil, NPG 4529(222). SIR M.BEERBOHM, 1931, tql seated, pencil, ink and w/c, The Columbus Gallery of Fine Arts, Columbus, Ohio, USA; study chalk, NPG 4665. SIR BERNARD PARTRIDGE, 1923-31, various cartoons for *Punch*, pen and ink, NPG.
PH SIR BENJAMIN STONE, 1907, wl, print, NPG. G.C.BERESFORD c1920, 3 hs portraits, print and 2 negs, NPG X6541-42. WALTER STONEMAN, 1923, hs, NPG (NPR). OLIVE EDIS, c1920-30?, hs, 2 prints and 2 autochromes, NPG. CENTRAL PRESS PHOTOS LTD c1932-34, wl with Lord Londonderry, print, NPG.

MacDONALD, Sir Murdoch (1866-1957) engineer.
P SIR JAMES GUNN, tql seated, Institution of Civil Engineers London.
SC GLADYS BARRON, c1933, bronze head, Town Hall, Inverness.
PH WALTER STONEMAN, 1932, hs, NPG (NPR).

McDOUGALL, William (1871-1938) psychologist.
PH WALTER STONEMAN, 1917, hs in uniform, NPG (NPR).

McEVOY, (Arthur) Ambrose (1878-1927) painter.
P AUGUSTUS JOHN, hs, Durban Art Gallery, South Africa.
D A.JOHN, c1894-98, tql seated, chalk, NPG 3056. Self-portrait 1900, head, pencil and pen and ink, TATE 5832. Self-portrait c1912, hl, pencil, NPG 2790. ALBERT RUTHERSTON, pencil Ashmolean Museum, Oxford.

G SIR WILLIAM ORPEN, 'The Selecting Jury of the New English Art Club, 1909', oil, NPG 2556.
SC F.D.WOOD, 1915, bronze bust, NPG 2958, and Royal Academy, London.

McEWEN, Sir John Blackwood (1868-1948) principal of the Royal Academy of Music, London.
P R.G.EVES, hs, Royal Academy of Music.

McFADYEAN, Sir Andrew (1887-1974) diplomat, businessman and politician.
PH WALTER STONEMAN, 1947, hs, NPG (NPR).

MacFARLANE, Sir (Frank) Noel Mason-, see Mason-MacFarlane.

McGOWAN, Sir Harry Duncan McGowan, 1st Baron (1874-1961) industrialist.
P SIR WILLIAM ORPEN, 1928, tql seated, Imperial Chemical Industries Ltd, London.
PH WALTER STONEMAN, 2 hs portraits, 1931 and 1953, NPG (NPR). HOWARD COSTER, various sizes and negs, NPG.

McGRIGOR, Sir Rhoderick Robert (1893-1959) admiral.
PH WALTER STONEMAN, 2 hs portraits in uniform, 1942 and 1952, NPG (NPR).

McINDOE, Sir Archibald Hector (1900-1960) plastic surgeon.
P M.EASTON, Queen Victoria Hospital, East Grinstead. E.I.HALLIDAY, Royal College of Surgeons, London.
G ANNA ZINKEISEN, operating theatre scene, oil, 1944, IWM.
PH WALTER STONEMAN, 1948, hs, NPG (NPR). LENARE, 1949, 2 hs portraits, negs, NPG x3984-85.

MacIVER, David Randall-, see Randall-MacIver.

MACKAIL, Denis (George) (1892-1971) novelist.
PH HOWARD COSTER, c1932, various sizes and negs, NPG.

McKENNA, Reginald (1863-1943) statesman and banker.
P SIR JAMES GUNN, 1935, tql seated, Midland Bank, Poultry, London.
C SIR LESLIE WARD ('Spy'), wl, lith, for *Vanity Fair*, 31 Oct 1906, NPG. 'Owl', wl, mechanical repro, for *Vanity Fair*, 23 April 1913, NPG. SIR BERNARD PARTRIDGE, 3 cartoons for *Punch*, 22 April 1908; 6 June 1923; and 21 May 1928, NPG.
PH G.C.BERESFORD, 1909, hs and tql seated, print and 2 negs, NPG x6544-45. JOHN RUSSELL & SONS, c1915, hs, print, for *National Photographic Record*, vol 2, NPG.

MACKENNAL, Sir (Edgar) Bertram (1863-1931) sculptor.
PH JOHN RUSSELL & SONS, c1915, hl with statuette, print, for *National Photographic Record*, vol 1, NPG. WALTER STONEMAN, 1924, hs, NPG (NPR). UNKNOWN, hs, print, NPG.

McKENZIE, Alexander (1869-1951) professor of chemistry.
PH WALTER STONEMAN, 1932, hl, NPG (NPR).

MACKENZIE, Sir (Edward Montague) Compton (1883-1972) writer.
P SIR W.O.HUTCHISON, hl seated, SNPG 2377. R.H.WESTWATER, 1954, University of Texas, Austin, USA.
D DAVID FOGGIE, 1933, pencil, SNPG 2003. HELEN WILSON, 1963, hs, pastel, NPG 4948.
SC MICHAEL KATZ, 1919, bronze head, University of Texas.
C R.S.SHERRIFFS, hs, ink and wash, NPG.
PH G.C.BERESFORD, 1912, hs, print and neg, NPG x6540. A.L.COBURN, 1914, hs, profile, photogravure, NPG AX7826. HOWARD COSTER, 1934 and 1954, various sizes, prints and negs, NPG x2000-04, AX3493 and x3776-89. ELLIOTT & FRY, c1949, hs, profile, print, NPG. ROBIN ADLER, c1950s, hs, profile, print, NPG

x7764. WALTER BIRD, 1965, hs, profile, NPG (NPR).

MACKENZIE, William Warrender, see 1st Baron Amulree.

McKERROW, Ronald Brunlees (1872-1940) scholar and bibliographer.
PH WALTER STONEMAN, 1933, hs, NPG (NPR).

MACKESY, Pierse Joseph (1883-1956) major-general.
PH WALTER STONEMAN, 1937, hs in uniform, NPG (NPR).

MACKINDER, Sir Halford John (1861-1947) geographer and politician.
P 'M.R.', 1908, tql seated, University of Reading.
D SIR WILLIAM ROTHENSTEIN, hs, sanguine and chalk, NPG 4785. SIR W.ROTHENSTEIN, 1933, London School of Economics.

MacKINNON, Sir Frank Douglas (1871-1946) judge and author.
D SIR GERALD KELLY, pencil, Holdsworth Club, University of Birmingham.
PH WALTER STONEMAN, 1927, hs, NPG (NPR).

MACKINTOSH, Charles Rennie (1868-1928) architect and painter.
P F.H.NEWBERY, wl, SNPG 1205.

MACKINTOSH, Hugh Ross (1870-1936) Scottish theologian.
PH UNKNOWN, print, New College, Edinburgh.

MACLAGAN, Sir Eric Robert Dalrymple (1879-1951) director of the Victoria and Albert Museum, London.
D FRANCIS DODD, 1944, hl, profile, charcoal, V & A.
PH WALTER STONEMAN, 1940, hs, NPG (NPR). HOWARD COSTER, various sizes and negs, NPG.

MacLAREN, Archibald Campbell (1871-1944) cricketer.
P GERALD REYNELL, posthumous, Old Trafford, Manchester.

McLAREN, Henry Duncan, see 2nd Baron Aberconway.

MACLEAN, Sir Donald (1864-1932) politician.
PH JOHN RUSSELL & SONS, c1915, hs, print, for *National Photographic Record*, vol 2, NPG. WALTER STONEMAN, 1925, hs, NPG (NPR).

McLENNAN, Sir John Cunningham (1867-1935) Canadian physicist.
P AUGUSTUS JOHN, Physics Department, University of Toronto, Canada.
PH WALTER STONEMAN, 1933, hs, profile, NPG (NPR).

MACLEOD, John James Rickard (1876-1935) physiologist and biochemist.
SC EMANUEL HAHN, 1928, bronze portrait medallion, Medical Faculty, University of Toronto, Canada.
PH WALTER STONEMAN, 1931, hs, NPG (NPR).

McLINTOCK, Sir William, 1st Bart (1873-1947) chartered accountant.
C FRED MAY, hs, gouache, NPG.

McLINTOCK, William Francis Porter (1887-1960) geologist.
PH INSTITUTE OF GEOLOGICAL SCIENCES, tql, print, Geological Museum, London.

McMAHON, Sir (Arthur) Henry (1862-1949) military political officer.
PH WALTER STONEMAN, 1920, hs, NPG (NPR).

MacMICHAEL, Sir Harold (Alfred) (1882-1969) diplomat.
PH WALTER STONEMAN, 1932, hs, NPG (NPR).

MACMILLAN, Daniel (de Mendi) (1886-1965) publisher.
PR ROBERT LUTYENS, c1961-62, hl, profile, seated at table with

Stanley Morison, one of set of 'Old Burgundians', type of lith, NPG.

MACMILLAN, Hugh Pattison Macmillan, Baron (1873-1952) judge.
P L.CAMPBELL TAYLOR, c1945, Senate House, University of London.
D SIR WILLIAM ROTHENSTEIN, 1937?, hs, chalk, The Athenaeum, London.
PH WALTER STONEMAN, hs and hl seated, 1937 and 1948, NPG (NPR).

McMILLAN, Margaret (1860-1931) educationist.
P JOHN MANSBRIDGE, posthumous, hl with two children, Rachel McMillan College of Education, London.

MACMILLAN, (Maurice) Harold (b1894) prime minister.
P SIR JAMES GUNN, 1960, tql seated in chancellor's robes, Carlton Club, London.
D MARCUS POWELL, 1972, head, pencil, Hertford College, Oxford.
SC ANGELA CONNER, 1973, bronze bust, NPG 5133.
C GEOFFREY DAVIEN, plaster head, 'sculptoon', NPG. DAVID LEVINE, 1966, wl, ink, NPG.
PH WALTER STONEMAN, 1947, hs, NPG (NPR). ARNOLD NEWMAN, 1954, tql, print, NPG P44. MARK GERSON, 1967, tql with Lord and Lady Snow, print, NPG.

McNAIR, Arnold Duncan McNair, 1st Baron (1885-1975) judge.
P MRS P.DODD, 1959, hs in robes, Gray's Inn, London. UNKNOWN, University of Liverpool.
PH WALTER BIRD, 1964, hs, NPG (NPR).

MACNAMARA, Thomas James (1861-1931) politician.
C SIR LESLIE WARD ('Spy'), wl, w/c study for *Vanity Fair*, 9 Oct 1907, NPG 2975.
PH SIR BENJAMIN STONE, 1901, wl, print, NPG. WALTER STONEMAN, 1920, hs, NPG (NPR).

McNEILE, (Herman) Cyril ('Sapper') (1888-1937) soldier and novelist.
PH HOWARD COSTER, various sizes and negs, NPG.

McNEILL, Sir James (McFadyen) (1892-1964) naval architect and engineer.
PH WALTER BIRD, 1963, hs, NPG (NPR).

MACNEILL, John ('Eoin') (1867-1945) Irish scholar and politician.
P SÉAMAS O'SULLIVAN, University College, Belfast, N Ireland.

MACPHERSON, (James) Ian, see 1st Baron Strathcarron.

MACPHERSON, Sir John (Stuart) (1898-1971) diplomat.
PH WALTER STONEMAN, 1957, hs, NPG (NPR).

MACREADY, Sir (Cecil Frederick) Nevil, 1st Bart (1862-1946) general.
P PERCIVAL ANDERSON, Royal Coll.
D FRANCIS DODD, 1917, charcoal and w/c, IWM.
PH WALTER STONEMAN, c1915, 2 hs portraits in uniform, NPG (NPR).

M'TAGGART, John M'Taggart Ellis (1866-1925) philosopher.
P ROGER FRY, hs, Trinity College, Cambridge.
D SIR WILLIAM ROTHENSTEIN, 1916, head, pencil, Trinity College.
C R.FRY, w/c, Trinity College.
PH WALTER STONEMAN, 1917, hs, NPG (NPR).

MADDEN, Sir Charles Edward, 1st Bart (1862-1935) admiral.
P R.G.EVES, 1922, IWM.
D FRANCIS DODD, 1917, charcoal and w/c, IWM.
G SIR A.S.COPE, 'Naval Officers of World War I, 1914-18', oil,

1921, NPG 1913.
PH WALTER STONEMAN, 1924, hs in uniform, NPG (NPR).

MAFFEY, John Loader, see 1st Baron Rugby.

MAGEE, William Kirkpatrick (1868-1961) Irish essayist 'John Eglinton'.
D J.B.YEATS, 1905, hl seated, pencil, James Augustine Healy Coll of Irish Literature, Colby College, Waterville, Maine, USA.

MAITLAND, Sir Arthur Herbert Drummond Ramsay-Steel-, see Steel-Maitland.

MALCOLM, Sir Dougal Orme (1877-1955) scholar and imperialist.
P By or after SIR OSWALD BIRLEY, hs in Highland dress, All Souls College, Oxford. SIR JAMES GUNN, c1954-55, tql seated, Althorp, Northants, study for Society of Dilettanti conversation group.
G SIR J.GUNN, 'Society of Dilettanti Conversation Piece', oil, c1954-59, Society of Dilettanti, Brooks's Club, London.
PH WALTER STONEMAN, 2 hs portraits, 1938 and 1947, NPG (NPR).

MALLESON, (William) Miles (1888-1969) actor.
PH HOWARD COSTER, 3 negs, NPG.

MALLON, James Joseph (1875-1961) warden of Toynbee Hall, London.
SC SIR JACOB EPSTEIN, bronze bust, Toynbee Hall.

MALLORY, George Leigh (1886-1924) mountaineer.
D SIMON BUSSY, head, pastel, NPG 3918.

MALLORY, Sir Trafford Leigh Leigh-, see Leigh-Mallory.

MALLOWAN, Agatha, Lady, see Dame Agatha Christie.

MANDER, Sir Geoffrey Le Mesurier (1882-1962) politician.
PH WALTER STONEMAN, 2 hs portraits, 1937 and 1945, NPG (NPR).

MANN, Sir James Gow (1897-1962) director of the Wallace Collection and master of the armouries, Tower of London.
D A.K.LAWRENCE, c1955, chalk, Society of Antiquaries, London.
PH HOWARD COSTER, various sizes and negs, NPG.

MANNERS, Diana, Lady, see 1st Viscountess Norwich.

MANNING, Frederic (1882-1935) novelist and poet.
D SIR WILLIAM ROTHENSTEIN, 1921, hs, profile, chalk, NPG 4417.

MANSBRIDGE, Albert (1876-1952) founder of the Workers' Educational Association.
P JOHN MANSBRIDGE, 1947, tql seated, NPG 3987.
PH WALTER STONEMAN, 1932, hs, profile, NPG (NPR). HOWARD COSTER, 1930s, various sizes and negs, NPG. Various photographs, Workers' Educational Association, London.

MANSERGH, Sir Maurice (James) (1896-1966) admiral.
PH WALTER STONEMAN, 1946, hl in uniform, NPG (NPR).

MANSFIELD Sir John Maurice (1893-1949) vice-admiral.
PH WALTER STONEMAN, 1943, hs in uniform, NPG (NPR).

MANSFIELD, Katherine, see Kathleen Murry.

MANSON, James Bolivar (1879-1945) painter and director of the Tate Gallery, London.
P Self-portrait, c1912, hs, TATE 4929.
SC ANDREW O'CONNOR, bronze bust?, Municipal Gallery of Modern Art, Dublin.
PH HOWARD COSTER, various sizes and negs, NPG.

MANSON, Thomas Walter (1893-1958) biblical scholar.
PH WALTER STONEMAN, 1946, hl, NPG (NPR).

MANSON-BAHR, Sir Philip (1881-1966) specialist in tropical medicine.

PH WALTER STONEMAN, 1947, hl, NPG (NPR).

MARETT, Robert Ranulph (1866-1943) philosopher and anthropologist.
P HENRY LAMB, 1935, hl in robes, Exeter College, Oxford.
PH WALTER STONEMAN, 1933, hs, NPG (NPR).

MARGESSON, (Henry) David (Reginald) Margesson, 1st Viscount (1890-1965) politician.
PH WALTER STONEMAN, 1930, hs, for NPR, NPG X484.

MARIE LOUISE of Schleswig-Holstein, Princess, real name Franziska Josepha Louise Augusta (1872-1956) grand-daughter of Queen Victoria.
SL H.L.OAKLEY, head, profile, NPG.
PH SIR CECIL BEATON, hl, print, NPG. LENARE, 1945, family? group, neg, NPG X1270.

MARKS of Broughton, Simon Marks, 1st Baron (1888-1964) businessman.
PH WALTER STONEMAN, 1933, hs, NPG (NPR).

MARLOW, Louis, see Wilkinson.

MARQUIS, Frederick James, see 1st Earl Woolton.

MARSH, Sir Edward Howard (1872-1953) patron of artists and writers.
P NEVILLE LEWIS, c1937, wl, Royal Society of Literature, London. SIR OSWALD BIRLEY, 1949, hl, NPG 3945.
D NICHOLAS EGON, 1951, hs, Trinity College, Cambridge.
SC FRANK DOBSON, c1938-39, bronze head, Doncaster Museum and Art Gallery.
PH HOWARD COSTER, various sizes, print and negs, NPG X2009 and others. KARL POLLAK, hs, print, NPG.

MARSHALL, Sir Guy Anstruther Knox (1871-1959) entomologist.
PH WALTER STONEMAN, 2 hs portraits, 1930 and 1946, NPG (NPR).

MARSHALL, Sir John Hubert (1876-1958) archaeologist.
PH WALTER STONEMAN, 1937, hs, NPG (NPR).

MARSHALL, Sir William Raine (1865-1939) lieutenant-general.
P FREDERIC WHITING, 1919, IWM.
G J.S.SARGENT, 'General Officers of World War I, 1914-18', oil, 1922, NPG 1954.
PH WALTER STONEMAN, 1919, hs in uniform, NPG (NPR).

MARTEL, Sir Giffard Le Quesne (1889-1958) lieutenant-general.
P UNKNOWN, Royal Engineers HQ Mess, Chatham.
PH WALTER STONEMAN, 1952, hs, NPG (NPR).

MARTEN, Sir (Clarence) Henry (Kennett) (1872-1948) provost of Eton.
P SIR GERALD KELLY, hl seated in robes, Eton College, Berks.
G R.E.EURICH, group when being knighted in College Chapel, Eton College.
PH WALTER STONEMAN, 1945, hs, NPG (NPR).

MARTIN, Sir Alec (1884-1971) fine art auctioneer and chairman of the National Art Collections Fund.
P W.R.SICKERT, 1935, nearly wl seated, TATE T221. JOHN WHEATLEY, tql seated, NPG 4850.
SC SIR JACOB EPSTEIN, bronze bust, Municipal Gallery of Modern Art, Dublin.

MARTIN, (Basil) Kingsley (1897-1969) journalist.
D EDMOND KAPP, 1956, Barber Institute, Birmingham University.
C SIR DAVID LOW, 2 heads and tql, pencil, NPG 4529(232-34).

MARTIN, Sir Charles James (1866-1955) physiologist and pathologist.
P M.LEWIS, copy, Lister Institute of Preventive Medicine, Elstree, Herts.
D A.J.MURCH, copy, Lister Institute.

MARTIN, Evelyn George (1871-1945) yachtsman.
D COR VISSER, 1937, hs, crayon, NPG 4227.

MARTIN, Violet Florence (1862-1915) novelist 'Martin Ross'.
P EDITH SOMERVILLE, 1886, tql seated, NPG 4655.

MARTIN-HARVEY, Sir John Martin (1863-1944) actor-manager.
P ARTHUR HACKER, c1917, hl as Hamlet, London Museum. F.O.SALISBURY, c1925, hs as Richard III, Garrick Club, London. BERNARD MUNNS, as Richard III, Royal Shakespeare Theatre, Stratford-Upon-Avon.
D CHARLES BUCHEL, 1918, head, profile, chalk, NPG 4694.
SC SIR GEORGE FRAMPTON, 1900, bronze bust as Sydney Carton, Royal Shakespeare Theatre.
PH WALTER STONEMAN, 1933, hs, NPG (NPR). HISTED, hl with dog, photogravure, NPG. ROTARY PHOTO, hl, postcard, NPG. Various photographs, NPG (Daily Herald).

MARY Victoria of Teck (1867-1953) Queen of George V.
P HEINRICH VON ANGELI, 1893, head, oval, Royal Coll. SIR LUKE FILDES, 1893, hs, Royal Coll. EDWARD HUGHES, 1890s, wl, Royal Coll. SIR WILLIAM LLEWELLYN, 1911, wl, state portrait, Royal Coll; versions, Queen's College, Oxford, and Liverpool Corporation. SIR JOHN LAVERY, 1913, head, Royal Coll, study for NPG 1745. F.O.SALISBURY, c1918, tql, Harewood House, W Yorks. ISAAC SNOWMAN, c1924?, Royal Coll. RICHARD JACK, c1926-27, wl, one of pair, Royal Coll. L.C.TAYLOR, 1928, tql seated, Royal College of Music, London. DAVID JAGGER, c1930, tql seated, Bethlem Royal Hospital, Beckenham, Kent, and Royal Coll. SIR OSWALD BIRLEY, 1934, hl seated, Royal Coll. M.L.WILLIAMS, 1938, hl, Nurse's Residence, St Thomas' hospital, London. SIMON ELWES, 1930s, tql seated, Royal Coll. A.T.NOWELL, c1937, hs, Royal Coll.
M M.H.CARLISLE, 1890s, hs, oval, NPG 2089.
G LAURITS TUXEN, marriage group, oil, 1893, Royal Coll. L.TUXEN, 'Marriage of Princess Maud and Prince Charles of Denmark', oil, 1896, Royal Coll. E.A.ABBEY, 'The Coronation of King Edward VII, 1902', oil, 1904, Royal Coll. SIR J.LAVERY, 'The Royal Family at Buckingham Palace, 1913', oil, NPG 1745. J.H.F.BACON, Coronation portrait, oil, 1912, Royal Coll. A.J.MUNNINGS, 'Their Majesties Return from Ascot', oil, 1925, TATE 4956. F.O.SALISBURY, 'Thanksgiving Service of the King's Silver Jubilee', oil, 1935, Guildhall, London. F.O.SALISBURY, 'Jubilee Service', oil, 1935, Royal Coll.
SC SYDNEY MARCH, 1905, bronze bust, Royal Coll. ALFRED DRURY, c1906, marble bust, Bradford City Art Gallery. SIR GEORGE FRAMPTON, 1912, marble bust, Royal Coll. SIR W.R.DICK, 1938, bronze bust, Royal Coll, and NPG 4164. SIR WILLIAM GOSCOMBE JOHN, 1939, bronze model for King George V memorial statues in Liverpool, National Museum of Wales, Cardiff. SIR W.R.DICK, marble tomb effigy with King George, St George's Chapel, Windsor.
PH Various photographs and postcards, singly and in groups, by BASSANO, MRS ALBERT BROOM, BYRNE & CO, W. & D.DOWNEY, ALICE HUGHES, JOHN RUSSELL & SONS, SPEAIGHT, J.THOMSON, F.THURSTON, VANDYK, H.R.WICKS, HAY WRIGHTSON and others, NPG and Royal Coll.

MARY Victoria Alexandra Alice, Countess of Harewood (1897-1965) princess royal, daughter of King George V.

P SOLOMON J.SOLOMON, 1911, hl, Harewood House, W Yorks. SIR JOHN LAVERY, c1913, head, Royal Coll, study for NPG 1745. SIR OSWALD BIRLEY, 1922, tql, Harewood House. RICHARD JACK, 1928, tql seated, Westminster Hospital, London. SIR A.J.MUNNINGS, 1930, wl on horseback with Earl of Harewood, Harewood House. SIR A.J.MUNNINGS, c1930, wl on horseback, Harewood House. SIMON ELWES, c1934, tql, The Royal Scots Regimental Museum, Edinburgh Castle. PETER GREENHAM, c1957, wl seated in Chancellor's robes, University of Leeds.

D J.S.SARGENT, 1925, hs, charcoal, Harewood House. MRS BLAKENEY WARD, hl, pastel, Harewood House.

G SIR J.LAVERY, 'The Royal Family at Buckingham Palace, 1913', oil, NPG 1745. F.O.SALISBURY, wedding portrait, oil, 1922, Harewood House, and Royal Coll.

PH Various photographs, singly and in groups, by SIR CECIL BEATON, CAMPBELL-GRAY, W. & D.DOWNEY, OLIVE EDIS, ELLIOTT & FRY, VANDYK, DOROTHY WILDING and others, NPG and Royal Coll.

MASEFIELD, John (1878-1967) poet.

P WILLIAM STRANG, 1909, tql with globe, Wolverhampton Art Gallery. W.STRANG, 1912, hl seated, Manchester City Art Gallery, related etch, NPG 4568.

D HENRY LAMB, c1910-15, head, pencil, NPG 4569. EDMOND KAPP, 1917, hs, Barber Institute, Birmingham University. SIR WILLIAM ROTHENSTEIN, 1920, hs, sanguine, Fitzwilliam Museum, Cambridge.

SC THEODORE SPICER-SIMSON, plasticine medallion, NPG 2053.

PH A.L.COBURN, 1913, hs, photogravure, NPG AX7796. HOWARD COSTER, 1940s, various sizes, prints and negs, NPG X3445-46 and others. FELIX MAN, c1945, hs, print, NPG X1154. MARK GERSON, 1961, tql, print, NPG.

MASON, Alfred Edward Woodley (1865-1948) novelist.

P SIR OSWALD BIRLEY, 1946, Trinity College, Oxford.

C SIR MAX BEERBOHM ('Max'), wl, Hentschel-Colourtype for Vanity Fair, 10 June 1908, NPG.

PH KARL POLLAK, hs and hl, prints, NPG.

MASON-MacFARLANE, Sir (Frank) Noel (1889-1953).

P R.G.EVES, 1940, 2 portraits, IWM.

PH WALTER STONEMAN, 3 hs portraits in uniform, 1940 and 1945, NPG (NPR) and NPG X482.

MASSINGBERD, Sir Archibald Armar Montgomery-, see Montgomery-Massingberd.

MASSON, Sir (James) Irvine (Orme) (1887-1962) scientist and vice-chancellor of University of Sheffield.

P SIR W.O.HUTCHISON, 1952, tql seated in robes, University of Sheffield.

PH WALTER STONEMAN, 1939, hs, NPG (NPR).

MASTERMAN, Charles Frederick Gurney (1874-1927) politician, author and journalist.

D EDMOND KAPP, 1914, Barber Institute, Birmingham University.

C SIR MAX BEERBOHM, 1911, drg, Ashmolean Museum, Oxford.

PH STEARN & SONS, 1899, family group, print, NPG.

MATHEW, Sir Theobald (1898-1964) solicitor and director of public prosecutions.

PH WALTER STONEMAN, 1946, hs, NPG (NPR).

MATHEWS, Dame Vera (Elvira Sibyl Maria) Laughton (1888-1959) director of the Women's Royal Naval Service.

P ANTHONY DEVAS, IWM.

PH WALTER STONEMAN, 1958, hs, NPG (NPR).

MATHIESON, William Law (1868-1938) historian.

P D.G.SHIELDS, 1934, SNPG 1407.

MATTHEWS, Walter Robert (1881-1973) dean of St Pauls.

P L.J.FULLER, tql seated in robes, The Deanery, St Paul's, London.

PH WALTER STONEMAN, 1945, hl, NPG (NPR). WALTER BIRD, 1962, hs, NPG (NPR).

MAUD Charlotte Mary Victoria (1869-1938) youngest daughter of Edward VII and Queen of Norway.

P HEINRICH VON ANGELI, 1875, head, Royal Coll.

G H.VON ANGELI, 'Prince and Princess of Wales with Albert Victor and Maud', oil, 1876. Royal Coll. S.P.HALL, hs with sisters Louise and Victoria, oil, 1883, NPG 4471. LAURITS TUXEN, 'The Royal Family at the Time of the Jubilee', oil, 1887, Royal Coll. L.TUXEN, 'Marriage of King George V and Queen Mary', oil, 1893, Royal Coll. L.TUXEN, 'Marriage of Princess Maud and Prince Charles of Denmark', oil, 1896, Royal Coll.

SC MARY THORNYCROFT, 1877, marble statue with her sister Princess Victoria, Royal Coll.

PH Various photographs, singly and in groups, by BYRNE & CO, W. & D.DOWNEY, ROBERT MILNE, JOHN RUSSELL & SONS and others, NPG and Royal Coll.

MAUDE, Cyril (Francis) (1862-1951) actor-manager.

C SIR LESLIE WARD ('Spy'), wl, profile, lith, for Vanity Fair, 11 March 1897, NPG. HARRY FURNISS, 1905, wl, pen and ink, for The Garrick Gallery, NPG 4095(8).

PH ALFRED ELLIS, 1894, hs, print, NPG. ROTARY PHOTO, c1905, hs as Captain Barley, postcard, NPG. LENARE, 1942, as Sir Peter Teazle in School for Scandal, neg, NPG X903.

MAUDE, Sir (Frederick) Stanley (1864-1917) lieutenant-general.

G J.S.SARGENT, 'General Officers of World War I, 1914-18', oil, 1922, NPG 1954.

PH MAULL & FOX, tql in uniform, cabinet, NPG. UNKNOWN, hs in uniform, cabinet, NPG.

MAUFE, Sir Edward (1883-1974) architect.

P J.L.WHEATLEY, c1956, hl, NPG 5155.

PH HOWARD COSTER, hs, print, NPG X2012. WALTER STONEMAN, 1950, hs, NPG (NPR). Various photographs, RIBA.

MAUGHAM, Frederic Herbert Maugham, 1st Viscount (1866-1958) lord chancellor.

P R.G.EVES, c1939, tql, seated in robes, Lincoln's Inn, London. SIR GERALD KELLY, c1939, tql in robes, Trinity Hall, Cambridge. SIR G.KELLY, tql seated in uniform, Lincoln's Inn. SIR JAMES GUNN, c1954-58, seated, Althorp, Northants, study for Society of Dilettanti group.

G SIR J.GUNN, 'Society of Dilettanti Conversation Piece', oil, c1954-59, Society of Dilettanti, Brooks's Club, London.

PH WALTER STONEMAN, 1936, 2 hs portraits, the 1st in robes, NPG X4143 and NPG (NPR).

MAUGHAM, (William) Somerset (1874-1965) novelist and playwright.

P SIR GERALD KELLY, 1907, hl, University of Texas, Austin, USA. SIR G.KELLY, 1911, wl seated, 'The Jester', TATE 4703. PHILIP STEEGMAN, 1931, tql seated, NPG 4524. SIR G.KELLY, 1934, hl seated, University of Texas. GRAHAM SUTHERLAND, 1949, wl seated, TATE 6034. G.SUTHERLAND, c1954-55, hs, Beaverbrook Art Gallery, Fredericton, Canada. SIR G.KELLY, 1960, tql seated, University of Texas.

D G.SUTHERLAND, head, studies for oil portraits, Fitzwilliam Museum, Cambridge, and Beaverbrook Art Gallery. B.E.WENDKOS, 1956, pastel, University of Texas.

SC FRITZ BEHN, terracotta head, Musée de la Ville, Nice, France. SIR JACOB EPSTEIN, 1951, bronze cast of head, TATE 6132. I.R.JONES, 1963, plaster bust?, Beaverbrook Art Gallery. SALLY RYAN,

plaster head, Walsall Museum and Art Gallery.
PR H.A.FREETH, 1946, hs, etch, NPG. G.SUTHERLAND, lith, Maidstone Museum and Art Gallery.
C SIR DAVID LOW, c1934, several sketches, pencil, NPG 4529(235–40).
PH SIR CECIL BEATON, hs, print, NPG. HOWARD COSTER, 1930, various sizes, print and negs, NPG X2014–16, AX2317, AX3460, X4081 and others. MARK GERSON, 1955, hs, print, NPG. WALTER STONEMAN, 1955, hs, NPG (NPR). MADAME YEVONDE, 1955, tql and wl with two grandsons, 2 prints, NPG. DOROTHY WILDING, 1958, 3 hs portraits, prints, NPG.

MAURICE, Sir Frederick Barton (1871-1951) major-general.
P HENRY LAMB, Queen Mary College, London.
D SIR WILLIAM ROTHENSTEIN, 1922, hs, sanguine, NPG 4786.
PH WALTER STONEMAN, 2 hs portraits, the 1st in uniform, 1917 and 1936, NPG (NPR).

MAVOR, Osborne Henry (1888-1951) physician and playwright 'James Bridie'.
G STANLEY CURSITER, 'Authors in Session 1950', oil. Glasgow City Art Gallery
SC LORIS REY, bronze bust, University of Glasgow. BENNO SCHOTZ, terracotta head, Scottish Arts Council, Edinburgh.

MAWER, Sir Allen (1879-1942) scholar.
D P.A.DE LÁSZLÓ, 1935, hs, crayon, University College, London.
PH WALTER STONEMAN, 1938, hs, NPG (NPR).

MAXSE, Sir (Frederick) Ivor (1862-1958) general.
D FRANCIS DODD, 1917, charcoal and w/c, IWM.
PH WALTER STONEMAN, 1919, hs in uniform, NPG (NPR). G.C.BERESFORD, c1921, hs in uniform, print, NPG.

MAXTON, James (1885-1946) politician.
P SIR JOHN LAVERY, c1933, tql, SNPG 1416.
D EDMOND KAPP, 1930, Barber Institute, Birmingham University. EMMANUEL LEVY, 1936, hs, charcoal, NPG 5097.
C SIR DAVID LOW, c1933, several sketches, pencil, NPG 4529(241–44).
SC LADY KATHLEEN KENNET, c1930, bronze bust, Glasgow City Art Gallery. BENNO SCHOTZ, 1938, bronze bust, Glasgow City Art Gallery.
PH ASSOCIATED SCOTTISH NEWSPAPERS LTD, c1938, wl seated with Benno Schotz modelling his bust, print, NPG.

MAXWELL, William (1873-1957) printer.
PH HOWARD COSTER, 1928, various sizes, print and negs, NPG AX2301 and others.

MAY, George Ernest May, 1st Baron (1871-1946) financial expert.
PH WALTER STONEMAN, 2 hs portraits, 1918 and 1932, NPG (NPR).

MAY, Philip William ('Phil') (1864-1903) humorous draughtsman.
P SIR JAMES SHANNON, c1902, tql, TATE 3825.
D Self-portrait, c1894, tql seated at easel, profile, pen and ink, NPG 3038. P.F.SPENCE, 1895, hs, pencil, NPG 1184A. R.P.STAPLES, 1898, hs, profile, with model, chalk, NPG 1659.
SL Self-portrait, 1894, hs, profile, NPG 3941.
C SIR LESLIE WARD ('Spy'), wl seated, profile, lith, for Vanity Fair, 21 Feb 1895, NPG. Self-portrait, 1896, hs, pencil, V & A. Self-portrait, c1900, hs, profile, charcoal, Leeds City Art Gallery. Self-portrait, c1900, wl, profile, as toy soldier, pencil, NPG 2661. Self-portrait, 1901, tql, profile, pencil, NPG 4149. ARTHUR COLLINS, hs, profile, pen and ink, NPG 2751.
SC UNKNOWN, portrait plaque, Leeds City Art Gallery.
PH BASSANO, 1898, various sizes, 4 negs, NPG X4228–31.

MAYBURY, Sir Henry Percy (1864-1943) civil engineer.
P SIR OSWALD BIRLEY, 1934, tql, Institution of Civil Engineers, London.
PH WALTER STONEMAN, 1919, hs in uniform, NPG (NPR).

MAYER, Sir Robert (b1879) musical philanthropist and planner.
P DEREK HILL, c1970, hs, The Robert Mayer Hall, Royal College of Music, London.
SC SIR JACOB EPSTEIN, bronze bust, Royal Festival Hall, London. HANS FREIBUSCH, 1979, bronze bust, BBC, Broadcasting House, London.
PH WALTER STONEMAN, 1946, hs, NPG (NPR). WALTER BIRD, 1967, hs, NPG (NPR). Various photographs, Youth and Music Ltd, London. Various photographs, Royal College of Music.

MEES, C(harles) E(dward) Kenneth (1882-1960) photographic researcher.
PH WALTER STONEMAN, 1947, hs, NPG (NPR).

MELBA, Dame Nellie (1861-1931) opera singer.
SC SIR BERTRAM MACKENNAL, 1899, bust, National Gallery of Victoria, Melbourne, Australia.
PH RAPHAEL TUCK & SONS, c1904, tql, postcard, NPG. UNKNOWN, hl, profile, postcard, NPG.

MELCHETT, Alfred Moritz Mond, 1st Baron (1868-1930) industrialist, financier and politician.
P RICHARD VON MARIENTREU, c1955, after Sir John Lavery, 1929, tql seated, profile, Imperial Chemical Industries Ltd, London.
D EDMOND KAPP, 1929, Barber Institute, Birmingham University. SIR WILLIAM ROTHENSTEIN, 1929, head, sanguine, Imperial Chemical Industries Ltd, and NPG 4788.
C POWYS EVANS ('Quiz'), 1926, hl, profile, pen and ink, NPG 5062. SIR BERNARD PARTRIDGE, tql, w/c and pen and ink, for Punch Almanack, 1 Nov 1926, NPG.
PH WALTER STONEMAN, 1917, hs, NPG (NPR).

MELLANBY, Sir Edward (1884-1955) medical scientist and administrator.
D H.A.FREETH, 1946, chalk, IWM.
PH WALTER STONEMAN, 1931, hs, NPG (NPR).

MELLANBY, John (1878-1939) physiologist.
PH WALTER STONEMAN, 1930, hs, NPG (NPR).

MENDL, Sir Charles Ferdinand (1871-1958) press attaché.
PH WALTER STONEMAN, 1930, hs, NPG (NPR).

MENZIES, Sir Frederick Norton Kay (1875-1949) medical officer of health.
PH WALTER STONEMAN, 1947, hs, NPG (NPR).

MENZIES, Sir Stewart Graham (1890-1968) major-general and head of Britain's Secret Intelligence Service (later MI6).
PH WALTER STONEMAN, 1953, hs, NPG (NPR).

MERCER, James (1883-1932) mathematician.
PH WALTER STONEMAN?, hs, print, Royal Society, London.

MERRIMAN, Frank Boyd Merriman, Baron (1880-1962) solicitor-general.
PH WALTER STONEMAN, 1955, hs, NPG (NPR).

MERRY DEL VAL, Rafael (1865-1930) cardinal.
P B.GEORGIEV, The Vatican, Rome. F.D'IGNAZIO, The Vatican.

MERZ, Charles Hesterman (1874-1940) electrical engineer.
P ARNOLD MASON, 1944, Institution of Electrical Engineers, London.

MESSERVY, Sir Frank Walter (1893-1974) general.
P BERNARD HAILSTONE, 1945, IWM.
D THOMAS HENNELL, 1945, w/c, IWM.

PH WALTER STONEMAN, 1946, hs in uniform, NPG (NPR). GODFREY ARGENT, 1968, hs, NPG (NPR).

MESTON, James Scorgie Meston, 1st Baron (1865-1943) Indian civil servant.
P M.F.DE MONTMORENCY, National Liberal Club, London.
PH WALTER STONEMAN, 1917, hs, NPG (NPR).

METHUEN, Paul Ayshford Methuen, 4th Baron (1886-1974) painter and public servant.
P P.A.DE LÁSZLÓ, hs in uniform, Corsham Court, Wilts.
D Self-portrait, pencil, BM.
SC DAVID McFALL, c1956, bronze bust, Corsham Court.
PH WALTER STONEMAN, 2 hs portraits, 1938 and 1951, NPG (NPR).

MEYER, Sir William Stevenson (1860-1922) Indian civil servant.
C 'SPY JUNIOR', crayon, India House, London.
PH WALTER STONEMAN, 1919, hs, NPG (NPR).

MEYERSTEIN, Edward Harry William (1889-1952) poet.
P PHILIP CONNARD, 1928, hs, NPG 4326.

MEYNELL, Sir Francis (Meredith Wilfrid) (1891-1975) writer and book designer.
P SIR WILLIAM ORPEN, with the artist's wife, 'The Chess Players', Ashmolean Museum, Oxford.

MIÉVILLE, Sir Eric Charles (1896-1971) assistant private secretary to King George VI.
G JOHN WARD, 'Directors of Westminster Bank, 1968', line and wash, 1969, National Westminster Bank, London.
PH WALTER STONEMAN, 1936, hs, NPG (NPR).

MILFORD, Sir Humphrey Sumner (1877-1952) publisher.
PH Several photographs, Oxford University Press, London.

MILL, Hugh Robert (1861-1950) geographer and meteorologist.
PH UNKNOWN, c1930, hs, print, Royal Geographical Society, London. UNKNOWN, c1930, hl in his garden, print, Royal Geographical Society. DEBENHAM & GOULD, c1930, hl seated, print and neg, Scott Polar Research Institute, University of Cambridge. UNKNOWN, c1940, hl, print, Scott Institute.

MILLAR, Gertie (1879-1952) actress.
PR HOWARD VAN DUSEN & HASSALL, hs and wl, lith, NPG.
PH Various postcards, NPG.

MILLER, Sir James Percy, 2nd Bart (1864-1906) sportsman.
C LIBERIO PROSPERI ('Lib'), wl, profile, lith, for *Vanity Fair*, 6 Sept 1890.

MILLIGAN, Sir William (1864-1929) laryngologist and otologist.
D WILLIAM WEATHERBY, w/c, Manchester City Art Gallery.

MILLS, Bertram Wagstaff (1873-1938) circus proprietor.
PH HOWARD COSTER, various sizes, print and 3 negs, NPG X2029 and others.

MILLS, Sir Percy Herbert Mills, 1st Viscount (1890-1968) politician.
PH WALTER STONEMAN, 1950, hs, NPG (NPR). WALTER BIRD, 1961, hs, NPG (NPR).

MILLS, William Hobson (1873-1959) organic chemist.
D RANDOLPH SCHWABE, 1945, pencil, Jesus College, Cambridge.
PH WALTER STONEMAN, 2 hs portraits, 1924 and 1943, NPG (NPR).

MILNE, Alan Alexander (1882-1956) author, playwright and journalist.
D HARRY FURNISS, c1910?, hs, pen and ink, NPG 3493. POWYS EVANS, c1930, hs, pen and ink, NPG 4399. HOMER EARL, 1952,

crayon and chalk, University of Texas, Austin, USA.
C H.FURNISS, c1910?, wl seated, profile, pen and ink, NPG 3494.
PH HOWARD COSTER, 1926, various sizes, prints and negs, some with son Christopher Robin, NPG X2030 and others.

MILNE, Edward Arthur (1896-1950) mathematician and natural philosopher.
PH WALTER STONEMAN, 2 hs portraits, 1943 and 1945, NPG (NPR).

MILNE, George Francis Milne, 1st Baron (1866-1948) field-marshal.
P J.S.SARGENT, c1922, hs in uniform, SNPG 1012, study for 'Generals', NPG 1954. MAURICE CODNER, 1936, tql in uniform, IWM.
G J.S.SARGENT, 'General Officers of World War I, 1914-18', oil, 1922, NPG 1954.
PH WALTER STONEMAN, 2 hs portraits in uniform, 1920 and 1931, NPG (NPR) and NPG X494. OLIVE EDIS, 1920, wl, autochrome, NPG X7198. O.EDIS, c1926?, 2 hs portraits in uniform, prints, NPG.

MILNE-WATSON, Sir David Milne, 1st Bart (1869-1945) businessman.
P After SIR JAMES GUNN, hl seated, North Thames Gas Board, Staines, Middx. HAROLD KNIGHT, c1937, hl seated, North Thames Gas.
SC ERIC SCHILSKY, c1940, bronze bust, British Gas Corporation, Watson House, Fulham, London. UNKNOWN, bronze bust, North Thames Gas.

MILNER of Leeds, James Milner, 1st Baron (1889-1967) politician.
PH WALTER STONEMAN, 1949, hs, NPG (NPR).

MILNER-WHITE, Eric (1884-1963) dean of York.
D H.A.FREETH, 1954, hs, King's College, Cambridge. W.GARROD, King's College.

MISSENDEN, Sir Eustace James (1886-1973) chairman of the Railway Executive.
PH UNKNOWN, c1948, hl seated, print, NPG.

MITCHELL, Sir Peter Chalmers (1864-1945) zoologist.
P SIR WILLIAM NICHOLSON, 1935, tql seated, Zoological Society of London.
PH HOWARD COSTER, 1930s, hs, 5 negs, NPG X10724-28. WALTER STONEMAN, 1935, hs, NPG (NPR).

MITCHELL, Sir William Gore Sutherland (1888-1944) air chief marshal.
PH WALTER STONEMAN, 1938, hl in uniform, for NPR, NPG X495.

MOBERLY, Sir Walter (Hamilton) (1881-1974) educationist and vice-chancellor of Manchester University.
PH WALTER STONEMAN, 1933, hs, profile, NPG (NPR). SELBY WHITTINGHAM, 1973, wl with Lady Moberly, print, NPG.

MOERAN, Ernest John (1894-1950) composer.
PH HOWARD COSTER, 1930s, various sizes and negs, NPG.

MOFFATT, James (1870-1944) divine and Biblical scholar.
PH OLIVE EDIS, hl seated, print, NPG.

MOFFET, Joseph (1885-1962) minister of the Crown Court Church of Scotland.
P SIR W.O.HUTCHISON, 1953, hs, Crown Court Church of Scotland, London.

MONASH, Sir John (1865-1931) Australian general.
P SIR JOHN LONGSTAFF, 1918, Australian War Memorial, Canberra. JAMES QUINN, c1919, Australian War Memorial. I.M.COHEN, c1920, wl, National Gallery of Victoria, Melbourne.
G J.S.SARGENT, 'General Officers of World War I, 1914-18', oil, 1922, NPG 1954.

c PAUL MONTFORD, bronze bust, Australian War Memorial.

H WALTER STONEMAN, 1918, hs in uniform, NPG (NPR).

MONCKTON, Sir Walter Turner Monckton, 1st Viscount (1891-1965) statesman.

P SIR JAMES GUNN, 1959, tql, Midland Bank Ltd, Poultry, London.

c SIR DAVID LOW, several heads, pencil, NPG 4529(250–52).

H SIR CECIL BEATON, hl seated in robes, print, NPG. WALTER STONEMAN, 1953, hs, NPG (NPR).

MOND, Alfred Moritz, see 1st Baron Melchett.

MOND, Sir Robert Ludwig (1867-1938) chemist, industrialist and archaeologist.

P F.O.SALISBURY, c1920, Westminster Hospital, London.

H WALTER STONEMAN, 1938, hs, NPG (NPR).

MONRO, Sir Charles Carmichael, Bart (1860-1929) general.

H WALTER STONEMAN, 1921, hs in uniform, NPG (NPR).

MONRO, Harold Edward (1879-1932) poet, editor and bookseller.

D JACOB KRAMER, 1923, head, ink and chalk, NPG 4705.

MONRO, Sir Horace Cecil (1861-1949) civil servant.

H WALTER STONEMAN, 1917, hs, NPG (NPR).

MONSELL, Bolton Meredith Eyres-Monsell, 1st Viscount (1881-1969) politician and first lord of the admiralty.

H FAYER, hs, print, NPG.

MONTAGU, Edwin Samuel (1879-1924) statesman.

G SIR WILLIAM ORPEN, 'The Signing of Peace in the Hall of Mirrors, Versailles, 1919', oil, IWM.

c LADY KATHLEEN KENNET, statue, Calcutta, India.

MONTAGU, George Charles, see 9th Earl of Sandwich.

MONTAGU of Beaulieu, John Walter Edward Douglas-Scott-Montagu, 2nd Baron (1866-1929) pioneer of motoring.

P JOHN COLLIER, c1921–22, tql in uniform, Palace House, Beaulieu, Hants.

D E.U.EDDIS, 1870, hl with musket, chalk, Palace House. SIR L.WARD, 1900, tql seated, Palace House.

c LADY WELBY, bronze bust, Palace House, Beaulieu.

c SIR LESLIE WARD ('Spy'), wl, lith, for *Vanity Fair*, 8 Oct 1896, NPG.

H WALTER STONEMAN, 1917, hs in uniform, NPG (NPR).

MONTAGUE, Charles Edward (1867-1928) man of letters and journalist.

D UNKNOWN, chalk, The Guardian, London.

MONTGOMERY of Alamein, Bernard Law Montgomery, 1st Viscount (1887-1976) field-marshal.

P AUGUSTUS JOHN, 1944, hs in uniform, Hunterian Museum and Art Gallery, University of Glasgow. F.O.SALISBURY, 1945, tql in uniform with map of Europe, NPG L165. JOHN WORSLEY, 1946, IWM. SIR OSWALD BIRLEY, 1948, tql seated in uniform, IWM. DWIGHT D.EISENHOWER, 1952, hs in uniform, DoE (British Embassy, Washington). DENNIS FILDES, 1956, tql in uniform, St Paul's School, London. TERENCE CUNEO, c1972, hl in battle dress, Staff College, Camberley.

D SYDNEY MORSE-BROWN, 1943, pencil, IWM. ANTHONY GROSS, 1944, pen and wash, IWM. J.B.STAFFORD-BAKER, 1945, w/c, IWM.

c OSCAR NEMON, c1976, bronze statuette, IWM. O.NEMON, 1980, bronze statue, Whitehall, London.

H WALTER STONEMAN, 2 hs portraits, the 2nd in uniform, 1939 and 1947, NPG (NPR) and NPG x4647. MARK GERSON, 1967, hl seated, print, NPG. GODFREY ARGENT, 1969, 2 hs portraits, NPG (NPR). Various photographs, IWM.

MONTGOMERY-MASSINGBERD, Sir Archibald Armar (1871-1947) field-marshal.

P SIR OSWALD BIRLEY, Gunby Hall (NT), Lincs. F.E.HODGE, Gunby Hall.

PH WALTER STONEMAN, 2 hs portraits in uniform, 1922 and 1933, NPG (NPR).

MOODY, Harold Arundel (1882-1947) medical practitioner and founder of the League of Coloured Peoples.

SC RONALD MOODY, bronze bust, London Missionary Society.

MOORE, George Edward (1873-1958) philosopher.

D PERCY HORTON, 1947, head, chalk, Trinity College, Cambridge. P.HORTON, 1947, 2 heads, pencil, pen and chalk, NPG 4087 and NPG 4135. H.A.FREETH, 1952, hs, pen and wash, Fitzwilliam Museum, Cambridge, related etch, 1952, NPG.

PH WALTER STONEMAN, 2 hs portraits, 1921 and 1945, NPG (NPR).

MOORE, Henry Charles Ponsonby, see 10th Earl of Drogheda.

MOORE, Sir Henry Monck-Mason (1887-1964) colonial governor.

PH WALTER STONEMAN, 1934, hs, profile, and hl in uniform, NPG x4667 and NPG (NPR).

MOORE, Sir Henry Ruthven (1886-1978) admiral.

PH WALTER STONEMAN, 3 hs portraits in uniform, 1940, 1942 and 1953, NPG (NPR) and NPG x4144.

MOORE, Henry (b1898) sculptor.

P R.J.COXON, 1924, hs, Manchester City Art Gallery.

D DAVID HOCKNEY, 1972, hl seated, pen and ink, Café Royal, London.

SC MARINO MARINI, 1969, bronze cast of head, NPG 4687. JEAN FRASER, 1973, life-size wax figure, Madame Tussauds Ltd, London. FRED KORMIS, 1978, plaster model for medallion portrait and bronze cast, Fitzwilliam Museum, Cambridge.

c SIR DAVID LOW, several sketches, pencil, NPG 4529(253–56).

PH SIR CECIL BEATON, hs, print, NPG. HOWARD COSTER, 1930s, various sizes, prints and negs, NPG x2037–39 and x11229–40. MARK GERSON, 1960, hs, print, NPG. WALTER BIRD, 1963, hs, NPG (NPR). J.S.LEWINSKI, 1964, hs, print, NPG. GODFREY ARGENT, 1970, hl, NPG (NPR). ARNOLD NEWMAN, 1978, hl seated, print, NPG.

MOORE, Mary, see Lady Wyndham.

MOORE, Thomas Sturge (1870-1944) poet and wood engraver.

D C.H.SHANNON, 1925, head, profile, chalk, NPG 4130.

PR C.H.SHANNON, 'The Modeller', 2 liths, Carlisle City Art Gallery.

PH G.C.BERESFORD, hs as young man, print, NPG. HECTOR MURCHISON, hs, print, NPG. WALTER STONEMAN, 1932, hs, NPG (NPR).

MOORE-BRABAZON, John Theodore, see 1st Baron Brabazon of Tara.

MORANT, Sir Robert Laurie (1863-1920) civil servant.

PH UNKNOWN, hs, print, NPG.

MORGAN, Charles Langbridge (1894-1958) novelist, critic and playwright.

D AUGUSTUS JOHN, 1944, head, chalk, NPG 4472.

PH HOWARD COSTER, 1934 and 1955, various sizes, prints and negs, NPG AX3504, X2042 and X10671–72. WALTER STONEMAN, 1948, hs, NPG (NPR). MARK GERSON, 1954, hs, print, NPG. ROGER MORGAN, 1950s, hs, profile, print, NPG. UNKNOWN, 1950s, hs, print, NPG.

MORISON, Stanley Arthur (1889-1967) typographer, scholar and historian of the press.

P ROBERT LUTYENS, Times Newspapers Ltd, London.

D R.LUTYENS, wash, Garrick Club, London. SIR WILLIAM ROT-
HENSTEIN, 1924, hl, charcoal, Cambridge University Press.
PR R.LUTYENS, *c*1961–62, hl seated at dinner, one of set of 'Old
Burgundians', type of lith, NPG.

MORISON, Sir Theodore (1863-1936) educationist and
writer.
P HAROLD KNIGHT, 1925, University of Newcastle-upon-Tyne.
T.B.GARVIE, 1930, University of Newcastle.
PH JOHN RUSSELL & SONS, *c*1915, hs, profile, print, for *National
Photographic Record*, vol 1, NPG.

MORLAND, Sir Thomas Lethbridge Napier (1865-1925)
general.
D FRANCIS DODD, 1917, charcoal and w/c, IWM.

MORLEY, Sir James Wycliffe Headlam-, see Headlam-
Morley.

MORLEY HORDER, Percy (Richard), see Horder.

MORRELL, Lady Ottoline Violet Anne (1873-1938)
patron of the arts.
P DUNCAN GRANT, *c*1913–14, hs, Leicestershire Museums and Art
Galleries, Leicester. SIMON BUSSY, *c*1920, head, profile, NPG L137.
D AUGUSTUS JOHN, chalk and wash, study for portrait, Manchester
City Art Gallery. HENRY LAMB, *c*1912, hs, pencil, NPG 4254.
PH SIR CECIL BEATON, tql, print, NPG. Various photographs, NPG
(Strachey Coll).

MORRIS, Alfred Edwin (1894-1971) archbishop of Wales.
P UNKNOWN, St David's University College, Lampeter, Wales.
PH WALTER BIRD, 1962, hl seated, NPG (NPR).

MORRIS, May (1863-1938) writer and craftswoman.
D SIR EDWARD BURNE-JONES, profile, pencil, V & A. D.G.ROSSETTI,
1871, hs, chalk, Kelmscott manor (Society of Antiquaries of
London), Glos. SIR WILLIAM ROTHENSTEIN, 1897, hl, profile,
silverpoint, NPG 3049.
G SIR E.BURNE-JONES, 'The Golden Stairs', model for 8th maiden,
oil, 1880, TATE 4005.
PH FREDERICK HOLLYER, 5 hl portraits, cabinet, NPG. Various cartes
and snapshots, singly and in groups, NPG.

MORRIS, Sir William Richard, see 1st Viscount Nuffield.

MORRIS-JONES, Sir John (1864-1929) Welsh poet and
grammarian.
SC R.L.GAPPER, University Library, Bangor.

MORRISON, William Shepherd, see 1st Viscount
Dunrossil.

**MORRISON of Lambeth, Herbert Stanley Morrison,
Baron (1888-1965)** statesman.
D JULIET PANNETT, 1961, hs, chalk, NPG 4476.
C SIR DAVID LOW, chalk, NPG 4559; study sketch, head, pencil,
NPG 4529(257). SIR BERNARD PARTRIDGE, wl, pen and ink, for
Punch, 30 Jan 1935, NPG.
PH WALTER STONEMAN, 1941, hs, NPG (NPR). HOWARD COSTER, 1953,
various sizes, print and negs, NPG X2043–51 and others. WALTER
BIRD, 1961, hl, NPG (NPR).

MORTON, Henry Canova Vollam ('H.V.') (1892-1979)
writer and journalist.
PH HOWARD COSTER, 1930s and 1950s, various sizes, prints and negs,
NPG AX3470, X3395–3400 and X10147–49. Various photographs,
NPG (*Daily Herald*).

**MORTON, John Cameron Andrieu Bingham Michael
('J.B.') (1893-1979)** journalist.
PH HOWARD COSTER, 1933, various sizes, print and negs, NPG AX3470
and others.

**MORTON of Henryton, Fergus Dunlop Morton, Baron
(1887-1973)** lord of appeal.
PH WALTER STONEMAN, 2 hs portraits, 1938 and 1954, NPG (NPR).
WALTER BIRD, 1962, hl, NPG (NPR).

MOSLEY, Sir Oswald (Ernald), 6th Bart (*b*1896) politician.
C SIR MAX BEERBOHM, 1931, tql, drg, The Spectator, London, lith,
NPG.
PH WALTER STONEMAN, 1931, hs, NPG (NPR). Various photographs,
NPG (*Daily Herald*).

**MOTTISTONE, Henry John Alexander Seely, 2nd Baron
(1899-1963)** architect.
PH HOWARD COSTER, 1934, tql, print, NPG AX3496. WALTER
STONEMAN, 1945, hs, NPG (NPR).

**MOTTISTONE, John Edward Bernard Seely, 1st Baron
(1868-1947)** politician and soldier.
P SIR A.J.MUNNINGS, wl in uniform on horseback, National
Gallery of Canada, Ottawa, Ontario. SIR WILLIAM ORPEN, 1918,
IWM.
C SIR LESLIE WARD ('Spy'), wl, profile, w/c study for *Vanity Fair*,
23 Feb 1905, NPG 2967.
PH WALTER STONEMAN, 1924, hs in uniform, NPG (NPR).

MOTTRAM, Ralph Hale (1883-1971) novelist.
PH HOWARD COSTER, 1930s, various sizes and negs, NPG.

MOULE, Arthur Christopher (1873-1957) professor of
Chinese language and history.
D H.A.FREETH, 1947, wl, pen and wash, Institute of Oriental
Studies, University of Cambridge. H.A.FREETH, 1947, pen and
wash, Trinity College, Cambridge.

MOULLIN, Eric Balliol (1893-1963) electrical engineer.
PH UNKNOWN, *c*1949–50, hs, print, Institution of Electrical Engineers, London.

**MOUNTBATTEN of Burma, Louis Mountbatten, Earl
(1900-1979)** admiral.
P P.A.DE LÁSZLÓ, 1925, hs in uniform, Broadlands, Hants.
BERNARD HAILSTONE, *c*1944–45, tql in uniform, IWM. SIR
OSWALD BIRLEY, 1946, hs in uniform, Royal Naval College,
Greenwich; and tql, Broadlands. E.I.HALLIDAY, *c*1949, wl in state
robes, Government House, New Delhi, India. F.O.SALISBURY,
1957, tql in uniform, DoE (British Embassy, Rangoon). JOHN
ULBRICHT, 1968, head, NPG 4617. GEORGE LONN, 1972, hs in
uniform, Broadlands. JOHN GILROY, 1978, hl seated in uniform,
Royal Marines Museum, Southsea, Hants. CARLOS SANCHA,
1978, hl, Trinity House, London; and wl, Broadlands.
PH OLIVE EDIS, 1920, 3 hs portraits, 2 autochromes and 1 print, NPG
X7199 and X8004. MADAME YEVONDE, 1922, hl seated with
Edwina Ashley, engagement portrait, print, NPG. DOROTHY
WILDING, 1930s, hs in uniform, print, NPG. MADAME YEVONDE,
1937, wl in coronation robes, colour print, NPG. WALTER
STONEMAN, 3 hs portraits in uniform, 1939, 1942 and 1955, NPG
(NPR). SIR CECIL BEATON, 1940s, hl in uniform, print, NPG.
HOWARD COSTER, *c*1944–45, various sizes, print and negs, NPG
X2072 and others. ARNOLD NEWMAN, 1978, tql in uniform, print,
NPG. Various photographs, Broadlands.

**MOUNTEVANS, Edward Ratcliffe Garth Russell Evans,
1st Baron (1880-1957)** admiral.
P SYDNEY MORSE-BROWN, 1937, hs, National Museum of Wales
475, Cardiff.
PH WALTER STONEMAN, 1947, hl in uniform, NPG (NPR). Various
photographs, Scott Polar Research Institute, University of
Cambridge.

MOUNT TEMPLE, Wilfrid William Ashley, Baron

(1867-1938) politician.
P EDWARD CLIFFORD, c1874, Broadlands, Hants. EMIL FUCHS, 1904, tql, Broadlands. MRS BLAKENEY WARD, Broadlands.
D EVA SAWYER, crayon, Broadlands.
PH WALTER STONEMAN, 2 hs portraits, 1917 and 1927, NPG (NPR). Various photographs, Broadlands.

MOYNE, Walter Edward Guinness, 1st Baron (1880-1944) statesman and traveller.
PH WALTER STONEMAN, 4 hs portraits, 1919, 1929, 1939 and 1941, NPG (NPR).

MOYNIHAN, Berkeley George Andrew Moynihan, 1st Baron (1865-1936) surgeon.
P RICHARD JACK, 1927, tql seated in robes, Leeds General Infirmary; copy, Royal College of Surgeons, London.
G MOUSSA AYOUB, 'Members of the Council of Royal College of Surgeons, 1926-27', oil, 1927-29, Royal College of Surgeons.
SC SIR W.R.DICK, marble bust, Leeds General Infirmary. F.J.WILCOXSON, 1926, marble bust, Royal College of Surgeons; another, bronze, Leeds Medical School.
PH WALTER STONEMAN, 1929, hs, NPG (NPR).

MUIR, Edwin (1887-1959) writer.
G STANLEY CURSITER, 'Authors in Session, 1950', oil, Glasgow City Art Gallery.
SC MAREK SZWARC, bust, Saltire Society, Edinburgh.
PH HOWARD COSTER, various sizes and negs, NPG. MARK GERSON, 1955, hl seated, print, NPG.

MUIR, Sir Robert (1864-1959) pathologist.
P G.FIDDES WATT, 1931, University of Glasgow.
SC G.H.PAULIN, bust, Pathological Institute, University of Glasgow.
PH WALTER STONEMAN, 1932, NPG (NPR).

MUNNINGS, Sir Alfred James (1878-1959) painter and PRA.
P Self-portrait, 1930, wl with Lady Munnings who is mounted on Master Munn, Sir Alfred Munnings Art Museum, Castle House, Dedham, Essex.
D JOHN GILROY, hl, Garrick Club, London. Self-portrait, wl, ink, NPG 4136. Self-portrait, 2 portraits, pen and ink and pencil, V & A. A.R.THOMSON, with Augustus John and Sir William Orpen, ink, The Athenaeum, London.
SC FRANK KOVACKS, c1948, plaster medallion, NPG 4120, and bronze cast, NPG 4120A.
PH A.C.COOPER, 1945, 2 hs portraits, prints, NPG. PAUL LAIB, wl seated at easel with his dog, print, NPG.

MUNNINGS, Hilda, see Lydia Sokolova.

MUNRO, Robert, see 1st Baron Alness.

MUNRO-FERGUSON, Ronald Crauford, see 1st Viscount Novar.

MURRAY, Sir Archibald James (1860-1945) general.
PH WALTER STONEMAN, 1919, hs in uniform, NPG (NPR).

MURRAY, Sir (George) Evelyn (Pemberton) (1880-1947) civil servant.
PH WALTER STONEMAN, 1930, hs, NPG (NPR).

MURRAY, (George) Gilbert (Aimé) (1866-1957) classicist and man of letters.
P F.A.NEWBERY, c1924, tql seated, on loan to the University of Glasgow. L.L.TOYNBEE, 1950, hl seated, NPG 4037. L.L.TOYNBEE, 1954, hl, Library of the Prime Minister's Office, Canberra, Australia.
D EDMOND KAPP, 1928, Barber Institute, Birmingham University. FRANCIS DODD, c1939, tql, charcoal, St John's College, Oxford. H.A.FREETH, 1950s, University of Leicester. AUGUSTUS JOHN, 1957, head, chalk, NPG 4170.
SC MELNIKOFF, bronze head, National Liberal Club.
PR SIR WILLIAM ROTHENSTEIN, hl, lith, NPG.
PH G.C.BERESFORD, 1916, 4 hs portraits, prints and neg, NPG X6549 and others. OLIVE EDIS, hs, print, NPG. WALTER STONEMAN, 1917, hs, NPG (NPR). UNKNOWN, 1934, hs profile, photogravure, NPG.

MURRAY, Sir John (1884-1967) publisher.
PH WALTER STONEMAN, 1932, hs, NPG (NPR).

MURRAY, Margaret Alice (1863-1963) Egyptologist.
SC STEPHEN RICKARD, c1965, bronze bust, Department of Egyptology, University College, London.
PH Various photographs, Department of Egyptology, University College.

MURRAY, Sir Oswyn Alexander Ruthven (1873-1936) civil servant.
PH WALTER STONEMAN, 1920, hs, NPG (NPR).

MURRY, John Middleton (1889-1957) author.
PH HOWARD COSTER, 1934, various sizes, print and negs, NPG AX3503 and others.

MURRY, Kathleen (1888-1923) writer 'Katherine Mansfield'.
P A.E.RICE, 1920?, hl, National Art Gallery, Wellington, New Zealand.

MYERS, Charles Samuel (1873-1946) psychologist.
PH WALTER STONEMAN, 1933, hs, profile, NPG (NPR).

MYERS, Leopold Hamilton (1881-1944) novelist.
D SIR WILLIAM ROTHENSTEIN, c1936, head, sanguine and chalk, NPG 4790.
PH MRS EVELYN MYERS, c1892, hs with his father, photogravure, NPG. MRS E.MYERS, 1892, hs, print, NPG. HOWARD COSTER, 1930s, various sizes and negs, NPG.

MYRDDIN-EVANS, Sir Guildhaume (1894-1964) chairman of the International Labour Organization.
PH WALTER STONEMAN, 1949, hs, NPG (NPR).

MYRES, Sir John Linton (1869-1954) archaeologist and historian.
D ALBERT RUTHERSTON, pencil, New College, Oxford. A.RUTHERSTON, School of Geography, Oxford University.
PH WALTER STONEMAN, 2 hs portraits, 1923 and 1930, NPG (NPR).

N

NAIRNE, Alexander (1863-1936) scholar, theologian and mystic.
D FRANCIS DODD, c1934, hs, Jesus College, Cambridge.

NAPIER, Sir Trevylyan Dacres Willes (1867-1920) vice-admiral.
D FRANCIS DODD, 1917, charcoal and w/c, IWM.
G SIR A.S.COPE, 'Naval Officers of World War I, 1914-18', oil, 1921, NPG 1913.
PH WALTER STONEMAN, 1919, hs in uniform, NPG (NPR).

NASH, John Northcote (1893-1977) artist.
D PETER COKER, hs, pencil and chalk, NPG CP16.
PH EDWARD MORGAN, 1970, tql and wl, prints, NPG X1596-97. S.S.WALIA, hs, print, NPG X1522.

NASH, Paul (1889-1946) artist.
D RUPERT LEE, 1913, head, profile, pencil, NPG 4134.
PH FELIX MAN, 1943, various sizes, prints, NPG X11804-07. HELEN MUSPRATT, hs, print, NPG X4085. RAMSEY & MUSPRATT, 2 hl portraits, prints, NPG X4086-87. LANCE SIEVELING, hs, snapshot, NPG X4090. Various prints by unknown photographers, NPG X4084, X4088, X4089, X4091.

NASMITH, Sir Martin (Eric) Dunbar- (1883-1965) admiral.
P AMBROSE MCEVOY, 1918, IWM. A.D.WALES-SMITH, after a photograph, tql seated in uniform, NMM, Greenwich.
PH WALTER STONEMAN, 3 hs portraits in uniform, 1931, 1942 and 1955, NPG (NPR).

NATHAN, Harry Louis Nathan, 1st Baron (1889-1963) politician.
PH WALTER STONEMAN, 1943, hs in uniform, NPG (NPR). WALTER BIRD, 1959, hs, NPG (NPR).

NATHAN, Sir Matthew (1862-1939) soldier and civil servant.
PH WALTER STONEMAN, 2 hs portraits, 1920 and 1931, NPG (NPR).

NEALE, Sir John Ernest (1890-1975) Elizabethan scholar.
PH WALTER STONEMAN, 1949, hs, NPG (NPR).

NEILL, Alexander Sutherland (1883-1973) child psychologist and writer.
P ISHBEL MCWHIRTER, 1964, wl seated, Summerhill School, Leiston, Suffolk.
D I.MCWHIRTER, 1965, hs, ink, NPG 5111.
SC ALAN THORNHILL, bronze head, SNPG 2204.

NEILSON, Julia Emilie, Mrs Fred Terry (1868-1957) actress.
PR CHARLES BUCHEL & HASSALL, hs and wl, lith, NPG.
C SIR MAX BEERBOHM, hs, pencil and pen, V & A.
PH Various prints, cabinets, postcards, some in character, by BARRAUD, W. & D.DOWNEY, ALFRED ELLIS, SARONY and MADAME YEVONDE, NPG.

NEILSON-TERRY, Phyllis (1892-1977) actress.
P CHARLES BUCHEL, 1909, tql, Royal Academy of Music, London.
PH MRS ALBERT BROOM, theatrical group, neg, NPG X1141. ALEXANDER CORBETT, tql seated at piano, print, NPG X3828. ELLIS & WALERY, hs, profile, postcard, NPG X4873. UNKNOWN, wl seated at piano with Frank Freeman, in character, print, NPG X3827.

NELSON, Sir Frank (1883-1966) head of the Special Operations Executive.
PH ELLIOTT & FRY, hs, print, NPG.

NELSON of Stafford, Sir George (Horatio) Nelson, 1st Baron (1887-1962) businessman.
PH WALTER STONEMAN, 2 hs portraits, 1947 and 1958, NPG (NPR).

NETHERSOLE, Olga (Isabel) (1870?-1951) actress and theatre manager.
PH W. & D.DOWNEY, tql, print, NPG. ALFRED ELLIS, 1894, hl, print, NPG. ROTARY PHOTO, tql seated, postcard, NPG.

NEVINSON, Christopher Richard Wynne (1889-1946) artist.
P Self-portrait, 1911, hs, NPG L151.
SL HUBERT LESLIE, 1936, hs, profile, NPG.
PH HOWARD COSTER, 1935, various sizes, prints and negs, NPG X2056-57 and others.

NEVINSON, Evelyn, Mrs Henry Woodd Nevinson, see Sharp.

NEWALL, Dame Bertha Surtees, Mrs Hugh Frank Newall, see Phillpotts.

NEWALL, Cyril Louis Norton Newall, 1st Baron (1886-1963) air marshal.
P R.G.EVES, 1940, hs in uniform, NPG 4356; version?, IWM.
PH SIR CECIL BEATON, 1942, hl, print, NPG.

NEWBERRY, Percy Edward (1869-1949) Egyptologist.
G ALBERT LIPCZINSKI, staff group, oil, 1915, Faculty of Arts, University of Liverpool.

NEWBOLD, Sir Douglas (1894-1945) civil secretary to the Sudan government.
P UNKNOWN, posthumous, Newbold memorial Library, University College, Khartoum.

NEWBOLT, Sir Henry John (1862-1938) poet.
P MEREDITH FRAMPTON, 1931, tql seated, NPG 4664.
D WILLIAM STRANG, 1897, hl, pencil, TATE 2079. EDMOND KAPP, 1913, Barber Institute, Birmingham University.
SC THEODORE SPICER-SIMSON, c1922, plasticine medallion, NPG 2054.
PR W.STRANG, c1898, tql seated, etch, NPG.
PH WALTER STONEMAN, 1917, hs, NPG (NPR). UNKNOWN, hs, profile, print, NPG.

NEWMAN, Sir George (1870-1948) pioneer in public and child health.
P MARGARET LINDSAY WILLIAMS, c1935, hl, London School of Hygiene and Tropical Medicine.
PH WALTER STONEMAN, 1918, hs, NPG (NPR).

NEWSAM, Sir Frank (Aubrey) (1893-1964) civil servant.
PH WALTER STONEMAN, 2 hs portraits, 1943 and 1954, NPG (NPR).

NEWTON, Algernon (1880-1968) painter.
PH WALTER STONEMAN, 1950, hs, NPG (NPR).

NICHOLS, (John) Beverley (b1898?) author and composer.
PH SIR CECIL BEATON, 1920s, tql seated, print, NPG. HOWARD COSTER, 1929, various sizes, print and negs, NPG AX2273, AX2346 and X10582-613. GODFREY ARGENT, 1969, hs and hl, profile, NPG

(NPR).

NICHOLS, Robert Malise Bowyer (1893-1944) poet.
D AUGUSTUS JOHN, 1921, hs, chalk, NPG 3825.

NICHOLSON, Ben (b1894) artist.
G SIR WILLIAM ORPEN, 'A Bloomsbury Family', oil, 1907, Scottish National Gallery of Modern Art, Edinburgh.
PH BILL BRANDT, 1956, print, Museum of Modern Art, New York. H.SPENDER, hl reflected in mirror, print, NPG P42.

NICHOLSON, Charles Ernest (1868-1954) yacht designer.
C 'OWL', wl, profile, mechanical repro, for *Vanity Fair*, 13 Aug 1913, NPG.

NICHOLSON, Reynold Alleyne (1868-1945) orientalist.
PH WALTER STONEMAN, 2 hs portraits, 1922 and 1930, NPG (NPR).

NICHOLSON, Sir Sydney Hugo (1875-1947) organist, church musician and founder of the Royal School of Church Music.
PH G.C.BERESFORD, 1922, hs, neg, NPG X6551. WALTER STONEMAN, 1940, hs, NPG (NPR).

NICHOLSON, Sir William Newzam Prior (1872-1949) artist.
P AUGUSTUS JOHN, c1914?, wl seated, Fitzwilliam Museum, Cambridge. DIANA LOW, c1934, wl reclining, Wolverhampton Art Gallery.
D D.MORRIS, 1914, hs, pencil, Whitworth Art Gallery, University of Manchester.
G SIR WILLIAM ORPEN, 'A Bloomsbury Family', oil, 1907, Scottish National Gallery of Modern Art, Edinburgh. SIR W.ORPEN, group in the Café Royal, oil, 1911-12, Musée d'Art Moderne, Paris; copy, Café Royal, London.
C SIR MAX BEERBOHM, w/c, Castle Museum, Nottingham.
PH A.L.COBURN, 1908, hs, profile, photogravure, NPG AX7787. A.C.COOPER, 1943, 2 hs portraits, prints, NPG X11841-42.

NICOLSON, Sir Harold (George) (1886-1968) diplomat and writer.
PH HOWARD COSTER, 1930s, various sizes, prints and negs, NPG X2059-60, X2371 and others. WALTER STONEMAN, 1955, hs, NPG (NPR).

NICOLSON, Vita, Mrs Harold Nicolson, see Sackville-West.

NIEMEYER, Sir Otto (Ernst) (1883-1971) director of the Bank of England.
PH WALTER STONEMAN, 1937, hs, NPG (NPR).

NOBLE, Sir Percy Lockhart Harnam (1880-1955) admiral.
P SIR OSWALD BIRLEY, c1945-48, hs in uniform, Royal Naval College, Greenwich.
D JAN ROSCIWEWSKI, pen and ink, IWM.
PH WALTER STONEMAN, 1942, hs in uniform, NPG (NPR).

NOEL-BAKER, Philip John Noel-Baker, Baron (b1889) politician and Nobel peace prize winner.
PH HOWARD COSTER, 1930s, various sizes and negs, NPG X2677-81. WALTER STONEMAN, 1947, hs, NPG (NPR). WALTER BIRD, 1963, hs, NPG (NPR).

NOEL-BUXTON, Noel Edward Noel-Buxton, 1st Baron (1869-1948) politician and philanthropist.
PH G.C.BERESFORD, 1906, hs, neg, NPG X6454. WALTER STONEMAN, 1924, hs, NPG (NPR).

NORMAN, Montagu Collet Norman, Baron (1871-1950) governor of the Bank of England.
P A.K.LAWRENCE, c1928, wl, Bank of England, London. SIR JAMES GUTHRIE, 1929, wl, profile, Bank of England. AUGUSTUS JOHN,

1931, tql seated, Bank of England.
G A.K.LAWRENCE, 'Committee of Treasury, 1928', mural, c1927-30, Bank of England.
SC LADY KATHLEEN KENNET, c1937-38, bronze head, Bank of England. SIR CHARLES WHEELER, c1945-46, bronze bust, Bank of England; stone statue, Bank of England.
PH WALTER STONEMAN, 1930, hs, NPG (NPR).

NORRISH, Ronald George Wreyford (1897-1978) physical chemist and Nobel prize winner.
P WILLIAM EVANS, 1969, hs in academic robes, Emmanuel College, Cambridge.
PH WALTER STONEMAN, 1945, hs, NPG (NPR). GODFREY ARGENT, 1970, hs, NPG (NPR). Various photographs, Emmanuel College.

NORTH, Sir Dudley Burton Napier (1881-1961) admiral.
PH WALTER STONEMAN, 2 hs portraits in uniform, 1932 and 1942, NPG (NPR).

NORTHCLIFFE, Alfred Charles William Harmsworth, 1st Viscount (1865-1922) journalist and newspaper proprietor.
P After P.A.DE LÁSZLÓ, 1911, tql, Times Newspapers Ltd, London. SIR JOHN LAVERY, c1921, Municipal Gallery of Modern Art, Dublin.
SC EDITH ANNA BELL, 1900, copper medallion, NPG 4101. LADY KATHLEEN KENNET, bronze bust, St Dunstan-in-the-West, London.
C SIR LESLIE WARD ('Spy'), wl seated, profile, lith, for *Vanity Fair*, 16 May 1895, NPG. SIR BERNARD PARTRIDGE, wl seated, w/c and pen and ink, for *Punch Almanack*, 1922, NPG.

NORTHUMBERLAND, Alan Ian Percy, 8th Duke of (1880-1930) landowner.
P P.A.DE LÁSZLÓ, 1927, hl in Garter robes, Alnwick Castle, Northd.

NORTON, Edward Felix (1884-1954) lieutenant-general and mountain climber.
PH WALTER STONEMAN, 1952, hs, NPG (NPR).

NORTON-GRIFFITHS, Sir John, 1st Bart (1871-1930) engineer.
D J.K.LAWSON, posthumous, hs in uniform, pencil and w/c, NPG 4333.

NORWAY, Maud, Queen of, see MAUD Charlotte Mary Victoria.

NORWICH, Alfred Duff Cooper, 1st Viscount (1890-1954) politician, diplomat and author.
C POWYS EVANS ('Quiz'), hs, mechanical repro, for *Saturday Review*, 13 Feb 1926, NPG. SIR DAVID LOW, wl with wife, Lady Diana, chalk, NPG 4560.
PH WALTER STONEMAN, 1938, hs, NPG (NPR). HOWARD COSTER, c1939-40, various sizes, print and negs, NPG X11431-34 and X2062.

NORWICH, Lady Diana Cooper, née Manners, 1st Viscountess (b1892) society beauty and actress.
SC BORIS ANREP, 1952, wl as 'Britannia crowning Punch', mosaic, National Gallery, London.
PR VIOLET, DUCHESS OF RUTLAND, 1899, hs, when Lady Manners, lith, NPG.
C SIR DAVID LOW, wl with husband, chalk, NPG 4560.
PH G.C.BERESFORD, 1906, hl as St Joan, neg, NPG X6488. MRS ALBERT BROOM, 1913, 'Elizabethan Tourney at Earls Court', neg, NPG. SIR CECIL BEATON, 1929, hs in costume as a 'madonna', print, NPG X6368.

NORWOOD, Sir Cyril (1875-1956) educationist.
P SIR OSWALD BIRLEY, c1934, tql in academic robes, St John's

College, Oxford. R.G.Eves, Marlborough College, Wilts.
George Harcourt, tql, Marlborough College.
ph Walter Stoneman, 1945, hs, npg (npr).

NOVAR, Ronald Crauford Munro-Ferguson, 1st Viscount (1860-1934) politician.
ph Walter Stoneman, 2 hs portraits, 1921 and 1931, npg (npr).

NOVELLO, Ivor (1893-1951) actor-manager, dramatist and composer.
sc Clemence Dane, bronze bust, Drury Lane Theatre, London.
ph Sir Cecil Beaton, hl, print, npg. Foulsham & Banfield, hs, postcard, npg. Angus McBean, 1937, hl, print, npg p65. Sasha, hs, profile, postcard, npg. Paul Tanqueray, 1932 and 1934, 4 hs portraits, prints, npg.

NOYES, Alfred (1880-1958) poet.
d Sir Bernard Partridge, 1929, tql seated, chalk and pencil, npg 3673.
pr Walter Tittle, 1922, hs, lith, Frick Art Reference Library, New York.
ph Howard Coster, 1929, various sizes, print and negs, npg ax2264 and others. Walter Stoneman, 1953, hs, npg (npr).

NUFFIELD, Sir William Richard Morris, Viscount (1877-1963) industrialist and philanthropist.
p P.A.de László, c1937, tql seated in robes, St Peter's Hall, Oxford. Mrs Beatrice Enes, c1937, Guy's Hospital, London. John Wheatley, 1949, after a photograph, hl seated, Royal College of Surgeons, London. Sir Oswald Birley, before 1952, tql seated, The Nuffield Foundation, London.
d Flora Lion, hs in uniform, pencil, The Nuffield Foundation. Sir Bernard Partridge, 1927, hl, chalk and pencil, npg 3674.
sc Maurice Lambert, c1948, bronze statue, Guy's Hospital.
ph Howard Coster, 1930s, hl, neg, npg. Walter Stoneman, 1934, hs, npg (npr). Unknown, 2 hs portraits, prints, npg.

NUGENT, George Colborne (1864-1915) soldier.
c Sir Leslie Ward ('Spy'), wl in uniform, w/c study for *Vanity Fair*, 12 Aug 1897, npg 2999.

NUGENT, Terence Edmund Gascoigne Nugent, 1st Baron (1895-1973) lieutenant-colonel and lord-in-waiting to Queen Elizabeth II.
ph Walter Bird, 1960, hl, npg (npr).

NUNN, Sir (Thomas) Percy (1870-1944) educationist.
p Henry Lamb, 1937, wl seated, Institute of Education, London.

NUTTALL, George Henry Falkiner (1862-1937) bacteriologist.
p P.A.de László, 1935, pencil, Magdalene College, Cambridge.
ph Walter Stoneman, 1917, hs, npg (npr). Unknown, 1920, tql in academic robes, print, npg.

NYE, Sir Archibald Edward (1895-1967) lieutenant-general.
p Henry Lamb, 1942, iwm.
d William Dring, 1942, pastel, iwm.

OAKLEY, Sir John Hubert (1867-1946) surveyor.
P R.G.EVES, tql, Royal Institution of Chartered Surveyors, London.

OAKSEY, Geoffrey Lawrence, 3rd Baron Trevethin and 1st Baron (1880-1971) judge.
P J.M.CREALOCK, tql seated in robes, Inner Temple, London. DEREK FOWLER, hl, Haileybury and Imperial Service College, Herts.

OATES, Lawrence Edward Grace (1880-1912) Antarctic explorer.
P J.NEWMAN HOLROYD, after a photograph, c1951-52, hs in uniform, Scott Polar Research Institute, University of Cambridge.
SC A.G.WALKER, bronzed plaster group of statues with R.F.Scott and E.A.Wilson, Scott Institute.
PH J.WESTON & SON, c1900, 2 hs portraits, prints, Scott Institute. UNKNOWN, c1907-08, 3 army groups in Cairo, prints, Scott Institute. FRANK DEBENHAM, c1911, wl in Antarctic, neg, Scott Institute. H.G.PONTING, c1911, wl seated with Cecil Meares, print, NPG P121. H.G.PONTING, c1911-12, various prints and negs, Scott Institute.

O'BRIEN, Kate (1897-1974) novelist and playwright.
PH HOWARD COSTER, various sizes and negs, NPG x11722-34.

O'BRIEN, Sir Tom (1900-1970) trade unionist.
PH WALTER STONEMAN, 1950, hs, NPG (NPR). WALTER BIRD, 1960, hs, NPG (NPR).

O'CASEY, Sean (1880-1964) playwright and author.
P AUGUSTUS JOHN, 1927, tql seated, Metropolitan Museum of Art, New York.
D PATRICK TUOHY, 1926, pencil, Municipal Gallery of Modern Art, Dublin. POWYS EVANS, c1927, head, pen and ink, NPG 4402. HARRY KERNOFF, 1930, hs, pastel, NGI 2935.

O'CONNOR, John (1870-1952) divine and writer.
PH HOWARD COSTER, various sizes and negs, NPG.

O'DWYER, Sir Michael Francis (1864-1940) Indian administrator.
PH WALTER STONEMAN, 1920, hs, NPG (NPR).

OGILVIE, Sir Frederick Wolff (1893-1949) economist and university vice-chancellor.
D DAVID FOGGIE, 1932, pencil, SNPG 1800.
PH WALTER STONEMAN, 1938, hs, for NPR, NPG x496.

OGILVY, David Lyulph Gore Wolseley, see 12th Earl of Airlie.

O'HIGGINS, Kevin Christopher (1892-1927) Irish statesman.
P SIR JOHN LAVERY, 1921, tql seated, Municipal Gallery of Modern Art, Dublin.
SC OLIVER SHEPPARD, 1932, marble bust, NGI 8046.

OLIPHANT, Sir Lancelot (1881-1965) diplomat.
PH WALTER STONEMAN, 2 hs portraits, 1931 and 1948, NPG (NPR).

OLIVER, Francis Wall (1864-1951) palaeobotanist and ecologist.

D FRANCES DE BIDEN FOOTNER, hs, profile, crayon, University College, London.

OLIVER, Sir Henry Francis (1865-1965) admiral.
P J.BLAIR LEIGHTON, hl seated in uniform, Royal Naval Navigation School, Portsmouth.
D FRANCIS DODD, 1917, charcoal and w/c, IWM.
PR W.G.BURN-MURDOCH, c1923, lith, IWM.
PH WALTER STONEMAN, 1928, hs in uniform, NPG (NPR).

OLIVER, Sir Roland Giffard (1882-1967) judge.
PH WALTER STONEMAN, 1939, hl seated in robes, for NPR, NPG x4138.

OLIVER, Vic (1898-1964) actor and musician.
C R.S.SHERRIFFS, c1939, wl with violin, ink and blue wash, NPG.

OLSSON, Julius (1864-1942) painter.
PH ELLIOTT & FRY, c1915, hs, cabinet, NPG. JOHN RUSSELL & SONS, c1915, hs, print, for National Photographic Record, vol 1, NPG. WALTER STONEMAN, 1931, hs, NPG (NPR).

O'MALLEY, Sir Owen St Clair (1887-1974) diplomat.
PH WALTER STONEMAN, 1945, hs, NPG (NPR).

OMAN, Sir Charles William Chadwick (1860-1946) historian.
D J.B.SOUTER, hs, All Souls College, Oxford.
PH WALTER STONEMAN, 1920, hs, NPG (NPR).

OMAN, John Wood (1860-1939) divine.
P H.G.RIVIERE, c1934, Westminster and Cheshunt College, Cambridge.
PH WALTER STONEMAN, 1938, hs, NPG (NPR).

ONIONS, Berta, Mrs Oliver Onions, see Ruck.

ONIONS, Charles Talbut (1873-1965) editor of the Oxford English Dictionary.
D WILLIAM DRING, 1948, pastel, Magdalen College, Oxford.
PH UNKNOWN, 2 portraits, prints, Magdalen College. UNKNOWN, hs, profile, snapshot, NPG.

ONIONS, Oliver (1873-1961) novelist.
PH JOHN RUSSELL & SONS, c1915, hs, print, for National Photographic Record, vol 1, NPG.

OPPÉ, Adolph Paul (1878-1957) art historian and collector.
SC ULI NIMPTSCH, 1949, bronze bust, BM.
PH WALTER STONEMAN, 1954, hs, NPG (NPR). UNKNOWN, hs, print, NPG.

OPPENHEIM, Edward Phillips (1866-1946) novelist.
PH OLIVE EDIS, early 1900s, wl with wife and daughter, print, NPG. HOWARD COSTER, 1929, various sizes, print and negs, NPG.

ORCHARD, William Edwin (1877-1955) Roman Catholic priest and theologian.
P A.P.COLE, 1941, tql seated, NPG 4466.

ORMSBY-GORE, William George Arthur, see 4th Baron Harlech.

ORPEN, Sir William (Newenham Montague) (1878-1931) painter.
P Self-portrait, various portraits including: 1891, aged 13, Ashmolean Museum, Oxford; c1901, wl, Glasgow City Art Gallery;

1908, wl with white handkerchief around head, Laing Art Gallery and Museum, Newcastle; c1908, Municipal Gallery of Modern Art, Dublin; c1909, hl, 'The Dead Ptarmigan', NGI 945; 1910, 'Myself and Venus', The Carnegie Institute, Pittsburg, USA; 1910, hl, 'The Jockey', National Museum, Stockholm; 1914, wl, 'Leading the Life in the West', Metropolitan Museum of Art, New York; 1917, 2 portraits, 'Ready to Start', IWM; c1923–24, hs, 4 images reflected in mirrors, Fitzwilliam Museum, Cambridge; 1925, hl, 'The Man with the Brush', Uffizi, Florence; hs, Ulster Museum, Belfast, N Ireland. CHARLES CONDER, before c1907, NGI 1327. JAMES SLEATOR, c1937–38, Municipal Gallery of Modern Art.

D Self-portrait, various drawings, including: c1898, hs pencil, NPG 5267; c1899, hs, ink, Scottish National Gallery of Modern Art, Edinburgh; 1903, pencil and w/c, Ashmolean Museum; 1910, tql seated, oval, pencil and wash, NPG 2638; 'Orpsie Boy', w/c, Oldham Art Galleries, Greater Manchester; ink, SNPG 1447.

G Sir WILLIAM ORPEN, 'The Selecting Jury of the New English Art Club', oil, 1909, NPG 2556. SIR W.ORPEN, group in the Café Royal, oil, 1911–12, Musée d'Art Moderne, Paris; copy, Café Royal, London.

C Sir MAX BEERBOHM, 1914, 'Bravura', drg, TATE 6043. Self-portrait, 1919, 2 caricatures, ink and wash, Birmingham City Art Gallery. A.R.THOMSON, with Augustus John and Sir Alfred Munnings, ink, The Athenaeum, London.

PH G.C.BERESFORD, 1902, various hs portraits, prints and negs, NPG x6554–56 and others. A.L.COBURN, 1908, hs, photogravure, NPG AX7782. WALTER STONEMAN, 1921, hs, NPG (NPR). HOWARD COSTER, 1927, various sizes, print and negs, NPG AX3436 and others.

ORR, John (1885-1966) philologist.

D DAVID FOGGIE, 1939, pencil, SNPG 2007.
PH WALTER BIRD, 1965, tql seated, NPG (NPR).

ORR, John Boyd, see Boyd Orr.

ORSBORN, Albert William Thomas (1886-1967) head of the Salvation Army.

P F.O.SALISBURY, 1954, hl in uniform, Salvation Army, London.
PH Various photographs, Salvation Army.

ORTON, Charles William Previté-, see Previté-Orton.

ORWIN, Charles Stewart (1876-1955) agricultural economist.

P RICHARD MURRAY, 1929, tql seated, Institute of Agricultural Economics, Oxford.

OSBORNE, Malcolm (1880-1963) engraver and teacher.
D DOROTHY HAWKSLEY, 1959, tql, chalk and w/c, NPG 4357.

OWEN, (William) Harold (1897-1971) artist and author.
PH MICHAEL WARD, 1970, hs, print, NPG.

OXFORD and ASQUITH, Emma Alice Margaret ('Margot') Asquith, née Tennant, Countess of (1864-1945) society beauty and woman of affairs.

D J.S.SARGENT, c1895, hs, NPG 4155. McLURE HAMILTON, c1921, head, profile, National Liberal Club, London.

G H.J.BROOKS, 'Private View of the Old Masters Exhibition, Royal Academy, 1888', oil, 1889, NPG 1833.

C Sir BERNARD PARTRIDGE, 1922, with five others, drawing for Punch's Almanack, 1922, caricature of the Countess was not published, V & A.

PH Sir CECIL BEATON, 1930s, tql seated, print, NPG. LUCIA MOHOLY, 1935, hs, profile, print (1978), NPG P128. HOWARD COSTER, c1938–39, various sizes, print and negs, NPG.

P

PAGE, Sir Archibald (1875-1949) engineer and administrator in electricity supply.
PH WALTER STONEMAN, 1940, hs, NPG (NPR).

PAGE, Sir Frederick Handley (1885-1962) aviation pioneer.
P UNKNOWN, hl, Royal Aero Club on loan to RAF Museum, Hendon.
C FRED MAY, 1936, pen and wash, RAF, Hendon.
PH DOUGLAS GLASS, hs, print, NPG.

PAGE, Sir Leo Francis (1890-1951) magistrate.
PH WALTER STONEMAN, 1948, hs, NPG (NPR).

PAGE, William (1861-1934) historian and antiquary.
P H.J.STOCK, 1926, hs, Institute of Historical Research, University of London.

PAGET, Sir Bernard (Charles Tolver) (1887-1961) general.
P KENNETH GREEN, 1939, Staff College, Camberley, Surrey.
D HENRY LAMB, 1941, pencil and chalk, IWM.

PAKENHAM, Sir William Christopher (1861-1933) admiral.
P SIR WILLIAM NICHOLSON, 1920, IWM.
D FRANCIS DODD, 1917, charcoal and w/c, IWM.
G SIR A.S.COPE, 'Naval Officers of World War I, 1914-18', oil, 1921, NPG 1913.
PH WALTER STONEMAN, 1919, hs in uniform, NPG (NPR).

PALAIRET, Sir (Charles) Michael (1882-1956) diplomat.
PH UNKNOWN, c1907, hs, print, NPG.

PALMER, Roundell Cecil, see 3rd Earl of Selborne.

PALMER, Sir William (1883-1964) civil servant.
PH WALTER STONEMAN, 1943, hs, NPG (NPR).

PANETH, Friedrich Adolf (1887-1958) scientist.
PH WALTER STONEMAN, 1953, hs, NPG (NPR).

PANKHURST, Dame Christabel (Harriette) (1880-1958) militant suffragette.
D JESSIE HOLLIDAY, wl, pencil, NPG 4207.
SC PETER HILLS, 1959, bronze medallion, Victoria Tower Gardens, London.
PR SIR LESLIE WARD ('Spy'), wl, Hentschel-Colourtype, for Vanity Fair, 15 June 1910, NPG.
PH OLIVE EDIS, 2 tql portraits, print and autochrome, NPG x6196 and x7200. Various prints and postcards, Fawcett Library, City of London Polytechnic.

PANKHURST, (Estelle) Sylvia (1882-1960) militant suffragette.
D HERBERT COLE, c1925, hs, chalk, NPG 4244. Self-portrait, hs, chalk, NPG 4999.
PH HOWARD COSTER, various sizes and negs, NPG. UNKNOWN, 1935, wl addressing Anti-Nazi demonstration in Hyde Park, NPG (Daily Herald). Several prints and postcard, Fawcett Library, City of London Polytechnic.

PANTIN, Carl Frederick Abel (1899-1967) zoologist.
D CLAUDE ROGERS, 1959, Trinity College, Cambridge.
PH WALTER STONEMAN, 2 hs portraits, 1937 and 1953, NPG (NPR).

PARES, Sir Bernard (1867-1949) historian of Russia.
G ALBERT LIPCZINSKI, staff group, oil, 1915, Faculty of Arts, University of Liverpool.
SC PAUL VINCZE, c1942, bronze plaque, School of Slavonic and East European Studies, University of London.
PH WALTER STONEMAN, 1920, hs, NPG (NPR).

PARIS, Sir Archibald (1861-1937) major-general.
P H.DONALD SMITH, 1920, hl in uniform, Royal Marines Museum, Eastney, Southsea, Hants.
PH WALTER STONEMAN, 1917, hs in uniform, profile, NPG (NPR).

PARK, Bertram (1883-1972) photographer.
PH YVONNE PARK, hs, print, NPG x5605. STUART BLACK, hs, profile, print, NPG x5604. UNKNOWN, 1933, 3 special constabulary groups, prints, NPG x5606-08.

PARKER, Cecil (1897-1971) actor.
C R.S.SHERRIFFS, 1938, hs, profile, ink and wash, NPG.

PARKER, Sir (Horatio) Gilbert (George), Bart (1862-1932) author and politician.
P SIR HUBERT VON HERKOMER, 1910, tql seated, National Gallery of Canada, Ottawa.
C HARRY FURNISS, wl, pen and ink, NPG 3498. SIR LESLIE WARD ('Spy'), wl, Hentschel-Colourtype, 23 June 1909, NPG.
PH JOHN RUSSELL & SONS, c1915, hs, print, for National Photographic Record, vol 1, NPG. WALTER STONEMAN, 1919, hs, NPG (NPR).

PARKER of Waddington, Hubert (Lister) Parker, Baron (1900-1972) judge.
P SIR W.O.HUTCHISON, c1962, tql seated in robes, Lincoln's Inn, London.
G NORMAN HEPPLE, 'A Short Adjournment', oil, 1958, Lincoln's Inn.
PH GODFREY ARGENT, 1968, tql seated in robes, NPG (NPR).

PARRY, Sir David Hughes (1893-1973) professor of law.
P KYFFIN WILLIAMS, c1965, University College of Wales, Aberystwyth.

PARRY, Sir (William) Edward (1893-1972) admiral.
PH WALTER STONEMAN, 1947, hs in uniform, NPG (NPR).

PARSONS, Sir John Herbert (1868-1957) ophthalmologist and physiologist.
P JOHN GILROY, hl seated, Institute of Ophthalmology, University of London.
PH WALTER STONEMAN, 1931, hs, NPG (NPR).

PARSONS, Sir Leonard Gregory (1879-1950) paediatrician.
PH WALTER STONEMAN, 1946, hs, NPG (NPR).

PARSONS, Richard Godfrey (1882-1948) bishop of Hereford.
P T.BINNEY GIBBS, 1942, tql seated, Bishop's Palace, Hereford.
PH WALTER STONEMAN, 2 hs portraits, 1940 and 1945, NPG (NPR). UNKNOWN, hs, print, NPG (Anglican Bishops).

PARTRIDGE, Sir Bernard (1861-1945) cartoonist.
P RALPH PEACOCK, head, profile, NPG 4234.
D Self-portrait, hs, chalk and wash, NPG 3948.
PH JOHN RUSSELL & SONS, c1885?, hs, cabinet, NPG. BASSANO, c1885-86?, hs and tql seated, prints, NPG. ELLIOTT & FRY, c1886?, hs, cabinet, NPG. E.O.HOPPÉ, 1915, tql seated in his studio, print,

NPG X4170. HOWARD COSTER, 1930, various sizes, print and negs, NPG AX3445 and others.

PATCH, Sir Edmund Leo Hall-, see Hall-Patch.

PATERSON, Sir Alexander Henry (1884-1947) prison reformer.
D E.I.HALLIDAY, University College, Oxford.

PATERSON, Sir William (1874-1956) mechanical engineer.
PH WALTER STONEMAN, 1949, hl seated, NPG (NPR).

PATERSON, William Paterson (1860-1939) Scottish divine.
P H.W.KERR, 1903, hs in robes, University of Edinburgh. G.FIDDES WATT, tql in academic robes, University of Edinburgh.

PATTERSON, Sir Wilfrid Rupert (1893-1954) admiral.
PH WALTER STONEMAN, 1943, hs in uniform, NPG (NPR).

PEACOCK, Sir Edward Robert (1871-1962) director of the Bank of England.
P SIR JAMES GUNN, hl seated, Baring Brothers & Co Ltd, London.
PH WALTER STONEMAN, hs and tql seated portraits, 1934 and 1948, NPG (NPR).

PEAKE, Sir Charles Brinsley Pemberton (1897-1958) diplomat.
PH WALTER STONEMAN, 1950, hs, NPG (NPR).

PEAKE, Frederick Gerard (1886-1970) 'Peake Pasha', founder of the Arab Legion.
PH WALTER STONEMAN, 1951, hs, NPG (NPR).

PEAKE, Harold John Edward (1867-1946) archaeologist.
PH LAFAYETTE, c1926–28, tql seated, print, Royal Anthropological Institute, London.

PEARCE, Ernest Harold (1865-1930) bishop of Worcester.
P ARNOLD HYNDMAN, Christ's Hospital, Horsham, Sussex. SOLOMON J.SOLOMON, c1927, Hartlebury Castle, Worcs.
PH WALTER STONEMAN, 1919, hs, NPG (NPR). UNKNOWN, hs in uniform, print, NPG (Anglican Bishops).

PEARSALL SMITH, (Lloyd) Logan, see Smith.

PEARSON, Alfred Chilton (1861-1935) classical scholar.
D A.K.LAWRENCE, 1927, head, semi-profile, chalk, Trinity College, Cambridge.

PEARSON, Sir Cyril Arthur, 1st Bart (1866-1921) newspaper proprietor and philanthropist.
C SIR LESLIE WARD ('Spy'), wl, profile, lith, for *Vanity Fair*, 17 Nov 1904, NPG.
PH JOHN RUSSELL & SONS, hs, print, St Dunstan's, London.

PEARSON, Sir Robert Barclay (1871-1952) chairman of the London Stock Exchange.
PH WALTER STONEMAN, 1944, hs, NPG (NPR).

PEASE, Joseph Albert, see 1st Baron Gainford.

PEEL, Beatrice Lillie, Lady, see Lillie.

PEEL, William Robert Wellesley Peel, 2nd Viscount and 1st Earl (1867-1937) statesman.
P SIR WILLIAM NICHOLSON, County Hall, London.
PH OLIVE EDIS, tql seated, print, NPG. WALTER STONEMAN, 2 hs portraits, 1919 and 1929, NPG (NPR).

PEERS, Sir Charles Reed (1868-1952) antiquary.
D FRANCIS DODD, c1939, hs, pencil, Society of Antiquaries, London.

PEET, Thomas Eric (1882-1934) Egyptologist.
C UNKNOWN, 'Digging in Egypt', Queen's College, Oxford.

PEIRSE, Sir Richard Edmund Charles (1892-1970) air chief marshal.
P SIR OSWALD BIRLEY, 1940, IWM.
PH HOWARD COSTER, various sizes and negs, NPG. WALTER STONEMAN, 1938, hs, NPG (NPR).

PEMBER, Francis William (1862-1954) warden of All Souls College, Oxford.
PH WALTER STONEMAN, 1921, hs, profile, NPG (NPR).

PENROSE FRY, Sheila, see Kaye-Smith.

PENSON, Dame Lillian Margery (1896-1963) educationist.
PH UNKNOWN, print, Vice-Chancellor's Office, University of London.

PENTLAND, John Sinclair, 1st Baron (1860-1925) governor of Madras.
C HARRY FURNISS, c1905, hl seated, pen and ink, NPG 3408.
PH WALTER STONEMAN, 1921, hs, NPG (NPR).

PEPLER, Sir George Lionel (1882-1959) town planner.
P SIR ROBIN DARWIN, 1959, posthumous, Royal Town Planning Institute, London.
PH WALTER STONEMAN, 1949, hs, NPG (NPR).

PERCIVAL, Arthur Ernest (1887-1966) lieutenant-general.
PH WALTER STONEMAN, 1949, hs in uniform, NPG (NPR).

PERCY, Alan Ian, see 8th Duke of Northumberland.

PERCY, (Saville) Esmé (1887-1957) actor and producer.
C R.S.SHERRIFFS, head, profile, ink and charcoal?, for *The Sketch*, 9 Dec 1936, NPG.

PERCY of Newcastle, Eustace Sutherland Campbell Percy, Baron (1887-1958) politician and educationist.
P LAWRENCE GOWING, c1953, University of Newcastle. UNKNOWN, University of Newcastle.
PH WALTER STONEMAN, 1924, hs, NPG (NPR).

PEREIRA, George Edward (1865-1923) soldier and traveller.
PH WALTER STONEMAN, 1918, hs in uniform, NPG (NPR).

PERKIN, Arthur George (1861-1937) organic chemist.
P RICHARD JACK, c1926, tql, University of Leeds.
PH WALTER STONEMAN, 1932, hs, NPG (NPR).

PERKIN, William Henry (1860-1929) organic chemist.
SC E.G.GILLICK, 1930, relief medallion portrait on bronze plaque, The Chemical Society, London.
PH Various photographs, The Chemical Society.

PEROWNE, Freya, Mrs Stewart Perowne, see Stark.

PERRING, William George Arthur (1898-1951) director of the Royal Aircraft Establishment.
P H.J.PROCTOR, Royal Aircraft Establishment, Farnborough, Hants.

PERRINS, Charles William Dyson (1864-1958) art collector and benefactor.
P ARTHUR HACKER, c1907, wl, Perrins Hall, Worcester Royal Grammar School.

PERRY, Sir Percival Lea Dewhurst Perry, Baron (1878-1956) businessman.
PH WALTER STONEMAN, 1921, hs, NPG (NPR).

PERTH, James Eric Drummond, 16th Earl of (1876-1951) first secretary-general of the League of Nations.
PH WALTER STONEMAN, 2 hs portraits, 1917 and 1939, NPG (NPR) and NPG X4141.

PETAVEL, Sir Joseph Ernest (1873-1936) engineer and physicist.

P ALFRED HAYWARD, 1954, hl, DoE (Bushy House, Teddington, Middx).
PH UNKNOWN, hl, print, National Physical Laboratory, Teddington.

PETERSON, Sir Maurice Drummond (1889-1952) diplomat.
PH WALTER STONEMAN, hs, for NPR, NPG x498.

PETHICK-LAWRENCE, Emmeline, née Pethick, Lady (1867-1954) suffragette.
P JOHN BAKER, posthumous, hl with Lord Pethick-Lawrence, Peaslake Village Hall, Surrey.
PH Various prints and postcards, Fawcett Library, City of London Polytechnic.

PETHICK-LAWRENCE, Frederick William Pethick-Lawrence, Baron (1871-1961) politician and women's suffragist.
P HENRY COLLER, 1933, tql seated, NPG 4275. JOHN BAKER, posthumous, hl seated with Lady Pethick-Lawrence, Peaslake Village Hall, Surrey.
SC ALBIN MORODER, 1949, wooden head, NPG 4280.
PH WALTER STONEMAN, 1945, hs, NPG (NPR). Various postcards, Fawcett Library, City of London Polytechnic.

PHILBY, Harry St John Bridger (1885-1960) explorer and orientalist.
PH Various photographs, some in Arab dress, Royal Geographical Society, London.

PHILIPPS, Sir Ivor (1861-1940) major-general and businessman.
PH WALTER STONEMAN, 1918, hs in uniform, NPG (NPR).

PHILIPPS, Sir John Wynford, 13th Bart, see 1st Viscount ST DAVIDS.

PHILLIMORE, John Swinnerton (1873-1926) classical scholar and poet.
P MAURICE GREIFFENHAGEN, c1925, University of Glasgow.

PHILLIMORE, Sir Richard Fortescue (1864-1940) admiral.
D FRANCIS DODD, 1917, charcoal and w/c, IWM.
PH WALTER STONEMAN, 2 hs portraits in uniform, 1919 and 1933, NPG (NPR).

PHILLIPS, Stephen (1864-1915) poet and dramatist.
D PERCY ANDERSON, 1902, hs, w/c, NPG 4338.
PR SIR WILLIAM ROTHENSTEIN, 1898, hs, lith, NPG.
PH ELLIOTT & FRY, hs, profile, cabinet, NPG x4623.

PHILLIPS, Sir Thomas Williams (1883-1966) civil servant.
PH WALTER STONEMAN, 3 hs portraits, 1934, 1947 and 1958, NPG (NPR).

PHILLIPS, Sir Tom Spencer Vaughan (1888-1941) admiral.
PH WALTER STONEMAN, 1940, 2 hl portraits in uniform, NPG (NPR) and NPG x499.

PHILLPOTTS, Dame Bertha Surtees, Mrs Hugh Frank Newall (1877-1932) educationist and Scandinavian scholar.
P P.A.DE LÁSZLÓ, 1921, Westfield College, University of London. HOWARD SOMERVILLE, 1927, Girton College, Oxford.
PH UNKNOWN, c1932, hs, print, NPG.

PHILLPOTTS, Eden (1862-1960) writer.
P BERYL TRIST, 1937, hl, University of Exeter.
C ALICK P.F.RITCHIE, wl with flower pots, mechanical repro, for Vanity Fair, 11 June 1913, NPG.
PH JOHN RUSSELL & SONS, 1915, hs, print, for National Photographic

Record, vol 1, NPG.

PHILPOT, Glyn (Warren) (1884-1937) painter.
P Self-portrait, 1908, hl with palette, NPG 4681. SIR OSWALD BIRLEY, 1920, hl, NPG 3651.
PH F.J.GUTMAN, 1937, hs and wl seated, prints, NPG.

PHIPPS, Sir Eric Clare Edmund (1875-1945) diplomat.
PH WALTER STONEMAN, 1932, hs, NPG (NPR).

PICK, Frank (1878-1941) vice-chairman of the London Passenger Transport Board.
PH HOWARD COSTER, 1930s, various sizes and negs, NPG.

PICKARD, Sir Robert Howson (1874-1949) chemist.
PH UNKNOWN, print, University of Surrey.

PIERCY, William Piercy, 1st Baron (1886-1966) economist.
PH WALTER STONEMAN, 1945, hs, NPG (NPR). WALTER BIRD, 1965, hs, NPG (NPR).

PIGOU, Arthur Cecil (1877-1959) economist.
P E.H.NELSON, c1948-49, tql seated, King's College, Cambridge; study, 1948, hs, Marshall Library of Economics, Cambridge.
D E.H.NELSON, w/c, King's College.

PILCHER, Sir Gonne (St Clair) (1890-1966) judge.
PH WALTER STONEMAN, 1942, hs, NPG (NPR).

PISSARRO, Lucien (1863-1944) painter, engraver and printer.
P CAMILLE PISSARRO, 1882, wl seated, Phoenix Art Museum, Arizona, USA. WILLIAM STRANG, 1920, tql seated, National Gallery of Canada, Ottawa. J.B.MANSON, 1939, hl seated, Manchester City Art Gallery. DAME ETHEL WALKER, c1944, hl, Scottish National Gallery of Modern Art, Edinburgh.
D C.PISSARRO, various drawings, Ashmolean Museum, Oxford.
SC DORA GORDINE, bronze bust, Ashmolean Museum.
PR C.PISSARRO, 1890, hs, etch, NPG 4103. C.PISSARRO, hs, lith, Art Institute of Chicago, USA.

PISSARRO, Orovida (Camille) (1893-1968) artist.
P CAREL WEIGHT, 1956, wl seated, TATE T139. C.WEIGHT, 1957, nearly wl seated, Ashmolean Museum, Oxford.

PLATNAUER, Maurice (1887-1974) principal of Brasenose College, Oxford.
D SIR STANLEY SPENCER, head, 2 drgs, Brasenose College.

PLAYFAIR, Sir Nigel Ross (1874-1934) actor-manager.
P W.R.SICKERT, 1928, as Tony Lumpkin in She Stoops to Conquer, on loan to the Garrick Club, London.
D EDMOND KAPP, 1927, Barber Institute, Birmingham University.
C HARRY FURNISS, wl, profile, pen and ink, NPG 3504.

PLENDER, William Plender, Baron (1861-1946) accountant.
P SIR WILLIAM LLEWELLYN, 1929, hl seated, Institute of Chartered Accountants, London.
PH WALTER STONEMAN, 1932, hs, NPG (NPR). KETURAH-COLLINGS, c1932, hs, print, NPG.

PLUMMER, Henry Crozier Keating (1875-1946) astronomer and mathematician.
PH UNKNOWN, c1939-41, hs, print, Royal Astronomical Society, London.

PLUNKETT, Edward John Moreton Drax, see 18th Baron of Dunsany.

POCOCK, Ruby Mildred, Mrs R.W.Pocock, see Ayres.

POLLARD, Albert Frederick (1869-1948) historian.
PH BLAKE, tql seated, print, NPG.

POLLITT, George Paton (1878-1964) colonel and director of Imperial Chemical Industries Ltd.

PH HOWARD COSTER, hl seated, print, Imperial Chemical Industries Ltd, London.

POLLITT, Harry (1890-1960) general secretary and later chairman of the British Communist Party.

PH HOWARD COSTER, c1935, various sizes and negs, NPG X10164–71.

POLLOCK, Bertram (1863-1943) headmaster and bishop of Norwich.

P EDMOND BROCK, hl, Wellington College, Berks.

C SIR LESLIE WARD ('Spy'), wl, lith, for *Vanity Fair*, 9 Oct 1902, NPG.

PH JOHN RUSSELL & SONS, c1915, hs, print, for *National Photographic Record*, vol 1, NPG. J.RUSSELL & SONS, c1915, tql seated, print, NPG. VANDYK, hs, print, NPG (Anglican Bishops). WALTER STONEMAN, 1938, hs, NPG (NPR). UNKNOWN, tql seated, print, NPG.

POLLOCK, Ernest Murray, see 1st Viscount Hanworth.

PONSONBY, Vere Brabazon, see 9th Earl of Bessborough.

PONSONBY of Shulbrede, Arthur Augustus William Harry Ponsonby, 1st Baron (1871-1946) politician and writer.

D SIR WILLIAM ROTHENSTEIN, 1925, hs, sanguine, NPG 4792.

PH WALTER STONEMAN, 2 hs portraits, 1924 and 1934, NPG (NPR) and NPG X4153.

PONTING, Herbert George (1870-1935) photographer.

PH Various self-portrait photographs, c1910–12, Scott Polar Research Institute, University of Cambridge.

POOLE, Austin Lane (1889-1963) historian.

PH WALTER STONEMAN, 1952, hs, NPG (NPR).

POPE, Sir William Jackson (1870-1939) chemist.

PH WALTER STONEMAN, 1921, NPG (NPR).

POPHAM, Arthur Ewart (1889-1970) art historian and keeper of prints and drawings at the British Museum.

D DAVID BELL, hs, pencil, BM.

PH WALTER STONEMAN, 1949, hs, NPG (NPR).

POPHAM, Sir (Henry) Robert (Moore) Brooke-, see Brooke-Popham.

PORTAL, Sir Wyndham Raymond Portal, 3rd Bart and Viscount (1885-1949) industrialist and public servant.

PH WALTER STONEMAN, 1935, hs, NPG (NPR).

PORTAL of Hungerford, Charles Frederick Algernon Portal, 1st Viscount (1893-1971) marshal of the Royal Air Force.

P SIR OSWALD BIRLEY, 1942, hl in uniform, RAF Museum, Hendon, London. A.E.COOPER, c1945, RAF Museum. SIR O.BIRLEY, 1948, tql in Garter robes, Christ Church, Oxford.

D SIR WILLIAM ROTHENSTEIN, 1939, sanguine, IWM. ERIC KENNINGTON, 1940, pastel, IWM.

SC SIR JACOB EPSTEIN, bronze head, IWM, and RAF Museum.

PH HOWARD COSTER, 1941, various sizes, print and negs, NPG X10676 and others. WALTER STONEMAN, 2 hs portraits, the 1st in uniform, 1941 and 1952, NPG (NPR). WALTER BIRD, 1965, hs, NPG (NPR).

PORTER, Samuel Lowry Porter, Baron (1877-1956) judge.

D HENRY LAMB, 1948, pastel, Emmanuel College, Cambridge.

PH WALTER STONEMAN, 2 hs portraits, the 1st in robes, 1935 and 1952, NPG (NPR).

POSTGATE, Raymond William (1896-1971) writer.

PH GODFREY ARGENT, 1970, 2 hl portraits, NPG (NPR).

POTTER, (Helen) Beatrix, Mrs William Heelis (1866-1943) writer of books for children.

P DELMAR BANNER, tql as young woman, National Book League, London. D.BANNER, 1938, replica, tql, NPG 3635.

POTTER, Stephen (1900-1969) author and broadcaster.

C SIR DAVID LOW, various sketches, pencil, NPG 4529(272–76).

POUND, Sir (Alfred) Dudley (Pickman Rogers) (1877-1943) admiral.

P SIR OSWALD BIRLEY, c1945-48, hs in uniform, Royal Naval College, Greenwich. DAVID EWART, hl in uniform, formerly the United Service Club, London (c/o Crown Commissioners).

D ERIC KENNINGTON, 1940, pastel, IWM.

PH WALTER STONEMAN, 3 hs portraits in uniform, 1920 and c1940, for NPR, NPG X500–02.

POWER, Sir Arthur John (1889-1960) admiral.

P SIR OSWALD BIRLEY, c1945-48, hs in uniform, Royal Naval College, Greenwich.

PH WALTER STONEMAN, 1947, hs in uniform, NPG (NPR) and NPG X4156.

POWER, Sir John Cecil, 1st Bart (1870-1950) company director and public benefactor.

P SIR OSWALD BIRLEY, 1934, wl, Royal Institute of International Affairs, Chatham House, London.

SC SIEGFRIED CHAROUX, 1944, bronze bust, Royal Institute of International Affairs.

POWICKE, Sir (Frederick) Maurice (1879-1963) medieval historian.

PH WALTER STONEMAN, 1945, hs, NPG (NPR). RAMSEY & MUSPRATT, c1947, hs, print, NPG.

POWNALL, Sir Henry Royds (1887-1961) lieutenant-general.

PH WALTER STONEMAN, 1941, hs in uniform, NPG (NPR).

POWYS, John Cowper (1872-1963) author and poet.

D AUGUSTUS JOHN, hs, chalk, NPG 4668. IVAN OPFFER, charcoal, University of Texas, Austin, USA.

SC HUGH OLOFF DE WET, 1963, bronze head, University of Texas. H.O.DE WET, terracotta study head?, University of Texas.

POWYS, Theodore Francis (1875-1953) novelist.

P AUGUSTUS JOHN, c1932, hs, TATE T194.

D POWYS EVANS, c1929, hs, pen and ink, NPG 4461.

SC ELIZABETH MUNTZ, 1949, marble bust, Bristol City Art Gallery.

PH HOWARD COSTER, 1934, various sizes, prints and negs, NPG X2087, AX3487 and X10425·34.

POYNDER, Sir John Poynder Dickson-, see 1st Baron Islington.

PREEDY, George, see Gabrielle Margaret Vere LONG.

PRESTAGE, Edgar (1869-1951) historian and professor of Portuguese.

PH WALTER STONEMAN, 1943, hs, NPG (NPR).

PREVITÉ-ORTON, Charles William (1877-1947) historian and editor.

PH WALTER STONEMAN, 1945, hs, NPG (NPR).

PRICE THOMAS, Sir Clement (1893-1973) surgeon.

PH WALTER STONEMAN, 1952, hl seated, NPG (NPR).

PRICHARD, Harold Arthur (1871-1947) philosopher.

PH WALTER STONEMAN, 2 hs portraits, 1933 and 1945, NPG (NPR).

PRIESTLEY, John Boynton (b1894) writer.

P J.P.BARRACLOUGH, 1932, hl seated, Bradford City Art Gallery. HENRY CARR, 1950, University of Texas, Austin, USA. MICHAEL

NOAKES, 1970, hl seated, Bradford City Art Gallery.

D JACOB KRAMER, 1930, head, profile, charcoal, NPG CP17. WYNDHAM LEWIS, 1932, head, profile, pencil, Graves Art Gallery, Sheffield. POWYS EVANS, early 1930s, hs, ink, NPG 5109. EDMOND KAPP, 1947, Barber Institute, Birmingham University. DAVID HOCKNEY, 1973, hl seated, ink, Bradford City Art Gallery.

SC SIR JACOB EPSTEIN, 1931, bronze bust, University of Texas. MAURICE LAMBERT, 1948, bronze head, University of Texas.

C SIR DAVID LOW, various sketches, pencil, NPG 4529(280–85).

PH HOWARD COSTER, 1926, 1937 and 1950s, various sizes, print and negs, NPG X2073–81, AX2243 and others. MARK GERSON, 1960, wl, print, NPG. GODFREY ARGENT, 1968, hs, NPG (NPR).

PRIESTLEY, Sir Raymond Edward (1886-1974) Antarctic explorer.

P A.R.MIDDLETON TODD, c1950, hl in robes, University of Birmingham.

PH H.G.PONTING, c1910–12, several photographs, Scott Polar Research Institute, University of Cambridge. WALTER STONEMAN, 1952, hs, NPG (NPR). WALTER BIRD, 1962, hs, NPG (NPR). SUSAN BUCHAN, 1972, hs, print, NPG X1473.

PRITCHETT, Sir Victor (Sawdon) (b1900) author and critic.

D CHRISTOPHER CORR, 1980, hl seated, Times Newspapers Ltd, London.

PH SIR CECIL BEATON, wl, print, NPG. HOWARD COSTER, various sizes, print and negs, NPG X2086 and others. GODFREY ARGENT, 1970, hs, NPG (NPR).

PRITT, Denis Nowell (1887-1972) lawyer.

PH HOWARD COSTER, 1930s, various sizes and negs, NPG. WALTER STONEMAN, 1949, hs, NPG (NPR).

PROUDMAN, Joseph (1888-1975) mathematician and oceanographer.

PH WALTER STONEMAN, 1931, hs, NPG (NPR).

PRYDE, James Ferrier (1866-1941) artist.

P Self-portrait, tql as 'Scarron', profile, Castle Museum, Nottingham.

D SIR W.O.HUTCHISON, charcoal, SNPG 1525.

G SIR WILLIAM ORPEN, group in the Café Royal, oil, c1911–12, Musée d'Art Moderne, Paris; copy, Café Royal, London.

M J.W.BROOKE, hs, profile, NPG 4006.

SC JO DAVIDSON, c1938, bronze head, Savage Club, London.

PR JOSEPH SIMPSON, c1928, hl, etch, NPG.

PUGH, Sir Arthur (1870-1955) trade unionist.

PH Various photographs, Trades Union Congress, London.

PULTENEY, Sir William Pulteney (1861-1941) lieutenant-general.

P P.A.DE LÁSZLÓ, 1917, hl in uniform, NPG 4236.

D FRANCIS DODD, 1917, charcoal and w/c, IWM.

PH WALTER STONEMAN, 1918, hs in uniform, NPG (NPR).

PURCELL, Albert Arthur William (1872-1935) trade unionist.

PH Various photographs, Trades Union Congress, London.

PURSE, Benjamin Ormond (1874-1950) blind social worker and expert on blind welfare.

PH JOHN RUSSELL & SONS, hs, print, Royal National Institute for the Blind, London. LONDON NEWS AGENCY PHOTOS LTD, tql seated with Vic Oliver, print, Royal National Institute for the Blind.

PYE, Sir David Randall (1886-1960) engineer and administrator.

D UNKNOWN, hl seated, University College, London.

PH WALTER STONEMAN, 1953, hs, NPG (NPR). UNKNOWN, c1952, hs, print, Institution of Mechanical Engineers, London.

Q

QUICKSWOOD, Hugh Richard Heathcote Gascoyne-Cecil, Baron (1869-1956) politician and provost of Eton.

P P.A.DE LÁSZLÓ, 1934, tql seated, Church House, Westminster, London.

D J.S.SARGENT, 1920, hs, charcoal, Hatfield House, Herts.

G F.H.SHEPHERD, family group, oil, 1928, University College, Oxford; version, Hatfield House.

C SIR LESLIE WARD ('Spy'), wl, profile, lith, for *Vanity Fair*, 18 Oct 1900, NPG. SIR MAX BEERBOHM, 1913, 'Cecils in Conclave', wash, Hatfield House. SIR M.BEERBOHM, 1921, wl with Lord Robert Cecil, pencil and wash, Ashmolean Museum, Oxford. SIR M.BEERBOHM, 1926, wl with Henry Brodribb, pencil and wash, Hatfield House.

PH G.C.BERESFORD, 1902, hs, print and neg, NPG X5730 and X6563. WALTER STONEMAN, 3 hs portraits, 1917, 1931 and 1945, NPG (NPR). HOWARD COSTER, 1936, various sizes, prints and negs, NPG X1786, X2386, AX3253 and X10626–32.

QUILLER-COUCH, Sir Arthur Thomas (1863-1944) Cornish man of letters.

P SIR WILLIAM NICHOLSON, 1934, hl, Jesus College, Cambridge. HENRY LAMB, 1938, tql, City Art Gallery, Truro, Cornwall; study sketch, chalk, NPG 4262.

D LOUIS PAUL, 1920, wl seated, w/c, NPG 4272.

PH HOWARD COSTER, various sizes, print and negs, NPG X2089 and others. STEREOSCOPIC COMPANY, 2 hs portraits as young man, cabinets, NPG.

QUILTER, Roger Cuthbert (1877-1953) composer.

P W.G.DE GLEHN, 1920, tql, NPG 3904.

PH HERBERT LAMBERT, c1922, hl seated, photogravure, NPG P110. HOWARD COSTER, 1930s, various sizes and negs, NPG.

R

RACKHAM, Arthur (1867-1939) illustrator.
P Self-portrait, 1919, hs, Art Workers Guild, London.

RADCLYFFE HALL, see Hall.

RADLEY, Sir (William) Gordon (1898-1970) director-general of the General Post Office.
PH WALTER STONEMAN, 1954, hs, NPG (NPR).

RAIKES, Humphrey Rivaz (1891-1955) chemist.
P R.BROADLEY, University of Witwatersrand, Johannesburg, S Africa.

RAISTRICK, Harold (1890-1971) biochemist.
PH WALTER STONEMAN, 1934, hs, NPG (NPR).

RAIT, Sir Robert Sangster (1874-1936) historian and principal of Glasgow University.
P SIR JAMES GUNN, posthumous, University of Glasgow.

RALEIGH, Sir Walter Alexander (1861-1922) critic and essayist.
P FRANCIS DODD, c1896, hs in Elizabethan dress, King's College, Cambridge.
W LAURA ANNING BELL, memorial window, Library, Merton College, Oxford.
PR M.EGERTON, after a photograph, hs, lith, NPG.
PH UNKNOWN, hs, oval, print, NPG XIIII.

RAM, Sir (Lucius Abel John) Granville (1885-1952) parliamentary draftsman.
PH WALTER STONEMAN, 4 hs portraits, for NPR, NPG X1406-09.

RAMBERT, Dame Marie, Marie Dukes (b1888) a founder of British ballet.
SC ASTRYD ZYDOWER, 1970, bronze cast of bust, NPG 4866.
PH WALTER BIRD, 1962, hs, NPG (NPR). J.S.LEWINSKI, 1967, wl, print, NPG.

RAMSAY, Sir Alexander Robert Maule (1881-1972) admiral.
PH ALEX CORBETT, 2 hs portraits in uniform, prints, NPG. PLATÉ LTD, c1935, hl in uniform, print, NPG.

RAMSAY, Allen Beville (1872-1955) master of Magdalene College, Cambridge.
P SIR GERALD KELLY, 1927, hl, Magdalene College.
PH WALTER STONEMAN, 1940, hs, NPG (NPR).

RAMSAY, Sir Bertram Home (1883-1945) admiral.
P SIR OSWALD BIRLEY, c1945-48, hs in uniform, Royal Naval College, Greenwich.
PH WALTER STONEMAN, 1944, hs in uniform, NPG (NPR).

RAMSAY, Lady Patricia, née Princess Patricia of Connaught (1886-1974) granddaughter of Queen Victoria.
P SIR JOHN LAVERY, before 1910, hl, National Gallery of Canada, Ottawa. CHARLES SHANNON, 1917-18, seated, profile, National Gallery of Canada.
PH W. & D.DOWNEY, c1906, wl with her sister Crown Princess Margaret of Sweden, postcard, NPG X6348. W. & D.DOWNEY, 1907, royal family group, print, NPG X1585.

RAMSAY-STEEL-MAITLAND, Sir Arthur Herbert Drummond, see Steel-Maitland.

RAMSBOTHAM, Herwald, see 1st Viscount Soulbury.

RANCE, Sir Hubert (Elvin) (1898-1974) major-general.
PH WALTER STONEMAN, 1946, 2 hs portraits in uniform, NPG (NPR).

RANDALL-MacIVER, David (1873-1945) archaeologist and anthropologist.
PH WALTER STONEMAN, 1939, hs, NPG (NPR).

RANK, Joseph Arthur Rank, Baron (1888-1972) a principal architect of the British film industry.
PH HOWARD COSTER, various sizes and negs, NPG. WALTER STONEMAN, 1957, hs, NPG (NPR).

RANKEILLOUR, James Fitzalan Hope, 1st Baron (1870-1949) parliamentarian.
PH WALTER STONEMAN, 1932, hs, NPG (NPR).

RANKIN, Sir George Claus (1877-1946) judge.
PH WALTER STONEMAN, 1939, hs, NPG (NPR).

RANKINE, Alexander Oliver (1881-1956) physicist.
PH WALTER STONEMAN, 1934, hs, NPG (NPR).

RANSOME, Arthur (1884-1967) author and journalist.
P DORA COLLINGWOOD, 1930, Abbot Hall Art Gallery, Kendal. JOHN GILROY, hl seated, Garrick Club, London.
PR ROBERT LUTYENS, c1961-62, hl seated at dinner, one of set of 'Old Burgundians', type of lith, NPG.
PH HOWARD COSTER, 1932, various sizes and negs, NPG X12267-78.

RAPSON, Edward James (1861-1937) Sanskrit scholar.
PH WALTER STONEMAN, 1932, hs, NPG (NPR).

RATHBONE, Basil (1892-1967) actor.
C R.S.SHERRIFFS, 1937, hs, ink and wash, NPG.
PH UNKNOWN, 2 portraits in character, prints, Theatre Museum, V & A.

RATHBONE, Eleanor Florence (1872-1946) social reformer.
P SIR JAMES GUNN, c1934, tql seated, NPG 4133.

RAVEN, Charles Earle (1885-1964) professor of divinity.
P EDMUND NELSON, 1949, Christ's College, Cambridge.
PH WALTER STONEMAN, 2 hs portraits, 1947 and 1957, NPG (NPR).

RAVEN-HILL, Leonard (1867-1942) artist, illustrator and cartoonist.
P MAURICE GREIFFENHAGEN, 1927, Glasgow City Art Gallery.
D Self-portrait, c1895, hs, pencil, NPG 3046.

RAVERAT, Gwendolen Mary (1885-1957) artist.
D ELISABETH VELLACOTT, pencil, Kettle's Yard, University of Cambridge.

RAWLINGS, Sir (Henry) Bernard (Hughes) (1889-1962) admiral.
P SIR OSWALD BIRLEY, c1945-48, hs in uniform, Royal Naval College, Greenwich.
PH WALTER STONEMAN, 1942, hs in uniform, NPG (NPR).

RAWLINSON, Sir Henry Seymour Rawlinson, Baron (1864-1925) general.
P SIR WILLIAM ORPEN, 1918, hl, IWM. J.S.SARGENT, c1919-22, hs in uniform, NPG 4181. SIR OSWALD BIRLEY, early 1920s, copy, tql in

uniform, Staff College, Camberley, Surrey.

D I.SHELDON-WILLIAMS, 1900, hl seated in uniform, profile, pencil and w/c, NPG 4039(4). FRANCIS DODD, 1917, charcoal and w/c, IWM.

G J.S.SARGENT, 'General Officers of World War I, 1914–18', oil, 1922, NPG 1954.

PH WALTER STONEMAN, 1918, hs in uniform, NPG (NPR).

RAYLEIGH, Robert John Strutt, 4th Baron (1875-1947) experimental physicist.

PH WALTER STONEMAN, 3 hs portraits, 1918, 1931 and 1943, NPG (NPR). HOWARD COSTER, 1930s, various sizes and negs, NPG.

READ, Sir Herbert (1893-1968) critic and writer on art.

P PATRICK HERON, 1950, hl, NPG 4654. BRYAN KNEALE, 1958, hl, York City Art Gallery. KARL APPEL, 1962, hs, Montreal Museum of Fine Arts, Canada.

G BARBARA HEPWORTH, family group, oil and pencil, Leeds City Art Gallery.

PH HOWARD COSTER, 1934, various sizes, prints and negs, NPG AX3520, X3438 and others. FELIX MAN, 1940, hl seated, print, NPG P13. MARK GERSON, 1965, hs print, NPG. WALTER BIRD, 1966, hs, NPG (NPR).

READ, Sir Herbert James (1863-1949) civil servant.

PH WALTER STONEMAN, 2 hs portraits, the 2nd in uniform, 1920 and 1931, NPG (NPR).

READING, Gerald Rufus Isaacs, 2nd Marquess of (1889-1960) politician.

PH WALTER STONEMAN, 2 hs portraits, 1936 and 1947, NPG (NPR). HOWARD COSTER, 1956, 2 hl portraits, prints, NPG X2168–69.

READING, Rufus Daniel Isaacs, 1st Marquess of (1860-1935) lord chief justice.

P SIR OSWALD BIRLEY, c1914, in chief justice's robes, Reading Municipal Art Gallery. SIR WILLIAM ORPEN, 1919, hs, NPG 4180. G.FIDDES WATT, c1920, tql in chief justice's robes, Middle Temple, on loan to Palace of Westminster, London. SIR O.BIRLEY, 1928, tql in viceroy's robes, Middle Temple.

D SIR WILLIAM ROTHENSTEIN, 1925, hs, chalk, NPG 2880. EDMOND KAPP, 1929, Barber Institute, Birmingham University.

SC LADY KATHLEEN KENNET, 1925, bronze bust, NPG 3643. C.S.JAGGER, c1928, statue, New Delhi, India. A.LOWENTAL, 1936, bronze plaque, NPG.

C SIR LESLIE WARD ('Spy'), tql in robes, lith, for *Vanity Fair*, 18 Feb 1904, NPG. 'Owl', wl, mechanical repro, for *Vanity Fair*, 18 June 1913, NPG. FRED MAY, 1930s, head, profile, gouache, NPG.

PH G.C.BERESFORD, 1903, 2 hs portraits, negs, NPG X6565–66. JOHN RUSSELL & SONS, c1915, hl in robes, print, for *National Photographic Record*, vol 1, NPG. WALTER STONEMAN, 1919, hs, NPG (NPR). F.BREMNER, c1926, wl in viceroy's robes, print, NPG X1109.

READING, Stella, née Charnaud, Baroness Swanborough and Marchioness of (1894-1971) founder of the Women's Royal Voluntary Service.

P SIR JAMES GUNN, hl, Women's Royal Voluntary Service, London. CYNTHIA BRANTS, posthumous, after a photograph, hl, WRVS.

PH HOWARD COSTER, 1940, various sizes, prints and negs, NPG X2166–67 and others. Various photographs, WRVS.

REBBECK, Sir Frederick (Ernest) (1877-1964) shipbuilder and marine engineer.

PH WALTER STONEMAN, 1947, hs, NPG (NPR).

REDMAYNE, Sir Richard Augustine Studdert (1865-1955) mining engineer.

P DOROTHY VICAJI, tql, Institution of Civil Engineers, London.

PH WALTER STONEMAN, 2 hs portraits, 1917 and 1943, NPG (NPR).

REDMOND, William Hoey Kearney (1861-1917) Irish nationalist.

D FREDERICK PEGRAM, c1888–89, at Parnell Special Commission session, pencil sketch, V & A.

G S.P.HALL, c1888–89, hs at Parnell Commission, pencil, NPG 2286.

PH JOHN RUSSELL & SONS, c1915, hl in uniform, print, for *National Photographic Record*, vol 1 NPG.

REDPATH, Anne (1895-1965) painter.

P LESZEK MUSZYNSKI, 1948, wl seated, NPG 5171.

D Self-portrait, c1958–60, hs, chalk, SNPG 2380.

REED, Austin Leonard (1873-1954) men's outfitter.

P SIR JAMES GUNN, copy, Austin Reed Ltd, Thirsk, Yorks.

C FRED MAY, wl, profile, gouache, NPG.

REED, Sir (Herbert) Stanley (1872-1969) journalist and politician.

PH WALTER STONEMAN, 2 hs portraits, 1930 and 1947, NPG (NPR).

REEVE, Ada (1874-1966) actress.

PH W.M.WHITELEY, hs in Oriental dress, postcard, NPG. WHITLOCK, tql, postcard, NPG.

REGAN, Charles Tate (1878-1943) zoologist and director of the British Museum (Natural History).

PH LAFAYETTE, c1935–36, hs, print, British Museum (Natural History), London. HOWARD COSTER, c1936, tql, print, NPG X2176.

REID, Forrest (1875-1947) novelist and critic.

P J.S.SLEATOR, Ulster Museum, Belfast. J.ARTHUR GREEVES, Royal Academical Institution, Belfast.

REID, James Scott Cumberland Reid, Baron (1890-1975) judge.

PH WALTER BIRD, 1959, hs, NPG (NPR).

REILLY, Sir Charles Herbert (1874-1948) professor of architecture.

P MARJORIE BROOKS, c1934, University Club, Liverpool. AUGUSTUS JOHN, University of Liverpool. T.A.WEST, 2 portraits, University of Liverpool.

G ALBERT LIPCZINSKI, staff group, Faculty of Arts, University of Liverpool.

PH WALTER STONEMAN, 1944, hs, NPG (NPR). KARL POLLAK, c1948, hl, print, NPG.

REITH, John Charles Walsham Reith, 1st Baron (1889-1971) first director-general of the BBC.

P SIR OSWALD BIRLEY, 1933, hl, SNPG L280.

D EDMOND KAPP, 1931, chalk, Barber Institute, Birmingham University. SIR WILLIAM ROTHENSTEIN, hs, chalk, NPG 4648. SIR W.ROTHENSTEIN, chalk, Laing Art Gallery, Newcastle-upon-Tyne.

C SIR DAVID LOW, tql, chalk, for *The New Statesman and Nation*, 11 Nov 1933, NPG 4566; related sketches, pencil, NPG 4529(294–97). SIR MAX BEERBOHM, 1938, drg, BBC, London.

PH OLIVE EDIS, 1925, 3 hs portraits, 1 autochrome (NPG X7201), and 2 prints, NPG. HOWARD COSTER, 1930s, various sizes and negs, NPG. WALTER STONEMAN, 2 hs portraits, 1934 and 1946, NPG (NPR). WALTER BIRD, 1962, hs, NPG (NPR). Various photographs, NPG (*Daily Herald*).

RENDALL, Montague John (1862-1950) headmaster of Winchester College.

P GLYN PHILPOT, 1925, tql seated in academic robes, Winchester College, Hants.

RENDEL, Harry Stuart Goodhart-, see Goodhart-Rendel.

RENDLE, Alfred Barton (1865-1938) botanist.
PH WALTER STONEMAN, 1931, hs, NPG (NPR).

RHONDDA, Margaret Haig Thomas, Viscountess (1883-1958) founder and editor of *Time and Tide*.
P ALICE M.BURTON, 1932, Trust Houses Forte Ltd, London.

RICARDO, Sir Harry Ralph (1885-1974) engineer.
PH WALTER STONEMAN, 2 hs portraits, 1931 and 1943, NPG (NPR).

RICHARDS, Ivor Armstrong (b1893) literary critic.
P RICHARD STONE, 1979, Magdalene College, Cambridge.

RICHARDSON, Sir Albert Edward (1880-1964) architect.
PH SIR CECIL BEATON, hl, print, NPG. WALTER STONEMAN, 1955, hs, NPG (NPR).

RICHARDSON, Ethel Florence Lindesay (1870-1946) novelist 'Henry Handel Richardson'.
D R.G.EVES, National Gallery of Victoria, Melbourne, Australia.

RICHARDSON, Henry Handel, see Ethel Florence Lindesay RICHARDSON.

RICHARDSON, Lewis Fry (1881-1953) physicist and meteorologist.
PH WALTER STONEMAN, 1931, hs, NPG (NPR).

RICHARDSON, Sir Owen Willans (1879-1959) physicist.
PH WALTER STONEMAN, 4 hs portraits, 1917, 1939 and 1955, NPG (NPR).

RICHMOND, Sir Bruce Lyttelton (1871-1964) journalist.
PH WALTER STONEMAN, 1946, hs, NPG (NPR).

RICHMOND, Sir Herbert William (1871-1946) admiral and master of Downing College, Cambridge.
P W.G.DE GLEHN, c1942, in admiral's uniform, Downing College. HENRY LAMB, 1944, in academic robes, Downing College.
PH WALTER STONEMAN, 3 hs portraits, the 1st two in uniform, 1921, 1931 and 1943, NPG (NPR).

RICKETTS, Charles (de Sousy) (1866-1931) painter and designer.
P C.H.SHANNON, 1898, hl, profile, 'The Man in the Inverness Cape', NPG 3106. J.E.BLANCHE, 1904, hl with C.H.Shannon, TATE 4907. C.H.SHANNON, 1916, hl seated, 'The Man with the Greek vase', Leamington Spa Museum and Art Gallery.
D ALPHONSE LEGROS, 1895, head, silverpoint, Fitzwilliam Museum, Cambridge. C.H.SHANNON, 1899, head, chalk, NPG 2631. FRANCIS DODD, 1905, hs, profile, chalk, BM. LAURA ANNING-BELL, c1920, head, profile, pencil, NPG 3108.
G CHARLES RICKETTS, self-portrait in group 'Fancy Dress Party', oil?, c1903, Carlisle City Art Gallery.
SC LADY KATHLEEN KENNET, bronze statuette, Leeds City Art Gallery.
PR C.H.SHANNON, 1894, wl seated, 'The Wood Engraver', lith, Carlisle City Art Gallery, and V & A. SIR WILLIAM ROTHENSTEIN, 1897, tql seated with Shannon, lith, NPG. Self-portrait, c1899, chiaroscuro woodcut, Fitzwilliam Museum.
C SIR MAX BEERBOHM, 1907, wl with Shannon in studio with 'John Bull', w/c and pen, Fitzwilliam Museum. SIR M.BEERBOHM, 1911, wl with Shannon, parody of Rossetti's painting 'Found', drg, Johannesburg Art Gallery, S Africa. EDMUND DULAC, 1914?, wl seated with Shannon as Oriental deities, w/c and pen, Fitzwilliam Museum. E.DULAC, 1920, wl with Shannon as medieval saints, tempera, Fitzwilliam Museum.
PH G.C.BERESFORD, 2 hs portraits, prints, NPG. G.C.BERESFORD, 1903, hs with Shannon, neg, NPG x6624.

RIDDELL of Walton Heath, George Allardice Riddell,

Baron (1865-1934) newspaper proprietor.
P SIR WILLIAM ORPEN, 1919, tql seated, SNPG 1283; version?, Stationers' Hall, London. M.L.WILLIAMS, after a photograph, hs, National Museum of Wales 673, Cardiff.
G SIR W.ORPEN, 'The Signing of Peace in the Hall of Mirrors, Versailles, 1919', oil, IWM.
SC SIR W.R.DICK, c1931, bust, Royal Free Hospital, London.
C SIR DAVID LOW, pencil sketch, NPG 4529(298).
PH LAFAYETTE, c1920, hs, print, NPG.

RIEU, Emile Victor (1887-1972) editor and publisher.
PH WALTER STONEMAN, 1957, hs, NPG (NPR).

ROBB, Sir James (Milne) (1895-1968) air chief marshal.
P WILLIAM DRING, 1945, IWM.
PH WALTER STONEMAN, 1948, hs, NPG (NPR).

ROBECK, Sir John Michael De, see De Robeck.

ROBERTON, Sir Hugh (Stevenson) (1874-1952) conductor and founder of the Glasgow Orpheus Choir.
D WILLIAM NIVEN, ink, SNPG 2063.
PH ELLIOTT & FRY, hs, print, NPG. WALTER STONEMAN, 2 hs portraits, 1940 and 1945, NPG (NPR) and NPG x5889.

ROBERTS, Sir Alfred (1897-1963) trade unionist.
PH Several photographs, Trades Union Congress, London.

ROBERTS, George Henry (1869-1928) politician and labour leader.
PH WALTER STONEMAN, 1918, hs, NPG (NPR).

ROBERTS, Sir Sydney (Castle) (1887-1966) master of Pembroke College, Cambridge.
P PETER GREENHAM, Pembroke College.
PH WALTER STONEMAN, 1949, hs, NPG (NPR).

ROBERTS, William (1895-1980) artist.
P Self-portrait, c1928, hs, TATE 5372.
D Self-portrait, c1965, head, pencil and w/c, NPG 5063.
G WILLIAM ROBERTS, self-portrait in group 'Vorticists at the Restaurant de la Tour Eifel: Spring 1915', oil, c1961-62, TATE T528.

ROBERTSON, Sir Charles Grant (1869-1948) historian and academic administrator.
P MEREDITH FRAMPTON, c1941, hl seated at desk, SNPG 1572.

ROBERTSON, Sir Dennis Holme (1890-1963) economist.
D FRANCIS DODD, 1939, hl, chalk, Marshall Library, University of Cambridge. CAREL WEIGHT, 1950, pencil, Trinity College, Cambridge.
PH WALTER STONEMAN, 1939, hs, NPG (NPR).

ROBERTSON, George Matthew (1864-1932) psychiatrist.
P SIR JAMES GUNN, 1930, tql seated, SNPG 2235.

ROBERTSON, Sir Howard (Morley) (1888-1963) architect.
P RODRIGO MOYNIHAN, c1954, tql, RIBA.
PH HOWARD COSTER, 1953, hs and tql, prints, NPG x2115 and x2320-21. WALTER STONEMAN, 1955, hs, NPG (NPR).

ROBERTSON, Sir Robert (1869-1949) explosives expert and government chemist.
PH WALTER STONEMAN, 2 hs portraits, 1921 and 1943, NPG (NPR).

ROBERTSON, Walford Graham (1866-1948) painter and playwright.
P J.S.SARGENT, 1894, wl, TATE 5066. Self-portrait, 1914, hl with young girl, Russell-Cotes Art Gallery and Museum, Bournemouth.
PH FREDERICK HOLLYER, early 1890s, hl, print, NPG P47.

ROBERTSON, Sir William Robert, 1st Bart (1860-1933) field-marshal.

P H.MEDIRIA, in uniform, Staff College, Camberley, Surrey. CUTHBERT ORDE, *c*1935, tql, Staff College. UNKNOWN, tql, Cavalry and Guards Club, London.

D FRANCIS DODD, 1918, charcoal and w/c, IWM.

G J.S.SARGENT, 'General Officers of World War I, 1914–18', oil, 1922, NPG 1954.

SC LADY FREDA FORRES, *c*1926, bronze bust, IWM.

PH MRS ALBERT BROOM, military and royal group on horseback in Hyde Park, neg, NPG x709. G.C.BERESFORD, 1916, hs in uniform, profile, neg, NPG x6571. G.C.BERESFORD, 1924, hs and tql in uniform, negs, NPG x6569–70. WALTER STONEMAN, 2 hs portraits in uniform, 1917 and 1928, NPG (NPR).

ROBERTSON SCOTT, John William (1866-1962) journalist.

PH HOWARD COSTER, 1930s, various sizes, prints and negs, NPG x2116–17 and others.

ROBERTSON of Oakridge, Sir Brian Hubert Robertson, Baron (1896-1974) general.

P WILLIAM EVANS, 1967, hl in uniform, Royal Engineers Head-quarters Mess, Chatham.

C SIR DAVID LOW, several pencil sketches, NPG 4529(304–06).

PH WALTER STONEMAN, 1947, hs in uniform, NPG (NPR). WALTER BIRD, 1960, hs, NPG (NPR).

ROBEY, Sir George Edward (1869-1954) comedian.

D EDMOND KAPP, 1932, as Menelaus, Barber Institute, Birmingham University.

C Self-portrait, 2 clown's heads, pen and ink, NPG 3939 and 3939A. Self-portrait, hs, pen and ink, NPG 4323. Self-portrait, 1944, head, pen and ink, NPG 5082. R.S.SHERRIFFS, 1936, wl, profile, ink and wash, NPG.

PR CHARLES BUCHEL & HASSALL, hs and wl, lith, NPG.

PH ROTARY PHOTO, hs as young man, postcard, NPG. UNKNOWN, *c*1937–38, hs, print, NPG. UNKNOWN, *c*1938, hs and hl in bowler hat, prints, NPG. UNKNOWN, *c*1940–41, tql as dame in pantomime, print, NPG. WALTER STONEMAN, 1954, 2 hs portraits, NPG (NPR).

ROBINSON, (Esmé Stuart) Lennox (1886-1958) Irish dramatist and theatre director.

P DERMOD O'BRIEN, 1918, Ulster Museum, Belfast. D.O'BRIEN, hl seated with cat, NGI 1862. JAMES SLEATOR, Abbey Theatre, Dublin.

D SIR WILLIAM ROTHENSTEIN, Municipal Gallery of Modern Art, Dublin.

ROBINSON, (George) Geoffrey, see Dawson.

ROBINSON, Harold Roper (1889-1955) scientist.

PH WALTER STONEMAN, 2 hs portraits, 1931 and 1954, NPG (NPR).

ROBINSON, Henry Wheeler (1872-1945) Baptist divine and Old Testament scholar.

P SIR JAMES GUNN, Regent's Park Baptist College, Oxford.

ROBINSON, Sir Robert (1886-1975) chemist and Nobel prize winner.

P A.K.LAWRENCE, *c*1950, tql seated in robes, Royal Society, London; related hl portrait, NPG 5112.

D JAMES GRANT, 1956, hs, Magdalen College, Oxford.

PH WALTER STONEMAN, 1933, hs, NPG (NPR). WALTER BIRD, 1963, hl, NPG (NPR).

ROBINSON, Roy Lister Robinson, Baron (1883-1952) forester.

PH WALTER STONEMAN, 1947, hs, NPG (NPR).

ROBINSON, Sir (William) Arthur (1874-1950) civil servant.

PH WALTER STONEMAN, 2 hs portraits, 1921 and 1942, NPG (NPR).

ROBINSON, William Heath (1872-1944) cartoonist and book illustrator.

SL H.L.OAKLEY, hs, profile, NPG.

ROBISON, Robert (1883-1941) biochemist.

PH WALTER STONEMAN, 1931, hs, NPG (NPR).

ROCHE, Alexander Adair Roche, Baron (1871-1956) judge.

P SIR JAMES GUNN, tql seated in robes, Wadham College, Oxford.

PH WALTER STONEMAN, 1931, hs, NPG (NPR).

ROE, Sir (Edwin) Alliott Verdon Verdon-, see Verdon-Roe.

ROGERS, Sir Leonard (1868-1962) major-general.

PH WALTER STONEMAN, 2 hs portraits in uniform, 1921 and 1933, NPG (NPR).

ROGERS, Leonard James (1862-1933) mathematician.

PH ERNEST HALL, hs, oval, print, NPG.

ROLLESTON, Sir Humphrey Davy, Bart (1862-1944) physician.

P SIR JAMES GUNN, St George's Hospital, London.

PH WALTER STONEMAN, 2 hs portraits, the 1st in uniform, 1917 and 1931, NPG (NPR).

ROLLS, Charles Stewart (1877-1910) engineer and aviator.

P UNKNOWN, hs in flying gear, Monmouth Museum.

D ELEANOR FORTESCUE-BRICKDALE, posthumous, 'The Guardian Angel', w/c, Monmouth Museum.

SC SIR WILLIAM GOSCOMBE JOHN, 1911, bronze statue, Monmouth. LADY KATHLEEN KENNET, 1912, bronze statuette, Monmouth Museum; bronze statue, Dover.

PH UNKNOWN, hs, print, NPG.

ROMER, Sir Charles Robert Ritchie (1897-1969) judge.

G NORMAN HEPPLE, 'A short Adjournment', oil, 1958, Lincoln's Inn, London.

ROMER, Mark Lemon Romer, Baron (1866-1944) judge.

PH WALTER STONEMAN, 1936, hs, NPG (NPR).

RONALD, Sir Landon (1873-1938) musician and conductor.

P JOHN COLLIER, 1928, tql, Guildhall School of Music, London.

D SIR BERNARD PARTRIDGE, hl seated, pencil, for *Punch*, 27 March 1929, NPG 3676. ERNEST PROCTER, 1929, 2 heads, pencil, at Delius Festival, Queen's Hall, London, NPG 4975(12–13).

C 'ASTL', wl, profile, mechanical repro, for *Vanity Fair*, 3 Dec 1913, NPG.

PH WALTER STONEMAN, 2 hs portraits, 1924 and 1934, NPG (NPR).

ROOTES, William Edward Rootes, 1st Baron (1894-1964) motor car manufacturer.

PH WALTER STONEMAN, 1942, hs, NPG (NPR).

ROSENBERG, Isaac (1890-1918) painter and poet.

P Self-portrait, 1911, hl, TATE T1550. Self-portrait, 1915, hs, NPG 4129.

PH Various photographs, Tower Hamlets Library, London.

ROSENHEIM, (Sigmund) Otto (1871-1955) organic chemist and biochemist.

PH WALTER STONEMAN, 1931, hs, NPG (NPR).

ROSS, Sir (Edward) Denison (1871-1940) orientalist.

P FRANK BERESFORD, 1937, tql in academic robes, School of Oriental and African Studies, University of London.

D SIR RICHARD PAGET, 1929, sketch, pencil, The Athenaeum,

London. HELEN M.CAMPBELL, 1939, hs, profile, pencil, NPG 3981. FRANK KOVACS, c1939, hs, profile, pencil, sketch for medallion, NPG 4203B. SIR WILLIAM ROTHENSTEIN, head, School of Oriental and African Studies.
SC F.KOVACS, c1939, plaster medallion and bronze cast, NPG 4203 and NPG 4203A.
C SIR DAVID LOW, 2 sketches, pencil, NPG 4529(308–09).

ROSS, Sir James Paterson, 1st Bart (b1895) surgeon.
P A.R.THOMSON, 1965, tql seated, St Bartholomew's Hospital, London.
PH WALTER STONEMAN, 1949, hs, NPG (NPR). WALTER BIRD, 1962, hs, NPG (NPR).

ROSS, Martin, see Violet Florence MARTIN.

ROSS, Sir (William) David (1877-1971) philosopher and vice-chancellor of Oxford University.
PH WALTER STONEMAN, 3 hs portraits, 1930, 1945 and 1955, NPG (NPR).

ROTHENSTEIN, Albert Daniel, see Rutherston.

ROTHENSTEIN, Sir William (1872-1945) artist and teacher of art.
P Self-portrait, c1895, fragment, Graves Art Gallery, Sheffield. AUGUSTUS JOHN, c1904, hs, Walker Art Gallery, Liverpool. Self-portrait, c1906, hl with palette, Bradford City Art Gallery. Self-portrait, 1917, hl, Carlisle City Art Gallery. Self-portrait, 1919, hl, Manchester City Art Gallery. Self-portrait, 1930, hs, NPG 5000.
D Self-portrait, various drawings: Leeds City Art Gallery, Manchester City Art Gallery, NPG 3880 and NPG 4433. EDMUND DULAC, sketch, pencil, RAF Museum, Hendon, London. A.K.LAWRENCE, head, charcoal and pencil, The Athenaeum, London. ALBERT RUTHERSTON, ink and wash, Manchester City Art Gallery.
G SIR WILLIAM ORPEN, 'The Selecting Jury of the New English Art Club, 1909', oil, NPG 2556. HENRY TONKS, 1903, family group, w/c, The Athenaeum.
PR J.S.SARGENT, 1897, tql, lith, BM and NPG 4414.
C SIR MAX BEERBOHM, various caricatures: University of Texas, Austin, USA; Royal College of Art, London; Merton College, Oxford; Art Gallery of New South Wales, Sydney, Australia; Lilly Library, University of Indiana, Bloomington, USA; and
V & A. H.TONKS, hl as Sancho Panza with D.S.MacColl as Don Quixote, pencil and w/c, BM.
PH HILLS & SAUNDERS, 1894, tql, cabinet, NPG. G.C.BERESFORD, c1900?, 2 hs portraits, print and neg, NPG. G.C.BERESFORD, 1920, 2 hs portraits, print and neg, NPG. HOWARD COSTER, 1930s, various sizes and negs, NPG. WALTER STONEMAN, 1940, hs, for NPR, NPG X4134.

ROTHERMERE, Harold Sidney Harmsworth, 1st Viscount (1868-1940) newspaper proprietor.
P P.A.DE LÁSZLÓ, c1936, tql in uniform, Middle Temple, London.
SC SIR JACOB EPSTEIN, bronze bust, RAF Museum, Hendon, London.

ROTHERWICK, Herbert Robin Cayzer, 1st Baron (1881-1958) shipowner, politician and soldier.
PH WALTER STONEMAN, 1939, hs, NPG (NPR).

ROTHSCHILD, Sir Lionel Walter Rothschild, 2nd Baron (1868-1937) banker and amateur scientist.
P RENÉ DE L'HÔPITAL, Manchester Great Synagogue.
C SIR LESLIE WARD ('Spy'), wl, lith, for Vanity Fair, 13 Sept 1900, NPG.
PH WALTER STONEMAN, c1915, hs, NPG (NPR).

ROUSE, William Henry Denham (1863-1950) schoolmaster and classical scholar.
P H.W.G.BETTERIDGE, The Perse School, Cambridge.
SC GEORGE THOMAS, 1928, bronze bust, Christ's College, Cambridge.
PH UNKNOWN, 1941, print, Christ's College.

ROWLEY, Arthur Henderson, Baron (1893-1968) politician.
PH WALTER STONEMAN, 2 hs portraits, 1942 and 1958, NPG (NPR).

ROWNTREE, Benjamin Seebohm (1871-1954) sociologist.
PH WALTER STONEMAN, 1931, hs, NPG (NPR).

ROXBURGH, John Fergusson (1888-1954) first headmaster of Stowe School.
P SIR JAMES GUNN, Stowe School, Bucks.

ROYCE, Sir (Frederick) Henry, Bart (1863-1933) engineer.
SC F.D.WOOD, 1922, bronze statue, The Arboretum, Derby. WILLIAM MCMILLAN, 1934, bust, Rolls-Royce Ltd, Derby.

ROYDEN, (Agnes) Maude, Mrs G.W.H.Shaw (1876-1956) preacher.
P P.A.DE LÁSZLÓ, 1932, tql, Lady Margaret Hall, Oxford.
PH HOWARD COSTER, various sizes and negs, NPG.

ROYDEN, Sir Thomas Royden, Baron (1871-1950) shipowner.
P SIR OSWALD BIRLEY, Cunard Steam-Ship Co Ltd, Liverpool.
PH WALTER STONEMAN, 1919, hs, NPG (NPR).

RUCK, Berta, Mrs Oliver Onions (1878-1978) writer.
PH JOHN RUSSELL & SONS, c1915, tql seated, print, for National Photographic Record, vol 1, NPG.

RUFFSIDE, Douglas Clifton Brown, 1st Viscount (1879-1958) speaker of House of Commons.
P SIR W.O.HUTCHISON, 1953, wl in robes, Palace of Westminster, London.
PH WALTER STONEMAN, 1947, hl, NPG (NPR).

RUGBY, John Loader Maffey, 1st Baron (1877-1969) governor-general of the Sudan and diplomat.
PH WALTER STONEMAN, 1947, hs, NPG (NPR).

RUMBOLD, Sir Horace George Montagu, 9th Bart (1869-1941) diplomat.
PH UNKNOWN, 1900, hs, print, NPG. WALTER STONEMAN, 2 hs portraits, 1919 and 1936, NPG (NPR).

RUNCIMAN of Doxford, Walter Runciman, 1st Viscount (1870-1949) statesman.
P R.G.EVES, c1937, hs, The General Council of British Shipping, London.
PR WILLIAM STRANG, 1913, tql seated, drypoint, NPG 5157.
C SIR BERNARD PARTRIDGE, 'The Cabinet Cherubs', ink, for Punch, 22 April 1908, NPG. 'MATT', 1924, hs, pen and ink, NPG 5141. EDMOND KAPP, 1929, hs, charcoal, Barber Institute, Birmingham University.
PH JOHN RUSSELL & SONS, c1915, hs, print, for National Photographic Record, vol 1, NPG. OLIVE EDIS, c1930s, hs, 2 prints, NPG X4096 and X4173. VANDYK, c1937, hs, profile, print, NPG.

RUSHBROOKE, James Henry (1870-1947) Baptist divine.
P L.D.M.PURSER, Hampstead Garden Suburb Free Church, London.

RUSHBURY, Sir Henry (George) (1889-1968) artist.
G T.C.DUGDALE, 'Lunch at the Chelsea Arts Club', oil, Chelsea Arts Club, London.
SC MAURICE LAMBERT, 1959, terracotta bust, Royal Academy, London.

RUSHCLIFFE, Henry Bucknall Betterton, Baron (1872-1949) politician.
PH WALTER STONEMAN, 1943, hs, NPG (NPR).

RUSSELL, Arthur Oliver Villiers, see 2nd Baron Ampthill.

RUSSELL, Bertrand Arthur William Russell, 3rd Earl (1872-1970) philosopher.
P ROGER FRY, c1923, hs, NPG 4832.
D JOHN WHEATLEY, 1947, pen and indian ink wash, Trinity College, Cambridge.
C SIR DAVID LOW, several sketches, pencil, NPG 4529(321). GEOFFREY DAVIEN, plaster bust, 'sculptoon', NPG. DAVID LEVINE, 1967, wl, ink, NPG.
SC BORIS ANREP, 1952, hl, profile, as 'Lucidity' in 'The Modern Virtues', mosaic, National Gallery, London.
PH WALTER STONEMAN, 1930, hs, NPG (NPR). HOWARD COSTER, 1935 and 1954, various sizes, prints and negs, NPG AX3519 and X2090-96. WALTER BIRD, 1960, hl, NPG (NPR). Various photographs, NPG (*Daily Herald*).

RUSSELL, Sir Charles, 1st Bart (1863-1928) solicitor.
C SIR LESLIE WARD ('Spy'), wl, w/c study, for *Vanity Fair*, 10 April 1907, NPG 2997.
PH LAFAYETTE, hs, print, NPG.

RUSSELL, Sir (Edward) John (1872-1965) agriculturalist.
PH WALTER STONEMAN, 3 hs portraits, 1923, 1933 and 1942, NPG (NPR).

RUSSELL, George William, 'AE' (1867-1935) Irish poet, economist and journalist.
P S.H.PURSER, c1902, NGI 1024. C.D.MARKIEWICZ, c1903, Municipal Gallery of Modern Art, Dublin. J.B.YEATS, 1903, tql seated, NGI 871. J.B.YEATS, 1905, Abbey Theatre, Dublin. DERMOD O'BRIEN, c1914, Abbey Theatre. HILDA ROBERTS, 1929, hs, Ulster Museum, Belfast. LILLIAN DAVIDSON, 2 portraits, University of Texas, Austin, USA. NIGEL NEWTON, NGI 1252.
D J.B.YEATS, 1898, pencil, NGI. J.B.YEATS, pencil, University of Texas. EDMOND KAPP, 1919, Barber Institute, Birmingham University. SIR WILLIAM ROTHENSTEIN, 1921, head, NGI. SEAN O'SULLIVAN, 1935, head on deathbed, chalk, Municipal Gallery of Modern Art and Public Art Gallery, Limerick.
G JOHN KEATING, 'Homage to Hugh Lane', oil, c1924, Municipal Gallery of Modern Art.
SC JOHN HUGHES, c1885-86, plaster bust, Municipal Gallery of Modern Art. OLIVER SHEPPARD, 1916, sandstone bust, NGI 8092. THEODORE SPICER-SIMSON, 1922, plasticine medallion, NGI 8138, and bronze cast, NGI 8219. JEROME CONNOR, c1926, bronze bust, Public Art Gallery, Limerick. JEANETTE HARE, c1931, bronze bust, NPG 3926. DONALD GILBERT, c1933, bronze bust, Ulster Museum.

PR MARY DUNCAN, c1912-13, hs, lith, NPG 3980. A.H.FISHER, c1934, hs, etch, Carlisle City Art Gallery.

RUSSELL, Mary du Caurroy, see Duchess of Bedford.

RUSSELL, Sir Thomas Wentworth, 'Russell Pasha' (1879-1954) Egyptian civil servant.
P JOHN WARD, 1956, Haileybury and Imperial Service College, Herts.
PH WALTER STONEMAN, 1949, hs, NPG (NPR).

RUSSELL, Sir Walter Westley (1867-1949) painter and teacher.
D AMBROSE MCEVOY, w/c, Royal Academy, London.
PH G.C.BERESFORD, 1922, 2 hs portraits, negs, NPG X6580-81.

RUSSELL of Killowen, Francis Xavier Joseph Russell, Baron (1867-1946) judge.
P R.G.EVES, 1937, hs, Lincoln's Inn, London.
PH WALTER STONEMAN, 1929, hs, NPG (NPR).

RUTHERFORD, Dame Margaret, Mrs Stringer Davis (1892-1972) actress.
D MICHAEL NOAKES, 1970, hs, pencil, NPG 4937.

RUTHERFORD of Nelson, Ernest Rutherford, Baron (1871-1937) physicist.
P P.A.DE LÁSZLÓ, 1924, hl in robes, Trinity College, Cambridge. SIR OSWALD BIRLEY, 1932, tql, Royal Society, London. SIR JAMES GUNN, 1932, hs, NPG 2935. F.L.EMANUEL, 1936, tql seated, Nelson College, Nelson, New Zealand.
D SIR WILLIAM ROTHENSTEIN, c1925, head, sanguine and pencil, NPG 4793. RANDOLPH SCHWABE, 1928, pencil, Trinity College. FRANCIS DODD, 1934, hs, chalk, NPG 4426. F.DODD, 1934, hs, charcoal, Fitzwilliam Museum, Cambridge.
SC ERIC GILL, c1933, relief portrait on stone plaque, Mond Laboratory, University of Cambridge. BORIS ANREP, 1952, hs splitting the atom, as 'Curiosity' in 'The Modern Virtues', mosaic, National Gallery, London.
PH WALTER STONEMAN, 1921, hs, NPG (NPR). OLIVE EDIS, c1920-30, hs, print, NPG.

RUTHERSTON, Albert Daniel, real name Rothenstein (1881-1953) artist.
P Self-portrait, c1898, wl, Ferens Art Gallery, Hull.
G GERARD CHOWNE, oil, 1910, Bradford City Art Gallery.

RUTHVEN, Alexander Gore Arkwright Hore-, see 1st Earl of Gowrie.

RYLE, Gilbert (1900-1976) philosopher.
P REX WHISTLER, Magdalen College, Oxford.
D H.A.FREETH, 1952, tql seated, sepia and w/c, NPG 5092.
G ALAN SORRELL, group in senior common room, oil, 1954, Magdalen College.

S

SACKVILLE, Charles John Sackville-West, 4th Baron (1870-1962) major-general.

P H.A.OLIVIER, 1919, IWM. SIR WILLIAM ORPEN, 1919, hl seated in uniform, NPG 4649.

SACKVILLE-WEST, Victoria Mary ('Vita'), Mrs Harold Nicolson (1892-1962) writer.

P WILLIAM STRANG, tql seated, Glasgow City Art Gallery.

PH SIR CECIL BEATON, wl seated in garden, print, NPG. HOWARD COSTER, 1930s, various sizes, prints and negs, NPG X10666-67 and X12029-31. WALTER STONEMAN, 1957, hs, NPG (NPR).

SADLER, Sir Michael Ernest (1861-1943) educational pioneer and art patron.

P MARK GERTLER, 1914, University of Leeds. JACOB KRAMER, 1917, Department of Extra-mural Studies, Oxford University. HENRY LAMB, University of Leeds.

D SIR WILLIAM ROTHENSTEIN, c1916, University of Leeds.

G F.H.SHEPHERD, group of master and fellows, oil, University College, Oxford.

SC LORIS REY, 1933, bronze bust, Brotherton Library, University of Leeds.

PH G.C.BERESFORD, 1914, hs, neg, NPG X6582. WALTER STONEMAN, 1921, hs, NPG (NPR).

ST DAVIDS, Sir John Wynford Philipps, 13th Bart and 1st Viscount (1860-1938) financier.

PH WALTER STONEMAN, 1917, hs, NPG (NPR).

ST JUST, Edward Charles Grenfell, 1st Baron (1870-1941) banker and politician.

C FRED MAY, hs, profile, gouache, NPG.

SALAMAN, Redcliffe Nathan (1874-1955) authority on the potato.

P CHATTIE SALAMAN, National Institute of Agricultural Botany, Cambridge.

SALISBURY, Frank O. (1874-1962) portrait painter.

P Self-portrait, 1924, tql seated in robes, Russell-Cotes Art Gallery, Bournemouth.

PH A.C.COOPER, hl with palette, print, NPG. KARL POLLAK, hl, print, NPG.

SALISBURY, James Edward Hubert Gascoyne-Cecil, 4th Marquess of (1861-1947) statesman.

P A.BISHOP, 1874, wl on a pony, Hatfield House, Herts. SIR W.B.RICHMOND, 1882, tql in uniform, Hatfield House. GLYN PHILPOT, 1917, wl in robes, Hatfield House.

D UNKNOWN, c1867, head, pencil, Hatfield House. SIR GEORGE RICHMOND, 1873, hs, profile, chalk, Hatfield House.

G F.H.SHEPHERD, family group, oil, 1928, University College, Oxford; version, Hatfield House.

SC BENNO ELKAN, 1949, bronze bust, Palace of Westminster, London.

C SIR LESLIE WARD, wl, w/c, Hatfield House. SIR MAX BEERBOHM, 1913, 'Cecils in Conclave', wash, Hatfield House.

PH ELLIOTT & FRY, hs, print, for *Our Conservative and Unionist Statesmen*, vol 2, NPG (Album 25). WALTER STONEMAN, 1917, hs, NPG (NPR). VIVIENNE, 1940, hs, print, NPG X6050.

SALISBURY, Robert Arthur James Gascoyne-Cecil, 5th Marquess of (1893-1972) statesman.

P SIR WILLIAM ORPEN, c1914-19, hs, Hatfield House, Herts. DEREK HILL, 1967, tql in Garter robes, Hatfield House.

D J.S.SARGENT, 1915, head, chalk, Hatfield House. J.S.SARGENT, 1915, head, pencil, Hatfield House. HENRY LAMB, 1950, hs, chalk, Hatfield House.

M UNKNOWN, hs as youth, ivory, Hatfield House.

G EDWARD HALLIDAY, family group, oil, 1951, Hatfield House. JOHN WARD, 'Directors of Westminster Bank, 1968', line and wash, 1969, Westminster Bank, London.

SC LORNE MCKEAN, 1965, bronze bust, Hatfield House. DAVID WYNNE, c1966-67, bronze head, Hatfield House.

PH HOWARD COSTER, 1930s, various sizes and negs, NPG X11086-88. WALTER STONEMAN, 3 hs portraits, 1936, 1941 and 1954, NPG (NPR). WALTER BIRD, 1962, hs, NPG (NPR).

SALMON, Sir Eric Cecil Heygate (1896-1946) administrator.

PH WALTER STONEMAN, 1945, hs, NPG (NPR).

SALMOND, Sir John (Maitland) (1881-1968) air chief marshal.

D FRANCIS DODD, 1917, charcoal and w/c, IWM.

SC L.F.ROSLYN, 1921, bronze bust, IWM.

PH HOWARD COSTER, 1929, various sizes, print and negs, NPG AX2278 and others. WALTER STONEMAN, 2 hs portraits, the 1st in uniform, 1928 and 1953, NPG (NPR).

SALTER, (James) Arthur Salter, 1st Baron (1881-1975) civil servant, politician and author.

PH WALTER STONEMAN, 3 portraits, 1930 and 1945, NPG (NPR) and NPG X511.

SAMMONS, Albert (1886-1957) violinist.

P ALEXANDER AKERBLADH, 1950, hs with violin, Royal College of Music, London.

SC PHYLLIS BLUNDELL, 1928, bronze bust, Royal College of Music. MARGARET WRIGHTSON, 1952, bronze bust, Royal College of Music.

PH OLIVE EDIS, hs with violin, print, NPG.

SAMSON, Charles Rumney (1883-1931) air commodore.

D DONALD MAXWELL, c1916, pen and w/c, IWM. C.R.FLEMING-WILLIAMS, 1916, 'An "OK" Bombing Chikaldir Bridge', w/c, IWM.

SAMUEL, Herbert Louis Samuel, 1st Viscount (1870-1963) statesman, administrator and philosopher.

P F.O.SALISBURY, 1949, tql seated in robes, National Liberal Club, London.

D EDMOND KAPP, 1920, Barber Institute, Birmingham University.

PH HOWARD COSTER, 1930s, various sizes and negs, NPG. OLIVE EDIS, c1932, hs, print and autochrome, NPG X7206. WALTER STONEMAN, 3 hs portraits, 1928, 1940 and 1948, NPG (NPR).

SANDERS, Sir Arthur Penrose Martyn (1898-1974) air chief marshal.

PH WALTER STONEMAN, 2 hs portraits in uniform, 1945 and 1950, NPG (NPR).

SANDERSON, Henry Sanderson Furniss, 1st Baron (1868-1939) principal of Ruskin College, Oxford.

P A.K.LAWRENCE, hs, Ruskin College.
PH WALTER STONEMAN, 1917, hs, NPG (NPR).

SANDWICH, George Charles Montagu, 9th Earl of (1874-1962) art collector and public servant.
P RODRIGO MOYNIHAN, c1946, tql seated, Cambridgeshire County Council.
PH WALTER STONEMAN, 3 hs portraits, 1920, 1930 and 1943, NPG (NPR).

SANGSTER, William Edwin Robert (1900-1960) Methodist minister.
PH WALTER STONEMAN, c1950, hs, NPG (Daily Herald). Various photographs, NPG (Daily Herald).

SANKEY, John Sankey, Viscount (1866-1948) lord chancellor.
P SIR OSWALD BIRLEY, 1930, tql seated in robes, Middle Temple, London. SIR O.BIRLEY, Jesus College, Oxford. E.J.WALTERS, 1937, hs, National Museum of Wales 472, Cardiff.
PH WALTER STONEMAN, 2 hs portraits, 1918 and 1939, NPG (NPR). HOWARD COSTER, 1930s, various sizes, print and negs, NPG X2118 and others. OLIVE EDIS, c1935, hs and tql in robes, print and autochrome, NPG X7207.

SAPPER, (Herman) Cyril, see McNeile.

SARGENT, Sir (Harold) Malcolm (Watts) (1895-1967) conductor.
P JOHN GILROY, hl conducting, Garrick Club, London; version?, Albert Hall, London. SIR GERALD KELLY, 1948, tql, Royal College of Music, London.
D EDMOND KAPP, 1930 and 1946, 2 studies conducting, Barber Institute, Birmingham University. HILDA WIENER, c1935, pencil, Royal College of Music. RUSSELL REEVE, 1939, hl, chalk, Royal College of Music.
SC W.E.NARRAWAY, bronze bust, Royal Festival Hall, London. WILLIAM TIMYN, bronze bust, Royal Albert Hall.
PR A.W.RISSIK, tql, lith, NPG 4657.
C SIR DAVID LOW, several sketches, pencil, NPG 4529(322-27). GEOFFREY DAVIEN, 1964, plaster bust, 'sculpton', NPG.
PH SIR CECIL BEATON, hs, print, NPG. KENNETH N.COLLINS, hs, print, NPG X1445. HOWARD COSTER, various sizes and negs, NPG. WALTER STONEMAN, 2 hs portraits, 1943 and 1955, NPG (NPR).

SARGENT, Sir Orme (1884-1962) permanent under-secretary of state for foreign affairs.
PH WALTER STONEMAN, 1941, hs, NPG (NPR).

SASSOON, Sir (Ellice) Victor, 3rd Bart (1881-1961) businessman.
PH HAMILTON STUDIOS, c1949, hs, print, NPG.

SASSOON, Sir Philip Albert Gustave David, 3rd Bart (1888-1939) politician and connoisseur.
P J.S.SARGENT, 1923, hl, TATE 5052.
C SIR MAX BEERBOHM, 1913, drg, Yale University Library, New Haven, USA.
PH WALTER STONEMAN, 2 hs portraits, 1921 and 1931, NPG (NPR). HOWARD COSTER, 1929, various sizes, print and negs, NPG AX2310, X2119 and others.

SASSOON, Siegfried (1886-1967) poet.
P GLYN PHILPOT, 1917, hs, semi-profile, Fitzwilliam Museum, Cambridge.
C SIR MAX BEERBOHM, 1931, tql, drg, The Spectator, London.
PH SIR CECIL BEATON, hs, print, NPG. HOWARD COSTER, various sizes and negs, NPG. WALTER STONEMAN, 1936, hs, NPG (NPR). UNKNOWN, hs in uniform, print, IWM.

SAUNDBY, Sir Robert Henry Magnus Spencer (1896-

1971) air chief marshal.
P T.C.DUGDALE, c1946, IWM.
PH HOWARD COSTER, various sizes and negs, NPG. WALTER STONEMAN, 1940s, 4 hl portraits in uniform, for NPR, NPG X1028-31.

SAUNDERS, Hilary (Aidan) St George (1898-1951) writer.
PH HOWARD COSTER, various sizes and negs, NPG.

SAXL, Friedrich ('Fritz') (1890-1948) art historian and co-founder of the Warburg Institute.
PH W.HÖFFERT, as a baby, neg, Warburg Institute, London. UNKNOWN, c1912?, hl as a student, neg, Warburg Institute. UNKNOWN, late 1920s, in Warburg Library, Hamburg, neg, Warburg Institute. UNKNOWN, c1930?, hs, neg, Warburg Institute. OTTO FEIN, c1946, head, print, Warburg Institute.

SAYERS, Dorothy Leigh, Mrs O.A.Fleming (1893-1957) writer.
P SIR W.O.HUTCHISON, tql seated, NPG 5146.
PH HOWARD COSTER, 1938, 3 hs portraits, prints, NPG X2322-24.

SCARBROUGH, Sir (Lawrence) Roger Lumley, 11th Earl of (1896-1969) lord chamberlain.
PH WALTER STONEMAN, 3 hs portraits, 1937, 1943 and 1958, NPG (NPR).

SCHILLER, Ferdinand Canning Scott (1864-1937) philosopher.
PH WALTER STONEMAN, 1930, hs, NPG (NPR).

SCHLESWIG-HOLSTEIN, Princess Marie Louise of, see MARIE LOUISE.

SCHOLES, Percy Alfred (1877-1958) musical writer and encyclopaedist.
PH UNKNOWN, hs, print, Oxford University Press, London.

SCHONLAND, Sir Basil Ferdinand Jamieson (1896-1972) director of the Atomic Energy Research Establishment.
PH WALTER STONEMAN, 1957, hs, NPG (NPR).

SCHUSTER, Sir Claud Schuster, Baron (1869-1956) civil servant.
PR SIR WILLIAM ROTHENSTEIN, hs as young man, lith, NPG.
PH WALTER STONEMAN, 3 hs portraits, 1920 and 1945, NPG (NPR) and NPG X5894.

SCHWABE, Randolph (1885-1948) etcher, draughtsman and teacher.
D FRANCIS DODD, chalk, Manchester City Art Gallery. Self-portrait, sketch, pencil, Slade School of Fine Art, University College, London.

SCOBIE, Sir Ronald MacKenzie (1893-1969) lieutenant-general.
PH WALTER STONEMAN, 1946, hs in uniform, NPG (NPR).

SCOONES, Sir Geoffry Allen Percival (1893-1975) general.
PH WALTER STONEMAN, 1953, hs in uniform, NPG (NPR).

SCOTT, Cyril (1879-1970) composer.
P GEORGE HALL NEALE, c1930, hl seated, NPG 5303.
PH HERBERT LAMBERT, c1922, hl seated, photogravure, NPG AX7750.

SCOTT, (Edith Agnes) Kathleen, see Lady Kennet.

SCOTT, Sir Giles Gilbert (1880-1960) architect.
P R.G.EVES, 1935, hs, NPG 4171. R.G.EVES, 1935, RIBA.
D POWYS EVANS, 1927, hs, pen and ink, NPG 4398. ROBIN GUTHRIE, 1937, hs, chalk, NPG 4162.
PH WALTER STONEMAN, 2 hs portraits, 1924 and 1944, NPG (NPR).

SCOTT, Sir Harold (Richard) (1887-1969) police

commissioner.

PH WALTER STONEMAN, 1945, hs, NPG (NPR).

SCOTT, John William Robertson, see Robertson Scott.

SCOTT, Sir Leslie Frederic (1869-1950) politician and judge..

PH WALTER STONEMAN, 1927, hs, NPG (NPR).

SCOTT, Robert Falcon (1868-1912) naval officer and Antarctic explorer.

P D.A.WEHRSCHMIDT, 1905, tql in uniform, NPG 2079. LANCE CALKIN, 1913, formerly United Service Club, London (c/o Crown Commissioners). J.C.LAWRENCE, 1913, hs in uniform, Scott Polar Research Institute, University of Cambridge. HAR-RINGTON MANN, posthumous, Royal Geographical Society, London. C.P.SMALL, posthumous, hs in uniform, NPG 1726.

D E.A.WILSON, 1901, hl seated in uniform, pencil, Scott Institute. E.A.WILSON, hs pencil, Scott Institute.

SL E.A.WILSON, 1902?, head, profile, Scott Institute.

SC LADY KATHLEEN KENNET, posthumous, bronze statue, Waterloo Place, London. LADY KENNET, posthumous, bronze bust, Scott Institute. A.G.WALKER, bronzed plaster group of statues with L.E.G.Oates and E.A.Wilson, Scott Institute.

PR 'HESTER', wl, mechanical repro, for *Vanity Fair*, 19 Feb 1913, NPG.

PH MAULL & FOX, tql in uniform, photogravure, NPG. ERNEST MILLS?, 2 hs portraits, prints, NPG. H.G.PONTING, 1911, wl seated, print, NPG P23. H.G.PONTING, various photographs, Scott Institute. THOMSON, tql in uniform, photogravure, NPG. Various photographs, Scott Institute.

SCOTT-ELLIS, Thomas Evelyn, see 8th Baron Howard de Walden.

SEAFORD, Thomas Evelyn Scott-Ellis, 4th Baron, see 8th Baron Howard de Walden.

SEAL, Sir Eric (Arthur) (1898-1972) civil servant.

PH WALTER STONEMAN, 1955, hs, NPG (NPR).

SEAMAN, Sir Owen, Bart (1861-1936) poet, satirist and parodist.

P H.A.OLIVIER, hl seated, *Punch*, London.

PH A.L.COBURN, 1914, hl seated, profile, photogravure, NPG AX7823. HOWARD COSTER, 1930s, various sizes and negs, NPG.

SEELY, Henry John Alexander, see 2nd Baron Mottistone.

SEELY, John Edward Bernard, see 1st Baron Mottistone.

SELBIE, William Boothby (1862-1944) Congregational divine.

P ERNEST MOORE, Mansfield College, Oxford.

PH JOHN RUSSELL & SONS, c1917, hs, print, for *National Photographic Record*, vol 1, NPG.

SELBORNE, Roundell Cecil Palmer, Viscount Wolmer and 3rd Earl of (1887-1971) politician.

D UNKNOWN, hs, pencil, Church House, London.

PH WALTER STONEMAN, 2 hs portraits, c1917 and 1942, NPG (NPR).

SELBY, Sir Walford Harmood Montague (1881-1965) diplomat.

PH WALTER STONEMAN, 1938, hs, NPG (NPR).

SELIGMAN, Charles Gabriel (1873-1940) ethnologist.

D SIR WILLIAM ROTHENSTEIN, head, pencil, NPG 4833.

PH WALTER STONEMAN, 1933, hs, NPG (NPR).

SELINCOURT, Ernest de (1870-1943) scholar and literary critic.

P FRED YATES, Department of English, Birmingham University.

PH WALTER STONEMAN, 1930, hs, NPG (NPR).

SETON-WATSON, Robert William (1879-1951) historian.

SC IVAN MESTROVIC, portrait on bronze tablet, School of Slavonic and East European Studies, University of London.

SEWARD, Sir Albert Charles (1863-1941) botanist and geologist.

P SIR JAMES GUNN, 1933, Downing College, Cambridge. HAROLD KNIGHT, 1937, hs, Department of Botany, University of Cambridge.

PH OLIVE EDIS, tql, print, NPG.

SEYLER, Athene (b1889) actress.

P FLORENCE GREY-EDWARDS, Garrick Club, London.

D PERCIVAL SMALL, head, pastel, Royal Academy of Dramatic Art, London.

PH GODFREY ARGENT, 1968, 2 hs portraits, NPG (NPR). SIR CECIL BEATON, hl, print, NPG. MADAME YEVONDE, print, NPG.

SHACKLETON, Sir David James (1863-1938) labour leader, politician and civil servant.

PH GEORGE LORD, hs, print, NPG. WALTER STONEMAN, 2 hs portraits, 1917 and 1933, NPG (NPR).

SHACKLETON, Sir Ernest Henry (1874-1922) Antarctic explorer.

P R.G.EVES, 1921, hs, NPG 2608; 2 studies, charcoal, Scott Polar Research Institute, University of Cambridge. R.G.EVES, 1921, hl, NMM, Greenwich; study, oil, Scott Institute.

D E.A.WILSON, 1902, 2 heads, profile, pencil, Scott Institute.

SL E.A.WILSON, 1902, head, profile, Scott Institute.

SC C.J.JAGGER, c1932, statue, Royal Geographical Society, London.

C 'KITE', wl, Hentschel-Colourtype, for *Vanity Fair*, 6 Oct 1909, NPG.

PH SIR BENJAMIN STONE, 1904, wl with the Earl of Balfour, print, NPG. G.C.BERESFORD, 1909, hs, neg, NPG X6585. OLIVE EDIS, 1910, hs, print, NPG. Various photographs, Scott Institute.

SHANNON, Charles Haslewood (Hazelwood) (1863-1937) painter and lithographer.

P Self-portrait, 1897, hl, 'The Man in the Black Shirt', NPG 3107. J.E.BLANCHE, 1904, hl seated with Charles Ricketts, TATE 4907. Self-portrait, 1917, hl, Fitzwilliam Museum, Cambridge; related lith, 1918, NPG 3081, and BM.

D ALPHONSE LEGROS, 1896, hs, profile, silverpoint, Fitzwilliam Museum. A.LEGROS, 1896, hs, chalk, Fitzwilliam Museum. A.LEGROS, 1897, head, profile, pencil, Fitzwilliam Museum. SIR WILLIAM ROTHENSTEIN, 1903, hs, pastel, BM. FRANCIS DODD, 1905, hl, chalk, Fitzwilliam Museum.

SC LADY KATHLEEN KENNET, bronze statuette, Leeds City Art Gallery. R.F.WELLS, bronze head, Fitzwilliam Museum.

PR SIR WILLIAM ROTHENSTEIN, 1897, tql seated, lith, BM, NPG. SIR W.ROTHENSTEIN, 1897, tql seated with Ricketts, lith, NPG. Self-portrait, lith, Carlisle City Art Gallery.

C SIR MAX BEERBOHM, 1907, wl with Ricketts in studio with 'John Bull', w/c and pen, Fitzwilliam Museum. SIR M.BEERBOHM, 1911, wl with Ricketts, parody of Rossetti's painting 'Found', drg, Johannesburg Art Gallery, S Africa. EDMUND DULAC, 1914?, wl seated with Ricketts as oriental deities, w/c and pen, Fitzwilliam Museum. E.DULAC, 1920, wl with Ricketts as medieval saints, tempera, Fitzwilliam Museum.

PH G.C.BERESFORD, 1903, 4 hs portraits, 3 prints and 1 neg, NPG X6586. G.C.BERESFORD, 1903, hs with Ricketts, neg, NPG X6624. A.L.COBURN, 1907, hs, profile, photogravure, NPG AX7780. ELLIOTT & FRY, hs, profile, cabinet, NPG.

SHANNON, Sir James Jebusa (1862-1923) painter.

P Self-portrait, c1919, hl seated, NPG 4412.

SHARP, Evelyn, Mrs H.W.Nevinson (1869-1955) sociologist and suffragette.

D SIR WILLIAM ROTHENSTEIN, 1933, hs, pencil, NPG 4001.

SHAW, (Agnes) Maude, Mrs G.W.H.Shaw, see Royden.

SHAW, Thomas ('Tom') (1872-1938) labour leader and politician.
P WALTER STONEMAN, 1924, hs, NPG (NPR).

SHAW, William Arthur (1865-1943) archivist and historian.
PH UNKNOWN, wl seated in garden, snapshot, NPG.

SHEEPSHANKS, Sir Thomas Herbert (1895-1964) civil servant.
PH WALTER STONEMAN, 1948, hs, NPG (NPR).

SHEPARD, Ernest Howard (1879-1976) artist and illustrator.
PH HOWARD COSTER, 1932, various sizes, print and negs, NPG AX3448 and others. GWEN MORGAN, wl, print, NPG. DAVID MONTGOMERY, 1969, wl seated, cibachrome print, NPG X1455. PATHÉ NEWS PICTORIAL, hs, print, NPG.

SHEPPARD, Hugh Richard Lawrie ('Dick') (1880-1937) dean of Canterbury.
P SIR GERALD KELLY, c1932, tql seated, St Martin-in-the-Fields, London. UNKNOWN, The Deanery, Canterbury.
C SIR DAVID LOW, c1927, head, pencil, NPG 4529(334). SIR D.LOW, 1938, with Aldous Huxley, pencil, chalk and ink, TATE 5464.
PH HOWARD COSTER, 1937, various sizes, prints and negs, NPG X2100–03 and others.

SHEPPARD, Sir John Tressider (1881-1968) provost of King's College, Cambridge.
P JILL CROCKFORD, hl seated, King's College. JOAN HORSLEY, monochrome, King's College. HENRY LAMB, 1944, King's College.
D DUNCAN GRANT, head, pencil, King's College.
PH WALTER STONEMAN, 1947, hs, NPG (NPR).

SHIELS, Sir (Thomas) Drummond (1881-1953) physician and politician.
PH WALTER STONEMAN, 2 hs portraits, 1930 and 1943, NPG (NPR).

SHINWELL, Emanuel ('Manny') Shinwell, Baron (b1884) politician.
C GEOFFREY DAVIEN, plaster head, 'sculptoon', NPG.
PH HOWARD COSTER, 1930s, various sizes and negs, NPG. WALTER STONEMAN, 3 hs portraits, 1924, 1945 and 1958, NPG (NPR). GODFREY ARGENT, 1968, hs, NPG (NPR).

SHIPLEY, Sir Arthur Everett (1861-1927) zoologist.
P P.A.DE LÁSZLÓ, 1925, hs in robes, Christ's College, Cambridge. J.NICHOLSON, Imperial College of Agriculture, Trinidad, West Indies. WINIFRED RIEBER, c1926–27, hs, Department of Zoology, University of Cambridge.
PH OLIVE EDIS, hl seated, print, NPG. WALTER STONEMAN, 1917, hs, NPG (NPR). UNKNOWN, hs, print, NPG.

SHORT (Hugh) Oswald (1883?-1969) aviation pioneer.
PH Various photographs, Short Brothers & Harland Ltd, Queen's Island, Belfast.

SHORTT, Edward (1862-1935) home secretary.
D R.G.EVES, 1922, 3 heads, pencil, NPG 4368A, B and C.
PH WALTER STONEMAN, 1920, hs, NPG (NPR).

SHUCKBURGH, Sir John Evelyn (1877-1953) civil servant.
PH G.C.BERESFORD, 1929, tql in uniform, neg, NPG X6588.

SIBLY, Sir (Thomas) Franklin (1883-1948) geologist and University administrator.
P WILLIAM DRING, 1947, hl seated in robes, University of Reading. W.DRING, University College of Swansea, Wales.

PH WALTER STONEMAN, 1931, hs, NPG (NPR).

SICKERT, Walter Richard (1860-1942) painter.
P Self-portrait, various portraits including: c1896, hs, Leeds City Art Gallery; c1887, wl with palette, Art Gallery of New South Wales, Sydney. Australia; 1907, hs, 'The Juvenile Lead', Southampton Art Gallery; 1907, hl, 'The Painter in his studio', Hamilton Art Gallery, Ontario, Canada; 1929, hs, 'The Servant of Abraham', TATE T259; 1930s?, wl, NPG 3134; 'The Raising of Lazarus', National Gallery of Victoria, Melbourne, Australia. J.A.MCNEILL WHISTLER, 1886?, hs, Municipal Gallery of Modern Art, Dublin. J.E.BLANCHE, 1898, hl, NPG 4761. P.W.STEER, 1890s?, wl, NPG 3142. SYLVIA GOSSE, c1923–25, TATE 4364. HENRY TONKS, 1930, 'Sodales', wl seated with P.W.Steer, TATE T40. J.E.BLANCHE, 1935, wl, Manchester City Art Gallery.
D Self-portrait, 1882, hs, ink, Islington Public Libraries, London. SIR CHARLES HOLROYD, 1897, head, profile, metal-point, BM. Self-portrait, c1903–04, hs, charcoal, pen and ink, Ashmolean Museum, Oxford. EDMOND KAPP, 1940, tql seated, pen and ink, NPG 3547. E.KAPP, pen and indian ink, Fitzwilliam Museum, Cambridge. THERESE LESSORE, w/c, Manchester City Art Gallery. P.W.STEER, sketch, V & A.
G SIR WILLIAM ORPEN, 'Homage to Manet', oil, 1909, Manchester City Art Gallery. SIR W.ORPEN, 'The Selecting Jury of the New English Art Club', oil, 1909, NPG 2556.
SC F.D.WOOD, 1925, bronze bust, Royal Academy, London.
PR HENRY RAYNER, 1931, head, profile, drypoint, NPG and V & A.
C SIR MAX BEERBOHM, various drgs, BM and University of Texas, Austin, USA.
PH G.C.BERESFORD, 1911, 2 hs portraits, negs, NPG X6589–90. Various photographs, Islington Public Libraries. H.WALTER BARNETT, c1910–20, 3 tql portraits, prints, V & A. SIR CECIL BEATON, 1940, tql with wife, print, NPG.

SIDGWICK, Nevil Vincent (1873-1952) chemist.
P J.R.MERTON, Lincoln College, Oxford.
PH WALTER STONEMAN, 1933, hs, NPG (NPR).

SIEFF, Israel Moses Sieff, Baron (1889-1972) businessman.
PH HOWARD COSTER, various sizes and negs, NPG. UNKNOWN, print, Marks & Spencer, London.

SIEPMANN, Otto (1861-1947) teacher of modern languages.
P FRITZ VON KAMPTZ, Clifton College, Bristol.

SILKIN, Lewis Silkin, 1st Baron (1889-1972) politician and administrator.
PH HOWARD COSTER, various sizes and negs, NPG. WALTER STONEMAN, 1945, hs, NPG (NPR). WALTER BIRD, 1962, hs, NPG (NPR).

SILLITOE, Sir Percy (Joseph) (1888-1962) director-general of the Security Service.
PH WALTER STONEMAN, 1947, hs, NPG (NPR).

SILVERMAN, (Samuel) Sidney (1895-1968) politician and opponent of capital punishment.
PH DAILY HERALD, hs, print, NPG.

SIM, Alastair (1900-76) actor.
P EDWARD SEAGO, hs, Garrick Club, London.
PH HOWARD COSTER, various sizes, prints and negs, NPG X2120–21 and others.

SIMON, John Allsebrook Simon, 1st Viscount (1873-1954) statesman and lord chancellor.
P SIR OSWALD BIRLEY, 1933, tql seated, Inner Temple, London. SIR GERALD KELLY, c1924, tql in uniform, Wadham College, Oxford. SIR G.KELLY, National Liberal Club, London. P.A.DE LÁSZLÓ, All Souls College, Oxford. F.O.SALISBURY, c1945–46,

tql in lord chancellor's robes, DoE (Privy Council, London).
SC LADY KATHLEEN KENNET, bust, All Souls.
PR FRANK DICKSEE, 1922, hs, line, NPG.
C WALLACE HESTER ('WH'), wl, mechanical repro, for *Vanity Fair*, 18 Oct 1911, NPG. SIR MAX BEERBOHM, 1932, drg, All Souls College.
PH SIR CECIL BEATON, hl seated, print, NPG. HOWARD COSTER, *c*1935, various sizes, print and negs, NPG x2186 and others. WALTER STONEMAN, 1937, hs, NPG (NPR).

SIMON, Oliver Joseph (1895-1956) printer.
P BRIAN ROBB, *c*1950, wl, Curwen Press, London.

SIMON of Wythenshawe, Ernest Emil Darwin Simon, 1st Baron (1879-1960) industrialist and public servant.
P T.C.DUGDALE, 1944, hs, Simon Engineering Ltd, Stockport, Cheshire.
SC SIR JACOB EPSTEIN, bronze bust, Simon Engineering.
PH Various photographs, Simon Engineering.

SIMONDS, Gavin Turnbull Simonds, Viscount (1881-1971) lord chancellor.
P SIR GERALD KELLY, *c*1953, tql seated in lord chancellor's robes, Lincoln's Inn, London.
G LORD METHUEN, 'The Lord Chancellor on the Woolsack', oil, *c*1954, Palace of Westminster, London.
PH WALTER STONEMAN, 1946, hs, NPG (NPR). SIR CECIL BEATON, 1953, hl seated in Lord chancellor's robes, print, NPG.

SIMONSEN, Sir John Lionel (1884-1957) organic chemist.
PH WALTER STONEMAN, 1945, hs, NPG (NPR).

SIMPSON, Bertram Fitzgerald (1883-1971) bishop of Southwark.
PH UNKNOWN, hl, print, NPG (Anglican Bishops).

SIMPSON, Frederick Arthur (1883-1974) divine and historian.
D J.K.GREEN, 1924, Trinity College, Cambridge. AIDAN SAVAGE, 1929, pencil, Trinity College. GERALD LEET, 1947, pencil, Trinity College.

SIMPSON, Sir George (Clarke) (1878-1965) meteorologist.
C D.G.LILLIE, 1911, wl, w/c, Scott Polar Research Institute, University of Cambridge.
PH H.G.PONTING, *c*1911-12, various photographs, Scott Institute. WALTER STONEMAN, 2 hs portraits, 1943 and 1954, NPG (NPR).

SIMPSON, Sir John Hope (1868-1961) Indian civil servant.
PH WALTER STONEMAN, 1922, hs, NPG (NPR).

SIMPSON, Percy (1865-1962) librarian and literary scholar.
D PERCY HORTON, 1952, English Library, Oxford.

SIMS, Charles (1873-1928) painter.
PH ELLIOTT & FRY, hs, cabinet, NPG. WALTER STONEMAN, 1924, hs, NPG (NPR).

SINCLAIR, Archibald Henry Macdonald, see 1st Viscount Thurso.

SINCLAIR, Sir Edwyn Sinclair Alexander-, see Alexander-Sinclair.

SINCLAIR, John, see 1st Baron Pentland.

SINCLAIR of Cleeve, Robert John Sinclair, 1st Baron (1893-1979) president of the Federation of British Industries.
P SIR JAMES GUNN, 1951, hs, Confederation of British Industry.
PH WALTER STONEMAN, 1942, hs, NPG (NPR).

SINGER, Charles Joseph (1876-1960) historian of medicine and science.
PH UNKNOWN, *c*1914-18?, hs in uniform, print, Wellcome Institute,

London. E.A.UNDERWOOD?, hs at desk, print, Wellcome Institute.

SINGLETON, Sir John Edward (1885-1957) judge.
PH WALTER STONEMAN, 1935, hs in robes, NPG (NPR).

SISAM, Kenneth (1887-1971) publisher.
PH PROFESSOR MUSTANOJA, wl, print, Oxford University Press, London.

SITWELL, Dame Edith (1887-1967) poet.
P ROGER FRY, 1918, hs, Sheffield City Art Galleries. ALVARO GUEVARA, *c*1919, wl seated, TATE 3509. WYNDHAM LEWIS, *c*1923-35, tql seated, TATE 5437. PAVEL TCHELITCHEW, 1937, wl seated, on loan to the Tate. FELIKS TOPOLSKI, 1959, hl, University of Texas, Austin, USA. P.TCHELITCHEW, University of Texas.
D NINA HAMNETT, 1918, pencil, University of Texas. W.LEWIS, 1921, hs, pencil, NPG 4464. W.LEWIS, 1921, tql seated, pencil and colour wash, National Gallery of South Australia, Adelaide. W.LEWIS, 1923, hl seated, pencil, NPG 4465. W.LEWIS, *c*1922-28, hl, pencil and w/c, Cecil Higgins Art Gallery, Bedford. ALBERT RUTHERSTON, 1928, hs, charcoal, University of Texas. MERVYN LEVY, 1959, hl, pencil, University of Texas. POWYS EVANS, hs, pencil, University of Texas.
SC BORIS ANREP, 1952, wl, as 'Sixth Sense' in 'The Modern Virtues', mosaic, National Gallery, London.
PR A.RUTHERSTON, 1928, with Osbert and Sacheverell, lith, Scarborough Borough Council.
C SIR CECIL BEATON, 3 Sitwells in a triptych, ink, University of Texas. Z.CZERMANSKI, hl with Gertrude Stein and Marianne Moore, gouache, University of Texas. SIR BERNARD PARTRIDGE, with 5 others, for Summer Number of *Punch*, 21 May 1928, pencil, ink and w/c, V & A. R.S.SHERRIFFS, 3 Sitwells with G.B.Shaw, ink, NPG.
PH SIR C.BEATON, 1927, tql seated with harp, print, NPG x4082. HORST P.HORST, 1930s, hs and tql seated, prints, NPG. HOWARD COSTER, 1937, various sizes and negs, NPG x1639, x4296 and x10964. BILL BRANDT, 1945, wl, print, NPG. UNKNOWN, 1951, Edith and Osbert in group in New Orleans, USA, print, NPG x4295. SIR C.BEATON, 1962, hl, print, NPG. MARK GERSON, 1962, hs, print, NPG. Various photographs, University of Texas.

SITWELL, Sir (Francis) Osbert Sacheverell, 5th Bart (1892-1969) poet and novelist.
P DESMOND HARMSWORTH, 1938, University of Texas, Austin, USA.
D ALBERT RUTHERSTON, 1927, hs, charcoal, Ashmolean Museum, Oxford. A.RUTHERSTON, 1927, pencil and ink, University of Texas. REX WHISTLER, 1935, profile head as a medallion, pencil and w/c, NPG 5009.
SC FRANK DOBSON, 1923, polished brass head, TATE 5938. BORIS ANREP, 1933, as Apollo in 'The Awakening Muses', mosaic, National Gallery, London.
PR A.RUTHERSTON, 1928, with Edith and Sacheverell, lith, Scarborough Borough Council.
C SIR CECIL BEATON, 3 Sitwells in a triptych, ink, University of Texas. R.S.SHERRIFFS, 3 Sitwells with G.B.Shaw, ink, NPG.
PH SIR C.BEATON, hl seated, print, NPG. HOWARD COSTER, 1927, various sizes, print and negs, NPG AX3439 and others. MAURICE BECK & HELEN MACGREGOR, tql, print, NPG. UNKNOWN, 1951, with Edith in group in New Orleans, USA, print, NPG x4295.

SITWELL, Sir Sacheverell, 6th Bart (*b*1897) writer.
PR ALBERT RUTHERSTON, 1928, with Edith and Osbert, lith, Scarborough County Council.
C SIR CECIL BEATON, 3 Sitwells in a triptych, ink, University of Texas. R.S.SHERRIFFS, 3 Sitwells with G.B.Shaw, ink, NPG.

PH DENYS, hs as youth, print, NPG. SIR C.BEATON, hl with cape, print, NPG. MAURICE BECK & HELEN MACGREGOR, hs, profile, oval, print, NPG.

SLADE, Sir Gerald Osborne (1891-1962) judge.
PH WALTER STONEMAN, 1949, hs, NPG (NPR).

SLATER, Sir William (Kershaw) (1893-1970) agriculturalist.
PH WALTER STONEMAN, 1951, hs, NPG (NPR).

SLATTER, Sir Leonard Horatio (1894-1961) air marshal.
P After WILLIAM DRING, hl in uniform, on loan to RAF Museum, Hendon, London.

SLIM, William Joseph Slim, 1st Viscount (1891-1970) field-marshal.
P T.C.DUGDALE, c1947, hl in uniform, on loan to the Staff College, Camberley, Surrey.
PH WALTER STONEMAN, 1945, hs in uniform, NPG (NPR). WALTER BIRD, 1964, hs, NPG (NPR).

SMART, Sir Morton Warrack (1877-1956) manipulative surgeon.
PH WALTER STONEMAN, 1933, hs in uniform, NPG (NPR).

SMITH, Sir Benjamin ('Ben') (1879-1964) politician.
PH HOWARD COSTER, various sizes and negs, NPG. WALTER STONEMAN, 1945, hs, NPG (NPR).

SMITH, Charles William Dyson-, see Dyson-Smith.

SMITH, David Nichol (1875-1962) literary scholar.
PH WALTER STONEMAN, 1940, hs, NPG (NPR).

SMITH, Sir Ernest Woodhouse (1884-1960) fuel technologist.
PH WALTER STONEMAN, 1947, hs, NPG (NPR).

SMITH, Sir Frank (Edward) (1879-1970) scientist.
P DUDLEY HEATH, 1937, hs, profile, National Physical Laboratory, Teddington, Middx.
PH WALTER STONEMAN, 1933, hs, NPG (NPR). UNKNOWN, hs, print, National Physical Laboratory.

SMITH, Frederick Edwin, see 1st Earl of Birkenhead.

SMITH, Sir Grafton Elliot (1871-1937) anatomist and anthropologist.
PH WALTER STONEMAN, 1920, hs, NPG (NPR).

SMITH, Sir Henry Babington (1863-1923) civil servant and financier.
PH WALTER STONEMAN, 1917, hs, NPG (NPR).

SMITH, Herbert (1862-1938) Yorkshire miners' leader.
SC JACOBI, 1931, bust, Miners' Hall, Barnsley.
PH Various photographs, Trades Union Congress, London.

SMITH, Sir Hubert Llewellyn (1864-1945) civil servant and social worker.
PH WALTER STONEMAN, 1917, hs, NPG (NPR). UNKNOWN, c1921-22, hs, print, NPG.

SMITH, John Alexander (1863-1939) philosopher and classical scholar.
D GILBERT SPENCER, 1936, pencil, Balliol College, Oxford.

SMITH, (Lloyd) Logan Pearsall (1865-1946) writer.
P ROGER FRY, hl seated, Haverford College, Haverford, Pennsylvania, USA.
D EDMOND KAPP, 1922, Chinese ink, Barber Institute, Birmingham University.

SMITH, Sir Matthew Arnold Bracy (1879-1959) painter.
P Self-portrait, 1909, hl, Guildhall Art Gallery, London. Self-

portrait, 1932, head, NPG 4190. AUGUSTUS JOHN, 1944, hs, TATE 5929. CATHLEEN MANN, 1952, hl seated, NPG 4161.
PH SIR CECIL BEATON, hl, print, NPG.

SMITH, Sir Ross Macpherson (1892-1922) airman.
SC F.BROOK HITCH, posthumous, statue, Adelaide, Australia.

SMITH, Vivian Hugh, see Baron Bicester.

SMITH, William Frederick Danvers, see 2nd Viscount Hambleden.

SMITH, Wilson (1897-1965) bacteriologist.
PH UNKNOWN, 2 portraits, prints, Royal Society, London.

SMITHELLS, Arthur (1860-1939) chemist.
P G.FIDDES WATT, c1925, hl, University of Leeds.
PH WALTER STONEMAN, 1921, hs, NPG (NPR).

SMUTS, Jan Christian (1870-1950) statesman and field-marshal.
P SIR WILLIAM ORPEN, c1917-19, University of Cape Town, S Africa. J.S.SARGENT, c1920, hs, NPG 4187, study sketch for 'Generals', NPG 1954. SIR WILLIAM NICHOLSON, 1923, hs, Fitzwilliam Museum, Cambridge. SIR W.NICHOLSON, hl in uniform, Johannesburg Art Gallery, S Africa. J.BLAIR LEIGHTON, 1924, tql in uniform, Palace of Westminster, London. ADRIAN JONES, c1933, cut down equestrian portrait, Royal Commonwealth Society, London. SIMON ELWES, c1943?, hl in uniform, National Art Gallery, Cape Town. JOSSELIN BODLEY, 1949, head, Rhodes House, Oxford. ARTHUR PAN, hs in uniform, South Africa House, London; version?, Christ's College, Cambridge. F.O.SALISBURY, hs, University of St Andrews, Scotland.
D FRANCIS DODD, 1917, tql, charcoal and w/c, IWM. SIR WILLIAM ROTHENSTEIN, head, chalk, NPG 4645.
G SIR W.ORPEN, 'A Peace Conference at the Quai d'Orsay', oil, c1918-19, IWM. J.S.SARGENT, 'General Officers of World War I, 1914-18', oil, 1922, NPG 1954.
SC MOSES KOTTLER, 1949, bronze bust, NPG 4004. SIR JACOB EPSTEIN, 1956, bronze statue, Parliament Square, London.
PH WALTER STONEMAN, 3 hs portraits, the 1st in uniform, 1917, 1931 and 1947, NPG (NPR). HOWARD COSTER, 1941, various sizes, print and negs, NPG X2122 and others.

SNELL, Henry Snell, Baron (1865-1944) politician.
P FRANCIS DODD, c1935, hl, County Hall, London. M.M.C.URQUHART, 1939, tql seated, Royal Institute of International Affairs, Chatham House, London.
D F.DODD, charcoal, The Athenaeum, London.
PH WALTER STONEMAN, 2 hs portraits, 1931 and 1943, NPG (NPR).

SNELL, Sir John Francis Cleverton (1869-1938) electrical engineer.
PH WALTER STONEMAN, 1930, hs, NPG (NPR).

SNOWDEN, Philip Snowden, Viscount (1864-1937) statesman.
D COLIN GILL, chalk, Manchester City Art Gallery.
M W.C.DONGWORTH, c1920-30, hs, oval, NPG 5028.
SC SIGISMOND DE STROBL, bronze bust, Leeds University Library, and DoE, London.
C SIR MAX BEERBOHM, 1920, drg, Ashmolean Museum, Oxford, and Cornell University, Ithaca, New York, USA. SIR DAVID LOW, c1927-28, wl, chalk, NPG 4563; related pencil sketch, NPG 4529(335). SIR BERNARD PARTRIDGE, wl, pen and ink, for Punch, 25 Dec 1929, NPG.
PH WALTER STONEMAN, 1924, hs, NPG (NPR). OLIVE EDIS, 1920s, hs, print, NPG X5189.

SODDY, Frederick (1877-1956) chemist.
PH WALTER STONEMAN, 1920, hs, NPG (NPR).

SOKOLOVA, Lydia, real name Hilda Munnings (1896-1974) ballet dancer.
D DEREK HILL, 1954, hl, profile, pen and ink, NPG CP20.

SOLOMON, Solomon Joseph (1860-1927) painter.
D Self-portrait, tql seated at easel, pen and ink, NPG 3044.
G SIR HUBERT VON HERKOMER, 'The Council of the Royal Academy', oil, 1908, TATE 2481.
C HARRY FURNISS, hs, profile, with palette, pen and ink, NPG 3515.
PH ELLIOTT & FRY, hs, cabinet, NPG. JOHN RUSSELL & SONS, c1915, hs in uniform, print, for *National Photographic Record*, vol 1, NPG. WALTER STONEMAN, c1917, hs, NPG (NPR).

SOMERS, Arthur Herbert Tennyson Somers-Cocks, 6th Baron (1887-1944) Chief scout and governor of Victoria, Australia.
P SIR OSWALD BIRLEY, 1944, tql in scout uniform, The Scout Association, London. SIR O.BIRLEY, Eastnor Castle, Herefords.
PH WALTER STONEMAN, 3 hs portraits, 1926 and 1939, NPG X514 and NPG (NPR).

SOMERVELL, Theodore Howard (1890-1975) mountaineer.
PH HOWARD COSTER, various sizes and negs, NPG.

SOMERVELL of Harrow, Donald Bradley Somervell, Baron (1889-1960) politician and judge.
PH WALTER STONEMAN, 2 hs portraits, 1934 and 1945, NPG (NPR).

SOMERVILLE, Sir James Fownes (1882-1949) admiral.
P SIR OSWALD BIRLEY, c1945-48, hs in uniform, Royal Naval College, Greenwich.
PH WALTER STONEMAN, 1942, hs in uniform, NPG (NPR).

SOMERVILLE, Sir William (1860-1932) agriculturalist.
P G.HALL NEALE, 1924, hl seated, School of Rural Economy, Oxford; copy, St John's College, Oxford.

SORLEY, Charles Hamilton (1895-1915) poet.
D CECIL JAMESON, 1916, hs, chalk, NPG 5012.

SORLEY, Sir Ralph Squire (1898-1974) air marshal.
PH WALTER STONEMAN, 1942, hs in uniform, NPG (NPR).

SOULBURY, Herwald Ramsbotham, 1st Viscount (1887-1971) politician and governor-general of Ceylon.
P E.I.HALLIDAY, 1965, hl seated in uniform, Carlton Club, London.
PH WALTER STONEMAN, 3 hs portraits, 1937, 1941 and 1955, NPG (NPR).

SOUTHBOROUGH, Francis John Stephens Hopwood, 1st Baron (1860-1947) civil servant.
P F.O.SALISBURY, Tilbury Contracting Group Ltd, London.
PH WALTER STONEMAN, 1918, hs in robes, NPG (NPR).

SOUTHOUSE-CHEYNEY, Reginald Evelyn Peter (1896-1951) crime novelist 'Peter Cheyney'.
PH HOWARD COSTER, late 1930s, various sizes and negs, NPG X10781-10800.

SOUTHWELL, Sir Richard Vynne (1888-1970) engineer.
P HENRY LAMB, 1954, hl seated, Imperial College of Science and Technology, London.
D ROBIN GUTHRIE, 1962, Trinity College, Cambridge.
PH WALTER STONEMAN, 3 hs portraits, 1930, 1943 and 1953, NPG (NPR).

SOUTHWOOD, Julius Salter Elias, Viscount (1873-1946) newspaper proprietor.
P T.C.DUGDALE, c1938, Printers Charitable Corporation, London.
SC A.F.HARDIMAN, c1948-49, statue, Garden of Remembrance, St James Church, Piccadilly, London.

PH HOWARD COSTER, various sizes and negs, NPG.

SPARE, Austin Osman (1886-1956) artist.
D Self-portrait, pastel, Manchester City Art Gallery.

SPEARMAN, Charles Edward (1863-1945) psychologist.
PH WALTER STONEMAN, 1931, hs, NPG (NPR).

SPEARS, Sir Edward Louis, 1st Bart (1886-1974) soldier and politician.
P MARY BORDEN (LADY SPEARS), hs, NPG 5099.
PH WALTER STONEMAN, 3 hs portraits, 1922, 1932 and 1953, NPG (NPR). WALTER BIRD, 1965, hs, NPG (NPR).

SPEARS, Mary, Lady, see Mary Borden.

SPEED, Harold (1872-1957) portrait painter.
P Self-portrait, hl, Art Workers Guild, London.

SPENCER, Albert Edward John Spencer, 7th Earl (1892-1975) connoisseur and patron of the arts.
P NELLIE HARVEY, 1909, Althorp, Northants. LIONEL EDWARDS, 1929, wl on his horse 'Miss Magtart', Althorp. AUGUSTUS JOHN, c1930, tql seated in uniform, Althorp. MURRAY URQUHART, 1939, seated in hunt dress, Althorp. SIR JAMES GUNN, c1954-59, seated, Althorp, study for Society of Dilettanti conversation group.
D J.S.SARGENT, 1915, hs in uniform, charcoal, Althorp. JOHN WARD, 1972, hl seated, chalk and wash, Althorp.
G SIR J.GUNN, 'Society of Dilettanti Conversation Piece', oil, c1954-59, Society of Dilettanti, Brooks's Club, London.
PH UNKNOWN, c1923, tql with Lady Spencer and daughter Anne, print, NPG X4095. WALTER STONEMAN, 2 hs portraits, 1930 and 1949, NPG (NPR). LENARE, 1953, various portraits in peer's robes some with his wife, NPG X5394-97.

SPENCER, Gilbert (1892-1979) artist.
P Self-portrait, 1919, hs, NPG 5290. Self-portrait, 1928, hs, TATE T2012.
PH HOWARD COSTER, 1932 and 1954, various sizes, prints and negs, NPG AX3447, X2290-92 and others.

SPENCER, Leonard James (1870-1959) mineralogist and geologist.
PH WALTER STONEMAN, 1930, hs, NPG (NPR).

SPENCER, Sir Stanley (1891-1959) painter.
P Self-portrait, various portraits including: 1913, hs, TATE 6188; 1936, hs, Stedelijk Museum, Amsterdam; 1936, 'Double Nude Portrait: the artist and his second wife', TATE T1863; c1936-37, hs with Patricia (his second wife), Fitzwilliam Museum, Cambridge; 1939, hs with palette, Fitzwilliam Museum; 1944, hs, National Gallery of Canada, Ottawa, Ontario. HENRY LAMB, 1928, hs, NPG 4527. H.LAMB, hs, The Art Gallery of Western Australia, Perth.
D Self-portraits: c1912-13, sanguine, Williamson Art Gallery and Museum, Birkenhead; 1919, hs, pencil, NPG 4306; c1926, head, pencil, Arts Council of Great Britain, London. HILDA SPENCER, 1931, hs, pencil, Scottish National Gallery of Modern Art, Edinburgh.
G SIR STANLEY SPENCER, 'The Resurrection, Cookham', oil, c1923-27, TATE 4239.
PH Various photographs, Stanley Spencer Gallery, Cookham, Berks.

SPENCER, Sir Walter Baldwin (1860-1929) biologist and ethnographer.
P W.B.McINNES, Exeter College, Oxford. W.B.McINNES, University of Melbourne, Australia.

SPENCER-CHURCHILL of Chartwell, Clementine Ogilvy Spencer-Churchill, Baroness (1885-1977) wife of Sir

Winston Churchill.

P SIR JOHN LAVERY, 1915, wl, Chartwell (NT), Kent. SIR J.LAVERY, c1915, wl reclining with daughter Sarah, NPG 5184. DOUGLAS CHANDOR, 1946, hl, Chartwell.

PH SIR CECIL BEATON, 1940, wl seated at tea with portrait of Sir Winston behind, print, NPG. DOROTHY WILDING, 1943, hl and tql profile, prints, NPG X6144–45. UNKNOWN, 1957, tql seated, print, NPG X6141. GODFREY ARGENT, 1968, hl, for NPR, NPG X6142 and X6146.

SPENDER, John Alfred (1862-1942) journalist and author.

P CLIVE GARDINER, Reform Club, London.

D SIR MUIRHEAD BONE, pencil, IWM.

SPENS, Sir William (1882-1962) master of Corpus Christi College, Cambridge.

P SIR W.O.HUTCHISON, c1955, tql seated, Rugby School, Warwicks.

SQUIRE, Sir John Collings (1884-1958) poet, critic and journalist.

P JOHN MANSBRIDGE, c1932–33, tql seated, NPG 4110.

D SIR WILLIAM ROTHENSTEIN, c1920, head, sanguine, NPG 4794.

STACK, Sir Lee Oliver Fitzmaurice (1868-1924) soldier and administrator.

PH WALTER STONEMAN, c1918, hs in uniform, NPG (NPR).

STACPOOLE, Henry de Vere (1863-1951) novelist.

PH JOHN RUSSELL & SONS, c1915, hs, print, for National Photographic Record, vol 1, NPG.

STALLYBRASS, William Teulon Swan (1883-1948) principal of Brasenose College and vice-chancellor of the University of Oxford.

D HUMPHREY SEARLE, hs, pencil, Brasenose College.

STAMP, Sir Josiah Charles Stamp, 1st Baron (1880-1941) statistician and administrator.

P J.A.A.BERRIE, Abbey National Building Society, London. S.P.KENDRICK, posthumous, The Leys School, Cambridge.

C FRED MAY, 1934, hs, gouache, NPG.

PH WALTER STONEMAN, 1920, hs, NPG (NPR).

STAMP, Sir (Laurence) Dudley (1898-1966) geographer.

PH WALTER BIRD, 1965, hs, NPG (NPR).

STANHOPE, James Richard Stanhope, 7th Earl (1880-1967) statesman and public servant.

P SIR JAMES GUNN, 1946, tql seated, NMM, Greenwich.

PH WALTER STONEMAN, 1917, hs in uniform, NPG (NPR). HAY WRIGHTSON, c1926, hs, print, NPG.

STANIER, Sir William Arthur (1876-1965) engineer.

P WILLIAM DRING, c1959, Institution of Mechanical Engineers, London.

PH WALTER STONEMAN, 1945, hs, NPG (NPR).

STANLEY, Albert Henry, see Baron Ashfield.

STANLEY, Sir Arthur (1869-1947) philanthropist.

P HUGH DE T.GLAZEBROOK, c1919, St Thomas' Hospital, London. SOLOMON J.SOLOMON, c1922, tql seated, Royal Automobile Club, London.

PH UNKNOWN, hs, print, NPG.

STANLEY, Edward George Villiers, see 17th Earl of Derby.

STANLEY, Sir Herbert James (1872-1955) colonial administrator.

P UNKNOWN, Queen's House, Colombo, Ceylon.

PH WALTER STONEMAN, 1927, hs, NPG (NPR).

STANLEY, Oliver Frederick George (1896-1950) politician.

PH WALTER STONEMAN, 4 hs portraits, 1937 and 1943, NPG (NPR).

STANSFELD, Margaret (1860-1951) pioneer in physical training for women.

P ARTHUR MILLS, after a photograph, hl, Bedford College of Higher Education.

PH Various photographs, Bedford College.

STANSGATE, William Wedgwood Benn, 1st Viscount (1877-1960) parliamentarian.

PH OLIVE EDIS, tql seated, print, NPG. WALTER STONEMAN, 1917, hs in uniform, NPG (NPR).

STAPLEDON, Sir (Reginald) George (1882-1960) pioneer of grassland science.

P ALLAN GWYNNE-JONES, c1958, hl, Grassland Research Station, Hurley, Berks.

PH WALTER STONEMAN, 2 hs portraits, 1940 and 1946, NPG (NPR).

STARK, Freya (Madeline), Mrs Stewart Perowne (b1893) traveller and writer.

PH Various photographs, Royal Geographical Society, London.

STARLING, Ernest Henry (1866-1927) physiologist.

P A.H.SHORE, 1921, hl, Department of Physiology, University of Cambridge. W.W.RUSSELL, c1926, tql in laboratory, University College, London.

STEED, Henry Wickham (1871-1956) editor of The Times.

P CHARLES SHANNON, c1920, tql, Times Newspapers Ltd, London.

PH HOWARD COSTER, various sizes and negs, NPG.

STEEL-MAITLAND, Sir Arthur Herbert Drummond Ramsay- (formerly Arthur Herbert Drummond Steel), 1st Bart (1876-1935) politician and economist.

PH WALTER STONEMAN, 1918, hs, NPG (NPR).

STEER, Philip Wilson (1860-1942) painter.

P W.R.SICKERT, c1895, wl seated, NPG 3116. Self-portrait, 1905, hl, Uffizi, Florence. Self-portrait, 1920, hl, Fitzwilliam Museum, Cambridge. HENRY TONKS, 1930, 'Sodales', wl seated with W.R.Sickert, TATE T40.

D SIR WILLIAM ROTHENSTEIN, 1928, hs, chalk, NPG 4643. INA SHELDON-WILLIAMS, pencil, BM. HENRY TONKS, 5 heads, pencil, NPG 5088 and NPG 3072 (1, 3 and 6).

G SIR WILLIAM ORPEN, 'The Selecting Jury of the New English Art Club, 1909', oil, NPG 2556. SIR W.ORPEN, 'Homage to Manet', oil, 1909, Manchester City Art Gallery. WILLIAM ROBERTS, 'The Vorticists at the Restaurant de la Tour Eiffel: Spring 1915', oil, 1961–62, TATE T528. H.TONKS, 'Steer at Home on Christmas Day', oil, Slade School of Fine Art, University of London.

C SIR MAX BEERBOHM, 1904, 'Mr P.W.Steer, prospecting', w/c, Ashmolean Museum, Oxford. SIR M.BEERBOHM, 1907, 'The New English Art Club', w/c, TATE 6075. SIR M.BEERBOHM, 1913, 'Annual Banquet: a suggestion to the New English Art Club', w/c, TATE 4332. AUGUSTUS JOHN, wl in a letter to Ursula Tyrwhitt, National Library of Wales, Aberystwyth. D.G.MACLAREN, 'Some Members of the New English Art Club', w/c, NPG 2663.

PH G.C.BERESFORD, 1922, hs, neg, NPG X6594. WALTER STONEMAN, 1934, hs, NPG (NPR).

STEIN, Sir (Mark) Aurel (1862-1943) scholar, explorer and archaeologist.

D SIR WILLIAM ROTHENSTEIN, 1920, head, chalk, NPG 3881. SIR W.ROTHENSTEIN, sanguine, Manchester City Art Gallery.

PH WALTER STONEMAN, 1925, hs, print, NPG. WYKEHAM, c1933, hs, print, NPG. UNKNOWN, 1942, tql, print, NPG.

STENTON, Sir Frank Merry (1880-1967) medieval scholar.

P WILLIAM DRING, 1948, hl, seated in robes, University of Reading.

STEPHENS, James (1880?-1950) poet and novelist.
P PATRICK TUOHY, hl seated, NGI 1126. SIR WILLIAM ROTHENSTEIN, 1941, TATE 5349. ESTELLA SOLOMONS, Municipal Gallery of Modern Art, Dublin.
D MARY DUNCAN, Municipal Gallery of Modern Art. A.H.FISHER, 1941, 2 heads, pencil, BM.
SC E.T.QUINN, bronze bust, NGI 8002, and Municipal Gallery of Modern Art. THEODORE SPICER-SIMSON, 1913, bronze medallion, NGI 8220.
PR M.DUNCAN, c1915, tql seated, lith, NPG 3989.

STEPHENSON, Sir Gilbert Owen (1878-1972) vice-admiral.
PH WALTER STONEMAN, 1919, hs in uniform, NPG (NPR).

STEPHENSON, Marjory (1885-1948) biochemist.
D CATHARINE DODGSON, Newnham College, Cambridge.
PH WALTER STONEMAN, 1945, hs, NPG (NPR).

STERN, Gladys Bertha, Mrs G.L.Holdsworth (1890-1973) novelist.
D EDMOND KAPP, 1930, Barber Institute, Birmingham University.

STEVENSON, James Stevenson, Baron (1873-1926) administrator.
PH WALTER STONEMAN, 1917, hs, NPG (NPR).

STEWART, Charles Stewart Henry Vane-Tempest-, see 7th Marquess of Londonderry.

STEWART, Sir (Percy) Malcolm, 1st Bart (1872-1951) industrialist.
SC SIR W.R.DICK, c1948, bronze head, on loan to the Community Hall, Stewartby, Beds.

STEWART, Sir (Samuel) Findlater (1879-1960) civil servant.
PH WALTER STONEMAN, 1931, hs, NPG (NPR).

STEWART-MURRAY, Katharine Marjory, see Duchess of Atholl.

STILES, Sir Harold Jalland (1863-1946) surgeon.
P FREDERIC WHITING, Royal Hospital for Sick Children, Edinburgh.
PH WALTER STONEMAN, 1933, hs, NPG (NPR).

STILL, Sir (George) Frederic (1868-1941) paediatrician.
P SIR GERALD KELLY, c1935, hs, King's College Hospital, London.
PH WALTER STONEMAN, 1937, hs, NPG (NPR).

STOCKDALE, Sir Frank Arthur (1883-1949) tropical agriculturalist.
PH WALTER STONEMAN, 2 hs portraits, 1940 and 1947, NPG (NPR).

STOCKS, Mary Danvers Stocks, Baroness (1891-1975) economist, writer and broadcaster.
P PHILIP CONNARD, c1952, hl, Westfield College, University of London.
PH WALTER BIRD, 1967, hs, NPG (NPR).

STOKES, Sir Frederick Wilfrid Scott (1860-1927) civil engineer and inventor.
PH OLIVE EDIS, c1915-20, hs and tql seated, prints, NPG.

STOLL, Sir Oswald (1866-1942) theatrical impresario.
C 'APE JUNIOR', wl, profile, Hentschel-Colourtype, for *Vanity Fair*, 4 Jan 1911, NPG. 'OWL', wl, mechanical repro, for *Vanity Fair*, 8 Oct 1913, NPG.

STONEY, George Gerald (1863-1942) engineer.
P T.B.GARVIE, C.A.Parsons and Co, Newcastle-upon-Tyne.

PH WALTER STONEMAN, 1917, hs, NPG (NPR).

STOPES, Marie Charlotte Carmichael (1880-1958) palaeobotanist and founder of family planning clinics.
P SIR GERALD KELLY, 1953, hl seated, NPG 4111.
D EDMOND KAPP, 1929, Barber Institute, Birmingham University.
C SIR DAVID LOW, c1933, hs and wl, pencil, NPG 4529(340-41).
PH UNKNOWN, c1911-18, tql, print, University College, London.

STOPFORD, Sir Montagu George North (1892-1971) general.
P BERNARD HAILSTONE, 1945, IWM.

STOPFORD of Fallowfield, John Sebastian Bach Stopford, Baron (1888-1961) anatomist.
PH WALTER STONEMAN, 2 hs portraits, 1931 and 1955, NPG (NPR).

STORRS, Sir Ronald Henry Amherst (1881-1955) Near Eastern expert and governor.
PH WALTER STONEMAN, 2 hs portraits, in uniform, 1919 and 1931, NPG (NPR).

STOUT, George Frederick (1860-1944) philosopher.
D After JAMES PATERSON, 1921, pencil, University of St Andrews, Fife, Scotland.
PH WALTER STONEMAN, 1930, hs, NPG (NPR).

STRACHAN, John (1862-1907) classical and Celtic scholar.
SC UNKNOWN, bronze bust, University of Manchester.

STRACHEY, (Giles) Lytton (1880-1932) critic and biographer.
P DUNCAN GRANT, c1909, TATE 5764. HENRY LAMB, 1914, wl seated, TATE T118; oil study, hs, Fitzwilliam Museum, Cambridge, and pencil study, wl, V & A. ROGER FRY, 1917, hl seated, University of Texas, Austin, USA. DORA CARRINGTON, tql seated, King's College, Cambridge.
D SIMON BUSSY, 1904, wl seated, pastel, NPG 4595. NINA HAMNETT, wl seated, NPG 2215. EDMOND KAPP, 1928, Barber Institute, Birmingham University.
SC STEPHEN TOMLIN, c1928-30, bronze head, TATE 4616.
C SIR MAX BEERBOHM, tql, profile, drg, Ashmolean Museum, Oxford. SIR M.BEERBOHM, 'Twenty-one Prominent Men', oil, University of Texas.
PH Various photographs, NPG (Strachey Coll).

STRACHEY, John St Loe (1860-1927) journalist.
D SIR WILLIAM ROTHENSTEIN, 1924, hs, sanguine and chalk, NPG 4795.
PH Various photographs, NPG (Strachey Coll).

STRACHEY, Philippa (1872-1968) pioneer of the women's rights movement.
P HENRY LAMB, 1957, hs, Fawcett Library, City of London Polytechnic.
PH Various photographs, NPG (Strachey Coll).

STRADLING, Sir Reginald Edward (1891-1952) civil engineer.
P R.J.BURN, IWM.
PH WALTER STONEMAN, 1947, hs, NPG (NPR).

STRAKOSCH, Sir Henry (1871-1943) financier.
PH WALTER STONEMAN, 1927, hs, NPG (NPR).

STRANGWAYS, Giles Stephen Holland Fox-, see 6th Earl of Ilchester.

STRATHCARRON, (James) Ian Macpherson, 1st Baron (1880-1937) politician.
PH WALTER STONEMAN, 1920, hs, NPG (NPR).

STRATTON, Frederick John Marrian (1881-1960) astrophysicist.

P SIR OSWALD BIRLEY, Gonville and Caius College, Cambridge.
PH WALTER STONEMAN, 1953, hs, NPG (NPR).

STREET, Sir Arthur William (1892-1951) civil servant.
P HENRY CARR, 1942, IWM.
PH WALTER STONEMAN, 1938, 5 hl portraits, for NPR, NPG X1427-30 and X5908. HOWARD COSTER, 1930s, various sizes and negs, NPG.

STREETER, Burnett Hillman (1874-1937) divine.
P D.H.BANNER, 1929, Queen's College, Oxford.
C 'DRAW', drg, Queen's College, Oxford.
PH PIRIE MACDONALD, c1900-05, print, Pembroke College, Oxford.

STRICKLAND, Gerald Strickland, Baron (1861-1940) colonial administrator and politician.
P C.THORP, Sizergh Castle (NT), Kendal, Cumbria.
SC ANTON SCIORTINO, statue, Valetta, Malta.
C 'HAY', wl in racing colours, lith, for *Vanity Fair*, 4 May 1893, NPG.

STRONG, Eugénie, née Sellers (1860-1943) classical archaeologist and art historian.
P CONSTANCE PHILLOTT, 1890, hs, Girton College, Cambridge.
SC DAVID EVANS, bronze head, Girton College.
PH UNKNOWN, hs, print, Girton College.

STRONG, Leonard Alfred George (1896-1958) author and journalist.
D WYNDHAM LEWIS, 1932, hs, pencil and wash, NPG 5143.
C SIR DAVID LOW, various sketches, pencil, NPG 4529(345-48).
PH HOWARD COSTER, 1930s, various sizes and negs, NPG. MARK GERSON, 1955, hl seated, print, NPG.

STRONG, Sandford Arthur (1863-1904) orientalist and art historian.
D ALPHONSE LEGROS, 1896, hs, silverpoint, Fitzwilliam Museum, Cambridge. A.LEGROS, 1897, head, profile, silverpoint, Fitzwilliam Museum. SIR CHARLES HOLROYD, 1904, head, profile, after death, pencil, NPG 3633.

STRONG, Thomas Banks (1861-1944) bishop of Ripon and Oxford.
P SIR WILLIAM ORPEN, 1923, tql seated, Christ Church, Oxford.
D SIR WILLIAM ROTHENSTEIN, 1916, hs, pencil, NPG 4805. SIR W.ROTHENSTEIN, 1916, hs, pencil, Christ Church. JOHN WHEATLEY, chalk and w/c, The Athenaeum, London.
PH T. & E.COX, hs, print, NPG (Anglican Bishops).

STRUTT, Robert John, see 4th Baron Rayleigh.

STUART, Sir Campbell (1885-1972) journalist.
PH WALTER STONEMAN, 1921, hs, NPG (NPR).

STUART, Sir John Theodosius Burnett-, see Burnett-Stuart.

STUART-JONES, Sir Henry (1867-1939) classical scholar, Roman historian and lexicographer.
PH WALTER STONEMAN, 1918, hs, NPG (NPR).

STUART of Findhorn, James Gray Stuart, 1st Viscount (1897-1971) politician.
PH WALTER STONEMAN, 3 hs portraits, 1930 and 1943, NPG (NPR).

STUBBS, Sir Reginald Edward (1876-1947) colonial governor.
PH UNKNOWN, 1920, Sir Reginald and Lady Stubbs visiting a silkworm farm at Kowloon, print, NPG. WALTER STONEMAN, 1935, hs, for NPR, NPG X5903.

SUETER, Sir Murray Frazer (1872-1960) rear-admiral.
P SIR WILLIAM RUSSELL FLINT, 1928, hs in uniform, NMM, Greenwich.

SULLIVAN, Alexander Martin (1871-1959) barrister.

G SIR JOHN LAVERY, 'Trial of Roger Casement, 1915', oil, on loan to the Society of King's Inn, Dublin.

SUMNER, Benedict Humphrey (1893-1951) historian.
D AUGUSTUS JOHN, hs, unfinished, All Souls College, Oxford.
SC DAVID WYNNE, bronze head, All Souls College.
PH WALTER STONEMAN, 1950, hs, NPG (NPR).

SUTHERLAND, George Granville Sutherland-Leveson-Gower, 5th Duke of (1888-1963) statesman and public servant.
PH WALTER STONEMAN, 3 hs portraits, 1926 and 1936, NPG (NPR) and NPG X5891-92.

SUTRO, Alfred (1863-1933) playwright and translator.
C HARRY FURNISS, wl seated, pen and ink, NPG 3521.

SUTTON, Sir Bertine Entwisle (1886-1946) air marshal.
PH WALTER STONEMAN, 1944, hs in uniform, NPG (NPR).

SWANBOROUGH, Stella, Baroness, see Marchioness of Reading.

SWINTON, Alan Archibald Campbell (1863-1930) electrical engineer.
PH WALTER STONEMAN, 1917, hs, NPG (NPR).

SWINTON, Sir Ernest Dunlop (1868-1951) major-general.
D ERIC KENNINGTON, hs in uniform, pastel, The Tank Museum, Bovington Camp, Wareham, Dorset.

SWINTON, Sir Philip Cunliffe-Lister, 1st Earl of (1884-1072) politician.
PH HOWARD COSTER, 1930s, various sizes and negs, NPG. WALTER STONEMAN, 3 hs portraits, 1931, 1943 and 1955, NPG (NPR).

SYFRET, Sir (Edward) Neville (1889-1972) admiral.
P SIR OSWALD BIRLEY, c1945-48, hs in uniform, Royal Naval College, Greenwich.
D WILLIAM DRING, 1942, pastel, IWM.
PH WALTER STONEMAN, 1942, hs in uniform, NPG (NPR).

SYKES, Sir Frederick Hugh (1877-1954) chief of air staff and governor of Bombay.
SC L.F.ROSLYN, 1920, bronze bust, IWM.
PH WALTER STONEMAN, 1919, hs in uniform, NPG (NPR).

SYKES, Sir Mark, 6th Bart (1879-1919) traveller, soldier and politician.
P LEOPOLD PILICHOWSKI, Sledmere House, Driffield, N Humberside.
SC BRYANT BAKER, bust, Sledmere House.
C WALLACE HESTER ('WH'), wl seated on bookcase, mechanical repro, for *Vanity Fair*, 26 June 1912, NPG.

SYKES, Sir Percy Molesworth (1867-1945) soldier and administrator.
PH WALTER STONEMAN, 1919, hs in uniform, NPG (NPR).

SYMONS, Arthur William (1865-1945) poet, translator and critic.
P J.E.BLANCHE, 1895, tql seated, TATE 4862. R.H.SAUTER, 1935, hs, NPG 4172; version?, DoE, London.
D AUGUSTUS JOHN, c1909, 2 hs portraits, pencil, TATE 4863.
PH FREDERICK H.EVANS, c1900, hs, print, NPG P104. A.L.COBURN, 1906, hs, photogravure, NPG X7778.

SYNGE, John Millington (1871-1909) dramatist.
P J.B.YEATS, c1905, hl seated, Municipal Gallery of Modern Art, Dublin.
D ROBERT GREGORY, 1904, chalk, NGI. J.B.YEATS, 1905, tql, pencil, NGI 2937. HAROLD OAKLEY, 1905, hs, Municipal Gallery of Modern Art.
SL J.B.YEATS, head, profile, Royal Coll.
C SIR WILLIAM ORPEN, 1907, wl with Lady Gregory, Sir Hugh Lane and W.B.YEATS, ink, NPG 4676.

T

TAGORE, Sir Rabindranath (1861-1941) Indian writer.
D SIR WILLIAM ROTHENSTEIN, 1912, tql seated, pencil, TATE 3190.
SIR W.ROTHENSTEIN, 2 drgs, pencil, Manchester City Art
Gallery. EDMOND KAPP, 1921, hs and wl, chalk, Barber Institute,
Birmingham University. SIR MUIRHEAD BONE, c1930, hl, pencil,
Airlie Castle, Tayside region, Scotland.
PR SIR W.ROTHENSTEIN, 1912, lith, Carlisle City Art Gallery.
SC SIR JACOB EPSTEIN, c1926, bronze bust, Salford Museum and Art
Gallery.

TAIT, James (1863-1944) historian.
D RONALD ALLAN, Manchester University Press.

TAIT, Sir (William Eric) Campbell (1886-1946) admiral.
P EDWARD ROWARTH, c1942-44, hl seated in uniform, NMM,
Greenwich.
PH WALTER STONEMAN, 1941, hs in uniform, NPG (NPR).

TALBOT, Sir George John (1861-1938) judge.
PH WALTER STONEMAN, 1926, hs, NPG (NPR).

TALLENTS, Sir Stephen George (1884-1958) civil servant.
PH WALTER STONEMAN, 2 hs portraits, 1932 and 1942, NPG (NPR).
HOWARD COSTER, 1940s?, hs, print, NPG X2325.

TANNER, Jack (1889-1965) president of the Amalgamated
Engineering Union.
C SIR DAVID LOW, hs, pencil, NPG 4529(358).

TANSLEY, Sir Arthur George (1871-1955) plant ecologist.
C D.G.LILLIE, 1908, wl with F.F.Blackman, w/c, NPG.

TATLOW, Tissington (1876-1957) general secretary of the
Student Christian Movement.
P DELMAR BANNER, hs, Student Christian Movement Head-
quarters, Birmingham.

TAWNEY, Richard Henry (1880-1962) economist.
D JOHN MANSBRIDGE, 1953, hl seated, pencil, NPG 4258.
PH WALTER STONEMAN, 3 hs portraits, 1934, 1945 and 1956, NPG
(NPR).

TAYLOR, Alfred Edward (1869-1945) philosopher.
D DAVID FOGGIE, 1934, pencil, SNPG 1795.
PH DRUMMOND YOUNG, c1935, hs, print, NPG.

TAYLOR, Eva Germaine Rimington (d1966) professor of
geography.
PH ELLIOTT & FRY, 1947, hs, print, Royal Geographical Society,
London. UNKNOWN, hs, print, Geography Department, Birkbeck College, University of London.

TAYLOR, Frank Sherwood (1897-1956) chemist, historian
of science and director of the Science Museum, London.
PH UNKNOWN, c1940, hl seated at desk, print, Museum of the
History of Science, Oxford.

TAYLOR, Sir Geoffrey (Ingram) (1886-1975) physicist and
meteorologist.
D T.C.DUGDALE, 1949, pencil, Trinity College, Cambridge.
PH WALTER STONEMAN, 2 hs portraits, 1933 and 1958, NPG (NPR).
HOWARD COSTER, 1950s, various sizes, print and negs, NPG X1108
and X10960-63.

TAYLOR, Sir Gordon Gordon-, see Gordon-Taylor.

TAYLOR, Leonard Campbell (1874-1969) artist.
D BRENDA MOORE, 1966, hs, charcoal, NPG 4936.
PH WALTER STONEMAN, 1937, hs, NPG (NPR).

TAYLOR, Samuel Coleridge-, see Coleridge-Taylor.

TAYLOR, Sir Thomas Murray (1897-1962) principal and
vice-chancellor of the University of Aberdeen.
SC GLADYS BARRON, c1958, bronze bust, University of Aberdeen.

TAYLOR, Sir Thomas Weston Johns (1895-1953) scientist
and academic administrator.
P HECTOR WHISTLER, University of the West Indies, Jamaica.

TAYLOR, William (1865-1937) designer of scientific
instruments.
PH WALTER STONEMAN, 1935, hs, NPG (NPR).

TEDDER, Arthur William Tedder, 1st Baron (1890-1967)
air marshal.
P HENRY CARR, 1943, IWM. H.CARR, 1949, Magdalene College,
Cambridge.
D H.A.FREETH, 1943, chalk, IWM. ROBERT TOLLAST, Churchill
College, Cambridge.
PH WALTER STONEMAN, 1946, hs in uniform, NPG (NPR). WALTER
BIRD, 1961, hs in uniform, NPG (NPR).

TEGART, Sir Charles Augustus (1881-1946) Indian police
officer.
PH WALTER STONEMAN, 1937, hs, NPG (NPR).

TEMPERLEY, Harold William Vazeille (1879-1939)
historian.
PH RAMSEY & MUSPRATT, 3 hs portraits, prints, NPG.

TEMPEST, Dame Marie (1864-1942) actress.
P J.E.BLANCHE, 1903, tql seated, Garrick Club, London. SIR
WILLIAM NICHOLSON, 1903, hl seated with a Blenheim spaniel,
NPG 5191. SIR W.NICHOLSON, 1908, Municipal Gallery of
Modern Art, Dublin.
D GEORGE SHERINGHAM, in 'Midsummer Madness', pencil, Garrick
Club.
PR JULES O. DE BAN, c1910, tql seated, lith, V & A.
PH HISTED, hs as young woman, photogravure, NPG. STAGE PHOTO
CO, 1930s?, tql seated at piano, print, NPG. GORDON ANTHONY,
1935, hs, print, NPG. UNKNOWN, 3 postcards, NPG.

TEMPEST-STEWART, Charles Stewart Henry Vane-,
see 7th Marquess of Londonderry.

TEMPLE, William (1881-1944) archbishop of Canterbury.
P J.W.NICHOL, 1917, Queen's College, Oxford. T.C.DUGDALE,
c1929, tql seated, Manchester City Art Gallery. T.C.DUGDALE,
hl, Lambeth Palace, London. P.A.DE LÁSZLÓ, 1934, tql, Lambeth
Palace; study, Balliol College, Oxford. SIR OSWALD BIRLEY,
1943, tql seated, Bishopthorpe Palace, York.
PH HOWARD COSTER, 1942?, wl, print, NPG X2363. WALTER
STONEMAN, 1943, hs, NPG (NPR). UNKNOWN, tql, print, NPG
(Anglican Bishops).

TEMPLER, Sir Gerald (Walter Robert) (1898-1979)
general.
G TERENCE CUNEO, 'Visit of the Queen and Prince Philip to the
Staff College', oil, 1958, Staff College, Camberley, Surrey.

PH WALTER STONEMAN, 2 hs portraits, 1942 and 1945, NPG (NPR).
MARK GERSON, 1966, hl seated, print, NPG.

TEMPLEWOOD, Sir Samuel John Gurney Hoare, 1st Viscount (1880-1959) statesman.
P PATRICK PHILLIPS, c1953, tql seated in chancellor's robes, University of Reading.
D EDMOND KAPP, 2 studies, 1934 and 1935, Barber Institute, Birmingham University.
PH WALTER STONEMAN, 1921, hs, NPG (NPR).

TENBY, Gwilym Lloyd George, 1st Viscount (1894-1967) politician.
P WALTER STONEMAN, 1942, hs in uniform, NPG (NPR).

TENNANT, Sir William George (1890-1963) admiral.
PH WALTER STONEMAN, 1946, hs in uniform, NPG (NPR).

TENNYSON-D'EYNCOURT, Sir Eustace Henry William, 1st Bart (1868-1951) naval architect.
PH WALTER STONEMAN, 1918, 2 hs portraits, NPG (NPR).

TERRISS, Ellaline, Lady Hicks (1871-1971) actress.
D 'P.M.', tql as young girl, pen and ink sketch, NPG.
PH ALFRED ELLIS, 1894, wl as Cinderella, print, NPG. A.ELLIS, hs, cabinet, NPG. ELLIS & WALERY, tql seated, photogravure, NPG. ELLIS & WALERY, hs, 2 postcards, NPG. S.GEORGES LTD, tql seated, profile, print, NPG. VAUGHAN & FREEMAN, hs, print, NPG.

TERRY, Charles Sanford (1864-1936) historian and musician.
P ALLAN SUTHERLAND, King's College, Aberdeen.

TERRY, Fred (1863-1933) actor.
PR CHARLES BUCHEL & HASSALL, 1916, hs and wl, lith, NPG.
PH ALFRED ELLIS, 1894, hs, print, NPG. ELLIS & WALERY, 3 postcards in character, NPG. HISTED, hs, photogravure, NPG.

TERRY, Julia Emilie, Mrs Fred Terry, see Neilson.

TERRY, Phyllis Neilson, see Neilson-Terry.

TERTIS, Lionel (1876-1975) musician.
D EDMOND KAPP, 1933, Barber Institute, Birmingham University.
PH HOWARD COSTER, various sizes and negs, NPG.

THANKERTON, William Watson, Baron (1873-1948) judge.
PH WALTER STONEMAN, 1935, hs, for NPR, NPG x4661.

THESIGER, Ernest (1879-1961) actor.
P W.B.E.RANKEN, 1918, tql, Manchester City Art Gallery.
D SIR W.R.FLINT, c1945, hs as Voltaire, chalk, BM.
SC ERIC SCHILSKY, 1925, bronze bust, V & A.
PH KARL POLLAK, print, NPG. UNKNOWN, hs, print, NPG (Daily Herald).

THESIGER, Frederic John Napier, see 1st Viscount Chelmsford.

THIRKELL, Angela Margaret, née Mackail (1890-1961) novelist.
P JOHN COLLIER, 1912, tql, National Gallery of Victoria, Melbourne, Australia.
PH HOWARD COSTER, various sizes, print and negs, NPG x2129 and others. WALTER STONEMAN, 1957, hs, NPG (NPR).

THOMAS, Bert (Herbert Samuel) (1883-1966) cartoonist.
P UNKNOWN, 1913, tql seated, NPG 4510.
SL HUBERT LESLIE, 1930, wl, profile, NPG. H.L.OAKLEY, 1937, hs, profile, NPG.
PH UNKNOWN, 1936, hs, print, NPG x1540. UNKNOWN, 1963, hl, print, NPG x1541.

THOMAS, Bertram Sidney (1892-1950) explorer.

PH UNKNOWN, 1930, hs, print, Royal Geographical Society, London.

THOMAS, Sir Clement Price, see Price Thomas.

THOMAS, Frederick William (1867-1956) orientalist.
PH UNKNOWN, hs, print, India Office Library, London.

THOMAS, Freeman Freeman-, see 1st Marquess of Willingdon.

THOMAS, Sir (Gwilym) Ivor (1893-1972) general.
PH WALTER STONEMAN, 1944, hs in uniform, NPG (NPR).

THOMAS, Sir Henry (1878-1952) Hispanologist and bibliographer.
PH WALTER STONEMAN, 2 hs portraits, 1938 and 1948, NPG (NPR).

THOMAS, Sir Hugh Evan-, see Evan-Thomas.

THOMAS, James Henry (1874-1949) trade unionist and politician.
D SYDNEY MORSE-BROWN, hs, chalk, National Museum of Wales, Cardiff.
C SIR DAVID LOW, c1926, wl, chalk, NPG 4564; related sketch, hs, pencil, NPG 4529(362). SIR BERNARD PARTRIDGE, wl, w/c and pen and ink, for Punch, 1 Nov 1926, NPG.
PH UNKNOWN, 1932, group with 1st Earl Baldwin of Bewdley and Mayor of Southampton, print, NPG x371. WALTER STONEMAN, 2 hs portraits, 1924 and 1934, NPG (NPR) and NPG x4136.

THOMAS, Margaret Haig, see Viscountess Rhondda.

THOMAS, Sir Percy Edward (1883-1969) architect.
P SIR JAMES GUNN, c1946, tql seated, RIBA.

THOMAS, (Philip) Edward (1878-1917) poet.
D E.H.THOMAS, 1905, hs, profile, pencil, NPG 2892. JOHN WHEATLEY, 1915, head, pencil, NPG 4459.
PR J.WHEATLEY, 1916, hl, etch, NPG.

THOMAS, Sir William Beach (1868-1957) journalist and author.
D SIR MUIRHEAD BONE, chalk, IWM.
PH G.C.BERESFORD, 1917, 2 hs portraits in uniform, negs, NPG x6597-98.

THOMPSON, Alexander Hamilton (1873-1952) historian
PH WALTER STONEMAN, 1945, hs, NPG (NPR).

THOMPSON, Sir D'Arcy Wentworth (1860-1948) zoologist and classical scholar.
P D.S.EWART, wl in academic robes, Royal Society, Edinburgh. D.S.EWART, tql, Zoology Department, University of St Andrews.
SC ALFRED FORREST, bronze head, University of St Andrews.
PH WALTER STONEMAN, 1933, hs, NPG (NPR).

THOMPSON, Edward John (1886-1946) writer.
PH HOWARD COSTER, various sizes, print and negs, NPG.

THOMPSON, James Matthew (1878-1956) scholar.
D RANDOLPH SCHWABE, 1938, pencil, Magdalen College, Oxford.

THOMPSON, Sir (John) Eric Sidney (1898-1975) archaeologist.
M GERTRUDE MASSEY, as a boy, Fitzwilliam Museum, Cambridge

THOMPSON, Reginald Campbell (1876-1941) Assyriologist.
PH WALTER STONEMAN, 1934, hs, NPG (NPR).

THOMSON, Sir Basil Home (1861-1939) colonial governor and assistant commissioner of the Metropolitan Police.
PH WALTER STONEMAN, 1920, hs, NPG (NPR). UNKNOWN, c1910-20, hs, print, NPG.

THOMSON, Christopher Birdwood Thomson, Baron (1875-1930) soldier and politician.
M W.C.DONGWORTH, c1920-30, hs, oval, NPG 5031.
PH WALTER STONEMAN, 1924, hs, NPG (NPR).

THOMSON, Sir George Paget (1892-1975) physicist.
P EDMUND NELSON, c1953, hl seated in robes, Corpus Christi College, Cambridge.
D MICHAEL AYRTON, c1961-62, hs, pencil, Corpus Christi College.
PH WALTER STONEMAN, 1946, hs, NPG (NPR). GODFREY ARGENT, 1970, hs, NPG (NPR).

THOMSON of Fleet, Roy Herbert Thomson, 1st Baron (1894-1976) newspaper proprietor.
P WILLIAM COLDSTREAM, Times Newspapers Ltd, London.
C SIR DAVID LOW, several sketches, pencil, NPG 4529(363-65).
PH WALTER BIRD, 1964, hs, NPG (NPR).

THORNDIKE, Dame Sybil, Lady Casson (1882-1976) actress.
P KENNETH GREEN, 1961, tql, Sybil Thorndike Theatre, Leatherhead.
D EDMOND KAPP, 1926, in 'Trojan Women', Barber Institute, Birmingham University.
SC SIR JACOB EPSTEIN, bronze bust, Doncaster Museum and Art Gallery.
PH PAUL TANQUERAY, 1926, hl, print, NPG. FELIX MAN, 1943, tql in 'Peer Gynt', print, NPG X1156. WALTER STONEMAN, 1958, hs, NPG (NPR). J.S.LEWINSKI, 1967, tql, print, NPG. GODFREY ARGENT, 1968, tql seated with Sir Lewis Casson, for NPR, NPG X5707. N.VOGEL, c1968, 2 hs portraits, prints, NPG. SIR CECIL BEATON, hs, print, NPG. KARL POLLAK, hs, print, NPG. UNKNOWN, hl seated, print, NPG.

THORNHILL, Dame Rachel Eleanor, see Crowdy.

THRELFALL, Sir Richard (1861-1932) physicist and chemical engineer.
PH WALTER STONEMAN, 2 hs portraits, 1920 and 1931, NPG (NPR).

THURSO, Archibald Henry Macdonald Sinclair, 1st Viscount (1890-1970) politician.
D WILLIAM DRING, pastel, IWM. DAVID FOGGIE, 1939, chalk, SNPG 2009.
PH WALTER STONEMAN, 3 hs portraits, 1936, 1940 and 1943, NPG (NPR). NORMAN PARKINSON, c1955, hl seated, print, NPG.

TILLETT, Benjamin ('Ben') (1860-1943) labour leader.
SC J.A.STEVENSON, c1924, bronze bust, Bristol City Art Gallery.
C SIR LESLIE WARD ('Spy'), wl with John Ward, mechanical repro, for *Vanity Fair*, 29 July 1908, NPG.

TILLEY, Vesta, Lady de Frece (1864-1952) male impersonator.
PR HOWARD VAN DUSEN & HASSALL, wl and hs, lith, NPG.
PH ROTARY PHOTO, hs, postcard, NPG.

TILLYARD, Eustace Mandeville Wetenhall (1889-1962) literary scholar and master of Jesus College, Cambridge.
P ERIC KENNINGTON, c1952, Jesus College.
PH WALTER STONEMAN, 1947, hs, NPG (NPR).

TIZARD, Sir Henry Thomas (1885-1959) scientist and administrator.
P BERNARD HAILSTONE, IWM. CUTHBERT ORDE, hl seated in robes, Imperial College of Science and Technology, University of London.
D WILLIAM DRING, 1956, pastel, Magdalen College, Oxford.
PH HOWARD COSTER, various sizes and negs, NPG.

TOLKIEN, John Ronald Reuel (1892-1973) Anglo-Saxon scholar and writer.

PH JOHN WYATT, 1968, hs, print, NPG.

TOMLINSON, George (1890-1952) politician.
PH WALTER STONEMAN, 1945, hs, NPG (NPR).

TOMLINSON, Henry Major (1873-1958) writer.
P RICHARD MURRY, 1927, hs, NPG 4597.
D POWYS EVANS, 1926, head, ink, BM.
PH HOWARD COSTER, various sizes, print and negs, NPG X2130 and others.

TONKS, Henry (1862-1937) painter and teacher.
P Self-portrait, 1909, wl seated, TATE 3231.
D HELEN M.CAMPBELL, hs, pencil, Manchester City Art Gallery. G.W.LAMBERT, head, profile, with Percy Grainger, pencil, NPG 3137A. THOMAS MONNINGTON, 1937, head on deathbed, pencil, Slade School of Fine Art, University College, London. J.S.SARGENT, 1918, tql reclining in uniform, pencil and ink, Fitzwilliam Museum, Cambridge. Self-portrait, tql seated, 2 pencil sketches, NPG 3072(4-5).
G SIR WILLIAM ORPEN, 'Homage to Manet', oil, 1909, Manchester City Art Gallery. SIR W.ORPEN, 'The Selecting Jury of the New English Art Club, 1909', oil, NPG 2556. WILLIAM ROBERTS, 'The Vorticists at the Restaurant de la Tour Eiffel: Spring 1915', oil, c1961-62, TATE T528.
PR JOHN MANSBRIDGE, wl seated, etch, NPG.
C D.G.MACLAREN, 'Some Members of the New English Art Club', w/c, NPG 2663. E.HEBER THOMPSON, 1923, hs and nearly wl, ink and wash, NPG 5089 and 5089A.
PH G.C.BERESFORD, 1902, 2 hs portraits, negs, NPG X6599-600. G.C.BERESFORD, 1922, hs, neg, NPG X6601.

TOPLEY, William Whiteman Carlton (1886-1944) bacteriologist.
PH WALTER STONEMAN, 2 hs portraits, 1931 and 1943, NPG (NPR).

TOVEY, Sir Donald Francis (1875-1940) musician.
P P.A.DE LÁSZLÓ, 1913, hl, Edinburgh University.
D DAVID FOGGIE, 1933, hs, pencil, Edinburgh University. SIR WILLIAM ROTHENSTEIN, c1936, hs, sanguine and pencil, NPG 5277. OTTO SCHLAPP, wl, gouache, Edinburgh University.

TOVEY of Langton Matravers, John Cronyn Tovey, Baron (1885-1971) admiral.
P SIR OSWALD BIRLEY, c1945-46, hs in uniform, Royal Naval College, Greenwich.
D WILLIAM DRING, pastel, IWM.
PH WALTER STONEMAN, 1943, hs in uniform, NPG (NPR).

TOWSE, Sir (Ernest) Beachcroft (Beckwith) (1864-1948) soldier and pioneer of blind welfare.
PH WALTER STONEMAN, tql in uniform, for NPR, NPG X5909.

TOYNBEE, Arnold Joseph (1889-1975) historian.
P LAWRENCE TOYNBEE, Royal Institute of International Affairs, Chatham House, London.
SC EFFIE STILLMAN, 1893, hs, profile, wax medallion, NPG 5208.
PH WALTER STONEMAN, 1945, hs, NPG (NPR). WALTER BIRD, 1959, hs, NPG (NPR). GODFREY ARGENT, 1969, 2 hs portraits, NPG (NPR).

TRAVERS, Ben (1886-1980) dramatist and novelist.
P E.I.HALLIDAY, hs, Garrick Club, London.
PH HOWARD COSTER, 1938, various sizes, prints and negs, NPG X2133-34 and others. TARA HEINEMANN, 1979, hs, print, NPG X8017.

TRAVERS, Morris William (1872-1961) chemist.
PH WALTER STONEMAN, 1917, hs, NPG (NPR).

TREFUSIS, Violet, née Keppel (1894-1972) writer.
P J.E.BLANCHE, 1926, tql seated, NPG 5229.

TREMAYNE, Sir John Tremayne, real name Babington (1891-1979) air marshal.
PH HOWARD COSTER, 1940s, various sizes and negs, NPG x2892–2900. WALTER STONEMAN, 1940s, 5 hs portraits in uniform, for NPR, NPG x1036–40.

TRENCH, Frederick Herbert (1865-1923) poet and playwright.
D SIR WILLIAM ROTHENSTEIN, 1921, head, charcoal, Keble College, Oxford.
PH A.L.COBURN, 1910, hs, photogravure, NPG AX7792.

TRENCHARD, Hugh Montague Trenchard, 1st Viscount (1873-1956) air marshal.
P SIR WILLIAM ORPEN, 1917, IWM. SIR OSWALD BIRLEY, c1926, tql seated in uniform, RAF Club, London. E.VERPILLEUX, 1936, wl in uniform, RAF College, Cranwell, Lincs. A.R.THOMSON, c1943, RAF Staff College, Bracknell, Berks. FRANK BERESFORD, wl in uniform, HQ 11 Group, RAF Bentley Priory, Stanmore, Middx.
D FRANCIS DODD, 1917, charcoal and w/c, IWM. KENNETH GREEN, 1930, pencil, RAF Staff College, Bracknell.
SC WILLIAM MCMILLAN, bronze statue, Victoria Embankment Gardens, London; plaster statuette and bronze cast, RAF Museum, Hendon.
C SIR BERNARD PARTRIDGE, 1927, wl in uniform, chalk, NPG 3677.
PH WALTER STONEMAN, 2 hs portraits in uniform, 1919 and 1932, NPG (NPR).

TREVELYAN, Sir Charles Philips, 3rd Bart (1870-1958) politician.
D SIR WILLIAM ROTHENSTEIN, 1924, hs, sanguine and chalk, NPG 4797.
SC GERTRUDE HERMES, bronze bust, Wallington, Northd.
PH WALTER STONEMAN, 1930, hs, NPG (NPR).

TREVELYAN, George Macaulay (1876-1962) historian.
P EDMUND NELSON, c1947, Trinity College, Cambridge.
D SIR WILLIAM ROTHENSTEIN, 1913, pencil, Trinity College. SIR W.ROTHENSTEIN, c1913, head, chalk, NPG 4286. FRANCIS DODD, 1933, pencil, NPG 4287. F.DODD, 1933, hl, charcoal, Fitzwilliam Museum, Cambridge.
PH SIR CECIL BEATON, tql, print, NPG. WALTER STONEMAN, 2 hs portraits, 1930 and 1948, NPG (NPR).

TREVELYAN, Hilda, Mrs Sydney Blow (1877-1959) actress.
PR CHARLES BUCHEL & HASSALL, wl and hs, lith, NPG.
PH UNKNOWN, tql seated, postcard, NPG.

TREVETHIN, Geoffrey Lawrence, 3rd Baron, see 1st Baron Oaksey.

TRIBE, Sir Frank Newton (1893-1958) comptroller and auditor general of the Exchequer.
PH WALTER STONEMAN, 2 hs portraits, 1941 and 1953, NPG (NPR).

TROTTER, Wilfred Batten Lewis (1872-1939) surgeon, physiologist and philosopher.
P H.A.OLIVIER, 1940, copy, hl, Royal College of Surgeons, London.
G MOUSSA AYOUB, 'Council of the Royal College of Surgeons, 1926–27', oil, c1927–29, Royal College of Surgeons.
PH WALTER STONEMAN, 1931, hs, NPG (NPR).

TROUBRIDGE, Sir Thomas Hope (1895-1949) vice-admiral.
PH WALTER STONEMAN, 1946, hs in uniform, NPG (NPR).

TROUP, Robert Scott (1874-1939) forestry expert.
P P.A.HEY, 1932, The Forestry School, University of Oxford.

TRUEMAN, Sir Arthur Elijah (1894-1956) geologist and administrator.
PH WALTER STONEMAN, 1946, 2 hs portraits, prints, Royal Society London.

TURNBULL, Hubert Maitland (1875-1955) pathologist.
P WILHELM KAUFMANN, Bernhard Baron Institute of Pathology Middlesex Hospital, London. EDMUND NELSON, Medical College, London Hospital.
PH WALTER STONEMAN, 1942, hs, NPG (NPR).

TURNER, Sir Ben (1863-1942) trade unionist.
P R.H.BLACKHAM, 1917, Council Chambers, Batley, Yorks.
C SIR DAVID LOW, 2 heads, pencil, NPG 4529(366–67).
PH Various photographs, Trades Union Congress, London.

TURNER, George Grey (1877-1951) surgeon.
G MOUSSA AYOUB, 'Council of the Royal College of Surgeons 1926–27', oil, c1927–29, Royal College of Surgeons, London. HENRY CARR, 'Council of the Royal College of Surgeons 1946–47', oil, Royal College of Surgeons.

TURNER, Sir George Wilfred (1896-1974) civil servant.
PH WALTER STONEMAN, 1948, hl seated, NPG (NPR).

TURNER, Herbert Hall (1861-1930) astronomer.
D CATHARINE DODGSON, chalk, Royal Astronomical Society London. SIR WILLIAM ROTHENSTEIN, 1916, hs, pencil, Trinity College, Cambridge.
PH WALTER STONEMAN, 1918, hs, NPG (NPR).

TURNER, Sir Ralph Lilley (b1888) orientalist and director of the School of Oriental and African Studies.
P LEONARD BODEN, 1957, hl seated in robes, School of Oriental and African Studies, London.
PH WALTER STONEMAN, 2 hs portraits, 1945 and 1953, NPG (NPR).

TURNER, Walter James Redfern (1889-1946) poet, musical critic, journalist and playwright.
PH HOWARD COSTER, 1930s, various sizes and negs, NPG.

TURNER, William Ernest Stephen (1881-1963) glass technology expert.
PH WALTER STONEMAN, 1938, hs, NPG (NPR).

TURNOUR, Edward, see 6th Earl Winterton.

TUTTON, Alfred Edwin Howard (1864-1938) crystallographer and alpinist.
PH WALTER STONEMAN, 1918, hs, NPG (NPR).

TWEED, John (1869-1933) sculptor.
PH G.C.BERESFORD, 1922, 3 hs portraits, 2 prints and 1 neg, NPG.

TWEEDSMUIR, John Buchan, 1st Baron (1875-1940) novelist and governor-general of Canada.
SC T.J.CLAPPERTON, 1935, bronze head, SNPG 1400; bronze cast, NPG 3636.
PH G.C.BERESFORD, 1906, hs, neg, NPG x6452. HOWARD COSTER 1931, various sizes, print and negs, NPG AX3437, x3288 and x10485. WALTER STONEMAN, 1935, hs and tql seated in uniform, NPG (NPR) and NPG x519.

TWYMAN, Frank (1876-1959) designer of optical instruments.
PH WALTER STONEMAN, 1938, hs, NPG (NPR).

TYNAN, Katharine, see Hinkson.

TYRRELL, Sir William George Tyrrell, Baron (1866-1947) diplomat.
PH WALTER STONEMAN, 1918, hs, NPG (NPR).

TYRWHITT, Sir Reginald Yorke, 1st Bart (1870-1951) admiral.

P GLYN PHILPOT, 1918, IWM.
D FRANCIS DODD, 1917, charcoal and w/c, IWM.
G SIR A.S.COPE, 'Naval Officers of World War I, 1914–18', oil,

1921, NPG 1913.
PH WALTER STONEMAN, 1918, 2 hs portraits in uniform, NPG (NPR).

TYRWHITT-WILSON, Sir Gerald, see 14th Baron Berners.

U

UNDERWOOD, (George Claude) Leon (1890-1975) artist.
D SIR WILLIAM ROTHENSTEIN, 1922, hs, chalk, NPG 4798.
PR Self-portrait, etch, Bradford City Art Gallery.

UNWIN, Sir Raymond (1863-1940) architect.
P SIR GEORGE CLAUSEN, 1933, hl seated, RIBA.
PH G.C.BERESFORD, 1922, hs, neg, NPG X6603. UNKNOWN, several photographs, First Garden City Museum, Letchworth, Herts.

UNWIN, Sir Stanley (1884-1968) publisher.
PH WALTER STONEMAN, 1946, hs, NPG (NPR). GODFREY ARGENT, 1968, hs, NPG (NPR). UNKNOWN, 2 hs portraits, prints, NPG.

UTHWATT, Augustus Andrewes Uthwatt, Baron (1879-1949) judge.
PH WALTER STONEMAN, 1942, hs, NPG (NPR).

UVAROV, Sir Boris (Petrovitch) (1889-1970) entomologist.
PH UNKNOWN, hs, print, Royal Entomological Society of London.

VACHELL, Horace Annesley (1861-1955) novelist.
c HARRY FURNISS, hs, ink, NPG 3531.
PH JOHN RUSSELL & SONS, *c*1915, hs, print, for *National Photographic Record*, vol 1, NPG.

VALERA, Eamon de, see de Valera.

VALOIS, Dame Ninette de, see de Valois.

VANBRUGH, Dame Irene (1872-1949) actress.
P SIR OSWALD BIRLEY, *c*1907, National Gallery of Victoria, Melbourne, Australia. CHARLES BUCHEL, 1923, wl as Lady Mary in Sir J.M.Barrie's *The Admirable Crichton*, Royal Academy of Dramatic Art, London.
PR C.BUCHEL & HASSALL, wl and hs, lith, NPG. FLORA LION, 1913, tql seated, lith, NPG 4102.
PH Mrs ALBERT BROOM, tql, neg, NPG x928. HOWARD COSTER, various sizes and negs, NPG.

VANBRUGH, Violet (1867-1942) actress.
P CHARLES BUCHEL, wl as Queen Katherine in Shakespeare's *Henry VIII*, Royal Academy of Dramatic Art, London.
D C.BUCHEL, wl as Lady Macbeth, chalk and wash, Royal Shakespeare Theatre, Stratford-upon-Avon. EDMOND KAPP, 1919, Barber Institute, Birmingham University.
PR C.BUCHEL, wl and hs, lith, NPG.
PH BASSANO, hs, postcard, NPG. HISTED, hl, photogravure, NPG.

VANE-TEMPEST-STEWART, Charles Stewart Henry, see 7th Marquess of Londonderry.

VANSITTART, Robert Gilbert Vansittart, Baron (1881-1957) diplomat.
PH SIR CECIL BEATON, hs, print, NPG. HOWARD COSTER, various sizes and negs, NPG. WALTER STONEMAN, 3 hs portraits, 1930, 1940 and 1952, NPG (NPR).

VAUGHAN, Dame Helen Charlotte Isabella Gwynne-, see Gwynne-Vaughan.

VAUGHAN, William Wyamar (1865-1938) schoolmaster.
P GEORGE HARCOURT, hl seated, Wellington College, Berks. GLYN PHILPOT, Rugby School, Warwicks.
D SIR WILLIAM ROTHENSTEIN, Wellington College.

VAUGHAN WILLIAMS, Ralph (1872-1958) composer.
P SIR GERALD KELLY, 1952, Royal College of Music, London. SIR G.KELLY, 1959, tql seated, Glasgow City Art Gallery. SIR G.KELLY, 1958-61, tql seated, NPG 4829.
D EDMOND KAPP, 1915, wl, Barber Institute, Birmingham University. SIR WILLIAM ROTHENSTEIN, *c*1915, chalk, Royal College of Music. JOYCE FINZI, 1947, head, profile, pencil and chalk, NPG 4086. J.FINZI, 1947, pencil, Trinity College, Cambridge. JULIET PANNETT, 1957, hs, profile, chalk, NPG 4073. J.PANNETT, 1958, head, profile, chalk, NPG 4074.
SC SIR JACOB EPSTEIN, 1950, bronze cast of head, NPG 4762, Royal College of Music, and Arts Council of Great Britain, London. DAVID MCFALL, bronze head, NPG 4088, and Royal Festival Hall, London.
PH HERBERT LAMBERT, *c*1923, hs, photogravure, NPG AX7744. WALTER STONEMAN, 1936, hs, for NPR, NPG X4127. HOWARD

COSTER, 1938 and 1954, various sizes, prints and negs, NPG X2203-05, X2143, X2369, X2377 and others.

VEALE, Sir Douglas (1891-1973) civil servant and registrar of Oxford University.
SC MARK BATTEN, 1953, stone bust, Bodleian Library, Oxford.
PH WALTER STONEMAN, 1955, hs, NPG (NPR).

VELLACOTT, Paul Cairn (1891-1954) master of Peterhouse, Cambridge.
P RUSKIN SPEAR, 1949, hs, Peterhouse.
PH HOWARD COSTER, various sizes, print and negs, NPG X2331 and others. WALTER STONEMAN, 1947, hl, NPG (NPR).

VENN, John Archibald (1883-1958) president of Queens' College, Cambridge.
P T.S.LA FONTAINE, *c*1948, Queens' College.
D E.J.ROSENBERG, 1885, chalk, Queens' College.
PH WALTER STONEMAN, 1947, hl, NPG (NPR).

VENNING, Sir Walter King (1882-1964) general.
PH WALTER STONEMAN, 1935, hl in uniform, NPG (NPR).

VERDON-ROE, Sir (Edwin) Alliott Verdon (1877-1958) aircraft designer and manufacturer.
P FRANK EASTMAN, 1949, hl seated, Royal Aero Club on loan to RAF Museum, Hendon, London. F.EASTMAN, hl, British Aerospace, Manchester.

VEREKER, John Standish Surtees Prendergast, see 1st Viscount Gort.

VERNEY, Richard Greville, see 19th Baron Willoughby de Broke.

VIAN, Sir Philip (1894-1968) admiral.
P SIR OSWALD BIRLEY, *c*1945-48, hs in uniform, Royal Naval College, Greenwich.
PH WALTER STONEMAN, 1942, hs in uniform, NPG (NPR).

VICKERS, Kenneth Hotham (1881-1958) historian and principal of University College, Southampton.
P A.S.HILL, University of Southampton.

VICTORIA Alexandra Olga Mary, Princess (1868-1935) second daughter of King Edward VII.
P HEINRICH VON ANGELI, 1878, head, oval, Royal Coll. K.W.F.BAUERLE, 1871, wl with sister Louise, Royal Coll.
G S.P.HALL, 'Daughters of Edward VII', oil, 1883, NPG 4471. LAURITS TUXEN, 'The Royal Family at the Time of the Jubilee', oil, 1887, Royal Coll. L.TUXEN, 'Marriage of King George and Queen Mary', oil, 1893, Royal Coll. L.TUXEN, 'Marriage of Princess Maud and Prince Charles of Denmark', oil, 1896, Royal Coll.
SC MARY THORNYCROFT, 1877, marble statue with her sister Princess Maud, Royal Coll.
PH Various photographs, singly and in groups, by Mrs ALBERT BROOM, BYRNE & CO, W. & D.DOWNEY, R.MILNE and JOHN RUSSELL & SONS, NPG. Various photographs, Royal Coll.

VILLIERS, George Herbert Hyde, see 6th Earl of Clarendon.

W

WADSWORTH, Edward Alexander (1889-1949) painter.
D WYNDHAM LEWIS, 1920, tql seated, chalk, Pembroke College, Oxford.
G WILLIAM ROBERTS, 'The Vorticists at the Restaurant de la Tour Eiffel: Spring 1915', oil, *c*1961–62, TATE T528.
PH A.L.COBURN, 1916, hs, photogravure, NPG AX7831.

WAKE-WALKER, Sir William Frederic (1888-1945) admiral.
P MAURICE CODNER, *c*1945–46, Haileybury and Imperial Service College, Herts.
PH WALTER STONEMAN, 3 hs portraits in uniform, 1940 and 1942, NPG (NPR) and NPG X534.

WALEY, Arthur (David) (1889-1966) poet and translator.
D MICHAEL AYRTON, 1957, tql seated, pencil, King's College, Cambridge. REX WHISTLER, head, profile, pencil, NPG 4598.
PH WALTER STONEMAN, 1946, hs, NPG (NPR). SIR CECIL BEATON, 1956, hl, print, NPG.

WALKDEN, Alexander George Walkden, Baron (1873-1951) railway trade unionist.
SC E.J.CLACK, bronze bust, Transport Salaried Staffs Association, London.
PH Various photographs, Transport Salaried Staffs Association.

WALKER, Charles Clement (1877-1968) pioneer aviator.
PH YOUSUF KARSH, *c*1954–55, hs, print, British Aerospace, Aircraft Group, Hatfield, Herts.

WALKER, Ernest (1870-1949) musician.
D FRANCIS DODD, 1934, Balliol College, Oxford.

WALKER, Dame Ethel (1861-1951) painter and sculptor.
P Self-portrait, *c*1925, hs, NPG 5301. Self-portrait, *c*1930?, TATE 6006.

WALKER, Frederic John (1896-1944) Royal Navy captain.
P A.R.SIMS, hs in uniform, Creasy Building, HMS *Vernon*, Portsmouth.

WALKER, Sir Gilbert Thomas (1868-1958) applied mathematician and meteorologist.
PH MAULL & FOX, tql seated, print, Royal Society, London. JOHN RUSSELL & SONS, hs, print, Royal Society.

WALKER, Sir James (1863-1935) chemist.
PH WALTER STONEMAN, 1918, hs, NPG (NPR).

WALKER, Sir Norman Purvis (1862-1942) dermatologist and president of the General Medical Council.
P JOHN BOWIE, *c*1931–39, General Medical Council, London.

WALKER, Sir William Frederic Wake-, see Wake-Walker.

WALLACE, Sir Cuthbert Sidney, Bart (1867-1944) surgeon.
P GEORGE HARCOURT, *c*1931, hl, St Thomas' Hospital, London.
G MOUSSA AYOUB, 'Council of the Royal College of Surgeons, 1926–27', oil, 1927–29, Royal College of Surgeons, London.
PH WALTER STONEMAN, 1918, hs in uniform, NPG (NPR).

WALLACE, (Richard Horatio) Edgar (1875-1932) novelist, playwright and journalist.
P TENNYSON COLE, hl, Press Club, London.

D EDMOND KAPP, 4 drgs, 1931, 1932 and 1940, Barber Institute, Birmingham University.
SC UNKNOWN, relief portrait on bronze plaque, Ludgate Circus, London.
C R.S.SHERRIFFS, wl stealing crown jewels, ink, NPG.
PH HOWARD COSTER, 1930, various sizes, print and negs, NPG AX2263 and X10204–11.

WALLER, Lewis (1860-1915) actor-manager.
P ARTHUR HACKER, 1900, as Henry V, Royal Shakespeare Theatre, Stratford-upon-Avon. JOHN COLLIER, 1903, wl as Monsieur Beaucaire, Russell-Cotes Art Gallery, Bournemouth.
SC EDWARD ONSLOW FORD, 1900, bronze bust as Brutus, Royal Shakespeare Theatre.
C SIR MAX BEERBOHM, brush and indian ink, V & A. 'IMP', wl as a musketeer, lith, for *Vanity Fair*, 13 Oct 1904, NPG. J.ROSS, wl on horseback, w/c, NPG.
PH BARRAUD, 1887, hl, print, NPG. ALFRED ELLIS, 1894, hl, print, NPG. HISTED, hs, profile, photogravure, NPG. LANGFIER, hl and 2 wl portraits as Henry V, photogravures, NPG. LANGFIER, various theatrical postcards, NPG.

WALLIS, Sir Barnes (Neville) (1887-1979) inventor and aeronautical engineer.
SC M.M.KAYE, 1970, bronze bust, RAF Club, London, and Christ's Hospital, Horsham, Sussex. DAVID NORRIS, 1974, bronze head, RAF Museum, Hendon, London.
PH WALTER STONEMAN, 1945, hs, NPG (NPR). GODFREY ARGENT, 1968, hs, NPG (NPR).

WALPOLE, Sir Hugh Seymour (1884-1941) novelist.
P AUGUSTUS JOHN, *c*1926, hl, King's School, Canterbury. W.R.SICKERT, 1928, hs, Fitzwilliam Museum, Cambridge. W.R.SICKERT, 1929, hs, Glasgow City Art Gallery. R.G.EVES, *c*1940, hl, National Book League, London. STEPHEN BONE, nearly wl seated, NPG 3841.
D R.J.SWAN, 1925, sepia pencil, University of Texas, Austin, USA. A.JOHN, 1926, head, chalk, Fitzwilliam Museum.
SC BENNO SCHOTZ, *c*1925, bronze bust, SNPG 1489. DAVID EVANS, 1929, bronze head, NPG 4282. SIR JACOB EPSTEIN, bronze head, Fitz Park Museum and Art Gallery, Keswick, Cumbria.
C SIR DAVID LOW, 2 heads, pencil, NPG 4529(377–78).
PH UNKNOWN, *c*1929, hs with sculptor David Evans at work on his bust, print, NPG. HOWARD COSTER, 1931, various sizes, print and negs, NPG. WALTER STONEMAN, 1939, hs and tql, NPG (NPR).

WALTER, John (1873-1968) newspaper proprietor.
P P.A.DE LÁSZLÓ, *c*1924, tql seated, Times Newspapers Ltd, London.

WARD, Francis ('Frank') Kingdon-, see Kingdon-Ward.

WARD, John (1866-1934) politician and soldier.
C SIR LESLIE WARD ('Spy'), wl with Ben Tillett, mechanical repro, for *Vanity Fair*, 29 July 1908, NPG.
PH WALTER STONEMAN, 1921, hs in uniform, NPG (NPR).

WARD, William Humble, see 2nd Earl of Dudley.

WARDE, Beatrice (1900-1969) authority on typography.
PR ERIC GILL, 1926, hs, profile, 2 engrs, V & A.
PH HOWARD COSTER, 1956, hl, print, NPG X2144.

WARDLAW, William (1892-1958) chemist and university teacher.
PH UNKNOWN, hs, print, Royal Society of Chemistry, London.

WARE, Sir Fabian Arthur Goulstone (1869-1949) editor and originator of the Imperial War Graves Commission.
PH WALTER STONEMAN, 2 hs portraits in uniform, 1919 and 1942, NPG (NPR).

WARING, Sir Holburt Jacob, 1st Bart (1866-1953) surgeon.
G MOUSSA AYOUB, 'Council of the Royal College of Surgeons, 1926-27', oil, 1927-29, Royal College of Surgeons, London.

WARLOCK, Peter, see Philip Arnold HESELTINE.

WARMAN, (Frederic Sumpter) Guy (1872-1953) bishop of Manchester.
PH WALTER STONEMAN, 1933, hs, NPG (NPR). SCOTT, print, Pembroke College, Oxford. UNKNOWN, hl seated, print, NPG (Anglican Bishops).

WARNEFORD, Reginald Alexander John (1891-1915) airman.
PR SIR W.R.FLINT, 1915, lith, IWM.

WARNER, Sir Pelham Francis (1873-1963) writer on cricket.
PH WALTER STONEMAN, 2 hs portraits, 1940 and 1953, NPG (NPR).

WARNER, Sylvia Townsend (1893-1978) poet and novelist.
D JOYCE FINZI, 1960, head, profile, The Library, University of Reading.
PH HOWARD COSTER, various sizes and negs, NPG X3370-75.

WARWICK, Frances Evelyn Greville, Countess of (1861-1938) society beauty.
P ELLIS ROBERTS, 1899, hs, Warwick Castle, Warwicks. J.S.SARGENT, 1905, wl with son, Worcester Art Museum, Mass, USA.
SC SIR EDGAR BOEHM?, marble bust, St Mary's Church, Little Easton, Essex.
PH BARRAUD, c1888, tql seated, print, NPG X5464. ELLIS & WALERY, hl, cabinet, NPG. WALERY, hl, profile, cabinet, NPG. UNKNOWN, wl, seated with infant, cabinet, NPG.

WATERHOUSE, Paul (1861-1924) architect.
P SIR WILLIAM ORPEN, 1923, hs, RIBA.

WATSON, David Meredith Seares (1886-1973) zoologist and palaeontologist.
PH WALTER STONEMAN, 1949, hs, NPG (NPR).

WATSON, Sir David Milne Milne-, see Milne-Watson.

WATSON, Sir James Anderson Scott (1889-1966) agriculturalist.
PH WALTER STONEMAN, 1949, hs, NPG (NPR).

WATSON, Sir Malcolm (1873-1955) malariologist.
PH Various photographs, Ross Institute of Tropical Hygiene, London School of Hygiene and Tropical Medicine.

WATSON, Robert William Seton-, see Seton-Watson.

WATSON, Samuel ('Sam') (1898-1967) miners' leader.
PH UNKNOWN, group, print, Trades Union Congress, London.

WATSON, William, see Baron Thankerton.

WATSON-WATT, Sir Robert (1892-1973) inventor of radar.
P LEONARD APPLEBEE, hs in robes, IWM.
PH WALTER STONEMAN, 1943, hs, NPG (NPR).

WATT, George Fiddes (1873-1960) portrait painter.
SC THOMAS HUXLEY-JONES, c1943, bronze head, Aberdeen Art Gallery.

WATT, Margaret Rose (1868-1948) founder of Women's Institute movement in England and Wales.
PH Several photographs, National Federation of Women's Institutes, London.

WATT, Sir Robert Watson-, see Watson-Watt.

WATTS, John (1861-1902) jockey.
C LIBERIO PROSPERI ('Lib'), wl, profile, lith, for *Vanity Fair*, 25 June 1887, NPG.

WAUCHOPE, Sir Arthur Grenfell (1874-1947) soldier and administrator.
D UNKNOWN, hs in uniform, crayon, The Black Watch Regimental Museum, Balhousie Castle, Perth.

WAVELL, Archibald Percival Wavell, 1st Earl (1883-1950) field-marshal.
SC SIR JACOB EPSTEIN, bronze bust, IWM.
C JAN ROSCIWEWSKI ('Tom Tit'), pen and ink, IWM.
PH SIR CECIL BEATON, tql, print, NPG. WALTER STONEMAN, 2 hs portraits in uniform, 1920 and 1933, NPG (NPR) and NPG X528. E.G.SPENCER CHURCHILL, 1940s, hs and tql, snapshots, NPG.

WAVELL, Arthur John Byng (1882-1916) soldier and explorer.
SC UNKNOWN, statue, Mombasa, Kenya.

WAVERLEY, Ava, Viscountess (1895-1974) political hostess.
P NAPOLEONE PARISANI, 1902, hl, NPG 5026.

WAVERLEY, John Anderson, 1st Viscount (1882-1958) administrator and statesman.
D AUGUSTUS JOHN, 1944, hs, chalk, NPG 5025.
SC SIR JACOB EPSTEIN, 1945, bronze bust, IWM; version, Port of London Authority.
PH WALTER STONEMAN, 3 hs portraits, 1930, 1941 and 1952, NPG (NPR). HOWARD COSTER, 1940s, various sizes, prints and negs, NPG X2327-28, X2364 and X2573-79. SIR CECIL BEATON, 1950s, tql seated, print, NPG.

WEAVER, Sir Lawrence (1876-1930) architectural critic.
PH WALTER STONEMAN, 1920, hs, NPG (NPR).

WEBB, Clement Charles Julian (1865-1954) theologian, philosopher and historian.
P D.H.BANNER, 1929, Oriel College, Oxford.
D SIR WILLIAM ROTHENSTEIN, 1933, chalk, Magdalen College, Oxford.
PH WALTER STONEMAN, 1930, hs, NPG (NPR).

WEBB, Mary Gladys (1881-1927) novelist, essayist and poet.
PH Various photographs, Local Studies Department, Shropshire Libraries, Shrewsbury.

WEBB-JOHNSON, Alfred Edward Webb-Johnson, 1st Baron (1880-1958) surgeon.
P FRANCIS HODGE, 1943, tql in robes, Royal College of Surgeons, London. F.HODGE, c1948, Middlesex Hospital, London. T.C.DUGDALE, c1952, hl, The Royal Society of Medicine, London.

WEBSTER, Benjamin (1864-1947) actor.
C SIR LESLIE WARD ('Spy'), wl in character, pencil, NPG.
PH ALFRED ELLIS, 1893, tql, print, NPG. A.ELLIS, 1895, tql seated with wife, print, NPG.

WEBSTER, Sir Charles Kingsley (1886-1961) historian.
PH WALTER STONEMAN, 2 hs portraits, 1937 and 1953, NPG (NPR).

WEBSTER, (Gilbert) Tom (1890-1962) cartoonist.

PH HOWARD COSTER, 1930s, various sizes, print and negs, NPG X2145 and others. UNKNOWN, 1934, tql seated, print, NPG X1544. UNKNOWN, 1937, hl seated, print, NPG X1545.

WEBSTER, Dame Mary Louise ('May'), née Whitty (1865-1948) actress.

PH ALFRED ELLIS, 1895, tql seated with husband, print, NPG.

WEDGWOOD, Josiah (1899-1968) master potter.

SC DAVID MCFALL, 1975, bronze bust, Josiah Wedgwood & Sons Ltd, Barlaston, Stoke-on-Trent, Staffs.

PH HOWARD COSTER, various sizes and negs, NPG. Various photographs, Josiah Wedgwood & Sons.

WEDGWOOD, Josiah Clement Wedgwood, 1st Baron (1872-1943) politician.

PH SIR BENJAMIN STONE, 1911, 2 wl portraits, prints, NPG. WALTER STONEMAN, 1920, hs, NPG (NPR). HOWARD COSTER, 1930s, various sizes and negs, NPG. LONDON STEREOSCOPIC CO, hs, print, NPG.

WEDGWOOD, Sir Ralph Lewis, 1st Bart (1874-1956) railway administrator.

PH WALTER STONEMAN, 2 hs portraits, 1940 and 1948, NPG (NPR).

WEDGWOOD BENN, William, see Viscount Stansgate.

WEEKS, Ronald Morce Weeks, Baron (1890-1960) industrialist and soldier.

P HERBERT HOLT, 1959, hl seated, Imperial College of Science and Technology, University of London.

WEIR, Andrew, see 1st Baron Inverforth.

WEIR, Sir Cecil McAlpine (1890-1960) industrialist and public servant.

PH WALTER STONEMAN, 2 hs portraits, 1938 and 1952, NPG (NPR).

WEIR, Sir John (1879-1971) physician.

PH WALTER STONEMAN, 1949, hs, NPG (NPR).

WEIR, William Douglas Weir, 1st Viscount (1877-1959) industrialist and public servant.

P T.C.DUGDALE, c1939, wl seated, Weir Group Ltd, Glasgow.

PH WALTER STONEMAN, 1919, hl, NPG (NPR). UNKNOWN, c1917–19, hl seated at desk, print, NPG.

WELCH, Adam Cleghorn (1864-1943) Scottish divine and biblical scholar.

P DAVID ALISON, c1935, New College, Edinburgh.

WELCHMAN, Harry (1886-1966) actor.

PH FOULSHAM & BANFIELD, hs, postcard, NPG.

WELDON, Walter Frank Raphael (1860-1906) zoologist.

SC R.H.HOPE PINKER, 1908, marble bust, The University Museum, Oxford.

WELLESLEY, Dorothy Violet, see Duchess of Wellington.

WELLESLEY, Gerald, see 7th Duke of Wellington.

WELLESZ, Egon Joseph (1885-1974) composer and musicologist.

P JEAN E.COOKE, c1970, wl seated, Lincoln College, Oxford.

WELLINGTON, Dorothy Violet Wellesley, Duchess of (1889-1956) poet.

D SIR WILLIAM ROTHENSTEIN, 2 drgs, Stratfield Saye, Hants. REX WHISTLER, 1933, hl seated, pencil, Stratfield Saye.

PH MADAME YEVONDE, hs as Hecate, print, NPG.

WELLINGTON, Gerald Wellesley, 7th Duke of (1885-1972) architect and public servant.

P ROBERT BUHLER, tql seated in chancellor's robes, University of Southampton. PETER GREENHAM, wl seated in Garter robes, Stratfield Saye, Hants. SIR JAMES GUNN, c1954–58, hs, Stratfield

Saye, study for Society of Dilettanti group.

G SIR J.GUNN, 'Society of Dilettanti Conversation Piece', oil, 1954–59, Society of Dilettanti, Brooks's Club, London.

PH HARLIP LTD, hs in uniform, print, NPG. UNKNOWN, hs, print, NPG.

WELLS, Herbert George (1866-1946) writer.

P UNKNOWN, c1915, hs, University of Texas, Austin, USA.

D SIR WILLIAM ROTHENSTEIN, 1912, hl, chalk, NPG 4644. EDMOND KAPP, 1921 and 1930, wl and hs, Barber Institute, Birmingham University.

SC THEODORE SPICER-SIMSON, c1922, plasticine medallion, NPG 2055.

PR SIR W.ROTHENSTEIN, 1896, lith, Bradford City Art Gallery. SIR W.ROTHENSTEIN, 1904, hs, lith, NPG.

C SIR MAX BEERBOHM, 1903, 'Mr H.G.Wells and his patent mechanical New Republic', drg, Yale University Library, New Haven, USA. SIR M.BEERBOHM, 1931, 'Mr H.G.Wells foreseeing things', drg, The Spectator, London. C.L.FRASER, 'Mr H.G.Wells penetrates the Unknown', charcoal and wash, NPG 5071. SIR DAVID LOW, 2 heads, pencil, NPG 4529(384–85). R.S.SHERRIFFS, 1928, wl as a weather-vane on globe, ink, NPG 5224(3). R.S.SHERRIFFS, 1934, head, profile, pencil and ink, NPG 5224(2). BERT THOMAS, wl, 'Motley's the only wear', ink, NPG 4543.

PH A.L.COBURN, 1905, hs, photogravure, NPG AX7773. G.C.BERESFORD, c1920, 4 hs portraits, 2 prints and 2 negs, NPG. WALTER STONEMAN, 3 hs portraits, 1925, 1935 and 1943, NPG (NPR). HOWARD COSTER, 1934, various sizes, prints and negs, NPG X2146–47, AX3515 and others. UNKNOWN, hs as young man, print, NPG. UNKNOWN, tql seated as young man, print, NPG.

WEMYSS, Rosslyn Erskine, see Baron Wester Wemyss.

WEST, Charles John Sackville-, see 4th Baron Sackville.

WEST, Dame Rebecca (b1892) writer.

PH SIR CECIL BEATON, hl, print, NPG. G.C.BERESFORD, 1912, hs, neg, NPG X6611. WALTER BIRD, 1964, hs, NPG (NPR). HOWARD COSTER, various sizes and negs, NPG. MARK GERSON, 1957, tql seated, print, NPG. J.S.LEWINSKI, 1968, hl, print, NPG. MADAME YEVONDE, hs, print, NPG.

WEST, Victoria Mary ('Vita') Sackville-, see Sackville-West.

WESTER WEMYSS, Rosslyn Erskine Wemyss, Baron (1864-1933) admiral.

P SIR WILLIAM ORPEN, 1919, tql seated in uniform, NPG 4182.

D FRANCIS DODD, 1917, tql in uniform, charcoal and w/c, IWM.

G SIR A.S.COPE, 'Naval Officers of World War I, 1914–18', oil, 1921, NPG 1913.

PH WALTER STONEMAN, 1918, hs in uniform, NPG (NPR).

WESTON, Sir Aylmer Gould Hunter-, see Hunter-Weston.

WESTON, Frank (1871-1924) bishop of Zanzibar.

PH UNKNOWN, hs, print, NPG (Anglican Bishops).

WHEATLEY, Dennis (Yates) (1897-1977) writer.

PH GODFREY ARGENT, 1970, hs, NPG (NPR).

WHEATLEY, John (1869-1930) politician.

C SIR BERNARD PARTRIDGE, wl as Apache dancer, ink and w/c, for *Punch Almanack*, 1 Nov 1926, NPG.

PH HUTCHINSON & RUSSELL, c1924, hl seated, print, NPG. WALTER STONEMAN, 1924, hs, NPG (NPR).

WHEELER, Sir Charles (Thomas) (1892-1974) sculptor.

SC LADY MURIEL WHEELER, 1931, lead bust, NPG 5132.

WHEELER, Sir (Robert Eric) Mortimer (1890-1976) archaeologist.

D J.A.GRANT, 1960, hs, charcoal, Society of Antiquaries, London.
PH UNKNOWN, 1932, wl on a dig, NPG (*Daily Herald*). E.G.MALINDINE, 1934, wl on a dig, NPG (*Daily Herald*). WALTER STONEMAN, 1951, hs, NPG (NPR). HOWARD COSTER, 1956, various sizes, prints, NPG X2148 and X2365–67. WALTER BIRD, 1961, hs, NPG (NPR). GODFREY ARGENT, 1970, hs and hl, NPG (NPR). LAFAYETTE, hs, print, NPG.

WHETHAM, Sir William Cecil, see Dampier.

WHIBLEY, Leonard (1863-1941) classical scholar.
D DOROTHY HAWKSLEY, pencil, Pembroke College, Cambridge.

WHIPPLE, Robert Stewart (1871-1953) manufacturer and collector of scientific instruments and books.
SC MARY GILLICK, bronze relief portrait, Whipple Museum of the History of Science, Cambridge.

WHISTLER, Sir Lashmer (Gordon) (1898-1963) general.
PH WALTER STONEMAN, 1950, hs in uniform, NPG (NPR).

WHITAKER, Sir (Frederick) Arthur (1893-1968) civil engineer.
P JOHN and MAURICE CODNER, c1958, tql seated, Institution of Civil Engineers, London.
PH WALTER STONEMAN, 1945, hs, NPG (NPR).

WHITBY, Sir Lionel Ernest Howard (1895-1956) medical scientist and regius professor of physic.
P WALDRON WEST, Bromsgrove School, Worcs; copy, Downing College, Cambridge.
PH WALTER STONEMAN, 2 hs portraits, the 1st in uniform, 1945 and 1955, NPG (NPR).

WHITE, Claude Grahame-, see Grahame-White.

WHITEHEAD, Alfred North (1861-1947) mathematician and philosopher.
D PAUL DRURY, 1928, pencil, Trinity College, Cambridge.
PH WALTER STONEMAN, 1917, hs, NPG (NPR).

WHITELEY, Sir John Francis Martin (1896-1970) general.
PH WALTER STONEMAN, 1947, hs, NPG (NPR).

WHITELEY, William (1881-1955) politician.
PH WALTER STONEMAN, 3 hs portraits, 1930 and 1945, NPG (NPR).

WHITLEY, John Henry (1866-1935) speaker of the House of Commons.
P GLYN PHILPOT, 1929, wl in robes, Palace of Westminster, London.
D SIR WILLIAM ROTHENSTEIN, 1924, hl in robes, sanguine and crayon, NPG 4799.
PH G.C.BERESFORD, 1903, 2 hs portraits, negs, NPG X6612–13. WALTER STONEMAN, 1917, hs, NPG (NPR).

WHITTAKER, Sir Edmund Taylor (1873-1956) mathematician, astronomer and philosopher.
P TREVOR HADDON, 1933, hs, NPG 4299.
SC BENNO SCHOTZ, c1944, bronze head, Royal Society of Edinburgh.
PH WALTER STONEMAN, 1933, hs, NPG (NPR).

WHITTEN BROWN, Sir Arthur, see Brown.

WHITTINGHAM, Sir Harold (Edward) (b1887) air marshal and pathologist.
PH WALTER STONEMAN, c1940s, 4 hs portraits in uniform, for NPR, NPG X4147–50.

WHITTY, Dame Marie Louise ('May'), see Webster.

WHITWORTH, Geoffrey Arundel (1883-1951) founder of the British Drama League.
P ROGER FRY, hl, British Theatre Association, London.

SC JAMES BUTLER, bronze bust, British Theatre Association. OSCAR NEMON, bronze head, British Theatre Association.

WILBRAHAM, Sir Philip Wilbraham Baker, 6th Bart (1875-1957) ecclesiastical lawyer and administrator.
P SIR OSWALD BIRLEY, 1940, tql seated in robes, Church House, Westminster, London.

WILD, (John Robert) Francis (1873-1939) Antarctic explorer.
PH Various photographs, Scott Polar Research Institute, Cambridge.

WILKIE, Sir David Percival Dalbreck (1882-1938) surgeon.
D DAVID FOGGIE, 1933, pencil, SNPG 1808.

WILKINSON, Ellen Cicely (1891-1947) trade unionist and politician.
D EDMOND KAPP, 1930, chalk, Barber Institute, Birmingham University.
PH HOWARD COSTER, various sizes and negs, NPG. WALTER STONEMAN, 1945, hl, NPG (NPR).

WILKINSON, Louis Umfreville (1881-1966) novelist 'Louis Marlow'.
PH WALTER STONEMAN, 1948, tql seated, NPG (NPR).

WILKINSON, Sir Nevile Rodwell (1869-1940) soldier, herald and artist.
PH WALTER STONEMAN, 1931, hs, NPG (NPR).

WILKINSON, Norman (1878-1971) marine artist.
PH HOWARD COSTER, various sizes and negs, NPG.

WILLCOX, Sir William Henry (1870- 1941) physician and toxicologist.
PH WALTER STONEMAN, hs, for NPR, NPG X531.

WILLERT, Sir Arthur (1882-1973) journalist and public servant.
PH WALTER STONEMAN, 1930, hs, NPG (NPR).

WILLEY, Basil (1897-1978) literary scholar.
PH IAN FLEMING, head, print, Pembroke College, Cambridge. WALTER STONEMAN, 1948, hs, NPG (NPR).

WILLIAMS, Alwyn Terrell Petre (1888-1968) bishop of Winchester.
P SIR GERALD KELLY, 1936, tql, Winchester College, Hants. RODRIGO MOYNIHAN, c1952, tql seated, Christ Church, Oxford.
D WILLIAM DRING, c1961, hl, pastel, Bishop's Palace, Winchester.
PH J.K.EDIS, c1939, hs, print, NPG (Anglican Bishops). WALTER BIRD, 1961, hs, NPG (NPR).

WILLIAMS, (Arthur Frederic) Basil (1867-1950) historian.
PH WALTER STONEMAN, 1935, hs, NPG (NPR).

WILLIAMS, Charles Walter Stansby (1886-1945) author and scholar.
PH UNKNOWN, c1904, tql seated, snapshot, NPG X6951. UNKNOWN, c1944, hl, snapshot, NPG X6952.

WILLIAMS, E.G.Harcourt (1880-1957) actor and producer.
PH HOWARD COSTER, various sizes and negs, NPG. ROTARY PHOTO, hl in character, postcard, NPG.

WILLIAMS, Henry Herbert (1872-1961) bishop of Carlisle.
PH WALTER STONEMAN, 1933, hs, NPG (NPR). UNKNOWN, hs, print, NPG (Anglican Bishops).

WILLIAMS, Sir Ifor (1881-1965) Welsh scholar and author.
PH WALTER STONEMAN, 1938, hs, NPG (NPR).

WILLIAMS, Sir John Coldbrook Hanbury-, see Hanbury-Williams.

WILLIAMS, Margaret Lindsay (1888–1960) artist.
P A.J.LYDDON, hl, National Museum of Wales 360, Cardiff.

WILLIAMS, Ralph Vaughan, see Vaughan Williams.

WILLIAMS-ELLIS, Sir (Bertram) Clough (1883–1978) architect.
PH HOWARD COSTER, 1936, hs, profile, print, NPG x2392. BRUNO DE HAMEL, c1969, hl seated, print, NPG. KARL POLLAK, hl, print, NPG.

WILLIAMS of Barnburgh, Thomas Williams, Baron (1888–1967) politician.
PH HOWARD COSTER, various sizes and negs, NPG. WALTER STONEMAN, 1944, hs, NPG (NPR).

WILLIAMSON, Henry (1895–1977) writer.
D POWYS EVANS, 1928, head, ink, NPG 5110.

WILLINGDON, Freeman Freeman-Thomas, 1st Marquess of (1866–1941) governor-general of Canada and viceroy of India.
P SIR OSWALD BIRLEY, c1936, wl seated, Viceroy's House, New Delhi, India.
SC SIR W.R.DICK, statue, New Delhi.
PH WALTER STONEMAN, 2 hs portraits, 1924 and 1934, NPG (NPR) and NPG x1044.

WILLINK, Sir Henry Urmston (1894–1973) politician and master of Magdalene College, Cambridge.
P A.R.MIDDLETON TODD, c1957, hl seated, Magdalene College.
C SIR DAVID LOW, 4 sketches, pencil, NPG 4529(392–95).
PH HOWARD COSTER, various sizes and negs, NPG. WALTER STONEMAN, 1944, hs, NPG (NPR).

WILLIS, Sir Algernon Usborne (1889–1976) admiral.
P SIR OSWALD BIRLEY, c1945, hs in uniform, Royal Naval College, Greenwich.
PH WALTER STONEMAN, 2 hs portraits, the 1st in uniform, 1944 and 1955, NPG (NPR).

WILLOUGHBY de Broke, Richard Greville Verney, 19th Baron (1869–1923) huntsman and politician.
C SIR LESLIE WARD ('Spy'), wl, w/c study for *Vanity Fair*, 23 Nov 1905, NPG 4946.
PH BASSANO, 1898, 4 portraits, negs, NPG x4232–35.

WILMOT of Selmeston, John Wilmot, Baron (1895–1964) politician.
PH HOWARD COSTER, various sizes and negs, NPG. WALTER STONEMAN, 1953, hs, NPG (NPR).

WILSHAW, Sir Edward (1879–1968) communications engineer.
PH WALTER STONEMAN, 3 hl portraits, 1940 and 1953, NPG (NPR) and NPG x530.

WILSON, Sir Arnold Talbot (1884–1940) soldier, politician, administrator and author.
D SIR RICHARD PAGET, 1929, sketch, ink, The Athenaeum, London.
PH WALTER STONEMAN, 1921, 2 hs portraits, NPG (NPR).

WILSON, Charles Thomson Rees (1869–1959) physicist.
P SIR JAMES GUNN, Sidney Sussex College, Cambridge.
PH WALTER STONEMAN, 1933, hs, NPG (NPR).

WILSON, Edward Adrian (1872–1912) naturalist and Antarctic explorer.
D A.U.SOORD, 1909, tql seated, w/c, Scott Polar Research Institute, Cambridge.
SC LADY KATHLEEN KENNET, bronze bust, St George's Hospital, London, and bronze statue, Cheltenham. A.G.WALKER, bronzed plaster group of statues with R.F.Scott and L.E.G.Oates, Scott Institute.
PH H.G.PONTING, various photographs, Scott Institute.

WILSON, Sir Gerald Hugh Tyrwhitt-, see 14th Baron Berners.

WILSON, Henry Albert (1876–1961) bishop of Chelmsford.
PH WALTER STONEMAN, 1939, hs, NPG (NPR).

WILSON, Sir Henry Hughes, Bart (1864–1922) field-marshal.
P SIR WILLIAM ORPEN, 1919, hl seated in uniform, NPG 4183. J.S.SARGENT, c1921, head, NPG 2889, study for 'Generals', NPG 1954. After SIR OSWALD BIRLEY, 1922, tql seated in uniform, Staff College, Camberley, Surrey.
D INGLIS SHELDON-WILLIAMS, 1900, tql seated in uniform, pencil and w/c, NPG 4039(7). FRANCIS DODD, 1917, charcoal and w/c, IWM.
G J.S.SARGENT, 'General Officers of World War I, 1914–18', oil, 1922, NPG 1954.
PH G.C.BERESFORD, 1920, 2 hs and 1 wl portrait in uniform, prints and negs, NPG x6614–16. WALTER STONEMAN, c1918, hs in uniform, NPG (NPR).

WILSON, Henry Maitland Wilson, 1st Baron (1881–1964) field-marshal.
PH FREDERIC ROBINSON, 1939, hs in uniform, NPG. WALTER STONEMAN, 1945, hs in uniform, NPG (NPR).

WILSON, Sir Horace John (1882–1972) civil servant.
PH WALTER STONEMAN, 1941, 5 hl portraits, NPG (NPR) and NPG x8389–92.

WILSON, John Dover (1881–1969) Shakespearian scholar.
D ROBERT LYON, 1959, pencil, The Shakespeare Centre, Stratford-upon-Avon.
PH WALTER STONEMAN, 2 hs portraits, 1932 and 1945, NPG (NPR).

WILSON, John Leonard (1897–1970) bishop of Birmingham.
P HENRY CARR, c1964, tql seated, Bishop's Palace, Birmingham.

WILSON, Sir Samuel Herbert (1873–1950) colonial administrator.
PH WALTER STONEMAN, 1920, hs in uniform, NPG (NPR).

WIMBORNE, Ivor Churchill Guest, 1st Viscount (1873–1939) politician.
PH WALTER STONEMAN, 1921, hs, NPG (NPR). OLIVE EDIS, 1931, tql seated, print, NPG.

WINDSOR, Edward Duke of (1894–1972) Edward VIII, reigned 1936.
P SIR A.S.COPE, 1912, wl in robes, Royal Coll. FRANÇOIS FLAMENG, 1912, hs, oval, Royal Coll. SIR JOHN LAVERY, c1913, head, sketch, Royal Coll, study for NPG 1745. FRANK BROOKS, 1921, hs in naval uniform, DoE, Britannia Royal Naval College, Dartmouth, S Devon. JOHN COLLIER, 1921, Hall of Princes, Delhi. JOHN ST HELIER LANDER, c1922, wl, Manchester City Art Gallery. J.ST HELIER LANDER, 1925, tql with dog, Leeds City Art Gallery. SIR WILLIAM ORPEN, 1928, wl as young man in golfing dress, Royal and Ancient Golf Club of St Andrews. J.ST HELIER LANDER, 1936, wl in Garter robes, Master Mariners Company, London. F.O.SALISBURY, 1936, hs in uniform, Belton House, Grantham, Lincs. W.R.SICKERT, after photograph by Harold J.Clemens, 1936, wl in Welsh Guards' uniform, Beaverbrook Art Gallery, Fredericton, New Brunswick, Canada. SIR JAMES GUNN, 1954, hs, study for group, NPG 4949. SIR J.GUNN, c1954, hs in Garter robes, Royal Coll.
D SIR W.Q.ORCHARDSON, c1897, head, pencil, Royal Coll, study for 'The Four Generations'. WILLIAM STRANG, 1909, hs in naval

cadet uniform, Royal Coll. R.G.Eves, c1920, hs, chalk, NPG 4169. Sir William Rothenstein, 1929, crayon, Cheltenham Art Gallery. Vandyk, (after photograph?), hs chalk, Royal College of Music, London.
M R.G.Eves, c1920, hl in uniform, NPG 4138.
SL H.L.Oakley, 1919, wl, profile, NPG 4534.
G Sir W.Q.Orchardson, 'Four Generations', oil, c1897–99, Royal Agricultural Society, London; study, NPG 4536. Sir J.Lavery, 'The Royal Family at Buckingham Palace, 1913', oil, NPG 1745. F.O.Salisbury, 'Burial of Unknown Warrior', oil, 1920, Palace of Westminster, London. F.O.Salisbury, 'Marriage of Princess Mary', oil, 1922, Harewood House, W Yorks, and Royal Coll. F.O.Salisbury, 'Jubilee Service, for George V', oil, 1935, Royal Coll; related 'Thanksgiving Service', oil, Guildhall, London.
SC Charles S.Jagger, 1922, bronze statuette, National Museum of Wales, Cardiff; version?, Graves Art Gallery, Sheffield. Charles Hartwell, c1920–24, marble bust, Corporation of London. F.W.Doyle-Jones, c1932, Master Mariners Company. Fred Kormis, 1936, bronze medal, NPG 5051.
PR Edmond Kapp, 1932, hl in evening dress, lith, NPG 4908.
C 'Nibs', wl, Hentschel-Colourtype, for Vanity Fair, 21 June 1911, NPG. O.H.Mavor, 1943, 'The Duke of Windsor as Hamlet', w/c, Dundee City Art Gallery.
PH Various photographs as infant and child, singly and in groups, by W. & D.Downey, Hughes & Mullins, Dunham and Mrs Albert Broom, NPG and Royal Coll. Various photographs as young man by Olive Edis, Hugh Cecil, Mrs Broom, J.Russell & Sons and Vandyk, NPG and Royal Coll. Various photographs when king and after abdication, alone and with the Duchess of Windsor, Sir Cecil Beaton and Dorothy Wilding, NPG.

WINDSOR, Wallis Simpson, Duchess of (b1896) wife of Edward VIII, Duke of Windsor.
PH Sir Cecil Beaton, hs with Duke of Windsor, print, NPG. Various photographs singly and with Duke, Dorothy Wilding, NPG. Various photographs, NPG (Daily Herald).

WINFIELD, Sir Percy Henry (1878-1953) lawyer and legal scholar.
D John Hookham, 1945, St John's College, Cambridge.
PH Walter Stoneman, 2 hs portraits, 1934 and 1945, NPG (NPR).

WINGATE, Sir (Francis) Reginald, 1st Bart (1861-1953) soldier and governor-general of the Sudan.
D Sir Leslie Ward, hs in uniform, pencil, NPG.
C Sir L.Ward ('Spy'), wl, lith, for Vanity Fair, 9 Sept 1897, NPG.
PH Walter Stoneman, 1920, hs in uniform, NPG (NPR).

WINSTANLEY, Denys Arthur (1877-1947) historian.
D Francis Dodd, 1933, pencil, Trinity College, Cambridge.

WINSTER, Reginald Thomas Herbert Fletcher, Baron (1885-1961) governor of Cyprus.
PH Howard Coster, various sizes and negs, NPG. Walter Stoneman, 1945, hs, NPG (NPR).

WINTERTON, Edward Turnour, 6th Earl (1883-1962) statesman.
C Sir Leslie Ward ('Spy'), wl, Hentschel-Colourtype, for Vanity Fair, 16 Sept 1908, NPG.
PH Walter Stoneman, 2 hs portraits, 1921 and 1936, NPG (NPR).

WITT, Sir Robert Clermont (1872-1952) art collector.
P Sir Oswald Birley, 1931, hl seated, Witt Library, Courtauld Institute of Art, London. T.C.Dugdale, 1931, wl seated with Lady Witt, Witt Library.

WITTGENSTEIN, Ludwig Josef Johann (1889-1951) philosopher.

PH Unknown, hs, print and neg, Trinity College, Cambridge.

WODEHOUSE, Helen Marion (1880-1964) mistress of Girton College, Cambridge.
PH Unknown, print, Girton College.

WODEHOUSE, Sir Pelham Grenville ('P.G.') (1881-1975) writer.
C Sir David Low, tql, mechanical repro, for The New Statesman and Nation, 23 Dec 1933, NPG.
PH Unknown, hs in old age, postcard, NPG.

WOLFE, Humbert, real name Umberto Wolff (1886-1940) poet and civil servant.
D William Shackleton, 1924, hs, Bradford City Art Gallery. Ivan Opffner, 1930, hs, chalk, NPG. Sir William Rothenstein, 2 hs portraits, profile, sanguine, NPG L168(10–11).
C Sir David Low, head, pencil, NPG 4529(396).
PH Howard Coster, 1934, various sizes, prints and negs, NPG AX3498, X2154 and others.

WOLFSON, Sir Isaac, 1st Bart (b1897) businessman and public servant.
SC Sir W.R.Dick, 1953, bronze cast of bust, Royal College of Physicians, London, and Wolfson College, Oxford.
PH Godfrey Argent, 1969, hs, NPG (NPR).

WOLMARK, Alfred (Aaron) (1877-1961) artist.
P Self-portrait, Southampton Art Gallery.
D Henri Gaudier-Brzeska, c1913, 2 heads, profile, pencil, Southampton Art Gallery. Self-portrait, 1926, head, ink, NPG 4884.
SC H.Gaudier-Brzeska, 1913, plaster bust, Walker Art Gallery, Liverpool, and bronze cast, Southampton Art Gallery.

WOLMER, Roundell Cecil Palmer, Viscount, see 3rd Earl of Selborne.

WOMERSLEY, Sir Walter James, 1st Bart (1878-1961) politician.
PH Walter Stoneman, 2 hs portraits, 1930 and 1942, NPG (NPR).

WOOD, Edward Frederick Lindley, see 1st Earl of Halifax.

WOOD, Francis Derwent (1871-1926) sculptor.
P G.W.Lambert, 1906, hl seated, NPG 4416.
C H.M.Bateman, hs, Chelsea Arts Club, London.
PH G.C.Beresford, 1922, 3 hs portraits, prints and negs, NPG X6617–19 and others.

WOOD, Sir Henry Joseph (1869-1944) conductor.
P Meredith Frampton, c1930, wl, Savage Club, London. Flora Lion, 1937, tql conducting, Savage Club on loan to the Royal Albert Hall, London. F.O.Salisbury, 1943, tql seated in robes, NPG 3688.
D C.P.Hawkes, ink and wash, Royal College of Music, London. Edmond Kapp, 1929–44, 8 sketches, Barber Institute, Birmingham University. Sir William Rothenstein, hs, profile, sanguine, NPG L168(7). H.E.Wiener, 1938, tql, profile, pencil, NPG 3818.
SC Donald Gilbert, bronze bust, Royal Academy of Music, London.
C Sir Leslie Ward ('Spy'), wl, mechanical repro, for Vanity Fair, 17 April 1907, NPG. W.K.Haselden, 1933, wl, profile, ink, NPG 4078.
PH Howard Coster, print and 3 negs, NPG X2385 and others. Alfred Ellis, hs, cabinet, NPG. Claude Harris, hs, print, NPG. Felix Man, 1938, wl, print, NPG X1157. Walter Stoneman, 1940, hs, NPG (NPR).

WOOD, Sir (Howard) Kingsley (1881-1943) politician.
PH Walter Stoneman, 5 portraits, 1921 and c1941, NPG (NPR) and

NPG X8385–88. HOWARD COSTER, 1938, various sizes, print and negs, NPG X2387 and others.

WOOD, Matilda Alice Victoria, see Marie LLOYD.

WOODS, Edward Sydney (1877-1953) bishop of Lichfield.
PH WALTER STONEMAN, 1939, hs, for NPR, NPG X1046. UNKNOWN, tql, print, NPG (Anglican Bishops).

WOODS, Sir John (Harold Edmund) (1895-1962) civil servant.
PH WALTER STONEMAN, 1948, hl, NPG (NPR).

WOODWARD, Sir Arthur Smith (1864-1944) palaeontologist.
G JOHN COOKE, 'Group at the Royal College of Surgeons examining the Piltdown Skull, 1913', oil, c1915, Geological Society of London.
PH WALTER STONEMAN, 1918, hs, NPG (NPR).

WOODWARD, Clifford Salisbury (1878-1959) bishop of Gloucester.
P SIMON ELWES, 1952, hs, Church House, Diocese of Gloucester.
PH WALTER STONEMAN, 2 hs portraits, 1938 and 1940, NPG (NPR). UNKNOWN, hs, print, NPG (Anglican Bishops).

WOODWARD, Sir Ernest Llewellyn (1890-1971) historian.
PH WALTER STONEMAN, 1948, hl, NPG (NPR).

WOOLF, (Adeline) Virginia, née Stephen (1882-1941) novelist and critic.
P J.E.BLANCHE, 1927?, hs, Museum of Art, Rhode Island School of Design, Providence, USA.
D FRANCIS DODD, 1908, head, chalk, NPG 3802. WYNDHAM LEWIS, 1921, tql seated, pencil, pen and wash, V & A.
SC BORIS ANREP, 1933, as Clio in 'The Awakening of the Muses', mosaic, National Gallery, London. STEPHEN TOMLIN, c1935, lead cast of bust, 1953, NPG 3882.
PH G.C.BERESFORD, c1902, hs with her father Sir Leslie Stephen, print, NPG X4600. Various photographs, NPG (Strachey Coll).

WOOLF, Leonard Sidney (1880-1969) journalist and publisher.
P VANESSA BELL, 1912, wl seated with Adrian Stephen, 'Conversation Piece', University of Hull. V.BELL, c1938, wl seated, NPG 4695.
SC CHARLOTTE HEWER, 1968, bronze bust, NPG 4938.
PH Various photographs, NPG (Strachey Coll).

WOOLLARD, Frank George (1883-1957) pioneer of mass production in the motor industry.
PH UNKNOWN, c1945, hs, print, Institution of Mechanical Engineers, London.

WOOLLEY, Sir (Charles) Leonard (1880-1960) archaeologist.
PH WALTER STONEMAN, 1954, hs, NPG (NPR).

WOOLTON, Frederick James Marquis, 1st Earl (1883-1964) statesman.
P A.C.DAVIDSON-HOUSTON, 1954, hl, The Salters' Company, London.
C GEOFFREY DAVIEN, plaster bust, 'sculptoon', NPG. SIR DAVID LOW, head, profile, pencil, NPG.
PH HOWARD COSTER, various sizes and negs, NPG. WALTER STONEMAN, 3 hs portraits, 1939, 1941 and 1952, NPG (NPR).

WOOTTON of Abinger, Barbara Frances Wootton, Baroness (b1897) educationist.
PH WALTER BIRD, 1964, hs, NPG (NPR).

WORNUM, George Grey (1888-1957) architect.

SC UNKNOWN, bronze bust, RIBA.

WORTHINGTON-EVANS, Sir (Worthington) Laming, 1st Bart (1868-1931) politician.
PH WALTER STONEMAN, 1925, hs, NPG (NPR).

WRENCH, Sir (John) Evelyn (Leslie) (1882-1966) founder of the Overseas League and the English-Speaking Union.
P SIR OSWALD BIRLEY, 1921, tql, Royal Over-Seas League, London. M.L.WILLIAMS, wl, English-Speaking Union, London.
SC UNKNOWN, plaster bust, English-Speaking Union.
PH WALTER STONEMAN, 2 hs portraits, 1945 and 1955, NPG (NPR). Various photographs, The English Speaking Union, London.

WRIGHT, Sir Almroth Edward (1861-1947) bacteriologist.
P SIR GERALD KELLY, 1933, tql seated in laboratory, Wright-Fleming Institute of Microbiology, St Mary's Hospital, Paddington, London.
D FRANCIS DODD, 1932, hl seated, charcoal, NPG 4127.
SC DONALD GILBERT, c1935, bronze bust, St Mary's Hospital.
PH Various photographs, Wright-Fleming Institute.

WRIGHT, Sir Charles Theodore Hagberg (1862-1940) librarian.
P SIR WILLIAM ORPEN, hl seated, London Library.

WRIGHT, Robert Alderson Wright, Baron (1869-1964) judge.
P SIR GERALD KELLY, hs, Inner Temple, London.
PH WALTER STONEMAN, 1936, hs in robes, NPG (NPR).

WRIGHT, Sir (William) Charles, 2nd Bart (1876-1950) ironmaster and steelmaker.
P SIR OSWALD BIRLEY, 1944, tql seated, British Steel Corporation, East Midlands Regional Records Centre, Irthlingborough, near Wellingborough, Northants.

WROTTESLEY, Sir Frederic John (1880-1948) judge.
D ERIC KENNINGTON, hs, pastel, Skinners' Company, London.
PH WALTER STONEMAN, 1938, hs in robes, NPG (NPR).

WYCHERLEY, Sir (Robert) Bruce (1894-1965) first president of the Abbey National Building Society.
P SIR JAMES GUNN, wl seated, Abbey National Building Society Head Office, London.
PH WALTER STONEMAN, 1955, hs, NPG (NPR).

WYLD, Henry Cecil Kennedy (1870-1945) English philologist and lexicographer.
G ALBERT LIPCZINSKI, staff group, oil, 1915, Faculty of Arts, University of Liverpool.

WYLIE, Sir Francis James (1865-1952) first warden of Rhodes House, Oxford.
P E.I.HALLIDAY, 1952, wl seated, Rhodes House.
D F.A.DE BIDEN FOOTNER, 1935, hs, pencil, Rhodes House.

WYNDHAM, George (1863-1913) statesman.
P HAROLD SPEED, 1914, wl in robes, Dover Town Hall.
SC AUGUSTE RODIN, 1904, bronze bust, TATE 6059, and Municipal Gallery of Modern Art, Dublin. UNKNOWN, 1913, plaster cast of death-mask, NPG 3814.
C SIR LESLIE WARD ('Spy'), wl, lith, for *Vanity Fair*, 20 Sept 1900, NPG. SIR BERNARD PARTRIDGE, wl with J.E.Redmond and 1st Earl Balfour, ink, for *Punch*, 6 May 1903, NPG.
PH SIR BENJAMIN STONE, 1902, wl, print, NPG. G.C.BERESFORD, 1903, 3 hs portraits, negs, NPG X6620–22. ELLIOTT & FRY, hs, print, for *Our Conservative and Unionist Statesmen*, vol 2, NPG (Album 25). UNKNOWN, hl in uniform, print, NPG.

WYNDHAM, Mary, Lady (1861-1931) actress 'Mary Moore' and theatre-manager.

D S.P.HALL, 1887, 3 sketches, pencil, NPG 2370–72.
PR HOWARD VAN DUSEN & HASSALL, hs and wl, lith, NPG.
C SIR MAX BEERBOHM, wl as doll with Sir Charles Wyndham, drg, V & A.
PH BARRAUD, *c*1889, tql seated, 2 prints, NPG AX 5449 and another.

ALFRED ELLIS, 1895, hs, profile, print, NPG. A.ELLIS, *c*1895, hs, profile, cabinet, NPG. ELLIS & WALERY, hl, oval, print, NPG.

WYNN, Harold Edward (1889-1956) bishop of Ely.
PH WALTER STONEMAN, 1948, hl, NPG (NPR).

Y

YARROW, Sir Harold (Edgar), 2nd Bart (1884-1962) businessman.

PH WALTER STONEMAN, 1958, hs, NPG (NPR).

YEATS, Jack Butler (1871-1957) painter.

P JOHN BUTLER YEATS, as a boy, NGI 1142. ESTELLA SOLOMONS, 1922, hl seated, Sligo County Library and Museum. SEAN O'SULLIVAN, 1942, oil?, Sligo County Library and Museum. JAMES SLEATOR, 1942, Cork Municipal Art Gallery. LILIAN DAVIDSON, NGI 1289. SARAH PURSER, hs, NGI. J.B.YEATS, hs, NGI 4040.

D J.B.YEATS, 1899, hl, pencil, NGI. PAMELA COLEMAN SMITH, 1901, hs, 2 pen and ink sketches on the title page of Lady Gregory's copy of *Samhain I*, New York Public Library, USA. Self-portrait, *c*1920, wl, pencil, NGI 3319. S.O'SULLIVAN, 1929, hs, charcoal, NGI. S.O'SULLIVAN, 1943, seated, pencil, NGI.

PH HOWARD COSTER, 1939, various sizes, prints and negs, NPG X2155-57 and others.

YEATS, William Butler (1865-1939) poet and dramatist.

P H.M.PAGET, 1889, hs, Ulster Museum, Belfast. J.B.YEATS, *c*1890s, hl, Municipal Gallery of Modern Art, Dublin. J.B.YEATS, 1900, hs, NGI 872. AUGUSTUS JOHN, 1907, hl, Manchester City Art Gallery; related etch, NPG 3061. A.JOHN, 1907, hs, TATE 5218; related drg, hs, pencil, TATE 5298. J.B.YEATS, *c*1907, hl, Abbey Theatre, Dublin. A.JOHN, 1930, tql seated, Glasgow City Art Gallery. SEAN O'SULLIVAN, 1934, tql seated, Abbey Theatre.

D SIR WILLIAM ROTHENSTEIN, 1897, pencil, University of Texas, Austin, USA. Attrib SIR W.ROTHENSTEIN, hl, pen and ink, University of Texas. SIR W.ROTHENSTEIN, 1898, hs, Municipal Gallery of Modern Art; related lith, NPG. SARAH PURSER, 1898?, hs, pastel, Municipal Gallery of Modern Art. J.B.YEATS, 1898, tql seated, w/c, NGI 2942. J.B.YEATS, 1899, hs, pencil, Birmingham City Art Gallery. ALTHEA GYLES, *c*1900, head, profile, ink, BM. UNKNOWN, *c*1900?, hs, pastel, NGI 2933. WILLIAM STRANG, 1903, hs, NGI 2729. W.STRANG, 1903, hs, chalk, Fitzwilliam Museum, Cambridge. GEORGE RUSSELL ('AE'), 1903, hs, NGI 2988. A.JOHN, *c*1907, tql, pencil and wash, NPG 4105. J.S.SARGENT, 1908?, charcoal, Abbey Theatre. EDMOND KAPP, 1914, Barber Institute, Birmingham University. SIR W.ROTHENSTEIN, 1916, hs, chalk, Municipal Gallery of Modern Art. SIR W.ROTHENSTEIN, 1916, hs, pencil, Leeds City Art Gallery. SIR W.ROTHENSTEIN, 1923, head, profile, Laing Art Gallery, Newcastle-upon-Tyne. S.O'SULLIVAN, 1933, hs, NGI 3537. IVAN OPFFER, 1935?, head, chalk, NPG 3965. HARRY KERNOFF, pastel and tempera, University of Texas.

G JOHN KEATING, 'Homage to Hugh Lane', oil, *c*1924, Municipal Gallery of Modern Art.

SC AUGUSTUS JOHN, *c*1907, bronze bust, Abbey Theatre. LADY KATHLEEN KENNET, 1907, plaster mask, NPG 3644; bronze cast, NPG 3644A. ALBERT POWER, 1918, bronze bust, University of Texas. THEODORE SPICER-SIMSON, 1922, bronze medallion, NGI 8215. A.POWER, 1939, bronze bust, NGI 8048.

C SIR MAX BEERBOHM, *c*1904, 'W.B.Yeats introducing George Moore to the Queen of the Fairies', pen and wash, Municipal Gallery of Modern Art. SIR M.BEERBOHM, nearly wl, ink and w/c, NGI 3773. SIR M.BEERBOHM, 'Some Persons of the 90s', drg, Ashmolean Museum, Oxford. SIR WILLIAM ORPEN, 1907, wl with Lady Gregory, Sir Hugh Lane and J.M.Synge, pen and ink, NPG 4676. EDMUND DULAC, 1915, wl seated as a marionette, w/c, Abbey Theatre.

PH G.C.BERESFORD, hs, print and neg, NPG X6397 and X6623. A.L.COBURN, 1908, hs, photogravure, NPG AX7786. HOWARD COSTER, 1935, various sizes, prints and negs, NPG AX3510, X1961-65 and others. Various photographs, The Huntingdon Library, San Marino, USA.

YORKE, Albert Edward Philip Henry, see 6th Earl of Hardwicke.

YOUNG, (Edith Agnes) Kathleen Hilton, see Lady Kennet.

YOUNG, Edward Hilton, see 1st Baron Kennet.

YOUNG, Francis Brett (1884-1954) novelist.

P CATHLEEN MANN, 1922, hl, Medical Faculty, University of Birmingham.

PH HOWARD COSTER, 1930s, various sizes and negs, NPG X10456-61 and X3138-41.

YOUNG, George Malcolm (1882-1959) historian.

D HENRY LAMB, *c*1935, head, pencil, NPG 4255. H.LAMB, 1938, head, pencil, NPG 4292.

YOUNG, Sir Hubert Winthrop (1885-1950) soldier and administrator.

PH WALTER STONEMAN, 1934, hs, for NPR, NPG X4669.

YOUNG, William Henry (1863-1942) mathematician.

PH WALTER STONEMAN, 2 hs portraits, 1920 and 1933, NPG (NPR).

YOUNGER, Robert, see Baron Blanesburgh.

YOUNGHUSBAND, Sir Francis Edward (1863-1942) soldier, explorer and mystic.

P SIR W.Q.ORCHARDSON, 1906, hs, NPG 3184. HAROLD SPEED, *c*1937, hs, World Congress of Faiths, London.

SC J.E.HYETT, *c*1917, bronze bust, Royal Geographical Society, London.

PH WALTER STONEMAN, 1929, hs, NPG (NPR).

YULE, George Udny (1871-1951) statistician.

D HENRY LAMB, St John's College, Cambridge.

Z

ZANGWILL, Israel (1864-1926) novelist.

P W.R.SICKERT, 1904, hl seated, Scottish National Gallery of Modern Art, Edinburgh. C.R.POLOWETSKI, 1909, hl seated, profile, NPG 3318.

D EDMOND KAPP, 1924, Barber Institute, Birmingham University. ALFRED WOLMARK, 1925, head, semi-profile, ink, NPG 2808.

C 'SIC', wl, profile, lith, for *Vanity Fair*, 25 Feb 1897, NPG. SIR BERNARD PARTRIDGE, wl, chalk, NPG 4003.

PH ELLIOTT & FRY, 1901, hl seated, photogravure, NPG. A.L.COBURN, 1913, hs, photogravure, NPG AX7818.

ZETLAND, Lawrence John Lumley Dundas, 2nd Marquess of (1876-1961) secretary of state for India and governor of Bengal.

PH WALTER STONEMAN, 2 hs portraits, 1927 and 1943, NPG (NPR).

ZIMMERN, Sir Alfred Eckhard (1879-1957) scholar and authority on international institutions.

PH WALTER STONEMAN, 1944, hl, NPG (NPR).

ZULUETA, Francis de (Francisco Maria José) (1878-1958) academic lawyer.

PH WALTER STONEMAN, 1945, hl, NPG (NPR).

INDEX

Each subject is listed here by the name under which his or her entry appears in the text (e.g. peers are listed under their titles rather than their family names). It was decided that the inclusion of cross references and name variants in the index would have made it unwieldy but these appear in full in the individual volumes.

INDEX

Each subject is listed here by the name under which his or her entry appears in the text (e.g. peers are listed under their titles rather than their family names). It was decided that the inclusion of cross references and name variants in the index would have made it unwieldy but these appear in full in the individual volumes.

Abbey, E.A. (1852–1911) III *1*
Abbot, George (1562–1633) I *1*
Abbot, Robert (1560–1617) I *1*
Abbot, William (1789–1843) II *1*
Abbot, E.A. (1838–1926) III *1*
Abbott, Evelyn (1843–1901) III *1*
Abbot, Sir James (1807–1896) III *1*
Abbot, Lemuel (1760–1803) II *1*
À Beckett, A.W. (1844–1909) III *1*
À Beckett, G.A. (1811–1856) III *1*
À Beckett, G.A. (1837–1891) III *1*
Abel, C.F. (1725–1787) II *1*
Abel, Sir F.A., Bart (1827–1902) III *1*
Abell, William (fl 1640) I *1*
Aberconway, 1st Baron (1850–1934) III *1*
Aberconway, 2nd Baron (1879–1953) IV *1*
Abercorn, 6th Earl of (1656–1734) I *1*
Abercorn, 8th Earl of (1712–1789) II *1*
Abercorn, 1st Duke of (1811–1885) III *1*
Abercorn, 2nd Duke of (1838–1913) III *1*
Abercorn, 3rd Duke of (1869–1953) IV *1*
Abercrombie, John (1726–1806) II *1*
Abercrombie, John (1780–1844) II *1*
Abercrombie, Lascelles (1881–1938) IV *1*
Abercrombie, Sir L.P. (1879–1957) IV *1*
Abercromby, Sir Ralph (1734–1801) II *1*
Aberdare, 1st Baron (1815–1895) III *1*
Aberdare, 3rd Baron (1885–1957) IV *1*
Aberdeen, 1st Earl of (1637–1720) I *1*
Aberdeen, 4th Earl of (1784–1860) II *1*
Aberdeen and Temair, 1st Marquess of (1847–1934) III *1*
Aberdeen and Temair, 1st Marchioness of (1857–1939) III *1*
Abergavenny, 3rd or 5th Baron (1461?–1535?) I *1*
Abernethy, John (1764–1831) II *1*
Abingdon, 4th Earl of (1740–1799) II *1*
Abinger, 1st Baron (1769–1844) II *1*
Abington, Frances (1737–1815) II *1*
Abney, Sir Thomas (1640–1722) I *1*
Abney, Sir William (1843–1920) III *1*
Abraham, C.J. (1814–1903) III *1*
Abraham J.J. (1876–1963) IV *1*
Abraham, William (1842–1922) III *1*
Abrahams, B.L. (1870–1908) IV *1*
Accum, F.C. (1769–1838) II *1*
Ackerley, J.R. (1896–1967) IV *1*
Acland, Sir A.H.D., 13th Bart (1847–1926) III *1*
Acland, Lady C.H.C. (1750–1815) II *2*
Acland, Sir H.W. (1815–1900) III *1*
Acland, J.D. (*d*1778) II *2*
Acland, Sir T.D., 10th Bart (1787–1871) II *2*
Acontius, Jacobus (1500?–1566?) I *1*
Acton, 1st Baron (1834–1902) III *2*
Acton, C.J.E. (1803–1847) II *2*
Acton, Sir Edward (1865–1945) IV *1*
Acton, Sir J.F.E., Bart (1736–1811) II *2*
Acton, 2nd Baron (1870–1924) IV *1*
Acworth, Sir W.M. (1850–1925) III *2*
Adair, James (*d*1798) II *2*
Adair, Robert (1711–1790) II *2*
Adair, Robert (1763–1855) II *2*
Adam, Alexander (1741–1809) II *2*
Adam, Sir Charles (1780–1853) II *2*
Adam, Sir Frederick (1781–1853) II *2*
Adam, James (*d*1794) II *2*
Adam, John (1721–1792) II *2*
Adam, P.W. (1854–1929) III *2*
Adam, Robert (1728–1792) II *2*
Adam, William (1688–1748) I *1*
Adam, William (1751–1839) II *2*
Adam, W.P. (1823–1881) III *2*
Adami, J.G. (1862–1926) IV *1*
Adams, Bernard (*d*1965) IV *1*
Adams, J.W. (1839–1903) III *2*
Adams, John (1764–1829) II *2*
Adams, J.C. (1819–1892) III *2*
Adams, Sarah Flower (1805–1848) III *2*
Adams, William (1772–1851) II *2*
Adams, William (1706–1789) II *2*
Adams, William (1814–1848) III *2*
Adams, W.D. (1851–1904) III *2*
Adamson, Patrick (1537–1592) I *1*
Adamson, Robert (1821–1848) III *2*
Adamson, William (1863–1936) IV *1*
Adcock, A.St J. (1864–1930) IV *1*
Addington, 1st Baron (1805–1889) III *2*
Addington, Anthony (1713–1790) II *2*

Addington, Stephen (1729–1796) II *2*
Addis, Sir C.S. (1861–1945) IV *1*
Addison, 1st Viscount (1869–1951) IV *1*
Addison, John (1766?–1844) II *2*
Addison, Joseph (1672–1719) I *1*
Addison, Lancelot (1632–1703) I *1*
Addison, Laura (1827–1852) III *2*
Addison, Thomas (1793–1860) II *2*
Addy, William (fl 1685) I *1*
Adelaide, Queen (1792–1849) II *2*
Adolphus Frederick (1774–1850) II *2–3*
Adolphus, John (1768–1845) II *3*
Adler, Hermann (1839–1911) II *2*
Adler, N.M. (1803–1890) III *2*
Adrian, E.G., Lord (1889–1977) IV *1*
Adye, Sir J.M. (1819–1900) III *2*
Affleck, Philip (1726–1799) II *3*
Agar, J.S. (1770–1858) II *3*
Agate, J.E. (1877–1947) IV *1*
Agnew, Sir Andrew, Bart (1793–1849) II *3*
Agnew, Sir William, 1st Bart (1825–1910) III *2*
Agnew, Sir W.G. (1898–1960) IV *1*
Aguilar, Grace (1816–1847) III *2*
Aickin, Francis (*d*1805) II *3*
Aickin, James (1740–1803) II *3*
Aikenhead, Mary (1787–1858) II *3*
Aikin, Arthur (1773–1854) II *3*
Aikin, John (1747–1822) II *3*
Aikman, William (1682–1731) I *1*
Ailesbury, 1st Earl of (*d*1685) I *1*
Ailesbury, 2nd Earl of (1655–1741) I *1*
Ailesbury, Sir Thomas (1576–1657) I *1*
Ailesbury, William (1615–1656) I *1*
Ainley, H.H. (1879–1945) IV *1*
Ainslie, G.R. (1776–1839) II *3*
Ainsworth, Harrison (1888–1965) IV *1*
Ainsworth, W.H. (1805–1882) III *2*
Airay, Henry (1560?–1616) I *1*
Aird, Sir John, 1st Bart (1833–1911) III *2*
Airedale, 1st Baron (1835–1911) III *2*
Airey, Sir J.T. (1812–1898) III *2*
Airey, Richard Airey, Lord (1803–1881) III *3*
Airlie, 1st Earl of (1586–1664) I *1*
Airlie, 2nd Earl of (1615?–1703?) I *1*
Airlie, 6th Earl of (1725–1803) II *3*
Airlie, 11th Earl of (1893–1968) IV *1*
Aitchison, C.M. Aitchison, Lord (1882–1941) IV *1*
Aitchison, George (1825–1910) III *3*
Aitken, Charles (1869–1936) IV *1*
Aitken, James (1752–1777) II *3*
Aitken, John (1793–1833) II *3*
Aitken, Sir William (1825–1892) III *3*
Aiton, William (1731–1793) II *3*
Aiton, W.T. (1766–1849) II *3*
Akenside, Mark (1721–1770) II *3*
Akerman, J.Y. (1806–1873) III *3*
Akers, Sir W.A. (1888–1954) IV *1*
Alabaster, William (1567–1640) I *1*
Alanbrooke, 1st Viscount (1883–1963) IV *2*
Albani, Dame Marie (1852–1930) III *3*
Albany, John Stewart, Duke of (1481–1536) I *1*
Albany, Prince Leopold, 1st Duke of (1853–1884) III *3*
Albany, Louisa, Countess of (1753–1824) II *3*
Albemarle, 1st Duke of (1608–1670) I *1–2*
Albemarle, 2nd Duke of (1653–1688) I *1*
Albemarle, 1st Earl of (1669–1718) I *1*
Albemarle, 2nd Earl of (1702–1754) II *3*
Albemarle, 3rd Earl of (1724–1772) II *3*
Albemarle, 4th Earl of (1772–1849) II *3*
Albemarle, 6th Earl of (1799–1891) II *3*
Albemarle, 7th Earl of (1832–1894) III *3*
Albert, Prince Consort (1819–1861) III *3–4*
Albertazzi, Emma (1813–1847) III *4*
Albery, Sir B.J. (1881–1971) IV *2*
Albery, James (1838–1889) III *4*
Alcester, F.B.P. Seymour, Baron (1821–1895) III *4*
Alcock, John (1430–1500) I *2*
Alcock, John (1715–1806) II *3*
Alcock, Sir J.W. (1892–1919) IV *2*
Alcock, Sir Rutherford (1809–1897) III *4*
Alcock, Thomas (1784–1833) II *3*
Alcuin (735–804) I *2*
Aldborough, 2nd Earl of (*d*1801) II *3–4*
Aldenham, 1st Baron (1819–1907) III *4*
Aldenham, 4th Baron (1886–1969) IV *2*
Alderson, Sir E.A.H. (1859–1927) III *4*

Alderson, Sir E.H. (1787–1857) II *4*
Alderson, Sir John (1757–1829) II *4*
Aldington, Richard (1892–1962) IV *2*
Aldis, Sir Charles (1775?–1863) II *4*
Aldrich, Henry (1647–1710) I *2*
Aldrich-Blake, Dame Louisa (1865–1925) IV *2*
Aldridge, William (1737–1797) II *4*
Alemoor, Andrew Pringle, Lord (*d*1776) II *4*
Alexander, Mrs Cecil Frances (1818–1895) III *4*
Alexander, D.A. (1768–1846) II *4*
Alexander, Sir George (1858–1918) III *4*
Alexander, Sir J.E. (1803–1885) III *4*
Alexander, M.S. (1799–1845) III *4*
Alexander, Robert (1840–1923) III *4*
Alexander, Samuel (1859–1938) III *4*
Alexander, William (1767–1816) II *4*
Alexander, William (1824–1911) III *4*
Alexander, W.L. (1808–1884) III *4*
Alexander of Hillsborough, 1st Earl (1885–1965) IV *2*
Alexander of Tunis, 1st Earl (1891–1969) IV *2*
Alexander-Sinclair, Sir E.S. (1865–1945) IV *2*
Alexandra, Queen (1844–1925) III *4–5*
Aleyn, Charles (*d*1640) I *2*
Alford, Henry (1810–1871) III *5*
Alford, Viscountess (1817–1888) III *5*
Alfred (849–901) I *2*
Alfred, Duke of Edinburgh (1844–1900) III *5*
Alice, Princess (1843–1878) III *5*
Alington, 1st Baron (1825–1904) III *5*
Alison, Archibald (1757–1839) II *4*
Alison, Sir Archibald, Bart (1792–1867) II *4*
Alison, Sir Archibald, 2nd Bart (1826–1907) III *5*
Alison, W.P. (1790–1859) II *4*
Allan, David (1744–1796) II *4*
Allan, George (1736–1800) II *4*
Allan, Sir William (1782–1850) II *4*
Allan, Sir William (1837–1903) III *5*
Allardice, R.B. (1779–1854) II *4*
Allbutt, Sir T.C. (1836–1925) III *5*
Allen, C.G.B. (1848–1899) III *5*
Allen, George (1832–1907) III *5*
Allen, Sir H.P. (1869–1946) IV *2*
Allen, Sir James (1855–1942) III *5*
Allen, John (1660?–1741) I *2*
Allen, John (1771–1843) II *4*
Allen, P.S. (1869–1933) IV *2*
Allen, Ralph (1694–1764) I *2*
Allen, Thomas (1542–1632) I *2*
Allen, Thomas (1681–1755) I *2*
Allen, William (1770–1843) II *4*
Allen, William (1793–1864) II *4*
Allen, W.G. (*b*1891) IV *2*
Allen, William (1532–1594) I *2*
Allen of Hurtwood, Baron (1889–1939) IV *2*
Allenby of Megiddo, 1st Viscount (1861–1936) IV *2*
Allerton, 1st Baron (1840–1917) III *5*
Allestree, Richard (1619–1681) I *2*
Alleyn, Edward (1566–1626) I *2*
Allin, Sir Thomas (1612–1685) I *2*
Allingham, J.T. (fl 1799–1810) II *4*
Allingham, William (1824–1889) III *5–6*
Allix, Peter (1641–1717) I *2*
Allman, G.J. (1812–1898) III *6*
Allon, Henry (1818–1892) III *6*
Alloway, David Catchcart, Lord (*d*1829) II *4*
Allport, Sir J.J. (1811–1892) III *6*
Alma-Tadema, Laura, Lady (*d*1909) III *6*
Alma-Tadema, Sir Lawrence (1836–1912) III *6*
Alness, 1st Baron (1868–1955) IV *2*
Alsop, Vincent (*d*1703) I *2*
Alten, Sir Charles, Count von (1764–1840) II *4*
Altrincham, 1st Baron (1879–1955) IV *2*
Alvanley, 1st Baron (1744–1804) II *4*
Alverstone, Viscount (1842–1915) III *6*
Ambrose, Isaac (1604–1663) I *2*
Amelia, Princess (1711–1786) II *4–5*
Amelia, Princess (1783–1810) II *4*
Amery, L.C.M.S. (1873–1955) IV *2*
Ames, Joseph (1689–1759) I *2*
Ames, William (1576–1633) I *2*
Amesbury, Charles Dundas, Baron (1751–1822) II *5*
Amherst, 1st Baron (1717–1797) II *5*
Amherst of Arracan, 1st Earl (1773–1857) II *5*
Amherst of Hackney, 1st Baron (1835–1909) III *6*
Amhurst, Nicholas (1697–1742) I *2*

Amory, Thomas (1701–1774) II 5
Amos, Andrew (1791–1860) II 5
Amphlett, Sir R.P. (1809–1883) III 6
Ampthill, 1st Baron (1829–1884) III 6
Ampthill, 2nd Baron (1869–1935) IV 2–3
Amulree, 1st Baron (1860–1942) IV 3
Amyot, Thomas (1775–1850) II 5
Ancaster, 1st Earl of (1830–1910) III 6
Ancram, 1st Earl of (1578–1654) I 2
Anderson, Adam (d1846) II 5
Anderson, Dame Adelaide (1863–1936) IV 3
Anderson, Alexander (1845–1909) III 6
Anderson, Sir A.G. (1877–1952) IV 3
Anderson, Christopher (1782–1852) II 5
Anderson Sir Edmund (1530–1605) I 2
Anderson, Elizabeth Garrett (1836–1917) III 6
Anderson, Sir G.W. (1791–1857) II 5
Anderson, Sir H.K. (1865–1928) IV 3
Anderson, James (1739–1808) II 5
Anderson, James (d1809) II 5
Anderson, John (1726–1796) II 5
Anderson, John (1805–1855) III 7
Anderson, J.H. (1815–1874) III 7
Anderson, J.R. (1811–1895) III 6
Anderson, Sir K.A.H. (1891–1959) IV 3
Anderson, Lucy (1790–1878) II 5
Anderson, Mary (1859–1940) III 7
Anderson, Robert (1750–1830) II 5
Anderson, Thomas (1832–1870) III 7
Anderson, William (1805–1866) III 7
Anderson, Sir W.H. (1872–1930) IV 3
André, John (1751–1780) II 5
Andrewes, Sir F.W. (1859–1932) IV 3
Andrewes, G.T. (1750–1825) II 5
Andrewes, Lancelot (1555–1626) I 2
Andrews, Henry (1743–1820) II 5
Andrews, Sir James, Bart (1877–1951) IV 3
Andrews, J.P. (1737?–1797) II 5
Andrews, M.P. (d1814) II 5
Andrews, Thomas (1813–1885) III 7
Andrews, W.E. (1773–1837) II 5
Angell, Sir Norman (1874–1967) IV 3
Angelo, Henry (c1755–1835?) II 5
Angerstein, J.J. (1735–1823) II 5–6
Anglesey, Arthur Annesley, 1st Earl of (1614–1686) I 2
Anglesey, Christopher Villiers, 1st Earl of (1593?–1630) I 2
Anglesey, 1st Marquess of (1768–1854) II 6
Angwin, Sir A.S. (1883–1959) IV 3
Annandale, 1st Marquess (d1721) I 2
Annandale, Thomas (1838–1907) III 7
Anne of Bohemia, Queen (1366–1394) I 2
Anne, Queen (1456–1485) I 2–3
Anne Boleyn, Queen (1507–1536) I 3
Anne of Cleves, Queen (1515–1557) I 3
Anne of Denmark, Queen (1574–1619) I 3
Anne, Queen (1665–1714) I 3
Anne, Princess Royal (1709–1759) I 6
Annesley, James (1715–1760) II 6
Annesley, Samuel (1620?–1696) I 3
Annet, Peter (1693–1769) I 3
Anrep, Boris (1883–1969) IV 3
Ansdell, Richard (1815–1885) III 7
Anson, George (1697–1762) I 3
Anson, George (1797–1857) II 6
Anson, Peter F. (1889–1975) IV 3
Anson, Sir W.R., 3rd Bart (1843–1914) III 7
Anspach, Elizabeth, Margravine of (1750–1828) II 6
Ansted, D.T. (1814–1880) III 7
Anstey, Christopher (1724–1805) II 6
Anstie, F.E. (1833–1874) III 7
Anstis, John (1669–1744) I 3
Anstruther, Sir John, Bart (1753–1811) II 6
Anstruther, Sir William, Lord (d1711) I 3
Anthony, John (1585–1655) I 3
Apperley, C.J. (1779–1843) II 6
Appleton, Sir E.V. (1892–1965) IV 3
Apsley, Sir Allen (1616–1683) I 3
Aram, Eugene (1704–1759) II 6
Arbuthnot, Charles (1767–1850) II 6
Arbuthnot, John (1667–1735) II 3
Arbuthnot, Marriot (1711?–1794) II 6
Arbuthnot, Sir R.K., 4th Bart (1864–1916) IV 3
Arch, Joseph (1826–1919) III 7
Archer, Edward (1717–1789) II 6
Archer, Frederick (1857–1886) III 7
Archer, F.S. (1813?–1857) III 7
Archer, James (fl 1820) II 6
Archer, James (1823–1904) III 7
Archer, John (fl 1660–1684) I 3
Archer, William (1856–1924) III 7
Archibald Sir T.D. (1817–1876) III 7
Ardagh, Sir J.C. (1840–1907) III 7
Arden-Close, Sir C.F. (1865–1952) IV 3
Ardilaun, 1st Baron (1840–1915) III 7
Ardizzone, E.J.I. (1900–1979) IV 3
Ardmillan, James Craufurd, Lord (1805–1876) III 7
Argyll, 7th Earl of (1576?–1638) I 3

Argyll, 8th Earl and 1st Marquess of (1607?–1661) I 3
Argyll, 9th Earl of (1629–1685) I 3
Argyll, 1st Duke of (d1703) I 3
Argyll, 2nd Duke of (1680–1743) I 3
Argyll, 3rd Duke of (1682–1761) I 3
Argyll, 8th Duke of (1823–1900) III 7–8
Argyll, 9th Duke of (1845–1914) III 8
Arkwright, Sir J.A. (1864–1944) IV 3
Arkwright, Sir Richard (1732–1792) II 6–7
Arlen, Michael (1895–1956) IV 3
Arlington, 1st Earl of (1618–1685) I 3
Arliss, George (1868–1946) IV 3
Armes, Philip (1836–1908) III 8
Armin, Robert (fl 1610) I 3
Armine, Mary, Lady (1589–1676) I 3–4
Armine, Sir William (1593–1651) I 4
Armitage, Edward (1817–1896) III 8
Armstead, H.H. (1828–1905) III 8
Armstrong, Sir Alexander (1818–1899) III 8
Armstrong, Archibald (d1672) I 4
Armstrong, Sir G.C.H. 1st Bart (1836–1907) III 8
Armstrong, H.E. (1848–1937) III 8
Armstrong, John (1674?–1742) I 4
Armstrong, John (1709–1779) II 7
Armstrong, Sir Thomas (1674?–1742) I 4
Armstrong, Thomas (1832–1911) III 8
Armstrong, Walter (1850–1918) III 8
Armstrong, William (1602?–1658?) I 4
Armstrong, William (1882–1952) IV 3
Armstrong of Cragside, Baron (1810–1900) III 8
Arnaud, Yvonne (1893–1958) IV 3
Arne, T.A. (1710–1778) II 7
Arniston, Robert Dundas, Lord (1713–1787) II 7
Arnold, Benedict (1741–1801) II 7
Arnold, Sir Edwin (1832–1904) III 8
Arnold, John (1736?–1799) II 7
Arnold, Matthew (1822–1888) III 8
Arnold, Samuel (1740–1802) II 7
Arnold, S.J. (1774–1852) II 7
Arnold, Thomas (1742–1816) II 7
Arnold, Thomas (1795–1842) II 7
Arnold, Thomas (1823–1900) III 8–9
Arnold, Tom (1897?–1969) IV 3
Arnold-Forster, H.O. (1855–1909) III 8
Arnot, Hugo (1749–1786) II 7
Arnot, William (1808–1875) III 9
Arnott, Neil (1788–1874) II 7
Arran, 2nd Earl of (d1575) I 4
Arran, 4th Earl of (1589–1625) I 4
Arrol, Sir William (1839–1913) III 9
Arrowsmith, Aaron (1750–1823) II 7
Arrowsmith, Edmund (1585–1628) I 4
Arrowsmith, John (1790–1873) II 7
Artaud, William (1763–1823) II 7
Arthur, Sir George (1784–1854) II 7
Arthur, William (1819–1901) III 9
Arundel, 7th Earl of (1408–1435) I 4
Arundel, 12th Earl of (1511–1580) I 4
Arundel, 1st Earl of (1557–1595) I 4
Arundel, 3rd Earl of (1608–1652) I 4
Arundel, Thomas (1353–1414) I 4
Arundel and Surrey, 5th Earl of (1381–1415) I 4
Arundel and Surrey, 2nd Earl of (1585–1646) I 4
Arundell, Blanche, Lady (1583–1649) I 4
Arundell, F.V.J. (1780–1846) II 7
Arundell of Wardour, 1st Baron (1560–1639) I 4
Arundell of Wardour, 2nd Baron (1584–1643) I 4
Arundell of Wardour, 3rd Baron (1606?–1694) I 4
Asbury, Francis (1745–1816) II 7
Asche, T.S.H.O. (1871–1936) IV 3
Asgill, Sir Charles, Bart (1763–1823) II 7
Ash, John (1723–1798) II 7
Ashbee, C.R. (1863–1942) IV 3
Ashbourne, 1st Baron (1837–1913) III 9
Ashbridge, Sir Noel (1889–1975) IV 3
Ashburnham, John (1603–1671) I 4
Ashburton, 1st Baron (1731–1783) II 7
Ashburton, 1st Baron (1774–1848) II 7
Ashburton, 2nd Baron (1799–1864) II 7
Ashby, A.W. (1886–1953) IV 3
Ashby, Harry (1744–1818) II 7
Ashby, Thomas (1874–1931) IV 3–4
Ashe, Simeon (d1662) I 4
Asher, Alexander (1835–1905) III 9
Ashfield, Baron (1874–1948) IV 4
Ashford, William (1746–1824) II 7
Ashmead Bartlett, Sir Ellis (1849–1902) III 9
Ashmole, Elias (1617–1692) I 4
Ashton, Charles (1665–1752) I 4
Ashton, Hugh (d1522) I 4
Ashton, John (d1691) I 4
Ashton, Thomas (1716–1775) II 7–8
Ashton of Hyde, 1st Baron (1855–1933) III 9
Ashurst, Sir W.H. (1725–1807) II 8
Ashwell, Lena Margaret (1872–1957) IV 4
Ashworth, Henry (1794–1880) III 8

Askew, Anthony (1722–1774?) II 8
Askwith, Baron (1861–1942) IV 4
Aslin, C.H. (1893–1959) IV 4
Aspland, Robert (1782–1845) II 8
Aspull, George (1813–1832) III 9
Asquith, C.M.A., Lady (1887–1960) IV 4
Asquith of Bishopstone, Baron (1890–1954) IV 4
Asquith of Yarnborough, Baroness (1887–1969) IV 4
Astbury, Sir J.M. (1860–1939) IV 4
Astell, William (1774–1847) II 8
Astle, Thomas (1735–1803) II 8
Astley, Baron (1579–1652) I 4
Astley, Sir John Dugdale, 3rd Bart (1828–1894) III 9
Astley, Philip (1742–1814) II 8
Aston, F.W. (1877–1945) IV 4
Aston, Sir Thomas (1600–1645) I 4
Aston, W.G. (1841–1911) III 9
Aston of Forfar, Baron (1584–1639) I 4–5
Astor, Viscountess (1880–1964) IV 4
Astor, 2nd Viscount (1879?–1952) IV 4
Astor of Hever, 1st Baron (1886–1971) IV 4
Athelstan (895–940) I 5
Atherton, William (1776–1850) II 8
Athlone, 1st Earl of (1644–1703) I 5
Athlone, 2nd Earl of (1668–1719) I 5
Athlone, 1st Earl of (1874–1957) IV 4
Athlone, Countess of (1883–1981) IV 4
Atholl, 1st Duke of (1659/60–1724) I 5
Atholl, 2nd Duke of (1690?–1764) I 5
Atholl, 3rd Duke of (1729–1774) I 6
Atholl, 1st Marquess of (1635?–1703) I 5
Atholl, Duchess of (1874–1960) IV 4
Atkin, Baron (1867–1944) IV 4
Atkins, Sir I.A. (1869–1953)
Atkinson, Baron (1844–1932) III 9
Atkinson, Sir E.H.T. (1878–1957) IV 4
Atkinson, James (1759–1839) II 8
Atkinson, James (1780–1852) II 8
Atkinson, Miles (1741–1811) II 8
Atkinson, Paul (1656–1729) I 5
Atkinson, Peter (1776–1842) II 8
Atkinson, Thomas (1801?–1833) III 9
Atkyns, Sir Edward (1587–1669) I 5
Atkyns, Richard (1615–1677) I 5
Atkyns, Sir Robert (1647–1711) I 5
Atlay, James (1817–1894) III 9
Atmore, Charles (1759–1826) II 8
Atterbury, Francis (1662–1732) I 5
Atterbury, Lewis (1656–1731) I 5
Attlee, 1st Earl (1883–1967) IV 4–5
Attwood, Thomas (1765–1838) II 8
Attwood, Thomas (1783–1856) II 8
Aubert, Alexander (1730–1805) II 8
Aubrey, John (1626–1697) I 5
Aubrey, M.E. (1885–1957) IV 5
Aubrey, William (1529–1595) I 5
Auchinleck, Lord (1706–1782) II 8
Auchinleck, Sir Claude (b1884) IV 5
Auchmuty, Sir Samuel, Bart (1756–1822) II 8
Auckland, 1st Baron (1744–1814) II 8
Auckland, 1st Earl of (1784–1849) II 8
Audley of Walden, Baron (1488–1544) I 5
Augusta, Princess of Wales (1719–1772) I 6
Augusta Sophia, Princess (1768–1840) II 8–9
Aumonier, Stacy (1887–1928) IV 5
Austen, Jane (1775–1817) II 9
Austin, Baron (1866–1941) IV 5
Austin, Alfred (1835–1913) III 9
Austin, Sir H.T. (1801–1865) III 9
Austin, John (1717–1784) II 9
Austin, John (fl 1820) II 9
Austin, Sarah (1793–1867) II 9
Austin, William (1587–1634) I 5
Austin, William (fl 1662) I 5
Austin, William (1721–1820) II 9
Auverquerque, Count of (1641–1708) II 5
Avebury, 1st Baron (1834–1913) III 9
Avershawe, L.J. (1773?–1795) II 9
Avery, Benjamin (d1764) I 5
Avery, John (fl 1695) I 5
Avery, John (1807–1855) III 9
Avon, 1st Earl of (1897–1977) IV 5
Avonmore, 1st Viscount (1736–1805) II 9
Avory, Sir H.E. (1851–1935) III 9
Axtel(l), Daniel (d1660) I 5
Aylesford, 1st Earl of (1647?–1719) I 5
Aylett, Robert (1583–1655?) I 5
Aylmer, Baron (1655–1720) I 5
Aylmer, Sir Felix (1899–1979) IV 5
Ayres, John (fl 1680–1700) I 5
Ayres, Ruby Mildred (1883–1955) IV 5
Ayrton, A.S. (1816–1886) III 9
Ayrton, W.E. (1847–1908) III 9
Ayscough, Francis (1700–1763) II 9
Ayscough, G.E. (d1779) II 9
Ayscough, Samuel (1745–1804) II 9
Ayscue, Sir George (fl 1646–1671) I 5

Ayton, Richard (1786–1823) II 9
Ayton, Sir Robert (1570–1638) I 5
Aytoun, W.E. (1813–1865) III 10

Babbage, Charles (1792–1871) II 10
Baber, H.H. (1775–1869) II 10
Babington, B.G. (1794–1866) II 10
Babington, C.C. (1808–1895) III 11
Babington, Gervase (1550?–1610) I 7
Babington, John (fl 1635) I 7
Babington, Sir Philip (1894–1965) IV 6
Babington, William (1765–1833) II 10
Bache, Sarah (1771?–1844) II 10
Back, Sir George (1796–1878) II 10
Backhouse, Sir R.R.C. (1878–1939) IV 6
Backwell, Edward (d1683) I 7
Bacon, Anne, Lady (1528–1610) I 7
Bacon, Sir James (1798–1895) II 10
Bacon, John (1740–1799) II 10
Bacon, John (1777–1859) II 10
Bacon, Sir Nathaniel (1585–1627) I 7
Bacon, Sir Nicholas (1509–1579) I 7
Bacon, Sir R.H.S. (1863–1947) IV 6
Baddeley, Robert (1733–1794) II 10
Baddeley, Sophia (1745–1786) II 10
Badeley, Baron (1874–1951) IV 6
Baden-Powell, 1st Baron (1857–1941) III 11
Bagehot, Walter (1826–1877) III 11
Bagford, John (1650–1716) I 7
Baggallay, Sir Richard (1816–1888) III 11
Baggs, C.M. (1806–1845) III 11
Bagot, 2nd Baron (1773–1856) II 10
Bagot, Sir Charles (1781–1843) II 10
Bagot, Lewis (1740–1802) II 10
Bagot, Richard (1782–1854) II 10
Bagster, Samuel (1772–1851) II 10
Bagwell, William (fl 1655) I 7
Baikie, W.B. (1825–1864) III 11
Bailey, Sir Abe, 1st Bart (1864–1940) IV 6
Bailey, Cyril (1871–1957) IV 6
Bailey, H.C. (1878–1961) IV 6
Bailey, Nathan (d1742) I 7
Bailey, P.J. (1816–1902) III 11
Baillie, Lady Grizel (1665–1746) I 7
Baillie, Joanna (1762–1851) II 10
Baillie, John (1772–1833) II 10
Baillie, Sir J.B. (1872–1940) IV 6
Baillie, Matthew (1761–1823) II 10
Baillie, Robert (d1684) I 7
Baillie, Thomas (c1725–1802) II 11
Baillie, William (1723–1810) II 11
Baily, E.H. (1788–1867) II 11
Baily, Francis (1774–1844) II 11
Bain, Sir F.W. (1889–1950) IV 6
Bainbridge, Christopher (1464?–1514) I 7
Baine, James (1710–1790) II 11
Baines, Edward (1774–1848) II 11
Baines, Sir Edward (1800–1890) II 11
Baines, M.T. (1799–1860) II 11
Baines, Sir Thomas (1622–1680) I 7
Baines, Thomas (1806–1881) III 11
Baines, Thomas (1822–1875) III 11
Baird, Sir David, Bart (1757–1829) II 11
Baird, G.H. (1761–1840) II 11
Baird, J.L. (1888–1946) IV 6
Bairstow, Sir Leonard (1880–1963) IV 6
Baker, Sir Benjamin (1840–1907) III 11
Baker, C.H.C. (1880–1959) IV 6
Baker, David (1575–1641) I 7
Baker, David Erskine (1730–1767) II 11
Baker, George (1540–1600) I 7
Baker, Sir George, Bart (1722–1809) II 11
Baker, George (1781–1851) II 11
Baker, Henry (1698–1774) I 7
Baker, Sir Herbert (1862–1946) IV 6
Baker, H.B. (1862–1935) IV 6
Baker, Sir Richard (1568–1645) I 7
Baker, Richard St Barbe (b1889) IV 6
Baker, Sir S.W. (1821–1893) III 11
Baker, Thomas (1656–1740) I 7
Baker, Valentine (1827–1887) III 11
Baker, William (1668–1732) I 7
Baker, William (1841–1905) III 11
Bakewell, Robert (1725–1795) II 11
Balcarres, 3rd Earl of (1654?–1722) I 7
Balchen, Sir John (1670–1744) I 7
Balcon, Sir Michael (1896–1977) IV 6
Baldwin, Robert (1804–1858) III 11
Baldwin of Bewdley, 1st Earl (1867–1947) IV 6
Bale, John (1495–1563) I 7
Balfe, M.W. (1808–1870) III 11–12
Balfe, Victoire (1837–1871) III 12
Balfour, 1st Earl of (1848–1930) III 12
Balfour, 2nd Earl of (1853–1945) III 12
Balfour, Sir Andrew (1873–1931) IV 6–7
Balfour, Clara Lucas (1808–1878) III 12
Balfour, E.G. (1813–1889) III 12

Balfour, F.M. (1851–1882) III 12
Balfour, Henry (1863–1939) IV 7
Balfour, Sir James (1600–1657) I 7
Balfour, J.H. (1808–1884) III 12
Balfour, J.S. (1843–1916) III 12
Balfour, T.G. (1813–1891) III 12
Balfour, Sir William (d1660) I 7
Balfour of Burleigh, 6th Baron (1849–1921) III 12
Balguy, Thomas (1716–1795) II 11
Ball, Albert (1896–1917) IV 7
Ball, Sir A.J. (1757–1809) II 11
Ball, John (1818–1889) III 12
Ball, John (1861–1940) IV 7
Ball, J.T. (1815–1898) III 12
Ball, Robert (1802–1857) III 12
Ball, Sir R.S. (1840–1913) III 12
Ballance, John (1839–1893) III 12
Ballantine, William (1812–1887) III 12–13
Ballantyne, James (1772–1833) II 11
Ballantyne, James (1808–1877) III 13
Ballantyne, John (1774–1821) II 11
Ballantyne, R.M. (1825–1894) III 13
Balmer, Robert (1787–1844) II 11
Balmerino, 6th Baron (1688–1746) I 7
Balmuto, Lord (1742–1824) II 11
Baltimore, 1st Baron (1580?–1632) I 7
Baltimore, 6th Baron (1731–1771) II 11
Balvaird, 1st Baron (1597?–1644) I 7
Baly, William (1814–1861) III 13
Bambridge, Thomas (d1741) I 7
Bampfylde, J.C.W. (1754–c1796) II 11
Banbury, 1st Earl of (1547–1632) I 7
Banbury of Southam, 1st Baron (1850–1936) III 13
Bancroft, Lady (1839–1921) III 13
Bancroft, Edward (1744–1821) II 11
Bancroft, John (1574–1640) I 8
Bancroft, Richard (1544–1610) I 7
Bancroft, Sir Squire (1841–1926) III 13
Bandinel, Bulkeley (1781–1861) II 11
Bandinel, James (1783–1849) II 11
Banim, John (1798–1842) II 11
Banim, Michael (1796–1874) II 11
Banister, Richard (d1626) I 8
Bankes, Sir John (1589–1644) I 8
Bankes, Sir J.E. (1854–1946) III 13
Bankes, W.J. (d1855) II 11
Banks, Sir Edward (1769?–1835) II 11
Banks, G.L. (1821–1881) III 13
Banks, Sir Joseph, Bart (1743–1820) II 12
Banks, Sir J.T. (1815?–1908) III 13
Banks, L.J. (1890–1952) IV 7
Banks, Sarah Sophia (1744–1818) II 12
Banks, Thomas (1735–1805) II 12
Bannatyne, Sir W.M. (1743–1833) II 12
Bannister, Charles (1738?–1804) II 12
Bannister, Elizabeth (1752–1844) II 12
Bannister, John (1760–1836) II 12
Bannister, Saxe (1790–1877) II 12
Bantock, Sir G.R. (1868–1946) IV 7
Barbauld, Anna Letitia (1743–1825) II 12
Barbirolli, Sir John (1899–1970) IV 7
Barbon, Praise God (1596?–1697) I 8
Barbow, Sir D.M. (1841–1928) III 13
Barcaple, Lord (1803?–1870) III 13
Barclay, John (1582–1621) I 8
Barclay, John (1758–1826) II 12
Barclay, Robert (1774–1811) II 12
Barclay, William (1546/7–1608) I 8
Barcroft, Sir Joseph (1872–1947) IV 7
Bardsley, Sir J.L. (1801–1876) III 13
Bardsley, J.W. (1835–1904) III 13
Bardsley, S.A. (1764–1851) II 12
Baretti, G.M.A. (1719–1789) II 12
Bargeny, 1st Baron (d1658) I 8
Barger, George (1878–1939) IV 7
Bargrave, Isaac (1586–1643) I 8
Barham, 1st Baron (1726–1813) II 12
Barham, Henry (1670?–1726) I 8
Barham, Richard Harris (1788–1845) II 12
Baring, Sir Francis, Bart (1740–1810) II 12
Baring, Maurice (1874–1945) IV 7
Baring, Thomas (1799–1873) III 12–13
Baring-Gould, Sabine (1834–1924) III 13
Barker, Sir Ernest (1874–1960) IV 7
Barker, Frederick (1808–1882) III 13
Barker, Hugh (d1632) I 8
Barker, Sir H.A. (1869–1950) IV 7
Barker, Robert (1739–1806) II 13
Barker, Thomas (1769–1847) II 13
Barkla, C.G. (1877–1944) IV 7
Barkly, Sir Henry (1815–1898) III 13
Barkstead, John (d1662) I 8
Barling, Sir H.G., Bart (1855–1940) III 13
Barlow, Sir G.H., Bart (1762–1846) II 13
Barlow, H.C. (1806–1876) III 13
Barlow, Peter (1776–1862) II 13
Barlow, Thomas (1607–1691) I 8

Barlow, Sir Thomas, 1st Bart (1845–1945) III 13
Barlow, T.O. (1824–1889) III 13–14
Barlow, W.H. (1812–1902) III 14
Barman, Christian (b1898) IV 7
Barnard, Lady Anne (1750–1825) II 13
Barnard, Sir A.F. (1773–1855) II 13
Barnard, Frederick (1846–1896) III 14
Barnard, Sir John (1685–1764) I 8
Barnard, Thomas (1728–1806) II 13
Barnardiston, Sir Nathaniel (1588–1653) I 8
Barnardiston, Sir Samuel (1620–1707) I 8
Barnardiston, Sir Thomas (d1669) II 13
Barnardiston, Thomas (d1752) II 13
Barnardo, T.J. (1845–1905) III 14
Barnato, B.I. (1852–1897) III 14
Barnby, Sir Joseph (1838–1896) III 14
Barnes, Sir Edward (1776–1838) II 13
Barnes, E.W. (1874–1953) IV 7
Barnes, G.N. (1859–1940) III 14
Barnes, Joshua (1654–1712) I 8
Barnes, Sir K.R. (1878–1957) IV 7
Barnes, S.F. (1876–1967) IV 7
Barnes, Thomas (1747–1810) II 13
Barnes, Thomas (1785–1841) III 13
Barnett, Curtis (d1746) I 8
Barnett, Dame H.O.W. (1851–1936) III 14
Barnett, John (1802–1890) III 14
Barnett, L.D. (1871–1960) IV 7
Barnett, Morris (1800–1856) III 14
Barnett, S.A. (1844–1913) III 14
Baron, Bartholomew (d1696) I 8
Baron, Bernard (1696–1762) I 8
Baron, Bernhard (1850–1929) III 14
Baron, John (1786–1851) II 13
Baron, Robert (fl 1645) I 9
Barr, Archibald (1855–1931) III 14
Barratt, Sir A.S. (1891–1966) IV 7
Barré, Isaac (1726–1802) II 13
Barret, George (1728?–1784) II 13
Barret, George (1774–1842) II 13
Barrett, John (1753–1821) II 13
Barrett, Lucas (1837–1862) III 14
Barrett, William (1733–1789) II 13
Barrett, Wilson (1846–1904) III 14
Barrie, Sir J.M. (1860–1937) IV 7
Barrington, 1st Viscount (1678–1734) I 8
Barrington, 2nd Viscount (1717–1793) II 13
Barrington, Daines (1727–1800) II 13
Barrington, George (1755–1804) II 13
Barrington, Sir Jonah (1760–1834) II 13
Barrington, Rutland (1853–1922) III 14
Barrington, Shute (1734–1826) II 13
Barrow, Isaac (1630–1677) I 8
Barrow, Sir John, Bart (1764–1848) II 13–14
Barrow, John (1808–1898) III 14
Barrowby, William (1682–1751) I 8
Barry, Alfred (1826–1910) III 14
Barry, Mrs Ann Spranger (1734–1801) II 14
Barry, Sir Charles (1795–1860) III 14
Barry, Edward (1759–1822) II 14
Barry, Elizabeth (1658–1713) I 8
Barry, E.M. (1830–1880) III 14
Barry, Henry (1750–1822) II 14
Barry, James (1741–1806) II 14
Barry, James (1795–1865) II 14
Barry, Martin (1802–1855) III 14
Barry, Sir Redmond (1813–1880) III 14
Barry, Spranger (1719–1777) II 14
Bartholomew, J.G. (1860–1920) IV 7
Bartleman, James (1769–1821) II 14
Bartlett, W.H. (1809–1854) III 14
Bartley, George (1782?–1858) II 14
Bartley, Sir G.C.T. (1842–1910) III 14–15
Bartley, Sarah (1783–1850) II 14
Bartolozzi, Francesco (1727–1815) II 14
Bartolozzi, G.S. (1757–1821) II 14
Barton, Bernard (1784–1849) II 14
Barton, Sir D.P., 1st Bart (1853–1937) III 15
Barton, Sir Edmund (1849–1920) III 15
Barton, Sir Sidney (1876–1946) IV 7
Barwell, Richard (1741–1804) II 14
Barwick, John (1612–1664) I 8
Barwick, Peter (1619–1705) I 8
Bascvi, George (1794–1845) II 14
Basham, W.R. (1804–1877) III 15
Basing, 1st Baron (1826–1894) III 15
Baskerville, John (1706–1775) II 14
Bass, M.T. (1799–1884) III 15
Bastard, J.P. (1756–1816) II 15
Bastwick, John (1593–1654) I 8
Bateman, H.M. (1887–1970) IV 7
Bateman, Thomas (1821–1861) III 15
Bates, H.W. (1825–1892) III 15
Bates, Joah (1741–1799) II 14
Bates, Joshua, (1788–1864) II 14
Bates, Sir P.E., 4th Bart (1879–1946) IV 7
Bates, Sarah (d1811) II 14–15

Bates, William (1625–1699) I 8
Bateson, William (1861–1926) IV 7
Bath, 7th Earl of (1628–1701) I 8
Bath, 1st Earl of (1684–1764) I 9
Bath, 1st Marquess of (1734–1796) II 15
Bath, 2nd Marquess of (1765–1837) II 15
Bather, Edward (1779–1847) II 15
Batsford, Harry (1880–1951) IV 7
Batteley, John (1646–1708) I 9
Battell, Ralph (1649–1713) I 9
Batten, Sir William (d1667) I 9
Battenberg, Henry Maurice, Prince of (1858–1896) III 15
Battie, William (1704–1776) II 15
Battishill, Jonathan (1738–1801) II 15
Batty, Robert (1763–1849) II 15.
Bax, Sir Arnold (1883–1953) IV 7–8
Bax, Clifford (1886–1962) IV 8
Baxter, Charles (1809–1879) III 15
Baxter, Sir David (1793–1872) II 15
Baxter, Richard (1615–1691) I 9
Baxter, William (1650–1723) I 9
Bayes, Joshua (1671–1746) I 9
Bayfield, Robert (fl 1668) I 9
Baylee, Joseph (1808–1883) III 15
Bayley, F.W.N. (1808–1853) III 15
Bayley, Sir John, Bart (1763–1841) II 15
Bayley, Sir S.C. (1836–1925) III 15
Bayley, W.B. (1782–1860) II 15
Baylis, Lilian Mary (1874–1937) IV 8
Bayliss, Sir W.M. (1860–1924) IV 8
Bayly, Ada Ellen (1857–1903) III 15
Bayly, Benjamin (1671–1720) I 9
Bayly, T.H. (1797–1839) II 15
Baynes, T.S. (1823–1887) III 15
Bayning, 1st Baron (1728–1810) II 15
Bayntun, Sir H.W. (1766–1840) II 15
Bazalgette, Sir J.W. (1819–1891) III 15
Bazley, Sir Thomas (1797–1885) II 15
Beach, Thomas (1738–1806) II 15
Beach, T.M. (1841–1894) III 15
Beaconsfield, 1st Earl of (1804–1881) III 15–16
Beadon, Richard (1737–1824) II 15
Beale, Charles (1631–1705) I 9
Beale, Charles (1660–1774) I 9
Beale, Dorothea (1831–1906) III 16
Beale, L.S. (1828–1906) III 16
Beale, Mary (1633–1699) I 9
Beale, William (d1651) I 9
Beard, Charles (1827–1888) III 16
Beard, John (1716?–1791) II 15
Beard, Thomas (d1632) I 9
Beard, William (1772–1868) II 15
Beardsley, A.V. (1872–1898) IV 8
Bearsted, 1st Viscount (1853–1927) III 16
Beaton, David (1494–1546) I 9
Beatson, Alexander (1759–1833) II 15
Beattie, James (1735–1803) II 15
Beattie, J.H. (1768–1790) II 15–16
Beattie, William (1793–1875) II 16
Beatty, 1st Earl (1871–1936) IV 8
Beatty, Sir William (c1770–1842) II 16
Beauchamp, Baron (1561–1612) I 9
Beauchamp, 6th Earl (1830–1891) III 16
Beauchamp, 7th Earl (1872–1938) IV 8
Beauclerk, Lord Amelius (1771–1846) II 16
Beauclerk, Lord Aubrey (1711–1741) II 16
Beauclerk, Lady Diana (1734–1808) II 16
Beauclerk, Topham (1739–1780) II 16
Beaufort, 1st Duke of (1629–1700) I 9
Beaufort, 2nd Duke of (1684–1714) I 9
Beaufort, 7th Duke of (1792–1853) II 16
Beaufort, Sir Francis (1774–1857) II 16
Beaufort, Henry (d1447) I 9
Beaufoy, Henry (d1795) II 16
Beaufoy, Mark (1764–1827) II 16
Beaumont, Basil (1669–1703) I 9
Beaumont, Francis (1584–1616) I 9
Beaumont, Sir G.H., Bart (1753–1827) II 16
Beaumont, John (d1701) I 9
Beaumont, Joseph (1616–1699) I 9
Beaumont, J.T.B. (1774–1841) II 16
Beaumont, T.W. (1792–1848) II 16
Beaver, Sir Hugh (1890–1967) IV 8
Beaverbrook, 1st Baron (1879–1964) IV 8
Beck, Cave (1623–1706?) I 10
Becker, Lydia Ernestine (1827–1890) III 16
Becket, William (1684–1738) I 10
Beckett, Isaac (1653–1719) I 10
Beckett, Thomas à (1118?–1170) I 10
Beckford, Peter (1740–1811) II 16
Beckford, William (1709–1770) II 16
Beckford, William (1759–1844) II 16
Beckford, William (d1799) II 16
Beckington, Thomas (1390?–1465) I 10
Beckwith, Sir George (1753–1823) II 16

Beckwith, J.C. (1750–1809) II 16
Becon, Thomas (1512–1567) I 10
Beddoes, Thomas (1760–1808) II 16
Bedell, William (1571–1642) I 10
Bedford, 1st Earl of (1486?–1555) I 10
Bedford, 2nd Earl of (1527?–1585) I 10
Bedford, 4th Earl of (1593–1641) I 10
Bedford, 1st Duke of (1613–1700) I 10
Bedford, 4th Duke of (1710–1771) II 17
Bedford, 5th Duke of (1765–1802) II 16–17
Bedford, 6th Duke of (1766–1839) II 17
Bedford, 9th Duke of (1819–1891) III 16
Bedford, 11th Duke of (1858–1940) III 16
Bedford, Countess of (d1627) I 10
Bedford, Duchess of (1781–1853) II 17
Bedford, Duchess of (1767?–1937) IV 8
Bedford, John (1810–1879) III 16
Bedford, Paul (1792?–1871) II 17
Bedford, W.K.R. (1826–1905) III 16
Bedingfield, Sir Henry (1511–1583) I 10
Bedingfield, Sir Henry (1633–1687) I 10
Bedloe, William (1650–1680) I 10
Beecham, John (1787–1856) II 17
Beecham, Sir Thomas, 2nd Bart (1879–1961) III 8
Beechey, F.W. (1796–1856) II 17
Beechey, Sir William (1753–1839) II 17
Beerbohm, Sir H.M. (1872–1956) IV 8
Beeton, Isabella Mary (1836–1865) III 16
Begbie, J.W. (1826–1876) III 16
Begg, James (1808–1883) III 16
Behn, Aphra (1640–1689) I 10
Beilby, Sir G.T. (1850–1924) III 16
Beit, Alfred (1853–1906) III 16
Beit, Sir O.J., 1st Bart (1865–1930) IV 8
Beith, J.H. (1876–1952) IV 8
Belasyse of Worlaby, Baron (1614–1689) I 10
Belcher, Sir Edward (1799–1877) II 17
Belcher, James (1781–1811) II 17
Belcher, John (1841–1913) III 16
Belcher, Thomas (1783–1854) II 17
Belchier, John (1706–1785) II 17
Belfast, Earl of (1827–1853) III 16
Belfrage, Henry (1744–1835) II 17
Belhaven, 2nd Baron (1656–1679) I 10
Belhaven, Viscount (1574?–1639) I 10
Bell, Andrew (1726–1809) II 17
Bell, Andrew (1753–1832) II 17–18
Bell, Archibald (1755–1854) II 18
Bell, A.G. (1847–1922) III 16
Bell, Beaupré (1704–1745) II 18
Bell, Benjamin (1749–1806) II 18
Bell, Sir Charles (1774–1842) II 18
Bell, Clive (1881–1964) IV 9
Bell, C.F.M. (1847–1911) III 16
Bell, Enid Moberly (1881–1967) IV 9
Bell, Francis (1590–1643) I 10
Bell, Sir F.H.D. (1851–1936) III 16–17
Bell, G.J. (1770–1843) II 18
Bell, G.K.A. (1883–1958) IV 9
Bell, Gertrude Margaret (1868–1926) IV 9
Bell, Henry (1767–1830) II 18
Bell, H.G. (1803–1874) III 17
Bell, H.N. (1792–1822) II 18
Bell, Jacob (1810–1859) III 17
Bell, John (1745–1831) II 18
Bell, John (1763–1820) II 18
Bell, John (1764–1836) II 18
Bell, Sir John (1782–1876) II 18
Bell, Maria, Lady (d1825) II 18
Bell, Patrick (1799–1869) II 18
Bell, Sir Robert (d1577) I 10
Bell, Robert (c1800–1867) III 17
Bell, Thomas (1792–1880) II 18
Bell, Vanessa (1879–1961) IV 9
Bellamy, Daniel (1718–1788) II 18
Bellamy, G.A. (1731?–1788) II 18
Bellamy, James (1819–1909) III 17
Bellamy, Thomas (1745–1800) II 18
Bellamy, T.L. (1770–1843) II 18
Bellew, J.C.M. (1823–1874) III 17
Belloc, Hilaire (1870–1953) IV 9
Bellot, J.R. (1826–1852) III 17
Bellwood, Bessie (d1896) III 17
Belsham, Thomas (1750–1829) II 18
Belzoni, G.B. (1778–1823) II 18
Benazech, Charles (1767?–1794) II 18
Benbow, John (1653–1702) I 10
Bendall Cecil (1856–1906) III 17
Bendlowes, William (1516–1584) I 10
Benedict, Sir Julius (1804–1885) III 17
Benger, Elizabeth Ogilby (1778–1827) II 18
Benjamin, J.P. (1811–1884) III 17
Benlowes, Edward (1603?–1676) I 10
Benn, Sir E.J.P., 2nd Bart (1875–1954) IV 9
Benn, William (1600–1680) I 10
Bennet, Agnes Maria (d1808) II 18
Bennet, Benjamin (1674–1726) I 10

Bennet, Christopher (1617–1655) I 10
Bennet, William (1746–1820) II 18
Bennett, C.H. (1829–1867) III 17
Bennett, E.A. (1867–1931) IV 9
Bennett, E.H. (1837–1907) III 17
Bennett, G.J. (1800–1879) III 17
Bennett, G.M. (1892–1959) IV 9
Bennett, James (1774–1862) II 18
Bennett, Sir John (1814–1897) III 17
Bennett, J.G. (1800–1872) III 17
Bennett, J.H. (1812–1875) III 17
Bennett, J.J. (1801–1876) III 17
Bennett, Sir J.R. (1809–1891) III 17
Bennett, W.M. (1778–1858) II 18
Bennett, Sir W.S. (1816–1875) III 17
Bennett of Edgbaston, Baron (1880–1957) IV 9
Bensley, Robert (1738?–1817) II 18
Benson, A.C. (1862–1925) IV 9
Benson, Christopher (1789–1868) II 18
Benson, E.F. (1867–1940) IV 9
Benson, E.W. (1829–1896) III 17
Benson, Sir F.R. (1858–1939) III 17–18
Benson, George (1699–1762) I 11
Benson, Joseph (1749–1821) II 19
Benson, Martin (1689–1752) I 11
Benson, R.H. (1871–1914) IV 9
Benson, R.M. (1824–1915) III 18
Benson, Stella (1892–1933) IV 9
Bentham, George (1800–1884) III 18
Bentham, James (1708–1794) II 19
Bentham, Jeremy (1748–1832) II 19
Bentham, Sir Samuel (1757–1831) II 19
Bentham, Thomas (1513–1578) I 10
Bentinck, Lord G.C. (1802–1848) III 19
Bentinck, Sir H.J.W. (1796–1878) II 19
Bentinck, J.A. (1737–1775) I 19
Bentinck, Lord W.C. (1774–1839) II 19
Bentley, E.C. (1875–1956) IV 9
Bentley, George (1828–1895) III 18
Bentley, J.F. (1839–1902) III 18
Bentley, Nathaniel (1735?–1809) II 19
Bentley, Richard (1662–1742) I 11
Bentley, Richard (1708–1782) I 19
Bentley, Richard (1794–1871) II 19
Bentley, Robert (1821–1893) III 18
Bentley, Thomas (1693?–1742) I 11
Bentley, Thomas (1731–1780) II 19
Benwell, Mary (fl 1761–1800) II 19
Berdmore, Samuel (1740–1802) II 19
Berengaria, Queen (d after 1230) I 11
Beresford, Baron (1846–1919) III 18
Beresford, Viscount (1768–1854) II 19
Beresford, G.C. (1864–1938) IV 9
Beresford, John (1738–1805) II 19
Beresford, J.D. (1873–1947) IV 9
Beresford, Lord J.G. de la Poer (1773–1862) II 19
Beresford, Sir J.P., Bart (1766–1844) II 19
Beresford, M.G. (1801–1885) II 18
Berkeley, 1st Earl of (1628–1698) I 11
Berkeley, 3rd Earl of (1679–1736) I 22
Berkeley, 8th Earl of (1865–1942) IV 9
Berkeley, 17th Baron (1753–1818) II 19
Berkeley, F.H.F. (1794–1870) II 19
Berkeley, George (1685–1753) I 11
Berkeley, G.C.G.F. (1800–1881) II 18
Berkeley, G.M. (1763–1793) II 19
Berkeley, M.J. (1803–1889) III 18
Berkeley, Sir Robert (1584–1656) I 11
Berkeley, Sir William (1639–1666) I 11
Berkeley of Stratton, 1st Baron (d1678) I 11
Berkeley of Stratton, 3rd Baron (1663–1697) I 11
Berkenhout, John (1730?–1791) II 19
Bernal, Ralph (d1854) II 19–20
Bernard, Sir Charles (1650–1711) I 11
Bernard, Francis (1627–1698) I 11
Bernard, Sir Francis (1712–1779) II 20
Bernard, John (1756–1828) II 20
Bernard, J.H. (1860–1927) IV 9–10
Bernard, Mountague (1820–1882) III 18
Bernard, Sir Thomas (1750–1818) II 20
Bernardi, John (1657–1736) I 11
Bernays, A.J. (1823–1892) III 18
Berners, 2nd Baron (1467–1533) I 11
Berners, 14th Baron (1883–1950) IV 10
Bernstein of Leigh, 1st Baron (b1899) IV 10
Berridge, John (1716–1793) II 20
Berriman, William (1688–1750) I 11
Berry, Sir Edward, Bart (1768–1831) II 20
Berry, Sir Graham (1822–1904) III 18
Berry, Mary (1763–1852) II 20
Bertie, Sir Albemarle (1755–1824) II 20
Bertie, Sir Thomas (1758–1825) II 20
Bertie of Thame, 1st Viscount (1844–1919) III 18
Berwick, 1st Duke of (1670–1734) I 11
Berwick, 3rd Baron (1773–1842) II 20
Besant, Annie (1847–1933) III 18
Besant, Sir Walter (1836–1901) III 18

essborough, 2nd Earl of (1704–1793) II 20
essborough, 4th Earl of (1781–1847) II 20
essborough, 5th Earl of (1809–1880) III 18
essborough, 6th Earl of (1815–1895) III 18
essborough, 9th Earl of (1880–1956) IV 10
essemer, Sir Henry (1813–1898) III 18
est, Samuel (1738–1825) II 20
est, W.T. (1826–1897) III 18–19
etagh, Thomas (1739–1811) II 20
etham, William (1749–1839) II 20
etham, Sir William (1779–1853) II 20
ethel, Slingsby (1617–1697) I 11
ethell, Christopher (1773–1859) II 20
ethune-Baker, J.F. (1861–1951) IV 10
etterton, Thomas (1635–1710) I 11
ettesworth, G.E.B. (1780–1808) II 20
etty, W.H.W. (1791–1874) II 20
evan, Aneurin (1897–1960) IV 10
evan, A.A. (1859–1933) III 19
evan, Edward (1770–1860) II 20
evan, R.P. (1865–1925) IV 10
everidge, 1st Baron (1879–1963) IV 10
everidge, William (1637–1708) I 11
everley, H.R. (1796–1863) II 20
everley, John (1743–1827) II 20
everley, W.R. (1814?–1889) III 20
evin, Ernest (1881–1951) IV 10
ewick, Thomas (1753–1828) II 20
ewick, William (1795–1866) II 20
exley, 1st Baron (1766–1851) II 20–21
hownaggree, Sir M.M. (1851–1933) III 19
icester, Baron (1867–1956) IV 10
icheno, J.E. (1785–1851) II 21
ickersteth, Edward (1786–1850) II 21
ickersteth, Edward (1850–1897) III 19
ickersteth, E.H. (1825–1906) III 19
ickersteth, Robert (1816–1884) III 19
ickerton, Sir R.H. (1759–1832) II 21
ickham, George (d 1769) I 11
ickley, Thomas (1518–1596) I 11
idder, G.P. (1806–1878) III 19
idder, G.P. (1863–1953) IV 10
iddulph, Sir M.A.S. (1823–1904) III 19
iddulph, Sir Robert (1835–1918) III 19
iddulph, Sir T.M. (1809–1878) III 19
iddulph, T.T. (1763–1838) II 21
idlake, John (1755–1814) II 21
iffen, Sir R.H. (1874–1949) IV 10
iffin, Sarah (1784–1850) II 21
igg, Charles (1840–1908) III 19
igg, W.R. (1755–1828) II 21
iggar, J.G. (1828–1890) III 19
igland, John (1750–1832) II 21
igland, Ralph (1711–1784) II 21
ikaner, Maharaja of (1880–1943) IV 10
ill, William (d 1561) I 11
illing, Archibald (1791–1881) II 21
illingsley, Martin (fl 1618–1637) I 11
illington, Elizabeth (1768–1818) II 21
ilson, Thomas (1547–1616) I 11
indley, Charles (1795–1859) II 21
indley, James (1619–1683) II 21
ingham, Sir G.R. (1777–1833) II 21
ingham, Sir Richard (1528–1599) I 11
ingley, Baron (1676–1731) I 11
ingley, William (1774–1823) II 21
inney, Thomas (1798–1874) II 21
innie, W.J.E. (1867–1949) IV 10
inning, Charles Hamilton, Lord (1697–1733) I 11
inns, John (1772–1860) II 21
inyon, Laurence (1869–1943) IV 10
irch, C.B. (1832–1893) III 19
irch, John (1745?–1815) II 21
irch, Sir J.F.N. (1865–1939) IV 10
irch, Lamorna (1869–1955) IV 10
irch, Samuel (1813–1885) III 19
irch, Thomas (1705–1766) II 21
ird, C.K. (1887–1965) IV 10
ird, Edward (1772–1819) II 21
ird, E.J. (1799–1881) II 21
ird, H.E. (1830–1908) III 19
ird, Sir James (1883–1946) IV 10
ird, John (1709–1776) II 21
irdwood, 1st Baron (1865–1951) IV 10
irdwood, Sir G.C.M. (1832–1917) III 19
irkbeck, George (1776–1841) II 21
irkenhead, 1st Earl of (1872–1930) IV 10–11
irkett, 1st Baron (1883–1962) IV 11
irks, T.R. (1810–1883) III 19
irley, Sir O.H.J. (1880–1952) IV 11
irmie, Sir Richard (1760?–1832) II 21
irrell, Augustine (1850–1933) III 19
ishop, Ann (1814–1884) II 21
ishop, George (1785–1861) II 21
ishop, Sir H.R. (1786–1855) II 21
ishop, Isabella Lucy (1831–1904) III 19
ishop, Samuel (1731–1795) II 21

Bishop, William (1554–1624) I 11
Bisse, Philip (1667–1721) I 12
Bisset, William (1758–1834) II 22
Blaauw, W.H. (1793–1870) II 22
Blachford, Baron (1811–1889) III 19
Black, Adam (1784–1874) II 22
Black, John (1783–1855) II 22
Black, Joseph (1728–1799) II 22
Black, William (1749–1829) II 22
Black, William (1841–1898) III 19–20
Blackadder, John (1664–1729) I 12
Blackall, John (1771–1860) II 22
Blackall, Offspring (1654–1716) I 12
Blackburn, Baron (1813–1896) III 20
Blackburne, Francis (1705–1787) I 12
Blackburne, Francis (1782–1867) II 22
Blackburne, J.H. (1841–1924) III 20
Blackburne, Lancelot (1658–1743) I 12
Blackerby, Richard (1574–1648) I 12
Blacket, Joseph (1786–1810) II 22
Blackett, 1st Baron (1897–1974) IV 11
Blackett, Sir B.P. (1882–1935) IV 11
Blackie, J.S. (1809–1895) III 20
Blacklock, Thomas (1721–1791) II 22
Blacklock, W.J. (c1815–1858) III 20
Blackman, F.F. (1866–1947) IV 11
Blackman, V.H. (1872–1967) IV 11
Blackmore, Sir Richard (d 1729) I 12
Blackmore, R.D. (1825–1900) III 20
Blackner, John (1770–1816) II 22
Blackstone, Sir William (1723–1780) II 22
Blackwall, Anthony (1674–1730) I 12
Blackwell, Sir B.H. (b 1889) IV 11
Blackwell, Elizabeth (1821–1910) III 20
Blackwell, Thomas (1701–1757) II 22
Blackwood, Adam (1539–1613) I 12
Blackwood, A.H. (1869–1951) IV 11
Blackwood, Sir Henry, Bart (1770–1832) II 22
Blackwood, John (1818–1879) III 20
Blackwood, William (1776–1834) II 22
Blades, William (1824–1890) III 20
Blagden, Sir Charles (1748–1820) II 22
Blagrave, John (d 1611) I 12
Blagrave, Joseph (1610–1682) I 12
Blagrave, Thomas (d 1688) I 12
Blagrove, H.G. (1811–1872) III 20
Blaikie, W.G. (1829–1899) III 20
Blair, Hugh (1718–1800) II 22
Blair, James (1656–1743) I 12
Blair, Sir J.H. (1741–1787) II 22
Blair, Robert (1741–1811) II 22
Blair, William (1766–1822) II 22
Blake, J.B. (1745–1773) II 22
Blake, Robert (1599–1657) I 12
Blake, William (1757–1827) II 22
Blake, William (1773–1821) II 22
Blakely, Johnston (1781–1814) II 22
Blakeney, Lord (1672–1761) I 12
Blakeney, Sir Edward (1778–1868) II 22–23
Blakesley, J.W. (1808–1885) III 20
Blakeway, J.B. (1765–1826) II 23
Blakiston, H.E.D. (1862–1942) IV 11
Blanchard, E.L.L. (1820–1889) III 20
Blanchard, S.L. (1804–1845) II 23
Blanchard, William (1769–1835) II 23
Bland, G.N. (1886–1972) IV 11
Bland, Maria Theresa (1769–1838) II 23
Bland-Sutton, Sir John, Bart (1855–1936) III 20
Blandford, Walter (1619–1675) I 12
Blandy, Mary (1719–1752) II 23
Blane, Sir Gilbert (1749–1834) II 23
Blanesburgh, Baron (1861–1946) IV 11
Blantyre, 5th Lord (d 1704) I 12
Blatchford, R.P.G. (1851–1943) III 20
Blathwayt, William (1649?–1717) I 12
Bledisloe, Viscount (1867–1958) IV 11
Blencowe, Sir John (1642–1726) I 12
Blessington, 1st Earl of (1782–1829) II 23
Blessington, Countess of (1789–1849) II 23
Bligh, Sir R.R. (1737–1821) II 23
Bligh, Thomas (1685–1775) I 12
Bligh, William (1754–1817) II 23
Blight, William (c1780–1762) II 23
Bliss, Sir Arthur (1891–1975) IV 11
Bliss, Philip (1787–1857) II 23
Blith, Walter (fl 1649) I 12
Blizard, Sir William (1743–1835) II 23
Blochmann, H.F. (1838–1878) III 20
Blogg, H.G. (1876–1954) IV 11
Blome, Richard (d 1705) I 12
Blomfield, Sir A.W. (1829–1899) III 20
Blomfield, C.J. (1786–1857) II 23
Blomfield, Ezekiel (1778–1818) II 23
Blomfield, Sir R.T. (1856–1942) III 20
Blood, Sir Bindon (1842–1940) III 20
Blood, Thomas (1618?–1680) I 12
Bloomfield, 1st Baron (1768–1846) II 23

Bloomfield, 2nd Baron (1802–1879) III 20
Bloomfield, Robert (1766–1823) II 23
Blore, Edward (1787–1879) II 23
Blouet, L.P. (1848–1903) III 20–21
Blount, Sir Henry (1602–1682) I 12
Blount, Martha (1690–1762) I 12
Blow, John (1648–1708) I 12
Bloxam, Andrew (1801–1878) III 21
Bloxam, J.R. (1807–1891) III 21
Bloxam, M.H. (1805–1888) III 21
Blumenfeld, R.D. (1864–1948) IV 11
Blumenthal, Jacques (1829–1908) III 21
Blundell, Henry (1724–1810) II 23
Blundell, James (1790–1877) II 23
Blunden, Edmund (1896–1974) IV 11
Blunt, Henry (1794–1843) II 23
Blunt, J.J. (1794–1855) II 23
Blunt, W.S. (1840–1922) III 21
Boaden, James (1762–1839) II 23
Bobart, Jacob (1599–1680) I 12
Bobart, Jacob (1641–1719) I 12
Bodichon, Barbara (1827–1891) III 21
Bodington, Sir Nathan (1848–1911) III 21
Bodkin, Sir A.H. (1862–1957) IV 11
Bodkin, Thomas (1887–1961) IV 11
Bodkin, Sir W.H. (1791–1874) II 23–24
Bodley, G.F. (1827–1907) III 21
Bodley, J.E.C. (1853–1925) III 21
Bodley, Sir Thomas (1545–1613) I 12
Body, George (1840–1911) III 21
Boehm, Sir J.E., 1st Bart (1834–1890) III 21
Bogue, David (1750–1825) II 24
Boileau, Sir J.P., Bart (1794–1869) II 24
Boit, Charles (d 1726?) I 12
Boldero, Sir H.E.A. (1889–1960) IV 11
Bolingbroke, 1st Earl of (1580?–1646) I 12
Bolingbroke, 1st Viscount (1678–1751) I 12
Bolitho, H.H. (1898–1974) IV 11
Bolland, Sir William (1772–1840) II 24
Bols, Sir L.J. (1867–1930) IV 11
Bolton, 1st Duke of (1625?–1699) I 12
Bolton, 6th Duke of (1719–1794) II 24
Bolton, 1st Baron (1746–1807) II 24
Bolton, 3rd Baron (1818–1895) III 21
Bolton, Duchess of (1708–1760) II 24
Bolton, Sir F.J. (1831–1887) III 21
Bolton, Robert (1572–1631) I 13
Bolton, Samuel (1606–1654) I 13
Bomberg, D.G. (1890–1957) IV 11–12
Bompas, W.C. (1834–1906) III 21
Bonar, James (1852–1941) III 21
Bond, Sir C.H. (1870–1945) IV 12
Bond, Sir E.A. (1815–1898) III 21
Bond, J.L. (1766–1837) II 24
Bond, Martin (1558–1643) I 13
Bond, W.B. (1815–1906) III 21
Bondfield, Margaret Grace (1873–1953) IV 12
Bone, Henry (1755–1834) II 24
Bone, Sir Muirhead (1876–1953) IV 12
Bone, R.T. (1790–1840) II 24
Bonham-Carter, Sir Edgar (1870–1956) IV 12
Bonington, R.P. (1802–1828) II 24
Bonnar, William (1800–1853) III 21
Bonnell, James (1653–1699) I 13
Bonner, Edmund (1500?–1569) I 13
Bonney, W.F.V. (1872–1953) IV 12
Bonomi, Joseph (1739–1808) II 24
Bonomi, Joseph (1796–1878) II 24
Booker, John (1603–1667) I 13
Booker, Luke (1762–1835) II 24
Boole, George (1815–1864) III 21
Boone, J.S. (1799–1859) II 24
Boorde, Andrew (1490?–1549) I 13
Booth, Abraham (1734–1806) II 24
Booth, Barton (1681–1733) I 13
Booth, Catherine (1829–1890) III 21
Booth, Charles (1840–1916) III 21
Booth, J.B. (1796–1852) II 24
Booth, Sarah (1793–1867) II 24
Booth, William (1829–1912) III 21–22
Booth, W.B. (1856–1929) III 22
Boothby, Sir Brooke, 7th Bart (1744–1824) II 24
Boothroyd, Benjamin (1768–1836) II 24
Boott, Francis (1792–1863) II 24
Borclen, Mary, Lady Spears (1886–1968) IV 12
Borden, Sir R.L. (1854–1937) III 22
Borlase, Sir John (1576–1648)
Borrow, George (1803–1881) III 22
Borthwick, Peter (1804–1852) III 22
Borton, Sir Arthur (1814–1893) III 22
Boruwlaski, Joseph (1739–1837) II 24
Bosanquet, Bernard (1848–1923) III 22
Bosanquet, Sir F.A. (1837–1923) III 22
Bosanquet, Sir J.B. (1773–1847) II 24
Bosanquet, R.C. (1871–1935) IV 12
Boscawen, Edward (1711–1761) II 24
Bostock, John (1773–1846) II 24

Boston, Thomas (1677–1732) I *13*
Boswell, James (1740–1795) II *24–25*
Boswell, P.G.H. (1886–1960) IV *12*
Bosworth, Joseph (1789–1876) II *25*
Botfield, Beriah (1807–1863) III *22*
Botha, Louis (1862–1919) IV *12*
Bothwell, 4th Earl of (1535?–1578) I *13*
Botley, Samuel (1642–1696?) I *13*
Bottomley, Gordon (1874–1948) IV *12*
Bottomley, H.W. (1860–1933) IV *12*
Bottomley, Sir N.H. (1891–1970) IV *12*
Bouch, Sir Thomas (1822–1880) IV *22*
Boucher, Jonathan (1738–1804) II *25*
Boucicault, Dion (1820?–1890) III *22*
Boucicault, Dion (1859–1929) III *22*
Bough, Samuel (1822–1878) III *22*
Boughton, G.H. (1833–1905) III *22*
Boughton, Rutland (1870–1960) IV *12*
Boult, Sir Adrian (*b*1889) IV *12*
Boulter, Hugh (1672–1742) I *13*
Boulton, Matthew (1728–1809) II *25*
Bourchier, Arthur (1863–1927) IV *12*
Bourchier, J.D. (1850–1920) III *22*
Bourchier, Thomas (1404?–1486) I *13*
Bourchier, Sir Thomas (1791–1849) II *25*
Bourdillon, Sir B.H. (1883–1948) IV *12*
Bourgeois, Sir P.F. (1756–1811) II *25*
Bourke, Sir Richard (1777–1855) II *25*
Bourn, Samuel (1648–1719) I *13*
Bourn, Thomas (1771–1832) II *25*
Bourne, Sir A.G.B. (1882–1967) IV *12*
Bourne, F.A. (1861–1935) IV *12*
Bourne, Hugh (1772–1852) II *25*
Bourne, R.C. (1888–1938) IV *12*
Bouverie, E.P. (1818–1889) III *22*
Bovill, Sir William (1814–1873) III *22*
Bowater, Sir Edward (1787–1861) II *25*
Bowater, Sir E.V. (1895–1962) IV *12*
Bowden, J.W. (1798–1844) II *25*
Bowdich, T.E. (1791–1824) II *25*
Bowdler, Henrietta Maria (1754–1830) II *25*
Bowdler, Jane (1743–1784) II *25*
Bowdler, John (1746–1823) II *25*
Bowdler, John (1783–1815) II *25*
Bowen, Baron (1835–1894) III *22*
Bowen, Elizabeth (1899–1973) IV *12–13*
Bowen, James (1751–1835) II *25*
Bowe, Archibald (1686–1766) I *13*
Bower, F.O. (1855–1948) III *22–23*
Bowerbank, J.S. (1797–1877) II *25*
Bowes, Baron (1690–1767) I *13*
Bowes, Sir George (1527–1580) I *13*
Bowes, Sir Jerome (*d*1616) I *13*
Bowes, Sir Martin (1500?–1566) I *13*
Bowes, Sir Robert (1495?–1554) I *13*
Bowhill, Sir F.W. (1880–1960) IV *13*
Bowlby, Sir A.A., 1st Bart (1855–1929) III *—23*
Bowle, John (1725–1788) II *25*
Bowles, T.G. (1842–1922) III *23*
Bowles, W.L. (1762–1850) II *25*
Bowley, Sir A.L. (1869–1957) IV *13*
Bowly, Samuel (1802–1884) III *23*
Bowman, Sir James (*b*1898) IV *13*
Bowman, Sir William (1816–1892) III *23*
Bowra, Sir Maurice (1898–1971) IV *13*
Bowring, Sir John (1792–1872) II *25*
Bowyer, Sir George, Bart (1740–1800) II *25*
Bowyer, Sir George, 7th Bart (1811–1883) III *23*
Bowyer, William (1663–1737) I *13*
Bowyer, William (1699–1777) I *13*
Boxall, Sir William (1800–1879) III *23*
Boyce, G.P. (1826–1897) III *23*
Boyce, Sir R.W. (1863–1911) IV *13*
Boyce, William (1711–1779) II *25*
Boycott, A.E. (1877–1938) IV *13*
Boycott, C.C. (1832–1897) III *23*
Boyd, Archibald (1803–1883) III *23*
Boyd, A.K.H. (1825–1899) III *23*
Boyd, Henry (*d*1832) II *25*
Boyd, Henry (1831–1922) III *23*
Boyd, Hugh (1746–1794) II *25–26*
Boyd, M.A. (1563–1601) I *13*
Boyd, Sir Robert (1710–1794) II *26*
Boyd, Sir T.J. (1818–1902) III *23*
Boyd, Zachary (1585?–1653) I *13*
Boyd-Carpenter, William (1841–1918) III *23*
Boyd-Orr, 1st Baron (1880–1971) IV *13*
Boyd of Trochrig, Robert (1578–1627) I *13*
Boydell, John (1719–1804) II *26*
Boydell, Josiah (1752–1817) II *26*
Boyer, Abel (1667–1729) I *13*
Boyle, Lord (1772–1853) II *26*
Boyle, Michael (1609?–1702) I *13*
Boyle, Robert (1627–1691) I *13*
Boys, Sir C.V. (1855–1944) III *23*
Boys, Edward (1599–1667) I *14*
Boys, John (1571–1625) I *14*

Boys, T.S. (1803–1874) III *23*
Brabazon, H.B. (1821–1906) III *23*
Brabazon of Tara, 1st Baron (1884–1964) IV *13*
Brabourne, 1st Baron (1829–1893) III *23*
Bracegirdle, Anne (1663?–1748) I *14*
Brackenbury, C.B. (1831–1890) III *23*
Brackenbury, Sir Henry (1837–1914) III *23*
Brackley, 1st Viscount (1540?–1617) I *14*
Bradburn, Samuel (1751–1816) II *26*
Bradbury, 1st Baron (1872–1950) IV *13*
Bradbury, Thomas (1677–1759) I *14*
Bradford, 1st Earl of (1620–1708) I *14*
Bradford, Sir E.R.C., 1st Bart (1836–1911) IV *23*
Bradford, John (1510?–1555) I *14*
Bradford, Sir J.R., Bart (1863–1935) IV *13*
Bradford, Samuel (1652–1731) I *14*
Bradford, Sir Thomas (1777–1853) II *26*
Bradlaugh, Charles (1833–1891) III *23*
Bradley, A.C. (1851–1935) III *23*
Bradley, G.G. (1821–1903) III *24*
Bradley, Henry (1845–1923) III *24*
Bradley, James (1693–1762) I *14*
Bradley, Thomas (1751–1813) II *26*
Bradshaw, Ann Maria (1801–1862) III *24*
Bradshaw, George (1801–1853) III *24*
Bradshaw, Henry (1831–1886) III *24*
Bradshaw, John (1602–1659) I *14*
Bradshaw, William (1671–1732) I *14*
Brady, H.B. (1835–1890) III *24*
Brady, Sir Maziere (1796–1871) II *26*
Brady, Nicholas (1659–1726) I *14*
Brady, Robert (*d*1700) I *14*
Bragg, Sir W.H. (1862–1942) IV *13*
Bragg, Sir W.L. (1890–1971) IV *13*
Bragge, William (1823–1884) III *24*
Braham, John (1774?–1856) II *26*
Braid, James (1870–1950) IV *13*
Brain of Eynsham, 1st Baron (1895–1966) IV *13*
Braithwaite, John (1797–1870) II *26*
Braithwaite, Dame Lilian (1873–1948) IV *13*
Braithwaite, Warwick (1896–1971) IV *13*
Braithwaite, Sir W.P. (1865–1945) IV *13*
Bramah, Joseph (1748–1814) II *26*
Bramhall, John (1594–1663) I *14*
Bramley-Moore, John (1800–1886) III *24*
Brampton, 1st Baron (1817–1907) III *24*
Bramston, Sir John (1577–1654) I *14*
Bramston, J.Y. (1763–1836) II *26*
Bramwell, Baron (1808–1892) III *24*
Bramwell, Sir Byrom (1847–1931) III *24*
Bramwell, Sir F.J., Bart (1818–1903) III *24*
Brancker, Sir W.S. (1877–1930) IV *13*
Brand, John (1743/4–1806) II *26*
Brand, John (*d*1808) II *26*
Brand, Sir J.H. (1823–1888) III *24*
Brande, W.T. (1788–1866) II *26*
Brander, Gustavus (1720–1787) II *26*
Brandram, Samuel (1824–1892) III *24*
Brandreth, Jeremiah (*d*1817) II *26*
Brandreth, Joseph (1746–1815) II *26*
Brangwyn, Sir Frank (1867–1956) IV *13–14*
Branthwaite, William (*d*1620) I *14*
Branwhite, Charles (1817–1880) III *24*
Brassey, Baroness Anna (1839–1887) III *24*
Brassey, 1st Earl (1836–1918) III *24*
Brassey, Thomas (1805–1870) III *24*
Brathwaite, Richard (1588?–1673) I *14*
Braxfield, Lord (1722–1799) II *26*
Bray, Anna Eliza (1790–1883) II *26*
Bray, Charles (1811–1884) III *24*
Bray, E.A. (1778–1857) II *26*
Bray, Sir Reginald (*d*1503) I *14*
Bray, Sir R.M. (1842–1923) III *24*
Bray, William (1736–1832) II *26*
Braybrooke, 2nd Baron (1750–1825) II *26*
Braybrooke, 3rd Baron (1783–1858) II *26*
Braybrooke, 4th Baron (1820–1861) III *24*
Brayton, Lily (1876–1953) IV *14*
Breadalbane, 1st Earl of (1635–1716) I *14*
Breadalbane, 3rd Earl of (1696–1782) I *14*
Breadalbane, 2nd Marquess of (1796–1862) II *26–27*
Breeks, J.W. (1830–1872) III *24*
Brenan, Gerald (*b*1894) IV *14*
Brenchley, J.L. (1816–1873) III *24*
Brent, Charlotte (*d*1802) II *27*
Brentford, Earl of (1573?–1651) I *14*
Brentford, 1st Viscount (1865–1932) IV *14*
Brenton, E.P. (1774–1839) II *27*
Brereton, O.S. (1715–1798) II *27*
Brereton, Sir William (1604–1661) I *14*
Bressey, Sir C.H. (1874–1951) IV *14*
Bretland, Joseph (1742–1819) II *27*
Brett, John (1831–1902) III *24*
Brett, Sir Peircy (1709–1781) II *27*
Bretterg, Katherine (1579–1601) I *14*
Brettingham, Matthew (1699–1769) I *14*
Brewer, Jehoiada (1752?–1818) II *27*

Brewster, Abraham (1796–1874) II *27*
Brewster, Sir David (1781–1868) II *27*
Brewster, John (1753–1842) II *27*
Brewster, Patrick (1788–1859) II *27*
Brian, Havergal (1876–1972) IV *14*
Briant, Alexander (1553–1581) I *14*
Brice, Andrew (1690–1773) I *14*
Brideoake, Ralph (1613–1678) I *14*
Bridge, Frank (1879–1941) IV *14*
Bridge, Sir J.F. (1844–1924) III *25*
Bridge, William (1600?–1670) I *14*
Bridgeman, John (1577–1652) I *14*
Bridgeman, Sir Orlando, 1st Bart (1606?–1674) I *14*
Bridges, 1st Baron (1892–1969) IV *14*
Bridges, Charles (1794–1869) II *27*
Bridges, John (1666–1724) I *14*
Bridges, J.H. (1832–1906) III *25*
Bridges, Noah (fl 1661) I *14*
Bridges, R.S. (1844–1930) III *25*
Bridges, Thomas (fl 1760–1775) II *27*
Bridges, Sir Tom (1871–1939) IV *14*
Bridgewater, 1st Earl of (1579–1649) I *14*
Bridgewater, 2nd Earl of (1622–1686) I *15*
Bridgewater, 3rd Earl of (1646–1701) I *15*
Bridgewater, 8th Earl of (1756–1829) II *27*
Bridgewater, 3rd Duke of (1736–1803) II *27*
Bridgman, Charles (*d*1738) I *15*
Bridport, 1st Viscount (1727–1814) II *27*
Brierley, Benjamin (1825–1896) III *25*
Brierly, Sir O.W. (1817–1895) III *25*
Briggs, H.P. (1791?–1844) II *27*
Briggs, John (1788–1861) II *27*
Briggs, William (1642–1704) I *15*
Bright, Sir C.T. (1832–1888) III *25*
Bright, Henry (1814–1873) III *25*
Bright, Jacob (1821–1899) III *25*
Bright, John (1811–1889) III *25*
Bright, J.F. (1832–1920) III *25*
Bright, Mynors (1818–1883) III *25*
Bright, Richard (1789–1858) II *27*
Brightman, F.E. (1856–1923) III *25*
Brightman, Thomas (1562–1607) I *15*
Brindley, James (1716–1772) II *27*
Brinkley, John (1763–1835) II *27*
Brinton, William (1823–1867) III *25*
Brisbane, Sir Charles (1769?–1829) II *27*
Brisbane, Sir T.M. (1773–1860) II *27*
Bristol, 1st Earl of (1580–1653) I *15*
Bristol, 1st Earl of (1665–1751) I *15*
Bristol, 2nd Earl of (1612–1677) I *15*
Bristol, 2nd Earl of (1721–1775) II *28*
Bristol, 3rd Earl of (1724–1779) II *27*
Bristol, 4th Earl of (1730–1803) II *27–28*
Bristol, 3rd Countess of (1720–1788) II *27*
Bristowe, J.S. (1827–1895) III *25*
Brittain, Vera Mary (1894–1970) IV *14*
Britton, John (1771–1857) II *28*
Britton, Thomas (1654?–1714) I *15*
Broad, C.D. (1887–1971) IV *14*
Broadbent, T.B. (1793–1817) II *28*
Broadbent, Sir W.H., 1st Bart (1835–1907) III *25*
Broadhurst, Henry (1840–1911) III *25*
Broadwood, John (1732–1812) II *28*
Brocas, Sir Bernard (1330?–1395) I *15*
Brock, Sir Isaac (1769–1812) II *28*
Brock, Sir O. de B. (1869–1947) IV *14*
Brock, Sir Thomas (1847–1922) III *25*
Brock, William (1807–1875) III *26*
Brockedon, William (1787–1854) II *28*
Brockhurst, G.L. (*b*1890) IV *14*
Brocklesby, Richard (1722–1797) II *28*
Broderip, W.J. (1789–1859) II *28*
Brodie, Sir B.C., Bart (1783–1862) II *28*
Brodie, William (*d*1788) II *28*
Brodie, William (1815–1881) III *26*
Brodsky, Adolf (1851–1929) III *26*
Brodzky, Horace (1885–1969) IV *14*
Brogan, Sir D.W. (1900–1974) IV *14*
Broke, Sir P.B.V. (1776–1841) II *28*
Bromby, Charles Henry (1814–1907) III *26*
Brome, Alexander (1620–1666) I *15*
Brome, Richard (*d*1652?) I *15*
Bromfield, William (1712–1792) II *28*
Bromfield, W.A. (1801–1851) III *26*
Bromley, Sir Thomas (1530–1587) I *15*
Bromley, V.W. (1848–1877) III *26*
Bromley, William (1664–1732) I *15*
Bromley, William (1699?–1737) I *15*
Brontë, Anne (1820–1849) III *26*
Brontë, Charlotte (1816–1855) III *26*
Brontë, Emily (1818–1848) III *26*
Brontë, Patrick (1777–1861) II *28*
Brook, Sir Basil (1576–1646?) I *15*
Brook, Benjamin (1776–1848) II *28*
Brook, Clive (1887–1974) IV *14*
Brooke, 2nd Baron (1608–1643) I *15*
Brooke, A.E. (1863–1939) IV *14*

rooke, Sir C.A.J. (1829–1917) III 26
rooke, Lady Elizabeth (1601–1683) I 15
rooke, Frances (1724–1789) II 28
rooke, Henry (1703?–1783) II 28
rooke, G.V. (1818–1866) IV 26
rooke, Sir James (1803–1868) IV 26
rooke, J.C. (1748–1794) II 28
rooke, Ralph (1553–1625) I 15
rooke, R.C. (1887–1915) IV 14
rooke, S.A. (1832–1916) III 26
rookeborough, 1st Viscount (1888–1973) IV 14
rooke-Popham, Sir H.R.M. (1878–1953) IV 14
rookes, Joshua (1754–1821) II 28
rookes, Joshua (1761–1833) II 28
rookfield, W.H. (1809–1874) III 26
rooks, Sir R.A.D. (1896–1966) IV 14
rooks, W.C. (1887–1959) IV 14
roome, Sir F.N. (1843–1896) III 26
roome, William (1689–1745) I 15
rophy, John (1899–1965) IV 14
rothers, Richard (1757–1824) II 28
rotherton, Joseph (1783–1857) II 28
rough, Lionel (1836–1909) III 26
rough, Robert (1872–1905) IV 14
rougham, John (1814–1880) II 26
rougham and Vaux, 1st Baron (1778–1868) II 28–29
rougham and Vaux, 2nd Baron (1795–1886) II 29
roughton, Hugh (1549–1612) I 15
roughton, John (1705–1789) II 29
roughton, Rhoda (1840–1920) III 26
roughton, W.G. (1788–1853) II 29
roughton de Gyfford, Baron (1786–1869) II 29
rouncker, 2nd Viscount (1620?–1684) I 15
rouncker, 3rd Viscount (d 1688) I 15
rown, Sir A.W. (1886–1948) IV 14
rown, Charles (d 1753) I 15
rown, Ernest (1881–1962) IV 15
rown, F.G. (1887–1941) IV 15
rown, F.M. (1821–1893) III 26–27
rown, Frederick (1851–1941) III 27
rown, George (1650–1730) I 15
rown, George (1818–1880) III 27
rown, Sir George (1790–1865) II 29
rown, G.B. (1849–1932) III 27
rown, H.S. (1823–1886) III 27
rown, I.J.C. (1891–1974) IV 15
rown, John (d 1532) I 15
rown, John (1722–1787) II 29
rown, John (1735–1788) II 29
rown, John (1754–1832) II 29
rown, John (1784–1858) II 29
rown, John (1810–1882) III 27
rown, Sir John (1816–1896) III 27
rown, John (1826–1883) III 27
rown, Sir John (1880–1958) IV 15
rown, J.B. (1785–1843) II 29
rown, Lancelot (1715–1783) II 29
rown, O.M. (1855–1874) III 27
rown, Sir Robert (d 1760) I 15
rown, Robert (1773–1858) II 29
rown, Robert (1842–1895) III 27
rown, Samuel (1817–1856) III 27
rown, Thomas (1663–1704) I 15
rown, Thomas (1778–1856) III 27
rown, T.E. (1830–1897) III 27
rown, U.M. von (1705–1757) II 29
rown, William (1777–1857) II 29
rown, Sir William, Bart (1784–1864) II 29
rown, W.F. (1862–1951) IV 15
rown, W.H. (1823–1907) III 27
rown, W.J. (1894–1960) IV 15
rowne, Alexander (fl 1660) I 15
rowne, Sir Anthony (d 1548) I 15
rowne, Edward (1644–1708) I 15
rowne, E.G. (1862–1926) IV 15
rowne, E.H. (1811–1891) III 27
rowne, G.F. (1833–1930) III 27
rowne, H.K. (1815–1882) III 27
rowne, I.H. (1705–1760) II 29
rowne, I.H. (1745–1818) II 29
rowne, John (1642–1700?) I 15
rowne, Sir J.C. (1849–1938) III 27
rowne, Sir J.F.M. (1823–1911) III 27
rowne, Moses (1704–1787) II 29
rowne, Peter (d 1735) I 15
rowne, Sir Richard (d 1669) I 16
rowne, Sir Richard (1605–1683) I 16
rowne, Samuel (d 1668) I 15
rowne, Sir S.J. (1824–1901) III 27–28
rowne, Sir Thomas (1605–1682) I 16
rowne, Sir William (1692–1774) I 16
Browning, Elizabeth Barrett (1806–1861) III 28
Browning, Sir F.A.M. (1896–1965) IV 15
Browning, Sir M.E. (1863–1947) IV 15
Browning, Oscar (1837–1923) III 28
Browning, Robert (1812–1889) III 28
Brownlow, Richard (1553–1638) I 16

Brownrig, Ralph (1592–1659) I 16
Brownrigg, Elizabeth (d 1767) II 29
Brownrigg, Sir Robert, Bart (1759–1833) II 29–30
Brownrigg, William (1711–1800) II 30
Bruce, Sir David (1855–1931) III 28
Bruce, Sir G.B. (1821–1908) III 28
Bruce, Sir H.H. (1862–1948) IV 15
Bruce, James (1730–1794) II 30
Bruce, John (1745–1826) II 30
Bruce, J.C. (1805–1892) III 28
Bruce, Sir William (d 1710) I 16
Bruce, William (1757–1841) II 30
Bruce of Kinloss, 1st Baron (1549?–161:) I 16
Brudenell, Sir Robert (1461–1531) I 16
Bruen, John (1560–1625) I 16
Brugis, Thomas (fl 1640?) I 16
Brühl, Count of (1736–1809) II 30
Brummell, G.B. (1778–1840) II 30
Brundrett, Sir Frederick (1894–1974) IV 15
Brunel, I.K. (1806–1859) III 28
Brunel, Sir M.I. (1769–1849) II 30
Brunton, Alexander (1772–1854) II 30
Brunton, Mary (1778–1818) II 30
Brunton, Sir T.L., 1st Bart (1844–1916) III 28
Bryan, Margaret (fl 1790–1815) II 30
Bryan, Michael (1757–1821) II 30
Bryant, Sir Arthur (b 1899) IV 15
Bryant, Jacob (1715–1804) II 30
Bryce, 1st Viscount (1838–1922) II 28–29
Bryce, David (1803–1876) III 28
Brydges, Sir H.J. (1764–1847) II 30
Brydges, Sir S.E., Bart (1762–1837) II 30
Brydon, William (1811–1873) II 30
Brydone, Patrick (1736–1818) II 30
Buccleuch, 3rd Duke of (1746–1812) II 30
Buccleuch, 5th Duke of (1806–1884) III 29
Buccleuch, Countess of (1651–1731/2) I 16
Bucer, Martin (1491–1551) I 16
Buchan, 6th Earl of (d 1640) I 16
Buchan, 11th Earl of (1742–1829) II 30
Buchan, C.M. (1891–1960) IV 15
Buchan, William (1729–1805) II 30
Buchanan, Claudius (1766–1815) II 30
Buchanan, George (1506–1582) I 16
Buchanan, Sir George (1831–1895) III 29
Buchanan, George (1890–1954) IV 15
Buchanan, Sir G.C. (1865–1940) IV 15
Buchanan, Sir G.W. (1854–1924) III 29
Buchanan, James (1804–1870) III 29
Buchanan, Robert (1802–1875) III 29
Buchanan, R.W. (1841–1901) III 29
Buchman, F.N.D. (1878–1961) IV 15
Buck, Adam (1759–1833) II 30
Buck, Charles (1771–1815) II 30
Buck, Samuel (1696–1779) I 16
Buck, Zachariah (1798–1879) II 30
Buckeridge, John (1562?–1631) I 16
Buckingham, 1st Duke of (1592–1628) I 16
Buckingham, 2nd Duke of (1628–1687) I 16
Buckingham, 3rd Duke of (1478–1521) I 16
Buckingham, 1st Marquess of (1753–1816) II 31
Buckingham, J.S. (1786–1855) II 31
Buckingham and Chandos, 1st Duke of (1776–1839) II 31
Buckingham and Chandos, 2nd Duke of (1797–1861) II 31
Buckingham and Chandos, 3rd Duke of (1823–1889) III 29
Buckingham and Normanby, 1st Duke of (1648–1721) I 16–17
Buckinghamshire, 1st Earl of (1694?–1756) I 17
Buckinghamshire, 2nd Earl of (1723–1793) II 31
Buckinghamshire, 4th Earl of (1760–1816) II 31
Buckland, F.T. (1826–1880) III 29
Buckland, William (1784–1856) II 31
Buckland, W.W. (1859–1946) III 29
Buckle, G.E. (1854–1935) III 29
Buckler, Benjamin (1718–1780) II 31
Buckler, John (1770–1851) II 31
Buckmaster, 1st Viscount (1861–1934) IV 15
Bucknill, Sir A.T. (1880–1963) IV 15
Bucknill, Sir J.C. (1817–1897) III 29
Buckstone, J.B. (1802–1879) III 29
Budd, Henry (1774–1853) II 31
Budd, Richard (1746–1821) II 31
Budge, Sir Wallis (1857–1934) IV 15
Budgell, Eustace (1686–1737) I 17
Bufton, Eleanor (1840?–1893) III 29
Bugg, Francis (1640–1724?) I 17
Buissière, Paul (d 1739) I 17
Buist, George (1805–1860) III 29
Bulfin, Sir E.S. (1862–1939) IV 15
Bulkeley, Lady Sophia (fl 1688) I 17
Bulkley, Peter (1583–1659) I 17
Bull, George (1634–1710) I 17
Bull, John (1563?–1628) I 17
Bull, John (d 1642) I 17
Bull, William (1738–1814) II 31
Bullaker, Thomas (1604?–1642) I 17
Bullein, William (d 1576) I 17

Bullen, Sir Charles (1769–1853) II 31
Bullen, George (1816–1894) III 29
Buller, Charles (1806–1848) III 29
Buller, Sir Francis, Bart (1746–1800) II 31
Buller, Sir R.H. (1839–1908) III 29
Bullett, G.W. (1893–1958) IV 15
Bullingham, Nicholas (1512?–1576) I 17
Bulloch, William (1868–1941) IV 15
Bullock, William (1657?–1740) I 17
Bullough, Elsie (1886–1962) IV 15
Bulmer, William (1757–1830) II 31
Bulstrode, Whitelocke (1650–1724) I 17
Bulwer, John (fl 1654) I 17
Bunbury, H.W. (1750–1811) II 31
Bunn, Alfred (1796?–1860) II 31
Bunn, Margaret Agnes (1799–1883) II 31
Bunting, Edward (1773–1843) II 31
Bunting, Jabez (1779–1858) II 31
Bunyan, John (1628–1688) I 17
Burbage, Richard (1567?–1619) I 17
Burch, Edward (fl 1771) II 31
Burchell, W.J. (1782?–1863) II 31
Burchett, Josiah (1666?–1746) I 17
Burchett, Richard (1815–1875) III 30
Burckhardt, J.L. (1784–1817) II 31
Burder, George (1752–1832) II 32
Burder, H.F. (1783–1864) II 32
Burder, Samuel (1773–1837) II 32
Burdett, Sir Francis, Bart (1770–1844) II 32
Burdett-Coutts, Baroness Angela (1814–1906) III 30
Burdon, J.S. (1826–1907) III 30
Burdon, William (1764–1818) II 32
Burdon-Sanderson, Sir J.S., Bart (1828–1905) III 30
Burge, H.M. (1862–1925) IV 15
Burges, William (1827–1881) III 30
Burgess, Daniel (1645–1713) I 17
Burgess, J.B. (1830–1897) III 30
Burgess, Richard (1796–1881) II 32
Burgess, Thomas (1756–1837) II 32
Burgess, Thomas (1791–1854) II 32
Burgh, Sir John (1587–1627) I 17
Burgh, William (1741–1808) II 32
Burgh, W.H. (1742–1783) II 32
Burghersh, Baron (d 1355) I 17
Burghersh, Henry (1292–1340) I 17
Burghley, 2nd Baron (1542–1623) I 17
Burgon, J.W. (1813–1888) III 30
Burgon, Thomas (1787–1858) II 32
Burgoyne, John (1722–1792) II 32
Burgoyne, Sir J.F., Bart (1782–1871) II 32
Burke, Edmund (1729–1797) II 32
Burke, Sir J.B. (1814–1892) III 30
Burke, R. O'Hara (1820–1861) III 30
Burke, T.H. (1829–1882) III 30
Burke, T.N. (1830–1883) III 30
Burke, William (1792–1829) II 32
Burkitt, F.C. (1864–1935) IV 15
Burkitt, William (1650–1703) I 17
Burley, Sir Simon (1336–1388) I 17
Burlington, 1st Earl of (1612–1697) I 17
Burlington, 3rd Earl of (1695–1753) I 17
Burn, Edward (1762–1837) II 32
Burn, Richard (1709–1785) II 32
Burn, Robert (1829–1904) III 30
Burnaby, F.G. (1842–1885) III 30
Burnand, Sir F.C. (1836–1917) III 30
Burne-Jones, Sir E.C., 1st Bart (1833–1898) III 30
Burnes, Sir Alexander (1805–1841) III 30
Burnet, Elizabeth (1661–1709) I 18
Burnet, Gilbert (1643–1715) I 18
Burnet, John (1784–1868) II 32
Burnet, John (1863–1928) IV 15
Burnet, Thomas (c 1635–1715) I 18
Burnet, Sir Thomas (1694–1753) I 18
Burnet, William (d 1729) I 18
Burnett, Frances Eliza Hodgson (1849–1924) III 30
Burnett, Sir R.L. (1887–1959) IV 15
Burnett-Stuart, Sir J.T. (1875–1958) IV 15
Burney, Sir Cecil, 1st Bart (1858–1929) III 30–31
Burney, Charles (1726–1814) II 32–33
Burney, Charles (1757–1817) II 33
Burney, C.R. (1747–1819) II 33
Burnham, 1st Baron (1833–1916) III 31
Burnham, 1st Viscount (1862–1933) IV 15
Burnham, Richard (1711–1752) II 33
Burnham, Richard (1749?–1810) II 33
Burns, Sir George, 1st Bart (1795–1890) II 33
Burns, Jabez (1805–1876) III 31
Burns, James (1789–1871) II 33
Burns, John (1774–1850) II 33
Burns, J.E. (1858–1943) III 31
Burns, Robert (1759–1796) II 33
Burns, Robert (1789–1869) II 33
Burns, W.C. (1815–1868) III 31
Burnside, William (1852–1927) III 31
Burrell, Sir William (1732–1796) II 33
Burrell, Sir William (1861–1958) IV 15

Burrough, Sir James (1750–1839) II 33
Burrough, Sir James (1691–1764) I 18
Burroughes, Jeremiah (1599–1646) I 18
Burroughs, Joseph (1685–1761) I 18
Burrow, Sir James (1701–1782) II 33
Burrowes, Peter (1753–1841) II 33
Burrows, Christine Mary Elizabeth (1872–1959) IV 15–16
Burrows, Sir Frederick (1887–1973) IV 16
Burrows, Sir George, 1st Bart (1801–1887) III 31
Burrows, G.M. (1771–1846) II 33
Burrows, Sir J.C. (1813–1876) III 31
Burt, Sir Cyril (1883–1971) IV 16
Burt, Thomas (1837–1922) III 31
Burton, 1st Baron (1837–1909) III 31
Burton, Decimus (1800–1881) III 31
Burton, Edward (1794–1836) II 33
Burton, Sir F.W. (1816–1900) III 31
Burton, Henry (1578–1648) I 18
Burton, Hezekiah (d1681) I 18
Burton, Lady Isabel (1831–1896) III 31
Burton, John (1696–1771) I 18
Burton, J.H. (1809–1881) III 31
Burton, Sir M.M. (1885–1952) IV 16
Burton, Robert (1577–1640) I 18
Burton, Sir R.F. (1821–1890) III 31
Burton, William (1575–1645) I 18
Burton, William (1609–1657) I 18
Burton, W.E. (1804–1860) III 31
Burton, W.S. (1825–1916) III 31
Bury, Lady Charlotte Susan Maria (1775–1861) II 33
Bury, Mrs Elizabeth (1644–1720) I 18
Bury, J.B. (1861–1927) IV 16
Bury, Thomas (1655–1722) I 18
Busby, Richard (1606–1695) I 18
Busby, Thomas (1755–1838) II 33
Bushe, C.K. (1767–1843) II 33
Bushell, Thomas (1594–1674) I 18
Busk, George (1807–1886) III 31
Busk, Hans (1815–1882) III 31
Butchell, Martin van (1735–1812?) II 33
Butcher, Richard (1583–1665?) I 18
Butcher, S.H. (1850–1910) III 31
Bute, 3rd Earl of (1713–1792) II 33
Bute, 3rd Marquess of (1847–1900) III 32
Butler, Alban (1711–1773) II 33
Butler, A.G. (1831–1909) III 32
Butler, Charles (1750–1832) II 33
Butler, E.J.A. (1858–1934) III 32
Butler, Lady Eleanor Charlotte (1745?–1829) II 33
Butler, Elizabeth Southerden, Lady (1846–1933) III 32
Butler, F.H. (1855–1928) III 32
Butler, George (1774–1853) II 33
Butler, Sir H.B. (1883–1951) IV 16
Butler, H.M. (1833–1918) III 32
Butler, Sir James (1889–1975) IV 16
Butler, John (1717–1802) II 33
Butler, Joseph (1692–1752) I 18
Butler, Josephine Elizabeth (1828–1906) III 32
Butler, Sir M.S.D. (1873–1952) IV 16
Butler, Sir N.M. (1893–1973) IV 16
Butler, Samuel (1612–1680) I 18
Butler, Samuel (1774–1839) II 33
Butler, Samuel (1835–1902) III 32
Butler, Simon (1757–1797) II 34
Butler, Sir S.H. (1869–1938) IV 16
Butler, William (1535–1618) I 18
Butler, W.A. (1814?–1848) III 32
Butler, Sir W.F. (1838–1910) III 32
Butler, W.J. (1818–1894) III 32
Butlin, Sir H.T., 1st Bart (1845–1912) III 32
Butlin, Sir W.E. (1899–1977) IV 16
Butt, Sir Alfred, 1st Bart (1878–1962) IV 16
Butt, Dame Clara Ellen (1872–1936) IV 16
Butt, Sir C.P. (1830–1892) III 32
Butt, George (1741–1795) II 34
Butt, Isaac (1813–1879) III 32
Butterfield, William (1814–1900) III 32
Butterworth, G.S.K. (1885–1916) IV 16
Butterworth, John (1727–1803) II 34
Butts, Sir William (d1545) I 18
Buxton, Earl (1853–1934) III 32
Buxton, Jedidiah (1707–1772) II 34
Buxton, P.A. (1892–1955) IV 16
Buxton, Sir T.F., Bart (1786–1845) II 34
Byfield, Adoniram (d1660) I 18
Byfield, Nicholas (1579–1622) I 18
Byng, John (1704–1757) II 34
Byng of Vimy, 1st Viscount (1862–1935) IV 16
Byrd, William (1538?–1623) I 18
Byres, James (1734–1817) II 34
Byrne, Charles (1761–1783) II 34
Byrne, Sir E.W. (1844–1904) III 32
Byrne, William (1743–1805) II 34
Byrom, John (1692–1763) I 18
Byron, 1st Baron (d1652) I 18
Byron, George Gordon, 6th Baron (1788–1824) II 34
Byron, Henry James (1834–1884) III 32

Byron, John (1723–1786) II 34
Byron, Sir Thomas (d1644) I 18
Bywater, Ingram (1840–1914) III 32

Cabbell, B.B. (1781–1874) II 35
Cable, Alice Mildred (1878–1952) IV 17
Cadbury, George (1839–1922) III 33
Cade, Sir Stanford (1895–1973) IV 17
Cadell, Thomas (1742–1802) II 34
Cadman, 1st Baron (1877–1941) IV 17
Cadogan, 1st Earl (1675–1726) I 19
Cadogan, 5th Earl (1840–1915) II 33
Cadogan, Sir A.G.M. (1884–1968) IV 17
Cadogan, Henry (1780–1813) II 35
Cadogan, William (1711–1797) II 35
Caesar, Sir Charles (1590–1642) I 19
Caesar, Henry (1562–1636) I 19
Caesar, Sir Julius (1558–1636) I 19
Caesar, Sir Thomas (1561–1621) I 19
Caillard, Sir V.H.P. (1856–1930) III 33
Caine, Sir T.H.H. (1853–1931) III 33
Caine, W.S. (1842–1903) III 33
Caird, Edward (1835–1908) III 33
Caird, Sir James (1816–1892) III 33
Caird, Sir James, 1st Bart (1864–1954) IV 17
Caird, John (1820–1898) III 33
Cairns, 1st Earl (1819–1885) III 33
Cairns, D.S. (1862–1946) IV 17
Cairns, Sir H.W.B. (1896–1952) IV 17
Cairns, John (1818–1892) III 33
Caithness, 14th Earl of (1821–1881) III 33
Caius, John (1510–1573) I 19
Calamy, Benjamin (1642–1686) I 19
Calamy, Edmund (1600–1666) I 19
Calamy, Edmund (1671–1732) I 19
Calcraft, John (1765–1831) II 35
Caldecote, 1st Viscount (1876–1947) IV 17
Caldecott, Randolph (1846–1886) III 33
Calder, Sir Robert (1745–1818) II 35
Calderon, P.H. (1833–1898) III 33
Calderwood, Henry (1830–1897) III 33
Caldwell, Sir Benjamin (1737?–1820) II 35
Caldwell, Sir J.L. (1770–1863) II 35
Call, Sir John (1732–1801) II 35
Callaghan, Sir G.A. (1852–1920) III 33
Callander, 1st Earl of (d1674) I 19
Callcott, J.W. (1766–1821) II 35
Callcott, Sir A.W. (1779–1844) II 35
Callcott, Maria, Lady (1785–1842) II 35
Callender, Sir G.A.R. (1875–1946) IV 17
Callow, John (1822–1878) III 33
Callow, William (1812–1908) III 33
Calman, W.T. (1871–1952) IV 17
Calthorpe, Sir S.A. Gough (1864–1937) IV 17
Calveley, Sir Hugh (d1393) I 19
Calver, Edward (fl 1649) I 19
Calverley, C.S. (1831–1884) III 33
Calverley, Henry (1604–1661) I 19
Calvert, Sir Harry (1763–1826) II 35
Cambell, Sir James (1570–1642) I 19
Cambridge, 2nd Duke of (1819–1904) III 33–34
Cambridge, Richard Owen (1717–1802) II 35
Camden, 1st Earl and 1st Baron (1714–1794) II 35
Camden, 2nd Earl and 1st Marquess of (1759–1840) II 35
Camden, William (1551–1623) I 19
Camelford, 1st Baron (1737–1793) II 35
Camelford, 2nd Baron (1775–1804) II 35
Cameron, Alexander (1747–1828) II 35
Cameron, Archibald (1707–1753) II 35
Cameron, C.H. (1795–1880) III 36
Cameron, Sir D.C. (1872–1948) IV 17
Cameron, Sir D.Y. (1865–1945) IV 17
Cameron, Sir Ewen (1629–1719) I 19
Cameron, G.B. (1884–1975) IV 17
Cameron, John (1771–1815) II 36
Cameron, Julia Margaret (1815–1879) III 34
Cameron, V.L. (1844–1894) III 34
Camidge, John (1790–1859) II 36
Camm, Sir Sydney (1893–1966) IV 17
Campbell, Alexander (1764–1824) II 36
Campbell, Sir Archibald (1739–1791) II 36
Campbell, Sir Archibald (1769–1843) II 36
Campbell, Sir Colin (1776–1847) II 36
Campbell, Duncan (1680–1730) I 19
Campbell, Lord Frederick (1729–1816) II 36
Campbell, George (1719–1796) II 36
Campbell, Sir George (1824–1892) III 34
Campbell, Sir Gerald (1879–1964) IV 17
Campbell, Gertrude Elizabeth, Lady (1858–1911) III 34
Campbell, Gordon (1886–1953) IV 17
Campbell, H.C.M. (1887–1970) IV 17
Campbell, Sir Ilay, Bart (1734–1823) II 36
Campbell, Sir James (1745–1832) II 36
Campbell, Sir James, Bart (1763–1819) II 36
Campbell, 1st Baron (1779–1861) II 36
Campbell, John (1766–1840) II 36
Campbell, Sir John (1780–1863) II 36

Campbell, John (1794–1867) II 36
Campbell, John (1817–1904) III 34
Campbell, Lewis (1830–1908) III 34
Campbell, Sir Malcolm (1885–1948) IV 17
Campbell, Sir Neil (1776–1827) II 36
Campbell, Mrs Patrick (1865–1940) IV 17
Campbell, Sir R.H. (1883–1953) IV 17
Campbell, Thomas (1777–1844) II 36
Campbell-Bannerman, Sir Henry (1836–1908) III 34
Campeggio, Lorenzo (1472–1539) I 19
Campion, 1st Baron (1882–1958) IV 17
Campion, Edmund (1540–1581) I 19
Camrose, 1st Viscount (1879–1954) IV 17
Candlish, R.S. (1806–1873) III 34
Cann, Abraham (fl 1820) II 36
Cannan, Charles (1858–1919) III 34
Canning, Earl (1812–1862) III 34
Canning, Elizabeth (1730–1773) I 19
Canning, George (1770–1827) II 36
Canning, Richard (1708–1775) I 19
Canning, Sir Samuel (1823–1908) III 34
Cannon, Richard (1779–1865) II 37
Cant, Andrew (1590?–1663) I 19
Canterbury, 1st Viscount (1780–1845) II 37
Canterbury, 3rd Viscount (1814–1877) III 34
Canton, John (1718–1772) II 37
Canton, William (1845–1926) III 34
Canute, King (994?–1035) I 19
Canynge, William (1399?–1474) I 19
Cape, H.J. (1879–1960) IV 17
Capel, T.J. (1836–1911) III 34–35
Capell, Edward (1713–1781) II 37
Capell of Hadham, 1st Baron (1610–1649) I 19
Capon, William (1757–1827) II 37
Cappe, Newcome (1733–1800) II 37
Capper, Joseph (1727–1804) II 37
Caradori-Allan, Maria (1800–1865) III 35
Carbery, 3rd Earl of (1640?–1713) I 19
Card, Henry (1779–1844) II 37
Carden, Sir R.W., Bart (1801–1888) III 35
Cardigan, 7th Earl of (1797–1868) II 37
Cardmaker, John (d1555) I 20
Cardon, Anthony (1772–1813) II 37
Cardonnel, Adam de (d1820) II 37
Cardross, 2nd Baron (1616–1671) I 20
Cardross, 3rd Baron (1649?–1693) I 20
Cardwell, Viscount (1813–1886) III 35
Cardwell, Edward (1787–1861) II 37
Carew, Sir Alexander, 2nd Bart (1609–1644) I 20
Carew, Sir B.H. (1760–1834) II 37
Carew, B.M. (1693–1770?) I 20
Carew, Sir John (d1660) I 20
Carew, J.E. (1782–1868) II 37
Carew, Sir Nicholas (d1539) I 20
Carew, Sir Peter (1514–1575) I 20
Carew, Richard (1555–1620) I 20
Carew, Thomas (1595?–1639?) I 20
Carcy, F.C.S. (1883–1968) IV 17
Carey, G.S. (1743–1807) II 37
Carey, Henry (d1743) I 20
Carey, William (1761–1834) II 37
Carey, William (1769–1846) II 37
Cargill, Anne (1748?–1784) II 37
Carhampton, 2nd Earl of (1743–1821) II 37
Carleill, Christopher (1551?–1593) I 20
Carleton, Viscount (1739–1826) II 37
Carleton, Baron (d1725) I 20
Carleton, George (1559–1628) I 20
Carleton, Mary (1642?–1673) I 20
Carleton, William (1798–1869) II 37
Carlile, James (1784–1854) II 37
Carlile, Richard (1790–1843) II 37
Carlile, Wilson (1847–1942) III 35
Carling, Sir E.R. (1877–1960) IV 17
Carlingford, Baron (1823–1898) III 35
Carlini, Agostino (d1790) II 38
Carlisle, 1st Viscount Doncaster and 1st Earl of (d1636) I 20
Carlisle, 1st Earl of (1629–1685) I 20
Carlisle, 3rd Earl of (1669–1738) I 20
Carlisle, 5th Earl of (1748–1825) II 38
Carlisle, 6th Earl of (1773–1848) II 38
Carlisle, 7th Earl of (1802–1864) III 35
Carlisle, 9th Earl of (1843–1911) III 35
Carlisle, Countess of (1599–1660) I 20
Carlisle, Countess of (1845–1921) III 35
Carlisle, Sir Anthony (1768–1840) II 38
Carlisle, Nicholas (1771–1847) II 38
Carlos, Major William (d1689) I 20
Carlyle, Alexander (1722–1805) II 38
Carlyle, Jane (1801–1866) III 35
Carlyle, J.A. (1801–1879) III 35
Carlyle, Sir R.W. (1859–1934) III 35
Carlyle, Thomas (1795–1881) II 38
Carmichael, 1st Baron (1578?–1672) I 20
Carmichael, 11th Bart, Baron (1859–1926) III 35
Carnaby, William (1772–1839) II 38
Carnac, John (1716–1800) II 38

Carnac, Sir J.R., 1st Bart (1785–1846) II 38
Carnarvon, 1st Earl of (1607?–1643) I 20
Carnarvon, 3rd Earl of (1800–1849) III 35
Carnarvon, 4th Earl of (1831–1890) III 35
Carnarvon, 5th Earl of (1866–1923) IV 17
Carnegie, Andrew (1835–1919) III 35–36
Carnock, 1st Baron (1849–1928) III 36
Carnwath, 6th Earl of (d 1737) I 20
Caroline, Queen (1683–1737) I 20
Caroline, Princess (1713–1757) II 38
Caroline, Queen (1768–1821) II 38
Carpenter, Baron (1657–1732) I 20
Carpenter, A.F.B. (1881–1955) IV 17
Carpenter, Edward (1844–1929) III 36
Carpenter, Sir H.C.H. (1875–1940) IV 18
Carpenter, J.E. (1844–1927) III 36
Carpenter, Lant (1780–1840) II 38
Carpenter, Margaret (1793–1872) II 38–39
Carpenter, Mary (1807–1877) III 36
Carpenter, Richard (d 1670?) I 20
Carpenter, W.B. (1813–1885) III 36
Carpenter, W.H. (1792–1866) II 39
Carpue, J.C. (1764–1846) II 39
Carr, John (1723–1807) I 20
Carr, Sir John (1772–1832) II 39
Carr, Robert James (1774–1841) II 39
Carr-Saunders, Sir A.M. (1886–1966) IV 18
Carrick, T.H. (1802–1875) III 36
Carrington, Lord (1616–1679) I 20
Carrington, 1st Baron (1752–1838) I 39
Carrington, 1st Earl (1843–1928) III 36
Carrington, Sir C.E. (1769–1849) II 39
Carrington, Dora (1893–1932) IV 18
Carrington, Sir Frederick (1844–1913) III 36
Carrington, N.T. (1777–1830) I 39
Carrodus, J.T. (1836–1895) III 36
Carruthers, Douglas (1882–1962) IV 18
Carruthers, Robert (1799–1878) I 39
Carson, Baron (1854–1935) III 36
Carstares, William (1649–1715) I 20–21
Carte, Richard D'Oyly (1844–1901) III 36
Carter, Elizabeth (1717–1806) I 39
Carter, Francis (1741–1783) I 39
Carter, George (1737–1794) II 39
Carter, Howard (1874–1939) IV 18
Carter, John (1554–1635) I 21
Carter, John (1748–1817) II 39
Carter, Lawrence (1672–1745) I 21
Carter, R.B. (1828–1918) III 36
Carter, T.T. (1808–1901) III 36
Carton, R.C. (1856–1928) III 36
Cartwright, Edmund (1743–1823) I 39
Cartwright, John (1740–1824) II 39
Cartwright, Samuel (1788–1864) II 39
Cartwright, Thomas (1535–1603) I 21
Cartwright, Thomas (1634–1689) I 21
Cartwright, William (1611–1643) I 21
Cartwright, William (d 1687) I 21
Carve, Thomas (1590–1672) I 21
Carver, A.J. (1826–1909) III 36
Cary, A.J.L. (1888–1957) IV 18
Cary, F.S. (1808–1880) III 36
Cary, H.F. (1772–1844) II 39
Caryl, Joseph (1602–1673) I 21
Carysfort, 1st Earl of and 2nd Baron (1751–1828) II 39
Casaubon, Isaac (1559–1614) I 21
Casaubon, Meric (1599–1671) I 21
Case, John (d 1600) I 21
Case, Thomas (1598–1682) I 21
Casement, Sir R.D. (1864–1916) IV 18
Casey, W.F. (1884–1957) IV 18
Caslon, William (1692–1766) I 21
Cass, Sir John (1666–1718) I 21
Cassan, S.H. (1789–1841) II 39
Cassel, Sir E.J. (1852–1921) III 36
Cassell, John (1817–1865) III 36
Cassels, Sir J.D. (1877–1972) IV 18
Cassels, Sir R.A. (1876–1959) IV 18
Casson, Sir Lewis (1875–1969) IV 18
Castell, Edmund (1606–1685) I 21
Castlemaine, Earl of (1634–1705) I 21
Caswall, Edward (1814–1878) III 36
Catalani, Angelica (1780–1849) II 39
Cates, W.L.R. (1821–1895) III 36
Catesby, Robert (1573–1605) I 21
Catesby, William (d 1485) I 21
Cathcart, 9th Baron (1721–1776) II 39
Cathcart, 10th Baron and 1st Earl of (1755–1843) II 39
Cathcart, E.P. (1877–1954) IV 18
Cathcart, Sir George (1794–1854) II 39
Catherine of Valois (1401–1437) I 21
Catherine of Aragon (1485–1536) I 21
Catherine Parr (1512–1548) I 21
Catherine of Braganza (1638–1705) I 21
Catley, Anne (1745–1789) I 39
Cattermole, George (1800–1868) III 36
Catto, 1st Baron (1879–1959) IV 18

Catton, Charles (1728–1798) II 39
Caulfield, James (1764–1826) II 39–40
Cavallo, Tiberius (1749–1809) II 40
Cavagnari, Sir P.L.N. (1841–1879) III 36
Cavan, 7th Earl of (1763–1836) II 40
Cavan, 10th Earl of (1865–1946) IV 18
Cave, Viscount (1856–1928) III 36–37
Cave, Sir Ambrose (d 1568) I 21
Cave, Edward (1691–1754) I 21
Cave, Sir L.W. (1832–1897) III 37
Cave, Sir Stephen (1820–1880) III 37
Cavell, Edith (1865–1915) IV 18
Cavendish, Ada (1839–1895) III 37
Cavendish, Sir Charles (1591–1654) I 21
Cavendish, Charles (1620–1643) I 21
Cavendish, Lord F.C. (1836–1882) III 37
Cavendish, George (1500–1561) I 21
Cavendish, Henry (d 1616) I 21
Cavendish, Henry (1731–1810) II 40
Cavendish, Sir Henry, Bart (1732–1804) II 40
Cavendish, Lord John (1732–1796) II 40
Cavendish, Thomas (1560–1592) I 21–22
Cavendish, Sir William (1505?–1557) I 22
Cawdor, 3rd Earl (1847–1911) III 37
Cawley, William (1602–1667) I 22
Cawton, Thomas (1605–1659) I 22
Caxton, William (1422?–1491) I 22
Cayley, Arthur (1821–1895) III 37
Cayley, Cornelius (1729–1780?) II 40
Cayley, Sir George, Bart (1773–1857) II 40
Cecil, Lord (1867–1918) IV 18
Cecil, Arthur (1843–1896) III 37
Cecil, James (1748–1823) II 40
Cecil, Richard (1748–1810) II 40
Cecil of Chelwood, 1st Viscount (1864–1958) IV 18
Céleste-Elliott, Celine (1814?–1882) III 37
Cellier, Alfred (1844–1891) III 37
Cennick, John (1718–1755) II 40
Centlivre, Susannah (1667?–1723) I 22
Cervetto, Giacomo (1682?–1783) I 22
Cervetto, Giacomo (1747?–1837) II 40
Chaderton, William (1540?–1608) I 22
Chadwick, Sir Edwin (1801–1890) III 37
Chadwick, Sir James (1891–1974) IV 18
Chadwick, Roy (1893–1947) IV 18
Chaffers, Richard (1731–1762) II 40
Chaffers, William (1811–1892) III 37
Chafy, William (1779–1843) II 40
Challoner, Richard (1691–1781) I 22
Chalmers, Alexander (1759–1834) II 40
Chalmer, George (1742–1825) II 40
Chalmers, G.P. (1826–1878) III 37
Chalmers, James (1782–1853) II 40
Chalmers, Sir M.D. (1847–1927) III 37
Chalmers, Thomas (1780–1847) II 40
Chalmers of Northiam, Baron (1858–1938) III 37
Chalon, A.E. (1780–1860) II 40
Chalon, J.J. (1778–1854) II 40
Chaloner, Sir Thomas (1521–1565) I 22
Chamberlain, Joseph (1836–1914) III 37
Chamberlain, Sir J.A. (1863–1937) IV 19
Chamberlain, Neville (1869–1940) IV 18–19
Chamberlain, Robert (fl 1678) I 22
Chamberlain, Thomas (1810–1892) III 37
Chamberlayne, William (1619–1689) I 22
Chamberlen, Hugh (1664–1728) I 22
Chamberlen, Paul (1635–1717) I 22
Chamberlin, Mason (d 1787) II 40
Chambers, Sir E.K. (1866–1954) IV 19
Chambers, George (1803–1840) III 37
Chambers, Sir Robert (1737–1803) II 40
Chambers, Robert (1802–1871) III 37–38
Chambers, R.W. (1874–1942) IV 19
Chambers, Sir Thomas (1814–1891) III 38
Chambers, Sir William (1726–1796) II 40
Chambers, William (1800–1883) III 38
Chambers, W.F. (1786–1855) II 40–41
Chambré, Sir Alan (1739–1823) II 41
Chambre, John (1470–1549) I 22
Chamier, Anthony (1725–1780) II 41
Chamier, Frederic (1796–1870) II 41
Champion, Anthony (1725–1801) II 41
Champion, Joseph (b 1709) II 41
Champneys, Basil (1842–1935) III 38
Champneys, Sir F.H., 1st Bart (1848–1930) III 38
Champneys, W.W. (1807–1875) III 38
Chance, Sir J.T., 1st Bart (1814–1902) III 38
Chancellor, Sir J.R. (1870–1952) IV 19
Chandler, Edward (1668?–1750) I 22
Chandler, H.W. (1828–1889?) III 38
Chandler, Samuel (1693–1766) I 22
Chandos, 3rd Baron (1547–1594) I 22
Chandos, 1st Duke of (1673–1744) I 22
Chandos, 3rd Viscount (1893–1972) IV 19
Channell, Sir A.M. (1838–1928) III 38
Channon, Sir Henry (1897–1958) IV 19
Chantrey, Sir F.L. (1781–1841) II 41

Chaplin, 1st Viscount (1840–1923) III 38
Chaplin, Sir Charles (1889–1977) IV 19
Chapman, D.L. (1869–1958) IV 19
Chapman, Sir F.E. (1815–1893) III 38
Chapman, George (1559?–1634) I 22
Chapman, John (1822–1894) III 38
Chapman, R.W. (1881–1960) IV 19
Chapman, Sydney (1888–1970) IV 19
Chapman, Sir S.J. (1871–1951) IV 19
Chapman, William (1749–1832) II 41
Chapone, Hester (1727–1801) II 41
Chard, J.R.M. (1847–1897) III 38
Chardin, Sir John (1643–1713) I 22
Charke, Charlotte (1713–1760?) I 41
Charlemont, 1st Earl of (1728–1799) II 41
Charles I (1600–1649) I 22–23
Charles II (1630–1685) I 23
Charles, Prince (1720–1788) II 41
Charles, David (1762–1834) II 41
Charles, Elizabeth (1828–1896) III 38
Charles, Sir J.A. (1893–1971) IV 19
Charles, Thomas (1755–1814) II 41
Charlesworth, E.P. (1783–1853) II 41
Charlesworth, M.P. (1895–1950) IV 19
Charleton, Rice (1710–1789) II 41
Charleton, Walter (1619–1707) I 23
Charley, Sir W.T. (1833–1904) III 38
Charlotte, Queen (1744–1818) II 42
Charlotte, Princess Royal (1766–1828) II 41–42
Charlotte, Princess (1796–1817) II 41
Charlton, Sir Job, Bart (1614–1697) I 23
Charnock, John (1756–1807) II 42
Charnock, Stephen (1628–1680) I 23
Charnwood, 1st Baron (1864–1945) IV 19
Charrington, F.N. (1850–1936) III 38
Charteris, A.H. (1835–1908) III 38
Charteris, Francis (1675–1732) I 23
Chase, D.P. (1820–1902) III 38
Chase, F.H. (1853–1925) III 38
Chatfield, 1st Baron (1873–1967) IV 19
Chatham, 1st Earl of (1708–1778) II 42
Chatham, 2nd Earl of (1756–1835) II 42
Chatterley, W.S. (1787–1822) II 42
Chatterton, J.B. (1802?–1871) III 38
Chatterton, Thomas (1752–1770) II 42
Chaucer, Geoffrey (1340?–1400) I 23
Chaucer, Thomas (1367?–1434) I 23
Chauncey, Charles (1706–1777) II 42
Chauncy, Sir Henry (1632–1719) I 23
Chavasse, C.M. (1884–1962) IV 19
Chavasse, F.J. (1846–1928) III 38
Chedworth, 4th Baron (1754–1804) II 42
Cheesman, R.E. (1878–1962) IV 19
Cheesman, Thomas (1760–1835) II 42
Cheke, Sir John (1514–1557) I 23
Chelmsford, 1st Baron (1794–1878) II 42
Chelmsford, 2nd Baron (1827–1905) III 38
Chelmsford, 1st Viscount (1868–1933) IV 19
Chelsum, James (1740?–1801) II 42
Chenery, Thomas (1826–1884) III 38
Chenevix, Richard (1698–1779) I 23
Chenevix, Richard (1774–1830) II 42
Chéron, Louis (1655–1725) I 23
Cherry, Andrew (1762–1812) II 42
Cherry-Garrard, A.G.B. (1886–1959) IV 19
Cherwell, 1st Viscount (1886–1957) IV 19
Cheselden, William (1688–1752) I 23
Chesney, C.C. (1826–1876) III 38–39
Chesney, F.R. (1789–1872) II 42
Chesney, Sir G.T. (1830–1895) III 39
Chesser, Elizabeth Sloan (d 1940) IV 19
Chester, Sir William (1509?–1595?) I 23
Chesterfield, 2nd Earl of (1633–1713) I 23
Chesterfield, 4th Earl of (1694–1773) I 23
Chesterfield, 5th Earl of (1755–1815) II 42
Chesterfield, Countess of (d 1667) I 23
Chesterton, G.K. (1874–1936) IV 19–20
Chetham, Humphrey (1580–1653) I 23
Chetwode, 1st Baron (1869–1950) IV 20
Chetwynd, Walter (d 1693) I 23
Chevalier, Thomas (1767–1824) II 42
Chevallier, Temple (1794–1873) II 42
Cheylesmore, 3rd Baron (1848–1925) III 39
Cheyne, George (1671–1743) I 23
Cheyne, John (1777–1836) II 42–43
Cheyne, T.K. (1841–1915) III 39
Cheyne, Sir W.W., 1st Bart (1852–1932) IV 19
Chichele, Henry (1362?–1443) I 23
Chicheley, Sir John (c 1640–1691) I 24
Chicheley, Sir Thomas (1618–1699) I 24
Chichester, 1st Earl of (1728–1805) II 43
Chichester, 2nd Earl of (1756–1826) II 43
Chichester, 3rd Earl of (1804–1886) III 39
Chiffinch, Thomas (1600–1666) I 24
Chiffinch, William (1602?–1688) I 24
Chifney, Samuel (1753?–1807) II 43
Chifney, Samuel (1786–1854) II 43

Child, Sir Francis (1642–1713) I 24
Child, Sir Francis (1684?–1740) I 24
Child, Sir Josiah, Bart (1630–1699) I 24
Child, William (1606?–1697) I 24
Childe, V.G. (1892–1957) IV 20
Childers, H.C.E. (1827–1896) III 39
Childers, R.E. (1870–1922) IV 20
Children, George (1742–1818) II 43
Children, J.G. (1777–1852) II 43
Childs, W.M. (1869–1939) IV 20
Chillingworth, William (1602–1644) I 24
Chilston, 1st Viscount (1851–1926) III 39
Chilston, 2nd Viscount (1876–1947) IV 20
Chinnery, George (1774–1852) II 43
Chippendale, Mary Jane (d1888) III 39
Chippendale, W.H. (1801–1888) III 39
Chirol, Sir I.V. (1852–1929) III 39
Chisenhale, Edward (d1654) I 24
Chisholm, Caroline (1808–1877) III 39
Chisholm, Hugh (1866–1924) IV 20
Chitty, Sir J.W. (1828–1899) III 39
Cholmondeley, 1st Marquess of (1749–1827) II 43
Chorley, H.F. (1808–1872) III 39
Christian, Sir H.C. (1747–1798) II 43
Christie, Dame Agatha (1890–1976) IV 20
Christie, James (1730–1803) II 43
Christie, James (1773–1831) II 43
Christie, John (1882–1962) IV 20
Christie, S.H. (1784–1865) II 43
Christie, Sir W.H.M. (1845–1922) III 39
Christy, Henry (1810–1865) III 39
Christison, Sir Robert (1797–1882) II 43
Chrystal, George (1851–1911) III 39
Chubb, Thomas (1679–1747) I 24
Church, Richard (1893–1972) IV 20
Church, R.W. (1815–1890) III 39
Church, Sir W.S., 1st Bart (1837–1928) III 39
Churchill, Arabella (1648–1730) I 24
Churchill, Charles (1731–1764) II 43
Churchill, George (1654–1710) I 24
Churchill, Jennie, Lady (1854–1921) III 39
Churchill, Lord Randolph (1849–1895) III 39–40
Churchill, Sir Winston (1874–1965) IV 20
Chute, Chaloner (d1659) I 24
Chuter-Ede, Baron (1882–1965) IV 20
Cibber, Colley (1671–1757) I 24
Cibber, C.G. (1630–1700) I 24
Cibber, Susannah Maria (1714–1766) II 43
Cibber, Theophilus (1703–1758) II 43
Cipriani, G.B. (1727–1785) II 43
Citrine, 1st Baron (b1887) IV 20
Clairmont, Clara (1798–1879) II 43
Clanricarde, 15th Earl and 2nd Marquess of (1832–1916) III 40
Clanwillian, 3rd Earl of (1795–1879) II 43
Clanwillian, 4th Earl of (1832–1907) III 40
Clapham, Sir A.W. (1883–1950) IV 20
Clapham, Sir J.H. (1873–1946) IV 20
Clapperton, Hugh (1788–1827) II 43
Clare, 1st Earl of (1564?–1637) I 24
Clare, 1st Earl of (1749–1802) II 44
Clare, John (1793–1864) II 43–44
Clarence and Avondale, Duke of (1864–1892) IV 20–21
Clarendon, 1st Earl of (1609–1674) I 24
Clarendon, 2nd Earl of (1638–1709) I 24
Clarendon, 1st Earl of (1709–1786) II 44
Clarendon, 2nd Earl of (1753–1824) II 44
Clarendon, 4th Earl of (1800–1870) III 40
Clarendon, 6th Earl of (1877–1955) IV 21
Clarendon, Countess of (d1725) I 24
Clarina, 1st Baron (1719–1804) II 44
Clark, Sir Andrew, Bart (1826–1893) III 40
Clark, A.C. (1859–1937) III 40
Clark, Edwin (1814–1894) III 40
Clark, Sir James (1788–1870) II 44
Clark, John (1688–1736) I 24
Clark, J.L. (1822–1898) III 40
Clark, J.W. (1833–1910) III 40
Clark, Sir W.E. Le Gros (1895–1971) IV 21
Clark, W.G. (1821–1878) III 40
Clark, Sir W.H. (1876–1952) IV 21
Clarke, Adam (1762?–1832) II 44
Clarke, Alured (1696–1742) I 24
Clarke, Sir Alured (1745?–1832) II 44
Clarke, Sir Andrew (1824–1902) III 40
Clarke, Sir Charles (d1750) I 24
Clarke, C.C. (1787–1877) II 44
Clarke, Sir C.M., Bart (1782–1857) II 44
Clarke, Sir C.P. (1846–1911) III 40
Clarke, E.D. (1769–1822) II 44
Clarke, Sir E.G. (1841–1931) III 40
Clarke, Sir Fred (1880–1952) IV 21
Clarke, George (1661–1736) I 24
Clarke, John (1582–1653) I 24
Clarke, John (1761–1815) II 44
Clarke, J.S. (1765?–1834) II 44
Clarke, L.C.G. (1881–1960) IV 21

Clarke, Mary Anne (1776–1852) II 44
Clarke, Mary Victoria Cowden (1809–1898) III 40
Clarke, Maude Violet (1892–1935) IV 21
Clarke, Matthew (1664–1726) I 24
Clarke, Samuel (1599–1683) I 24
Clarke, Samuel (1625–1669) I 24
Clarke, Samuel (1626–1701) I 24
Clarke, Samuel (1675–1729) I 24
Clarke, Sir T.E. (1871–1962) IV 21
Clarkson, David (1622–1686) I 24
Clarkson, Thomas (1760–1846) I 24
Clater, Francis (1756–1823) II 44
Claughton, P.C. (1814–1884) III 40
Claughton, T.L. (1808–1892) III 40
Clausen, Sir George (1852–1944) III 40
Clauson, Baron (1870–1946) IV 21
Clavel, John (1603–1642) I 25
Clavering, Robert (1671–1747) I 25
Clay, Frederick (1839–1889) III 40–41
Clay, Sir Henry (1883–1954) IV 21
Clay, Sir William, Bart (1791–1869) II 44
Clayden, P.W. (1827–1902) III 41
Claypole, Elizabeth (1629–1658) I 25
Claypole, John (d1688) I 25
Clayton, Sir G.F. (1875–1929) IV 21
Clayton, John (1754–1843) II 44
Clayton, John (1780–1865) II 44
Clayton, John (1843–1888) III 41
Clayton, P.T.B. (1885–1972) IV 21
Clayton, Sir Robert (1629–1707) I 25
Cleasby, Sir Anthony (1804–1879) III 41
Cleaver, Euseby (1746–1819) II 44
Cleaver, William (1742–1815) II 44
Clegg, Samuel (1781–1861) II 44–45
Cleghorn, George (1716–1789) II 45
Clein, Francis (1590?–1658) I 25
Clement, Gregory (d1660) I 25
Clement, W.I. (d1852) II 45
Clementi, Sir Cecil (1875–1947) IV 21
Clench, Sir John (d1607) I 25
Clennell, Luke (1781–1840) II 45
Clérisseau, C.L. (1721–1820) II 45
Clerk, Sir Dugald (1854–1932) III 41
Clerk, Sir George (1787–1867) II 45
Clerk, Sir G.R. (1874–1951) IV 21
Clerk, Sir John, 2nd Bart (1676–1755) I 25
Clerk, John (1728–1812) II 45
Clerk, Josiah (1639–1714) I 25
Clerk-Maxwell, James (1831–1879) III 41
Clerke, Charles (1741–1779) II 45
Clerke, Henry (d1687) I 25
Clerke, T.H.S. (1792–1849) II 45
Cleveland, 1st Duke of (1662–1730) I 25
Cleveland, 1st Earl of (1591–1667) I 25
Cleveland, 1st Duke of (1766–1842) II 45
Cleveland, Duchess of (1640–1709) I 25
Cleveland, John (1613–1658) I 25
Cleveley, Robert (1747–1809) II 45
Clifford, Sir A.W.J., Bart (1788–1877) II 45
Clifford, Sir E.G.A. (1900–1964) IV 21
Clifford, Sir H.H. (1826–1883) III 41
Clifford, John (1836–1923) III 41
Clifford, Martin (d1677) I 25
Clifford, W.K. (1845–1879) III 41
Clifford of Chudleigh, 1st Baron (1630–1673) I 25
Clifford of Chudleigh, 7th Baron (1790–1858) I 25
Clift, William (1775–1849) II 45
Cline, Henry (1750–1827) II 45
Clint, Alfred (1807–1883) III 41
Clint, George (1770–1854) II 45
Clinton, Sir Henry (1738?–1795) II 45
Clinton, Sir Henry (1771–1829) II 45
Clitherow, Sir Christopher (d1641) I 25
Clive, 1st Baron (1725–1774) II 45
Clive, Catherine (1711–1785) II 45
Clive, Sir R.H. (1887–1948) IV 21
Clobery, R.G. (1719–1800) II 45
Clodd, Edward (1840–1930) III 41
Clonmell, 1st Earl of (1739–1798) II 45
Clonmore, 1st Baron (d1786) II 45
Close, Sir Barry (1756–1813) II 45
Close, Francis (1797–1882) II 45–46
Clough, A.H. (1819–1961) III 41
Clough, Anne Jemima (1820–1892) III 41
Clough, Richard (d1570) I 25
Cloutt, Thomas (1781?–1846) II 46
Clowes, Butler (d1782) II 46
Clowes, John (1743–1831) II 46
Clowes, William (1780–1851) II 46
Clutterbuck, Henry (1767–1856) II 46
Clutterbuck, Robert (1772–1831) II 46
Clutton-Brock, Arthur (1868–1924) IV 21
Clyde, Baron (1792–1836) II 46
Clyde, Lord (1863–1944) IV 21
Clydesmuir, 1st Baron (1894–1954) IV 21
Clynes, J.R. (1869–1949) IV 21
Coates, Eric (1886–1957) IV 22

Coates, Robert (1772–1848) II 46
Coates, W.W. (1895–1958) IV 22
Cobb, James (1756–1818) II 46
Cobbe, Charles (1687–1765) I 25
Cobbett, William (1763–1835) II 46
Cobbin, Ingram (1777–1851) II 46
Cobbold, Elizabeth (1767–1824) II 46
Cobden, Richard (1804–1865) III 41
Cobden-Sanderson, T.J. (1840–1922) III 41
Cobham, 1st Viscount (1675–1749) I 25
Cobham, Sir Alan (1894–1973) IV 22
Cobham, Thomas (1786–1842) II 46
Coburn, A.L. (1882–1966) IV 22
Cochran, Sir C.B. (1872–1951) IV 22
Cochrane, Sir A.F.I. (1758–1832) II 46
Cochrane, J.D. (1780–1825) II 46
Cochrane, Sir T.J. (1789–1872) II 46
Cockburn, Lord (1779–1854) II 46
Cockburn, Archibald (fl 1722) I 25
Cockburn, Sir A.J.E. (1802–1880) III 41–42
Cockburn, Catharine (1679–1749) I 25
Cockburn, Sir George (1772–1853) II 46
Cockburn, Sir James, Bart (1771–1852) II 46
Cockburn, Sir William (1768–1835) II 46
Cockcroft, Sir J.D. (1897–1967) IV 22
Cocker, Edward (1631–1675) I 25
Cockerell, C.R. (1788–1863) II 46
Cockerell, D.B. (1870–1945) IV 22
Cockerell, Sir S.C. (1867–1962) IV 22
Cockerell, S.P. (1754–1827) II 46–47
Cockerill, William (1759–1832) II 47
Cockin, F.A. (1888–1969) IV 22
Cockings, George (d1802) II 47
Codington, Christopher (1668–1710) I 25
Codrington, Sir Edward (1770–1851) II 47
Codrington, Sir H.J. (1808–1877) III 42
Codrington, Sir W.J. (1804–1884) III 42
Coffin, Sir Isaac, Bart (1759–1839) II 47
Cogan, Eliezer (1762–1855) II 47
Cogan, Thomas (1736–1818) II 47
Cogan, William (d1774) I 25–26
Cohen, Lord (1888–1973) IV 22
Cohen, Harriet (d1967) IV 22
Cohen, Sir R.W. (1877–1952) IV 22
Cokayne, Sir Aston (1608–1684) I 26
Coke, D.P. (1745–1825) II 47
Coke, Sir Edward (1552–1634) I 26
Coke, George (d1646) I 26
Coke, Sir John (1563–1644) I 26
Coke, Thomas (1747–1814) II 47
Coker, E.G. (1869–1946) IV 22
Colby, T.F. (1784–1852) II 47
Colchester, 1st Baron (1757–1829) II 47
Colden, Cadwallader (1688–1776) I 26
Cole, Abdiah (1610?–1670?) I 26
Cole, Sir Christopher (1770–1837) II 47
Cole, George (1810–1883) III 42
Cole, G.D.H. (1889–1959) IV 22
Cole, Sir G.L. (1772–1842) II 47
Cole, G.V. (1833–1893) III 42
Cole, Sir Henry (1808–1882) III 42
Cole, Dame Margaret Isabel (1893–1980) IV 22
Cole, Sir Ralph, 2nd Bart (1625?–1704) I 26
Cole, William (1635–1716) I 26
Cole, William (1714–1782) II 47
Colebrooke, H.T. (1765–1837) II 47
Colenso, J.W. (1814–1883) III 42
Colepepper, William (d1726) I 26
Coleraine, 2nd Baron (1636–1708) I 26
Coleraine, 3rd Baron (1693–1749) I 26
Coleraine, 4th Baron (1751?–1824) II 47
Coleridge, 1st Baron (1820–1894) III 42
Coleridge, 2nd Baron (1851–1927) III 42
Coleridge, Derwent (1800–1883) III 42
Coleridge, Sir J.T. (1790–1876) II 47
Coleridge, S.T. (1772–1834) II 47
Coleridge, Sara (1802–1852) III 42
Coleridge, S.W.B. (1854–1936) III 42
Coleridge, W.H. (1789–1849) II 47
Coleridge-Taylor, Samuel (1875–1912) IV 22
Coles, C.P. (1819–1870) III 42
Colet, John (1467?–1519) I 26
Coley, Henry (1633–1695?) I 26
Collard, F.W. (1772–1860) II 47
Collard, W.F. (1776–1866) II 47
Colledge, T.R. (1796–1879) II 47
College, Stephen (1635?–1681) I 26
Colles, Abraham (1773–1843) II 47
Colles, H.C. (1879–1943) IV 22
Colley, Sir G.P. (1835–1881) III 42
Collier, Jeremy (1650–1726) I 26
Collier, John (1708–1786) II 47
Collier, John (1850–1934) III 42
Collier, J.P. (1789–1883) II 47
Colling, Charles (1751–1836) II 47
Collinges, John (1623–1690) I 26
Collings, Jesse (1831–1920) III 42

Collings, Samuel (fl 1780–1790?) II 48
Collingwood, Baron (1748–1810) II 48
Collingwood, George (d 1716) I 26
Collingwood, R.G. (1889–1943) IV 22
Collins, Baron (1842–1911) III 42
Collins, C.A. (1828–1873) III 42
Collins, David (1756–1810) II 48
Collins, John (1743–1808) I 26
Collins, Josephine (1887–1958) IV 22
Collins, Michael (1890–1922) IV 22
Collins, Richard (1755–1831) II 48
Collins, Samuel (1576–1651) I 26
Collins, Samuel (1618–1710) I 26
Collins, Thomas (1775–1806) II 48
Collins, William (1721–1759) II 48
Collins, William (1788–1847) II 48
Collins, W.W. (1824–1889) III 48–49
Collinson, Peter (1694–1768) I 26
Collinson, Sir Richard (1811–1883) III 43
Collyer, W.B. (1782–1854) II 48
Colman, George (1732–1794) II 48
Colman, George (1762–1836) II 48
Colman, Walter (d 1645) I 26
Colnaghi, D.P. (1790–1879) II 48
Colnaghi, M.H. (1821–1908) III 43
Colnaghi, Paul (1751–1833) II 48
Colomb, Sir J.C.R. (1838–1909) III 43
Colonsay and Oronsay, Baron (1793–1874) II 48
Colpoys, Sir John (1742?–1821) II 48
Colquhoun, A.C. (d 1820) II 48
Colquhoun, Janet, Lady (1781–1846) II 48
Colquhoun, John (1748–1827) II 48
Colquhoun, Patrick (1745–1820) II 48
Colson, John (1680–1760) I 26
Colson, Lancelot (fl 1668) I 26
Colston, Edward (1636–1721) I 26
Colston, William (1762–1836) II 48
Colum, Padraic (1881–1972) IV 22
Colville, Sir Charles (1770–1843) II 48
Colville, Sir S.C.J. (1861–1939) IV 22
Colvin, Sir Sidney (1845–1927) III 43
Colwall, Daniel (d 1690) I 26
Combe, Andrew (1797–1847) II 48
Combe, Charles (1743–1817) II 48
Combe, George (1788–1858) II 48
Combe, Taylor (1774–1826) II 48
Combe, Thomas (1797–1872) II 48–49
Combe, William (1741–1823) II 49
Comber, Thomas (1575–1654) I 26
Comber, Thomas (1645–1699) I 26
Combermere, Sir S.C. (1773–1865) II 49
Comerford, John (1762?–1832?) II 49
Commerell, Sir J.E. (1829–1901) III 43
Common, A.A. (1841–1903) III 43
Comper, Sir J.N. (1864–1960) IV 22
Compton, Lord A.F. (1825–1906) III 43
Compton, Henry (1632–1713) I 26
Compton, Sir H.A.D. (1770–1846) II 49
Compton, H.C.M. (801805–1877) III 43
Compton, Sir William (1625–1663) I 26
Compton-Burnett, Dame Ivy (1892–1969) IV 22–23
Comyns, Sir John (d 1740) I 26
Conant, John (1608–1694) I 26
Conder, Charles (1868–1909) IV 23
Conder, John (1714–1781) II 49
Conder, Josiah (1789–1855) II 49
Conduitt, John (1688–1737) I 26
Congreve, William (1670–1729) I 26
Congreve, Sir William, Bart (1772–1828) II 49
Congreve, W.N. (1862–1927) IV 23
Coningham, Sir Arthur (1895–1948) IV 23
Coningsby, Earl of (1656?–1729) I 27
Coningsby, Sir Thomas (1551–1625) I 27
Conington, John (1825–1869) III 43
Connard, Philip (1875–1958) IV 23
Connaught, Arthur, Prince of (1883–1938) IV 23
Connaught, Princess Arthur of (1891–1959) IV 23
Connaught and Strathearn, 1st Duke of (1850–1942) III 43
Connemara, 1st Baron (1827–1902) III 43
Connor, Charles (d 1826) I 49
Conny, Robert (1645?–1723) I 27
Conolly, Arthur (1807–1842) III 43
Conolly, John (1794–1866) II 49
Conolly, Thomas (1738–1803) II 49
Conolly, William (1662–1729) I 27
Conquest, G.A. (1837–1901) III 43
Conquest, J.T. (1789–1866) II 49
Conrad, Joseph (1857–1924) III 43–4
Conroy, Sir John, Bart (1786–1854) II 49
Const, Francis (1751–1839) II 49
Constable, Archibald (1774–1827) II 49
Constable, John (1776–1837) II 49
Constable, Thomas (1812–1881) III 44
Constable, W.G. (1887–1976) IV 23
Conway, H.S. (1721–1795) II 49
Conway, R.S. (1864–1933) IV 23
Conway, W.A. (1789–1828) II 49
Conway of Allington, Baron (1856–1937) III 44

Conybeare, John (1692–1755) I 27
Conybeare, J.J. (1779–1824) II 49
Conybeare, W.D. (1787–1857) II 49
Coode, Sir John (1816–1892) III 44
Cook, A.B. (1868–1952) IV 23
Cook, A.J. (1883–1931) IV 23
Cook, Eliza (1818–1889) III 44
Cook, Sir E.T. (1857–1919) III 44
Cook, Sir Francis, 1st Bart (1817–1901) III 44
Cook, James (1728–1779) II 49–50
Cook, John (d 1660) I 27
Cook, Sir Joseph (1860–1947) IV 23
Cook, J.M. (1834–1899) III 44
Cook, Sir J.W. (1900–1975) IV 23
Cook, Samuel (1806–1859) III 44
Cook, S.A. (1873–1949) IV 23
Cook, Thomas (1808–1892) III 44
Cook, William (d 1824) II 50
Cooke, Sir Anthony (1504–1576) I 27
Cooke, Benjamin (1734–1793) II 50
Cooke, Edward (1755–1820) II 50
Cooke, E.W. (1811–1880) III 44
Cooke, Sir George (1768–1837) II 50
Cooke, G.A. (1865–1939) IV 23
Cooke, G.F. (1756–1811) II 50
Cooke, G.W. (1814–1865) III 44
Cooke, Henry (1788–1868) II 50
Cooke, John (1765–1805) II 50
Cooke, Thomas (1722–1783) II 50
Cooke, T.P. (1786–1864) II 50
Cooke, T.S. (1782–1848) II 50
Cooke, William (1711–1797) II 50
Cooke, Sir W.F. (1806–1879) III 44
Cookworthy, William (1705–1780) II 50
Cooling, Richard (d 1697) I 27
Cooper, Abraham (1787–1868) II 50
Cooper, Sir Alfred (1838–1908) III 44
Cooper, C.H. (1808–1866) II 50
Cooper, Sir Daniel, 1st Bart (1821–1902) III 44
Cooper, Sir D'Arcy, Bart (1882–1941) IV 23
Cooper, Dame Gladys (1888–1971) IV 23
Cooper, Sir Grey (d 1801) II 50
Cooper, John (1790–1870) II 50
Cooper, Richard (d 1764) II 50
Cooper, Richard (c 1740–c 1814) II 50
Cooper, Samuel (1609–1672) I 27
Cooper, Samuel (1781–1848) II 50
Cooper, Thomas (1805–1892) III 44
Cooper, Sir T.E. (1874–1942) IV 23
Cooper, T.S. (1803–1902) III 44
Cooper of Culross, Baron (1892–1955) IV 23
Coote, Sir Eyre (1762–1823) II 50
Cope, Sir A.S. (1857–1940) III 44
Cope, C.W. (1811–1890) III 44
Cope, Richard (1776–1856) II 50
Cope, Sir V.Z. (1881–1974) IV 23
Copeland, Ralph (1837–1905) III 44
Copeland, Thomas (1781–1855) II 50
Copeland, W.T. (1797–1868) II 50
Copland, James (1791–1870) II 50
Copleston, Edward (1776–1849) II 50
Copley, Sir Godfrey, 2nd Bart (d 1709) I 27
Copley, J.S. (1737–1815) II 50–51
Coppard, A.E. (1878–1957) IV 23
Coppock, Sir Richard (1885–1971) IV 23
Coram, Thomas (1668?–1751) I 27
Corbet, Miles (d 1662) I 27
Corbet, M.R. (1850–1902) III 44
Corbet, Richard (1582–1635) I 27
Corbet, William (1779–1842) II 51
Corbett, William (d 1748) I 27
Corbett-Ashby, Dame Margery (b 1882) IV 23
Corbould, Henry (1787–1844) II 51
Corbould, Richard (1757–1831) II 51
Cordell, Sir William (d 1580) I 27
Corder, William (1804–1828) III 44
Cordiner, James (1775–1836) II 51
Corehouse, Lord (d 1850) II 51
Cork, 1st Earl of (1566–1643) I 27
Cork and Orrery, 5th Earl of (1706/7–1762) II 51
Cork and Orrery, 12th Earl of (1873–1967) IV 23–24
Cork and Orrery, Countess of (1746–1840) II 51
Cornbury, Viscount (1710–1753) II 51
Cornelius, John (1557–1594) I 27
Cornewall, F.H.W. (1754–1831) II 51
Corn(e)wall, James (1699–1744) I 27
Cornford, F.M. (1874–1943) IV 24
Cornish, Henry (d 1685) I 27
Cornwall, C.W. (1735–1789) II 51
Cornwallis, 1st Marquess (1738–1805) II 51
Cornwallis, 2nd Marquess (1774–1823) II 51
Cornwallis, 4th Earl of (1742–1824) II 51
Cornwallis, Sir Charles (d 1629) I 27
Cornwallis, Frederick (1713–1783) II 51
Cornwallis, Sir Kinahan (1883–1959) IV 24
Cornwallis, Sir Thomas (1519–1604) I 27
Cornwallis, Sir William (1744–1819) II 51

Corrie, Daniel (1777–1837) II 51
Corrie, G.E. (1793–1885) II 51
Corrigan, Sir D.J. (1802–1880) III 44 45
Corry, H.T.L. (1803–1873) III 45
Corry, Isaac (1755–1813) II 51
Cort, Henry (1740–1800) II 51
Cory, John (1828–1910) III 45
Coryate, Thomas (1577?–1617) I 27
Cosin, John (1594–1672) I 27
Costa, Sir M.A.A. (1810–1884) III 45
Costard, George (1710–1782) II 51
Coster, Howard (1885–1959) IV 24
Cosway, Maria (1759–1838) II 51–52
Cosway, Richard (1740–1821) II 52
Cotes, Francis (1726?–1770) II 52
Cotes, Samuel (1734–1818) II 52
Cotman, J.S. (1782–1842) II 52
Cottam, Thomas (1549–1582) I 27
Cottenham, 1st Earl of (1781–1851) II 52
Cotter, Patrick (1761?–1806) II 52
Cotterell, Sir C. (1612?–1702) I 27
Cotterell, Sir C.L. (1654–1710) I 27
Cottesloe, 1st Baron (1798–1890) II 52
Cottesloe, 3rd Baron (1862–1956) IV 24
Cottesloe, 4th Baron (b 1900) IV 24
Cottington, 1st Baron (1578–1652) I 27
Cottle, A.S. (1766–1800) II 52
Cotton, Charles (1630–1687) I 27
Cotton, Sir Charles, Bart (1753–1812) II 52
Cotton, G.E.L. (1813–1866) III 45
Cotton, Sir Henry (1821–1892) III 45
Cotton, Sir John, 3rd Bart (1621–1701) I 27
Cotton, Joseph (1745–1825) II 52
Cotton, Nathaniel (1705–1788) II 52
Cotton, Sir R.B., 1st Bart (1571–1631) I 27–28
Cotton, R.L. (1794–1880) II 52
Cotton, Sir St Vincent, Bart (1801–1863) III 45
Cotton, Sir S.J. (1792–1874) II 52
Cotton, William (1786–1866) II 52
Cotton, Sir Willoughby (1783–1860) II 52
Cotton, Sir W.J.R. (1822–1902) III 45
Couch, Sir Richard (1817–1905) III 45
Coulson, Walter (1794?–1860) II 52
Coulton, G.G. (1858–1947) III 45
Coupland, Sir Reginald (1884–1952) IV 24
Courayer, P.F. le (1681–1776) I 28
Courtauld, Samuel (1876–1947) IV 24
Courten, William (1342?–1396) I 28
Courtenay, John (1741–1816) II 52
Courtenay, T.P. (1782–1841) II 52
Courtenay, William (1342?–1396) I 28
Courtney, Dame Kathleen (1878–1974) IV 24
Courtney, W.L. (1850–1928) III 45
Courtney of Penwith, 1st Baron (1832–1918) III 45
Cousins, Samuel (1801–1887) III 45
Coutts, John (1699–1751) I 28
Coutts, Thomas (1735–1822) II 52
Covell, John (1638–1722) I 28
Coventry, 1st Baron (1578–1640) I 28
Coventry, Countess of (1733–1760) II 52–53
Coventry, Andrew (1764–1832) II 53
Coventry, Henry (1619–1686) I 28
Coventry, Sir John (d 1682) I 28
Coventry, Sir William (1628?–1686) I 28
Cowan, H.V. (1854–1918) III 45
Cowan, Sir W.H., Bart (1871–1956) IV 24
Cowans, Sir J.S. (1862–1921) IV 24
Coward, Sir Noel (1899–1973) IV 24
Coward, William (d 1738) I 28
Cowdray, 1st Viscount (1856–1927) III 45
Cowell, E.B. (1826–1903) III 45
Cowell, S.H. (1820–1864) III 45
Cowen, Sir Joseph (1800–1873) III 45
Cowen, Joseph (1831–1900) III 45
Cowie, B.M. (1816–1900) III 45
Cowie, W.G. (1831–1902) III 45
Cowley, 1st Baron (1773–1847) II 53
Cowley, 1st Earl (1804–1884) III 46
Cowley, Abraham (1618–1667) I 28
Cowley, Sir A.E. (1861–1931) IV 24
Cowley, Hannah (1743–1809) II 53
Cowper, 1st Earl of (1665?–1723) I 28
Cowper, 7th Earl (1834–1905) III 46
Cowper, 1st Countess of (1685–1724) I 28
Cowper, C.S. (1816–1879) III 46
Cowper, F.C. (1877–1958) IV 24
Cowper, Henry (1758–1840) II 53
Cowper, Spencer (1669–1728) I 28
Cowper, William (1666–1709) I 28
Cowper, William (1731–1800) II 53
Cox, Alfred (1866–1954) IV 24
Cox, David (1783–1859) II 53
Cox, E.A. (1876–1955) IV 24
Cox, E.W. (1809–1879) III 46
Cox, F.A. (1783–1853) II 53
Cox, Harold (1859–1936) III 46

Cox, Richard (1500–1581) I 28
Cox, Sir P.Z. (1864–1937) IV 24
Cox, Sir Richard (1650–1733) I 28
Coxe, H.O. (1811–1881) III 46
Coxe, Peter (d1844) II 53
Coxe, William (1747–1828) II 53
Coxwell, H.T. (1819–1900) III 46
Cozens-Hardy, 1st Baron (1838–1920) III 46
Crab, Roger (1621?–1680) I 28
Crabbe, George (1754–1832) II 53
Cracherode, C.M. (1730–1799) II 53
Crackenthorpe, Richard (1567–1624) I 28
Craddock, Sir R.H. (1864–1937) IV 24
Cradock, Sir C.G.F. (1862–1914) IV 24
Cradock, Joseph (1742–1826) II 53
Cradock, Samuel (1621?–1706) I 28
Cradock, Zachary (1633–1695) I 28
Craggs, James (1657–1721) I 28
Craggs, James (1686–1721) I 28
Craig, Lord (1745–1813) II 53
Craig, E.G. (1872–1966) IV 24
Craig, James (1740–1795) II 53
Craig, John (d1655) I 28
Craig, Sir John (1874–1957) IV 24
Craig, Sir J.G. (1765–1850) II 53
Craig, Sir J.H. (1748–1812) II 53
Craig, Robert (1730–1823) II 53
Craig, Sir Thomas (1538–1608) I 28
Craig, Sir W.G. (1797–1878) II 53
Craig, W.M. (fl 1788–1828) II 53
Craigavon, 1st Viscount (1871–1940) IV 24
Craighall, Lord (1605?–1654) I 28
Craigie, Pearl (1867–1906) IV 24
Craigie, Sir W.A. (1867–1957) IV 24–25
Craigmyle, 1st Baron (1850–1937) III 46
Craik, Dinah Maria (1826–1887) III 46
Craik, Sir Henry, 1st Bart (1846–1927) III 46
Cramer, Franz (1772–1848) II 53
Cramer, J.A. (1793–1848) II 53
Cramer, J.B. (1771–1858) II 53
Cramer, Wilhelm (1745?–1799) II 53
Crampton, Sir Philip, Bart (1777–1858) II 53
Cranbrook, 1st Earl of (1814–1906) III 46
Cranch, John (1751–1821) II 53
Crane, Sir Francis (d1636) I 28
Crane, Walter (1845–1915) III 46
Cranley, Thomas (1337?–1417) I 28
Cranmer, Thomas (1489–1556) I 28
Cranstoun, Helen d'Arcy (1765–1838) II 54
Cranstoun, W.H. (1707–1752) II 54
Cranworth, Baron (1790–1868) II 54
Craster, Sir H.H.E. (1879–1959) IV 25
Craven, 1st Earl of (1606–1697) I 28
Craven, Countess of (1785?–1860) II 54
Craven, H.T. (1818–1905) III 46
Craven, K.R. (1779–1851) II 54
Craven of Ryton, Baron (1610–1648) I 28
Crawford, 17th Earl of (1596–1678) I 28
Crawford, 20th Earl of (1702–1749) II 54
Crawford, 25th Earl of (1812–1880) III 46
Crawford, 26th Earl of (1847–1913) III 46
Crawford, W.S. (1781–1861) II 54
Crawford and Balcarres, 27th Earl of (1871–1940) IV 25
Crawford and Balcarres, 28th Earl of (1900–1975) IV 25
Crawfurd, John (1783–1868) II 54
Crealock, H.H. (1831–1891) III 46
Creasy Sir E.S. (1812–1878) III 46
Creasy, Sir G.E. (1895–1972) IV 25
Creech, Thomas (1659–1700) I 29
Creech, William (1745–1815) II 54
Creed, J.M. (1889–1940) IV 25
Creed, Sir T.P. (1879–1969) IV 25
Creedy, Sir H.J. (1878–1973) IV 25
Cregan, Martin (1788–1870) II 54
Creighton, Mandell (1843–1901) III 46
Creighton, Robert (1593–1672) I 29
Cremer, Sir W.R. (1838–1908) III 47
Cresswell, Madam (fl 1670–1684) I 29
Creswick, Thomas (1811–1869) III 47
Creswick, William (1813–1888) III 47
Crew of Stene, 1st Baron (1598–1679) I 29
Crew of Stene, 3rd Baron (1633–1721) I 29
Crewdson, Isaac (1780–1844) II 54
Crewe, 1st Baron (1742–1829) II 54
Crewe, 1st Marquess of (1858–1945) III 47
Crewe, Lady (d1818) II 54
Cribb, Thomas (1781–1848) II 54
Crichton, James (1560–1583?) I 29
Cripps, Sir Stafford (1889–1952) IV 25
Crisp(e), Sir Nicholas (1599?–1666) I 29
Crisp(e), Tobias (1600–1643) I 29
Cristall, Joshua (1767–1847) II 54
Crocker, Sir J.T. (1896–1963) IV 25
Crockford, William (1775–1844) II 54
Croft, 1st Baron (1881–1947) IV 25

Croft, George (1747–1809) II 54
Croft, Herbert (1603–1691) I 29
Croft, Sir Herbert, 5th Bart (1751–1816) II 54
Croft, Sir James (d1590) I 29
Croft, John (1833–1905) III 47
Croft, Sir Richard, 6th Bart (1762–1818) II 54
Croft, William (1677?–1727) I 29
Crofts, Ernest (1847–1911) III 47
Croke, Sir George (1560–1642) I 29
Croke, Sir John (1553–1620) I 29
Croker, J.W. (1780–1857) II 54
Croker, Marianne (d1854) II 54
Croker, T.C. (1798–1854) II 54
Croly, George (1780–1860) II 54
Cromartie, 1st Earl of (1630–1714) I 29
Crome, John (1768–1821) II 54
Crome, J.B. (1794–1842) II 54
Cromek, R.H. (1771–1812) II 54
Cromer, 1st Earl of (1841–1917) III 47
Cromer, 2nd Earl of (1877–1953) IV 25
Crompton, Hugh (fl 1657) I 29
Crompton, R.E.B. (1845–1940) III 47
Crompton, Samuel (1753–1827) II 55
Cromwell, Henry (1628–1674) I 29
Cromwell, Oliver (1599–1658) I 29
Cromwell, Richard (1626–1712) I 29
Crookes, Sir William (1832–1919) III 47
Crooks, William (1852–1921) III 47
Crookshank, 1st Viscount (1893–1961) IV 25
Croone, William (1633–1684) I 29
Crosbie, Andrew (1733–1785) II 55
Crosby, Brass (1725–1793) II 55
Crosby, Sir John (d1475) I 29
Cross, 1st Viscount (1823–1914) III 47
Cross, Mary Ann (1819–1880) III 47
Cross, Sir R.H., 1st Baron (1896–1968) IV 25
Crosse, J.G. (1790–1850) II 55
Crosse, Richard (1742–1810) II 55
Crossley, Sir Francis (1817–1872) III 47
Crossley, James (1800–1883) III 47
Crossrig, Lord (1643–1707) I 29
Crotch, William (1775–1847) II 55
Crouch, Anna Maria (1763–1805) II 55
Crow, Sir A.D. (1894–1965) IV 25
Crowdy, Dame Rachel Eleanor (1884–1964) IV 25
Crowe, Eyre (1824–1910) III 48
Crowe, E.E. (1799–1868) II 55
Crowe, Sir E.T.F. (1877–1960) IV 25
Crowe, Sir J.A. (1825–1896) III 48
Crowe, Kate Josephine (1842–1917) III 48
Crowe, Mitford (d1719) I 29
Crowe, William (1745–1829) II 55
Crowther, Jonathan (1760–1824) II 55
Crowther, Jonathan (1794–1856) II 55
Crozier, F.R.M. (1796?–1848) II 55
Cruden, Alexander (1701–1770) II 55
Cruden, William (1725–1785) II 55
Cruikshank, George (1792–1878) II 55
Cruikshank, Robert (1899–1974) IV 25
Cruikshank, R.J. (1898–1956) IV 25
Cruikshank, W.C. (1745–1800) II 55
Crum, W.E. (1865–1944) IV 25
Crusius, Lewis (1701–1775) II 55
Cruso, Timothy (1656?–1697) I 29
Cruttwell, C.R.M.F. (1887–1941) IV 25
Cubbon, Sir Mark (1784–1861) II 55
Cubitt, Joseph (1811–1872) III 48
Cubitt, Lewis (b1799) II 55
Cubitt, Thomas (1788–1855) II 55
Cubitt, Sir William (1785–1861) II 55
Cubitt, William (1791–1863) III 48
Cubitt, W.G. (1835–1903) III 48
Cudworth, Ralph (1617–1688) I 29
Cuff, J.D. (1780–1853) II 55
Cuitt, George (1743–1818) II 55
Cuitt, George (1779–1854) II 55
Culbertson, Robert (1765–1823) II 55
Cullen, Lord (1658–1726) I 29
Cullen, Lord (d1810) II 55
Cullen, Paul (1803–1878) III 48
Cullen, William (1710–1790) II 55–56
Cullen of Ashbourne, 1st Baron (1864–1932) IV 25
Cullingworth, C.J. (1841–1908) III 48
Cullis, Winifred Clara (1875–1956) IV 25
Cullum, Sir John, 6th Bart (1733–1785) II 56
Cullum, Sir Thomas, Bart (1587?–1664) I 29
Cullum, Sir T.G., 7th Bart (1741–1831) II 56
Culpeper, Nicholas (1616–1654) I 30
Cumberland, 3rd Earl of (1558–1605) I 30
Cumberland, 5th Earl of (1591–1643) I 30
Cumberland, Duke of (1721–1765) II 56
Cumberland, King of Hanover and Duke of (1771–1851) II 56
Cumberland, Countess of (1560?–1616) I 30
Cumberland, George (1754?–1847) II 56
Cumberland, Richard (1631–1718) I 30
Cumberland, Richard (1732–1811) II 56

Cumberland and Strathearn, Duke of (1745–1790) II 56
Cuming, Hugh (1791–1865) II 56
Cuming, William (1769–1852) II 56
Cumming, Alexander (1733–1814) II 56
Cumming, James (d1827) II 56
Cumming, John (1807–1881) III 48
Cumming, Thomas (d1774) II 56
Cundall, Charles (1890–1971) IV 25
Cundell, Edric (1893–1961) IV 25
Cuningham, William (fl 1586) I 30
Cunliffe-Owen, Sir F.P. (1828–1894) III 48
Cunningham, Allan (1784–1842) II 56
Cunningham, Allan (1791–1839) II 56
Cunningham, Sir Charles (1755–1834) II 56
Cunningham, D.J. (1850–1909) III 48
Cunningham, Francis (1820–1875) III 48
Cunningham, John (1729–1773) II 56
Cunningham, John (1819–1893) III 48
Cunningham, Sir J.H.D. (1885–1962) IV 25
Cunningham, William (1805–1861) III 48
Cunningham, William (1849–1919) III 48
Cunningham of Hyndhope, 1st Viscount (1883–1963) IV 25
Cunnington, William (1754–1810) II 56–57
Cunynghame, Sir A.A.T. (1812–1884) III 48
Cureton, Sir Charles (1826–1891) III 48
Cureton, C.R. (1789–1848) II 57
Cureton, William (1808–1864) III 48
Curle, Walter (1575–1647) I 30
Curran, J.P. (1750–1817) II 57
Currie, Sir A.W. (1875–1933) IV 26
Currie, Sir Donald (1825–1909) III 48
Currie, James (1756–1805) II 57
Currie, Sir James (1868–1937) IV 26
Currie, Sir W.C. (1884–1961) IV 26
Curtis, John (1791–1862) II 57
Curtis, L.G. (1872–1955) IV 26
Curtis, Dame Myra (1886–1971) IV 26
Curtis, Sir Roger (1746–1816) II 57
Curtis, William (1746–1799) II 57
Curtis, Sir William, Bart (1752–1829) II 57
Curwen, John (1816–1880) III 48
Curzon, C.E. (1878–1954) IV 26
Curzon of Kedleston, Marquess (1859–1925) III 48–49
Cushny, A.R. (1866–1926) IV 26
Cust, H.J.C. (1861–1917) IV 26
Cust, Sir John, 3rd Bart (1718–1770) II 57
Cust, Sir L.H. (1859–1929) III 49
Cust, R.N. (1821–1909) III 49
Cutler, Sir John (1608?–1693) I 30
Cutler, Kate (1870–1955) IV 26
Cutts, Baron (1661–1707) I 30

D'Abernon, Viscount (1857–1941) III 51
Dacre, 9th Baron (1517?–1541) I 31
Dacre, 10th Baron (1539–1594) I 31
Dacres, Sir S.C. (1805–1884) III 51
Dadd, Richard (1817–1886) III 51
Dahl, Michael (1659?–1743) I 31
Dain, Sir H.G. (1870–1966) IV 27
Dalbiac, Sir J.C. (1776–1847) II 58
Dalby, Isaac (1744–1824) II 58
Dale, David (1739–1806) II 58
Dale, Sir H.H. (1875–1968) IV 27
Dale, R.W. (1829–1895) III 51
Dale, Samuel (1659?–1739) I 31
Dale, Thomas (1729–1816) II 58
Dale, Thomas (1797–1870) II 58
Dale, T.P. (1821–1892) III 51
Dalhousie, 10th Earl and 1st Marquess of (1812–1860) III 51
Dalhousie, 11th Earl of (1801–1874) III 51
Dalhousie, 13th Earl of (1847–1887) III 51
Dallas, A.R.C. (1791–1869) II 58
Dallas, Sir Robert (1756–1824) II 58
Dallas, Sir Thomas (d1839) II 58
Dalley, W.B. (1831–1888) III 51
Dalling and Bulwer, Baron (1801–1872) III 51
Dallinger, W.H. (1842–1909) III 51
Dalrymple, Alexander (1737–1808) II 58
Dalrymple, Sir Hew, Bart (1652–1737) I 31
Dalrymple, Sir H.W., Bart (1750–1830) II 58
Dalrymple, Sir John, 4th Bart (1726–1810) II 58
Dalrymple-Hamilton, Sir F.H.G. (1890–1974) IV 27
Dalton, 1st Baron (1887–1962) IV 27
Dalton, John (1766–1844) II 58
Dalton, Michael (d1648?) I 31
Dalton, O.M. (1866–1945) IV 27
Dalton, Richard (1715?–1791) II 58
Daly, Denis (1747–1791) II 58
Daly, Sir H.D. (1821–1895) III 51
Daly, Richard (d1813) II 58
Dalyell, Sir J.G., 6th Bart (1775–1851) II 58
Dalyell, Thomas (1599?–1685) I 31
Dalzel, Andrew (1742–1806) II 58
Dalzel, Robert (1662–1758) I 31
Dalziel, Edward (1817–1905) III 51
Dalziel, George (1815–1902) III 51
Damer, Anne Seymour (1749–1828) II 58

Dampier, Thomas (1748–1812) II 58
Dampier, William (1651–1715) I 31
Dampier, Sir W.C. (1867–1952) IV 27
Danby, Earl of (1573–1644) I 31
Danby, Francis (1793–1861) II 58
Danby, J.F. (1816–1875) III 51
Danby, William (1752–1833) II 58
Dance, George (1700–1768) II 59
Dance, George (1741–1825) II 59
Dance, Sir Nathaniel (1748–1827) II 59
Dance, William (1755–1840) II 59
Dance-Holland, Sir Nathaniel, 1st Bart (1735–1811)
Dancer, Daniel (1716–1794) II 59
Dane, Clemence (1888–1965) IV 27
Dane, Sir L.W. (1856–1946) IV 27
Daniel, C.H.O. (1836–1919) III 51–52
Daniel, George (1789–1864) II 59
Daniel, Samuel (1562–1619) I 31
Daniel, Sir William (d1610) I 31
Daniel, W.B. (1753?–1833) II 59
Daniell, E.T. (1804–1843) III 52
Daniell, J.F. (1790–1845) II 59
Daniell, Thomas (1749–1840) II 59
Daniell, William (1769–1837) II 59
Danvers, Sir John (1588?–1655) I 31
Darbishire, Dame Helen (1881–1961) IV 27
D'Arblay, Frances (1752–1840) II 59
Darby, George (d1790) II 59
Darby, J.N. (1800–1882) III 52
Darcie, Abraham (fl 1625) I 31
D'Arcy, C.F. (1859–1938) III 52
D'Arcy, M.C. (1888–1976) IV 27
Dare, Phyllis (1890–1975) IV 27
Dare, Zena (1887–1975) IV 27
Dargan, William (1799–1867) II 59
Darley, George (1795–1846) II 59
Darling, 1st Baron (1849–1936) III 52
Darling, Grace (1815–1842) III 52
Darly, Matthew (fl 1770) II 59
Darnley, Lord (1545–1567) I 31
Dart, John (d1730) I 31
Dartiquenave, Charles (1664–1737) I 31
Dartmouth, 1st Baron (1648–1691) I 31
Dartmouth, 1st Earl of (1672–1750) I 31
Dartmouth, 2nd Earl of (1731–1801) II 59
Dartmouth, 3rd Earl of (1755–1810) II 59
Darwin, Bernard (1876–1961) IV 27
Darwin, Sir C.G. (1887–1962) IV 27
Darwin, C.R. (1809–1882) III 52
Darwin, Erasmus (1731–1802) II 59
Darwin, Sir Francis (1848–1925) III 52
Darwin, Sir G.H. (1845–1912) III 52
Dashwood, Edmée Elizabeth Monica (1890–1943) IV 27
Daubeny, Charles (1745–1827) II 59
Daubeny, C.G.B. (1795–1867) II 59
Davenant, Sir Humphrey (1566–1645) I 31
Davenport, John (1597–1670) I 31
Davenport, Mary Ann (1765?–1843) II 59–60
Davey, Baron (1833–1907) IV 27
David, A.A. (1867–1950) IV 27
David, Sir T.W.E. (1858–1934) III 52
Davids, T.W.R. (1843–1922) III 52
Davidson, 1st Viscount (1889–1970) IV 27
Davidson, A.B. (1831–1902) III 52
Davidson, A.D. (1807–1872) III 52
Davidson, Charles (1824–1902) III 52
Davidson, John (d1797) II 60
Davidson, John (1797–1836) II 60
Davidson, John (1857–1909) III 52
Davidson, Sir J.H. (1876–1954) IV 27
Davidson, Samuel (1806–1898) III 52
Davidson, Thomas (1747–1827) II 60
Davidson of Lambeth, Baron (1848–1930) III 52–53
Davie, T.B. (1895–1955) IV 27
Davies, 1st Baron (1880–1944) IV 27
Davies, Christian (1667–1739) I 31
Davies, Clement (1884–1962) IV 27
Davies, Sir H.W. (1869–1941) IV 27
Davies, John (1565?–1618) I 32
Davies, John (1679–1732) I 32
Davies, J.L. (1826–1916) III 53
Davies, J.S. (fl 1841) II 60
Davies, Robert (1648–1728) I 32
Davies, R.R.H. (1866–1946) IV 27
Davies, (Sarah) Emily (1830–1921) III 53
Davies, Sneyd (1709–1769) II 60
Davies, Thomas (1712?–1785) II 60
Davies, Thomas (1837–1891) III 53
Davies, W.H. (1871–1940) IV 28
Davies, Sir W.L. (1887–1952) IV 28
Davis, C.E. (1827–1902) III 53
Davis, Sir Herbert (1891–1972) IV 28
Davis, H.W.B. (1833–1914) III 53
Davis, J.B. (1801–1881) III 53
Davis, Sir J.F., Bart (1795–1890) II 60
Davis, J.P. (1784–1862) II 60

Davis, Mary (fl 1663–1669) I 32
Davis, T.O. (1814–1845) III 53
Davis, William (1771–1807) II 60
Davison, Alexander (1750–1829) II 60
Davison, Maria Rebecca (1783–1858) II 60
Davison, Sir R.C. (1884–1958) IV 28
Davison, William (fl 1635–1660) I 32
Davitt, Michael (1846–1906) III 53
Davy, Sir Humphry, Bart (1778–1829) II 60
Davy, Martin (1763–1839) II 60
Davys, George (1780–1864) II 60
Dawber, Sir E.G. (1861–1938) IV 28
Dawe, George (1781–1829) II 60
Dawes, Richard (1793–1867) II 60
Dawes, Sir Willian, 3rd Bart (1671–1724) I 32
Dawkins, James (1722–1757) II 60
Dawkins, R. McG. (1871–1955) IV 28
Dawkins, Sir W.B. (1837–1929) III 53
Dawson, George (1821–1876) II 53
Dawson, G.G. (1874–1944) IV 28
Dawson, Henry (1811–1878) III 53
Dawson, John (1734–1820) II 60
Dawson, John (1827–1903) III 53
Dawson, Sir J.W. (1829–1899) III 53
Dawson, Matthew (1820–1898) III 53
Dawson, Nancy (1730?–1767) II 60
Dawson of Penn, 1st Viscount (1864–1945) IV 28
Day, Alexander (1773–1841) II 60
Day, John (1522–1584) I 32
Day, Sir J.C.F.S. (1826–1908) III 53
Day, L.F. (1845–1910) III 53
Day, Thomas (1748–1789) II 60
Day, William (1529–1596) I 32
Day, W.H. (1823–1908) III 53
Dayes, Edward (1763–1804) II 60
Deakin, Alfred (1856–1919) III 53
Deakin, Arthur (1890–1955) IV 28
Dealtry, Thomas (1796–1861) II 60
Dean, Basil (1888?–1978) IV 28
Dean, John (d1747) II 60
Deane, Sir Anthony (1638?–1721) I 32
Deane, Sir H.B. (1846–1919) III 53
Deane, Richard (1610–1653) I 32
Deane, Sir Thomas (1792–1871) II 60
Deane, Sir T.N. (1828–1899) III 53
Deane, W.W. (1825–1873) III 53
Deas, Lord (1804–1887) III 53
Dease, William (1752?–1798) II 60
De Beer, Sir G.R. (1899–1972) IV 28
De Begnis, Claudine (1800–1853) III 53
Debenham, Frank (1883–1965) IV 28
De Bunsen, Sir M.W.E., Bart (1852–1932) III 53
Deburgh, W.G. (1866–1943) IV 28
De Casalis, Jeanne (1898–1966) IV 28
De Chair, Sir D.R.S. (1864–1958) IV 28
De Coetlogon, C.E. (1746?–1820) II 60
De Dunstanville, Baron (1757–1835) II 60
Dee, John (1527–1608) I 32
Deeping, G.W. (1877–1950) IV 28
D'Egville, Sir Howard (1879–1965) IV 28
Defoe, Daniel (1661?–1731) I 32
De Gex, Sir J.P. (1809–1887) III 53
De Grey, 2nd Earl (1781–1859) II 61
De Havilland, Sir Geoffrey (1882–1965) IV 28
De Keyser, Sir Polydore (1832–1897) III 53
Dekker, Thomas (1570?–1641?) I 32
De la Beche, Sir H.T. (1796–1855) II 61
De la Mare, Walter (1873–1956) IV 28
Delamere, 1st Baron (1622–1684) I 32
DeLancey, Oliver (1749–1822) II 61
Delane, J.T. (1817–1879) III 54
Delane, Solomon (1727–1784?) II 61
Delany, Mary (1700–1788) II 61
Delany, Patrick (1685?–1768) I 32
De La Ramée, Marie Louise (1839–1908) III 54
De La Rue, Warren (1815–1889) III 54
Delatre, J.M. (1745–1840) II 61
Delaune, Gideon (1565?–1659?) I 32
Delavall, Sir Ralph (1645?–1707) I 32
De La Warr, 1st Baron (1519?–1595) I 32
De La Warr, 3rd Baron (1577–1618) I 32
De La Warr, 1st Earl (1693–1766) I 32
De La Warr, 2nd Earl (1729–1777) II 61
De La Warr, 5th Earl (1791–1869) II 61
De La Warr, 6th Earl (1815–1873) III 54
Delevingne, Sir Malcolm (1868–1950) IV 28
Delius, Frederick (1862–1934) IV 28–29
Deller, Sir Edwin (1883–1936) IV 29
De Lolme, J.L. (1740?–1807) II 61
Deloraine, 1st Earl of (1676–1730) I 32
Delpini, C.A. (d1828) II 61
De Luc, J.A. (1727–1817) II 61
Delvaux, Laurent (1695–1778) II 32
Demainbray, S.C.T. (1710–1782) II 61
De Morgan, Augustus (1806–1871) III 54
De Morgan, C.G. (1811–1876) III 54

De Morgan, W.F. (1839–1917) III 54
Dempsey, Sir M.C. (1896–1969) IV 29
Dempster, George (1732–1818) II 61
Denbigh, 1st Earl of (d1643) I 32
Denbigh, 2nd Earl of (d1674) I 32
Denham, Dixon (1786–1828) II 61
Denham, Sir J.S., Bart (1744–1839) II 61
Denham, Sir John (1615–1669) I 32
Denis, Sir Peter (d1778) II 61
Denison, Edward (1801–1854) III 54
Denison, Edward (1840–1870) III 54
Denison, G.A. (1806–1896) III 54
Denison, John (d1629) I 32
Denison, W.J. (1770–1849) II 61
Denman, 1st Baron (1779–1854) II 61
Denman, 2nd Baron (1805–1894) II 54
Denman, 3rd Baron (1874–1954) IV 29
Denman, George (1819–1896) III 54
Denman, Gertrude Mary, Lady (1884–1954) IV 29
Denman, Thomas (1733–1815) II 61
Denning, Baron (b1899) IV 29
Dennis, G.P. (1892–1963) IV 29
Dennis, John (1657–1734) I 32
Denniston, J.D. (1887–1949) IV 29
Dennistoun, James (1803–1855) III 54
Denny, Sir M.E., 2nd Bart (1886–1955) IV 29
Dent, E.J. (1876–1957) IV 29
Denville, A.A.H. (1876–1955) IV 29
D'Éon de Beaumont, Charles (1728–1810) II 61
De Quincey, Thomas (1785–1859) II 61–62
Derby, 3rd Earl of (1509–1572) I 32
Derby, 4th Earl of (1531–1593) I 32–33
Derby, 7th Earl of (1607–1651) I 33
Derby, 13th Earl of (1775–1851) II 62
Derby, 14th Earl of (1799–1869) II 62
Derby, 15th Earl of (1826–1893) III 54
Derby, 16th Earl of (1841–1908) III 54
Derby, 17th Earl of (1865–1948) IV 29
Derby, Countess of (1599–1664) I 32
Derby, Countess of (1759?–1829) II 62
Derham, William (1657–1735) I 33
Dering, Edward (1540?–1576) I 33
Dering, Sir Edward, 1st Bart (1598–1644) I 33
Dermody, Thomas (1775–1802) II 62
De Robeck, Sir J.M. (1862–1928) IV 28
Derrick, Samuel (1724–1769) II 62
Derrick, Thomas (1885–1954) IV 29
Derwentwater, 3rd Earl of (1689–1716) I 33
Desaguliers, J.T. (1683–1744) I 33
De Saumarez, Baron (1757–1836) II 62
Desbarres, J.F.W. (1722–1824) II 62
Desborough, 1st Baron (1855–1945) III 54–55
Desborough, John (1608–1680) I 33
Desenfans, N.J. (1745–1807) II 62
D'Espagne, Jean (1591–1659) I 33
Despard, Charlotte (1844–1939) III 55
Despard, E.M. (1751–1803) II 62
Despenser, Edward le (d1375) I 33
De Tabley, 1st Baron (1762–1827) II 62
Dethick, Sir Gilbert (1519?–1584) I 33
Detmold, C.M. (1883–1908) IV 29
Detmold, E.J. (1883–1957) IV 29
Deutsch, E.O.M. (1829–1873) III 55
De Valera, Eamon (1882–1975) IV 29
De Valois, Dame Ninette (b1898) IV 29
De Vere, A.T. (1814–1902) III 55
DeVerell, Sir C.J. (1874–1947) IV 29
De Villiers, 1st Baron (1842–1914) III 55
Devis, Arthur (1711?–1787) II 62
Devis, A.W. (1763–1822) II 62
Devisme, Louis (1720–1776) II 62
Devlin, Joseph (1871–1934) IV 29
Devon, Earl of (1526?–1556) I 33
Devon, 11th Earl of (1807–1888) III 55
Devonport, 1st Viscount (1856–1934) III 55
Devonshire, Earl of (1563–1606) I 33
Devonshire, 1st Earl of (d1626) I 33
Devonshire, 2nd Earl of (1591?–1628) I 33
Devonshire, 3rd Earl of (1617–1684) I 33
Devonshire, 1st Duke of (1640–1707) I 33
Devonshire, 4th Duke of (1720–1764) II 62–63
Devonshire, 6th Duke of (1748–1811) II 63
Devonshire, 6th Duke of (1790–1858) II 63
Devonshire, 7th Duke of (1808–1891) III 55
Devonshire, 8th Duke of (1833–1908) III 55
Devonshire, 9th Duke of (1868–1938) IV 29
Devonshire, Duchess of (d1675) I 33
Devonshire, Duchess of (1757–1806) II 62
Devonshire, Duchess of (1759–1824) II 62
Dewar, Sir James (1842–1923) III 55
De Wet, C.R. (1854–1922) III 55
De Wiart, Sir A.C. (1880–1963) IV 29
De Wilde, Samuel (1748–1832) II 63
De Wint, Peter (17—84–1849) II 63
De Winton, Sir F.W. (1835–1901) III 55
Dewrance, Sir John (1858–1937) III 55
D'Eyncourt, C.T. (1784–1861) II 63

Diamond, H.W. (1809–1886) III 55
Dibbs, Sir G.R. (1834–1904) III 55
Dibdin, Charles (1745–1814) I 63
Dibdin, C.I.M. (1768–1833) II 63
Dibdin, T.F. (1776–1847) II 63
Dibdin, T.J. (1771–1841) II 63
Dicey, A.V. (1835–1922) III 55
Dick, Sir Alexander (1703–1785) I 63
Dick, Sir R.H. (1785?–1846) II 63
Dick, Thomas (1774–1857) II 63
Dick, Sir William, Bart (1580?–1655) I 33
Dick, Sir W.R. (1879–1961) IV 29–30
Dickens, Charles (1812–1870) III 55–56
Dickens, Sir H.F. (1849–1933) III 56
Dickinson, G.L. (1862–1932) IV 30
Dickinson, William (1756–1822) II 63
Dickons, Maria (1770?–1833) II 63
Dicksee, Sir F.B. (1853–1928) III 56
Dickson, Sir Alexander (1777–1840) II 63
Dickson, Alexander (1836–1887) III 56
Dickson, Sir Collingwood (1817–1904) III 56
Dickson, David (1754–1820) II 63
Dickson, David (1780–1842) II 63
Dickson, James (1737?–1822) II 63
Dickson, William (1745–1804) II 63
Digby, Sir Kenelm (1603–1665) I 33
Digby, Robert (1732–1815) II 63
Digby, William (1849–1904) III 56
Digby, Venetia, Lady (1600–1633) I 33–34
Digges, Sir Dudley (1583–1639) I 34
Digges, West (1720–1786) I 63
Dighton, Richard (fl 1795–1880) II 63
Dighton, Robert (1752?–1814) II 63
Dignum, Charles (1765?–1827) II 63–64
Dilke, C.W. (1789–1864) II 64
Dilke, Sir C.W., 1st Bart (1810–1869) III 56
Dilke, Sir C.W., 2nd Bart (1843–1911) III 56
Dilke, Lady Emilia Frances (1840–1904) III 56
Dilkes, Sir Thomas (1657?–1707) I 34
Dill, Sir J.G. (1881–1944) IV 30
Dillenius, J.J. (1687–1747) I 34
Dillon, 17th Viscount (1844–1932) III 56
Dillon, E.J. (1854–1933) III 56
Dillon, John (1851–1927) III 56
Dillon, J.B. (1816–1866) III 56
Dillon, Sir J.T. (1740?–1805) II 64
Dillon, R.C. (1795–1847) II 64
Dillwyn, L.W. (1778–1855) II 64
Dimsdale, Thomas (1712–1800) II 64
Dineley-Goodere, Sir John (1729?–1809) II 64
Dingley, Robert (1619–1660) I 34
Dircks, Henry (1806–1873) III 56
Disney, John (1677–1730) I 34
Disney, John (1746–1816) II 64
Disney, John (1779–1857) II 64
D'Israeli, Isaac (1766–1848) II 64
Dixie, Lady Florence Caroline (1857–1905) III 56
Dixie, Sir Wolstan (1525–1594) I 34
Dixon, Sir A.L. (1881–1969) IV 30
Dixon, H.N. (1869–1953) IV 30
Dixon, Robert (d 1688) I 34
Dixon, R.W. (1833–1900) III 56
Dixon, W.H. (1821–1879) III 56–57
Dobbie, Sir W.G.S. (1879–1964) IV 30
Dobbs, Sir H.R.C. (1871–1934) IV 30
Dobell, Bertram (1842–1914) III 57
Dobell, Sir C.M. (1869–1954) IV 30
Dobell, S.T. (1824–1874) III 57
Dobree, Bonamy (1891–1974) IV 30
Dobree, P.P. (1782–1825) II 64
Dobson, Frank (1888–1963) IV 30
Dobson, H.A. (1840–1921) III 57
Dobson, John (1787–1865) II 64
Dobson, Sir R.H. (1891–1968) IV 30
Dobson, William (1610–1646) I 34
Dobson, W.C.T. (1817–1898) III 57
Docwra, Sir Thomas (d 1527) I 34
Dod, John (1549?–1645) I 34
Dodd, C.H. (1884–1973) IV 30
Dodd, Francis (1874–1949) IV 30
Dodd, J.W. (1740?–1796) II 64
Dodd, P.S. (1775–1852) II 64
Dodd, Thomas (1771–1850) II 64
Dodd, William (1729–1777) II 64
Doddridge, Sir John (1555–1628) I 34
Doddridge, Philip (1702–1751) II 64
Dodgson, Campbell (1867–1948) IV 30
Dodgson, C.L. (1832–1898) III 57
Dodgson, G.H. (1811–1880) III 57
Dods, Marcus (1834–1909) III 57
Dodsley, Robert (1703–1764) II 64
Dodson, Sir John (1780–1858) II 64
Dodsworth, William (1798–1861) II 64
Dodwell, Edward (1767–1832) II 64
Dodwell, Henry (1641–1711) I 34
Doggett, Thomas (d 1721) I 34

Doherty, H.L. (1875–1919) IV 30
Doherty, John (1783–1850) II 64
Dolben, Sir Gilbert (1658–1722) I 34
Dolben, John (1625–1686) I 34
Dolben, John (1662–1710) I 34
Dolben, Sir John (1684–1756) I 34
Dolben, Sir William (1627?–1694) I 34
Dolben, Sir William, Bart (1727?–1814) II 64
Dolling, R.W.R. (1851–1902) III 57
Dollond, Peter (1730–1820) II 64
Dolmetsch, E.A. (1858–1940) III 57
Domett, Sir William (1754–1828) II 64
Dominis, M.A. de (1566–1624) I 34
Don, A.C. (1885–1966) IV 20
Don, Sir George (1754–1832) II 64
Don, Sir W.H. (1825–1862) III 57
Donald, Adam (1703–1780) II 64
Donald, Sir Robert (1860–1933) IV 30
Donaldson, Sir C.G.A. (1863–1935) IV 30
Donaldson, James (1751–1830) II 65
Donaldson, Sir James (1831–1915) III 57
Donaldson, John (d 1865) II 65
Donaldson, Sir S.A. (1812–1867) III 57
Donaldson, T.L. (1795–1885) II 65
Donkin, Bryan (1768–1855) II 65
Donkin, Sir R.S. (1773–1841) II 65
Donnan, F.G. (1870–1956) IV 30
Donoghue, Stephen (1884–1945) IV 30
Donoughmore, 1st Earl of (1756–1825) II 65
Donoughmore, 2nd Earl of (1757–1832) II 65
Donoughmore, 3rd Earl of (1787–1851) II 65
Donoughmore, 6th Earl of (1875–1948) IV 30
Doolittle, Thomas (1632?–1707) I 34
Dopping, Anthony (1643–1697) I 34
Doran, John (1807–1878) III 57
Dorchester, 1st Viscount (1573–1632) I 34
Dorchester, 1st Marquess of (1606–1680) I 34
Dorchester, 1st Baron (1724–1808) II 65
Dorchester, Countess of (1657–1717) I 34
Dorigny, Sir Nicholas (1658–1746) I 34
Dorislaus, Isaac (1595–1649) I 34
Dormer, James (1679–1741) I 34
Dormer, John (1669–1719) I 34–35
Dormer, Sir Robert (1649–1726) I 35
Dorrington, Theophilus (d 1715) I 35
D'Orsay, Alfred, Count (1801–1852) III 57
Dorset, 1st Earl of (1536–1608) I 35
Dorset, 2nd Earl of (1561–1609) I 35
Dorset, 3rd Earl of (1589–1624) I 35
Dorset, 4th Earl of (1591–1652) I 35
Dorset, 5th Earl of (1622–1677) I 35
Dorset, 6th Earl of (1638–1706) I 35
Dorset, 1st Duke of (1688–1765) I 35
Dorset, 2nd Duke of (1711–1769) II 65
Dorset, 3rd Duke of (1745–1799) II 65
Doubleday, Edward (1811–1849) III 57
Douce, Francis (1757–1834) II 65
Doughty, C.M. (1843–1926) III 57
Doughty, William (d 1782) II 65
Douglas, 1st Baron (1748–1821) II 65
Douglas, Lord A.B. (1870–1945) IV 30
Douglas, David (1798–1834) II 65
Douglas, F.S.N. (1791–1819) II 65
Douglas, Sir Howard, 3rd Bart (1776–1861) II 65
Douglas, James (1753–1819) II 65
Douglas, James (1867–1940) IV 31
Douglas, John (1721–1807) II 65
Douglas, Neil (1750–1823) II 65
Douglas, Sir Neil (1779–1853) II 65
Douglas, Norman (1868–1952) IV 30
Douglas, Percy (1876–1939) IV 31
Douglas, Philip (1758–1822) IV 31
Douglas, Sir W.F. (1822–1891) III 58
Douglas, Sir W.S. (1890–1953) IV 31
Douglas-Pennant, Sir C.E. (1894–1961) IV 31
Douglas of Kirtleside, 1st Baron (1893–1969) IV 31
Douglass, John (1743–1812) II 65
Doulton, Sir Henry (1820–1897) III 58
Dove, Dame (Jane) Frances (1847–1942) III 58
Dove, Thomas (1555–1630) I 35
Dover, 1st Baron (1636–1708) I 35
Dover, 1st Baron (1797–1833) II 65
Dover, Baron (1724–1792) II 66
Dover, Robert (1575?–1641) I 35
Dow, Alexander (d 1779) II 66
Dowden, Edward (1843–1913) III 58
Dowden, John (1840–1910) III 58
Dowdeswell, William (1761–1828) II 66
Dowding, 1st Baron (1882–1970) IV 31
Downes, 1st Baron (1752–1826) II 66
Downey, R.J. (1881–1953) IV 31
Downing, Sir George, 1st Bart (1623?–1684) I 35
Downing, Sir George, 3rd Bart (1684?–1749) I 35
Downman, Hugh (1740–1809) II 66
Downman, John (1750–1824) II 66
Downshire, 1st Marquess of (1718–1793) II 66

Downshire, 2nd Marquess of (1753–1801) II 66
Dowse, Richard (1824–1890) III 58
Dowson, Ernest (1867–1900) IV 31
Dowton, William (1764–1851) II 66
Doyle, Sir Arthur Conan (1859–1930) III 58
Doyle, Sir C.H. (1805–1883) III 58
Doyle, Sir C.W. (1770–1842) II 66
Doyle, Sir F.H.C., 2nd Bart (1810–1888) III 58
Doyle, H.E. (1827–1892) III 58
Doyle, Sir John, Bart (1750?–1834) II 66
Doyle, John (1797–1868) II 66
Doyle, J.W. (1786–1834) II 66
Doyle, Richard (1824–1883) III 58
D'Oyly, Sir John, 1st Bart (1774–1824) II 66
Dragonetti, Domenico (1755?–1846) II 66
Drake, Sir Francis (1540?–1596) I 35
Drake, Francis (1696–1771) I 35
Drake, James (1667–1707) I 35
Drake, Nathan (1766–1836) II 66
Drake, Samuel (1623–1673) I 35
Drake, William (1723–1801) II 66
Draper, J.W. (1811–1882) III 58
Draper, Sir William (1721–1787) II 66
Drayton, Michael (1563–1631) I 35
Drew, Samuel (1765–1833) II 66
Drew, Sir Thomas (1838–1910) III 58
Dreyer, F.G. (1878–1956) IV 31
Dreyer, Georges (1873–1934) IV 31
Drinkwater, John (1882–1937) IV 31
Driver, Sir G.R. (1892–1972) IV 31
Driver, S.R. (1846–1914) III 58
Drogheda, 6th Earl and 1st Marquess of (1730–1822) II 66
Drogheda, 10th Earl of (1884–1957) IV 31
Druce, G.C. (1850–1932) III 58
Druitt, Robert (1814–1883) III 58
Drummond, Flora (1879–1949) IV 31
Drummond, George (1687–1766) I 35
Drummond, Sir G.A. (1829–1910) III 58
Drummond, Henry (1786–1860) II 66
Drummond, Henry (1851–1897) III 58
Drummond, James (1816–1877) III 58
Drummond, Sir J.C. (1891–1952) IV 31
Drummond, Sir P.R.M. (1894–1945) IV 31
Drummond, R.H. (1711–1776) II 66
Drummond, Samuel (1765–1844) II 66
Drummond, Thomas (1797–1840) II 66
Drummond, Sir William (1770?–1828) II 66
Drummond-Hay, Sir J.H. (1816–1893) III 58
Drummond of Hawthornden, William (1585–1649) I 35–36
Drury, Alfred (1856–1944) III 58
Drury, Sir Dru (1531?–1617) I 36
Drury, H.J.T. (1778–1841) II 66–67
Drury, Sir Robert (d 1536) I 36
Drury, Sir William (1527–1579) I 36
Drury-Lowe, Sir D.C. (1830–1908) III 58
Dryander, Jonas (1748–1810) II 67
Dryden, John (1631–1700) I 36
Duane, Matthew (1707–1785) II 67
Dubois, Edward (1774–1850) II 67
Dubois, Simon (d 1708) I 36
Dubourdieu, Isaac (1597?–1692?) I 36
Dubourdieu, J.A. (1642?–1726) I 36
Ducarel, A.C. (1713–1785) II 67
Ducie, 2nd Earl of (1802–1853) III 58
Duck, Stephen (1705–1756) II 67
Duckworth, Sir Dyce, 1st Bart (1840–1928) III 58
Duckworth, Sir J.T. (1748–1817) II 67
Duckworth, W.L.H. (1870–1956) IV 31
Du Cros, Sir A.P., 1st Bart (1871–1955) IV 31
Ducrow, Andrew (1793–1842) II 67
Dudley, 1st Earl of (1781–1833) II 67
Dudley, 2nd Earl of (1867–1932) IV 31
Dudley, Duchess of (d 1669) I 36
Dudley, Edmund (1462?–1510) I 36
Dudley, Sir H.B., 1st Bart (1745–1824) II 67
Dudley, Lady Jane (Lady Jane Grey) (1537–1554) I 36
Dudley, Sir Robert (1574–1649) I 36
Duff, Alexander (1806–1878) III 58
Duff, Sir Alexander (1862–1933) IV 31
Duff, Sir J.F. (1898–1970) IV 31
Duff, Sir R.W. (1835–1895) III 58
Duff-Gordon, Lady Lucy (1821–1869) III 59
Dufferin and Ava, 1st Marquess of (1826–1902) III 59
Dufferin and Claneboye, Countess of (1807–1867) III 59
Duffy, Sir C.G. (1816–1903) III 59
Duffy, Sir F.G. (1852–1936) IV 19
Dugdale, Sir John (1628–1700) I 36
Dugdale, Richard (fl 1680–1697) I 36
Dugdale, Stephen (1640?–1683) I 36
Dugdale, T.C. (1880–1952) IV 31
Dugdale, Sir William (1605–1686) I 36
Duigenan, Patrick (1735–1816) II 67
Dukes, Ashley (1885–1959) IV 31
Dukes, Sir Paul (1889–1967) IV 31
Dulac, Edmund (1882–1953) IV 31
Du Maurier, George (1834–1896) III 59

Du Maurier, Sir Gerald (1873–1934) IV *31*
Dumbarton, Earl of (1636?–1692) I *36*
Dunbar, Earl of (*d* 1611) I *36*
Dunbar, Gavin (1455?–1532) I *36*
Dunbar, George (1774–1851) II *67*
Duncan, 1st Viscount (1731–1804) II *67*
Duncan, Andrew (1744–1828) II *67*
Duncan, Sir A.R. (1884–1952) IV *32*
Duncan, Edward (1804–1882) III *59*
Duncan, Francis (1836–1888) III *59*
Duncan, Henry (1774–1846) II *67*
Duncan, John (1805–1849) III *59*
Duncan, Jonathan (1756–1811) II *67*
Duncan, J.M. (1826–1890) III *59*
Duncan, J.S. (1769–1844) II *67*
Duncan, Sir Patrick (1870–1943) IV *32*
Duncan, P.B. (1772–1863) II *67*
Duncan, Thomas (1807–1845) III *59*
Dunch, Edmund (1657–1719) I *36*
Duncombe, John (1729–1786) II *67*
Duncombe, T.S. (1796–1861) II *67*
Duncombe, William (1690–1769) I *36*
Dundas, 1st Baron (1741–1820) II *68*
Dundas, Sir David (1735–1820) II *67*
Dundas, Francis (*d* 1824) II *67*
Dundas, Sir J.W.D. (1785–1862) II *67*
Dundas, Robert (1713–1787) II *67–68*
Dundas, Sir R.S. (1802–1861) III *59*
Dundas, William (1762–1845) II *68*
Dundas of Arniston, Sir James (*d* 1679) I *36*
Dundas of Arniston, Robert, Lord (1685–1753) I *36*
Dundas of Arniston, Robert, Lord (*d* 1727) I *36*
Dundas of Arniston, Robert (1758–1819) II *68*
Dundee, 1st Viscount (1649?–1689) I *36*
Dundonald, 9th Earl of (1747/8–1831) II *68*
Dundonald, 10th Earl of (1775–1860) II *68*
Dundrennan, Lord (1792–1851) I *68*
Dunedin, 1st Viscount (1849–1942) III *59*
Dunfermline, 1st Earl (1555–1622) I *36*
Dunfermline, 2nd Earl (1608–1672?) I *36*
Dunfermline, 1st Baron (1776–1858) II *68*
Dungannon, 3rd Viscount (1798–1862) II *68*
Dunhill, T.F. (1877–1946) IV *32*
Dunhill, Sir T.P. (1876–1957) IV *32*
Dunkin, A.J. (1812–1879) II *59*
Dunlop, John (1755–1820) II *68*
Dunlop, J.B. (1840–1921) III *59*
Dunlop, R.O. (1894–1973) IV *32*
Dunlop, William (1792–1848) II *68*
Dunmore, 4th Earl of (1732–1809) II *68*
Dunmore, 7th Earl of (1841–1907) III *59*
Dunn, Robert (1799–1877) II *68*
Dunn, Samuel (1798–1882) II *68*
Dunraven and Mount-Earl, 4th Earl of (1841–1926) III *59*
Dunrossil, 1st Viscount (1893–1961) IV *32*
Dunsany, 18th Baron of (1878–1957) IV *32*
Dunsinane, Lord (1731?–1811) II *68*
Dunstan, Saint (924–988) I *37*
Dunstan, Jeffrey (1759?–1797) II *68*
Dunstan, Sir W.R. (1861–1949) IV *32*
Dunster, Samuel (1675–1754) I *37*
Dunsterville, L.C. (1865–1946) IV *32*
Dunthorne, John (1770–1844) II *68*
Dunthorne, John (1798–1832) II *68*
Dunton, John (1659–1733) I *37*
Du Parcq, Baron (1880–1949) IV *32*
Dupont, Gainsborough (1754?–1797) II *68*
Duppa, Brian (1588–1662) I *37*
Duppa, Richard (1770–1831) II *68*
Dupré, August (1835–1907) III *59*
Dupuis, T.S. (1733–1796) II *68*
Durand, Sir H.M. (1812–1871) III *59*
Durand, Sir H.M. (1850–1924) III *60*
D'Urfey, Thomas (1653–1723) I *37*
Durham, 1st Earl of (1792–1840) II *68*
Durham, Joseph (1814–1877) III *60*
Durham, Sir P.C.H.C. (1763–1845) II *68–69*
Durie, Lord (*d* 1644) I *37*
Durnford, Richard (1802–1895) III *60*
Durnford, Sir Walter (1847–1926) III *60*
Dutens, Louis (1730–1812) II *69*
Duveen, Baron (1869–1939) IV *32*
Duveen, Sir J.J. (1843–1908) III *60*
Dwyer, Michael (1771–1826) II *69*
Dyce, Alexander (1798–1869) II *69*
Dyce, William (1806–1864) III *60*
Dyce-Sombre, D.O. (1808–1851) III *60*
Dyche, Thomas (fl 1719) I *37*
Dyer, Sir James (1512–1582) I *37*
Dyer, John (1700–1758) II *69*
Dyer, J.C. (1780–1871) II *69*
Dyer, Samuel (1725–1772) II *69*
Dyer, William (1636?–1696) I *37*
Dyke, Sir W.H. 7th Bart (1837–1931) III *60*
Dykes, J.B. (1823–1876) III *60*
Dykes, Thomas (1761–1847) II *69*

Dysart, 1st Earl of (1600?–1615) I *37*
Dyson, Sir Frank (1868–1939) IV *32*
Dyson, Sir George (1883–1964) IV *32*
Dyson-Smith, C.W. (*d* 1961) IV *32*
Dyve, Sir Lewis (1599–1669) I *37*

Eardley, Sir C.E., 3rd Bart (1805–1863) III *61*
Earle, Henry (1789–1838) II *70*
Earle, John (1601?–1665) I *39*
Earle, Sir Lionel (1866–1948) IV *33*
Earle, William (1833–1885) III *61*
Earle, William Benson (1740–1793) II *70*
Earlom, Richard (1743–1822) II *70*
Earnshaw, Thomas (1749–1829) II *70*
Earp, T.W. (1892–1958) IV *33*
East, Sir Alfred (1849–1913) III *61*
East, Sir E.H. (1764–1847) II *70*
East, Sir J.B. (1789–1878) II *70*
East, Sir Norwood (1872–1953) IV *33*
Easthope, Sir John, 1st Bart (1784–1865) II *70*
Eastlake, Sir C.L. (1793–1865) II *70*
Eastlake, Elizabeth, Lady (1809–1893) III *61*
Easton, Adam (*d* 1397) I *39*
Eaton, D.I. (*d* 1814) II *70*
Eaton, Sir Frederick (1838–1913) III *61*
Ebsworth, Joseph (1788–1868) II *70*
Ebury, 1st Baron (1801–1893) III *61*
Eccles, Sir J.A.S. (1898–1966) IV *33*
Echard, Laurence (1670?–1730) I *39*
Eckersley, P.P. (1892–1963) IV *33*
Eckersley, T.L. (1886–1959) IV *33*
Eddington, Sir A.S. (1882–1944) IV *33*
Eden, Sir Ashley (1831–1887) III *61*
Eden, Robert (1804–1886) III *61*
Edes, Richard (1555–1604) I *39*
Edgar (944–975) I *39*
Edgcumbe, 1st Baron (1680–1758) I *39*
Edgcumbe, 2nd Baron (1716–1761) II *70*
Edge, Sir John (1841–1926) III *61*
Edge, S.F. (1868–1940) IV *33*
Edgeworth, F.Y. (1845–1926) III *61*
Edgeworth, Maria (1767–1849) II *70*
Edgeworth, R.L. (1744–1817) II *70*
Edgeworth de Firmont, H.E. (1745–1807) II *70*
Edis, Olive (1872?–1955) IV *33*
Edmondes, Sir Thomas (1563?–1639) I *39*
Edmonds, Sir Clement (1564?–1622) I *39*
Edmonds, Sir J.E. (1861–1956) IV *33*
Edmondson, Joseph (*d* 1786) II *70*
Edmondstone, N.B. (1765–1841) II *70*
Edmund (841–870) I *39*
Edmund (922?–946) I *39*
Edmund of Langley (1341–1402) I *39*
Edouin, Willie (1846–1908) III *61*
Edward 'the Elder' (*d* 924) I *39*
Edward 'the Martyr' (963?–978) I *39*
Edward 'the Confessor' (*d* 1066) I *39*
Edward I (1239–1307) I *39*
Edward II (1284–1327) I *39*
Edward III (1312–1377) I *39*
Edward IV (1442–1483) I *39*
Edward V (1470–1483) I *39*
Edward VI (1537–1553) I *39–40*
Edward VII (1841–1910) III *61–62*
Edward, Prince of Wales, 'the Black Prince'
  (1330–1376) I *40*
Edward, Prince of Wales (1453–1471) I *40*
Edward of Saxe-Weimar, Prince (1823–1902) III *62*
Edward, Thomas (1814–1886) III *62*
Edwardes, Sir H.B. (1819–1868) III *62*
Edwards, Alfred (1888–1958) IV *33*
Edwards, A.G. (1848–1937) III *62*
Edwards, Amelia (1831–1892) III *62*
Edwards, Bryan (1743–1800) II *70*
Edwards, Edward (1738–1806) II *70*
Edwards, Edwin (1823–1879) III *62*
Edwards, George (1694–1773) I *40*
Edwards, John (1637–1716) I *40*
Edwards, John (1714–1785) II *70*
Edwards, J.P. (1823–1911) III *62*
Edwards, Ness (1897–1968) IV *33*
Edwards, Thomas (1652–1721) I *40*
Edwards, Thomas (1699–1757) I *40*
Edwards, T.C. (1837–1900) III *62*
Edwards, William (1719–1789) II *70*
Edwards, W.C. (1777–1855) II *70*
Edwards, W.J. (1900–1964) IV *33*
Edwin, John (1749–1790) II *70–71*
Edwin, John (1768–1805) II *71*
Effingham, 1st Earl of (1767–1845) II *71*
Egan, John (1750?–1810) II *71*
Egan, Pierce (1772–1849) II *71*
Egerton, Sir A.C.G. (1886–1959) IV *33*
Egerton, Daniel (1772–1835) II *71*
Egerton, John (1721–1787) II *71*

Egerton, Sarah (1782–1847) II *71*
Egg, Augustus (1816–1863) III *62*
Eginton, Francis (1737–1805) II *71*
Eglinton, 11th Earl of (1726–1796) II *71*
Eglinton, 12th Earl of (1739–1819) II *71*
Eglinton, 13th Earl of (1812–1861) III *62*
Egmont, 1st Earl of (1683–1748) I *40*
Egmont, 2nd Earl of (1711–1770) II *71*
Egremont, 2nd Earl of (1710–1763) II *71*
Egremont, 3rd Earl of (1751–1837) II *71*
Elchies, Lord (1690–1754) I *40*
Elcho, Lord (1721–1787) II *71*
Elder, Thomas (1737–1799) II *71*
Elder, William (fl 1680–1700) I *40*
Eldin, Lord (1757–1832) II *71*
Eldon, 1st Earl of (1751–1838) II *71*
Eldred, John (1552–1632) I *40*
Eldred, William (fl 1646) I **40*
Eleanor of Aquitaine (1122?–1204?) I *40*
Eleanor of Castile (*d* 1290) I *40*
Eleanor of Provence (*d* 1291) I *40*
Elers, J.P. (fl 1690–1730) I *40*
Elgar, Sir Edward, Bart (1857–1934) III *62–63*
Elgin, 7th Earl of (1766–1841) II *71*
Elgin, 8th Earl of (1811–1863) III *63*
Elgin, 9th Earl of (1849–1917) III *63*
Elias, John (1774–1841) II *71*
Elias, Ney (1844–1897) III *63*
Eliot, Sir C.N.E. (1862–1931) IV *33*
Eliot, Sir John (1592–1632) I *40*
Eliot, John (1604–1690) I *40*
Eliot, T.S. (1888–1965) IV *33*
Elizabeth Woodville (1437?–1492) I *40*
Elizabeth of York (1465–1503) I *40*
Elizabeth I (1533–1603) I *40–41*
Elizabeth, Queen of Bohemia (1596–1662) I *41*
Elizabeth, Princess (1635–1650) I *41*
Elizabeth, Princess (1770–1840) II *71–72*
Elizabeth, The Queen Mother (*b* 1900) IV *33*
Ellenborough, 1st Baron (1750–1818) II *72*
Ellenborough, 3rd Baron (1820–1890) III *63*
Ellenborough, 1st Earl of (1790–1871) II *72*
Ellenborough, Anne, Lady (1769–1843) II *72*
Ellenborough, Countess of (1807–1881) III *63*
Ellerman, Sir J.R. (1862–1933) IV *33*
Ellerton, Edward (1770–1851) II *72*
Elles, Sir H.J. (1880–1945) IV *34*
Elley, Sir John (*d* 1839) II *72*
Ellice, Edward (1781–1863) II *72*
Ellicott, C.J. (1819–1905) III *63*
Ellicott, John (1706?–1772) II *72*
Elliot, Sir George (1784–1863) II *72*
Elliot, Sir H.G. (1817–1907) III *63*
Elliot, Jane (1727–1805) II *72*
Elliotson, John (1791–1868) II *72*
Elliott, Ebenezer (1781–1849) II *72*
Elliott, Grace (1758?–1823) II *72*
Elliott, H.V. (1792–1865) II *72*
Ellis, A.J. (1814–1890) III *63*
Ellis, Clement (1630–1700) I *41*
Ellis, F.S. (1830–1901) III *63*
Ellis, Sir Henry (1777–1869) II *72*
Ellis, H.H. (1859–1939) III *63*
Ellis, Sir H.W. (1783–1815) II *72*
Ellis, John (1698–1791) I *41*
Ellis, John (1789–1862) II *72*
Ellis, Philip (1652–1726) I *41*
Ellis, Robinson (1834–1913) III *63*
Ellis, R.L. (1817–1859) III *63*
Ellis, Sarah (*d* 1872) II *72*
Ellis, T.E. (1796–1861) II *72*
Ellis, Welbore (1651?–1734) I *41*
Ellis, Sir William (1609–1680) I *41*
Ellis, William (1794–1872) II *72*
Ellis, Wynne (1790–1875) II *72*
Ellis, Sir W.H. (1860–1945) IV *34*
Elliston, R.W. (1774–1831) II *72*
Ellman, John (1753–1832) II *72*
Elmes, James (1782–1862) II *72*
Elmhirst, L.K. (1893–1974) IV *34*
Elmore, Alfred (1815–1881) III *63–64*
Elphinstone, James (1721–1809) II *72*
Elphinstone, 13th Baron (1807–1860) III *64*
Elphinstone, Sir H.C. (1829–1890) III *64*
Elphinstone, Keith (1865–1941) IV *34*
Elphinstone, Mountstuart (1779–1859) II *73*
Elphinstone, William (1431–1514) I *41*
Elrington, Thomas (1760–1835) II *73*
Elstob, Elizabeth (1683–1756) I *41*
Elton, Sir C.A. (1778–1853) II *73*
Elton, C.I. (1839–1900) III *64*
Elton, Oliver (1861–1945) IV *34*
Elton, Richard (fl 1650) I *41*
Elton of Headington, 1st Baron (1892–1973) IV *34*
Elvey, Sir G.J. (1816–1893) III *64*

Elvey, Maurice (1887–1967) IV 34
Elvin, Sir Arthur (1899–1957) IV 34
Elwes, G.H. (1866–1921) IV 34
Elwes, H.J. (1846–1922) III 64
Elwes, John (1714–1789) II 73
Elyot, Sir Thomas (d 1546) I 41
Elys, Edmund (fl 1707) I 41
Emerson, Sir H.W. (1881–1962) IV 34
Emerson, William (1701–1782) II 73
Emery, John (1777–1822) II 73
Emery, S.A. (1817–1881) III 64
Emly, Baron (1812–1894) III 64
Emlyn, Thomas (1663–1741) I 41
Emma, Queen (d 1052) I 41
Emmet, Robert (1778–1803) II 73
Emmet, T.A. (1764–1827) II 73
Emmott, 1st Baron (1858–1926) III 64
Empson, Sir Richard (d 1510) I 41
Empson, William (1791–1852) II 73
Endecott, John (1588?–1665) I 41
Enfield, William (1741–1797) II 73
England, Sir Richard (1793–1883) II 73
Englefield, Sir H.C. (1752–1822) II 73
Engleheart, George (1752–1839) II 73
Engleheart, J.C.D. (1783–1862) II 73
Ensor, George (1769–1843) II 73
Ent, Sir George (1604–1689) I 41
Entick, John (1703?–1773) II 73
Entwisle, Joseph (1767–1841) II 73
Entwistle, W.J. (1895–1952) IV 34
Epps, John (1805–1869) III 64
Epstein, Sir Jacob (1880–1959) IV 34
Erdeswicke, Sampson (d 1603) I 41
Erichsen, Sir J.E. (1818–1896) III 64
Erle, Thomas (1650?–1720) I 41
Erle, Sir William (1793–1880) II 73
Ernle, 1st Baron (1851–1937) III 64
Erpingham, Sir Thomas (1357–1428) I 41
Erskine, 1st Baron (1750–1823) II 73–74
Erskine, Ebenezer (1680–1754) I 41
Erskine, Henry (1746–1817) II 73
Erskine, James (1722–1796) II 73
Erskine, John (1695–1768) I 42
Erskine, John (1721–1803) II 73
Erskine, Ralph (1685–1752) I 42
Erskine, Thomas (1788–1864) II 74
Erskine, Thomas (1788–1870) II 74
Erskine, Sir William (1769–1813) II 74
Ervine, St J.G. (1883–1971) IV 34
Esdaile, William (1758–1837) II 74
Esher, 1st Viscount (1815–1899) III 64
Esher, 2nd Viscount (1852–1930) III 64
Esher, 3rd Viscount (1881–1963) IV 34
Eskgrove, Lord (1724?–1804) II 74
Esmond, H.V. (1869–1922) IV 34
Essex, 1st Earl of (d 1483) I 42
Essex, Thomas Cromwell, Earl of (1485?–1540) I 42
Essex, 2nd Earl of (1541?–1576) I 42
Essex, 2nd Earl of (1566–1601) I 42
Essex, 3rd Earl of (1591–1646) I 42
Essex, 1st Earl of (1631–1683) I 42
Essex, 5th Earl of (1757–1839) II 74
Essex, Countess of (1794–1882) II 74
Essex, James (1722–1784) II 74
Estcourt, J.B.B. (902–1855) III 64
Estcourt, T.H.S.S. (1801–1876) III 64
Este, Charles (1696–1745) I 42
Estlin, J.B. (1785–1855) II 74
Ethelbert (d 866) I 42
Ethelred I (d 871) I 42
Ethelred 'the Unready' (968?–1016) I 42
Ethelstan (893?–950) I 42
Etty, William (1787–1849) II 74
Euan-Smith, Sir C.B. (1842–1910) III 64
Eumorfopoulos, George (1863–1939) IV 34
Eusden, Laurence (1688–1730) I 42
Evan-Thomas, Sir Hugh (1862–1928) IV 34
Evans, Sir A.J. (1851–1941) III 64
Evans, B. Ifor (b 1899) IV 34
Evans, Christmas (1766–1838) II 74
Evans, Daniel (1797–1846) II 74
Evans, Dame Edith (1888–1976) IV 34
Evans, Edwin (1874–1945) IV 34
Evans, F.H. (1852–1943) III 64
Evans, Sir G. de Lacy (1787–1870) II 74
Evans, John (d 1724) I 42
Evans, John (1678–1730) I 42
Evans, John (1767–1827) II 74
Evans, John (1823–1908) III 64
Evans, John (1840–1897) III 64
Evans, Lewis (1755–1827) II 74
Evans, Philip (1645–1679) I 42
Evans, Richard (1784–1871) II 74
Evans, Robert (1773–1849) II 74
Evans, R.H. (1778–1857) II 74
Evans, Sir S.T. (1859–1918) III 64
Evans, T.S. (1777–1818) II 74

Evans, Sir Vincent (1851–1934) III 64
Evans, Sir W.D. (1767–1821) II 74
Eve, Sir H.T. (1856–1940) III 65
Eveleigh, John (1748–1814) II 74
Evelyn, John (1620–1705) I 42
Everard, John (1575?–1650?) I 42
Everest, Sir George (1790–1866) II 74
Everett, James (1784–1872) II 74
Everett, J.D. (1831–1904) III 65
Evershed, 1st Baron (1899–1966) IV 34
Eversley, Viscount (1794–1888) II 74–75
Eversley, Baron (1831–1928) III 65
Ewart, William (1798–1869) II 75
Ewen, John (1741–1821) II 75
Ewing, Sir Alfred (1855–1935) III 65
Ewing, Greville (1767–1841) II 75
Ewins, A.J. (1882–1957) IV 34
Exeter, Duke of (1352?–1400) I 42
Exley, Thomas (1775–1855) II 75
Exmouth, 1st viscount (1757–1833) II 75
Eyre, E.J. (1815–1901) III 65
Eyre, Sir James (1734–1799) II 75
Eyre, Sir James (1792–1857) II 75
Eyre, John (1754–1803) II 75
Eyre, Sir Robert (1666–1735) I 42
Eyre, Sir Samuel (1633–1698) I 42
Eyre, Sir Vincent (1811–1881) III 65

Faber, F.W. (1814–1863) III 67
Faber, Sir G.C. (1889–1961) IV 35
Faber, Oscar (1886–1956) IV 35
Faed, James (1856–1920) III 67
Faed, John (1819–1902) III 67
Faed, Thomas (1826–1900) III 67
Fagan, L.A. (1845–1903) III 67
Fagius, Paul (1504–1549) I 43
Fairbairn, A.M. (1838–1912) III 67
Fairbairn, Sir Peter (1799–1861) II 76
Fairbairn, Stephen (1862–1938) IV 35
Fairbairn, Sir William, Bart (1789–1874) II 76
Fairborne, Sir Stafford (d 1742) I 43
Fairbridge, K.O. (1885–1924) IV 35
Fairchild, Thomas (1667?–1729) I 43
Fairclough, Samuel (1594–1677) I 43
Fairey, Sir Richard (1887–1956) IV 35
Fairfax, Robert (1666–1725) I 43
Fairfax, Sir W.G. (1739–1813) II 76
Fairfax of Cameron, 1st Baron (1560–1640) I 43
Fairfax of Cameron, 2nd Baron (1584–1648) I 43
Fairfax of Cameron, 3rd Baron (1612–1671) I 43
Fairfield, 1st Baron (1863–1945) IV 35
Fairholt, F.W. (1814–1866) III 67
Fairley, Sir N.H. (1891–1966) IV 35
Faithfull, Lilian Mary (1865–1952) IV 35
Faithorne, William (1616?–1691) I 43
Falconer, Hugh (1808–1865) III 67
Falconer, William (1744–1824) II 76
Falconer, P.E. (1741–1791) II 76
Falkener, Edward (1814–1896) III 67
Falkland, 1st Viscount (1576–1633) I 43
Falkland, 2nd Viscount (1610?–1643) I 43
Falkland, Viscountess (1585–1639) I 43
Falkner, Sir Keith (b 1900) IV 35
Falkner, William (d 1682) I 43
Falls, Cyril (1888–1971) IV 35
Falmouth, 1st Viscount (c 1680–1734) I 43
Falmouth, 1st Earl of (1787–1841) II 76
Fane, Sir Henry (1778–1840) II 76
Fane, J.H.C. (1827–1870) III 67
Fanning, Edmund (1737–1818) II 76
Fanshawe, 1st Viscount (1596–1665) I 43
Fanshawe, 2nd Viscount (1630–1674) I 43
Fanshawe, Sir E.G. (1814–1906) III 67
Fanshawe, Henry (1506–1568) I 43
Fanshawe, Sir Richard (1608–1666) I 43
Fanshawe, Thomas (1533–1601) I 43
Faraday, Michael (1791–1867) II 76
Fargus, F.J. (1847–1885) III 67
Farington, Joseph (1747–1821) II 76
Farish, William (1759–1837) II 76
Farley, Charles (1771–1859) II 76
Farmer, George (1732–1779) II 76
Farmer, John (1835–1901) III 67
Farmer, Sir J.B. (1865–1944) IV 35
Farmer, Richard (1735–1797) II 76
Farnborough, 1st Baron (1761–1838) II 76
Farnborough, 1st Baron (1815–1886) III 67
Farnborough, Lady (1762–1837) II 76
Farnell, L.R. (1856–1934) III 67
Farnham, Richard (d 1642) I 43
Farquar, George (1678–1707) I 43
Farquhar, Sir Arthur (1772–1843) II 76
Farquhar, John (1751–1826) II 76
Farquhar, Sir R.T. (1776–1830) II 77
Farquhar, Sir Walter (1738–1819) II 77
Farr, William (1807–1883) III 67

Farrar, F.W. (1831–1903) III 67
Farrar, John (1802–1884) III 67
Farre, Arthur (1811–1887) III 67
Farren, Ellen (1848–1904) III 67
Farren, William (1786–1861) II 77
Farren, William (1825–1908) III 67–68
Farrer, 1st Baron (1819–1899) III 68
Farrington, Sir Anthony, Bart (1742–1823) II 77
Farwell, Sir George (1845–1915) III 68
Fauconberg, 1st Earl (1627–1700) I 43
Fauconberg, Thomas, the Bastard of (d 1471) I 43
Faulkner, George (1699?–1775) I 43
Faulkner, Thomas (1777–1855) II 77
Faulknor, Robert (1763–1795) II 77
Fauntleroy, Henry (1785–1824) II 77
Fauquier, Francis (1704?–1768) II 77
Fausset, Hugh l'Anson (1895–1965) IV 35
Fawcett, Henry (1833–1884) III 68
Fawcett, John (1740–1817) II 77
Fawcett, John (1768–1837) II 77
Fawcett, Sir Luke (1881–1960) IV 35
Fawcett, Dame Millicent (1847–1929) III 68
Fawcett, Sir William (1728–1804) II 77
Fawkener, Sir Everard (1694–1758) I 43
Fawkes, Guy (1570–1606) I 44
Fawkes, W.R. (1769–1825) II 77
Fay, Frank (1870–1931) IV 35
Fay, W.G. (1872–1947) IV 35
Fayrer, Sir Joseph, 1st Bart (1824–1907) III 68
Fazackerley, Nicholas (d 1767) I 44
Featley, Daniel (1582–1645) I 44
Featley, John (1605?–1666) I 44
Fechter, C.A. (1824–1879) III 68
Fegan, Ethel Sophia (1877–1975) IV 35
Feild, Edward (1801?–1876) III 68
Feilding, Robert (1651?–1712) I 44
Fell, John (1625–1686) I 44
Fell, Samuel (1584–1649) I 44
Fellowes, Sir Edward (1895–1970) IV 35
Fellowes, E.H. (1870–1951) IV 35
Fellowes, Robert (1770–1847) II 77
Fellows, Sir Charles (1799–1860) II 77
Felton, John (1595?–1628) I 44
Felton, Nicholas (1556–1626) I 44
Fenn, John (1831–1909) III 68
Fenn, Sir John (1739–1794) II 77
Fenn, J.F. (1820–1884) III 68
Fenner, Sir Edward (d 1612) I 44
Fenner, William (1600–1640) I 44
Fenning, Elizabeth (1792–1815) II 77
Fenton, Elijah (1683–1730) I 44
Fenton, Richard (1746–1821) II 77
Fenwick, John (1628–1679) I 44
Fenwick, Sir John, Bart (1645?–1697) I 44
Ferens, T.R. (1847–1930) III 68
Ferg, Francis de Paula (1689–1740) I 44
Ferguson, Adam (1723–1816) II 77
Ferguson, Sir Adam (1771–1855) II 77
Ferguson, James (1710–1776) II 77
Ferguson, Sir R.C. (1773–1841) II 77
Ferguson, R.S. (1837–1900) III 68
Fergusson, Sir Charles, 7th Bart (1865–1951) IV 35
Fergusson, James (1808–1886) III 68
Fergusson, Sir James, 6th Bart of Kilkerran (1832–1907) III 68
Fergusson, J.D. (1874–1961) IV 35
Fergusson, Robert (1750–1774) II 77
Fergusson, R.C. (1768–1838) II 77
Fergusson, Sir William, Bart (1808–1877) III 68
Feria, Duchess of (1538–1612) I 44
Fermor, Sir L.L. (1880–1954) IV 35
Ferneley, John (1782–1860) II 77
Ferranti, Sebastian Ziani de (1864–1930) IV 35
Ferrar, Nicholas (1592–1637) I 44
Ferrers, 4th Earl (1720–1760) II 77
Ferrers, N.M. (1829–1903) III 68
Ferriar, John (1761–1815) II 78
Ferrier, Sir David (1843–1928) III 68
Ferrier, J.F. (1808–1864) III 68
Ferrier, Susan Edmonstone (1782–1854) II 78
Festing, Sir F.W. (1833–1886) III 68
Festing, J.W. (1837–1902) III 68
Fettes, Sir William (1750–1836) II 78
Feversham, Earl of (1640?–1709) I 44
Ffoulkes, C.J. (1868–1947) IV 35
Ffrangcon-Davies, Gwen (b 1896) IV 35
Fiddes, Richard (1671–1725) I 44
Field, Baron (1813–1907) III 69
Field, E.W. (1804–1871) III 68–69
Field, Sir F.L. (1871–1945) IV 35
Field, Henry (1755–1837) II 78
Field, John (1782–1837) II 78
Field, Joshua (1787?–1863) II 78
Field, Sir Mostyn (1855–1950) III 68
Field, Nathaniel (1587–1633) I 44
Fielden, John (1784–1849) II 78
Fielding, A.V.C. (1787–1855) II 78

Fielding, Henry (1707–1754) II 78
Fielding, Sir John (d 1780) II 78
Fiennes, Nathaniel (1608?–1669) I 44
Fife, 2nd Earl of (1729–1809) II 78
Fife, 4th Earl of (1766–1857) II 78
Figg, James (d 1734) I 44
Figgis, J.N. (1866–1919) IV 35
Fildes, Sir Luke (1843/4–1927) III 69
Fildes, Sir Paul (1882–1971) IV 35
Filon, L.N.G. (1875–1937) III 35–36
Finch, 1st Baron (1584–1660) I 44
Finch, Edward (1664–1737?) I 44
Finch, G.I. (1888–1970) IV 36
Finch, F.O. (1802–1862) III 69
Finch, Sir Heneage (1580–1631) I 44
Finch, Sir John (1626–1682) I 44
Finch, Robert (1783–1830) II 78
Finch, R.P. (1724–1803) II 78
Finden, E.F. (1791–1857) II 78
Findlay, Sir George (1829–1893) III 69
Finet(t), Sir John (1571–1641) I 44
Finger, Gottfried (fl 1685–1717) I 44
Finlay, 1st Viscount (1842–1929) III 69
Finlay, 2nd Viscount (1875–1945) IV 36
Finlayson, John (1770–1854) II 78
Finnie, John (1829–1907) III 69
Firbank, Ronald (1886–1925) IV 36
Firth, Sir C.H. (1857–1936) III 69
Firth, J.R. (1890–1960) IV 36
Firth, Mark (1819–1880) III 69
Fischer, J.C. (1733–1800) II 78
Fisher, 1st Baron (1841–1920) III 69
Fisher, Daniel (1731–1807) II 78
Fisher, H.A.L. (1865–1940) IV 36
Fisher, James (1697–1775) I 44
Fisher, Jane, Lady (d 1689) I 44
Fisher, John (1459–1535) I 44
Fisher, John (1748–1825) II 78
Fisher, Sir J.W. (1788–1876) II 78
Fisher, Kitty (d 1767) II 78
Fisher, Sir Warren (1879–1948) IV 36
Fisher, Sir R.A. (1890–1962) IV 36
Fisher, Sir Warren (1879–1948) IV 36
Fisher, W.W. (1798?–1874) II 78
Fisher, Sir W.W. (1875–1937) IV 36
Fisher of Lambeth, Baron (1887–1972) IV 36
Fitch, W.S. (1793–1859) II 78
Fitchett, John (1776–1838) II 78
Fittler, James (1758–1835) II 78
Fitton, Mary (fl 1600) I 45
Fitzalan of Derwent, 1st Viscount (1855–1947) III 69
Fitzball, Edward (1792–1873) II 78
Fitzgerald, Lord (1763–1798) II 78
Fitzgerald, Lord (1816–1889) III 69
Fitzgerald, Edward (1809–1883) III 69
Fitzgerald, G.F. (1851–1901) III 69
Fitzgerald, G.R. (1748?–1786) II 78
Fitzgerald, James (1742–1835) II 78
Fitzgerald, Pamela (1776?–1831) II 78
Fitzgerald, Sir W.R.S.V. (1818–1885) III 69
Fitzgerald, W.T. (1759?–1829) II 79
Fitzgibbon, Gerald (1837–1909) III 69
Fitzhardinge, 1st Baron (1788–1867) II 79
Fitzherbert, Maria Anne (1756–1837) II 79
Fitzmaurice, Baron (1846–1935) III 69
Fitzmaurice, Sir Maurice (1861–1924) IV 36
Fitzpatrick, Sir Dennis (1837–1920) III 69
Fitzpatrick, Richard (1747–1813) II 79
Fitzpatrick, W.J. (1830–1895) III 69–70
Fitzroy, Sir C.A. (1796–1858) II 79
Fitzroy, E.A. (1869–1943) IV 36
Fitzroy, Robert (1805–1865) III 70
Fitzwilliam, 4th Earl (1748–1833) II 79
Fitzwilliam, 5th Earl of (1786–1857) II 79
Fitzwilliam, Edward (1788–1852) II 79
Fitzwilliam, Frances Elizabeth (1801–1854) III 70
Fitzwilliam, John (1651–1699) I 45
Fitzwilliam of Meryon, 7th Viscount (1745–1816) II 79
Flamsteed, John (1646–1719) I 45
Flatman, Thomas (1637–1688) I 45
Flavel, John (1630?–1691) I 45
Flaxman, Anne (d 1820) II 79
Flaxman, John (1755–1826) II 79
Flaxman, Mary Ann (1768–1833) II 79
Fleck, 1st Baron (1889–1968) IV 36
Fleetwood, Charles (d 1692) I 45
Fleetwood, George (1622?–after 1664) I 45
Fleetwood, Sir P.H., 1st Bart (1801–1866) III 70
Fleetwood, William (1656–1723) I 45
Fleming, Sir Alexander (1881–1955) IV 36
Fleming, Sir Ambrose (1849–1945) III 70
Fleming, Sir A.P.M. (1881–1960) IV 36
Fleming, Caleb (1698–1779) I 45
Fleming, Sir George, Bart (1667–1747) I 45
Fleming, George (1833–1901) III 70
Fleming, James (1682–1751) I 45
Fleming, James (1829–1908) III 70

Fleming, John (1785–1857) II 79
Fleming, Richard (d 1431) I 45
Fleming, Robert (1660?–1716) I 45
Fleming, Sir Thomas (1544–1613) I 45
Fletcher, Alexander (1787–1860) II 79
Fletcher, Sir B.F. (1866–1953) IV 36
Fletcher, Eliza (1770–1858) II 79
Fletcher, Sir Frank (1870–1954) IV 36
Fletcher, Hanslip (1874–1955) IV 36
Fletcher, Sir Henry (1727–1807) II 79
Fletcher, James (1852–1908) III 70
Fletcher, John (1579–1625) I 45
Fletcher, Joseph (1784–1843) II 79
Fletcher, Joseph (1816–1876) III 70
Fletcher, J.W. (1729–1785) II 79
Fletcher, Sir Richard (1768–1813) II 79
Fletcher, Sir W.M. (1873–1933) IV 36
Fletcher of Saltoun, Andrew (1655–1716) I 45
Flett, Sir J.S. (1869–1947) IV 36
Flexman, Roger (1708–1795) II 79
Flexmore, Richard (1824–1860) III 70
Flinders, Matthew (1774–1814) II 79
Flint, Robert (1838–1910) III 70
Flint, Sir W.R. (1880–1969) IV 36
Flitcroft, Henry (1697–1769) I 45
Flood, Henry (1732–1791) II 79–80
Florey, Baron (1898–1968) IV 36
Florio, John (1553?–1625) I 45
Flower, Benjamin (1755–1829) II 80
Flower, Sir C.T. (1879–1961) IV 36
Flower, R.E.W. (1881–1946) IV 36
Flower, Sir W.H. (1831–1899) III 70
Fludd, Robert (1574–1637) I 45
Fludyer, Sir Samuel (1705–1768) II 80
Fogerty, Elsie (1865–1945) IV 36
Fogg, Laurence (1623–1718) I 45
Foley, J.H. (1818–1874) III 70
Foley, Sir Thomas (1757–1833) II 80
Folkes, Martin (1690–1754) I 45
Follett, Sir W.W. (1798–1845) II 80
Fonblanque, A.W. (1793–1872) II 80
Foot, Isaac (1880–1960) IV 37
Foot, Jesse (1744–1826) II 80
Foote, Sir E.J. (1767–1833) II 80
Foote, Lydia (1844?–1892) III 70
Foote, Samuel (1720–1777) II 80
Forbes, 17th Baron (1765–1843) II 80
Forbes, Achibald (1838–1900) III 70
Forbes, Sir Charles, Bart (1774–1849) II 80
Forbes, Sir C.M. (1880–1960) IV 37
Forbes, David (1777?–1849) II 80
Forbes, Edward (1815–1854) III 70
Forbes, James (1749–1819) II 80
Forbes, James (1779–1837) II 80
Forbes, John (1571–1606) I 45
Forbes, John (1714–1796) II 80
Forbes, Sir John (1787–1861) II 80
Forbes, J.D. (1809–1868) III 70
Forbes, J.S. (1823–1904) III 70
Forbes, Patrick (1564–1635) I 45
Forbes, Rosita (1893–1967) IV 37
Forbes, S.A. (1857–1947) III 70
Forbes, William (1585–1634) I 45
Forbes, Sir William (1739–1806) II 80
Forbes of Culloden, Duncan (1685–1747) I 45
Forbes-Robertson, Sir Johnston (1853–1937) III 70–71
Forby, Robert (1759–1825) II 80
Ford, E.O. (1852–1901) III 71
Ford, Sir F.C. (1828–1899) III 71
Ford, Ford Madox (1873–1939) IV 37
Ford, James (1779–1850) II 80
Ford, Richard (1796–1858) II 80
Fordham, George (1837–1887) III 71
Fordyce, George (1736–1802) II 80
Fordyce, James (1720–1796) II 80
Forester, C.S. (1899–1966) IV 37
Forester-Walker, Sir F.W.E.F. (1844–1910) III 71
Forman, Simon (1552–1611) I 45
Forrest, 1st Baron (1847–1918) III 71
Forrest, Arthur (d 1770) II 80
Forrest, Theodosius (1728–1784) II 80
Forrest, Thomas (1729?–1802?) II 80
Forrester, A.H. (1804–1872) III 71
Forster, Edward (1730–1812) II 80
Forster, Edward (1765–1849) II 80–81
Forster, E.M. (1879–1970) IV 37
Forster, John (1812–1876) III 71
Forster, J.C. (1823–1886) III 71
Forster, Thomas (fl 1690–1710) I 45
Forster, Thomas (1675?–1738) I 46
Forster, Thomas (1761–1825) II 81
Forster, William (1784–1854) II 81
Forster, W.E. (1818–1886) III 71
Forsyth, A.R. (1858–1942) III 71
Forsyth, William (1737–1804) II 81
Forsyth, William (1812–1899) III 71
Fortescue, 3rd Earl (1818–1905) III 71

Fortescue, 4th Earl (1854–1932) III 71
Fortescue, Sir Edmund (1610–1647) I 46
Fortescue, Sir John (1394?–1476?) I 46
Fortescue, Sir John (1531?–1607) I 46
Fortescue, Sir J.W. (1859–1933) III 71
Fortescue, William (1687–1749) I 46
Fortescue of Credan, Baron (1670–1746) I 46
Fortnum, C.D.E. (1820–1899) III 71
Foss, H.J. (1899–1953) IV 37
Foster, Sir Gregory, 1st Bart (1866–1931) IV 37
Foster, James (1697–1753) I 46
Foster, John (1770–1843) II 81
Foster, Sir Michael (1689–1763) I 46
Foster, Sir Michael (1836–1907) III 71
Foster, M.B. (1825–1899) III 71–72
Foster, Robert (1589–1663) I 46
Foster, Thomas (1798–1826) II 81
Foster, V.H.L. (1819–1900) III 72
Fotherby, Martin (1549?–1619) I 46
Fothergill, Anthony (1732?–1813) II 81
Fothergill, George (1705–1760) II 81
Fothergill, John (1712–1780) II 81
Fothergill, J.R. (1876–1957) I* 37
Fotheringham, J.K. (1874–1936) IV 37
Foulis, Andrew (1712–1775) II 81
Foulis, Robert (1707–1776) II 81
Fountaine, Sir Andrew (1676–1753) I 46
Fourdrinier, Henry (1766–1854) II 81
Fowke, Francis (1823–1865) III 72
Fowke, John (d 1662) I 46
Fowle, T.W. (1835–1903) III 72
Fowler, Alfred (1868–1940) IV 37
Fowler, Edward (1632–1714) I 46
Fowler, Sir John, 1st Bart (1817–1898) III 72
Fowler, Robert (1726?–1801) II 81
Fowler, Sir R.H. (1889–1944) IV 37
Fowler, Sir R.N., 1st Bart (1828–1891) III 72
Fowler, Thomas (1832–1904) III 72
Fowler, William (1761–1832) II 81
Fowler, W.W. (1847–1921) III 72
Fownes, George (1815–1849) III 72
Fox, Charles (1794–1849) II 81
Fox, Sir Charles (1810–1874) III 72
Fox, Charles James (1749–1806) II 81
Fox, Sir C.F. (1882–1967) IV 37
Fox, C.R. (1796–1873) II 81
Fox, Dame Evelyn (1874–1955) IV 37
Fox, George (1624–1691) I 46
Fox, H.E. (1755–1811) II 81
Fox, Samson (1838–1903) III 72
Fox, Sir Stephen (1627–1716) I 46
Fox, William (1736–1826) II 81
Fox, Sir William (1812–1893) III 72
Fox, Wilson (1831–1887) III 72
Fox, W.J. (1786–1864) II 81
Foxe, John (1516–1587) I 46
Foxe, Richard (1448?–1528) I 46
Foxwell, H.S. (1849–1936) III 72
Foyle, G.S. (1886–1971) IV 37
Foyle, W.A. (1885–1963) IV 37
Frampton, Sir G.J. (1860–1928) IV 37
Frampton, Robert (1622–1708) I 46
Frampton, Tregonwell (1641–1727) I 46
Francatelli, C.E. (1805–1876) III 72
Francis, Sir Philip (1740–1818) II 81
Franck, Mark (1613–1664) I 46
Francklin, Thomas (1721–1784) II 81
Frankau, Gilbert (1884–1952) IV 37
Frankland, Joyce (1531–1587) I 46
Frankland, P.F. (1858–1946) III 72
Frankland, Richard (1630–1698) I 46
Franklin, Jane, Lady (1792–1875) II 81
Franklin, Sir John (1786–1847) II 81
Franks, Sir A.W. (1826–1897) III 72
Fraser, Sir Alexander (1537?–1623) I 46
Fraser, Lord (1819–1889) III 72
Fraser, Alexander (1827–1899) III 72
Fraser, Andrew (d 1792) II 82
Fraser, A.C. (1736–1815) II 82
Fraser, A.C. (1819–1914) III 72
Fraser, Sir A.H.L. (1848–1919) III 72
Fraser, A.M. (1756–1809) II 82
Fraser, C.L. (1890–1921) IV 37
Fraser, Donald (1826–1892) III 72
Fraser, James (d 1841) II 82
Fraser, James (1818–1885) III 72
Fraser, J.B. (1783–851856) II 82
Fraser, J.K. (1832–1895) III 72
Fraser, Lionel (1895–1965) IV 37
Fraser, Sir Ronald (1888–1974) IV 37
Fraser, Simon (d 1777) II 82
Fraser, Simon (1726–1782) II 82
Fraser, Sir T.R. (1841–1920) III 72
Fraser, Sir William (1816–1898) III 72–73
Fraser, Sir W.A., 4th Bart (1826–1898) III 73
Fraser of Lonsdale, 1st Baron (1897–1974) IV 37
Fraser of North Cape, 1st Baron (b 1888) IV 37

Frazer, Sir A.S. (1776–1835) II *82*
Frazer, Sir J.G. (1854–1941) III *73*
Fréchette, L.H. (1839–1908) III *73*
Frederica, Duchess of York (1767–1820) II *82*
Frederick V, King of Bohemia (1596–1632) I *46*
Frederick Lewis, Prince of Wales (1707–1751) II *82*
Freeling, Sir Francis, Bart (1764–1836) II *82*
Freeman, E.A. (1823–1892) III *73*
Freeman, John (1880–1929) IV *37*
Freeman, Sir W.R., 1st Bart (1888–1953) IV *37*
Freemantle, Sir E.R. (1836–1929) III *73*
Freeth, F.A. (1884–1970) IV *37*
Freind, John (1675–1728) I *46*
Freind, Robert (1667–1751) I *46*
Freind, William (1715–1766) II *82*
Freke, John (1688–1756) I *46*
Fremantle, Sir T.F. (1765–1819) II *82*
Fremantle, Sir W.H. (1766–1850) II *82*
French, Evangeline Frances (1869–1960) IV *37–38*
French, Francesca Law (1871–1960) IV *38*
French, Sir Henry (1883–1966) IV *38*
French, William (1786–1849) II *82*
Frend, William (1757–1841) II *82*
Frere, Sir H.B.E., 1st Bart (1815–1884) III *73*
Frere, J.H. (1769–1846) II *82*
Frere, William (1775–1836) II *82*
Frere, W.H. (1863–1938) IV *38*
Freshfield, D.W. (1845–1934) III *73*
Frewen, Accepted (1588–1664) I *46*
Frewen, John (1558–1628) I *46*
Frewen, Richard (1677?–1761) I *46*
Freyberg, 1st Baron (1889–1963) IV *38*
Fryer, Sir P.J. (1851–1921) III *73*
Frith, Mary (1584?–1659) I *47*
Frith, W.P. (1819–1909) III *73*
Fritsch, F.E. (1879–1954) IV *38*
Frobisher, Sir Martin (1535?–1594) I *47*
Frodsham, Bridge (1734–1768) II *82*
Frodsham, W.J. (1778–1850) II *82*
Frost, John (1626?–1656) I *47*
Frost, John (1781–1877) II *82–83*
Frost, W.E. (1810–1877) III *73*
Froude, J.A. (1818–1894) III *73*
Froude, Robert (1771?–1859) II *83*
Froude, William (1810–1879) III *73*
Frowde, Philip (d 1738) I *47*
Fry, C.B. (1872–1956) IV *38*
Fry, Sir Edward (1827–1918) III *73*
Fry, Elizabeth (1780–1845) II *83*
Fry, Margery (1874–1958) IV *38*
Fry, Roger (1866–1934) IV *38*
Fry, Ruth (1878–1962) IV *38*
Frye, Thomas (1710–1762) II *83*
Fryer, John (d 1733) I *47*
Fulford, Francis (1803–1868) III *73*
Fulke, William (1538–1589) I *47*
Fuller, Andrew (1754–1815) II *83*
Fuller, Sir Bampfylde (1854–1935) III *73–74*
Fuller, Sir C.T.M. (1874–1942) IV *38*
Fuller, Sir Isaac (1606?–1672) I *47*
Fuller, Thomas (1608–1661) I *47*
Fuller, Thomas (1654–1734) I *47*
Fuller, William (1608–1675) I *47*
Fuller, William (1670–1717?) I *47*
Fulleylove, John (1845–1908) III *74*
Furness, 1st Baron (1852–1912) III *74*
Furniss, Harry (1854–1925) III *74*
Furnivall, F.J. (1825–1910) III *74*
Furse, C.W. (1868–1904) IV *38*
Furse, Dame Katharine (1875–1952) IV *38*
Furse, M.B. (1870–1955) IV *38*
Furse, Sir R.D. (1887–1973) IV *38*
Fuseli, Henry (1741–1825) II *83*
Fust, Sir H.J. (1778–1852) II *83*
Fyfe, W.B.C. (1836?–1882) III *74*
Fyleman, Rose Amy (1877–1957) IV *38*

Gadbury, John (1627–1704) I *49*
Gadsby, William (1773–1844) II *84*
Gage, Sir Henry (1597–1645) I *49*
Gage, Sir John (1479–1556) I *49*
Gage, Thomas (1721–1787) II *84*
Gahan, William (1730–1804) II *84*
Gainford, 1st Baron (1860–1943) IV *39*
Gainsborough, Thomas (1727–1788) II *84*
Gairdner, James (1828–1912) III *75*
Gairdner, John (1790–1876) II *84*
Gairdner, Sir W.T. (1824–1907) III *75*
Gaisford, Thomas (1779–1855) II *84*
Gaitskell, Sir Arthur (b 1900) IV *39*
Gale, Sir H.M. (1890–1971) IV *39*
Gale, John (1680–1721) I *49*
Gale, Roger (1672–1744) I *49*
Gale, Samuel (1682–1754) I *49*
Gale, Thomas (1507–1587) I *49*
Gale, Thomas (1635?–1702) I *49*
Gale, William (1823–1909) III *75*

Gallacher, William (1881–1965) IV *39*
Gallenga, A.C.N. (1810–1895) III *75*
Galloway, 10th Earl of (1835–1901) III *75*
Galsworthy, John (1867–1933) IV *39*
Galt, Sir A.T. (1817–1893) III *75*
Galt, John (1779–1839) II *84*
Galton, Sir D.S. (1822–1899) III *75*
Galton, Sir Francis (1822–1911) III *75*
Galvin, George (1860–1904) IV *39*
Galway, 1st Earl of (1648–1720) I *49*
Gamage, Sir Leslie (1887–1972) IV *39*
Gambier, 1st Baron (1756–1833) II *84*
Gamble, John (d 1687) I *49*
Gambold, John (1711–1771) II *84*
Game, Sir P.W. (1876–1961) IV *39*
Gandon, James (1743–1823) II *84*
Gann, T.W.F. (1867–1938) IV *39*
Garancières, Theophilus (1610–1680) I *49*
Garbett, C.F. (1875–1955) IV *39*
Garbett, James (1802–1879) III *75*
Garcia, Manuel (1805–1906) III *75*
Gardelle, Theodore (1721–1761) II *84*
Gardenstone, Lord (1721–1793) II *84*
Gardiner, Arthur (1716?–1758) II *84*
Gardiner, A.G. (1865–1946) IV *39*
Gardiner, Sir A.H. (1879–1963) IV *39*
Gardiner, Clive (1891–1960) IV *39*
Gardiner, James (1637–1705) I *49*
Gardiner, James (1679?–1732) I *49*
Gardiner, James (1688–1745) I *49*
Gardiner, Sir R.W. (1781–1864) II *84*
Gardiner, Stephen (1483?–1555) I *49*
Gardiner, S.R. (1829–1902) III *75*
Gardiner, William (1748–1806) II *84*
Gardiner, William (1770–1853) II *84*
Gardiner, W.N. (1766?–1814) II *84*
Gardner, 1st Baron (1742–1809) II *84*
Gardner, 2nd Baron (1770–1815) II *84*
Gardner, 3rd Baron (1810–1883) III *75*
Gardner, E.A. (1862–1939) IV *39*
Gardner, Daniel (1750?–1805) II *84*
Gardner, Percy (1846–1937) III *75*
Gardner, Mrs (fl 1779–1790) II *84–85*
Gargrave, Sir Thomas (1495–1579) I *49*
Garner, W.E. (1889–1960) IV *39*
Garnett, David (b 1892) IV *39*
Garnett, Edward (1868–1937) IV *39*
Garnett, Henry (1555–1606) I *49*
Garnett, John (1709–1782) II *85*
Garnett, John (1748–1813) II *85*
Garnett, Maxwell (1880–1958) IV *39*
Garnett, Richard (1835–1906) III *75*
Garnett, Thomas (1766–1802) II *85*
Garnier, Thomas (1776–1873) II *85*
Garrard, Sir Samuel (1650–1724) I *49*
Garrett, J.L. (fl 1809) II *85*
Garrick, David (1717–1779) II *85*
Garrod, Sir A.B. (1819–1907) III *75*
Garrod, Sir A.E. (1857–1936) III *75*
Garrod, A.H. (1846–1879) III *75*
Garrod, H.W. (1878–1960) IV *39*
Garrow, Sir William (1760–1840) II *85*
Garstang, John (1876–1956) IV *39*
Garth, Sir Richard (1820–1903) III *75*
Garth, Sir Samuel (1661–1719) I *49*
Garthshore, William (1764–1806) II *85*
Garvey, Edmund (d 1813) II *85*
Garvie, A.E. (1861–1945) IV *39*
Garvin, J.L. (1868–1947) IV *39*
Gascoigne, George (1525?–1577) I *49*
Gascoigne, Richard (d 1716) I *49*
Gascoigne, Sir William (1350?–1419) I *49*
Gascoyne, Bamber (c 1729–1791) II *85*
Gascoyne, Sir Crisp (1700–1761) II *85*
Gaselee, Sir Stephen (1882–1943) IV *40*
Gask, G.E. (1875–1951) IV *40*
Gaskell, Elizabeth (1810–1865) III *75*
Gaskell, William (1805–1884) III *75*
Gaskell, W.H. (1847–1914) III *75*
Gaskin, George (1751–1829) III *85*
Gasquet, F.N. (1846–1929) III *75*
Gaster, Moses (1856–1939) III *75*
Gastineau, Henry (c 1791–1876) II *85*
Gastrell, Francis (1662–1725) I *49*
Gatacre, Sir W.F. (1843–1906) III *75*
Gatenby, J.B. (1892–1960) IV *40*
Gater, Sir G.H. (1886–1963) IV *40*
Gates, Bernard (1685?–1773) I *49*
Gates, Horatio (1728–1806) II *85*
Gattie, Henry (1774–1844) II *85*
Gatty, Margaret (1807–1873) III *75*
Gauden, John (1605–1662) I *49*
Gaudier-Brzeska, Henri (1891–1915) IV *40*
Gault, Hamilton (1882–1958) IV *40*
Gaultier, James (1600–1670?) I *49*
Gauntlett, Henry (1762–1833) II *85*
Gauntlett, H.J. (1805–1876) III *75–76*

Gauvain, Sir H.J. (1878–1945) IV *40*
Gay, John (1685–1732) I *49–50*
Gay, Noel (1898–1954) IV *40*
Gayton, Clark (c 1720–1787) II *85*
Geary, Sir Francis, Bart (1709–10–1796) II *85*
Geddes, 1st Baron (1879–1954) IV *40*
Geddes, Alexander (1737–1802) II *85*
Geddes, Andrew (1783–1844) II *85*
Geddes, Sir E.C. (1875–1937) IV *40*
Geddes, Sir Patrick (1854–1932) III *76*
Gee, Sir Orlando (d 1705) I *50*
Gee, S.J. (1839–1911) II *76*
Geffrey, Sir Robert (1613–1703?) I *50*
Geikie, Sir Archibald (1835–1924) III *76*
Geldorp, George (fl 1611–1660) I *50*
Gell, Frederick (1820–1902) III *76*
Gell, Sir John, Bart (1593–1671) I *50*
Gell, John (c 1740–1805) II *85*
Gell, Sir William (1777–1836) II *85*
Gellibrand, Sir John (1872–1945) IV *40*
Gemmell, Sir Arthur (1892–1960) IV *40*
Gendall, John (1790–1865) II *85*
Genée-Isitt, Dame Adeline (1878–1970) IV *40*
Gent, Thomas (1693–1778) I *50*
Gent-Tharp, W.M. (1837–1899) III *76*
Gentileschi, Artemisia (1590?–1642?) I *50*
Gentileschi, Orazio (1563–1647) I *50*
George I (1660–1727) I *50*
George II (1683–1760) I *50*
George III (1738–1820) II *85–86*
George IV (1762–1830) II *86*
George V (1865–1936) IV *40*
George VI (1895–1952) IV *40–41*
George of Denmark, Prince (1653–1708) I *50*
George, Dorothy (1878–1971) IV *41*
George, Sir Ernest (1839–1922) III *76*
Gerard, Alexander (1728–1795) II *86*
Gerard, John (1545–1612) I *50*
Gerbier, Sir Balthasar (1591?–1667) I *50*
Gere, C.M. (1869–1957) IV *41*
Germain(e), Lady Betty (1680–1769) I *50*
German, Sir Edward (1862–1936) IV *41*
Gerrald, Joseph (1763–1796) II *86*
Gertler, Mark (1891–1939) IV *41*
Gethin, Lady Grace (1676–1697) I *50*
Gething(e), Richard (1585?–1652?) I *50*
Gheeraerts, Marcus (1510?–1590?) I *51*
Gibb, Sir Alexander (1872–1958) IV *41*
Gibb, Sir C.D. (1898–1959) IV *41*
Gibbes, Sir G.S. (1771–1851) II *86*
Gibbings, R.J. (1889–1958) IV *41*
Gibbon, Edward (1737–1794) II *86–87*
Gibbons, Christopher (1615–1676) I *51*
Gibbons, Grinling (1648–1720) I *51*
Gibbons, Orlando (1583–1625) I *51*
Gibbons, Thomas (1720–1785) II *87*
Gibbons, William (1649–1728) I *51*
Gibbs, Armstrong (1889–1960) IV *41*
Gibbs, James (1682–1754) I *51*
Gibbs, Sir Philip (1877–1962) IV *41*
Gibbs, Joseph (1700?–1788) II *87*
Gibbs, Mrs Mary (1770–1844?) II *87*
Gibbs, Sir Vicary (1751–1820) II *87*
Gibbs, Vicary (1853–1932) III *76*
Gibbs, Mrs (1804–1854?) III *76*
Gibson, Edmund (1669–1748) I *51*
Gibson, Edward (1668–1701) I *51*
Gibson, John (d 1852) II *87*
Gibson, John (1790–1866) II *87*
Gibson, Patrick (c 1782–1829) II *87*
Gibson, Richard (1615–1690) I *51*
Giffard, Bonaventure (1642–1734) I *51*
Giffard, Sir G.J. (1886–1964) IV *41*
Giffard, Sir G.M. (1813–1870) III *76*
Gifford, 1st Baron (1779–1826) II *87*
Gifford, Lord (1820–1887) III *76*
Gifford, Andrew (1700–1784) II *87*
Gifford, William (1756–1826) II *87*
Gilbart, J.W. (1794–1863) II *87*
Gilbert, Sir Alfred (1854–1934) III *76*
Gilbert, A.T. (1786–1870) II *87*
Gilbert, Claudius (1670–1743) I *51*
Gilbert, Davies (1767–1839) II *87*
Gilbert, Sir Geoffrey (1674–1726) I *51*
Gilbert, Sir Humphrey (1539?–1583) I *51*
Gilbert, John (1693–1761) I *51*
Gilbert, Sir John (1817–1897) III *76*
Gilbert, Joseph (1779–1852) II *87*
Gilbert, J.H. (1817–1901) III *76*
Gilbert, Sir J.T. (1829–1898) III *76*
Gilbert, Marie Dolores Eliza Rosanna (1818–1861) III *76*
Gilbert, Samuel (d 1692?) I *51*
Gilbert, William (1540–1603) I *51*
Gilbert, Sir W.R. (1785–1853) II *87*
Gilbert, Sir W.S. (1836–1911) III *76*
Gilchrist, J.B. (1759–1841) II *87*
Gilchrist, O.G. (1779–1823) II *87*

Giles, Peter (1860–1935) IV *41*
Gilfillan, George (1813–1878) III *76*
Gilfillan, Robert (1798–1850) II *87*
Gill, Sir David (1843–1914) III *76*
Gill, Eric (1882–1940) IV *41*
Gill, John (1697–1771) I *51*
Gill, W.J. (1843–1882) III *76*
Gillespie, James (1726–1797) II *87*
Gillespie, Sir R.R. (1766–1814) II *87*
Gilliat, Sir William (1884–1956) IV *41*
Gillies, Lord (1760–1842) II *87*
Gillies, Duncan (1834–1903) III *76*
Gillies, Sir H.D. (1882–1960) IV *41*
Gillies, John (1747–1836) II *87*
Gilliland, Thomas (fl 1804) II *87*
Gillingwater, Edmund (1735?–1813) II *87*
Gillis, James (1802–1864) III *76*
Gillow, John (1753–1828) II *87*
Gillray, James (1756–1815) II *87–88*
Gilly, W.S. (1780–1855) II *88*
Gilmour, Sir John (*d*1671) I *51*
Gilmour, Sir John, 2nd Bart (1876–1940) IV *41*
Gilpin, Edward (1517–1583) I *51*
Gilpin, Sawrey (1733–1807) II *88*
Gilpin, William (1724–1804) II *88*
Ginner, Charles (1878–1952) IV *41*
Ginsberg, Morris (1889–1970) IV *41*
Ginsburg, C.D. (1831–1914) III *77*
Gipps, Sir George (1791–1847) II *88*
Gipps, Sir Richard (1659–1708) II *51*
Giraud, H.J. (1817–1888) III *77*
Girdlestone, G.R. (1881–1950) IV *41*
Girtin, Thomas (1775–1802) II *88*
Gisborne, Thomas (1758–1846) II *88*
Gissing, George (1857–1903) III *77*
Gladstone, Viscount (1854–1930) III *77*
Gladstone, Sir John (1764–1851) II *88*
Gladstone, J.H. (1827–1902) III *77*
Gladstone, W.E. (1809–1898) III *77*
Gladstone, W.H. (1840–1891) III *77*
Glaisher, James (1809–1903) III *77*
Glaisher, J.W.L. (1848–1928) III *77*
Glanvill, Joseph (1636–1680) I *51*
Glanville, Sir John (1542–1600) I *51*
Glanville, Sir John (1586–1661) I *51*
Glas, John (1695–1773) I *51*
Glass, Sir R.A. (1820–1873) III *77–78*
Glass, Thomas (*d*1780) II *88*
Glasse, Samuel (1735–1812) II *88*
Glassford, John (1715–1783) I *51*
Glazebrook, M.G. (1853–1926) III *78*
Glazebrook, Sir R.T. (1854–1935) III *78*
Gleichen, Count (1833–1891) III *78*
Gleig, George (1753–1840) II *88*
Gleig, G.R. (1796–1888) II *88*
Glenalmond, Lord (1803–1869) III *78*
Glenavy, 1st Baron (1851–1931) IV *41*
Glenbervie, Baron (1743–1823) II *88*
Glencairn, 9th Earl of (1610?–1664) I *51*
Glencairn, 14th Earl of (1749–1791) II *88*
Glencorse, Lord (1810–1891) II *88*
Glenelg, Baron (1778–1866) II *88*
Glenesk, 1st Baron (1830–1908) III *78*
Glenlee, Lord (1717–1789) II *88*
Glenlee, Lord (1755–1846) II *88*
Glenny, A.T. (1882–1965) IV *41*
Glenny, George (1793–1874) II *88*
Glenorchy, Viscountess (1741–1786) II *88*
Glisson, Francis (1597–1677) I *51*
Gloucester, Henry, Duke of 1640–1660) I *51*
Gloucester, Henry, Prince and Duke of (1900–1974) IV *41–42*
Gloucester, Maria, Duchess of (1739–1807) II *88*
Gloucester, William, Duke of (1689–1700) I *51–52*
Gloucester, William Frederick, 2nd Duke of (1776–1834) II *88*
Gloucester, William Henry, 1st Duke of (1743–1805) II *88–89*
Glover, John (1767–1849) II *89*
Glover, Julia (1779–1850) II *89*
Glover, Richard (1712–1785) II *89*
Glover, T.R. (1869–1943) IV *42*
Gluck, Helen (1896–1978) IV *42*
Glyn, Elinor (1864–1943) IV *42*
Glyn, Isabella Dallas (1823–1889) III *78*
Glyn, Sir R.C., 1st Bart (1755–1838) II *89*
Glynn, John (1722–1779) II *89*
Glynne, Sir John (1603–1666) I *52*
Glynne, Sir S.R., 9th Bart (1807–1874) III *78*
Goad, John (1616–1689) I *52*
Goddard, 1st Baron (1877–1971) IV *42*
Goddard, W.S. (1757–1845) II *89*
Godfrey, Ambrose (*d*1741) I *52*
Godfrey, Ambrose (*d*1756) I *52*
Godfrey, Daniel (1831–1903) III *78*
Godfrey, Sir E.B. (1621–1678) I *52*
Godfrey, J.H. (1888–1971) IV *42*
Godfrey, Peter (1899–1970) IV *42*

Godfrey, William (1889–1963) IV *42*
Godkin, E.L. (1831–1902) III *78*
Godlee, Sir R.J., Bart (1849–1925) III *78*
Godley, Sir A.J. (1867–1957) IV *42*
Godley, J.R. (1814–1861) III *78*
Godolphin, 1st Earl of (1645–1712) I *52*
Godolphin, 2nd Earl of (1678–1766) I *52*
Godolphin, Mrs Margaret (1652–1678) I *52*
Godolphin, Sidney (1610–1643) I *52*
Godolphin, Sir William (1634?–1696) I *52*
Godwin, Francis (1562–1633) I *52*
Godwin, George (1815–1888) III *78*
Godwin, Mrs Mary (1759–1797) II *89*
Godwin, Thomas (1517–1590) I *52*
Godwin, William (1756–1836) II *89*
Godwin-Austen, H.H. (1834–1923) III *78*
Gogarty, O.J. StJ. (1878–1957) IV *42*
Gold, Sir H.G. (1876–1952) IV *42*
Goldie, Sir G.D.T. (1846–1925) III *78*
Golding, Louis (1895–1958) IV *42*
Goldsalve, Sir John (*d*1556) I *52*
Goldsmid, Abraham (1756?–1810) III *89*
Goldsmid, Sir F.H. (1808–1878) III *78*
Goldsmid, Sir I.L., Bart (1778–1859) II *89*
Goldsmith, Francis (1613–1655) I *52*
Goldsmith, Oliver (1728–1774) II *89*
Gollancz, Sir Israel (1863–1930) IV *42*
Gollancz, Sir Victor (1893–1967) IV *42*
Gomm, Sir W.M. (1784–1875) II *89*
Gonne, Maud (1866–1953) IV *42*
Gooch, Sir Daniel (1816–1889) III *78*
Gooch, G.P. (1873–1968) IV *42*
Gooch, Robert (1784–1830) II *89*
Gooch, Sir Thomas, 2nd Bart (1674–1754) I *52*
Good, J.M. (1764–1827) II *89*
Good, T.S. (1789–1872) II *89*
Goodall, Charles (1642–1712) I *52*
Goodall, Charlotte (1765–1830) II *89*
Goodall, Frederick (1822–1904) III *78*
Goodall, Joseph (1760–1840) II *89*
Goodall, Thomas (1767–1832?) II *89*
Goode, Francis (1797–1842) II *89*
Goode, William (1762–1816) II *89*
Goode, Sir W.A.M. (1875–1944) IV *42*
Goodenough, F.C. (1866–1934) IV *42*
Goodenough, J.G. (1830–1875) III *78*
Goodenough, Samuel (1743–1827) II *89*
Goodenough, Sir W.E. (1867–1945) IV *42*
Goodenough, Sir W.M., 1st Bart (1899–1951) IV *42*
Goodere, Samuel (1687–1741) I *52*
Goodey, Tom (1885–1953) IV *42*
Goodford, C.O. (1812–1884) III *78–79*
Goodhart-Rendel, H.S. (1887–1959) IV *42*
Goodman, Gabriel (1529?–1601) I *52*
Goodrich, E.S. (1868–1946) IV *42*
Goodrich, Thomas (*d*1554) I *52*
Goodricke, Sir Henry, Bart (1642–1705) I *52*
Goodricke, John (1764–1786) II *89*
Goodsir, John (1814–1867) III *79*
Goodwin, Arthur (1593?–1643) I *52*
Goodwin, Harvey (1818–1891) III *79*
Goodwin, John (1594?–1665) I *52*
Goodwin, Thomas (1600–1680) I *52*
Goodwin, William (1555?–1620) I *52*
Goodyear, Joseph (1797–1839) II *89*
Goossens, Sir Eugene (1893–1962) IV *42*
Goossens, L.J. (*b*1897) IV *42*
Gordon, 1st Duke of (1643–1716) I *52*
Gordon, 4th Duke of (1743–1827) III *89–90*
Gordon, 5th Duke of (1770–1836) II *90*
Gordon, Baron (1814–1879) III *79*
Gordon, Duchess of (*c*1749–1812) II *90*
Gordon, Duchess of (1794–1864) II *90*
Gordon, Lord Adam (*c*1726–1801) II *89*
Gordon, Sir Alexander (1786–1815) II *89*
Gordon, Charles George (1833–1885) III *79*
Gordon, G.S. (1881–1942) IV *42*
Gordon, Lord George (1751–1793) II *90*
Gordon, John (1544–1619) I *52*
Gordon, Sir J.A. (1782–1869) II *90*
Gordon, Sir J.W., 1st Bart (1773–1851) II *90*
Gordon, Sir J.W. (1788–1864) II *90*
Gordon, M.H. (1872–1950) IV *42*
Gordon, Osborne (1813–1883) III *79*
Gordon, P.L. (fl 1834) II *90*
Gordon, Osborne (1813–1883) III *79*
Gordon, Robert (1580–1656) I *52*
Gordon, Robert (1665–1732) I *53*
Gordon, Robert (1786–1853) II *90*
Gordon, Sir Robert (1791–1847) II *90*
Gordon, Thomas (1788–1841) II *90*
Gordon, Sir William (1814–1870) III *79*
Gordon of Gordonstoun, Sir Robert (1647–1704) I *52*
Gordon of Straloch, Robert (1580–1661) I *52–53*
Gordon-Cumming, Sir W.G., 4th Bart (1848–1930) III *79*
Gordon-Taylor, Sir Gordon (1878–1960) IV *42*
Gore, Mrs Catherine (1799–1861) II *90*

Gore, Charles (1853–1932) III *79*
Gore, S.F. (1878–1914) IV *42*
Gorell, 1st Baron (1848–1913) III *79*
Gorell, 3rd Baron (1884–1963) IV *42–43*
Gorges, Sir Arthur (*d*1625) I *53*
Gorham, G.C. (1787–1857) II *91*
Goring, Baron (1608–1657) I *53*
Gorst, Sir J.E. (1835–1916) III *79*
Gorst, Sir J.E. (1861–1911) IV *43*
Gort, 2nd Viscount (1768–1842) II *90*
Gort, Viscount (1886–1946) IV *43*
Goschen, 1st Viscount (1831–1907) III *79*
Gosford, 2nd Earl of (1776–1849) II *90*
Gosling, Harry (1861–1930) IV *43*
Goss, Sir John (1800–1880) III *79*
Gossage, Sir Leslie (1891–1949) IV *43*
Gosse, Sir Edmund (1849–1928) III *79–80*
Gosse, Philip (1810–1888) III *80*
Gosset, Isaac (1735?–1812) II *90*
Gostlin, John (1566?–1626) I *53*
Gostling, William (1696–1777) I *53*
Gotch, J.A. (1852–1942) III *80*
Gott, John (1830–1906) III *80*
Gott, W.H.E. (1897–1942) IV *43*
Gouge, Sir Arthur (1890–1962) IV *43*
Gouge, Thomas (1609–1681) I *53*
Gouge, William (1578–1653) I *53*
Gough, 1st Viscount (1779–1869) II *90*
Gough, Sir H.H. (1833–1909) III *80*
Gough, H.J. (1890–1965) IV *43*
Gough, Sir Hubert (de la Poer) (1870–1963) IV *43*
Gough, J.B. (1817–1886) III *80*
Gough, Richard (1735–1809) II *90*
Goulburn, E.M. (1818–1897) III *80*
Goulburn, Henry (1784–1856) II *90*
Goulburn, Henry (1813–1843) III *80*
Gould, Sir F.C. (1844–1925) III *80*
Gould, Sir Henry (1710–1794) II *91*
Gould, John (1804–1881) III *80*
Goulding, Frederick (1842–1909) III *80*
Goupy, Joseph (*d*1763) I *53*
Goupy, Lewis (*d*1747) I *53*
Gow, Neil (1727–1807) II *91*
Gower, 1st Earl of (*d*1754) I *53*
Gower, Sir Erasmus (1742–1814) II *91*
Gower, Foote (1726?–1780) II *91*
Gower, George (fl 1575–1585) I *53*
Gower, Humphrey (1638–1711) I *53*
Gower, John (1325?–1408?) I *53*
Gower, R.H. (1767–1833) II *91*
Gower, Lord R.S. (1845–1916) III *80*
Gowers, Sir E.A. (1880–1966) IV *43*
Gowrie, 1st Earl of (1872–1955) IV *43*
Grabe, J.E. (1666–1711) I *53*
Grace, Mary (*d*1786?) II *91*
Grace, Richard (1620?–1691) I *53*
Grace, Sheffield (1788?–1850) II *91*
Grace, W.G. (1848–1915) III *80*
Gracey, Sir D.D. (1894–1964) IV *43*
Gradwell, Robert (1777–1833) II *91*
Grafton, 1st Duke of (1663–1690) I *53*
Grafton, 3rd Duke of (1735–1811) II *91*
Grafton, 4th Duke of (1760–1844) II *91*
Grafton, Richard (*d*1572?) I *53*
Graham, Clementina Stirling (1782–1877) II *91*
Graham, Sir Gerald (1831–1899) III *80*
Graham, James (1676–1746) I *53*
Graham, James (1745–1794) II *91*
Graham, James (1791–1845) II *91*
Graham, James (1799–1874) II *91*
Graham, John (1794–1865) II *91*
Graham, J.A. (1861–1942) IV *43*
Graham, Sir J.R.G., 2nd Bart (1792–1861) II *91*
Graham, Sir Robert (1744–1836) II *91*
Graham, Robert (1786–1845) II *91*
Graham, R.B. Cunninghame (1852–1936) III *80*
Graham, Sir R.W. (1870–1949) IV *43*
Graham, Thomas (1805–1869) III *80*
Graham, T.A.F. (1840–1906) III *80–81*
Graham-Gilbert, John (1794–1866) II *91*
Graham-Harrison, Sir W.M. (1871–1949) IV *43*
Graham-Little, Sir E.G.G. (1867–1950) IV *43*
Grahame, James (1765–1811) II *91*
Grahame, Kenneth (1859–1932) III *81*
Grahame-White, Claude (1879–1959) IV *43*
Grain, R.C. (1844–1895) III *81*
Grainger, Edward (1797–1824) II *91*
Grainger, P.A. (1882–1961) IV *43*
Grainger, Richard (1798–1861) II *91*
Grainger, R.D. (1801–1865) III *81*
Grainger, Thomas (1794–1852) II *91*
Grammont, Countess of (1641–1708) I *53*
Granard, 6th Earl of (1760–1837) II *91*
Granby, Marquess of (1721–1770) II *91*
Grandison, 1st Viscount (1559–1630) I *53*
Granet, Sir Guy (1867–1943) IV *43*
Grange, Lord (1679–1754) I *53*

Granger, James (1723–1776) II 92
Grant, Albert (1830–1899) III 81
Grant, Sir Alexander, 8th Bart (1826–1884) III 81
Grant, Anne (1755–1838) II 92
Grant, Charles (1746–1823) II 92
Grant, Colquhoun (d 1792) II 92
Grant, Duncan (1885–1978) IV 43
Grant, Sir Francis (1803–1878) III 81
Grant, G.M. (1835–1902) III 81
Grant, Sir Hamilton, 12th Bart (1872–1937) IV 43
Grant, James (1720–1806) II 92
Grant, Sir James, 8th Bart (1738–1811) II 92
Grant, James (1802–1879) III 81
Grant, J.A. (1827–1892) III 81
Grant, Sir J.H. (1808–1875) III 81
Grant, Sir J.P. (1807–1893) III 81
Grant, Sir Patrick (1804–1895) III 81
Grant, Sir Robert (1779–1838) II 92
Grant, R.E. (1793–1874) II 92
Grant, Thomas (1816–1870) III 81
Grant, Sir William (1752–1832) II 92
Grant-Duff, Sir M.E. (1829–1906) III 81
Grantham, 1st Baron (1695–1770) I 53
Grantham, 2nd Baron (1738–1786) II 92
Grantham, Sir William (1835–1911) III 81
Grantley, 1st Baron (1716–1789) II 92
Granton, Lord (1763–1851) II 92
Granville, 2nd Earl of (1690–1763) I 53
Granville, 1st Earl (1773–1846) II 92
Granville, 2nd Earl (1815–1891) III 81
Granville-Barker, Harley (1877–1946) IV 43
Grattan, Henry (1746–1820) II 92
Grattan, T.C. (1792–1864) II 92
Gravelot, H.F. (1699–1773) I 54
Graves, 1st Baron (1725?–1802) II 92
Graves, Algernon (1845–1922) III 82
Graves, Henry (1806–1892) III 82
Graves, Richard (1677–1729?) I 54
Graves, Richard (1715–1804) II 92
Graves, Richard (1763–1829) II 92
Graves, Robert (1798–1873) II 92
Graves, Robert (b 1895) IV 43
Graves, R.J. (1796–1853) II 92
Graves, Sir Thomas (1747?–1814) II 92
Gray, Andrew (1805–1861) III 82
Gray, E.D. (1845–1888) III 82
Gray, E.W. (1748–1806) II 93
Gray, Sir George, Bart (d 1773) II 93
Gray, G.R. (1808–1872) III 82
Gray, Sir James, Bart (d 1773) II 93
Gray, Sir James (1891–1975) IV 43
Gray, Sir John (1816–1875) III 82
Gray, John (1866–1934) IV 44
Gray, J.E. (1800–1875) III 82
Gray, J.M. (1850–1895) III 82
Gray, Maria Emma (1787–1876) II 93
Gray, Robert (1762–1834) II 93
Gray, Robert (1809–1872) III 82
Gray, Thomas (1716–1771) II 93
Gray, Thomas (1788–1848) II 93
Graydon, John (1660?–1726) I 54
Greathead, Henry (1757–1816) II 93
Greatrakes, Valentine (1629–1683) I 54
Greaves, John (1602–1652) I 54
Greaves, J.P. (1777–1842) II 93
Greaves, Walter (1846–1930) III 82
Green, Amos (1735–1807) II 93
Green, Charles (1785–1870) II 93
Green, C.A.H. (1864–1944) IV 44
Green, Curtis (1875–1960) IV 44
Green, James (1771–1834) II 93
Green, Jane (d 1791) II 93
Green, J.H. (1791–1863) II 93
Green, J.R. (1837–1883) III 82
Green, Mary Ann Everett (1818–1895) III 82
Green, Richard (1803–1863) III 82
Green, Thomas (1658–1738) I 54
Green, T.H. (1836–1882) III 82
Green, Valentine (1739–1813) II 93
Green, Sir William, 1st Bart (1725–1811) II 93
Green, Sir W.K.M. (1836–1891) III 82
Greenaway, Kate (1846–1901) III 82
Greene, Baron (1883–1952) IV 44
Greene, Sir Graham (1857–1950) III 82
Greene, H.P. (1865–1936) IV 44
Greene, Maurice (1696?–1755) I 54
Greene, Richard (1716–1793) II 93
Greenfield, William (1799–1831) II 93
Greenhalgh, John (d 1651) I 54
Greenhill, Henry (1646–1708) I 54
Greenhill, John (1644?–1676) I 54
Greenhill, W.A. (1814–1894) III 82
Greenough, G.B. (1778–1855) II 93
Greenwell, William (1820–1918) III 82
Greenwood, 1st Viscount (1870–1948) IV 44
Greenwood, Arthur (1880–1954) IV 44
Greenwood, Frederick (1830–1909) III 82

Greenwood, John (1727–1792) II 93
Greenwood, J.G. (1821–1894) III 82
Greg, Sir W.W. (1875–1959) IV 44
Gregg, John (1798–1878) II 93
Gregg, R.S. (1834–1896) III 82
Gregory, David (1661–1708) I 54
Gregory, Edmund (fl 1646) I 54
Gregory, E.J. (1850–1909) III 82
Gregory, F.G. (1893–1961) IV 44
Gregory, Isabella Augusta, Lady (1852–1932) III 82
Gregory, James (1638–1675) I 54
Gregory, James (1753–1821) II 93
Gregory, John (1724–1773) II 93
Gregory, J.W. (1864–1932) IV 44
Gregory, O.G. (1774–1841) II 93
Gregory, Robert (1819–1911) III 82
Gregory, Sir R.A., Bart (1864–1952) IV 44
Gregory, William (d 1663) I 54
Gregory, Sir William (1624–1696) I 54
Gregory, William (1803–1858) III 83
Gregory, Sir W.H. (1817–1892) III 83
Gregson, Matthew (1749–1824) II 93
Greiffenhagen, M.W. (1862–1931) IV 44
Greig, Sir Samuel (1735–1788) II 93
Grenfell, 1st Baron (1841–1925) III 83
Grenfell, B.P. (1869–1926) IV 44
Grenfell, D.R. (1881–1968) IV 44
Grenfell, Pascoe (1761–1838) II 93
Grenfell, Sir W.T. (1865–1940) IV 44
Grenville, 1st Baron (1759–1834) II 94
Grenville, Sir Bevil (1596–1643) I 54
Grenville, Denis (1637–1703) I 54
Grenville, George (1712–1770) II 93
Grenville, Sir Richard (1541?–1591) I 54
Grenville, Thomas (1755–1846) II 94
Gresham, Sir Thomas (1519?–1579) I 54
Gresley, William (1801–1876) III 83
Gresse, J.A. (1741–1794) II 94
Greswell, Richard (c 1801–1881) III 83
Gretton, William (1736–1813) II 94
Greville, 2nd Baron (1841–1910) III 83
Greville, A.F. (1798–1864) II 94
Greville, C.C.F. (1794–1865) II 94
Greville, H.W. (1801–1872) II 94
Greville, R.K. (1794–1866) II 94
Grew, Nehemiah (1641–1712) I 54
Grey, 1st Earl (1729–1807) II 94
Grey, 2nd Earl (1764–1845) II 94
Grey, 3rd Earl (1802–1894) III 83
Grey, 4th Earl (18511917) III 83
Grey, Charles (1804–1870) III 83
Grey, C.G. (1875–1953) IV 44
Grey, Sir George (1799–1882) II 94
Grey, Sir George (1812–1898) III 83
Grey, Henry (1778–1859) II 94
Grey, Zachary (1688–1766) I 54
Grey of Fallodon, 1st Viscount (1862–1933) IV 44
Grey de Wilton, 14th Baron (1536–1593) I 54
Grey-Egerton, Sir Philip de Malpas, Bart (1806–1881) III 83
Grierson, Sir H.J.C. (1866–1960) IV 44
Grierson, John (1898–1972) IV 44
Grierson, Sir J.M. (1859–1914) III 83
Grieve, C.M. (1892–1978) IV 44
Grieve, William (1800–1844) III 83
Griffier, John (1656–1718) I 54
Griffin, Benjamin (1680–1740) I 54
Griffin, B.W. (1880–1956) IV 44
Griffin, Gerald (1803–1840) III 83
Griffin, J.J. (1802–1877) III 83
Griffith, Arthur (1872–1922) IV 44
Griffith, A.A. (1893–1963) IV 44
Griffith, Elizabeth (1720?–1793) II 94
Griffith, F.L. (1862–1934) IV 44
Griffith, George (1601–1666) I 54
Griffith, John (1714–1798) II 94
Griffith, Moses (1747–1819) II 94
Griffiths, E.H. (1851–1932) III 83
Griffiths, James (1890–1975) IV 44
Griffiths, John (1806–1885) III 83
Griffiths, Ralph (1720–1803) II 95
Grigg, Sir James (1890–1964) IV 45
Grignion, Charles (1717–1810) II 95
Grimaldi, Joseph (1778–1837) II 95
Grimaldi, William (1751–1830) II 95
Grimshaw, William (1708–1763) II 95
Grimston, 1st Viscount (1683–1756) I 54
Grimston, Sir Edward (1528?–1599) I 54
Grimston, Sir Harbottle, 2nd Bart (1603–1685) I 54
Grimston, Robert (1816–1884) III 83
Grimston, Sir Samuel, 3rd Bart (1643–1700) I 54
Grimthorpe, 1st Baron (1816–1905) III 83
Grindal, Edmund (1519?–1583) I 54
Grindal, William (d 1548) I 54–55
Gronow, R.H. (1794–1865) II 95
Groome, R.H. (1810–1889) III 83
Grose, Francis (1731?–1791) II 95
Grose, Sir Nash (1740–1814) II 95

Grose, T.H. (1845–1906) III 83
Grossmith, George (1847–1912) III 83
Grossmith, George (1874–1935) I★ 45
Grossmith, Weedon (1854–1919) III 83–84
Grosvenor, 1st Earl (1731–1802) II 95
Grosvenor, Benjamin (1676–1758) I 55
Grosvenor, John (1742–1823) II 95
Grosvenor, Sir Thomas, 3rd Bart (1656–1700) I 55
Grosvenor, Thomas (1764–1851) II 95
Grote, Arthur (1814–1886) III 84
Grote, George (1794–1871) II 95
Grote, Harriet (1792–1878) II 95
Grove, Sir Coleridge (1839–1920) III 84
Grove, Sir George (1820–1900) III 84
Grove, Henry (1684–1738) I 55
Grove, Robert (1634–1696) I 55
Grove, Sir W.R. (1811–1896) III 84
Grozer, Joseph (fl 1784–1798) II 95
Grub, George (1812–1892) III 84
Grundy, John (1782–1843) II 95
Guedalla, Philip (1889–1944) IV 45
Guest, Edwin (1800–1880) III 84
Guest, Joshua (1660–1747) I 55
Guest, Sir J.J., Bart (1785–1852) II 95
Guildford, Sir Henry (1489–1532) I 55
Guilford, 1st Baron (1637–1685) I 55
Guilford, 2nd Earl of (1732–1792) II 95
Guilford, 4th Earl of (1761–1817) II 95
Guilford, 5th Earl of (1766–1827) II 95
Guillebaud, C.W. (1890–1971) IV 45
Guinness, Sir B.L., 1st Bart (1798–1868) II 95
Guinness, H.G. (1835–1910) III 84
Guise, John (d 1765) I 55
Gull, Sir W.W., 1st Bart (1816–1890) III 84
Gully, John (1783–1863) II 95–96
Gully, J.M. (1808–1883) III 84
Gulston, Joseph (1745–1786) II 96
Gunn, Sir James (1893–1964) IV 45
Gunn, William (1750–1841) II 96
Gunning, Henry (1768–1854) II 96
Gunning, Peter (1614–1684) I 55
Gunning, Sir Robert, Bart (1731–1816) II 96
Günther, Albert (1830–1914) III 84
Gunther, Robert (1869–1940) IV 45
Gurney, Hudson (1775–1864) II 96
Gurney, Sir H.L.G. (1898–1951) IV 45
Gurney, H.P. (1847–1904) III 84
Gurney, Sir John (1768–1845) II 96
Gurney, Sir J.J. (1788–1847) II 96
Gurney, Russell (1804–1878) III 84
Gurney, Samuel (1786–1856) II 96
Gurney, Thomas (1705–1770) II 96
Gurney, W.B. (1777–1855) II 96
Gurwood, John (1790–1845) II 96
Gutch, John (1746–1831) II 96
Gutch, J.M. (1776–1861) II 96
Gutch, Robert (1777–1851) II 96
Guthrie, Frederick (1833–1886) III 84
Guthrie, G.J. (1785–1856) II 96
Guthrie, James (1612?–1661) I 55
Guthrie, Sir James (1859–1930) III 84
Guthrie, Thomas (1803–1873) III 84
Guthrie, Sir Tyrone (1900–1971) IV 45
Guthrie, T.A. (1856–1934) III 84
Guthrie, William (1708–1770) II 96
Gutteridge, H.C. (1876–1953) IV 45
Guy, Sir H.L. (1887–1956) IV 45
Guy, Thomas (1644?–1724) I 55
Guyon, R.D. (1803–1856) III 84
Guyse, John (1680–1761) I 55
Gwilt, George (1775–1856) II 96
Gwyer, Barbara Elizabeth (1881–1974) IV 45
Gwyer, Sir M.L. (1878–1952) IV 45
Gwyn, Nell (1650–1687) I 55
Gwynn, John (d 1786) II 96
Gwynn, John (1827–1917) III 84
Gwynn, Mary (1754/5–1840) II 96
Gwynn, S.L. (1864–1950) IV 45
Gwynne, H.A. (1865–1950) IV 45
Gwynne-Jones, Allan (b 1892) IV 45
Gwynne-Vaughan, Dame Helen (1879–1967) IV 45
Gye, Frederick (1781–1869) II 96
Gye, Frederick (1810–1878) III 84
Gyles, Henry (1640?–1709) I 55

Haak, Theodore (1605–1690) I 57
Haast, Sir J.F.J. von (1824–1887) III 85
Hacker, Arthur (1858–1919) III 85
Hacker, Francis (d 1660) I 57
Hackett, John (1592–1670) I 57
Haddington, 1st Earl of (1563–1637) I 57
Haddington, 2nd Earl of (1600–1640) I 57
Haddington, 6th Earl of (1680–1735) I 57
Haddington, 9th Earl of (1780–1858) II 97
Haddock, Nicholas (1686–1746) I 57
Haddock, Sir Richard (1629–1715) I 57
Haddon, A.C. (1855–1940) III 85

Haden, Sir F.S. (1818–1910) III 85
Hadley, John (1731–1764) II 97
Hadow, Grace Eleanor (1875–1940) IV 46
Hadow, Sir Henry (1859–1937) III 85
Hadow, James (1670?–1747) I 57
Haggard, Sir H.R. (1856–1925) III 85
Haghe, Louis (1806–1885) III 85
Hague, Charles (1769–1821) II 97
Hahn, Kurt (1886–1974) IV 46
Haig, 1st Earl (1861–1928) IV 46
Haigh, M.G. (1887–1962) IV 46
Hailes, Lord (1726–1792) II 97
Hailey, 1st Baron (1872–1969) IV 46
Hailsham, 1st Viscount (1872–1950) IV 46
Hailstone, John (1759–1847) II 97
Haines, Sir F.P. (1819–1909) III 85
Haines, Herbert (1826–1872) III 85
Haining, Sir R.H. (1882–1959) IV 46
Haire, Norman (1892–1952) IV 46
Hake, T.G. (1809–1895) III 85
Hakewill, George (1578–1649) I 57
Haking, Sir R.C.B. (1862–1945) IV 46
Halcrow, Sir W.T. (1883–1958) IV 46
Haldane, Viscount (1856–1928) III 85
Haldane, Elizabeth Sanderson (1862–1937) IV 46
Haldane, J.A. (1768–1851) II 97
Haldane, J.B.S. (1892–1964) IV 46
Haldane, J.S. (1860–1936) IV 46
Haldimand, Sir Frederick (1718–1791) II 97
Hale, John (d 1806) II 97
Hale, Sir Matthew (1609–1676) I 57
Hale, Richard (1670–1728) I 57
Hale, W.H. (1795–1870) II 97
Hale, W.S. (1791–1872) II 97
Hale-White, Sir William (1857–1949) III 85
Hales, Sir Edward, 2nd Bart (d 1695) I 57
Hales, John (d 1572?) I 57
Hales, John (1584–1656) I 57
Hales, Stephen (1677–1761) I 57
Halford, F.B. (1894–1955) IV 46
Halford, Sir Henry, 1st Bart (1766–1844) II 97
Halford, Sir Henry St John, 3rd Bart (1828–1897) III 85
Halhed, N.B. (1751–1830) II 97
Haliburton, T.C. (1796–1865) II 97
Halifax, 1st Marquess of (1633–1695) I 57
Halifax, 2nd Marquess of (1665–1700) I 57
Halifax, 1st Earl of (1661–1715) I 57
Halifax, 2nd Earl of (1716–1771) II 97
Halifax, 1st Viscount (1800–1885) III 85–86
Halifax, 2nd Viscount (1839–1934) III 85
Halifax, 1st Earl of (1881–1959) IV 46
Halkett, Baron von (1783–1863) II 97
Halkett, Sir Colin (1774–1856) II 97
Hall, 1st Viscount (1881–1965) IV 47
Hall, Anna Maria (1800–1881) III 86
Hall, Anthony (1679–1723) I 57
Hall, A.H. (1876–1949) IV 47
Hall, Sir A.J. (1866–1951) IV 47
Hall, Basil (1788–1844) II 97
Hall, Chambers (1786–1855) II 97
Hall, Sir Charles (1814–1883) III 86
Hall, Sir Charles (1843–1900) III 86
Hall, C.N. (1816–1902) III 86
Hall, Sir Daniel (1864–1942) IV 47
Hall, Edna Clarke, Lady (1879–1979) IV 47
Hall, Sir E.M. (1858–1929) III 86
Hall, George (1613–1668) I 57
Hall, George (1753–1811) II 97
Hall, Jacob (fl 1668) I 57
Hall, James (1755–1826) II 97
Hall, Sir James, 4th Bart (1761?–1832) II 97
Hall, John (1529?–1566?) I 57
Hall, John (1627–1656) I 57
Hall, John (1633–1710) I 57
Hall, John (1739–1797) II 97
Hall, Joseph (1574–1656) I 57–58
Hall, Radclyffe (1886?–1943) IV 47
Hall, Sir Reginald (1870–1943) IV 47
Hall, Robert (1764–1831) II 97–98
Hall, S.C. (1800–1889) III 86
Hall, Sir W.H. (1797?–1878) II 98
Hall, Sir W.K. (1816–1886) III 86
Hall-Patch, Sir Edmund (1896–1975) IV 47
Hallam, Arthur (1811–1833) III 86
Hallam, Henry (1777–1859) II 98
Hallam, H.F. (1824–1850) III 86
Hallé, Sir Charles (1819–1895) III 86
Hallé, Wilma, Lady (1839–1911) III 86
Hallett, Sir T.J. (1878–1957) IV 47
Halley, Edmund (1656–1742) I 97
Halley, Robert (1796–1876) II 98
Halliburton, W.D. (1860–1931) IV 47
Halliday, Andrew (1830–1877) III 86
Halliday, Sir W.R. (1886–1966) IV 47
Hallifax, Samuel (1733–1790) II 98
Halliwell-Phillipps, J.O. (1820–1889) III 86
Halsbury, 1st Earl of (1823–1921) III 86

Halsey, Sir Lionel (1872–1949) IV 47
Halswelle, Keeley (1832–1891) III 86
Halton, Timothy (1632?–1704) I 58
Hambleden, 2nd Viscount (1868–1928) IV 47
Hambourg, Mark (1879–1960) IV 47
Hamerton, P.G. (1834–1894) III 86
Hamey, Baldwin (1568–1640) I 58
Hamey, Baldwin (1600–1676) I 58
Hamilton, 2nd Marquess of (1589–1625) I 58
Hamilton, 1st Duke of (1606–1649) I 58
Hamilton, 2nd Duke of (1616–1651) I 58
Hamilton, 3rd Duke of (1635–1694) I 58
Hamilton, 4th Duke of (1658–1712) I 58
Hamilton, 5th Duke of (1703–1743) II 98
Hamilton, 10th Duke of (1767–1852) II 98
Hamilton, 11th Duke of (1811–1863) III 87
Hamilton, 1st Duchess of (1613?–1638) I 58
Hamilton, 3rd Duchess of (1636?–1716) I 58
Hamilton, Alexander (1739–1802) II 98
Hamilton, Lady Anne (1766–1846) II 98
Hamilton, Anthony (1646?–1720) I 58
Hamilton, Lord Archibald (1769–1827) II 98
Hamilton, Sir Charles, 2nd Bart (1767–1849) II 98
Hamilton, Cicely (1872–1952) IV 47
Hamilton, David (1768–1843) II 98
Hamilton, Sir Edward, 1st Bart (1772–1851) II 98
Hamilton, Elizabeth (1757–1816) II 98
Hamilton, Emma, Lady (1761?–1815) II 98
Hamilton, Gavin (1723–1798) II 98
Hamilton, Sir George, 1st Bart (d 1676) I 58
Hamilton, G.A. (1802–1871) III 86
Hamilton, Lord G.F. (1845–1927) III 86
Hamilton, Hugh (1729–1805) II 98
Hamilton, H.D. (1739–1808) II 98
Hamilton, Sir I.S.M. (1853–1947) III 86–87
Hamilton, James (1749–1835) II 98
Hamilton, James (1814–1867) III 87
Hamilton, John (d 1755) I 98–99
Hamilton, Sir John, 1st Bart (1755–1835) II 99
Hamilton, John McLure (1853–1936) III 87
Hamilton, Robert (1743–1829) II 99
Hamilton, Robert (1743–1829) II 99
Hamilton, Sir R.G.C. (1836–1895) III 87
Hamilton, Sir R.N.C., 6th Bart (1802–1887) III 87
Hamilton, Sir R.V. (1829–1912) III 87
Hamilton, R.W. (1794–1848) II 99
Hamilton, Thomas (1784–1858) II 99
Hamilton, Thomas (1789–1842) II 99
Hamilton, William (1704–1754) II 99
Hamilton, Sir William (1730–1803) II 99
Hamilton, William (1751–1801) II 99
Hamilton, Sir William, Bart (1788–1856) II 99
Hamilton, W.A.B. (1803–1881) III 87
Hamilton, W.G. (1729–1796) II 99
Hamilton, W.K. (1808–1869) III 87
Hamilton, W.R. (1777–1859) II 99
Hamilton, Sir W.R. (1805–1865) III 87
Hamilton and Argyll, Duchess of (1733–1790) II 99
Hamley, Sir E.B. (1824–1893) III 87
Hammond, Baron (1802–1890) III 87
Hammond, Henry (1605–1660) I 58
Hammond, Sir John (1889–1964) IV 47
Hammond, J.L. Le Breton (1872–1949) IV 47
Hammond, Robert (1621–1654) I 58
Hamnett, Nina (1890–1956) IV 47
Hamond, Sir A.S., 1st Bart (1738–1828) II 99
Hamond, Sir E.A.C., 2nd Bart (1779–1862) II 99
Hampden, 1st Viscount (1706–1783) II 99
Hampden, 1st Viscount (1814–1892) III 87
Hampden, 2nd Viscount (1841–1906) III 87
Hampden, John (1594–1643) I 58
Hampden, John (1656–1696) I 58
Hampden, R.D. (1793–1868) II 99
Hamper, William (1776–1831) II 99
Hampson, John (1760–1817?) II 99
Hampton, 1st Baron (1799–1880) II 99
Hanbury, Daniel (1825–1875) III 87
Hanbury, John (1664–1734) I 58
Hanbury, R.W. (1845–1903) III 87
Hanbury, William (1725–1778) II 99
Hanbury-Williams, Sir J.C. (1892–1965) IV 47
Hancock, Dame Florence (1893–1974) IV 47
Hancock, Sir Henry (1895–1965) IV 47
Hancock, Robert (1730–1817) II 99
Hancock, Thomas (1786–1865) II 99
Hancock, Walter (1799–1852) II 99
Handasyde, Charles (fl 1760–1780) II 99–100
Handel, George Frederick (1685–1759) I 58–59
Handley, Tommy (1892–1949) IV 47
Hankey, 1st Baron (1877–1963) IV 47
Hankey, Thomson (1805–1893) III 87
Hanlan, Edward (1855–1908) III 87
Hanmer, Baron (1809–1881) III 87
Hanmer, Sir Thomas, 4th Bart (1677–1746) I 59
Hanna, William (1808–1882) III 87
Hannah, John (1792–1867) II 100
Hannay, Patrick (d 1629?) I 59

Hanneman, Adriaen (1601?–1671) I 59
Hannen, Baron (1821–1894) III 88
Hannen, N.J. (1881–1972) IV 47
Hannon, Sir P.J.H. (1874–1963) IV 47
Hansard, Luke (1752–1828) II 100
Hansom, J.A. (1803–1882) III 88
Hanson, 'Sir' Levett (1754–1814) II 100
Hanson, Sir R.D. (1805–1876) III 88
Hanway, Jonas (1712–1786) II 100
Hanworth, 1st Viscount (1861–1936) IV 47
Harben, Sir Henry (1823–1911) III 88
Harbin, George (fl 1713) I 59
Harcourt, 1st Viscount (1661?–1727) I 59
Harcourt, 1st Earl (1714–1777) II 100
Harcourt, 3rd Earl (1743–1830) II 100
Harcourt, 1st Viscount (1863–1922) IV 47–48
Harcourt, Charles (1838–1880) III 88
Harcourt, Sir C.H.J. (1892–1959) IV 47
Harcourt, E.V. (1757–1847) II 100
Harcourt, George (1868–1947) IV 47
Harcourt, Sir Simon (1603?–1642) I 59
Harcourt, Thomas (1618–1679) I 59
Harcourt, William (1827–1904) III 88
Harcourt, W.V. (1789–1871) II 100
Harcourt-Smith, Sir Cecil (1859–1944) III 88
Hardie, James Keir (1856–1915) III 88
Hardie, Martin (1875–1952) IV 48
Hardiman, A.F. (1891–1949) IV 48
Harding, Edward (1755–1840) II 100
Harding, G.P. (1781–1853) II 100
Harding, John (1805–1874) III 88
Harding, J.D. (1798–1863) II 100
Harding, Silvester (1745–1809) II 100
Hardinge, Sir A.E. (1828–1892) III 88
Hardinge, George (1743–1816) II 100
Hardinge, G.N. (1781–1808) II 100
Hardinge, Nicholas (1699–1758) I 59
Hardinge of Lahore, 1st Viscount (1785–1856) II 100
Hardinge of Penshurst, 1st Baron (1858–1944) III 88
Hardinge of Penshurst, 2nd Baron (1894–1960) IV 48
Hardwick, Thomas (1752–1829) II 100
Hardwicke, 1st Earl of (1690–1764) I 59
Hardwicke, 2nd Earl of (1720–1790) II 100
Hardwicke, 3rd Earl of (1757–1834) II 100–101
Hardwicke, 5th Earl of (1836–1897) III 88
Hardwicke, 6th Earl of (1867–1904) IV 48
Hardwicke, Sir Cedric (1893–1964) IV 48
Hardy, Sir Charles (1716?–1780) II 101
Hardy, Francis (1751–1812) II 101
Hardy, J.S. (1793–1849) II 101
Hardy, Sir Thomas (1666–1732) I 59
Hardy, Thomas (1752–1832) II 101
Hardy, Thomas (1840–1928) III 88–89
Hardy, Sir Thomas Duffus (1804–1878) III 89
Hardy, Sir Thomas Masterman, 1st Bart (1769–1839) II 101
Hardy, Sir W.B. (1864–1934) IV 48
Hare, Augustus (1792–1834) II 101
Hare, Augustus (1834–1903) III 89
Hare, Hugh (1668–1707) I 59
Hare, James (1749–1804) II 101
Hare, Sir John (1844–1921) III 89
Hare, Julius Charles (1795–1855) II 101
Hare, Thomas (1806–1891) III 89
Hare, William (fl 1829) II 101
Harewood, 2nd Earl of (1767–1841) II 101
Harewood, 6th Earl of (1882–1947) IV 48
Harford, J.S. (1785–1866) II 101
Hargood, Sir William (1762–1839) II 101
Hargrave, Francis (1741–1821) II 101
Hargreaves, John (1839–1895) III 89
Hargreaves, Thomas (1774–1846) II 101
Harington, Sir Charles (1872–1940) IV 48
Harington, E.C. (1804–1881) III 89
Harington, Henry (1727–1816) II 101
Harington, John (fl 1550) I 59
Harington, Sir John (1561–1612) I 59
Harington of Exton, 1st Baron (1541–1613) I 59
Harington of Exton, 2nd Baron (1592–1614) I 59
Harker, Alfred (1859–1939) III 89
Harkness, Robert (1816–1878) III 89
Harland, Henry (1861–1905) IV 48
Harland, Sir Robert, Bart (1715?–1796?) II 101
Harlech, 4th Baron (1885–1964) IV 48
Harley, Sir Edward (1624–1700) I 59
Harley, Edward (1664–1735) I 59
Harley, George (c 1762–1811) II 101
Harley, George (1829–1896) III 89
Harley, J.P. (1786–1858) II 101
Harley, Sir Robert (1579–1656) I 59
Harley, Thomas (1730–1804) II 101
Harlow, G.H. (1787–1819) II 101
Harlowe, Sarah (1765–1852) II 101
Harman, Sir G.B. (1830–1892) III 89
Harman, Sir John (1625?–1673) I 59
Harmer, James (1777–1853) II 101
Harmer, Thomas (1714–1788) II 101
Harness, Sir H.D. (1804–1883) III 89

Harness, William (1790–1869) II 102
Harold I (d1040) I 59
Harold II (1022?–1066) I 59
Harper, Sir G.M. (1865–1922) IV 48
Harper, John (d1742) I 59
Harper, Thomas (1787–1853) II 102
Harper, Sir William (1496?–1573) I 59
Harraden, Beatrice (1864–1936) IV 48
Harrel, Sir David (1841–1939) III 89
Harrington, 1st Earl of (1683?–1756) I 59
Harrington, 3rd Earl of (1753–1829) II 102
Harrington, 4th Earl of (1780–1851) II 102
Harrington, 5th Earl of (1784–1862) II 102
Harrington, Countess of (1797?–1867) II 102
Harrington, James (1611–1677) I 59
Harriot, John (1745–1817) II 102
Harris, 1st Baron (1746–1829) II 102
Harris, 2nd Baron (1782–1845) II 102
Harris, 3rd Baron (1810–1872) III 89
Harris, 4th Baron (1851–1932) III 89
Harris, Sir A.H.G. (1852–1896) III 89
Harris, Sir A.T., 1st Bart (b1892) IV 48
Harris, F.L. (1864–1926) IV 48
Harris, James (1709–1780) II 102
Harris, John (1588?–1658) I 59
Harris, John (1667?–1719) I 59
Harris, John (1802–1856) III 89
Harris, Joseph (fl 1660–1680) I 60
Harris, Joseph (1773–1825) II 102
Harris, J.R. (1852–1941) III 89
Harris, J.T. (1856–1931) III 89
Harris, Moses (fl 1766–1785) II 102
Harris, Robert (1581–1658) I 60
Harris, William (1675?–1740) I 60
Harris, William (1776?–1830) II 102
Harris, Sir W.C. (1807–1848) III 90
Harrison, Benjamin (1808–1887) III 90
Harrison, Frederic (1831–1923) III 90
Harrison, Sir George (d1841) II 102
Harrison, Henry (1867–1954) IV 48
Harrison, Jane Ellen (1850–1928) III 90
Harrison, John (1579–1656) I 60
Harrison, John (1693–1776) I 60
Harrison, Robert (1715–1802) II 102
Harrison, Samuel (1760–1812) II 102
Harrison, Thomas (1606–1660) I 60
Harrison, Thomas (1744–1829) II 102
Harrison, T.E. (1808–1888) III 90
Harrison, William (1812–1860) III 90
Harrison, William (1813–1868) III 90
Harrowby, 1st Earl of (1762–1847) II 102
Harrowby, 2nd Earl of (1798–1882) II 102
Harrowby, 3rd Earl of (1831–1900) III 90
Harsnett, Samuel (1561–1631) I 60
Hart, Aaron (1670–1756) I 60
Hart, Sir Anthony (1754?–1831) II 102
Hart, Sir A.S. (1811–1890) III 90
Hart, Sir Robert, 1st Bart (1835–1911) III 90
Hart, Sir R.G. (1899–1960) IV 48
Hart, S.A. (1806–1881) III 90
Hartgill, George (fl 1594) I 60
Hartley, A.C. (1889–1960) IV 48
Hartley, David (1705–1757) II 102
Hartley, David (1732–1813) II 102
Hartley, Elizabeth (1751–1824) II 102–103
Hartley, Sir Harold (1878–1972) IV 48
Hartley, James (1747–1800) II 103
Hartog, Sir P.J. (1864–1947) IV 48
Hartopp, Sir John, 3rd Bart (1637?–1722) I 60
Hartree, D.R. (1897–1958) IV 48
Hartrick, A.S. (1864–1950) IV 48
Harty, Sir Hamilton (1879–1941) IV 48
Harvey, D.W. (1786–1863) II 103
Harvey, Sir Eliab (1758–1830) II 103
Harvey, Sir E.M. (1867–1955) IV 48
Harvey, Gabriel (1545?–1630) I 60
Harvey, Sir George (1806–1876) III 90
Harvey, Gideon (1640?–1700?) I 60
Harvey, Sir Henry (1737–1810) II 103
Harvey, John (1740–1794) II 103
Harvey, William (1578–1657) I 60
Harvey, William (1796–1866) II 103
Harvey, W.H. (1811–1866) III 90
Harvey of Tasburgh, 1st Baron (1893–1968) IV 48
Harwood, Sir Busick (1745?–1814) II 103
Harwood, Sir H.H. (1888–1950) IV 48
Haselden, Thomas (d1740) I 60
Haslam, John (1764–1844) II 103
Haslett, Dame Caroline Harriet (1895–1957) IV 48–49
Hassall, John (1868–1948) IV 49
Hasted, Edward (1732–1812) II 103
Hastings, 1st Marquess of (1754–1826) II 103
Hastings, Sir Charles (1794–1866) II 103
Hastings, Lady Elizabeth (1682–1739) I 60
Hastings, Lady Flora Elizabeth (1806–1839) III 90
Hastings, Henry (1551–1650) I 60
Hastings, Sir Hugh (1307?–1347) I 60

Hastings, Sir P.G. (1880–1952) IV 49
Hastings, Warren (1732–1818) II 103
Hatcher, Henry (1777–1846) II 103
Hatchett, Charles (1765?–1847) II 103
Hatfield, John (1758?–1803) II 103
Hatfield, Martha (b1640) I 60
Hathaway, Dame Sybil (1884–1974) IV 49
Hatherley, Baron (1801–1881) III 90
Hatherton, 1st Baron (1791–1863) II 103
Hatherton, 3rd Viscount (1842–1930) III 90
Hatsell, Sir Henry (1641–1714) I 60
Hatsell, John (1743–1820) II 103
Hatton, 1st Viscount (1632–1706) I 60
Hatton, Sir Christopher (1540–1591) I 60
Hatton, Joseph (1841–1907) III 90
Hatton, J.L. (1809–1886) III 90
Hatton, Sir R.G. (1886–1965) IV 49
Haughton, J.C. (1817–1887) III 90
Haughton, Samuel (1821–1897) III 90
Havard, William (1710?–1778) II 103
Havelock, Sir Henry, 1st Bart (1795–1857) II 103–104
Havelock-Allan, Sir H.M., 1st Bart (1830–1897) III 90–91
Haward, Francis (1759–1797) II 104
Hawarden, Edward (1662–1735) I 60
Haweis, H.R. (1838–1901) III 91
Haweis, Thomas (1734–1820) II 104
Hawes, Sir Benjamin (1797–1862) II 104
Hawes, William (1736–1808) II 104
Hawke, 1st Baron (1705–1781) II 104
Hawke, Sir Anthony (1869–1941) IV 49
Hawke of Towton, 7th Baron (1860–1938) IV 49
Hawker, Peter (1786–1853) II 104
Hawker, Robert (1753–1827) II 104
Hawker, R.S. (1803–1875) III 91
Hawkesworth, John (1715?–1773) II 104
Hawkins, Sir A.H. (1863–1933) IV 49
Hawkins, Sir Caesar, Bart (1711–1786) II 104
Hawkins, C.H. (1798–1884) II 104
Hawkins, Edward (1780–1867) II 104
Hawkins, Edward (1789–1882) II 104
Hawkins, Francis (1628–1681) I 60
Hawkins, Sir John (1532–1595) I 60
Hawkins, Sir John (1719–1789) II 104
Hawkshaw, Sir John (1811–1891) III 91
Hawksley, Thomas (1807–1893) III 91
Hawksmoor, Nicholas (1661–1736) I 60
Hawkwood, Sir John de (d1394) I 60
Hawley, Sir J.H., 3rd Bart (1813–1875) III 91
Haworth, Samuel (fl 1683) I 60
Haworth, Sir W.N. (1883–1950) IV 49
Hawtrey, Sir C.H. (1858–1923) III 91
Hawtrey, E.C. (1789–1862) II 104
Hawtrey, R.G. (1879–1971) IV 49
Hay, Andrew (1762–1814) II 104
Hay, Sir A.L. (1785–1862) II 104
Hay, Sir George (1715–1778) II 104
Hay, George (1729–1811) II 104
Hay, Sir John (1816–1892) III 91
Haydock, Richard (fl 1600) I 61
Haydon, B.R. (1786–1846) II 104
Hayes, Catherine (1825–1861) III 91
Hayes, Sir J.M., 1st Bart (1750?–1809) II 104
Hayes, Philip (1738–1797) II 104
Hayes, William (1706–1777) II 104
Haygarth, John (1740–1827) II 104
Hayley, T.A. (1780–1800) II 104
Hayley, William (1745–1820) II 104
Hayls, John (d1679) I 61
Hayman, Francis (1708–1776) II 104
Hayne, Thomas (1582–1645) I 61
Haynes, Hopton (1672?–1749) I 61
Hayter, Charles (1761–1835) II 104
Hayter, Sir George (1792–1871) II 105
Hayter, Thomas (1702–1762) II 105
Hayter, Sir W.G., 1st Bart (1792–1878) II 105
Haythorne, Sir Edmund (1818–1888) III 91
Hayward, Abraham (1801–1884) III 91
Hayward, Sir John (1564?–1627) I 61
Haywood, Eliza (1693?–1756) I 61
Hazeldine, William (1763–1840) II 105
Hazlitt, William (1778–1830) II 105
Head, Sir E.W., Bart (1805–1868) III 91
Head, Sir F.B., 1st Bart (1793–1875) II 105
Head, Sir Henry (1861–1940) IV 49
Headlam, A.C. (1862–1947) IV 49
Headlam, T.E. (1813–1875) III 91
Headlam-Morley, Sir J.W. (1863–1929) IV 49
Heal, Sir Ambrose (1872–1959) IV 49
Healy, James (1824–1894) III 91
Healy, T.M. (1855–1931) III 91
Heaphy, Thomas (1813–1873) III 91
Heard, Sir Isaac (1730–1822) II 105
Heard, W.T. (1884–1973) IV 49
Hearle, F.T. (1886–1965) IV 49
Hearn, Mary Anne (1834–1909) III 91
Hearne, Samuel (1745–1792) II 105
Hearne, Thomas (1678–1735) I 61

Hearne, Thomas (1744–1817) II 105
Heath, Ambrose (1891–1969) IV 49
Heath, Benjamin (1704–1766) II 105
Heath, Charles (1785–1848) II 105
Heath, Christopher (1835–1905) III 91
Heath, D.D. (1811–1897) III 91
Heath, Henry (1599–1643) I 61
Heath, James (1757–1834) II 105
Heath, Nicholas (1501?–1578) I 61
Heath, Sir Robert (1575–1649) I 61
Heath, Sir T.L. (1861–1940) IV 49
Heathcote, Sir Gilbert (1651?–1733) I 61
Heather, William (1563?–1627) I 61
Heathfield, 1st Baron (1717–1790) II 105
Heaton, Sir J.H., 1st Bart (1848–1914) III 91
Heaviside, Oliver (1850–1925) III 91
Heber, Reginald (1783–1826) II 105
Heber, Richard (1773–1833) II 105
Heberden, William (1710–1801) II 105
Hector, Annie (1825–1902) III 91
Heemskerk, Egbert van (1645–1704) I 61
Heidegger, J.J. (1659?–1749) I 61
Heilbron, Sir I.M. (1886–1959) IV 49
Heinemann, William (1863–1920) IV 49
Helena, Princess (1846–1923) III 92
Hele-Shaw, H.S. (1854–1941) III 92
Hellmuth, Isaac (1817–1901) III 92
Helmore, Thomas (1811–1890) III 92
Helps, Sir Arthur (1813–1875) III 92
Helwys, Sir Gervase (1561–1615) I 61
Hely-Hutchinson, Christopher (1767–1826) II 105
Hely-Hutchinson, John (1724–1794) II 105
Hemans, Felicia Dorothea (1793–1835) II 105
Hemming, G.W. (1821–1905) III 92
Hemphill, 1st Baron (1822–1908) III 92
Henchman, Humphrey (1592–1675) I 61
Henderland, Lord A.M. (1736–1795) II 105–106
Henderson, Alexander (1583?–1646) I 61
Henderson, Andrew (1783–1835) II 106
Henderson, Arthur (1863–1935) IV 49
Henderson, Sir David (1862–1921) IV 49
Henderson, Ebenezer (1784–1858) II 106
Henderson, Sir E.Y.W. (1821–1896) III 92
Henderson, G.F.R. (1854–1903) III 92
Henderson, Sir H.D. (1890–1952) IV 49
Henderson, John (1747–1785) II 106
Henderson, John (1757–1788) II 106
Henderson, Sir N.M. (1882–1942) IV 49
Henderson, W.G. (1819–1905) III 92
Heneage, 1st Baron (1840–1922) III 92
Heneage, Sir Thomas (d1595) I 61
Henfrey, Arthur (1819–1859) III 92
Henley, Anthony (d1711) I 61
Henley, John (1692–1756) I 61
Henley, J.W. (1793–1884) II 106
Henley, W.E. (1849–1903) III 92
Henley, W.T. (1813?–1882) III 92
Hennessy, Sir John Pope (1834–1891) III 92
Henniker, 2nd Baron (1752–1821) II 106
Henning, John (1771–1851) II 106
Henrietta Maria, Queen (1609–1669) I 61
Henriques, Sir B.L.Q. (1890–1961) IV 49
Henry I (1068–1135) I 61
Henry II (1133–1189) I 61
Henry III (1207–1272) I 61
Henry IV (1367–1413) I 61
Henry V (1387–1422) I 61
Henry VI (1421–1471) I 61–62
Henry VII (1457–1509) I 62
Henry VIII (1491–1547) I 62
Henry Frederick, Prince (1594–1612) I 62
Henry, Sir E.R., Bart (1850–1931) III 92
Henry, Matthew (1662–1714) I 62
Henry, Mitchell (1826–1910) III 92
Henry, Philip (1631–1696) I 62
Henry, Robert (1718–1790) II 106
Henry, Sir Thomas (1807–1876) III 92
Henry, William (1774–1836) II 106
Henschel, Sir George (1850–1934) III 92
Hensey, Florence (fl 1758) I 60
Henslow, J.S. (1796–1861) II 106
Hensman, John (1780–1864) II 106
Henson, H.H. (1863–1947) IV 49
Henson, L.L. (1891–1957) IV 49
Henty, G.A. (1832–1902) III 92
Herbert, Sir A.P. (1890–1971) IV 50
Herbert, George (1593–1633) I 62
Herbert, J.R. (1810–1890) III 93
Herbert, Lady Lucy (1669–1744) I 62
Herbert, Sir P.E. (1822–1876) III 93
Herbert, Sir R.G.W. (1831–1905) III 93
Herbert, St Leger (1850–1885) III 93
Herbert, Sir Thomas, 1st Bart (1606–1682) I 62
Herbert, Sir Thomas (1793–1861) II 106
Herbert, Sir William (d1593) I 62
Herbert, William (1718–1795) II 106

Herbert, William (1778–1847) II *106*
Herbert of Cherbury, 1st Baron (1583–1648) I *62*
Herbert of Cherbury, 2nd Baron (1600?–1655) I *62*
Herbert of Cherbury, 3rd Baron (d1678) I *62*
Herbert of Cherbury, 4th Baron (d1691) I *62*
Herbert of Lea, 1st Baron (1810–1861) III *93*
Herdman, Robert (1829–1888) III *93*
Herdman, Sir W.A. (1858–1924) III *93*
Herdman, W.G. (1805–1882) III *93*
Herford, W.H. (1820–1908) III *93*
Herick(e), Sir William (1562–1653) I *62*
Heriot, George (1563–1624) I *62*
Herkomer, Sir Hubert von (1849–1914) III *93*
Heron, Sir Richard, Bart (1726–1805) II *106*
Heron, Sir Robert, 2nd Bart (1765–1854) II *106*
Herrick, Robert (1591–1674) I *63*
Herries, J.C. (1778–1855) II *106*
Herring, Ann (1795–1838) II *106*
Herring, J.F. (1795–1865) II *106*
Herring, Thomas (1693–1757) I *63*
Herringham, Sir W.P. (1855–1936) III *93*
Herschel, A.S. (1836–1907) III *93*
Herschel, Caroline (1750–1848) II *106*
Herschel, Sir J.F.W., 1st Bart (1792–1871) II *106*
Herschel, Sir William (1738–1822) II *106–107*
Herschel, 1st Baron (1837–1899) III *93*
Herschell, R.H. (1807–1864) III *93*
Hertford, Earl of (1539?–1621) I *63*
Hertford, 1st Marquess of (1719–1794) II *107*
Hertford, 2nd Marquess of (1743–1822) II *107*
Hertford, 3rd Marquess of (1777–1842) II *107*
Hertford, Countess of (1540?–1567?) I *63*
Hertz, J.H. (1872–1946) IV *50*
Hervey, Lord A.C. (1808–1894) III *93*
Hervey, James (1714–1758) I *107*
Hervey, John (1616–1679) I *63*
Hervey, Lady Mary (1700–1768) II *107*
Hervey, Thomas (1699–1775) I *63*
Hervey of Ickworth, Baron (1696–1743) I *63*
Heseltine, James (1690–1763) I *63*
Heseltine, P.A. (1894–1930) IV *50*
Hesilrige, Sir Arthur, 2nd Bart (d1661) I *63*
Hesketh, Harriet, Lady (1733–1807) II *107*
Hess, Dame Myra (1890–1965) IV *50*
Hessel, Phoebe (1713?–1821) II *107*
Hessey, J.A. (1814–1892) III *93*
Hetherington, Sir Hector (1888–1965) IV *15*
Heton, Martin (1552–1609) I *63*
Heugh, Hugh (1782–1846) II *107*
Hewart, 1st Viscount (1870–1943) II *50*
Hewett, Sir George, 1st Bart (1750–1840) II *107*
Hewett, Sir P.G., 1st Bart (1812–1891) III *93*
Hewett, Sir W.N.W. (1834–1888) III *93*
Hewit, John (1614–1658) I *63*
Hewlett, James (1768–1836) II *107*
Hewlett, John (1762–1844) II *107*
Hewlett, M.H. (1861–1923) IV *50*
Hewson, John (d1662) I *63*
Hewson, William (1739–1774) II *107*
Hey, John (1734–1815) II *107*
Hey, William (1736–1819) II *107*
Hey, William (1772–1844) II *107*
Heylin, Rowland (1562?–1631) I *63*
Heylyn, Peter (1600–1662) I *63*
Heytesbury, Baron (1779–1860) II *107*
Heywood, Sir Benjamin, 1st Bart (1793–1865) II *107*
Heywood, John (1497?–1580) I *63*
Heywood, Peter (1773–1831) II *107*
Heyworth, 1st Baron (1894–1974) IV *50*
Hibbert, George (1757–1837) II *107*
Hibbert, Henry (1600?–1678) I *63*
Hibbert, Sir J.T. (1824–1908) III *93–94*
Hichens, Lionel (1874–1940) IV *50*
Hichens, R.S. (1864–1950) IV *50*
Hickeringill, Edmund (1631–1708) I *63*
Hickes, George (1642–1715) I *63*
Hickes, John (1633–1685) I *63*
Hickey, William (1749–1830?) II *107*
Hickman, Charles (1648–1713) I *63*
Hicks, E.L. (1843–1919) III *94*
Hicks, G.E. (1879–1954) IV *50*
Hicks, William (1621–1660) I *63*
Hicks, William (1830–1883) III *94*
Higgins, E.J. (1864–1947) IV *50*
Higgins, Francis (1669–1728) I *63*
Higgins, Sir J.F.A. (1875–1948) IV *50*
Higgins, M.J. (1810–1868) III *94*
Highmore, Anthony (1719–1799) II *107*
Highmore, Joseph (1692–1780) I *63*
Hildersham, Arthur (1563–1632) I *63*
Hill, 1st Viscount (1772–1842) II *108*
Hill, Aaron (1685–1750) I *63*
Hill, Abraham (1635–1721) I *63*
Hill, A.S. (1825–1905) III *94*
Hill, A.V. (1886–1977) IV *50*
Hill, Sir A.W. (1875–1941) IV *50*

Hill, D.O. (1802–1870) III *94*
Hill, George (1716–1808) II *107*
Hill, George (1750–1819) II *107*
Hill, G.B.N. (1835–1903) III *94*
Hill, Sir G.F. (1867–1948) IV *50*
Hill, James (d1817?) II *107*
Hill, John (c1716–1775) II *107*
Hill, Sir L.E. (1866–1952) IV *50*
Hill, M.D. (1792–1872) II *107*
Hill, Octavia (1838–1912) III *94*
Hill, Richard (1655–1727) I *63*
Hill, Sir Richard, 2nd Bart (1732–1808) II *108*
Hill, Robert (d1628) I *63*
Hill, Sir Rowland (1492?–1561) I *63*
Hill, Rowland (1744–1833) II *108*
Hill, Sir Rowland (1795–1879) II *108*
Hill, Rowley (1836–1887) III *94*
Hill, Sir R.M. (1894–1954) IV *50*
Hill, Thomas (1760–1840) II *108*
Hill, T.W. (1763–1851) II *108*
Hilliard, Nicholas (1547–1619) I *64*
Hills, Robert (1769–1844?) II *108*
Hillsborough, Countess of (1729–1766) II *108*
Hilton, John (d1657) I *64*
Hilton, John (1804?–1878) II *108*
Hilton, William (1786–1839) II *108*
Hinchcliff, T.W. (1825–1882) III *94*
Hinchcliffe, John (1731–1794) I *108*
Hincks, Edward (1792–1866) II *108*
Hincks, Thomas (1818–1899) III *94*
Hind, A.M. (1880–1957) IV *50*
Hind, H.Y. (1823–1908) III *94*
Hind, James (d1652) I *64*
Hind, J.R. (1823–1895) III *94*
Hinderwell, Thomas (1744–1825) II *108*
Hindle, Edward (1886–1973) IV *50*
Hindley, Sir C.D.M. (1874–1944) IV *50*
Hindmarsh, Robert (1759–1835) II *108*
Hinds, Samuel (1793–1872) II *108*
Hine, H.G. (1811–1895) III *94*
Hingston, John (d1683) I *64*
Hinks, A.R. (1873–1945) IV *50*
Hinkson, Katharine (1861–1931) IV *50*
Hinshelwood, Sir Cyril (1897–1967) IV *50–51*
Hinsley, Arthur (1865–1943) IV *51*
Hinton, James (1822–1875) III *94*
Hinton, J.H. (1791–1873) II *108*
Hipkins, A.J. (1826–1903) III *94*
Hippisley, John (fl 1722–1748) I *64*
Hirschel, Solomon (1761–1841) II *108*
Hirst, F.W. (1873–1953) IV *51*
Hirst, G.H. (1871–1954) IV *51*
Hitcham, Sir Robert (1572?–1636) I *64*
Hitchcock, Sir Alfred (1899–1980) IV *51*
Hitchens, Ivon (1893–1979) IV *51*
Hoadley, John (1678–1746) I *64*
Hoadly, Benjamin (1676–1761) I *64*
Hoadly, Benjamin (1706–1757) II *108*
Hoadly, John (1711–1776) II *108*
Hoadly, Sarah (d1743) I *64*
Hoare, Prince (1755–1834) II *108*
Hoare, Sir Richard (1709–1754) II *108*
Hoare, Sir R.C., 2nd Bart (1758–1838) II *108*
Hoare, Sir R.H. (1882–1954) IV *51*
Hoare, William (1707?–1792) II *108–109*
Hobart, Sir Henry, 1st Bart (d1625) I *64*
Hobart, Sir James (d1507) I *64*
Hobart, Sir Miles (d1636?) I *64*
Hobart, Sir P.C.S. (1885–1957) IV *51*
Hobart-Hampden, A.C. (1822–1886) III *94*
Hobbes, Thomas (1588–1679) I *64*
Hobbs, Sir J.B. (1882–1963) IV *51*
Hobday, Sir F.T.G. (1869–1939) IV *51*
Hobday, W.A. (1771–1831) II *108*
Hobhouse, 1st Baron (1819–1904) III *94*
Hobhouse, Sir Benjamin, 1st Bart (1757–1831) II *109*
Hobhouse, Edmund (1817–1904) III *94*
Hobhouse, Henry (1854–1937) III *94*
Hobson, E.W. (1856–1933) III *94*
Hobson, Thomas (1544?–1631) I *64*
Hobson, W.R. (1831–1880) III *94*
Hoby, Sir Edward (1560–1617) I *64*
Hoby, Lady Elizabeth (1528–1609) I *64*
Hoby, Sir Philip (1505–1558) I *64*
Hoby, Sir Thomas (1530–1566) I *64*
Hocking, S.K. (1850–1935) III *94*
Hodder, James (fl 1661) I *64*
Hoddeson, John (b1632) I *64*
Hodge, John (1855–1937) III *94*
Hodges, C.H. (1764–1837) II *109*
Hodges, Sir William, 1st Bart (1645?–1714) I *64*
Hodges, William (1744–1797) II *109*
Hodgkin, Thomas (1831–1913) III *94*
Hodgkins, Frances Mary (1869–1947) IV *51*
Hodgson, B.H. (1800–1894) III *94–95*
Hodgson, Francis (1781–1852) II *109*
Hodgson, Sir H.K. Graham (1890–1960) IV *51*

Hodgson, James (1672–1755) I *64*
Hodgson, John (1779–1845) II *109*
Hodgson, Joseph (1788–1869) II *109*
Hodgson, J.E. (1831–1895) III *95*
Hodgson, Ralph (1871–1962) IV *51*
Hodgson, Sir R.M. (1874–1956) IV *51*
Hodgson, Studholme (1708–1798) II *109*
Hodsoll, Sir John (1894–1971) IV *51*
Hodson, Frodsham (1770–1822) II *109*
Hodson, Henrietta (1841–1910) III *95*
Hodson, J.L. (1891–1956) IV *51*
Hodson, Septimus (1768–1833) II *109*
Hodson, William (fl 1640) I *64*
Hody, Humphrey (1659–1707) I *64*
Hofland, Barbara (1770–1844) II *109*
Hofmeyr, J.H. (1845–1909) III *95*
Hogan, John (1800–1858) III *95*
Hogarth, D.G. (1862–1927) IV *51*
Hogarth, George (1783–1870) II *109*
Hogarth, William (1697–1764) I *64*
Hogben, Lancelot (1895–1975) IV *51*
Hogg, James (1770–1835) II *109*
Hogg, Sir J.W., 1st Bart (1790–1876) II *109*
Hogg, Quintin (1845–1903) III *95*
Hoghton, Daniel (1770–1811) II *109*
Holbein, Hans (1497–1543) I *64–65*
Holbrook, John (d1437) I *65*
Holbrooke, Josef (1878–1958) IV *51*
Holburne, Francis (1704–1771) II *109*
Holcroft, Thomas (1745–1809) II *109*
Holden, C.H. (1875–1960) IV *51*
Holden, Sir Isaac, 1st Bart (1807–1897) III *95*
Holden, Luther (1815–1905) III *95*
Holder, William (1616–1698) I *65*
Holderness, 4th Earl of (1718–1778) II *109*
Holderness, Sir T.W., 1st Bart (1849–1924) III *95*
Holdich, Sir T.H. (1843–1929) III *95*
Holdsworth, Sir W.S. (1871–1944) IV *51*
Hole, Matthew (d1730) I *65*
Hole, Richard (1746–1803) II *109*
Hole, S.R. (1819–1904) III *95*
Holgate, Robert (1481?–1555?) I *65*
Holiday, Henry (1839–1927) III *95*
Holker, Sir John (1828–1882) III *95*
Holl, Francis (1815–1884) III *95*
Holl, Frank (1845–1888) III *95*
Holl, William (1771–1838) II *109*
Holl, William (1807–1871) III *95*
Hollams, Sir John (1820–1910) III *95*
Holland, 1st Earl of (1590–1649) I *65*
Holland, 1st Baron (1705–1774) II *109*
Holland, 3rd Baron (1773–1840) II *109–110*
Holland, Charles (1733–1769) II *109*
Holland, Lady Elizabeth (1770–1845) II *109*
Holland, Henry (1746?–1806) II *109*
Holland, Sir Henry, 1st Bart (1788–1873) II *109*
Holland, Hezekiah (fl 1638–1661) I *65*
Holland, H.S. (1847–1918) III *95*
Holland, James (1800–1870) III *95*
Holland, John (1794–1872) II *109*
Holland, Philemon (1552–1637) I *65*
Holland, Thomas (d1612) I *65*
Holland, Sir T.E. (1835–1926) III *95*
Holland, Sir T.H. (1868–1947) IV *51*
Hollar, Wenceslaus (1607–1677) I *65*
Holles, 1st Baron (1599–1680) I *65*
Holles, Sir Frescheville (1641–1672) I *65*
Hollingshead, John (1827–1904) III *95*
Hollins, John (1798–1855) II *110*
Hollins, Peter (1800–1886) III *95*
Hollins, William (1754–1843) II *110*
Hollis, A.P. (1764–1844) II *110*
Hollis, Sir L.C. (1897–1963) IV *51*
Hollis, Thomas (1720–1774) II *110*
Hollond, Ellen Julia (1822–1884) III *95*
Hollond, H.A. (1884–1974) IV *51*
Hollond, Robert (1808–1877) III *95*
Holloway, Thomas (1800–1883) III *95*
Hollowell, J.H. (1851–1909) III *95*
Holman, James (1786–1857) II *110*
Holman, J.G. (1764–1817) II *110*
Holmes, Alfred (1837–1876) III *96*
Holmes, Sir Charles (1711–1761) II *110*
Holmes, Sir C.J. (1868–1936) IV *51*
Holmes, George (1662–1749) I *65*
Holmes, John (1800–1854) III *96*
Holmes, Sir M.G. (1885–1964) IV *51*
Holmes, Sir Robert (1622–1692) I *65*
Holmes, Robert (1765–1859) II *110*
Holmes, Sir R.R. (1835–1911) III *96*
Holmes, Timothy (1825–1907) III *96*
Holmes, T.R.E. (1855–1933) III *96*
Holmes, William (1689–1748) I *65*
Holmes, William (1779–1851) II *110*
Holmyard, E.J. (1891–1959) IV *51*
Holroyd, Sir Charles (1861–1917) IV *51*
Holroyd, Sir G.S. (1758–1831) II *110*

Holst, Gustav (1874–1934) IV *51*
Holt, Sir John (1642–1710) I *65*
Holt, John (1743–1801) II *110*
Holt, Joseph (1756–1826) II *110*
Holtby, Winifred (1898–1935) IV *51–52*
Holte, Sir Thomas, 1st Bart (1571–1654) I *65*
Holwell-Carr, William (1758–1830) II *110*
Holyoake, G.J. (1817–1906) III *96*
Home, D.D. (1833–1886) III *96*
Home, Sir Everard, 1st Bart (1756–1832) II *110*
Home, Francis (1719–1813) II *110*
Home, James (1760–1844) II *110*
Home, John (1722–1808) II *110*
Home, Robert (1752–1834) II *110*
Home, Robert (1837–1879) III *96*
Homer, Henry (1753–1791) II *110*
Hondius, Abraham (1638?–1691) I *65*
Hondius, Jodocus (1563–1611) I *65*
Hone, Evie (1894–1955) IV *52*
Hone, Horace (1756–1825) II *110*
Hone, J.C. (d 1837) II *110*
Hone, J.M. (1882–1959) IV *52*
Hone, Nathaniel (1718–1784) II *110*
Hone, William (1780–1842) II *110–111*
Honey, George (1822–1880) III *96*
Honey, Laura (1816?–1843) III *96*
Honner, Maria (1812–1870) III *96*
Honner, R.W. (1809–1852) III *96*
Honyman, Sir G.E., 4th Bart (1819–1875) III *96*
Honywood, Mrs Mary (1527–1620) I *65*
Honywood, Michael (1597–1681) I *65*
Hood, 1st Viscount (1724–1816) II *111*
Hood, Alexander (1758–1798) II *111*
Hood, Sir H.L.A. (1870–1916) IV *52*
Hood, Lady Maria (1783–1862) II *111*
Hood, Sir Samuel, 1st Bart (1762–1814) II *111*
Hood, Thomas (1799–1845) II *111*
Hood, Thomas (1835–1874) III *96*
Hood of Avalon, 1st Baron (1824–1901) III *96*
Hook, James (1746–1826) II *111*
Hook, James (1772?–1828) II *111*
Hook, J.C. (1819–1907) III *96*
Hook, T.E. (1788–1841) II *111*
Hook, W.F. (1798–1875) II *111*
Hooke, Nathaniel (d 1763) I *65*
Hooker, Sir J.D. (1817–1911) III *96*
Hooker, Richard (1554?–1600) I *65*
Hooker, Sir W.J. (1785–1865) II *111*
Hoole, Elijah (1798–1872) II *111*
Hoole, John (1727–1803) II *111*
Hooper, Sir F.C., 1st Bart (1892–1963) IV *52*
Hooper, George (1640–1727) I *65*
Hooper, J.S.M. (1882–1974) IV *52*
Hooper, Robert (1773–1835) II *111*
Hope, Sir Alexander (1769–1837) II *111*
Hope, A.J.B. (1820–1887) III *96*
Hope, F.W. (1797–1862) II *111*
Hope, George (1811–1876) III *96*
Hope, H.P. (d 1839) II *111*
Hope, James (1764–1846?) II *111*
Hope, James (1801–1841) III *96*
Hope, Sir James (1808–1881) III *96*
Hope, John (1725–1786) II *111*
Hope, John (1794–1858) II *111*
Hope, Sir Thomas, 1st Bart (d 1646) I *65*
Hope, Thomas (1770?–1831) II *111*
Hope, T.C. (1766–1844) II *111*
Hope, Sir W.J. (1766–1831) II *111–112*
Hope of Hopetoun, Sir James (1614–1661) I *65*
Hope-Scott, J.R. (1812–1873) III *96*
Hopetoun, 1st Earl of (1681–1742) I *65*
Hopetoun, 3rd Earl of (1741–1816) II *112*
Hopetoun, 4th Earl of (1765–1823) II *112*
Hopkins, Ezechiel (1634–1690) I *65*
Hopkins, Sir F.G. (1861–1947) IV *52*
Hopkins, G.M. (1845–1889) III *96–97*
Hopkins, John (fl 1700) I *65*
Hopkins, Matthew (d 1647) I *65*
Hopkins, Sir R.V.N. (1880–1955) IV *52*
Hopkins, William (fl 1674) I *66*
Hopkins, William (1793–1866) II *112*
Hopkinson, Sir Alfred (1851–1939) III *97*
Hopkinson, Bertram (1874–1918) IV *52*
Hopkinson, John (1849–1898) III *97*
Hopley, E.W.J. (1816–1869) III *97*
Hopper, Thomas (1776–1856) II *112*
Hoppner, John (1758–1810) II *112*
Hoppé, E.O. (1878–1972) IV *52*
Hoppus, John (1789–1875) II *112*
Hopsonn, Sir Thomas (1642–1717) I *66*
Hopton of Stratton, 1st Baron (1598–1652) I *66*
Hopwood, C.H. (1829–1904) III *97*
Hopwood, James (1752?–1819) II *112*
Horder, 1st Baron (1871–1955) IV *52*
Horder, Percy (1870–1944) IV *52*
Hore-Belisha, Baron (1893–1957) IV *52*
Horn, C.E. (1786–1849) II *112*

Hornby, Charles (1867–1946) IV *52*
Hornby, J.J. (1826–1909) III *97*
Hornby, Sir Phipps (1785–1867) II *112*
Horne, Baron (1861–1929) IV *52*
Horne, Viscount (1871–1940) IV *52*
Horne, George (1730–1792) I *66*
Horne, Robert (1519?–1580) I *66*
Horne, R.H. (1803–1884) III *97*
Horne, T.H. (1780–1862) II *112*
Horne, Sir William (1774–1860) II *112*
Horneck, Anthony (1641–1697) I *66*
Horner, Arthur (1894–1968) IV *52*
Horner, Francis (1778–1817) II *112*
Horner, Leonard (1785–1864) II *112*
Horniman, Annie (1860–1937) IV *52*
Horniman, F.J. (1835–1906) III *97*
Horridge, Sir T.G. (1857–1938) III *97*
Horsbrugh, Baroness (1889–1969) IV *52*
Horsey, Sir Edward (d 1582?) I *66*
Horsfield, Thomas (1773–1859) II *112*
Horsford, Sir A.H. (1818–1885) III *97*
Horsley, J.C. (1817–1903) III *97*
Horsley, Samuel (1733–1806) II *112*
Horsley, Sir V.A.H. (1857–1916) III *97*
Horsley, William (1774–1858) II *112*
Horsman, Edward (1807–1876) III *97*
Hort, F.J.A. (1828–1892) III *97*
Horton, Sir M.K. (1883–1951) IV *52*
Horton, R.F. (1855–1934) III *97*
Horton, Sir R.J.W., 3rd Bart (1784–1841) II *112*
Hosack, John (d 1887) II *112*
Hoskins, Sir A.H. (1828–1901) III *97*
Hoskins, John (d 1664) I *66*
Hoskins, Sir John, (b 1630?) I *66*
Hoskins, Sir John, 2nd Bart (1634–1705) I *66*
Hoste, Sir G.C. (1786–1845) II *112*
Hoste, Sir William, 1st Bart (1780–1828) II *112*
Hotham, 2nd Baron (1737–1814) II *112*
Hotham, 3rd Baron (1794–1870) II *112*
Hotham, Sir John, 1st Bart (d 1645) I *66*
Hotham, Sir William (1772–1848) II *112*
Houblon, Sir James (d 1700) I *66*
Houblon, Sir John (1630–1712) I *66*
Hough, John (1651–1743) I *66*
Houghton, 1st Baron (1809–1885) III *97*
Houldsworth, Sir H.S., 1st Bart (1889–1956) IV *52*
Housman, A.E. (1859–1936) III *97*
Housman, Laurence (1865–1959) IV *52*
Housman, Robert (1759–1838) II *112*
Houston, Sir William, 1st Bart (1766–1842) II *112–113*
Hovenden, Robert (1544–1614) I *66*
How, W.W. (1823–1897) III *98*
Howard, Sir Ebenezer (1850–1928) III *98*
Howard, Edward (d 1841) II *113*
Howard, E.C. (1774–1816) II *113*
Howard, E.H. (1829–1892) III *98*
Howard, Sir George (1720?–1796) II *113*
Howard, G.E. (1715–1786) II *113*
Howard, Henry (1757–1842) II *113*
Howard, Henry (1769–1847) II *113*
Howard, Hugh (1675–1737) I *66*
Howard, John (1726?–1790) II *113*
Howard, Leonard (1699?–1767) I *66*
Howard, Leslie (1893–1943) IV *52*
Howard, P.T. (1629–1694) I *66*
Howard, Sir Robert (1626–1698) I *66*
Howard, Robert (1683–1740) I *66*
Howard, Lord William (1563–1640) I *66*
Howard-Vyse, Sir R.G.H. (1883–1962) IV *52*
Howard de Walden, 4th Baron (1719–1797) II *113*
Howard de Walden, 8th Baron (1880–1946) IV *53*
Howard of Effingham, 1st Baron (1510?–1573) I *66*
Howard of Escrick, 3rd Baron (1626–1694) I *66*
Howard of Glossop, 1st Baron (1818–1883) III *98*
Howard of Penrith, 1st Baron (1863–1939) IV *53*
Howden, 2nd Baron (1762–1839) II *113*
Howe, 1st Earl (1725–1799) II *113*
Howe, 5th Earl (1884–1964) IV *53*
Howe, 5th Viscount (1729–1814) II *113*
Howe, E.S. (d 1709) I *67*
Howe, Henry (1812–1896) III *98*
Howe, James (1780–1836) II *113*
Howe, John (1630–1705) I *67*
Howell, George (1833–1910) III *98*
Howell, James (1594?–1666) I *67*
Howell, Laurence (1664?–1720) I *67*
Howells, H.N. (b 1892) IV *53*
Howitt, A.W. (1830–1908) III *98*
Howitt, Mary (1799–1888) II *113*
Howitt, William (1792–1879) II *113*
Howland, Sir W.P. (1811–1907) III *98*
Howley, William (1766–1848) II *113*
Howorth, Sir H.H. (1842–1923) III *98*
Howorth, Sir R.B. (1880–1964) IV *53*
Howson, John (1557?–1632) I *67*
Howson, J.S. (1816–1885) III *98*
Hoy, Thomas (1659–1718?) I *67*

Huddart, Joseph (1741–1816) II *113*
Huddesford, George (1749–1809) II *113*
Huddleston, John (1608–1698) I *67*
Huddleston, Sir J.W. (1815–1890) III *98*
Hudson, George (1800–1871) III *98*
Hudson, Sir James (1810–1885) III *98*
Hudson, Jeffrey (1619?–1682) I *67*
Hudson, John (1662–1719) I *67*
Hudson, Thomas (1701–1779) II *113*
Hudson, W.H. (1841–1922) III *98*
Hueffer, Francis (1845–1889) III *98*
Hugford, I.E. (1703–1778) II *113*
Huggins, William (1696–1761) I *67*
Huggins, William (1820–1884) III *98*
Huggins, Sir William (1824–1910) III *98*
Hughes, Arthur (1832–1915) III *98*
Hughes, Sir Edward (1720?–1794) II *113*
Hughes, E.H.B. (d 1863) II *113*
Hughes, George (1603–1667) I *67*
Hughes, H.P. (1847–1902) III *98*
Hughes, John (1677–1720) I *67*
Hughes, Joshua (1807–1889) III *98*
Hughes, Margaret (d 1719) I *67*
Hughes, Obadiah (1639–1704) I *67*
Hughes, Richard (1900–1976) IV *53*
Hughes, Sir Sam (1853–1921) III *98*
Hughes, Thomas (1822–1896) III *99*
Hughes, T.S. (1786–1847) II *114*
Hughes, W.M. (1862–1952) IV *53*
Hugo, Thomas (1820–1876) III *99*
Huish, Robert (1777–1850) II *114*
Hulke, J.W. (1830–1895) III *99*
Hull, Thomas (1728–1808) II *114*
Hullah, J.P. (1812–1884) III *99*
Hullmandel, C.J. (1789–1850) II *114*
Hulls, Jonathan (fl 1737) I *67*
Hulme, Nathaniel (1732–1807) II *114*
Hulse, Edward (1631–1711) I *67*
Hulse, Sir Edward, 1st Bart (1682–1759) I *67*
Hulse, Sir Samuel, 3rd Bart (1747–1837) II *114*
Hume, Sir Abraham, 2nd Bart (1749–1838) II *114*
Hume, Abraham (1814–1884) III *99*
Hume, David (1711–1776) II *114*
Hume, David (1757–1838) II *114*
Hume, Joseph (1777–1855) II *114*
Humphrey Plantagenet, Duke of Gloucester (1391–1447) I *67*
Humphrey, H.A. (1868–1951) IV *53*
Humphrey, Laurence (1527?–1590) I *67*
Humphrey, William (1740?–1810?) II *114*
Humphreys, Sir Travers (1867–1956) IV *53*
Humphry, Sir G.M. (1820–1896) III *99*
Humphry, Ozias (1742–1810) II *114*
Humphry, W.G. (1815–1886) III *99*
Hungerford, 2nd Baron (1409–1459) I *67*
Hungerford, Mrs Margaret (1855?–1897) III *99*
Hunsdon, 1st Baron (1524?–1596) I *67*
Hunsdon, 2nd Baron (1547–1603) I *67*
Hunt, Arabella (d 1705) I *67*
Hunt, A.S. (1871–1934) IV *53*
Hunt, A.W. (1830–1896) III *99*
Hunt, G.W. (1825–1877) III *99*
Hunt, Henry (1773–1835) II *114*
Hunt, James Henry Leigh (1784–1859) II *114*
Hunt, Robert (1807–1887) III 99
Hunt, Roger (fl 1533) I *67*
Hunt, Thornton Leigh (1810–1873) III *99*
Hunt, William Holman (1827–1910) III *99*
Hunter, Alexander (1729–1809) II *114*
Hunter, Andrew (1743–1809) II *114*
Hunter, Sir Archibald (1856–1936) III *99*
Hunter, Colin (1841–1904) III *99*
Hunter, Sir C.S. 1st Bart (1775–1851) II *114*
Hunter, Sir Ellis (1892–1961) IV *53*
Hunter, Sir G.B. (1845–1937) III *99*
Hunter, Henry (1741–1802) II *114*
Hunter, John (1728–1793) II *114*
Hunter, John (1738–1821) II *114*
Hunter, John (1745–1837) II *115*
Hunter, Joseph (1783–1861) II *115*
Hunter, P.V. (1883–1956) IV *53*
Hunter, Robert (d 1734) I *67*
Hunter, Sir Robert (1844–1913) III *99*
Hunter, Samuel (1769–1839) II *115*
Hunter, William (1718–1783) II *115*
Hunter, Sir W.W. (1840–1900) III *99*
Hunter-Weston, Sir A.G. (1864–1940) IV *53*
Hunting, Sir P.L. (1885–1973) IV *53*
Huntingdon, 1st Earl of (1488?–1545) I *67*
Huntingdon, 2nd Earl of (1514?–1561) I *67*
Huntingdon, 3rd Earl of (1535–1595) I *67*
Huntingdon, 7th Earl of (1650–1701) I *67*
Huntingdon, 11th Earl of (1779–1828) II *115*
Huntingdon, Countess of (1707–1791) II *115*
Huntingdon, William (1745–1813) II *115*
Huntingfotd, G.I. (1748–1832) II *115*
Huntly, 2nd Marquess of (d 1649) I *67–68*

Huntly, 9th Marquess of (1761–1853) II 115
Huquier, J.G. (1725–1805) II 115
Hurcomb, 1st Baron (1883–1975) IV 53
Hurd, Richard (1720–1808) II 115
Hurst, Sir A.F. (1866–1944) IV 53
Hurst, Sir Cecil (1870–1963) IV 53
Hussey, Giles (1710–1788) II 115
Hussey, Thomas (1741–1803) II 115
Hutcheson, Francis (1694–1746) I 68
Hutcheson, Thomas (1589–1641) I 68
Hutchins, John (1698–1773) I 68
Hutchinson, Arthur (1866–1937) IV 53
Hutchinson, A.S.M. (1879–1971) IV 53
Hutchinson, F.E. (1871–1947) IV 53
Hutchinson, H.D. (1847–1924) III 99
Hutchinson, H.G. (1859–1932) III 99–100
Hutchinson, John (1615–1664) I 68
Hutchinson, Sir Jonathan (1828–1913) III 100
Hutchinson, Lucy (b 1620) I 68
Hutchinson, William (1732–1814) II 115
Hutchinson, Sir Robert, 1st Bart (1871–1960) IV 53
Hutchison, Sir W.O. (1889–1970) IV 53
Huth, Henry (1815–1878) III 100
Hutt, John (1746–1794) II 115
Hutt, Sir William (1801–1882) III 100
Hutton, Alfred (1839–1910) III 100
Hutton, Catherine (1756–1846) II 115–116
Hutton, Charles (1737–1823) II 116
Hutton, G.C. (1825–1908) III 100
Hutton, James (1715–1795) II 116
Hutton, James (1726–1797) II 116
Hutton, Matthew (1529–1606) I 68
Hutton, Matthew (1693–1758) I 68
Hutton, Sir Richard (1561?–1639) I 68
Hutton, William (1723–1815) II 116
Huxham, John (1692–1768) I 68
Huxley, Aldous (1894–1963) IV 53–54
Huxley, Sir J.S. (1887–1975) IV 54
Huxley, T.H. (1825–1895) III 100
Hyatt, John (1767–1826) II 116
Hyde, Douglas (1860–1949) IV 54
Hyde, Sir Robert (1595–1665) I 68
Hyde, Sir Robert (1878–1967) IV 54
Hyde, Thomas (1636–1703) I 68
Hylton, 1st Baron (1800–1876) III 100
Hylton, Jack (1892–1965) IV 54
Hyndford, 3rd Earl of (1701–1767) II 116
Hyndley, 1st Viscount (1883–1963) IV 54
Hyndman, H.M. (1842–1921) III 100
Hysing, Hans (1678–1753?) I 68

Ibbetson, Bella (1783?–1817) II 117
Ibbetson, Sir D.C.J. (1847–1908) III 101
Ibbetson, J.C. (1759–1817) II 117
Ibbot, Benjamin (1680–1725) I 69
Iddesleigh, 1st Earl of (1818–1887) III 101
Ilbert, Sir C.P. (1841–1924) III 101
Ilchester, 6th Earl of (1874–1959) IV 55
Iliffe, 1st Baron (1877–1960) IV 55
Image, Selwyn (1849–1930) III 101
Imms, A.D. (1880–1949) IV 55
Impey, Sir Elijah (1732–1809) II 117
Ince, Sir G.H. (1891–1960) IV 55
Ince, William (1825–1910) III 101
Inchbald, Elizabeth (1753–1821) II 117
Inchbold, J.W. (1830–1888) III 101
Inchcape, 1st Earl of (1852–1932) III 101
Inchiquin, 1st Earl of (1614–1674) I 68
Incledon, Charles (1763–1826) II 117
Inderwick, F.A. (1836–1904) III 101
Inge, W.R. (1860–1954) IV 55
Ingelow, Jean (1820–1897) III 101
Ingenhousz, Jan (1730–1799) II 117
Ingham, Benjamin (1712–1772) II 117
Ingham, C.C. (1796–1863) II 117
Ingham, Sir J.T. (1805–1890) III 101
Inglefield, Sir E.A. (1820–1894) III 101
Inglefield, J.N. (1748–1828) II 117
Inglis, Charles (c 1731–1791) II 117
Inglis, Charles (1734–1816) II 117
Inglis, Sir C.E. (1875–1952) IV 55
Inglis, E.M. (1864–1917) IV 55
Inglis, John (1762–1834) II 117
Inglis, Sir J.E.W. (1814–1862) III 101
Inglis, Sir R.H., 2nd Bart (1786–1855) II 117
Ingram, Sir Arthur (d 1642) I 69
Ingram, Herbert (1811–1860) III 101
Ingram, James (1774–1850) II 117
Ingram, J.K. (1823–1907) III 101
Ingrams, W.H. (1897–1973) IV 55
Innes, Cosmo (1798–1874) II 117
Innes, J.D. (1887–1914) IV 55
Innes of Learney, Sir Thomas (1893–1971) IV 55
Innes-Ker, Lord C.J. (1842–1919) III 101
Inskipp, James (1790–1868) II 117
Inverforth, 1st Baron (1865–1955) IV 55

Ireland, John (d 1808) II 117
Ireland, John (1761–1842) II 117
Ireland, J.N. (1879–1962) IV 55
Ireland, Samuel (d 1800) II 117
Ireland, William (1636–1679) I 69
Ireland, W.H. (1777–1835) II 117
Ireton, Henry (1611–1651) I 69
Ironside, 1st Baron (1880–1959) IV 55
Ironside, Gilbert (1588–1671) I 69
Ironside, Gilbert (1632–1701) I 69
Irvine, Sir J.C. (1877–1952) IV 55
Irving, Edward (1792–1834) II 117–118
Irving, Sir Henry (1838–1905) III 101
Irwin, Eyles (1751?–1817) II 118
Irwin, N.M.S. (1892–1972) IV 55
Isaacs, Sir I.A. (1855–1948) III 102
Isaacson, Stephen (1798–1849) II 118
Isabella of Angoulême (d 1246) I 69
Isabella of France (1292–1358) I 69
Isham, Sir Justinian, 2nd Bart (1610–1674) I 69
Isham, Sir Thomas, 3rd Bart (1657–1681) I 69
Islington, 1st Baron (1866–1936) IV 55
Islip, John (d 1532) I 69
Ismay, T.H. (1837–1899) III 102
Ismay of Wormington, 1st Baron (1887–1965) IV 55
Iveagh, 1st Earl of (1847–1927) III 102
Iveagh, 2nd Earl of (1874–1967) IV 55
Ives, John (1751–1776) II 118
Ivimey, Joseph (1773–1834) II 118
Jack, Gilbert (1578?–1628) I 71
Jacks, L.P. (1860–1955) IV 56
Jackson, Arthur (1593?–1666) I 71
Jackson, Sir B.V. (1879–1961) IV 56
Jackson, Cyril (1746–1819) II 119
Jackson, Sir Cyril (1863–1924) IV 56
Jackson, F.G. (1860–1938) IV 56
Jackson, F.J. (1770–1814) II 119
Jackson, F.J.F. (1855–1941) III 103
Jackson, Henry (1831–1879) III 103
Jackson, Henry (1839–1921) III 103
Jackson, Sir Herbert (1863–1936) IV 56
Jackson, Holbrook (1874–1948) IV 56
Jackson, Sir H.B. (1855–1929) III 103
Jackson, John (1686–1763) I 71
Jackson, John (1769–1845) II 119
Jackson, John (1778–1831) II 119
Jackson, John (1811–1885) III 103
Jackson, John (1887–1958) IV 56
Jackson, Joseph (1733–1792) II 119
Jackson, J.H. (1835–1911) III 103
Jackson, Randle (1757–1837) II 119
Jackson, Samuel (1786–1861) II 119
Jackson, Sir Stanley (1870–1947) IV 56
Jackson, S.P. (1830–1904) III 103
Jackson, Sir T.G., 1st Bart (1835–1924) III 103
Jackson, William (1730–1803) II 119
Jackson, William (1737?–1795) II 119
Jackson, William (1751–1815) II 119
Jacob, Arthur (1790–1874) II 119
Jacob, Sir C.W. (1863–1948) IV 56
Jacob, Edgar (1844–1920) III 103
Jacob, Edward (1710?–1788) II 119
Jacob, E.F. (1894–1971) IV 56
Jacob, Hildebrand (1693–1739) I 71
Jacob, Sir Ian (b 1899) IV 56
Jacob, John (1812–1858) III 103
Jacob, William (1762?–1851) II 119
Jacobs, W.W. (1863–1943) IV 56
Jacobsen, Theodore (d 1772) II 119
Jacobson, William (1803–1884) III 103
Jacomb(e), Thomas (1622–1687) I 71
Jagger, C.S. (1885–1934) IV 56
James I (1394–1437) I 71
James II (1430–1460) I 71
James III (1451–1488) I 71
James IV (1473–1513) I 71
James V (1512–1542) I 71
James I (1566–1625) I 71
James II (1633–1701) I 71
James Stuart, Prince (1688–1766) I 71
James, Charles (d 1821) II 119
James, David (1839–1893) III 103
James, G.P.R. (1799–1860) II 119
James, Henry (1843–1916) III 103
James, John (1729–1785) II 119
James, J.A. (1785–1859) II 119
James, J.H. (1788–1869) II 119
James, J.T. (1786–1828) II 119
James, M.R. (1862–1936) IV 56
James, Thomas (1573?–1629) I 71
James, Thomas (1593?–1635?) I 72
James, Thomas (1748–1804) II 119
James, William (1542–1617) I 72
James, Sir William, 1st Bart (1721–1783) II 119
James, William (1771–1837) II 119
James, Sir W.M. (1807–1881) III 103
James of Hereford, 1st Baron (1828–1911) III 103–104

Jameson, Anna Brownell (1794–1860) II 119
Jameson, J.S. (1856–1888) III 104
Jameson, Sir L.S., Bart (1853–1917) III 104
Jameson, Robert (1774–1854) II 119
Jameson, Storm (b 1897) IV 56
Jameson, Sir Wilson (1885–1962) IV 56
Jamesone, George (1589?–1644) I 72
Jamieson, John (1759–1838) II 120
Jane Seymour (1509?–1537) I 72
Jane, William (1645–1707) I 72
Janeway, James (1636?–1674) I 72
Jardine, D.R. (1900–1958) IV 56
Jardine, James (1776–1858) II 120
Jardine, Sir Robert, 1st Bart (1825–1905) III 104
Jardine, Sir William (1800–1874) III 104
Jarman, Frances Eleanor (1803?–1873) III 104
Jarvie, Gibson (1883–1964) IV 56
Jay, William (1769–1853) II 120
Jayne, F.J. (1845–1921) III 104
Jeacocke, Caleb (1706–1786) II 120
Jeans, Sir J.H. (1877–1946) IV 56
Jebb, Eglantyne (1876–1928) IV 56
Jebb, John (1736–1786) II 120
Jebb, John (1775–1833) II 120
Jebb, Sir Joshua (1793–1863) II 120
Jebb, Sir Richard, Bart (1729–1787) II 120
Jebb, Sir R.C. (1841–1905) III 104
Jeffereys, James (1751–1784) II 120
Jefferies, Richard (1848–1887) III 104
Jeffery, Dorothy (1685–1777) I 72
Jeffery, G.B. (1891–1957) IV 56
Jeffery, John (1647–1720) I 72
Jeffreys, J.G. (1809–1885) III 104
Jeffreys of Wem, 1st Baron (1648–1689) I 72
Jeffry, Lord (1773–1850) II 120
Jegon, John (1550–1618) I 72
Jehner, Isaac (1750–1806?) II 120
Jekyll, Gertrude (1843–1932) III 104
Jekyll, Sir Joseph (1663–1738) I 72
Jekyll, Joseph (1753–1837) II 120
Jelf, R.W. (1798–1871) II 120
Jellett, J.H. (1817–1888) III 104
Jellicoe, 1st Earl (1859–1935) III 104
Jellicoe, Basil (1899–1935) IV 56
Jenkin, H.C.F. (1833–1885) III 104
Jenkins, Baron (1899–1969) IV 56–57
Jenkins, Claude (1877–1959) IV 56
Jenkins, David (1582–1663) I 72
Jenkins, E.E. (1820–1905) III 104
Jenkins, Henry (d 1670) I 72
Jenkins, Joseph (1743–1819) II 120
Jenkins, J.E. (1838–1910) III 104
Jenkins, J.J. (1811–1885) III 104
Jenkins, Sir Leoline (1623–1685) I 72
Jenkins, Sir L.H. (1857–1928) III 104
Jenkins, Thomas (1722–1798) II 120
Jenkinson, F.J.H. (1853–1923) III 104
Jenkinson, Sir G.S., Bart (1817–1892) III 104
Jenkinson, Sir Hilary (1882–1961) IV 57
Jenks, Edward (1861–1939) IV 57
Jenkyn, William (1613–1685) I 72
Jenkyns, Richard (1782–1854) II 120
Jenner, Edward (1749–1823) II 120
Jenner, Sir William, 1st Bart (1815–1898) III 104
Jenner-Fust, Herbert (1806–1904) III 104
Jennings, David (1691–1762) I 72
Jennings, H.C. (1731–1819) II 120
Jennings, Sir John (1664–1743) I 72
Jenyns, Soame (1704–1787) II 120
Jephson, A.J.M. (1858–1908) III 104–105
Jephson, Robert (1736–1803) II 120
Jerdan, William (1782–1869) II 120
Jeremie, Sir John (1795–1841) II 120
Jeremie, J.A. (1802–1872) III 105
Jermyn, Henry (1767–1820) II 120
Jerningham, Edward (1727–1812) II 120–121
Jerome, Jerome K. (1859–1927) III 105
Jerram, Sir Martyn (1858–1933) III 105
Jerrold, Douglas (1893–1964) IV 57
Jerrold, D.W. (1803–1857) III 105
Jerrold, W.B. (1826–1884) III 105
Jersey, 1st Earl of (1656–1711) I 72
Jersey, 2nd Earl of (1682?–1721) I 72
Jersey, 4th Earl of (1735–1805) II 121
Jersey, 5th Earl of (1773–1859) II 121
Jersey, 7th Earl of (1845–1915) III 105
Jersey, Countess of (1849–1945) III 105
Jervas, Charles (1675?–1739) I 72
Jervis, Thomas (1748–1833) II 121
Jervis, Sir W.F.D. (1821–1897) III 105
Jesse, Edward (1780–1868) II 121
Jesse, F.T. (1889–1958) IV 57
Jesse, J.H. (1815–1874) III 105
Jessel, Sir George (1824–1883) III 105
Jessey, Henry (1601–1663) I 72
Jessop, G.L. (1874–1955) IV 57

Jessop, William (1745–1814) II *105*
Jessopp, Augustus (1823–1914) III *105*
Jeune, Francis (1806–1868) III *105*
Jevons, W.S. (1835–1882) III *105*
Jewel, John (1522–1571) I *72*
Jewsbury, Maria Jane (1800–1833) III *105*
Jex-Blake, Sophia Louise (1840–1912) III *105*
Jex-Blake, T.W. (1832–1915) III *105*
Joachim, H.H. (1868–1938) IV *57*
Joachim, Joseph (1831–1907) III *105*
Joad, C.E.M. (1891–1953) IV *57*
Joan of Navarre, (1370?–1547) I *72*
Jobson, F.J. (1812–1881) III *105*
Jodrell, R.P. (1745–1831) II *121*
Jodrell, Sir R.P., 2nd Bart (1781–1861) II *121*
Joel, S.B. (1865–1931) IV *57*
John (1167?–1216) I *72*
John of Eltham, Earl of Cornwall (1316–1336) I *72*
John of Gaunt, Duke of Lancaster (1340–1399) I *72*
John of Lancaster, Duke of Bedford (1389–1435) I *72*
John, Augustus (1878–1961) IV *57*
John, Gwendolen (1876–1939) IV *57*
John, Sir William Goscombe (1860–1951) IV *57*
Johnes, Thomas (1748–1816) II *121*
Johns, C.H.W. (1857–1920) III *106*
Johnson, Benjamin (1665?–1742) I *72*
Johnson, Borough (1867–1949) IV *57*
Johnson, Cornelius (1593–1661) I *72–73*
Johnson, Esther (1681–1728) I *73*
Johnson, Sir George (1818–1896) III *106*
Johnson, G.H.S. (1808–1881) II *106*
Johnson, Sir Henry, 1st Bart (1748–1835) II *121*
Johnson, Hewlett (1874–1966) IV *57*
Johnson, Humphrey (fl 1713) I *73*
Johnson, James (1705–1774) II *121*
Johnson, James (1777–1845) II *121*
Johnson, John (1777–1848) II *121*
Johnson, John de Monins (1882–1956) IV *57*
Johnson, Joseph (1738–1809) II *121*
Johnson, Manuel John (1805–1859) III *106*
Johnson, Maurice (1688–1755) I *73*
Johnson, Sir N.K. (1892–1954) IV *57*
Johnson, Samuel (1709–1784) II *121*
Johnson, Sir William, 1st Bart (1715–1774) II *121*
Johnson, W.E. (1858–1931) III *106*
Johnston, Sir Alexander (1775–1849) II *121*
Johnston, Arthur (1587–1641) I *73*
Johnston, A.K. (1844–1879) III *106*
Johnston, David (1734–1824) II *121*
Johnston, Edward (1872–1944) IV *57*
Johnston, Francis (1761–1829) II *121*
Johnston, George (1797–1855) II *121*
Johnston H.E. (1777–1830?) II *121*
Johnston, Sir H.H. (1858–1927) III *106*
Johnston, Sir John, Bart (d 1690?) I *73*
Johnston, J.H. (1787–1851) II *121*
Johnston, Thomas (1881–1965) IV *57*
Johnston, Sir William (1802–1888) III *106*
Johnston, William (1829–1902) III *106*
Johnstone, George (1730–1787) II *121*
Johnstone, James (1754–1783) II *121*
Johnstone, James (1806–1869) III *106*
Johnstone, James (1815–1878) III *106*
Johnstone, J.H. (1749–1828) II *121*
Johnstone, W.B. (1804–1868) III *106*
Joicey, 1st Baron (1846–1936) III *106*
Jollie, Timothy (1659?–1714) I *73*
Jolly, Alexander (1756–1838) II *122*
Jolowicz, H.F. (1890–1954) IV *57*
Joly, John (1857–1933) III *106*
Jones, Avonia (1839?–1867) III *106*
Jones, A.C. (1891–1964) IV *67*
Jones, Sir A.L. (1845–1909) III *106*
Jones, B.M. (1882–1953) IV *58*
Jones, Daniel (1881–1967) IV *58*
Jones, David (1735–1810) II *122*
Jones, David (1895–1974) IV *58*
Jones, Ernest (1879–1958) IV *57*
Jones, George (1786–1869) II *122*
Jones, Henry (1605–1682) I *73*
Jones, Sir Henry (1852–1922) III *106*
Jones, Sir Horace (1819–1887) III *106*
Jones, H.A. (1851–1929) III *106*
Jones, H.B. (1814–1873) III *106*
Jones, H.C. (1818–1902) III *106*
Jones, Sir H.D. (1791–1866) II *122*
Jones, H.F. (1851–1928) III *106*
Jones, Sir H.S. (1890–1960) IV *58*
Jones, Inigo (1573–1652) I *73*
Jones, Ira (1896–1960) IV *58*
Jones, John (d 1660) I *73*
Jones, John (1745?–1797) II *122*
Jones, John (1796–1857) II *122*
Jones, J.D. (1865–1942) IV *58*
Jones, J.G. (1769–1838) II *122*
Jones, J.P. (1747–1792) II *122*
Jones, Sir J.T., 1st Bart (1783–1843) II *122*

Jones, J.V. (1856–1901) III *106*
Jones, J.W. (1805–1881) III *106*
Jones, L.G. (1779–1839) II *122*
Jones, Sir L.T. (1797–1895) II *122*
Jones, Owen (1741–1814) II *122*
Jones, Owen (1809–1874) III *106*
Jones, Owen (1878–1967) IV *58*
Jones, Parry (1891–1963) IV *58*
Jones, Richard (1779–1851) II *122*
Jones, Richard (1790–1855) II *122*
Jones, Sir Robert, 1st Bart (1857–1933) III *106*
Jones, Sir Roderick (1877–1962) IV *58*
Jones, R.R. (1780–1843) II *122*
Jones, Sir Thomas (1614–1692) I *73*
Jones, Thomas (1742–1803) II *122*
Jones, Thomas (1752–1845) II *122*
Jones, Thomas (c 1756–1807) II *122*
Jones, Thomas (1756–1820) II *122*
Jones, Thomas (1810–1875) III *106*
Jones, Thomas (1870–1955) IV *58*
Jones, Sir William (1566–1640) I *73*
Jones, Sir William (1631–1682) I *73*
Jones, William (1726–1800) II *122*
Jones, Sir William (1746–1794) II *122*
Jones, William (1784–1842) II *122*
Jones, W.B. (1822–1897) III *106*
Jones, W.W. (1838–1908) III *106–107*
Jones, Wood (1879–1954) IV *58*
Jonson, Benjamin (1573–1637) I *73*
Jopson, N.B. (1890–1969) IV *58*
Jordan, Dorothea (1762–1816) II *122*
Jordan, Sir Joseph (1603–1685) I *73*
Jordan, Sir J.N. (1852–1925) III *107*
Jordan, Karl (1861–1959) IV *58*
Jortin, John (1698–1770) I *73*
Joseph, H.W.B. (1867–1943) IV *58*
Joseph, Michael (1897–1958) IV *58*
Josi, Henry (1802–1845) III *107*
Joubert de la Ferte, Sir Philip (1887–1965) IV *58*
Joule, J.P. (1818–1889) III *107*
Jowett, Benjamin (1817–1893) III *107*
Jowitt, 1st Earl (1885–1957) IV *58*
Joy, William (1675?–1734) I *73*
Joyce, George (fl 1647–70) I *73*
Joyce, J.A. (1882–1941) IV *58*
Joyce, Sir M.I. (1839–1930) III *107*
Julien, L.A. (1812–1860) III *107*
Junius, Francis (1589–1677) I *73*
Jupp, R.W. (1767–1852) II *122*
Jurin, James (1684–1750) I *73*
Justel, Henri (1620–1693) I *73*
Jutsum, Henry (1816–1869) III *107*
Juxon, William (1582–1663) I *73*

Kames, Lord (1696–1782) I *75*
Kane, Richard (1666–1736?) I *75*
Kane, Sir R.J. (1809–1890) III *109*
Karslake, Sir J.B. (1821–1881) III *109*
Kater, Henry (1777–1835) II *123*
Katterfelto, Gustavus (d 1799) II *123*
Kauffer, E.M. (d 1954) IV *59*
Kauffmann, Angelica (1741–1807) II *123*
Kavanagh, Julia (1824–1877) III *109*
Kay, Sir E.E. (1822–1897) III *109*
Kay, John (fl 1733–1764) II *123*
Kay, John (1742–1826) II *123*
Kaye, John (1783–1853) II *123*
Kaye, Sir J.W. (1814–1876) III *109*
Kaye-Smith, Sheila (1887–1956) IV *59*
Keach, Benjamin (1640–1704) I *75*
Kean, C.J. (1811–1868) III *109*
Kean, Edmund (1787–1833) II *123*
Keate, George (1729–1797) II *123*
Keate, John (1773–1852) II *123*
Keate, Robert (1777–1857) II *123*
Keating, Sir H.S. (1775–1847) II *123*
Keating, Sir H.S. (1804–1888) III *109*
Keats, John (1795–1821) II *123*
Keay, J.S. (1839–1909) III *109*
Keble, John (1792–1866) II *123*
Keble, Richard (fl 1650) I *75*
Keats, Sir R.G. (1757–1834) II *123*
Keeble, Sir F.W. (1870–1952) IV *59*
Keeley, Mary Ann (1805?–1899) III *109*
Keeley, Robert (1793–1869) II *123*
Keeling, Josiah (fl 1691) I *75*
Keene, Sir Benjamin (1697–1757) I *75*
Keene, C.S. (1823–1891) III *109*
Keene, Edmund (1714–1781) II *123*
Keilin, David (1887–1963) IV *59*
Keir, Sir D.L. (1895–1973) IV *59*
Keir, James (1735–1820) II *123*
Keith, Viscount (1746–1823) II *124*
Keith, Viscountess (1762–1857) II *124*
Keith, Viscountess (1788–1867) II *124*
Keith, Alexander (1791–1880) II *123–124*
Keith, Sir Arthur (1866–1955) IV *59*

Keith, A.B. (1879–1944) IV *59*
Keith, J.F.E. (1696–1758) I *75*
Keith, Robert (1681–1757) I *75*
Keith, Sir R.M. (1730–1795) II *124*
Keith, Sir W.J. (1873–1937) IV *59*
Keith-Falconer, I.G.N. (1856–1887) III *109*
Kekewich, Sir Arthur (1832–1907) III *109*
Kelland, Philip (1808–1879) III *109*
Kellaway, C.H. (1889–1952) IV *52*
Kellett, Sir Henry (1806–1875) III *109*
Kellie, 6th Earl of (1732–1781) II *124*
Kelly, Sir D.V. (1891–1959) IV *59*
Kelly, Sir Gerald (1879–1972) IV *59*
Kelly, Sir Fitzroy (1796–1880) II *124*
Kelly, Frances (1790–1882) II *124*
Kelly, Sir Howard (1873–1952) IV *59*
Kelly, Hugh (1739–1777) II *124*
Kelly, Sir J.D. (1871–1936) IV *59*
Kelly, J.F. (1857–1923) III *110*
Kelly, Michael (1764?–1826) II *124*
Kelly, Patrick (1756–1842) II *124*
Kelly-Kenny, Sir Thomas (1840–1914) III *110*
Keltie, Sir J.S. (1840–1927) III *110*
Kelvin, 1st Baron (1824–1907) III *110*
Kelway, Joseph (d 1782) II *124*
Kelying, Sir John (d 1671) I *75*
Kem(e), Samuel (1604–1670) I *75*
Kemball, Sir A.B. (1820–1908) III *110*
Kemball-Cook, Sir B.A. (1876–1949) IV *59*
Kemble, Charles (1775–1854) II *124*
Kemble, Mrs Elizabeth (1763?–1841) II *124*
Kemble, Frances Anne (1809–1893) III *110*
Kemble, Henry (1848–1907) III *110*
Kemble, J.M. (1807–1857) III *110*
Kemble, J.P. (1757–1823) II *124*
Kemble, Maria Theresa (1774–1838) II *124*
Kemble, Priscilla (1756–1845) II *124*
Kemble, Roger (1721–1802) II *124*
Kemble, Stephen (1758–1822) II*125*
Kemp, G.M. (1795–1844) II*125*
Kemp, John (1380?–1454) I *75*
Kemp, S.W. (1882–1945) IV *59*
Kemp, T.R. (1781?–1844) II *125*
Kemp, William (fl 1600) I *75*
Kempe, A.J. (1785?–1846) II *125*
Kempenfelt, Richard (1718–1782) II *125*
Kempt, Sir James (1764–1854) II *125*
Kemsley, 1st Viscount (1883–1968) IV *59*
Ken, Thomas (1637–1711) I *75*
Kendal, Dame Margaret (1848–1935) III *110*
Kendal, W.H. (1843–1917) III *110*
Kendrick, James (1771–1847) II *125*
Kenealy, E.V.H. (1819–1880) III *110*
Kenmare, 4th Earl of (1825–1905) III *110*
Kenmare, 6th Earl of (1891–1943) IV *59*
Kenmure, 6th Viscount (d 1716) I *75*
Kennard, H.J. (1829–1896) III *110*
Kennard, Sir H.W. (1878–1955) IV *59*
Kennaway, Sir E.L. (1881–1958) IV *59*
Kennaway, Sir J.H., 3rd Bart (1837–1919) III *110*
Kennedy, Sir A.B.W. (1847–1928) III *110–111*
Kennedy, B.H. (1804–1889) III *111*
Kennedy, Sir J.N. (1893–1970) IV *59*
Kennedy, Sir J.S. (1788–1865) II *125*
Kennedy, Margaret (1896–1967) IV *59*
Kennedy, Patrick (1801–1873) III *111*
Kennedy, T.F. (1788–1879) II *125*
Kennedy, William (1813–1890) III *111*
Kennedy, Sir W.R. (1846–1915) III *111*
Kennedy of Dunure, Thomas (d 1759) I *75*
Kennet, 1st Baron (1879–1960) IV *59*
Kennet, Kathleen, Lady (1878–1947) IV *59*
Kennett, White (1660–1728) I *75*
Kenney, Annie (1879–1953) IV *59*
Kenney, James (1780–1849) II *125*
Kennicott, Benjamin (1718–1783) II *125*
Kennington, Eric (1880–1960) IV *59*
Kenny, C.S. (1847–1930) III *111*
Kenrick, Daniel (fl 1685) I *75*
Kenrick, John (1788–1877) II *125*
Kenrick, William (1727?–1779) II *125*
Kent, 10th Earl of (1594–1651) I *75*
Kent, 1st Duke of (1671–1740) I *75*
Kent, Duchess of (1581?–1651) I *75*
Kent, James (1700–1776) II *125*
Kent, Nathaniel (1737–1810) II *125*
Kent, William (1685?–1748) I *75*
Kent and Strathearn, Duke of (1767–1820) II *125*
Kent and Strathearn, Duchess of (1786–1861) II *125*
Kentish, John (1768–1853) II *125*
Kenton, Benjamin (1719–1800) II *125*
Kenyon, 1st Baron (1732–1802) II *125*
Kenyon, Sir F.G. (1863–1952) IV *59*
Kenyon, G.T. (1840–1908) III *111*
Kenyon, John (1784–1856) II *125*
Kenyon-Slaney, W.S. (1847–1908) III *111*
Keogh, Sir Alfred (1857–1936) III *111*

Keogh, W.N. (1817–1878) III *111*
Keppel, 1st Viscount (1725–1786) II *125*
Keppel, Frederick (1729–1777) II *125*
Keppel, Sir Henry (1809–1904) III *111*
Ker, John (1673–1726) I *75*
Ker, W.P. (1855–1923) III *111*
Kerr, Sir J.G. (1869–1957) IV *60*
Kerr, Munro (1868–1960) IV *60*
Kerr, Lord W.T. (1839–1927) III *111*
Kerrich, Thomas (1748–1828) II *126*
Kerrison, Sir Edward (1774–1853) II *126*
Kersey, John (1616–1690?) I *76*
Kershaw, James (1730?–1797) II *126*
Ketel, Cornelius (1548–1616) I *76*
Kett, Henry (1761–1825) II *126*
Kettell, Ralph (1563–1643) I *76*
Kettle, E.H. (1882–1936) IV *60*
Kettle, Sir R.A. (1817–1894) III *111*
Kettle, Tilly (1735–1786) II *126*
Kettlewell, John (1653–1695) I *76*
Key, C.A. (1793–1849) II *126*
Key, Sir John, 1st Bart (1794–1858) II *126*
Key T.H. (1799–1875) II *126*
Keyes, 1st Baron (1872–1945) IV *60*
Keyl F. W. (1823–1873) III *111*
Keynes, J.M. Keynes, Baron (1883–1946) IV *60*
Keynes, Florence Ada (1861–1958) IV *60*
Keynes, Sir Geoffrey (*b*1887) IV *60*
Keyse, Thomas (1722–1800) II *126*
Keyworth, Thomas (1782–1852) II *126*
Kiallmark, G.F. (1804–1887) III *111*
Kickham, C.J. (1826–1882) III *111*
Kidd, James (1761–1834) II *126*
Kidd, John (1775–1851) II *126*
Kidder, Richard (1633–1703) I *76*
Kidderminster, Baron (*d*1388) I *76*
Kiffin, William (1616–1701) I *76*
Kiggell, Sir L.E. (1862–1954) IV *60*
Kilbracken, 1st Baron (1847–1932) III *111*
Kilburne, Richard (1605–1678) I *76*
Kildare, 9th Earl of (1487–1534) I *76*
Killearn, 1st Baron (1880–1964) IV *60*
Killigrew, Anne (1660–1685) I *76*
Killigrew, Sir Thomas (1612–1683) I *76*
Killigrew, Sir William (1606–1695) I *76*
Kilmaine, C.E.S.J. (1751–1799) II *126*
Kilmarnock, 4th Earl of (1704–1746) II *126*
Kilmuir, Earl of (1900–1967) IV *60*
Kilvert, Richard (*d*1649) I *76*
Kilwarden, Viscount (1739–1803) II *126*
Kimber, Isaac (1692–1755) I *76*
Kimberley, 1st Earl of (1826–1902) III *111*
Kimmins, Dame Grace (1870–1954) IV *60*
Kindersley, 1st Baron (1871–1954) IV *60*
Kindersley, Sir R.T. (1792–1879) II *126*
King, C.W. (1818–1888) III *111*
King, David (1806–1883) III *111*
King, Sir Edmund (1629–1709) I *76*
King, Edward (1829–1910) III *111*
King, Frances Elizabeth (1757–1821) II *126*
King, Sir George (1840–1909) III *111–112*
King, Harold (1887–1956) IV *60*
King, Henry (1592–1669) I *76*
King, James (1732–1787) II *126*
King, John (1559?–1621) I *76*
King, Sir John (1639–1677) I *76*
King, J.G. (1732–1787) II *126*
King, P.G. (1758–1808) II *126*
King, P.J.L. (1811–1885) II *126*
King, P.P. (1793–1856) II *126*
King, Sir Richard, 1st Bart (1730–1806) II *126*
King, Sir Richard, 2nd Bart (1774–1834) II *126*
King, Robert (*d*1557) I *76*
King, Thomas (1730–1805) II *126*
King, William (1650–1729) I *76*
King, William (1663–1712) I *76*
King, William (1685–1763) I *76*
King of Ockham, 1st Baron (1669–1734) I *76*
King of Ockham, 7th Baron (1775–1833) II *126*
King-Hall, Baron (1893–1966) IV *60*
Kingdon-Ward, Francis (1885–1958) IV *60*
Kinghorn, Joseph (1766–1832) II *126*
Kinglake, A.W. (1809–1891) III *112*
Kingsburgh, Lord (1836–1919) III *112*
Kingsbury, William (1744–1818) II *126*
Kingscote, Sir R.N.F. (1830–1908) III *112*
Kingsdown, Baron (1793–1867) II *126*
Kingsford, C.L. (1826–1926) IV *60*
Kingsley, Charles (1819–1875) III *112*
Kingsley, Henry (1830–1876) III *112*
Kingsley, Mary Henrietta (1862–1900) IV *60*
Kingsley, William (1698?–1769) I *76*
Kingsmill, Sir R.B., 1st Bart (1730–1805) II *126–127*
Kingston, 1st Earl of (1584–1643) I *76*
Kingston, 1st Duke of (1665?–1726) I *76*
Kingston, Richard (fl 1700) I *76*

Kinnaird, 8th Baron (1780–1826) II *127*
Kinnaird, 9th Baron (1807–1878) III *112*
Kinnaird, 10th Baron (1814–1887) III *112*
Kinnaird, D.J.W. (1788–1830) II *127*
Kinneder, Lord (1769–1822) II *127*
Kinnear, Sir N.B. (1882–1957) IV *60*
Kinnoull, 1st Earl of (1572–1634) I *77*
Kinnoull, 9th Earl of (1710–1787) II *127*
Kinross, 1st Baron (1837–1905) III *112*
Kintore, 9th Earl of (1852–1930) III *112*
Kipling, Rudyard (1865–1936) IV *60*
Kipping, F.S. (1863–1949) IV *60*
Kippis, Andrew (1725–1795) II *127*
Kirby, John (1690–1753) I *77*
Kirby, J.J. (1716–1774) II *127*
Kirby, William (1759–1850) II *127*
Kirk, Sir John (1832–1922) III *112*
Kirk, K.E. (1886–1954) IV *60–61*
Kirke, Percy (1684–1741) I *77*
Kirkland, Thomas (1722–1798) II *127*
Kirkman, Francis (fl 1674) I *77*
Kirkpatrick, Sir Ivone (1897–1964) IV *61*
Kirkpatrick, John (1686?–1728) I *77*
Kirkup, S.S. (1788–1880) II *127*
Kirkwood, 1st Baron (1872–1955) IV *61*
Kirwan, Richard (1733–1812) II *127*
Kirwan, W.B. (1754–1805) II *127*
Kitchener, William (1775?–1827) II *127*
Kitchener of Khartoum and of Broome, 1st Earl
 (1850–1916) III *112*
Kitchin, G.W. (1827–1912) III *112*
Kitson Clark, G.S.R. (1900–1975) IV *61*
Klein, Melanie (1882–1960) IV *61*
Knapton, George (1698–1778) I *77*
Knapton, Philip (1762–1833) II *127*
Knatchbull, Sir Edward, 9th Bart (1781–1849) II *127*
Knatchbull, Sir Norton, 1st Bart (1602–1685) I *77*
Knatchbull-Hugessen, Sir H.M. (1886–1971) IV *61*
Kneller, Sir Godfrey, 1st Bart (1646–1723) I *77*
Kneller, J.Z. (1644–1702) I *77*
Knibb, William (1803–1845) III *112*
Knight, Charles (1791–1873) II *127*
Knight, Edward (1774–1826) II *127*
Knight, Ellis Cornelia (1757–1837) II *127*
Knight, Gowin (1713–1772) II *127*
Knight, Harold (1874–1961) IV *61*
Knight, H.G. (1786–1846) II *127*
Knight, Sir John (1748?–1831) II*127*
Knight, Joseph (1829–1907) III *113*
Knight, J.P. (1803–1881) III *112–113*
Knight, J.P. (1812–1887) III *113*
Knight, Dame Laura (1877–1970) IV *61*
Knight, R.P. (1750–1824) II *127*
Knight, Samuel (1759–1827) II *127*
Knight, Thomas (1764?–1820) II *127*
Knight, T.A. (1759–1838) II *127*
Knight-Bruce, G.W.H. (1852–1896) III *113*
Knight-Bruce, Sir J.L. (1791–1866) II *127–128*
Knighton, Sir William, 1st Bart (1776–1838) II *128*
Knipe, Thomas (1638–1711) I *77*
Knollys, 1st Viscount (1837–1924) III *113*
Knollys, 2nd Viscount (1895–1966) IV *61*
Knollys, Sir Francis (1514?–1596) I *77*
Knollys, Hanserd (1599–1691) I *77*
Knollys, Sir W.T. (1797–1883) II *128*
Knowles, Sir Charles, 1st Bart (1704?–1777) II *128*
Knowles, Sir C.H., 2nd Bart (1754–1831) II *128*
Knowles, Gilbert (fl 1723) I *77*
Knowles, James (1759–1840) II *128*
Knowles, John (1781–1841) II *128*
Knowles, J.S. (1784–1862) II *128*
Knowles, M.C. (1896–1974) IV *61*
Knox, Alexander (1757–1831) II *128*
Knox, E.A. (1847–1937) III *113*
Knox, E.G.V. (1881–1971) IV *61*
Knox, Sir H.H.S. (1873–1971) IV *61*
Knox, John (1505–1572) I *77*
Knox, Robert (1640?–1720) I *77*
Knox, Robert (1791–1862) II *128*
Knox, R.A. (1888–1957) IV *61*
Knox, R.B. (1889–1965) IV *61*
Knox, Sir R.U.E. (1889–1965) IV *61*
Knutsford, 1st Viscount (1825–1914) III *113*
Knutsford, 2nd Viscount (1855–1931) III *113*
Knyvett, Charles (1752–1822) II *128*
Knyvett, Charles (1773–1852) II *128*
Knyvett, William (1779–1856) II *128*
Knyvet(t) of Escrick, Baron (*d*1622) I *77*
Kokoschka, Oskar (1886–1980) IV *61*
König, C.D.E. (1774–1851) II *128*
Korda, Sir Alexander (1893–1956) IV *61*
Korda, Vincent (1897–1979) IV *61*
Kramer, Jacob (1892–1962) IV *61*
Kratzer, Nicholas (1487–1550?) I *77*
Krause, W.H. (1796–1852) II *128*
Kuper, Sir A.L. (1809–1885) III *113*
Kyd, Stewart (*d*1811) II *128*

Kynaston, Edward (1640?–1706) I *77*
Kynaston, Herbert (1809–1878) III *113*
Kyrle, John (1637–1724) I *77*

Lablache, Luigi (1794–1858) II *129*
Labouchere, H. du Pré (1831–1912) III *115*
Lacaita, Sir J.P. (1813–1895) III *115*
Lackington, James (1746–1815) II *129*
Lacroix, A.F. (1799–1859) II *129*
Lacy, Harriette (1807–1874) III *115*
Lacy, John (1622–1681) I *79*
Lacy, Maria Anne (1803–1877) III *115*
Lacy, M.R. (1795–1867) II *129*
Lacy, Walter (1809–1898) III *115*
Ladbrooke, Robert (1768–1841) II *129*
Laffan, Sir R.M. (1821–1882) III *115*
Laguerre, Louis (1663–1721) I *79*
Laidlaw, Sir P.P. (1881–1940) IV *62*
Laidlaw, William (1780–1845) II *129*
Laing, A.G. (1793–1826) II *129*
Laing, David (1793–1878) II *129*
Laing, Malcolm (1762–1818) II *129*
Laing, Samuel (1812–1897) III *115*
Laing, William (1764–1832) II *129*
Laird, John (1805–1874) III *115*
Laird, John (1887–1946) IV *62*
Lake, 1st Viscount (1744–1808) II *129*
Lake, Arthur (1569–1626) I *79*
Lake, Edward (1641–1704) I *79*
Lake, Sir H.A. (1808–1881) III *115*
Lake, John (1624–1689) I *79*
Lake, Kirsopp (1872–1946) IV *62*
Lake, Sir P.H.N. (1855–1940) III *115*
Lamb, Lady Caroline (1785–1828) II *129*
Lamb, Charles (1775–1834) II *129*
Lamb, George (1784–1834) II *129*
Lamb, Sir Horace (1849–1934) III *115*
Lamb, H.T. (1883–1960) IV *62*
Lamb, John (1789–1850) II *129*
Lamb, Sir J.B.B. (1752–1824) II *129*
Lamb, Mary (1764–1847) II *129*
Lamb, Sir Matthew, 1st Bart (1705–1768) II *129*
Lambarde, William (1536–1601) I *79*
Lambe, Sir C.E. (1900–1960) IV *62*
Lambe, John (*d*1628) I *79*
Lambe, William (1495–1580) I *79*
Lambert, 1st Viscount (1866–1958) IV *62*
Lambert, A.B. (1761–1842) II *129*
Lambert, Brooke (1834–1901) III *115*
Lambert, Daniel (1770–1809) II *129*
Lambert, George (1710–1765) II *129*
Lambert, G.W. (1873–1930) IV *62*
Lambert, Herbert (1881–1936) IV *62*
Lambert, James (1741–1823) II *129*
Lambert, James (1741–1823) II *129*
Lambert, John (1619–1684) I *79*
Lambert, Sir John (1772–1847) II *129–130*
Lambert, Sir John (1815–1892) III *115*
Lambourne, 1st Baron (1847–1928) III *115*
Lambton, John (1756–1823) I *79*
Lamington, 1st Baron (1816–1890) III *115*
Lamington, 2nd Baron (1860–1940) IV *62*
La Motte, John (1570?–1655) I *79*
Lampe, J.F. (1703?–1751) II*130*
Lamplugh, Thomas (1615–1691) I *79*
Lampson, Sir C.M., 1st Bart (1806–1885) III *115*
Lancaster, Earl of (1245–1296) I *79*
Lancaster, Sir James (*d*1618) I *79*
Lancaster, Joseph (1778–1838) II *130*
Lancaster, William (1650–1717) I *79*
Lance, George (1802–1864) III *115*
Lanchester, F.W. (1868–1946) IV *62*
Landells, R.T. (1833–1877) III *115*
Landmann, G.T. (1779–1854) II *130*
Lander, John (1807–1839) III *115*
Lander, R.L. (1804–1834) III *115–116*
Landmann, G.T. (1779–1854) II *130*
Landon, Letitia Elizabeth (1802–1838) III *116*
Landor, Walter Savage (1775–1864) II *130*
Landseer, Charles (1799–1879) II *130*
Landseer, Sir Edwin (1802–1873) III *116*
Landseer, John (1769–1852) II *130*
Landseer, Thomas (1795–1880) II *130*
Lane, Sir Arbuthnot, 1st Bart (1856–1943) III *116*
Lane, E.W. (1801–1876) III *116*
Lane, Sir H.P. (1875–1915) IV *62*
Lane, R.J. (1800–1872) III *116*
Laney, Benjamin (1591–1675) I *79*
Lang, Andrew (1844–1912) III *116*
Lang, Matheson (1877–1948) IV *62*
Lang of Lambeth, Baron (1864–1945) IV *62*
Langbaine, Gerard (1609–1658) I *79*
Langdale, 1st Baron (1598?–1661) I *79*
Langdale, Baron (1783–1851) II *130*
Langdon, S.H. (1876–1937) IV *62*
Langdon-Brown, Sir W.L. (1870–1946) IV *62*
Langford, Abraham (1711–1774) II *130*

Langford, J.A. (1823–1903) III *116*
Langham, Simon (1310–1376) I *79*
Langhorne, John (1735–1779) II *130*
Langhorne, Richard (*d*1679) I *79*
Langley, Batty (†1696–1751) I *79*
Langston, John (1641?–1704) I *79*
Langton, Bennet (1737–1801) II *130*
Langton, Sir G.P. (1881–1942) IV *62*
Langtry, Lily (1853–1929) III *116*
Langwith, Benjamin (1684?–1743) I *79*
Lanier, Nicholas (1588–1666) I *79*
Lankester, Edwin (1814–1874) III *116–117*
Lankester, Sir E. R. (1847–1929) III *117*
Lansbury, George (1859–1940) III *117*
Lansdowne, Baron (1667–1735) I *79*
Lansdowne, 1st Marquess of (1737–1805) II *130*
Lansdowne, 3rd Marquess of (1780–1863) II *130*
Lansdowne, 4th Marquess of (1816–1866) III *117*
Lansdowne, 5th Marquess of (1845–1927) III *117*
Lant, Thomas (1556?–1600) I *79*
Lanyon, Sir Charles (1813–1889) III *117*
Lanza, Gesualdo (1779–1859) II *130*
Lardner, Dionysius (1793–1859) II *130*
Lardner, Nathaniel (1684–1768) I *79*
Larke, Sir W.J. (1875–1959) IV *62*
Larkham, Thomas (1602–1669) I *80*
Larking, Cuthbert (*b*1842) III *117*
Larking, L.B. (1797–1868) II *130*
Larmor, Sir Joseph (1857–1942) III *117*
Laroon, Marcellus (1679–1772) I *80*
Larpent, F.S. (1776–1845) II *130*
Larpent, Sir G.G. de Hochepied, 1st Bart (1786–1855) II *130*
Lascelles, Sir F.C. (1841–1920) III *117*
Laski, H.J. (1893–1950) IV *62*
Laski, John (1499–1560) I *80*
László de Lombos, P.A. (1869–1937) IV *62*
Latewar, Richard (1560–1601) I *80*
Latey, John (1842–1902) III *117*
Latham, 1st Baron (1888–1970) IV *62*
Latham, Henry (1821–1902) III *117*
Latham, John (1761–1843) II *130*
Latham, R.G. (1812–1888) III *117*
Latimer, Hugh (1485?–1555) I *80*
Latrobe, C.I. (1758–1836) II *130*
Latrobe, C.J. (1801–1875) III *117*
Laud, William (1573–1645) I *80*
Lauder, Sir Harry (1870–1950) IV *62*
Lauder, J.E. (1811–1869) III *117*
Lauder, R.S. (1803–1869) III *117*
Lauder, Sir T.D., 7th Bart (1784–1848) II *130–131*
Lauderdale, 1st Duke of (1616–1682) I *80*
Lauderdale, 4th Earl of (1653–1695) I *80*
Lauderdale, 8th Earl of (1759–1839) II *131*
Lauderdale, 11th Earl of (1803–1878) III *117*
Lauderdale, Duchess of (*d*1698?) I *80*
Laugharne, Rowland (fl 1648) I *80*
Laughton, Charles (1899–1962) IV *63*
Laurence, John (*d*1732) I *80*
Laurie, Sir Peter (1779?–1861) II *131*
Laurie, S.S. (1829–1909) III *117*
Laurier, Sir Wilfred (1841–1919) III *117*
Laver, James (1899–1975) IV *63*
Lavery, Sir John (1856–1941) III *117–118*
Lavington, George (1684–1762) I *80*
Law, A.B. (1858–1923) III *118*
Law, C.E. (1792–1850) II *131*
Law, David (1831–1901) III *118*
Law, Edmund (1703–1787) II *131*
Law, G.H. (1761–1845) II *131*
Law of Lauriston, John (1671–1729) I *80*
Lawes, Sir C.B. 2nd Bart (1843–1911) III *118*
Lawes, Henry (2600–1662) I *80*
Lawes, Sir J.B., 1st Bart (1814–1900) III *118*
Lawes, William (*d*1645) I *80*
Lawless, John (1773–1837) II *131*
Lawless, M.J. (1837–1864) III *118*
Lawrence, 1st Baron (1811–1879) III *118*
Lawrence, D.H. (1885–1930) IV *63*
Lawrence, Gertrude (1898–1952) IV *63*
Lawrence, Sir G. St Patrick (1804–1884) III *118*
Lawrence, Henry (1600–1664) I *80*
Lawrence, Sir H.A. (1861–1943) IV *63*
Lawrence, Sir H.M. (1806–1857) III *118*
Lawrence, Sir P.O. (1861–1952) IV *63*
Lawrence, Sir Soulden (1751–1814) II *131*
Lawrence, Stringer (1697–1775) I *80*
Lawrence, Susan (1871–1947) IV *63*
Lawrence, Thomas (1711–1783) II *131*
Lawrence, Sir Thomas (1769–1830) II *131*
Lawrence, T.E. (1888–1935) IV *63*
Lawrence, Sir William, 1st Bart (1783–1867) II *131*
Lawrence, Sir W.R., 1st Bart (1857–1940) III *118*
Lawrenson, Thomas (fl 1760–1777) II *131*
Laws, Robert (1851–1934) III *118*
Lawson, C.G. (1849–1882) III *118*
Lawson, George (1749–1820) II *131*

Lawson, G.A. (1832–1904) III *118*
Lawson, Sir John (*d*1665) I *80*
Lawson, John (1712–1759) II *131*
Lawson, M.L. (1847–1918) III *118*
Lawson, Sir Wilfrid, 2nd Bart (1829–1906) III *118–119*
Layard, Sir A.H. (1817–1894) III *119*
Layer, Christopher (1683–1723) I *80*
Layton, 1st Baron (1884–1966) IV *63*
Layton, Sir Geoffrey (1884–1944) IV *63*
Leach, Bernard (1887–1979) IV *63*
Leach, Sir G.A. (1820–1913) III *119*
Leach, Sir John (1760–1834) II *131*
Leach, Thomas (1746–1818) II *131*
Leadbitter, Sir E.C.E. (1891–1971) IV *63*
Leader, B.W. (1831–1923) III *119*
Leader, J.T. (1810–1903) III *119*
Leaf, Walter (1852–1927) III *119*
Leahy, Arthur (1830–1878) III *119*
Leake, Sir John (1656–1720) I *80*
Leake, John (1729–1792) II *131*
Leake, S.M. (1702–1773) II *131*
Leake, W.M. (1777–1860) II *131*
Lear, Edward (1812–1888) III *119*
Leared, Arthur (1822–1879) III *119*
Learmonth, Sir James (1895–1967) IV *63*
Leask, William (1812–1884) III *119*
Leate, Nicholas (*d*1631) I *80*
Leathers, 1st Viscount (1883–1965) IV *63*
Leavis, F.R. (1895–1978) IV *63*
Le Brun, John (*d*1865) II *131*
Le Cène, Charles (1647?–1703) I *80*
Lechmere, Sir E.A.H., 3rd Bart (1826–1894) III *119*
Lechmere, Sir Nicholas (1613–1701) I *80*
Lecky, W.E.H. (1838–1903) III *119*
Leclercq, Carlotta (1840?–1893) III *119*
Leclercq, Rose (1845?–1899) III *119*
Le Despencer, 15th Baron (1708–1781) II *131*
Lediard, Thomas (1685–1743) I*80*
Ledingham, Sir J.C.G. (1875–1944) IV *63*
Ledwich, Edward (1738–1823) II *131*
Ledwidge, Francis (1891–1917) IV *63*
Lee, Charles (1731–1782) II *131*
Lee, F.H. (1699–1750) I *80*
Lee, F.R. (1799–1879) II *131*
Lee, Sir George (1700–1758) II *131*
Lee, Sir Henry (1533–1611) I*80*
Lee, James (1715–1795) II *131*
Lee, Sir James Lockhart, Lord (1594–1674) I *80*
Lee, John (1733–1793) II *131*
Lee, John (1779–1859) II *132*
Lee, John (1783–1866) II *132*
Lee, J.P. (1804–1869) III *119*
Lee, Matthew (1694–1755) I *81*
Lee, Nathaniel (1653?–1692) I *81*
Lee, Rachel (1774?–1829) II *132*
Lee, Robert (1804–1868) III *119*
Lee, R.W. (1868–1958) IV *63*
Lee, Samuel (1783–1852) II *132*
Lee, Sir Sidney (1859–1926) III *119*
Lee, Sophia (1750–1824) II *132*
Lee, Thomas (1552?–1601) I *81*
Lee, Sir Thomas, 1st Bart (1635–1691) I *81*
Lee, Sir William (1688–1754) I *81*
Lee of Fareham, Viscount (1868–1947) IV *63*
Leech, John (1817–1864) III *119*
Leechman, William (1706–1785) II *132*
Leeds, 1st Duke of (1631–1712) I *81*
Leeds, 2nd Duke of (1658–1729) I *81*
Leeds, 5th Duke of (1751–1799) II *132*
Leeper, Sir R.W.A. (1888–1968) IV *63*
Lees, G.M. (1898–1955) IV *63*
Lees, Sir Harcourt, 2nd Bart (1776–1852) II *132*
Leeson, S.S.G. (1892–1956) IV *63*
Le Fanu, J.T.S. (1814–1873) III *120*
Le Froy, T.L. (1776–1869) II *132*
Le Froy, William (1836–1909) III *120*
Le Galliene, R.T. (1866–1947) IV *63–64*
Legat, Francis (1755–1809) II*132*
Legge, H.B. (1708–1764) II *132*
Legge, Thomas (1535–1607) I *81*
Legge, William (1609–1672) I *81*
Le Grand, Antoine (*d*1699) I *81*
Legros, Alphonse (1837–1911) III *120*
Lehmann, Liza (1862–1918) IV *64*
Lehmann, Rudolph (1819–1905) III *120*
Leicester, Simon de Montfort, Earl of (1208?–1265) I *81*
Leicester, Earl of (1532?–1588) I *81*
Leicester, 1st Earl of (1563–1616) I *81*
Leicester, 2nd Earl of (1595–1677) I *81*
Leicester, 3rd Earl of (1619–1698) I *81*
Leicester, 1st Earl of (1752–1842) II *132*
Leicester, 2nd Earl of (1822–1909) III *120*
Leicester, Countess of (1545–1634) I *81*
Leifchild, John (1780–1862) II *132*
Leigh, 1st Baron (*d*1671) I *81*
Leigh, 1st Baron (1791–1850) II *132*
Leigh, Anthony (*d*1692) I *81*

Leigh, A.A. (1840–1905) III *120*
Leigh, Charles (1662–1701?) I *81*
Leigh, Edward (1602–1671) I *81*
Leigh, Egerton (1815–1876) III *120*
Leigh, Evan (1811–1876) III *120*
Leigh, H.S. (1837–1883) III *120*
Leigh, Samuel (fl 1686) I *81*
Leigh, Sir Thomas (1504?–1571) I *81*
Leigh-Mallory, Sir T.L., (1892–1944) IV *64*
Leighton, Baron (1830–1896) III *120*
Leighton, Alexander (1568–1649) I *81*
Leighton, Robert (1611–1684) I *81*
Leighton, Stanley (1837–1901) III *120*
Leiningen, Prince Ernest (1830–1904) III *120–121*
Leishman, Thomas (1825–1904) III *121*
Leishmann, Sir W.B. (1865–1926) IV *64*
Leitch, W.L. (1804–1883) III *121*
Leith, Sir James (1763–1816) II *132*
Leith, J.F. (1808–1887) III *121*
Leith Hay, Alexander (1758–1838) II *132*
Le Jeune, Henry (1819–1904) III *121*
Le Keux, J.H. (1812–1896) III *121*
Leland, John (1691–1766) I*81*
Leland, Thomas (1722–1785) II*132*
Lely, Sir Peter (1618–1680) I *81*
Leman, Sir John (1544–1632) I *81*
Le Marchant, Sir Denis, 1st Bart (1795–1874) II *132*
Le Marchant, J.G. (1766–1812) II *132*
Lemoine, Henry (1756–1812) II *132*
Lemon, Mark (1809–1870) III *121*
Lemon, Robert (1779–1835) II *132*
Lemprière, Charles (1818–1901) III *121*
Lemprière, John (1765?–1824) II *132*
Le Neve, Peter (1661–1729) I *82*
Leng, Sir John (1828–1906) III *121*
Leng, Sir W.C. (1825–1902) III *121*
Lennard, Samson (*d*1633) I *82*
Lennard-Jones, Sir J.E. (1894–1954) IV *64*
Lennox, 4th Earl of (1516–1571) I *82*
Lennox, 1st Duke of (1542?–1583) I *82*
Lennox, Countess of (1515–1578) I *82*
Lennox, Charlotte (1720–1804) II *133*
Lennox, G.H. (1737–1805) II *133*
Lennox, Lord H.C.G. Gordon- (1821–1886) III *121*
Lennox, Sir W.O. (1830–1897) III *121*
Lennox, Lord W.P. (1799–1881) II *133*
Lenox-Conyngham, Sir G.P. (1866–1956) IV *64*
Lens, A.B. (fl 1765–1770) II *133*
Lens, Bernard (1682–1740) I *82*
Lens, John (1756–1825) II *133*
Lenthall, William (1591–1662) I *82*
Le Piper, Francis (*d*1698) I *82*
Le Sage, Sir J.M. (1837–1926) III *121*
Leslie, Charles (1650–1722) I *82*
Leslie, C.R. (1794–1859) II *133*
Leslie, Frederick (1855–1892) III *121*
Leslie, G.D. (1835–1921) III *121*
Leslie, H.D. (1822–1896) III *121*
Leslie, John (1527–1596) I *82*
Leslie, Sir John (1766–1832) II *133*
Leslie, Sir J.R. (1885–1971) IV *64*
Leslie, Walter Leslie, Count (1606–1667) I*82*
Lester, Sean (1888–1959) IV *64*
Lestock, Richard (1679?–1746) I *82*
L'Estrange, Sir Roger (1616–1704) I *82*
Le Strange, Sir Thomas (1494–1545) I *82*
Lesueur, Robert (1580?–1670) I *82*
Lethaby, W.R. (1857–1931) III *121*
Lethbridge, J.S. (1897–1961) IV *64*
Letheby, Henry (1816–1876) III *121*
Lethieullier, Smart (1701–1760) II *133*
Lettsom, J.C. (1744–1815) II *133*
Leven, 1st Earl of (1580?–1661) I *82*
Leven, 3rd Earl of (1660–1728) I *82*
Leven and Melville, 12th Earl of (1817–1889) III *121*
Levens, Peter (fl 1587) I *82*
Lever, Sir Ashton (1729–1788) I *83*
Lever, C.J. (1806–1872) III *121*
Leverhulme, 1st Viscount (1851–1925) III *121*
Leveridge, Richard (1670?–1758) I *82*
Leverton, Thomas (1743–1824) II *133*
Leveson, Sir A.C. (1868–1929) IV *64*
Leveson, Sir Richard (1570–1605) I *82*
Leveson-Gower, Frederick (1819–1907) III *121–122*
Levi, David (1740–1799) II *133*
Levi, Leone (1821–1888) III *122*
Levinz, Sir Cresswell (1627–1701) I *82*
Levy, B.W. (1900–1973) IV *64*
Levy, J.M. (1812–1888) III *122*
Levy, Reuben (1891–1966) IV *64*
Lewes, C.L. (1740–1803) II *133*
Lewes, G.H. (1817–1878) III *122*
Lewis, Agnes (1843–1926) III *122*
Lewis, Sir A.J. (1900–1975) IV *64*
Lewis, Charles (1786–1836) III *133*
Lewis, C.G. (1808–1880) III *122*

Lewis, C.S. (1898–1963) IV *64*
Lewis, David (1617–1679) I *82*
Lewis, Elvet (1860–1953) IV *64*
Lewis, F.C. (1781–1856) II *133*
Lewis, Sir G.C., 2nd Bart (1806–1863) III *122*
Lewis, G.G. (1784–1859) II *133*
Lewis, Sir G.H., 1st Bart (1833–1911) III *122*
Lewis, J.F. (1805–1876) III *122*
Lewis, J.T. (1825–1901) III *122*
Lewis, Lady Maria Theresa (1803–1865) III *122*
Lewis, M.G. (1775–1818) II *133*
Lewis, (Percy) Wyndham (1882–1957) IV *64*
Lewis, Richard (1821–1905) III *122*
Lewis, S.S. (1836–1891) III *122*
Lewis, Sir Thomas (1881–1945) IV *64*
Lewis, Sir T.F., 1st Bart (1780–1855) II *133*
Lewis, William (1592–1667) I *82*
Lewis, Wyndham (1891–1969) IV *64*
Lewis, W.C.M. (1885–1956) IV *64*
Lewis, Sir W.H.P. (1881–1950) IV *64*
Lewis, W.T. (1748?–1811) III *133*
Lewson, Jane (1700–1816) II *133*
Lexington, 2nd Baron (1661–1723) I *82*
Leybourn, William (1626–1700?) I *82–83*
Leycester, Sir Peter, 1st Bart (1614–1678) I *83*
Leyden, John (1775–1811) II *133*
Lhuyd, Edward (1660–1709) I *83*
Liart, Matthew (1736–1782?) II *133*
Liberty, Sir A.L. (1843–1917) III *122*
Lichfield, Lord Bernard Stuart, titular Earl of (1680–1770) I *83*
Lichfield, 3rd Earl of (1718–1772) II *133–134*
Liddell, H.G. (1811–1898) III *122*
Liddell Hart, Sir Basil (1895–1970) IV *64*
Lidderdale, William (1832–1902) III *122*
Liddon, H.P. (1829–1890) III *122–123*
Lifford, 1st Viscount (1709–1789) II *134*
Light, William (1786–1839) II *134*
Lightfoot, John (1602–1675) I *83*
Lightfoot, J.B. (1828–1889) III *123*
Ligonier, 1st Earl of (1680–1770) I *83*
Ligonier, 1st Earl (*d*1782) II *134*
Lilburne, John (1614?–1657) I *83*
Lilburne, Robert (1613–1665) I *83*
Lillicrap, Sir C.S. (1887–1966) IV *64*
Lillie, Beatrice, Lady Peel (*b*1898) IV *64*
Lilly, William (1602–1681) I *83*
Lily, William (1468?–1522) I *83*
Limerick, 1st Earl of (1758–1844) II *134*
Linacre, Thomas (1460?–1524) I *83*
Lincoln, 3rd Earl of (1249?–1311) I*83*
Lincoln, 1st Earl of (1512–1585) I *83*
Lincolnshire, 1st Marquess of (1843–1928) III *123*
Lind, James (1716–1794) II *134*
Lind, James (1736–1812) II *134*
Lind, Jenny (1820–1887) III *123*
Lindgren, Baron (1900–1971) IV *64*
Lindley, Baron (1828–1921) III *123*
Lindley, Sir F.O. (1872–1950) IV *64*
Lindley, John (1799–1865) II *134*
Lindley, Robert (1776–1855) II *134*
Lindsay, Sir Coutts, 2nd Bart (1824–1913) III *123*
Lindsay, J.B. (1799–1862) II *134*
Lindsay, John (1737–1788) II *134*
Lindsay, Sir R.C. (1877–1945) IV *64*
Lindsay, T.M. (1843–1914) III *123*
Lindsay, W.M. (1858–1937) III *123*
Lindsay of Birker, 1st Baron (1879–1952) IV *64*
Lindsey, 1st Earl of (1582–1642) I *83*
Lindsey, 2nd Earl of (1608?–1666) I *83*
Lindsey, Theophilus (1723–1808) II *134*
Lingard, John (1771–1851) II *134*
Lingen, Baron (1819–1905) III *123*
Linklater, Eric (1899–1974) IV *64*
Linley, George (1798–1865) II *134*
Linley, O.T. (1766–1831) II *134*
Linley, Thomas (1733–1795) II *134*
Linley, Thomas (1756–1778) II *134*
Linley, William (1771–1835) II *134*
Linlithgow, 1st Marquess of (1860–1908) IV *65*
Linlithgow, 2nd Marquess of (1887–1952) IV *65*
Linnecar, Richard (1722–1800) II *134*
Linnell, John (1792–1882) II *134*
Linton, Eliza (1822–1898) III *123*
Linton, William (1791–1876) II *134*
Linton, Sir William (1801–1880) III *123*
Linton, W.J. (1812–1897) III *123*
Linwood, Mary (1755–1845) II *134*
Lionel of Antwerp, Duke of Clarence (1338–1368) I *83*
Lipscomb, Christopher (1781–1843) II *134*
Lipton, Sir T.J., Bart (1850–1931) III *123*
Lisgar, Baron (1807–1876) III *123*
Lisle, Sir George (*d*1648) I *83*
Lisle, John (1610?–1664) I*83*
Lisle, Samuel (1683?–1749) I *83*
Lister, Baron (1827–1912) III *123*
Lister, Sir Matthew (1571?–1656) I *83*

Lister, T.H. (1800–1842) III *124*
Liston, John (1776?–1846) II *134*
Liston, Sir Robert (1742–1836) II *134*
Liston, Robert (1794–1847) II *134–135*
Litchfield, Harriett (1777–1854) II *135*
Lithgow, Sir James, 1st Bart (1883–1952) IV *65*
Lithgow, William (1582–1645?) I *83*
Little, A.G. (1863–1945) IV *65*
Little, Sir C.J.C. (1882–1973) IV *65*
Littler, Sir J.H. (1783–1856) II *135*
Littler, Sir R.D.M. (1835–1908) III *124*
Littleton, 1st Baron (1589–1645) I *83*
Littleton, Sir Thomas (1422?–1481) I *83*
Littleton, Sir Thomas (1647?–1710) I *83*
Littlewood, J.E. (1885–1977) IV *65*
Littlewood, Sir Sydney (1895–1967) IV *65*
Litton, Marie (1847–1884) III *124*
Liverpool, 1st Earl of (1727–1808) II *135*
Liverpool, 2nd Earl of (1770–1828) II *135*
Liverseege, Henry (1803–1832) II *124*
Livesey, Sir G.T. (1834–1908) III *124*
Livesey, Joseph (1794–1884) II *135*
Livesey, Sir Michael, 1st Bart (1611–1663?) I *83*
Livingstone, Charles (1821–1873) III *124*
Livingstone, David (1813–1873) III *124*
Livingstone, Sir R.W. (1880–1960) IV *65*
Lizars, W.H. (1788–1859) II *135*
Llandaff, Viscount (1826–1913) III *124*
Llanover, 1st Baron (1802–1867) III *124*
Llewellin, 1st Baron (1893–1957) IV *65*
Llewellyn, Sir William (1858–1941) III *124*
Lloyd, 1st Baron (1879–1941) IV *65*
Lloyd, Bartholomew (1772–1837) II *135*
Lloyd, Charles (1748–1828) II *135*
Lloyd, Charles (1775–1839) II *135*
Lloyd, Charles (1784–1829) II *135*
Lloyd, C.D.C. (1844–1891) III *124*
Lloyd, Dorothy Jordan (1889–1946) IV *65*
Lloyd, Humphrey (1800–1881) II *124*
Lloyd, Sir J.E. (1861–1947) IV *65*
Lloyd, Marie (1870–1922) IV *65*
Lloyd, Sir Nathaniel (1669–1745) I *84*
Lloyd, Richard (1595–1659) I *84*
Lloyd, Sir T.I.K. (1896–1968) IV *65*
Lloyd, William (1627–1717) I *84*
Lloyd, William (1637–1710) I *84*
Lloyd, W.W. (1813–1893) III *124*
Lloyd-George, 1st Earl (1863–1945) IV *65*
Lloyd James, Arthur (1884–1943) IV *65*
Llwyd, Humphrey (1527–1568) I *84*
Loates, Thomas (1867–1910) IV *65*
Lobb, Theophilus (1678–1763) I *84*
Loch, James (1780–1855) II *135*
Lock, Walter (1846–1933) III *124*
Locke, John (1632–1704) I *84*
Locke, John (1805–1880) III *124*
Locke, Joseph (1805–1860) II *124*
Locke, Matthew (1630?–1677) I *84*
Locke, William (1732–1810) II *135*
Locke, William (1767–1847) II *135*
Locker, Arthur (1828–1893) III *124*
Locker, E.H. (1777–1849) II *135*
Locker, William (1731–1800) I *84*
Locker-Lampson, Frederick (1821–1895) III *125*
Lockey, Thomas (1602–1679) I *84*
Lockhart, J.G. (1794–1854) II *135*
Lockhart, Philip (1690?–1715) I *84*
Lockhart, Sir Robert Bruce (1887–1970) IV *65–66*
Lockhart, W.E. (1846–1900) III *125*
Lockhart, Sir W.S.A. (1841–1900) III *125*
Lockhart, Sir George (1630?–1689) I *84*
Lockhart of Carnwath, George (1673–1731) I *84*
Lockhart of Lee, Sir William (1621–1676) I *84*
Lockwood, Sir Frank (1846–1897) III *125*
Lockyer, Nicholas (1611–1685) I *84*
Lockyer, Sir Norman (1836–1920) III *125*
Locock, Sir Charles, 1st Bart (1799–1875) II *135*
Loder, J.D. (1791–1846) II *135*
Lodge, Edmund (1756–1839) II *135*
Lodge, Eleanor Constance (1869–1936) IV *66*
Lodge, Sir O.J. (1851–1940) III *125*
Lodge, Sir Richard (1855–1936) III *125*
Lodge, William (1649–1689) I *84*
Lofft, Capell (1751–1824) II *135*
Lofft, Capell (1806–1873) III *125*
Loftus, Adam (1533–1605) I *84*
Loftus, Lord Augustus (1817–1904) III *125*
Loftus, W.K. (1821?–1858) III *125*
Loftus of Ely, 1st Viscount (1568?–1643) I *84*
Logan, James (1674–1751) I *84*
Logan, John (1748–1788) II *135*
Logan, Sir W.E. (1798–1875) II*135*
Logier, J.B. (1780–1846) II *135*
Logue, Michael (1840–1924) III *125*
Lohmann, G.A. (1865–1901) IV *66*
Lombart, Peter (1620?–1681) I *84*
Londesborough, 1st Baron (1805–1860) III*125*

Londonderry, 2nd Marquess of (1769–1822) II *135–136*
Londonderry, 3rd Marquess of (1778–1854) II *135*
Londonderry, 5th Marquess of (1821–1884) III *125*
Londonderry, 6th Marquess of (1852–1915) III *125*
Londonderry, 7th Marquess of (1878–1949) IV *66*
Londonderry, 7th Marchioness of (1879–1959) IV *66*
Long, Lady Catherine (1797–1867) III *136*
Long, Edward (1734–1813) II *136*
Long, E.L. (1829–1891) III *125*
Long, Gabrielle (1886–1952) IV *66*
Long, Sir James (1617–1692) I *84*
Long, John St John (1798–1834) II *136*
Long, Sir Robert (*d*1673) I *84*
Long, Roger (1680–1770) I *84*
Long, R.B. (1771–1825) II *136*
Long of Wraxall, 1st Viscount (1854–1924) III *125–126*
Longley, C.T. (1794–1868) II *136*
Longman, T.N. (1771–1842) II *136*
Longmore, Sir A.M. (1885–1970) IV *66*
Longstaff, Sir John (1862–1941) IV *66*
Lonsdale, 1st Viscount (1655–1700) I *84*
Lonsdale, 1st Earl of (1757–1844) II *136*
Lonsdale, 2nd Earl of (1787–1872) II *136*
Lonsdale, 5th Earl of (1857–1944) III *126*
Lonsdale, James (1777–1839) II *136*
Lonsdale, John (1788–1867) II *136*
Lonsdale, J.G. (1816–1892) III *126*
Lopes, Sir L.M., 3rd Bart (1818–1908) III *126*
Loraine, Sir Percy (1880–1961) IV *66*
Loraine, Violet (1886–1956) IV *66*
Loreburn, 1st Earl (1846–1923) III *126*
Lorimer, James (1818–1890) III *126*
Lorimer, Sir R.S. (1864–1929) IV *66*
Lort, Michael (1725–1790) II *136*
Lothian, 3rd Earl of (1605?–1675) I *84*
Lothian, 1st Marquess of (1636–1703?) I *84*
Lothian, 2nd Marquess of (1662?–1722) I *84*
Lothian, 4th Marquess of (1710–1775) II *136*
Lothian, 9th Marquess of (1833–1900) III *126*
Lothian, 11th Marquess of (1882–1940) IV *66*
Loudon, 4th Earl of (1598–1663) I *85*
Loudoun, 4th Earl of (1705–1782) II *136*
Loudoun, J.C. (1783–1843) II *136*
Louis, Sir Thomas (1759–1807) II *136*
Louise, Princess (Duchess of Argyll) (1848–1939) III *126*
Louise, Princess Royal (Duchess of Fife) (1867–1931) IV *66*
Lovat, 11th Baron (1667?–1747) I *85*
Love, A.E.H. (1863–1940) IV *66*
Love, Christopher (1618–1651) I *85*
Love, James (1722–1774) II *136*
Love, John (1757–1825) II *136*
Love, Sir J.F. (1789–1866) II *136*
Love, Nicholas (1608–1682) I *85*
Love, Richard (1596–1661) I *85*
Love, W.E. (1806–1867) III *126*
Loveday, Robert (fl 1655) I *85*
Lovegrove, William (1778–1816) II *136*
Lovelace, Richard (1618–1658) I *85*
Lovelace of Hurley, 3rd Baron (1638?–1693) I *85*
Lovell, Sir L.B.B. (1786–1861) III *136*
Lovell, Sir Thomas (*d*1524) I *85*
Lover, Samuel (1797–1868) II *136–137*
Lovett, Neville, (1869–1951) IV *66*
Lovett, Richard, (1692–1780) I *85*
Lovett, William (1800–1877) III *126*
Low, Alexander Low, Lord (1845–1910) III *126*
Low, David (1768–1855) II *137*
Low, Sir David (1891–1963) IV *66*
Low, Sir Francis (1893–1972) IV *66*
Lowder, C.F. (1820–1880) III *126*
Lowe, Eveline Mary (1869–1956) IV *66*
Lowe, Sir Hudson (1769–1844) II *137*
Lowe, Peter (1550?–1612?) I *85*
Lowe, Thomas (*d*1783) II*137*
Lower, M.A. (1813–1876) III *126*
Lower, Sir William (1600?–1662) I *85*
Lowin, John (1576–1659) I *85*
Lowndes, William (1652–1724) I *85*
Lowry, L.S. (1887–1976) IV *66*
Lowry, T.M. (1874–1936) IV *66*
Lowry, Wilson (1762–1824) II *137*
Lowth, Robert (1710–1787) I *85*
Lowther, James (1840–1904) III *126*
Loyd, Sir H.C. (1891–1973) IV *66*
Luard, H.R. (1825–1891) III *126*
Luard, John (1790–1875) II *137*
Lubbock, Sir J.W., 3rd Bart (1803–1865) III *126–127*
Lucan, Patrick Sarsfield, titular Earl of (*d*1693) I *85*
Lucan, 3rd Earl of (1800–1888) III *127*
Lucan, Countess of (*d*1814) II *137*
Lucas, Charles (1713–1771) I *85*
Lucas, Sir C.P. (1853–1931) III *127*
Lucas, David (1802–1881) II *137*
Lucas, E.V. (1868–1938) IV *66*
Lucas, John (1807–1874) IV *127*
Lucas, J.S. (1849–1923) III *127*
Lucas, Richard (1648–1715) I *85*

Lucas, R.C. (1800–1883) III 127
Luckock, H.M. (1833–1909) III 127
Luckombe, Philip (d 1803) II 137
Lucy, Charles (1814–1873) III 127
Lucy, Sir H.W. (1845–1924) III 127
Lucy, Sir Thomas (1532–1600) I 85
Lucy, Sir Thomas (1585?–1640) I 85
Ludlam, William (1717–1788) II 137
Ludlow, 1st Baron (1828–1899) III 127
Ludlow, Edmund (1617?–1692) I 85
Ludlow-Hewitt, Sir E.R. (1886–1973) IV 66
Lugard, Baron (1858–1945) III 127
Luke, 1st Baron (1873–1943) IV 67
Luke, Sir H.C. (1884–1969) IV 67
Luke, Sir Samuel (d 1670) I 85
Lukin, Sir H.T. (1860–1925) IV 67
Lumby, J.R. (1831–1895) III 127
Lumisden, Andrew (1720–1801) II 137
Lumley, 1st Baron (1533?–1609) I 85
Lumley, Benjamin (1811–1875) III 127
Lumsden, Sir H.B. (1821–1896) III 127
Lunardi, Vincenzo (1759–1806) II 137
Lundgren, E.S. (1815–1875) III 127
Lunn, Sir H.S. (1859–1939) III 127
Lunsford, Sir Thomas (1610?–1653?) I 85
Lupton, T.G. (1791–1873) II 137
Lupton, William (1676–1726) I 85
Lush, Sir C.M. (1853–1930) III 127
Lush, Sir Robert (1807–1881) III 127
Lushington, E.L. (1811–1893) III 127
Lushington, Stephen (1782–1873) II 137
Lushington, S.R. (1776–1868) II 137
Lusk, Sir Andrew, 1st Bart (1810–1909) III 127
Luttrell, James (1751?–1788) II 137
Lutwyche, Sir Edward (d 1709) I 85
Lutyens, Sir E.L. (1869–1944) IV 67
Luxborough, Lady (d 1756) II 137
Luxmoore, Sir Fairfax (1876–1944) IV 67
Luxmoore, John (1756–1830) II 137
Lyall, Sir A.C. (1835–1911) III 127–128
Lyall, Robert (1790–1831) II 137
Lyall, W.R. (1788–1857) II 137
Lydgate, John (1370?–1451) I 85
Lye, Edward (1694–1767) I 85
Lye, Thomas (1621–1684) I 85
Lyell, Sir Charles, 1st Bart (1797–1875) II 137
Lyle of Westbourne, 1st Baron (1882–1954) IV 67
Lynam, Robert (1796–1845) II 137
Lynd, R.W. (1879–1949) IV 67
Lyndhurst, 1st Baron (1772–1863) II 137
Lyne, J.L. (1837–1908) III 128
Lynedoch, 1st Baron (1748–1843) II 137–138
Lynford, Thomas (1650–1724) I 85
Lynn, George (1707–1758) II 138
Lyon, Hart (1721–1800) II 138
Lyon of Carse, Sir Patrick (d 1695?) I 85
Lyons, 1st Baron (1790–1858) II 138
Lyons, 1st Earl (1817–1887) III 128
Lyons, Sir H.G. (1864–1944) IV 67
Lysons, Daniel (1727–1800) II 138
Lysons, Daniel (1762–1834) II 138
Lysons, Sir Daniel (1816–1898) III 128
Lysons, Samuel (1763–1819) II 138
Lyster, Sir Richard (d 1554) I 85
Lyte, Sir H.C.M. (1848–1940) III 128
Lyte, H.F. (1793–1857) II 138
Lyte, Thomas (1568?–1638) I 85
Lyttelton, 1st Baron (1709–1773) II 138
Lyttelton, 2nd Baron (1744–1779) II 138
Lyttelton, 1st Baron (1724–1808) II 138
Lyttelton, 3rd Baron (1782–1837) II 138
Lyttelton, Alfred (1857–1913) III 128
Lyttelton, A.T. (1852–1903) III 128
Lyttelton, Sir Charles, 3rd Bart (1629–1716) I 85
Lyttelton, Charles (1714–1768) II 138
Lyttelton, Edward (1855–1942) III 128
Lyttelton, Sir N.G. (1845–1931) III 128
Lyttelton, W.H. (1820–1884) III 128
Lyttelton of Frankley, 4th Baron (1817–1876) III 128
Lytton, 1st Baron (1803–1873) III 128
Lytton, 1st Earl of (1831–1891) III 128–129
Lytton, 2nd Earl of (1876–1947) IV 67
Lytton, 3rd Earl of (1879–1951) IV 67
Lytton, Sir H.A. (1865–1936) IV 67
Lytton, Lady (1802–1882) III 129
Lytton, 1st Baron (1800–1873) III 129

Mass, Joseph (1847–1886) III 131
Maberly, Catherine (1805–1875) III 131
Macadam, Sir Ivison (1894–1974) IV 68
McAdam, J.L. (1756–1836) II 139
MacAlister, Sir Donald, 1st Bart (1854–1934) III 131
McAlister, Sir Ian (1878–1957) IV 68
McAll, R.S. (1792–1838) II 139
Macara, Sir C.W., 1st Bart (1845–1929) III 131
Macardell, James (1729–1765) II 139
McArthur, John (1755–1840) II 139

McArthur, Sir William (1809–1887) III 131
Macartney, 1st Earl (1737–1806) II 139
Macartney, James (1770–1843) II 139
Macaulay, 1st Baron (1800–1859) III 131
Macaulay, Catharine (1731–1791) II 139
Macaulay, Dame Rose (1881–1958) IV 68
Macaulay, Zachary (1768–1838) II 139
McAuley, Catharine (1787–1841) II 139
McAvoy, Margaret (1800–1820) III 131
Macbeth, R.W. (1848–1910) III 131
McBey, James (1883–1959) IV 68
Macbride, David (1726–1778) II 139
Macbride, John (d 1800) II 139
Macbride, J.D. (1778–1868) II 139
M'Cabe, Edward (1816–1885) III 131
Maccall, William (1812–1888) III 131
MacCallum, Andrew (1821–1902) III 131
McCallum, R.B. (1898–1973) IV 68
McCalmont, H.L.B. (1861–1902) IV 68
McCardie, Sir H.A. (1869–1933) IV 68
MacCarrison, Sir Robert (1878–1960) IV 68
MacCarthy, Sir Desmond (1877–1952) IV 68
Maccarthy, D.F. (1817–1882) III 131
McCarthy, Justin (1830–1912) III 131
McCarthy, Lillah (1875–1960) IV 68
McCarthy, Dame Maud (1858–1949) III 131
McCaul, Alexander (1799–1863) II 139
McCheyne, R.M. (1813–1843) III 131–132
Macclesfield, 1st Earl of (1620?–1694) I 87
Macclesfield, 2nd Earl of (1697?–1764) I 87
Macclesfield, 1st Earl of (1667?–1732) I 87
Macclesfield, 9th Earl of (1811–1896) II 132
McClintock, Sir F.L. (1819–1907) III 132
McClure, Sir R.J. Le Mesurier (1807–1873) III 132
MacColl, D.S. (1859–1948) III 132
MacColl, Norman (1843–1904) III 132
MacCormac, Sir William, 1st Bart (1836–1901) III 132
McCormick, Robert (1800–1890) III 132
McCormick, W.P.G. (1877–1940) IV 68
McCormick, Sir W.S. (1859–1930) III 132
McCracken, H.J. (1767–1798) II 139
McCreery, Sir R.L. (1898–1967) IV 68
McCrie, Thomas (1772–1835) II 139
McCudden, J.T.B. (1895–1918) IV 68
McCullagh, James (1809–1847) III 132
McCulloch, Horatio (1805–1867) III 132
Macculloch, John (1773–1835) II 139
McCulloch, J.R. (1789–1864) II 139
MacCunn, Hamish (1868–1916) IV 68
MacDermot, H.H. O'Rorke (1834–1904) III 132
MacDermott, G.H. (1845–1901) III 132
M'Diarmid, John (1790–1852) II 139
Macdona, J.C. (1836–1907) III 132
Macdonald, Sir Archibald, 1st Bart (1747–1826) II 139
Macdonald, Sir C.M. (1852–1915) III 132
MacDonald, Flora (1722–1790) II 139
MacDonald, George (1824–1905) III 132
Macdonald, Sir George (1862–1940) IV 68
Macdonald, Hugh (1817–1860) III 132
Macdonald, Sir H.A. (1853–1903) III 132
Macdonald, H.M. (1865–1935) IV 68
Macdonald, John (1779–1849) II 139
Macdonald, Sir John (d 1850) II 139
Macdonald, Sir J.A. (1815–1891) III 132
McDonald, J.B. (1829–1901) III 133
MacDonald, J.R. (1866–1937) IV 68
Macdonald, Lawrence (1799–1878) II 139
MacDonald, Sir Murdoch (1866–1957) IV 68
Macdonald, Patrick (1729–1824) II 139–140
Macdonald, Sir R.J. (1820–1899) III 133
Macdonell, Alexander (1762–1840) II 140
Macdonell, A.A. (1854–1930) III 133
Macdonell, Sir James (d 1857) II 140
Macdonell, Sir John (1845–1921) III 133
Macdonell, John J. (1825–1900) III 133
Macdonnell, Baron (1844–1925) III 133
Macdonnell, Sir R.G. (1814–1881) III 133
Macdougall, Sir Duncan (1787–1862) II 140
McDougall, William (1871–1938) IV 68
Macdowell, Patrick (1799–1870) II 140
Macdowell, William (1590–1666) I 87
Mace, James (1831–1910) III 133
Mace, Thomas (1619?–1709?) I 87
Maceroni, Francis (1788–1846) II 140
McEvoy, Ambrose (1878–1927) IV 68–69
McEwen, Sir J.B. (1868–1948) IV 69
Macewen, Sir William (1848–1924) III 133
McFadyean, Sir Andrew (1887–1974) IV 69
Macfarlan, Walter (d 1767) II 140
Macfarlan of Macfarlan, Walter (d 1767) I 87
Macfarlane, Charles (d 1858) II 140
Macfarlane, John (1807–1874) III 133
Macfarren, Sir G.A. (1813–1887) III 133
M'Gavin, William (1773–1832) II 140
McGee, Thomas d'Arcy (1825–1868) III 133
McGowan, 1st Baron (1874–1961) IV 69
Macgowan, John (1726–1780) II 140

Macgregor, Sir C.M. (1840–1887) III 133
Macgregor, Sir Gregor (1786–1845) II 140
Macgregor, John (1825–1892) III 133
McGrigor, Sir James, 1st Bart (1771–1858) II 140
McGrigor, Sir R.R. (1893–1959) IV 69
Machale, John (1791–1881) II 140
Machell, J.O. (1837–1902) III 133
Machen, Thomas (1568–1614) I 87
Machray, Robert (1831–1904) III 133
McIan, R.R. (1803–1856) III 133
McIlwraith, Sir Thomas (1835–1900) III 133
Macintosh, Charles (1766–1843) II 140
McIntosh, W.C. (1838–1931) III 133
Mackail, Denis (1892–1971) IV 69
Mackail, J.W. (1859–1945) III 133
Mackarness, J.F. (1820–1889) III 133
Mackay, Alexander (1808–1852) III 133
Mackay, Andrew (1760–1809) II 140
Mackay, A.J.G. (1839–1911) III 133
Mackay, Charles (1814–1889) III 133
Mackay, Mary (1855–1924) III 133
McKenna, Reginald (1863–1943) IV 69
Mackennal, Alexander (1835–1904) III 133
Mackennal, Sir Bertram (1863–1931) IV 69
Mackenzie, Sir Alexander (1755?–1820) II 140
Mackenzie, Alexander (1822–1892) III 133
McKenzie, Alexander (1869–1951) IV 69
Mackenzie, Sir A.C. (1847–1935) III 133–134
Mackenzie, Colin (1753?–1821) II 140
Mackenzie, Colin (1806–1881) III 134
Mackenzie, Sir Compton (1883–1972) IV 69
Mackenzie, C.F. (1825–1862) III 134
Mackenzie, Sir G.S. (1844–1910) III 134
Mackenzie, Henry (1745–1831) II 140
Mackenzie, Henry (1808–1878) III 134
Mackenzie, Sir Morell (1837–1892) III 134
Mackenzie, Sir Stephen (1844–1909) III 134
Mackenzie, W.B. (1806–1870) III 134
Mackenzie, W.F. (1807–1862) III 134
Mackenzie, W.L. (1795–1861) II 140
Mackenzie of Rosehaugh, Sir George (1636–1691) I 87
McKerrow, R.B. (1872–1940) IV 69
Mackesy, P.J. (1883–1956) IV 69
Mackinder, Sir H.J. (1861–1947) IV 69
MacKinlay, Antoinette (1843?–1904) III 134
McKinlay, John (1819–1872) III 134
MacKinnon, Sir F.D. (1871–1946) IV 69
Mackinnon, Sir William, 1st Bart (1823–1893) III 134
Mackinnon, W.A. (1789–1870) II 140
Mackinnon, Sir W.H. (1852–1929) III 134
Mackintosh, C.R. (1868–1928) IV 69
Mackintosh, H.R. (1870–1936) IV 69
Mackintosh, Sir James (1765–1832) II 140
Macklin, Charles (1699?–1797) I 87
Macklin, Maria (d 1781) II 140
Mackonochie, A.H. (1825–1887) III 134
Maclagan, Sir E.R.D. (1879–1951) IV 69
Maclagan, W.D. (1826–1910) III 134
Maclaine, Archibald (1722–1804) II 140
Maclaren, Alexander (1826–1910) III 134
MacLaren, A.C. (1871–1944) IV 69
Maclaren, Charles (1782–1866) II 140
McLaren, Duncan (1800–1886) III 134
McLaren, John McLaren, Lord (1831–1910) III 134
Maclaurin, Colin (1698–1746) I 87
McLean, Archibald (1733–1812) II 140
Maclean, Sir Donald (1864–1932) IV 69
Maclean, Sir H.A. de Vere (1848–1920) III 134
Maclear, G.F. (1833–1902) III 134
Macleay, Alexander (1767–1848) II 140
Macleay, Kenneth (1802–1878) III 134
Macleay, W.S. (1792–1865) II 140
Maclehose, Mrs Agnes (1759–1841) II 140
McLellan, Archibald (1797–1854) II 141
McLennan, Sir J.C. (1867–1935) IV 69
McLennan, J.F. (1827–1881) III 134
Macleod, Sir D.F. (1810–1872) III 134
Macleod, Sir G.H.B. (1828–1892) III 134
Macleod, J.J.R. (1876–1935) IV 69
Macleod, Norman (1812–1872) III 134–135
McLintock, Sir William, 1st Bart (1873–1947) IV 69
McLintock, W.F.P. (1887–1960) IV 69
Maclise, Daniel (1806–1870) III 135
Maclure, E.C. (1833–1906) III 135
Maclure, Sir J.W., 1st Bart (1835–1901) III 135
McMahon, Sir Henry (1862–1949) IV 69
McMahon, P.A. (1854–1929) III 135
MacMichael, Sir Harold (1882–1969) IV 69
Macmichael, William (1784–1839) II 141
Macmillan, Baron (1873–1952) IV 70
Macmillan, Daniel (1813–1857) III 135
Macmillan, Daniel (1886–1965) IV 69–70
Macmillan, Sir F.O. (1851–1936) IV 70
Macmillan, Harold (b 1894) IV 70
McMillan, Margaret (1860–1931) IV 70
McMurrich, J.P. (1859–1939) III 135

Macnaghten, Baron (1830–1913) III *135*
Macnaghten, Sir W.H., 1st Bart (1793–1841) II *141*
McNair, 1st Baron (1885–1975) IV *70*
Macnamara, T.J. (1861–1931) IV *70*
Macnee, Sir Daniel (1806–1882) III *135*
McNeile, Cyril (1888–1937) IV *70*
McNeile, Hugh (1795–1879) II *141*
Macneill, Hector (1746–1818) II *141*
McNeill, Sir James (1892–1964) IV *70*
McNeill, Sir John (1795–1883) II *141*
Macneill, John (1867–1945) IV *70*
McNeill, Sir J.C. (1831–1904) III *135*
MacNeill, J.G.S. (1849–1926) III *135*
Macneven, W.J. (1783–1841) II *141*
Macnish, Robert (1802–1837) III *135*
Macpherson, Sir H.T. (1827–1886) III *135*
Macpherson, James (1736–1796) II *141*
Macpherson, Sir John (1745–1821) II *141*
Macpherson, Sir John (1898–1971) IV *70*
Macpherson, S.C. (1806–1860) III *135*
Macready, Sir Nevil, 1st Bart (1862–1946) IV *70*
Macready, W.C. (1793–1873) II *141*
Macrorie, W.K. (1831–1905) III *135*
Macsparran, James (d1757) I *87*
M'Taggart, J.M.E. (1866–1925) IV *70*
McTaggart, William (1835–1910) III *135*
Macward, Robert (1633?–1687) I *87*
MacWhirter, John (1839–1911) III *135*
McWilliam, J.O. (1808–1862) III *135*
Madan, Martin (1726–1790) II *141*
Madan, Spencer (1729–1813) II *141*
Madden, Sir C.E., 1st Bart (1862–1935) IV *70*
Madden, Sir Frederic (1801–1873) III *135*
Madden, R.R. (1798–1886) II *141*
Madden, Samuel (1686–1765) I *87*
Madocks, W.A. (1774–1828) II *141*
Magee, William (1766–1831) II *141*
Magee, W.C. (1821–1891) III *136*
Magee, W.K. (1868–1961) IV *70*
Magheramorne, 1st Baron (1823–1890) III *136*
Maginn, William (1793–1842) II *141*
Magrath, J.R. (1839–1930) III *136*
Maguire, J.F. (1815–1872) III *136*
Maguire, J.R. (1855–1925) III *136*
Maguire, Rochfort (d1867) III *136*
Maguire, Thomas (1792–1847) II *141*
Mahaffy, Sir J.P. (1839–1919) III *136*
Mahon, C.J.P. (1800–1891) III *136*
Mahony, F.S. (1804–1866) III *136*
Maidment, James (c1795–1879) II *141*
Maine, Sir H.J.S. (1822–1888) III *136*
Mainwaring, Sir Philip (1589–1661) I *87*
Mainzer, Joseph (1801–1851) II *138*
Mair, William (1830–1920) III *136*
Maitland, Agnes Catherine (1850–1906) III *136*
Maitland, F.W. (1850–1906) III *136*
Maitland, J.A.F. (1856–1936) III *136*
Maitland, Sir Peregrine (1777–1854) II *141*
Maitland, Sir Thomas (1759?–1824) II *141*
Maitland of Lethington, William (1528?–1573) I *87*
Maitland of Thirlestane, 1st Baron (1545?–1595) I *87*
Maittaire, Michael (1668–1747) I *87*
Majendie, H.W. (1754–1830) II *141*
Major, H.R. (1818–1891) III *136*
Major, Thomas (1720–1799) II *141*
Makin, Bathusa (fl 1673) I *87*
Malard, Michael (fl 1717–1720) I *87*
Malcolm, Sir D.O. (1877–1955) IV *70*
Malcolm, Sir George (1818–1897) III *136*
Malcolm, Sir John (1769–1833) II *141–142*
Malcolm, Sir Pulteney (1768–1838) II *142*
Malcolm, Sarah (1710?–1733) I *87*
Malden, Daniel (d1736) I *87*
Malden, Henry (1800–1876) III *136*
Malet, Sir E.B., 4th Bart (1837–1908) III *136*
Malet, Sir Thomas (1582–1665) I *87*
Malins, Sir Richard (1805–1882) III *136*
Malkin, B.H. (1769–1842) II *142*
Malkin, Sir B.H. (1797–1837) II *142*
Malleson, Miles (1888–1969) IV *70*
Mallet, Sir Louis (1823–1890) III *136*
Mallock, W.H. (1849–1923) III *136*
Mallon, J.J. (1875–1961) IV *70*
Mallory, G.L. (1886–1924) IV *70*
Malmesbury, 1st Earl of (1746–1820) II *142*
Malmesbury, 3rd Earl of (1807–1889) III *137*
Malone, Anthony (1700–1776) II *142*
Malone, Edmund (1741–1812) II *142*
Maltby, Edward (1770–1859) II *142*
Malthus, T.R. (1766–1834) II *142*
Malton, Thomas (1748–1804) II *142*
Manby, G.W. (1765–1854) II *142*
Manchester, 1st Earl of (1563?–1642) I *88*
Manchester, 2nd Earl of (1602–1671) I *88*
Manchester, 1st Duke of (1660?–1722) I *87–88*
Manchester, 4th Duke of (1737–1788) II *142*
Manchester, 5th Duke of (1771–1843) II *142*

Manchester, 7th Duke of (1823–1890) III *137*
Mander, Sir G. Le Mesurier (1882–1962) IV *70*
Mangan, James (1803–1849) III *137*
Mangin, Edward (1772–1852) II *142*
Mangles, R.D. (1801–1877) III *137*
Mangnall, Richmal (1769–1820) II *142*
Manisty, Sir Henry (1808–1890) III *137*
Manley, Thomas (1628–1690) I *88*
Manlove, Timothy (d1699) I *88*
Mann, Sir Horace, 1st Bart (1701–1786) II *142*
Mann, Sir J.G. (1897–1962) IV *70*
Mann, T.A. (1735–1809) II *142*
Manners, 1st Baron (1756–1842) II *142*
Manners, Lord Robert (1758–1782) II *142*
Manners-Sutton, Charles (1755–1828) II *142*
Manning, Frederic (1882–1935) IV *70*
Manning, H.E. (1808–1892) III *137*
Manns, Sir August (1825–1907) III *137*
Mansbridge, Albert (1876–1952) IV *70*
Mansel, H.L. (1820–1871) III *137*
Mansel, Sir Robert (1573–1656) I *88*
Mansel, W.L. (1753–1820) II *142*
Mansergh, Sir Maurice (1896–1966) IV *70*
Mansfield, 1st Earl of (1705–1793) II *143*
Mansfield, 2nd Earl of (1727–1796) II *142–143*
Mansfield, Sir James (1733–1821) II *143*
Mansfield, Sir J.M. (1893–1949) IV *70*
Manson, J.B. (1879–1945) IV *70*
Manson, Sir Patrick (1844–1922) III *137*
Manson, T.W. (1893–1958) IV *70*
Manson-Bahr, Sir Philip (1881–1966) IV *70–71*
Mant, Richard (1776–1848) II *143*
Mantell, G.A. (1790–1852) II *143*
Manton, Thomas (1620–1677) I *88*
Manwood, Sir Roger (1525–1592) I *88*
Maple, Sir J.B., Bart (1845–1903) III *137*
Mapleson, J.H. (1830–1901) III *137*
Mappin, Sir F.T., 1st Bart (1821–1910) III *137*
Mar, 1st Earl of (d1572) I *88*
Mar, 2nd Earl of (1562?–1634) I *88*
Mar, 6th Earl of (1675–1732) I *88*
Mara, Mrs Gertrude (1749–1833) II *143*
Marcet, A.J.G. (1770–1822) II *143*
March, John (1640–1692) I *88*
Marchant, Nathaniel (1739–1816) II *143*
Marchi, G.F.L. (1735?–1808) II *143*
Marchmont, 1st Earl of (1641–1724) I *88*
Marchmont, 2nd Earl of (1675–1740) I *88*
Marchmont, 3rd Earl of (1708–1794) II *143*
Marett, R.R. (1866–1943) IV *71*
Margaret, Queen (1282?–1318) I *88*
Margaret of Anjou, Queen (1430–1482) I *88*
Margaret of Denmark, Queen (1457?–1486) I *88*
Margaret Tudor, Queen (1489–1541) I *88*
Margaret of York, Duchess of Burgundy (1446–1503) I *88*
Margary, A.R. (1846–1875) III *137*
Margesson, 1st Viscount (1890–1965) IV *71*
Margoliouth, D.S. (1858–1940) III *137*
Maria Clementina Sobieska (1702–1735) II *143*
Marie Louise of Schleswig-Holstein, Princess (1872–1956) IV *71*
Marischal, 5th Earl of (1553?–1623) I *88*
Marischal, 7th Earl of (1614?–1661) I *88*
Marischal, 10th Earl of (1693?–1778) I *88*
Markham, Sir A.H. (1841–1918) III *138*
Markham, Sir C.R. (1830–1916) III *138*
Markham, Gervase (1568?–1637) I *88*
Markham, William (1719–1807) II *143*
Markland, Jeremiah (1693–1776) I *88*
Marks, D.W. (1811–1909) III *138*
Marks, H.S. (1829–1898) III *138*
Marks of Broughton, 1st Baron (1888–1964) IV *71*
Marlborough, 1st Earl of (1550–1629) I *88*
Marlborough, 1st Duke of (1650–1722) I *88–89*
Marlborough, 3rd Duke of (1706–1758) II *143*
Marlborough, 4th Duke of (1739–1817) II *143*
Marlborough, 5th Duke of (1766–1840) II *143*
Marlborough, 7th Duke of (1822–1883) III *138*
Marlborough, Duchess of (1660–1744) I *89*
Marnock, Robert (1800–1889) III *138*
Marochetti, Carlo, Baron (1805–1867) III *138*
Marr, J.E. (1857–1933) III *138*
Marriott, Charles (1811–1858) III *138*
Marriott, Sir J.A.R. (1859–1945) III *138*
Marriott, Sir W.T. (1834–1903) III *138*
Marryat, Florence (1838–1899) III *138*
Marryat, Frederick (1792–1848) II *143*
Marsden, Samuel (1764–1838) II *143*
Marsden, William (1754–1836) II *144*
Marsden, William (1796–1867) II *144*
Marsh, Catherine (1818–1912) III *138*
Marsh, Sir E.H. (1872–1953) IV *71*
Marsh, Sir Henry, 1st Bart (1790–1860) II *144*
Marsh, Herbert (1757–1839) II *144*
Marsh, Narcissus (1638–1713) I *89*
Marsh, William (1775–1864) II *144*
Marshall, Alfred (1842–1924) III *138*

Marshall, Benjamin (1767?–1835) II *144*
Marshall, Sir Frederick (1829–1900) III *138*
Marshall, Sir G.A.K. (1871–1959) IV *71*
Marshall, Henry (1775–1851) II *144*
Marshall, John (1818–1891) III *138*
Marshall, Sir J.H. (1876–1958) IV *71*
Marshall, Thomas (1621–1685) I *89*
Marshall, William (fl 1640) I *89*
Marshall, William (1748–1833) II *144*
Marshall, W.C. (1813–1894) III *138*
Marshall, Sir W.R. (1865–1939) IV *71*
Marsham, Sir John, 1st Bart (1602–1685) I *89*
Marshman, Joshua (1768–1837) II *144*
Marston, J.W. (1819–1890) III *138*
Marston, P.B. (1850–1887) III *138*
Martel, Sir G. Le Quesne (1889–1958) IV *71*
Marten, Sir Henry (1562?–1641) I *89*
Marten, Henry (1602–1680) I *89*
Marten, Sir Henry (1872–1948) IV *71*
Martin, Sir Alec (1884–1971) IV *71*
Martin, Alexander (1857–1946) III *138*
Martin, Benjamin (1704–1782) II *144*
Martin, Sir C.J. (1866–1955) IV *71*
Martin, David (1737–1798) II *144*
Martin, E.G. (1871–1945) IV *71*
Martin, Sir George (1764–1847) II *144*
Martin, Gregory (d1582) I *89*
Martin, G.W. (1828–1881) III *138*
Martin, Lady Helena (1817–1898) III *138–139*
Martin, John (1741–1820) II *144*
Martin, John (1789–1854) II *144*
Martin, John (1812–1875) III *139*
Martin, Jonathan (1782–1838) II *144*
Martin, Sir J.R. (1793–1874) II *144*
Martin, Kingsley (1897–1969) IV *71*
Martin, Matthew (1748–1838) II *144*
Martin, Sir Richard (1534–1617) I *89*
Martin, Richard (1570–1618) I *89*
Martin, Richard (1754–1834) II *144*
Martin, Sir Samuel (1801–1883) III *139*
Martin, Samuel (1817–1878) III *139*
Martin, Sir Theodore (1816–1909) III *139*
Martin, Thomas (1697–1771) I *89*
Martin, Sir T.B. (1773–1854) II *144*
Martin, Violet Florence (1862–1915) IV *71*
Martin, William (1772–1851) II *144*
Martin, Sir William (1807–1880) III *139*
Martin-Harvey, Sir J.M. (1863–1944) IV *71*
Martindale, Miles (1756–1824) II *144*
Martineau, Harriet (1802–1876) III *139*
Martineau, James (1805–1900) III *139*
Martineau,R.B. (1826–1869) III *139*
Martyn, Elizabeth (1813–1846) III *139*
Martyn, Henry (1781–1812) II *144*
Martyn, Thomas (1735–1825) II *144*
Marvell, Andrew (1621–1678) I *89*
Marwick, Sir J.D. (1826–1908) III *139*
Mary I (1516–1558) I *89*
Mary II (1662–1694) I *89*
Mary of Guise, Queen (1515–1560) I *89*
Mary of Modena, Queen (1658–1718) I *89*
Mary, Princess (1776–1857) II *144*
Mary, Princess of Hesse (1723–1772) II *144*
Mary, Princess of Orange (1631–1660) I *89–90*
Mary, Queen of Scots (1542–1587) I *90*
Mary Tudor, Queen (1496–1533) I *90*
Mary Victoria of Teck, Queen (1867–1953) IV *71*
Mary Victoria Alexandra Alice, Princess Royal (1897–1965) IV *71–72*
Mascall, Leonard (d1589) I *90*
Masefield, John (1878–1967) IV *72*
Maseres, Francis (1731–1824) II *144–145*
Masham, 1st Baron (1815–1906) III *139*
Maskelyne, Nevil (1732–1811) II *145*
Mason, A.E.W. (1865–1948) IV *72*
Mason, A.J. (1851–1928) III *139*
Mason, G.H. (1818–1872) III *139*
Mason, John (1503–1566) I *90*
Mason, Sir Josiah (1795–1881) II *145*
Mason, J.M. (1726–1809) II *145*
Mason, T.M. (1803–1889) III *139*
Mason, William (fl 1672–1709) I *90*
Mason, William (1725–1797) II *145*
Mason-MacFarlane, Sir Noel (1889–1953) IV *72*
Massereene, 1st Viscount (d1665) I *90*
Massereene, 2nd Viscount (d1695) I *90*
Massey, Sir Edward (1619?–1674?) I *90*
Massey, Gerald (1828–1907) III *139*
Massey, W.F. (1856–1925) III *139*
Massey, W.N. (1809–1881) III *139*
Massie, J.W. (1799–1869) II *145*
Massinger, Philip (1583–1640) I *90*
Masson, David (1822–1907) III *139–140*
Masson, Sir D.O. (1858–1937) IV *72*
Masson, Francis (1741–1805) II *145*
Masson, Sir Irvine (1887–1962) IV *72*
Massy, W.G.D. (1838–1906) III *140*

Master, Sir William (d1662) I 90
Masterman, C.F.G. (1874–1927) IV 72
Masters, M.T. (1833–1907) III 140
Masters, Robert (1713–1798) II 145
Mather, Cotton (1663–1728) I 90
Mather, Increase (1639–1723) I 90
Mather, Richard (1596–1669) I 90
Matheson, George (1842–1906) III 140
Mathew, Sir J.C. (1830–1908) III 140
Mathew, Theobald (1790–1856) II 145
Mathew, Sir Theobald (1898–1964) IV 72
Mathews, Charles (1776–1835) II 145
Mathews, C.J. (1803–1878) III 140
Mathews, Sir C.W., Bart (1850–1920) III 140
Mathews, Mrs Lucia Elizabeth (1797–1856) II 145
Mathews, Dame Vera (1888–1959) IV 72
Mathieson, W.L. (1868–1938) IV 72
Matilda, (1102–1167) I 90
Matilda, Duchess of Saxony (1156–1189) I 90
Maton, Robert (1607–1653?) I 90
Maton, W.G. (1774–1835) II 145
Matthew, Tobias (1546–1628) I 90
Matthew, Sir Tobias (1577–1655) I 90
Matthews, Henry (1789–1828) II 145
Matthews, John (1755–1826) II 145
Matthews, Sir William (1844–1922) III 140
Matthews, W.R. (1881–1973) IV 72
Mattocks, Isabella (1746–1826) II 145
Maturin, C.R. (1782–1824) II 145
Maty, Matthew (1718–1776) II 145
Maty, P.H. (1745–1787) II 145
Maud, Princess (1869–1938) IV 72
Maude, Cyril (1862–1951) IV 72
Maude, Sir Stanley (1864–1917) IV 72
Maudslay, Henry (1771–1831) II 145
Mauduit, Israel (1708–1787) II 145–146
Maufe, Sir Edward (1883–1974) IV 72
Maugham, 1st Viscount (1866–1958) IV 72
Maugham, Somerset (1874–1965) IV 72–73
Maule, Sir W.H. (1788–1858) II 146
Maunder, Samuel (1785–1849) II 146
Maurice, Sir F.B. (1871–1951) IV 73
Maurice, F.D. (1805–1872) III 140
Maurice, Sir J.F. (1841–1912) III 140
Maurice, Prince (1620–1652) I 90
Maurice, Thomas (1754–1824) II 146
Mavor, O.H. (1888–1951) IV 73
Mavor, W.F. (1758–1837) II 146
Mawbey, Sir Joseph, 1st Bart (1730–1798) II 146
Mawer, Sir Allen (1879–1943) IV 73
Mawson, Mathias (1683–1770) I 90
Maxim, Sir H.S. (1840–1916) III 140
Max-Müller, Friedrich (1823–1900) III 140
Maxse, Sir H.B. (1832–1883) III 140
Maxse, Sir Ivor (1862–1958) IV 73
Maxton, James (1885–1946) IV 73
Maxwell, Sir H.E., 7th Bart of Monreith (1845–1937) III 140
Maxwell, J.H. (1812–1866) III 140
Maxwell, Mary Elizabeth (1837–1915) III 140
Maxwell, Sir Murray (1775–1831) II 146
Maxwell, William (1873–1957) IV 73
Maxwell, W.H. (1792–1850) II 146
May, 1st Baron (1871–1946) IV 73
May, Baptist (1629–1698) I 90
May, Hugh (1622–1684) I 90–91
May, Sir Humphrey (1573–1630) I 91
May, P.W. (1864–1903) IV 73
May, Thomas (1595–1650) I 91
May, Sir W.H. (1849–1930) III 140–141
Maybury, Sir H.P. (1864–1943) IV 73
Mayer, Joseph (1803–1886) III 141
Mayer, Sir Robert (b1879) IV 73
Mayerne, Sir T.T. de (1573–1655) I 91
Mayhew, Henry (1812–1887) III 141
Mayhew, Horace (1816–1872) III 141
Maynard, Sir John (1602–1690) I 91
Mayne, Cuthbert (d1577) I 91
Mayne, Sir Richard (1796–1868) II 146
Mayne, R.C. (1835–1892) III 141
Mayne, William (1818–1855) III 141
Maynwaring, Arthur (1668–1712) I 91
Maynwaring, Everard (1628–1699?) I 91
Mayo, 6th Earl of (1822–1872) III 141
Mayo, John (1761–1818) II 146
Mayo, Richard (1631?–1695) I 91
Mayo, Thomas (1790–1871) II 146
Mayor, J.E.B. (1825–1910) III 141
Mayow, John (1640–1679) I 91
Mead, Matthew (1630?–1699) I 91
Mead, Richard (1673–1754) I 91
Meade, Sir R.H. (1835–1898) III 141
Meadowbank, 1st Lord (1748–1816) II 146
Meadowbank, 2nd Lord (1777–1861) II 146
Meadows, Drinkwater (1799–1869) II 146
Meadows, J.K. (1790–1874) II 146
Meagher, T.F. (1823–1867) III 141
Mears, John (1695?–1767) I 91

Meath, 12th Earl of (1841–1929) III 141
Mechi, J.J. (1802–1880) III 141
Medina, Sir J.B. (1659–1710) I 90
Medley, Henry (d1747) I 91
Medley, John (1804–1892) III 141
Medley, Samuel (1738–1799) II 146
Medows, Sir William (1738–1813) II 146
Medwyn, John Hay Forbes, Lord (1776–1854) II 146
Mee, Anne (1775?–1851) II 146
Mees, C.E. Kenneth (1882–1960) IV 73
Meggot, Richard (d1692) I 91
Meikle, Andrew (1719–1811) II 146
Meilan, M.A. (fl 1812) II 146
Melba, Dame Nellie (1861–1931) IV 73
Melbourne, 2nd Viscount (1779–1848) II 146
Melbourne, 3rd Viscount (1782–1853) II 146
Melchett, 1st Baron (1868–1930) IV 73
Melcombe, Baron (1691–1762) I 91
Meldola, Raphael (1754–1828) II 146
Meldola, Raphael (1849–1915) III 141
Meldrum, Sir John (d1645) I 91
Melfort, 1st Earl and titular Duke of (1649–1714) I 91
Mellanby, Sir Edward (1884–1955) IV 73
Mellanby, John (1878–1939) IV 73
Mellish, Sir George (1814–1877) III 141
Mellon, Alfred (1820–1867) III 141
Mellon, Sarah Jane (1824–1909) III 141
Mellor, Sir John (1809–1887) III 141
Melmoth, William (1666–1743) I 91
Melvill, Henry (1798–1871) II 146
Melvill, Lady Hester (d1864) II 147
Melvill, Sir J.C. (1792–1861) II 147
Melville, 1st Earl of (1634?–1707) I 91
Melville, 1st Viscount (1742–1811) II 147
Melville, 2nd Viscount (1771–1851) II 147
Melville, Robert (1723–1809) II 147
Mendes, Moses (d1758) II 147
Mendip, Baron (1713–1802) II 147
Mendl, Sir C.F. (1871–1958) IV 73
Mendoza, Daniel (1764–1836) II 147
Menken, Adah Isaacs (1835–1868) III 141
Mennes, Sir John (1599–1671) I 91
Menteith, Robert (d1660?) I 91
Menzies, Archibald (1754–1842) II 147
Menzies, Sir F.N.K. (1875–1949) IV 73
Menzies, Sir S.G. (1890–1968) IV 73
Mercer, Hugh (1726?–1777) II 147
Mercer, James (1883–1932) IV 73
Mercier, Philip (1689–1760) I 91
Meredith, George (1828–1909) III 141
Meredith, Sir William, 3rd Bart (1725?–1790) II 147
Merewether, H.A. (1780–1864) II 147
Merewether, John (1797–1850) II 147
Merewether, Sir W.L. (1825–1880) III 141–142
Merivale, Herman (1806–1874) III 142
Merivale, J.H. (1779–1844) II 147
Merke, Thomas (d1409) I 91
Merret(t), Christopher (1614–1695) I 91
Merriman, Baron (1880–1962) IV 73
Merriman, Samuel (1731–1818) II 147
Merriman, Samuel (1771–1852) II 147
Merrivale, 1st Baron (1855–1939) III 142
Merry, Robert (1755–1798) II 147
Merry, W.W. (1835–1918) III 142
Merry del Val, Rafael (1865–1930) IV 73
Mersey, 1st Viscount (1840–1929) III 142
Merthyr, 1st Baron (1837–1914) III 142
Meryon, C.L. (1783–1877) II 147
Merz, C.H. (1874–1940) IV 73
Messervy, Sir F.W. (1893–1974) IV 73–74
Meston, 1st Baron (1865–1943) IV 74
Metcalf, John (1717–1810) II 147
Metcalfe, 1st Baron (1785–1846) II 147
Metcalfe, Philip (1733–1818) II 147
Metcalfe, Theophilus (fl 1750) I 91
Methuen, 3rd Baron (1845–1932) III 142
Methuen, 4th Baron (1886–1974) IV 74
Methuen, David Smythe, Lord (1746–1806) II 147
Methuen, Sir A.M.M., 1st Bart (1856–1924) III 142
Methuen, John (1650?–1706) I 91
Methuen, Sir Paul (1672–1757) I 91–92
Meux, Sir Hedworth (1856–1929) III 142
Mews, Peter (1619–1706) I 92
Meyer, F.B. (1847–1929) III 142
Meyer, Jeremiah (1735–1789) II 147
Meyer, Sir W.S. (1860–1922) IV 74
Meyerstein, E.H.W. (1889–1952) IV 74
Meynell, Alice (1847–1922) III 142
Meynell, Sir Francis (1891–1975) IV 74
Meyrick, Edward (1854–1938) III 142
Meyrick, Frederick (1827–1906) III 142
Meyrick, Sir S.R. (1783–1848) II 147
Miall, Edward (1809–1881) III 142
Michelburn(e), John (1647–1721) I 92
Michell, Henry (1714–1789) II 147
Michell, Nicholas (1807–1880) III 142
Michell, Richard (1805–1877) III 142

Mickle, W.J. (1735–1788) II 147
Micklethwaite, Sir John (1612–1682) I 92
Micklethwaite, J.T. (1843–1906) III 142
Middlesex, 1st Earl of (1575–1645) I 92
Middleton, 1st Earl of (1608–1673) I 92
Middleton, Conyers (1683–1750) I 92
Middleton, Erasmus (1739–1805) II 148
Middleton, Jane (1645–1692) I 92
Middleton, John (1827–1856) III 142
Middleton, Richard (d1641) I 92
Middleton, Thomas (1570?–1627) I 92
Middleton, T.F. (1769–1822) II 148
Midleton, 9th Viscount and 1st Earl of (1856–1942) III 142
Miers, Sir H.A. (1858–1942) IV 74
Miéville, Sir E.C. (1896–1971) IV 74
Milborne, Luke (1649–1720) I 92
Mildmay, Sir Anthony (d1617) I 92
Mildmay, Sir Walter (1520?–1589) I 92
Milford, Sir H.S. (1877–1952) IV 74
Milford Haven, 1st Marquess of (1854–1921) III 142
Mill, Humphrey (fl 1646) I 92
Mill, H.R. (1861–1950) IV 74
Mill, John (1645–1707) I 92
Mill, John Stuart (1806–1873) III 142
Mill, W.H. (1792–1853) II 148
Millais, Sir J.E., Bart (1829–1896) III 142–143
Millar, Gertie (1879–1952) IV 74
Millar, James (1762–1827) II 148
Millar, John (1735–1801) II 148
Miller, Anna, Lady (1741–1781) II 148
Miller, Edward (1731–1807) II 148
Miller, George (1764–1848) II 148
Miller, Hugh (1802–1856) III 143
Miller, James (1812–1864) III 143
Miller, Joseph (1684–1738) I 92
Miller, J.C. (1814–1880) III 143
Miller, Sir J.P., 2nd Bart (1864–1906) IV 74
Miller, Patrick (1731–1815) II 148
Miller, Philip (1691–1771) I 92
Miller, R.W. (1762–1799) II 148
Miller, Thomas (1731–1804) II 148
Miller, William (1769–1845) II 148
Miller, William (1795–1861) II 148
Miller, William (1796–1882) II 148
Miller, W.A. (1817–1870) III 143
Miller, W.H. (1789–1848) II 148
Milles, Jeremiah (1714–1784) II 148
Milligan, William (1821–1893) III 143
Milligan, Sir William (1864–1929) IV 74
Millington, Sir Thomas (1628–1704) I 92
Mills, 1st Viscount (1890–1968) IV 74
Mills, B.W. (1873–1938) IV 74
Mills, Sir Charles (1825–1895) III 143
Mills, John (1670–1736) I 92
Mills, W.H. (1873–1959) IV 74
Milltown, 6th Earl of (1835–1890) III 143
Milman, H.H. (1791–1868) II 148
Milman, Robert (1816–1876) III 143
Milne, Sir Alexander, 1st Bart (1806–1896) III 143
Milne, A.A. (1882–1956) IV 74
Milne, Sir Berkeley, 2nd Bart (1855–1938) III 143
Milne, Colin (1743?–1815) II 148
Milne, Sir David (1763–1845) II 148
Milne, E.A. (1896–1950) IV 74
Milne, William (1785–1822) II 148
Milne, W.C. (1815–1863) III 143
Milne-Watson, Sir D.M., 1st Bart (1869–1945) IV 74
Milner, Viscount (1854–1925) III 143
Milner, Sir F.G., 7th Bart (1849–1931) III 143
Milner, Isaac (1750–1820) II 148
Milner, John (1752–1826) II 148
Milner, Joseph (1744–1797) II 148
Milner of Leeds, 1st Baron (1889–1967) IV 74
Milner-Gibson, Thomas (1806–1884) III 143–144
Milner-White, Eric (1884–1963) IV 74
Milton, Andrew Fletcher, Lord (1692–1766) I 92
Milton, John (1608–1674) I 92
Milton, John (1759–1805) II 148
Minto, 1st Earl of (1751–1814) II 148
Minto, 2nd Earl of (1782–1859) II 148
Minto, 4th Earl of (1845–1914) III 144
Minto, William (1845–1893) III 144
Misaubin, John (d1734) I 92
Missenden, Sir E.J. (1886–1973) IV 74
Mitchel, John (1815–1875) III 144
Mitchell, Alexander (1780–1868) II 148
Mitchell, Sir Andrew (1708–1771) II 148
Mitchell, Sir Andrew (1757–1806) II 148
Mitchell, Sir Arthur (1826–1909) III 144
Mitchell, A.F. (1822–1899) III 144
Mitchell, Sir Henry (1823–1898) III 144
Mitchell, J.M. (1815–1904) III 144
Mitchell, Sir P.C. (1864–1945) IV 74
Mitchell, Sir W.G.S. (1888–1944) IV 74
Mitford, Mary Russell (1787–1855) II 148–149
Mitford, William (1744–1827) II 149

Mivart, St George Jackson (1827–1900) III *144*
Moberly, George (1803–1885) III *144*
Moberly, Sir Walter (1881–1974) IV *74*
Mocatta, F.D. (1828–1905) III *144*
Mocket, Thomas (1602–1670?) I *92*
Moeran, E.J. (1894–1950) IV *74*
Moffat, Robert (1795–1883) II *149*
Moffatt, James (1870–1944) IV *74*
Moffet, Joseph (1885–1962) IV *74*
Moffet, Thomas (1553–1604) I *92*
Moir, D.M. (1798–1851) II *149*
Moivre, Abraham de (1667–1754) I *92*
Mole, J.H. (1814–1886) III *144*
Molesworth, 1st Viscount (1656–1725) I *92*
Molesworth, 2nd Viscount (1679–1726) I *92*
Molesworth, 3rd Viscount (1680–1758) I *92*
Molesworth, J.E.N. (1790–1877) II *149*
Molesworth, Mary Louisa (1839–1921) III *144*
Molesworth, Sir William, Bart (1810–1855) III *144*
Molesworth, W.N. (1816–1890) III *144*
Molteno, Sir J.C. (1814–1886) III *144*
Molyneux, Sir Thomas, 1st Bart (1661–1733) I *93*
Molyneux, William (1656–1698) I *93*
Molyneux of Maryborough, 3rd Viscount (1621?–1699) I *93*
Momerie, A.W. (1848–1900) III *144*
Mompesson, Sir Giles (1584–1651?) I *93*
Mompesson, William (1639–1709) I *93*
Monahan, J.H. (1804–1878) III *144*
Monamy, Peter (1670?–1749) I *93*
Monash, Sir John (1865–1931) IV *74–75*
Monboddo, James Burnett, Lord (1714–1799) II *149*
Monck, 4th Viscount and 1st Baron (1819–1894) III *144*
Monck, Nicholas (1610–1661) I *93*
Monckton, 1st Viscount (1891–1965) IV *75*
Monckton, Robert (1726–1782) II *149*
Moncrieff, Sir J.W. Moncrieff, Lord (1776–1851) II *149*
Moncreiff of Tulliebole, 1st Baron (1811–1895) III *144*
Moncrieff, Sir Alexander (1829–1906) III *144*
Moncrieff, W.T. (1794–1857) II *149*
Moncrieff-Wellwood, Sir Henry, Bart (1750–1827) II *149*
Mond, Ludwig (1839–1909) III *144*
Mond, Sir R.L. (1867–1938) IV *75*
Monier-Williams, Sir Monier (1819–1899) III *145*
Monk, J.H. (1784–1856) II *149*
Monk, W.H. (1823–1889) III *145*
Monkbretton, J.G.D. (1825–1897) III *145*
Monkhouse, W.C. (1840–1901) III *145*
Monkswell, 1st Baron (1817–1886) III *145*
Monmouth, 1st Earl (1560?–1639) I *93*
Monmouth, 2nd Earl (1596–1661) I *93*
Monmouth and Buccleuch, Duke of (1649–1685) I *93*
Monnoyer, J.B. (1634–1699) I *93*
Monro, Alexander (1697–1767) I *93*
Monro, Alexander (1733–1817) I *93*
Monro, Alexander (1773–1859) I *93*
Monro, Sir C.C., Bart (1860–1929) IV *75*
Monro, D.B. (1836–1905) III *145*
Monro, Henry (1791–1814) II *149*
Monro, Henry (1817–1891) III *145*
Monro, Sir H.C. (1861–1949) IV *75*
Monro, H.E. (1879–1932) IV *75*
Monro, James (1680–1752) I *93*
Monro, John (1715–1791) II *149*
Monro, Thomas (1759–1833) II *149*
Monsell, 1st Viscount (1881–1969) IV *75*
Monsey, Messenger (1693–1788) I *93*
Montagu, 1st Duke of (1638?–1709) I *94*
Montagu, 2nd Duke of (1690–1749) I *94*
Montagu, Duke of (1712–1790) II *149–150*
Montagu, Sir Edward (d 1557) I *93*
Montagu, Edward (1635–1655) I *93*
Montagu, Mrs Elizabeth (1720–1800) II *149*
Montagu, E.S. (1879–1924) IV *75*
Montagu, E.W. (1713–1776) II *149*
Moeran, Sir George (1750–1829) II *149*
Montagu, Sir James (1666–1723) I *93*
Montagu, James (1752–1794) II *150*
Montagu, John (1655?–1728) I *93*
Montagu, Lady Mary Wortley (1689–1762) I *93–94*
Montagu, Lord Robert (1825–1902) III *145*
Montagu, Sir Walter (1603?–1677) I *94*
Montagu of Beaulieu, 2nd Baron (1866–1929) IV *75*
Montagu of Boughton, 1st Baron (1562–1644) I *94*
Montagu of Boughton, 2nd Baron (1616–1684) I *94*
Montague, 1st Viscount (1526–1592) I *94*
Montague, C.E. (1867–1928) IV *75*
Montague, H.J. (1843?–1878) III *145*
Montague(e), James (1568?–1618) I *94*
Montague(e), Walter (1603?–1677) I *94*
Montaigne, George (1569–1628) I *94*
Monteage, Stephen (1623?–1687) I *94*
Monteagle, 1st Baron (1790–1866) II *150*
Montefiore, C.J. Goldsmid- (1858–1938) III *145*
Montefiore, Sir M.H., 1st Bart (1784–1885) II *150*
Montgomery, Henry (1788–1865) II *150*

Montgomery, James (1771–1854) II *150*
Montgomery, Sir J.W., 1st Bart (1721–1803) II *150*
Montgomery, Robert (1807–1855) III *145*
Montgomery, Sir Robert (1809–1887) III *145*
Montgomery of Alamein, 1st Viscount (1887–1976) IV *75*
Montgomery-Massingberd, Sir A.A. (1871–1947) IV *75*
Montresor, John (1736–1799) II *150*
Montrose, 1st Marquess and 5th Earl of (1612–1650) I *94*
Montrose, 3rd Duke of (1755–1836) II *150*
Montrose, 4th Duke of (1799–1874) II *150*
Montrose, 5th Duke of (1852–1925) III *145*
Moody, H.A. (1882–1947) IV *75*
Moody, J.L.N. (1727?–1812) II *150*
Moon, Sir F.G., 1st Bart (1796–1871) II *150*
Moor, Edward (1771–1848) II *150*
Moorcroft, William (1765?–1825) II *150*
Moore, Ann (fl 1813) II *150*
Moore, A.J. (1841–1893) III *145*
Moore, A.L. (1848–1890) III *145*
Moore, A.W. (1853–1909) III *145*
Moore, Edward (1712–1757) II *150*
Moore, Edward (1835–1916) III *145*
Moore, Francis (1657–1715?) I *94*
Moore, George (1806–1876) III *145*
Moore, George (1852–1933) III *145–146*
Moore, George (1873–1958) IV *75*
Moore, Sir Graham (1764–1843) II *150*
Moore, Henry (1751–1844) II *150*
Moore, Henry (1831–1896) III *146*
Moore, Henry (b 1898) IV *75*
Moore, Sir Henry Monck-Mason (1887–1964) IV *75*
Moore, Sir H.R. (1886–1978) IV *75*
Moore, John (1595?–1657) I *94*
Moore, Sir John (1620–1702) I *94*
Moore, John (1646–1714) I *94*
Moore, John (1729–1802) II *150*
Moore, John (1730–1805) II *150–151*
Moore, John (1761–1809) II *151*
Moore, Sir Jonas (1617–1679) I *94*
Moore, Joseph (1656–1732) I *94*
Moore, Sir J.H., 2nd Bart (1756–1780) II *151*
Moore, Thomas (1779–1852) II *151*
Moore, T.E.L. (1819–1872) III *146*
Moore, T.S. (1870–1944) IV *75*
Moorhouse, James (1826–1915) III *146*
Moorsom, C.R. (1792–1861) II *151*
Mor, Sir Anthony (1512?–1576?) I *94*
Morant, Sir R.L. (1863–1920) IV *75*
Moray, Earl of (1531?–1570) I *94*
Moray, 5th Earl of (1634–1700) I *94*
Moray, 15th Earl of (1840–1901) III *146*
Mordaunt, John (d 1506?) I *94*
Mordaunt, Sir John (1698–1780) I *94*
Mordaunt of Avalon, 1st Viscount (1627–1675) I *94*
Mordaunt of Turvey, 1st Baron (1490?–1560?) I *94*
Morden, Sir John, 1st Bart (1623–1708) I *94*
More, Alexander (1616–1670) I *94*
More, Anne (1511–1577) I *95*
More, Cresacre (1572–1649) I *95*
More, Sir George (1553–1632) I *95*
More, Gertrude (1606–1633) I *95*
More, Hannah (1745–1833) II *151*
More, Henry (1614–1687) I *95*
More, Jacob (1740–1793) II *151*
More, Sir John (1453?–1530) I *95*
More, John (1510–1547) I *95*
More, John (d 1592) I *95*
More, John (1557–1599?) I *95*
More, Maria (1534–1607) I *95*
More, Robert (1671–1727?) I *95*
More, Sir Thomas (1478–1535) I *95*
More, Thomas II (1531–1606) I *95*
More-Molyneux, Sir R.H. (1838–1904) III *146*
Morell, J.D. (1816–1891) III *146*
Morell, Thomas (1703–1784) II *151*
Mores, E.R. (1731–1778) II *151*
Moresby, Sir Fairfax (1786–1877) II *151*
Moreton, William (1641–1715) I *95*
Morfill, W.R. (1834–1909) III *146*
Morgan, Alice May (1850–1890) III *146*
Morgan, Sir Charles (1575?–1642) I *95*
Morgan, C.L. (1852–1936) III *146*
Morgan, C.L. (1894–1958) IV *75*
Morgan, F.C. (1834–1909) III *146*
Morgan, Sir G.O., 1st Bart (1826–1897) III *146*
Morgan, Sir Henry (1635?–1688) I *95*
Morgan, Sydney, Lady (1783?–1859) II *151*
Morgan, Sylvanus (1620–1693) I *95*
Morgan, Sir Thomas (d 1679?) I *95*
Morgan, Sir T.C. (1783–1843) II *151*
Mori, Nicolas (1797–1839) II *151*
Moriarty, David (1814–1877) III *146*
Moriarty, H.A. (1815–1906) III *146*
Morice, Humphry (1671?–1731) I *95*
Morice, Sir William (1602–1676) I *95*
Morier, D.R. (1784–1877) II *151*

Morier, J.J. (1780?–1849) II *151*
Morier, Sir R.B.D. (1826–1893) III *146*
Morison, Sir Alexander (1779–1866) II *151*
Morison, James (1770–1840) II *151*
Morison, John (1791–1859) II *151*
Morison, Robert (1620–1683) I *95*
Morison, S.A. (1889–1967) IV *75–76*
Morison, Sir Theodore (1863–1936) IV *76*
Morison, Thomas (d 1824) II *151*
Morland, George (1763–1804) II *151*
Morland, H.R. (1730?–1797) II *151*
Morland, Sir Samuel, 1st Bart (1625–1695) I *95*
Morland, Sir T.L.N. (1865–1925) IV *76*
Morley, 10th Baron (1476–1556) I *95*
Morley, 1st Earl of (1772–1840) II *151*
Morley, 2nd Earl of (1810–1864) III *146*
Morley, 3rd Earl of (1843–1905) III *146*
Morley, George (1597–1684) I *95*
Morley, Henry (1822–1894) III *146*
Morley, John (1656–1732) I *95*
Morley, Samuel (1809–1886) III *146*
Morley of Blackburn, 1st Viscount (1838–1923) III *146–147*
Mornington, 1st Baron (1690?–1758) I *95–96*
Mornington, 1st Earl of (1735–1781) II *152*
Mornington, 3rd Earl of (1763–1845) II *152*
Mornington, Countess of (1742–1831) II *151–152*
Morphett, Sir John (1809–1892) III *147*
Morrell, Lady Ottoline (1873–1938) IV *76*
Morris, Baron (1859–1935) III *147*
Morris, A.E. (1894–1971) IV *76*
Morris, Charles (1745–1838) II *152*
Morris, F.O. (1810–1893) III *147*
Morris, Jane (1839?–1914) III *147*
Morris, John (1617?–1649) I *96*
Morris, Sir Lewis (1833–1907) III *147*
Morris, May (1863–1938) IV *76*
Morris, P.R. (1836–1902) III *147*
Morris, Richard (1833–1894) III *147*
Morris, Tom (1821–1908) III *147*
Morris, William (1834–1896) III *147*
Morris, William O'Connor (1824–1904) III *147*
Morris-Jones, Sir John (1864–1929) IV *76*
Morris and Killanin, Baron (1826–1901) III *147–148*
Morrison, Alfred (1821–1897) III *148*
Morrison, James (1790–1857) II *152*
Morrison, Sir Richard (1767–1849) II *152*
Morrison, Robert (1782–1834) II *152*
Morrison of Lambeth, Baron (1888–1965) IV *76*
Morritt, J.B.S. (1772?–1843) II *152*
Morse, Henry (1595–1645) I *96*
Mortimer, Cromwell (d 1752) I *96*
Mortimer, Mrs Favell Lee (1802–1878) III *148*
Mortimer, G.F.W. (1805–1871) III *148*
Mortimer, John Hamilton (1740–1779) II *152*
Mortimer, Thomas (1730–1810) II *152*
Morton, 4th Earl of (d 1581) I *96*
Morton, 7th Earl of (1582?–1648?) I *96*
Morton, 14th Earl of (c 1702–1768) II *152*
Morton, Sir A.C. (1840–1923) III *148*
Morton, H.C.V. (1892–1979) IV *76*
Morton, John (1420?–1500) I *96*
Morton, J.C.A.B.M. (1893–1979) IV *76*
Morton, Richard (1637–1698) I *96*
Morton, Thomas (1564?–1659) I *96*
Morton, Thomas (1764?–1838) II *152*
Morton, Thomas (1814–1849) III *148*
Morton, Sir William (d 1672) I *96*
Morton of Henryton, Baron (1887–1973) IV *76*
Moseley, Benjamin (1742–1819) II *152*
Moseley, H.N. (1844–1891) III *148*
Moser, G.M. (1704–1783) II *152*
Moser, Joseph (1748–1819) II *152*
Moser, Mary (d 1819) II *152*
Mosley, Sir Oswald, 6th Bart (b 1896) IV *76*
Moss, Charles (1711–1802) II *152*
Moss, Charles (1763–1811) II *152*
Moss, Robert (1666–1729) I *96*
Mosse, Bartholomew (1712–1759) II *152*
Mossop, Henry (1729?–1774?) II *152*
Mostyn, Savage (d 1757) II *152*
Motherwell, William (1797–1835) II *152*
Mott, Sir Basil, 1st Bart (1859–1938) III *148*
Mott, C.G. (1833–1905) III *148*
Mott, Sir F.W. (1853–1926) III *148*
Mottershead, Joseph (1688–1771) I *96*
Motteux, P.A. (1660–1718) I *96*
Mottistone, 1st Baron (1868–1947) IV *76*
Mottistone, 2nd Baron (1899–1963) IV *76*
Mottram, R.H. (1883–1971) IV *76*
Moule, A.C. (1873–1957) IV *76*
Moule, G.E. (1828–1912) III *148*
Moule, H.C.G. (1841–1920) III *148*
Moullin, E.B. (1893–1963) IV *76*
Moulton, Baron (1844–1921) III *148*
Moulton, W.F. (1835–1898) III *148*
Mountain, Jacob (1749–1825) II *152*
Mountain, Mrs Rosoman (1768?–1841) II *152*

Mountbatten of Burma, Earl (1900–1979) IV 76
Mount-Edgcumbe, 1st Earl of (1721–1795) II 153
Mount-Edgcumbe, 2nd Earl of (1764–1839) II 153
Mountevans, 1st Baron (1880–1957) IV 76
Mountgarret, 1st Viscount (d1571) I 96
Mountnorris, Baron (1585–1660) I 96
Mount Stephen, 1st Baron (1829–1921) III 148
Mount-Temple, Baron (1811–1888) III 148
Mount Temple, Baron (1867–1938) IV 77
Mowat, Sir Oliver (1820–1903) III 148
Mowatt, Sir Francis (1837–1919) III 148
Mowbray, Sir J.R., 1st Bart (1815–1899) III 148
Moxon, John (1627–1700) I 96
Moylan, Francis (1735–1815) II 153
Moyle, Walter (1672–1721) I 96
Moyne, 1st Baron (1880–1944) IV 77
Moynihan, 1st Baron (1865–1936) IV 77
Mozley, J.B. (1813–1878) III 148
Mudford, William (1782–1848) II 153
Mudge, John (1721–1793) II 153
Mudge, Thomas (1717–1794) II 153
Mudge, Zachariah (1694–1769) I 96
Mudie, C.E. (1818–1890) III 148
Muggleton, Lodowicke (1609–1698) I 96
Muir, Edwin (1887–1959) IV 77
Muir, John (1810–1882) III 148
Muir, Sir Robert (1864–1959) IV 77
Muir, Thomas (1765–1798) II 153
Muir, William (1787–1869) III 153
Muir, Sir William (1819–1905) III 148
Muirhead, James (1831–1889) III 148
Muirhead, J.H. (1855–1940) III 148
Mulgrave, 1st Earl of (1564?–1646) I 96
Mulgrave, 2nd Earl of (1611?–1658) I 96
Mulgrave, 2nd Baron (1744–1792) II 153
Mulgrave, 1st Earl of (1755–1831) II 153
Mullens, Joseph (1820–1879) III 148
Müller, W.J. (1812–1845) III 148
Mulready, William (1786–1863) II 153
Mulvany, G.F. (1809–1869) III 148
Muncaster, 1st Baron (1737–1814) II 153
Mundella, A.J. (1825–1897) III 148
Munden, Sir John (d1719) I 96
Munden, J.S. (1758–1832) II 153
Mundy, Sir G.R. (1805–1884) III 148–149
Munk, William (1816–1898) III 149
Munnings, Sir A.J. (1878–1959) IV 77
Munro, Alexander (1825–1871) III 149
Munro, Sir Hector (1726–1805) II 153
Munro, H.A.J. (1819–1885) III 149
Munro, Sir Thomas, 1st Bart (1761–1827) II 153
Munster, 1st Earl of (1794–1842) II 153
Muntz, G.F. (1794–1857) II 153
Muntz, Sir P.A., Bart (1839–1908) III 149
Murchison, Charles (1830–1879) III 149
Murchison, Sir R.I., 1st Bart (1792–1871) II 153
Murcot, John (1625–1654) I 96
Murdock, William (1754–1839) II 153
Murlin, John (1722–1799) II 154
Murphy, Arthur (1727–1805) II 154
Murphy, Sir Francis (1809–1891) III 149
Murphy, F.S. (1810?–1860) III 149
Murphy, J.C. (1760–1814) II 154
Murphy, Robert (1806–1843) III 149
Murray, Alexander (1712–1778) II 154
Murray, Alexander (1775–1813) II 154
Murray, Sir A.J. (1860–1945) IV 77
Murray, Charles (1754–1821) II 154
Murray, Sir C.A. (1806–1895) III 149
Murray, Daniel (1768–1852) II 154
Murray, Sir David (1849–1933) III 149
Murray, D.C. (1847–1907) III 149
Murray, Mrs Elizabeth Leigh (d1892) III 149
Murray, Sir Evelyn (1880–1947) IV 77
Murray, Lord George (1700?–1760) II 154
Murray, Sir George (1759–1819) II 154
Murray, Sir George (1772–1846) II 154
Murray, George (1784–1860) II 154
Murray, Gilbert (1866–1957) IV 77
Murray, H.L. (1820–1870) III 149
Murray, James (1719–1794) II 154
Murray, James (1732–1782) II 154
Murray, Sir John, 8th Bart of Clermont (1768?–1827) II 154
Murray, John (1778–1843) II 154
Murray, John (1808–1892) III 149
Murray, Sir John (1841–1914) III 149
Murray, Sir John (1884–1967) IV 77
Murray, Sir J.A.H. (1837–1915) III 149
Murray, Sir J.A. Murray, Lord (1779–1859) II 154
Murray, Lindley (1745–1826) II 154
Murray, Margaret Alice (1863–1963) IV 77
Murray, Sir O.A.R. (1873–1936) IV 77
Murray, Thomas (1663–1734) I 96
Murray, W.H. (1790–1852) II 154
Murray of Gorthy, Sir David (1567–1629) I 96
Murray-Pulteney, Sir James, 7th Bart of Clermont (1751?–1811) II 154

Murry, John Middleton (1889–1957) IV 77
Murry, Kathleen (1888–1923) IV 77
Musgrave, Sir Anthony (1828–1888) III 149
Musgrave, Sir James, 1st Bart (1826–1904) III 149
Musgrave, Sir Thomas (1737–1812) II 154
Musgrave, Thomas (1788–1860) II 154
Muspratt, J.S. (1821–1871) III 149
Mutrie, Annie Feray (1826–1893) III 149
Mutrie, Martha Darley (1824–1885) III 149
Muybridge, Eadweard (1830–1904) III 149
Myddelton, Sir Hugh, 1st Bart (1560?–1631) I 96
Myddelton, Sir Thomas (1550–1631) I 96
Myddelton, Sir Thomas (1586–1666) I 96
Myers, C.S. (1873–1946) IV 77
Myers, F.W.H. (1834–1901) III 149
Myers, L.H. (1881–1944) IV 77
Mylne, John (1611–1667) I 96
Mylne, Robert (1734–1811) II 154
Mylne, W.C. (1781–1863) II 154
Myngs, Sir Christopher (1625–1666) I 96
Mynn, Alfred (1807–1861) III 149
Myrddin-Evans, Sir Guildhaume (1894–1964) IV 77
Myres, Sir J.L. (1869–1954) IV 77
Mytens, Daniel (1590?–1647?) I 96
Mytton, John (1796–1834) II 154
Mytton, Thomas (1597?–1656) I 96

Naftel, P.J. (1817–1891) III 151
Nagle, Sir Edmund (1757–1830) II 155
Nagle, Nano (1728–1784) II 155
Nagle, Sir Richard (fl 1689–1691) I 97
Nairne, Alexander (1863–1936) IV 78
Nairne, Baroness Carolina (1766–1845) II 155
Nairne, Sir C.E. (1833–1899) III 151
Nalton, James (1600?–1662) I 97
Napier, 1st Baron (1576–1645) I 97
Napier, 7th Baron (1758–1823) II 155
Napier, 10th Baron (1819–1898) III 151
Napier, Sir Charles (1786–1860) II 155
Napier, Sir C.J. (1782–1853) II 155
Napier, David (1790–1869) II 155
Napier, George (1751–1804) II 155
Napier, Sir G.T. (1784–1855) II 155
Napier, Sir Joseph, 1st Bart (1804–1882) III 151
Napier, Macvey (1776–1847) II 155
Napier, Mark (1798–1879) II 155
Napier, Richard (1559–1634) I 97
Napier, Robert (1791–1876) II 155
Napier, Sir T.D.W. (1867–1920) IV 78
Napier, Sir W.F.P. (1785–1860) II 155
Napier of Magdala, 1st Baron (1810–1890) III 151
Napier of Merchiston, John (1550–1617) I 97
Napleton, John (1738?–1817) II 155
Nares, Sir George (1716–1786) II 155
Nares, Sir G.S. (1831–1915) III 151
Nares, Robert (1753–1829) II 155
Nary, Cornelius (1660–1738) I 97
Nash, Frederick (1782–1856) II 155
Nash, John (1752–1835) II 155
Nash, Joseph (1809–1878) III 151
Nash, J.N. (1893–1977) IV 78
Nash, Paul (1889–1946) IV 78
Nash, Richard (1674–1762) I 97
Nash(e), Thomas (1567–1601) I 97
Nash, T.R. (1725–1811) I 97
Nasmith, David (1799–1839) II 155
Nasmith, Sir Martin Dunbar- (1883–1965) IV 78
Nasmyth, Alexander (1758–1840) II 155
Nasmyth, Charles (1826–1861) III 151
Nasmyth, James (1808–1890) III 151
Nasmyth, Patrick (1787–1831) II 155
Nathan, 1st Baron (1889–1963) IV 78
Nathan, Sir Matthew (1862–1939) IV 78
Natter, Lorenz (1705–1763) II 155
Naunton, Sir Robert (1563–1635) I 97
Nayler, Sir George (1764?–1831) II 156
Nayler, James (1617?–1660) I 97
Neal, Daniel (1678–1743) I 97
Neale, Sir H.B., 2nd Bart (1765–1840) II 156
Neale, Sir J.E. (1890–1975) IV 78
Neale, Thomas (d1699?) I 97
Neaves, Charles Neaves, Lord (1800–1876) III 151
Needham, J.T. (1713–1781) II 156
Neele, Henry (1798–1828) II 156
Neild, James (1744–1814) II 156
Neile, Richard (1562–1640) I 97
Neill, A.S. (1883–1973) IV 78
Neill, J.G.S. (1810–1857) III 151
Neill, Patrick (1776–1851) II 156
Neilson, Julia Emilie (1868–1957) IV 78
Neilson, Lilian Adelaide (1848–1880) III 151
Neilson, Samuel (1761–1803) II 156
Neilson-Terry, Phyllis (1892–1977) IV 78
Nelson, 1st Earl (1757–1835) II 156
Nelson, 3rd Earl (1823–1913) III 151
Nelson, Viscount (1758–1805) II 156
Nelson, Viscountess (1761–1831) II 156

Nelson, Sir Frank (1883–1966) IV 78
Nelson, Robert (1656?–1715) I 97
Nelson, Thomas (1822–1892) III 151
Nelson, William (1816–1887) III 151
Nelson, Wolfred (1792–1863) II 156
Nelson of Stafford, 1st Baron (1887–1962) IV 78
Nepean, Sir Evan, 1st Bart (1751–1822) II 156
Nesbit, J.C. (1818–1862) III 151
Nesbitt, John (1661–1727) I 97
Nesbitt, Robert (1700–1761) II 156
Nesfield, W.E. (1835–1888) III 151
Nesse, Christopher (1621–1705) I 97
Nethersole, Sir Francis (1587–1659) I 97
Nethersole, Olga (1870?–1951) IV 78
Nettleship, Henry (1839–1893) III 151
Nettleship, R.L. (1846–1892) III 151
Neubauer, Adolf (1832–1907) III 151
Neve, Cornelius (fl 1637–1664) I 97
Nevill, Lady Dorothy (1826–1913) III 151–152
Neville, Edmund (1605–1647) I 97
Neville, George (1789–1854) II 156
Nevill(e), Grey (1681–1723) I 97
Neville, Sir Henry (1562?–1615) I 97
Neville, H.G. (1837–1910) III 152
Neville, R.N.A. (1717–1793) II 156
Nevill(e), Sir Thomas (d1542) I 97
Neville, Thomas (1547?–1614) I 97
Nevinson, C.R.W. (1889–1946) IV 78
Nevinson, H.W. (1856–1941) III 152
Newall, 1st Baron (1886–1963) IV 78
Newall, H.F. (1857–1944) III 152
Newall, R.S. (1812–1889) III 152
Newark, 1st Baron (d1682) I 97
Newberry, P.E. (1869–1949) IV 78
Newbold, Sir Douglas (1894–1945) IV 78
Newbold, T.J. (1807–1850) III 152
Newbolt, Sir H.J. (1862–1938) IV 78
Newburgh, 1st Earl of (d1670) I 97–98
Newcastle, 1st Duke of (1592–1676) I 98
Newcastle, Duke of (1662–1711) I 98
Newcastle, 1st Duke of (1693–1768) I 98
Newcastle, Duchess of (1624?–1674) I 98
Newcastle-under-Lyme, 2nd Duke of (1720–1794) II 156
Newcastle-under-Lyme, 4th Duke of (1785–1851) II 156
Newcastle-under-Lyme, 5th Duke of (1811–1864) III 152
Newcomb, Thomas (1682?–1765?) I 98
Newcome, Henry (1627–1695) I 98
Newcome, Peter (1656–1738) I 98
Newcome, William (1729–1800) II 156
Newcomen, Elias (1550?–1614) I 98
Newcourt, Richard (d1716) I 98
Newdegate, C.N. (1816–1887) III 152
Newdigate, Sir Richard, 1st Bart (1602–1678) I 98
Newdigate, Sir Roger, 5th Bart (1719–1806) II 156
Newell, E.J. (1771–1798) II 156
Newenham, Sir Edward (1732–1814) II 156–157
Newhall, Sir Walter Pringle, Lord (1664?–1736) I 98
Newhaven, 2nd Viscount (1657–1728) I 98
Newland, Abraham (1730–1807) II 157
Newman, F.W. (1805–1897) III 152
Newman, Sir George (1870–1948) IV 78
Newman, John (1677?–1741) I 98
Newman, John Henry (1801–1890) III 152
Newman, Thomas (1692–1758) I 98
Newmarch, Rosa Harriet (1857–1940) III 152
Newnes, Sir George, 1st Bart (1851–1910) III 152
Newport, Earl of (1597?–1666) I 98
Newport, Andrew (1623–1699) I 98
Newport, Sir John, 1st Bart (1756–1843) II 157
Newsam, Sir Frank (1893–1964) IV 78
Newsholme, Sir Arthur (1857–1943) III 152
Newte, John (1655?–1716) I 98
Newton, 2nd Baron (1857–1942) III 153
Newton, Alfred (1829–1907) III 152
Newton, Algernon (1880–1968) IV 78
Newton, Ann Mary (1832–1866) III 152
Newton, A.P. (1830–1883) III 152
Newton, Benjamin (1677–1735) I 98
Newton, Charles Hay, Lord (1740?–1811) II 157
Newton, Sir C.T. (1816–1894) III 152–153
Newton, Ernest (1856–1922) III 153
Newton, F.M. (1720–1794) I 157
Newton, G.S. (1794–1835) II 157
Newton, Sir Henry (1651–1715) I 98
Newton, Sir Isaac (1642–1727) I 98
Newton, James (1670?–1750) I 98
Newton, John (1622–1678) I 98
Newton, John (1725–1807) II 157
Newton, Richard (1676–1753) I 98
Newton, Robert (1780–1854) II 157
Newton, Thomas (1704–1782) II 157
Newton, William (1735–1790) II 157
Newton, W.J. (1785–1869) II 157
Nias, Sir Joseph (1793–1879) II 157
Nichol, John (1833–1894) III 153
Nicholas, Abraham (1692–1744?) I 98
Nicholas, Sir Edward (1593–1669) I 98

Nicholas, William (1785–1812) II 157
Nicholl, Sir John (1759–1838) II 157
Nicholls, Sir George (1781–1865) II 157
Nichols, Beverley (b1898?) IV 78–79
Nichols, John (1745–1826) II 157
Nichols, J.B. (1779–1863) II 157
Nichols, R.M.B. (1893–1944) IV 79
Nicholson, Ben (b1894) IV 79
Nicholson, Charles (1795–1837) II 157
Nicholson, Sir Charles, 1st Bart (1808–1903) III 153
Nicholson, C.E. (1868–1954) IV 79
Nicholson, Francis (1753–1844) II 157
Nicholson, George (1787–1878) II 157
Nicholson, John (1730–1796) II 157
Nicholson, John (1790–1843) II 157
Nicholson, John (1821–1857) III 153
Nicholson, J.S. (1850–1927) III 153
Nicholson, Sir Lothian (1828–1893) III 153
Nicholson, Margaret (1750?–1828) II 157
Nicholson, Peter (1765–1844) II 157
Nicholson, Renton (1809–1861) III 153
Nicholson, R.A. (1868–1945) IV 79
Nicholson, Sir S.H. (1875–1947) IV 79
Nicholson, William (1753–1815) II 157
Nicholson, William (1781–1844) II 157
Nicholson, Sir W.N.P. (1872–1949) IV 79
Nicholson of Roundhay, Baron (1845–1918) III 153
Nicol, Erskine (1825–1904) III 153
Nicolas, Sir J.T. (1788–1851) II 157
Nicoll, Alexander (1793–1828) II 157
Nicoll, Sir W.R. (1851–1923) III 153
Nicolls, Sir Augustine (1559–1616) I 98–99
Nicolls, Sir Jasper (1778–1849) II 157
Nicolson, Sir Harold (1886–1968) IV 79
Nicolson, William (1655–1727) I 99
Niemann, E.J. (1813–1876) III 153
Niemeyer, Sir Otto (1883–1971) IV 79
Nightingale, Florence (1820–1910) III 153
Nimmo, Alexander (1783–1832) II 157
Nisbet of Dirleton, Sir John (1609?–1687) I 99
Nisbett, Louisa Cranstoun (1812?–1858) III 153
Nithsdale, 5th Earl of (1676–1744) I 99
Nithsdale, Countess of (d1749) I 99
Nixon, F.R. (1803–1879) III 153
Nobbs, G.H. (1799–1884) II 157
Noble, Mark (1754–1827) II 157
Noble, Matthew (1818–1876) III 153
Noble, Sir P.L.H. (1880–1955) IV 79
Noble, W.H. (1834–1892) III 152
Noel, B.W. (1798–1873) II 157–158
Noel, G.T. (1782–1851) II 158
Noel, William (1695–1762) I 99
Noel-Baker, Baron (b1889) IV 79
Noel-Buxton, 1st Baron (1869–1948) IV 79
Nollekens, Joseph (1737–1823) II 158
Norbury, 1st Earl of (1745–1831) II 158
Norden, F.L. (1708–1742) II 158
Norfolk, 1st Duke of (1430?–1485) I 99
Norfolk, 2nd Duke of (1443–1524) I 99
Norfolk, 3rd Duke of (1473–1554) I 99
Norfolk, 4th Duke of (1536–1572) I 99
Norfolk, 6th Duke of (1628–1684) I 99
Norfolk, 7th Duke of (1655–1701) I 99
Norfolk, 10th Duke of (1720–1786) II 158
Norfolk, 11th Duke of (1746–1815) II 158
Norfolk, 12th Duke of (1765–1842) II 158
Norfolk, 13th Duke of (1791–1856) II 158
Norfolk, 14th Duke of (1815–1860) II 158
Norfolk, 15th Duke of (1847–1917) III 153–154
Norfolk, Duchess of (1494–1558) I 99
Norford, William (1715–1793) II 158
Norie, J.W. (1772–1843) II 158
Norman, Baron (1871–1950) IV 79
Norman, Conolly (1853–1908) III 154
Norman, G.W. (1793–1882) II 158
Norman, Sir H.W. (1826–1904) III 154
Normanby, 1st Marquess of (1797–1863) II 158
Normanby, 2nd Marquess of (1819–1890) III 154
Normandy, A.R. Le Mire de (1809–1864) III 154
Norris, Antony (1711–1786) II 158
Norris, Charles (1779–1858) II 158
Norris, Sir John (1547?–1597) I 99
Norris, John (1657–1711) I 99
Norris, Sir John (1660?–1749) I 99
Norris, John (1734–1777) II 158
Norris, J.P. (1823–1891) III 154
Norris, Thomas (1741–1790) II 158
Norrish, R.G.W. (1897–1978) IV 79
North, 1st Baron (1496?–1564) I 99
North, 3rd Baron (1581–1666) I 99
North, 4th Baron (1602–1677) I 99
North, 6th Baron (1678–1734) I 99
North, Brownlow (1741–1820) II 158
North, Brownlow (1810–1875) III 154
North, Sir Dudley (1641–1691) I 99
North, Sir D.B.N. (1881–1961) IV 79
North, D.L. (1748–1829) II 158

North, Sir Ford (1830–1913) III 154
North, Sir John (1551?–1597) I 99
North, John (1645–1683) I 99
North, Marianne (1830–1890) III 154
North, Roger (1653–1734) I 99
Northampton, Marquess of (1513–1571) I 99
Northampton, 1st Earl of (1540–1614) I 99
Northampton, 2nd Earl of (1601–1643) I 99
Northampton, 2nd Marquess of (1790–1851) II 158
Northbrook, 1st Baron (1796–1866) II 158–159
Northbrook, 1st Earl of (1826–1904) III 154
Northcliffe, 1st Viscount (1865–1922) IV 79
Northcote, Baron (1846–1911) III 154
Northcote, James (1746–1831) II 159
Northcote, Sir John, 1st Bart (1599–1676) I 99
Northesk, 7th Earl of (1758–1831) II 159
Northington, 1st Earl of (1708?–1772) II 159
Northington, 2nd Earl of (1747–1786) II 159
Northmore, Thomas (1766–1851) II 159
Northumberland, 1st Earl of (1342–1408) I 100
Northumberland, 7th Earl of (1528–1572) I 100
Northumberland, 9th Earl of (1564–1632) I 100
Northumberland, 10th Earl of (1602–1668) I 99–100
Northumberland, 2nd Duke of (1665–1716) I 100
Northumberland, 2nd Duke of (1742–1817) II 159
Northumberland, 1st Duke of (1715–1786) II 159
Northumberland, 3rd Duke of (1785–1847) II 159
Northumberland, 4th Duke of (1792–1865) II 159
Northumberland, 8th Duke of (1880–1930) IV 79
Norton, 1st Baron (1814–1905) III 154
Norton, E.F. (1884–1954) IV 79
Norton, John (b1662) I 100
Norton-Griffiths, Sir John, 1st Bart (1871–1930) IV 79
Norwich, 1st Viscount (1890–1954) IV 79
Norwich, Lady Diana Cooper, 1st Viscountess (b1892) IV 79
Norwood, Sir Cyril (1875–1956) IV 79–80
Nott, Sir Thomas (1606–1681) I 100
Nott, Sir William (1782–1845) II 159
Nottingham, 1st Earl of (1536–1624) I 100
Nottingham, 1st Earl of (1621–1682) I 100
Nourse, Edward (1701–1761) II 159
Novar, 1st Viscount (1860–1934) IV 80
Novello, Clara Anastasia (1818–1908) III 154
Novello, Ivor (1893–1951) IV 80
Novello, Vincent (1781–1861) II 159
Nowell, Alexander (1507?–1602) I 100
Nowell, Thomas (1730–1801) II 159
Noy(e), Sir William (1577–1634) I 100
Noyes, Alfred (1880–1958) IV 80
Nuffield, Viscount (1877–1963) IV 80
Nugent, Earl (1702–1788) II 160
Nugent, Baron (1788–1850) II 159–60
Nugent, 1st Baron (1895–1973) IV 80
Nugent, Christopher (d1742) I 100
Nugent, Christopher (c1715–1807) II 159
Nugent, Sir C.E. (1759?–1844) II 159
Nugent, Sir George, 1st Bart (1757–1849) II 159
Nugent, G.C. (1864–1915) IV 80
Nugent, Thomas (1700?–1772) II 160
Nunburnholme, 1st Baron (1833–1907) III 154
Nunn, Sir Percy (1870–1944) IV 80
Nuthall, Thomas (d1775) II 160
Nuttall, Enos (1842–1916) III 154
Nuttall, G.H.F. (1862–1937) IV 80
Nuttall, Thomas (1786–1859) II 160
Nye, Sir A.E. (1895–1967) IV 80
Nye, Nathaniel (b1624) I 100

Oakeley, Sir Charles, 1st Bart (1751–1826) II 161
Oakeley, Sir H.S. (1830–1903) III 155
Oakes, Sir Hildebrand, 1st Bart (1754–1822) II 161
Oakes, J.W. (1820–1887) III 155
Oakley, John (1834–1890) III 155
Oakley, Sir J.H. (1867–1946) IV 81
Oaksey, 1st Baron (1880–1971) IV 81
Oastler, Richard (1789–1861) II 161
Oates, L.E.G. (1880–1912) IV 81
Oates, Titus (1649–1705) I 101
O'Brien, Cornelius (1843–1906) III 155
O'Brien, D.H. (1785–1857) II 161
O'Brien, Henry (1808–1835) III 155
O'Brien, James (1805–1864) III 155
O'Brien, J.F.X. (1828–1905) III 155
O'Brien, Kate (1897–1974) IV 81
O'Brien, Matthew (1814–1855) III 155
O'Brien, Nelly (d1768) II 161
O'Brien, Sir Tom (1900–1970) IV 81
O'Brien, William (d1815) II 161
O'Brien, William (1852–1928) III 155
O'Brien, W.S. (1803–1864) III 155
O'Bryen, Edward (1754?–1808) II 161
O'Callaghan, J.C. (1805–1883) III 155
O'Casey, Sean (1880–1964) IV 81
Occleve, Thomas (1370?–1450?) I 101
Ochterlony, Sir David, 1st Bart (1758–1825) II 161
O'Connell, Daniel (1775–1847) II 161
O'Connell, John (1810–1858) III 155

O'Connell, Morgan (1804–1885) III 155
O'Connor, Arthur (1763–1852) II 161
O'Connor, C.Y. (1843–1902) III 155
O'Connor, Feargus (1794–1855) II 161
O'Connor, James (1836–1910) III 155
O'Connor, John (1830–1889) III 155
O'Connor, John (1870–1952) IV 81
O'Connor, Roger (1762–1834) II 161
O'Connor, T.P. (1848–1929) III 155
O'Conor, Charles (1710–1791) II 161
O'Conor, Charles (1764–1828) II 161
O'Conor, Sir N.R. (1843–1908) III 155
Odger, George (1820–1877) III 155
O'Donovan, Edmund (1844–1883) III 155
O'Donovan, John (1809–1861?) III 155
O'Dwyer, Sir M.F. (1864–1940) IV 81
O'Ferrall, R.M. (1797–1880) II 161
Offaley, Baroness (1588?–1658) I 100
Offor, George (1787–1864) II 161
Ogden, Samuel (1716–1778) II 161
Ogilby, John (1580?–1615) I 101
Ogilby, John (1600–1676) I 101
Ogilvie, Sir F.W. (1893–1949) IV 81
Ogilvie, John (1733–1813) II 161
Oglander, Sir John (1585–1655) I 101
Ogle, Sir Chaloner (1681–1750) I 101
Ogle, C.C. (1851–1878) III 155
Ogle, George (1742–1814) II 161
Ogle, Sir John (1569–1640) I 101
Ogle, John (1647?–1685) I 101
Oglethorpe, J.E. (1696–1785) I 101
O'Hagan, 1st Baron (1812–1885) III 155
O'Hara, Kane (1714?–1782) II 161
O'Higgins, K.C. (1892–1927) IV 81
O'Keeffe, John (1747–1833) II 161
O'Kelly, Dennis (1720?–1787) II 161–162
Okes, Richard (1797–1888) II 162
Okey, John (d1662) I 101
Oldcorne, Edward (1561–1606) I 101
Oldenburg, Henry (1615?–1677) I 101
Oldfield, Anne (1683–1730) I 101
Oldfield, Joshua (1656–1729) I 101
Oldham, Hugh (d1519) I 101
Oldham, John (1653–1683) I 101
Oldham, Nathaniel (fl 1724) I 101
Oldys, William (1696–1761) I 101
O'Leary, Arthur (1729–1802) II 162
O'Leary, John (1830–1907) III 156
Oliphant, Sir Lancelot (1881–1965) IV 81
Oliphant, Laurence (1829–1888) III 156
Oliphant, Margaret (1828–1897) III 156
Oliver, Emma Sophia (1819–1885) III 156
Oliver, F.W. (1864–1951) IV 81
Oliver, George (1867–1867) II 162
Oliver, Sir H.F. (1865–1965) IV 81
Oliver, Isaac (1556–1617) I 101
Oliver, Peter (1594–1648) I 101
Oliver, Richard (1734?–1784) II 162
Oliver, Sir R.G. (1882–1967) IV 81
Oliver, Thomas (1734–1815) II 162
Oliver, Sir Thomas (1853–1942) III 156
Oliver, Tom (1789–1864) II 162
Oliver, Vic (1898–1964) IV 81
Oliver, William (1695–1764) I 100
Olivier, Baron (1859–1943) III 156
Ollivant, Alfred (1798–1882) II 162
O'Loghlen, Sir C.M., 2nd Bart (1819–1877) III 156
O'Loghlen, Sir Michael, 1st Bart (1789–1842) II 162
Olsson, Julius (1864–1942) IV 81
O'Malley, George (d1843) II 162
O'Malley, Sir O. St Clair (1887–1974) IV 81
Oman, Sir C.W.C. (1860–1946) IV 81
Oman, J.W. (1860–1939) IV 81
Ommanney, Sir Erasmus (1814–1904) III 156
Ommanney, Sir J.A. (1773–1855) II 162
O'Neil, H.N. (1817–1880) III 156
O'Neill, 2nd Viscount and 1st Earl (1779–1841) II 162
O'Neill, Sir Phelim (1604?–1653)) I 101
Onions, C.T. (1873–1965) IV 81
Onions, Oliver (1873–1961) IV 81
Onslow, 1st Baron (1654–1717) I 102
Onslow, 1st Earl of (1731–1814) II 162
Onslow, 2nd Earl of (1755–1827) II 162
Onslow, 4th Earl of (1853–1911) III 156
Onslow, Arthur (1691–1768) I 101–102
Onslow, George (1731–1792) II 162
Onslow, George(s) (1784–1853) II 162
Onslow, Richard (1528–1571) I 102
Onslow, Sir Richard, 1st Bart (1741–1817) II 162
Opie, Amelia (1769–1853) II 162
Opie, John (1761–1807) II 162
Oppé, A.P. (1878–1957) IV 81
Oram, Edward (fl 1770) II 162
Orchard, W.E. (1877–1955) IV 81
Orchardson, Sir W.Q. (1832–1910) III 156
Ord, W.M. (1834?–1902) III 156

Orde, Sir John, 1st Bart (1751–1824) II *162*
O'Reilly, J.B. (1844–1890) III *156*
Orford, Earl of (1653–1727) I *102*
Orford, 1st Earl of (1676–1745) I *102*
Orford, 4th Earl of (1717–1797) II *162*
Orger, Mrs Mary Ann (1788–1849) II *162*
Oriel, 1st Baron (1740–1828) II *162*
Orkney, 1st Earl of (1666–1737) I *102*
Orleans, Duchess of (1644–1670) I *102*
Orme, Robert (1728–1801) II *162*
Orme, William (1787–1830) II *162–163*
Ormerod, Eleanor Anne (1828–1901) III *156*
Ormerod, George (1785–1873) II *163*
Ormonde, 8th Earl of (d1539) I *102*
Ormonde, 1st Duke of (1610–1688) I *102*
Ormonde, 2nd Duke of (1665–1745) I *102*
Orpen, Sir William (1878–1931) IV *81–82*
Orr, Alexandra Sutherland (1828–1903) III *156*
Orr, John (1885–1966) IV *82*
Orrery, 1st Earl of (1621–1679) I *102*
Orrery, 4th Earl of (1674–1731) I *102*
Orsborn, A.W.T. (1886–1967) IV *82*
Ortelius, Abraham (1527–1598) I *102*
Orton, Arthur (1834–1898) III *156*
Orton, Job (1717–1783) II *163*
Orwin, C.S. (1876–1955) IV *82*
Osbaldeston, George (1787–1866) II *163*
Osbaldeston, Richard (1690–1764) I *102*
Osborn, Baron (1808–1891) III *156*
Osborn(e), Henry (1698?–1771) I *102*
Osborn, Sherard (1822–1875) III *156*
Osborne, Malcolm (1880–1963) IV *82*
Osborne, R.B. (1808–1882) III *156*
Osborne, Lord S.G. (1808–1889) III *156*
Osborne, W.F. (1859–1903) III *156*
O'Shea, W.H. (1840–1905) III *156–157*
Osler, Sir William, Bart (1849–1919) III *157*
Ossington, 1st Viscount (1800–1873) III *157*
Ossory, Earl of (1634–1680) I *102*
O'Sullivan, Mortimer (1791?–1859) II *163*
Oswald, James (1715–1769) II *163*
Otter, William (1768–1840) II *163*
Ottley, W.Y. (1771–1836) II *163*
Otway, Caesar (1780–1842) II *163*
Otway, Sir R.W., 1st Bart (1770–1846) II *163*
Otway, Thomas (1652–1685) I *102*
Oughton, Sir J.A.D. (1720–1780) II *163*
Oughtred, William (1575–1660) I *102*
Ouless, W.W. (1848–1933) III *157*
Ouseley, Sir F.A.G., 2nd Bart (1825–1889) III *157*
Ouseley, Gideon (1762–1839) II *163*
Ouseley, Sir Gore, 1st Bart (1770–1844) II *163*
Ouseley, Sir William (1767–1842) II *163*
Ouseley, Sir W.G. (1797–1866) II *163*
Outram, Sir James, 1st Bart (1803–1863) III *157*
Ouvry, Frederic (1814–1881) III *157*
Overall, John (1560–1619) I *103*
Overbury, Sir Thomas (1581–1613) I *103*
Overstone, 1st Baron (1796–1883) II *163*
Overton, John (1640–1708?) I *103*
Overtoun, 1st Baron (1843–1908) III *157*
Owen, Alice (d1613) I *103*
Owen, Sir E.C.R. (1771–1849) II *163*
Owen, Harold (1897–1971) IV *82*
Owen, Henry (1716–1795) II *163*
Owen, Hugh (1784–1861) II *163*
Owen, Sir Hugh (1804–1881) III *157*
Owen, James (1654–1706) I *103*
Owen, John (1560?–1622) I *103*
Owen, Sir John (1600–1666) I *103*
Owen, John (1616–1683) I *103*
Owen, John (1766–1822) II *163*
Owen, John (1854–1926) III *157*
Owen, Sir Richard (1804–1892) III *157*
Owen, Robert (1771–1858) II *163*
Owen, Samuel (1769–1857) II *163*
Owen, Thomas (d1598) I *103*
Owen, William (1769–1825) II *163*
Owen, W.F. (1774–1857) II *163*
Owtram, William (1626–1679) I *103*
Oxberry, William (1784–1824) II *163*
Oxenden, Henry (1609–1670) I *103*
Oxenford, John (1812–1877) III *158*
Oxford, 10th Earl of (1340?–1400) I *103*
Oxford, 11th Earl of (1490?–1540) I *103*
Oxford, 17th Earl of (1550–1604) I *103*
Oxford, 18th Earl of (1593–1625) I *103*
Oxford, 20th Earl of (1626–1703) I *103*
Oxford, 1st Earl of (1661–1724) I *103*
Oxford, 2nd Earl of (1689–1741) I *103*
Oxford and Asquith, 1st Earl of (1852–1928) III *158*
Oxford and Asquith, Countess of (1864–1945) IV *82*

Pack, Sir Denis (1772?–1823) II *164*
Packe, Sir Christopher (1593?–1682) I *105*
Packer, J.H. (1730–1806) II *164*
Packington, Sir John (1649–1625) I *105*

Paddy, Sir William (1554–1634) I *105*
Page, Sir Archibald (1875–1949) IV *83*
Page, Sir Francis (1661?–1741) I *105*
Page, Sir F.H. (1885–1962) IV *83*
Page, Sir L.F. (1890–1951) IV *83*
Page, T.E. (1850–1936) III *159*
Page, William (1861–1934) IV *83*
Paget, 1st Baron (1505–1563) I *105*
Paget, Baron (d1742) I *105*
Paget, Sir Arthur (1771–1840) II *164*
Paget, Sir A.B. (1823–1896) III *159*
Paget, Lord A.H. (1816–1888) III *159*
Paget, Sir Bernard (1887–1961) IV *83*
Paget, Charles (1560–1612) I *105*
Paget, Sir Charles (1778–1839) II *164*
Paget, Lord C.E. (1811–1895) III *159*
Paget, Sir Edward (1775–1849) II *164*
Paget, Francis (1851–1911) III *159*
Paget, Lord G.A.F. (1818–1880) III *159*
Paget, Sir G.E. (1809–1892) III *159*
Paget, Dame Rosalind (1855–1948) III *159*
Paget, Sir James, 1st Bart (1814–1899) III *159*
Paget, Stephen (1855–1926) III *159*
Paget, Violet (1856–1935) III *159*
Paine, James (1725–1789) II *164*
Paine, James (d1829) II *164*
Paine, Thomas (1737–1809) II *164*
Painter, Edward (1784–1852) II *164*
Paisley, Baron (1543?–1622) I *105*
Pakenham, Sir E.M. (1778–1815) II *164*
Pakenham, Sir H.R. (1781–1850) II *164*
Pakenham, Sir Thomas (1757–1836) II *164*
Pakenham, Sir W.C. (1861–1933) IV *83*
Pakington, Dorothy, Lady (d1679) I *105*
Pakington, Sir John, 4th Bart (1671–1727) I *105*
Palairet, Sir Michael (1882–1956) IV *83*
Paley, William (1743–1805) II *164*
Palgrave, Sir Francis (1788–1861) II *164*
Palgrave, F.T. (1824–1897) III *159*
Palgrave, Sir R.F.D. (1829–1904) III *159*
Palgrave, W.G. (1826–1888) III *159*
Palles, Christopher (1831–1920) III *159*
Palliser, Sir Hugh, 1st Bart (1723–1796) II *164*
Palliser, Sir William (1830–1882) III *159*
Palmer, C.J. (1805–1882) III *159*
Palmer, Sir C.M., 1st Bart (1822–1907) III *159*
Palmer, E.H. (1840–1882) III *159*
Palmer, Sir Geoffrey (1598–1670) I *105*
Palmer, George (1818–1897) III *159–160*
Palmer, G.W. (1851–1913) III *160*
Palmer, Herbert (1601–1647) I *105*
Palmer, James (1585–1660) I *105*
Palmer, John (1741?–1798) II *164*
Palmer, John (1742–1818) II *164*
Palmer, J.H. (1808–1884) III *160*
Palmer, Robert (1757–1805?) II *164*
Palmer, Samuel (1741–1813) II *164*
Palmer, Samuel (1805–1881) III *160*
Palmer, Sir T.F. (1747–1802) II *164*
Palmer, Sir William (1883–1964) IV *83*
Palmerston, 3rd Viscount (1784–1865) II *164–165*
Palmerston, Viscountess (1787–1869) II *164*
Paneth, F.A. (1887–1958) IV *83*
Panizzi, Sir Anthony (1797–1879) II *165*
Pankhurst, Dame Christabel (1880–1958) IV *83*
Pankhurst, Emmeline (1858–1928) III *160*
Pankhurst, Sylvia (1882–1960) IV *83*
Panmure, 4th Earl of (1659?–1723) I *105*
Panmure, 1st Baron (1771–1852) II *165*
Pantin, C.F.A. (1899–1967) IV *83*
Panton, Thomas (d1685) I *105*
Paoli, Pascal (1725–1807) II *165*
Papillon, David (1581–1655?) I *105*
Papillon, Thomas (1623–1702) I *105*
Papineau, L.J. (1786–1871) II *165*
Papworth, J.B. (1775–1847) II *165*
Papworth, W.A. Van Sandau (1822–1894) III *160*
Pardoe, Julia (1806–1862) III *160*
Parepa-Rosa, E.P. de Boyesku (1836–1874) III *160*
Pares, Sir Bernard (1867–1949) IV *83*
Paris, Sir Archibald (1861–1937) IV *83*
Paris, J.A. (1785–1856) II *165*
Parish, Sir Woodbine (1796–1882) II *165*
Park, Bertram (1883–1972) IV *83*
Park, Sir J.A. (1763–1838) II *165*
Park, Mungo (1771–1806) II *165*
Park, Patric (1811–1855) III *160*
Park, Thomas (1759–1834) II *165*
Parke, Daniel (1669–1710) I *105*
Parke, John (1745–1829) II *165*
Parke, T.H. (1857–1893) III *105*
Parker, Cecil (1897–1971) IV *83*
Parker, Sir C.C., 5th Bart (1792–1869) II *165*
Parker, C.S. (1829–1910) III *160*
Parker, George (1651–1743) I *105*
Parker, George (1732–1800) II *165*
Parker, Sir Gilbert, Bart (1862–1932) IV *83*

Parker, Sir Hyde, 5th Bart (1714–1782) II *165*
Parker, Sir Hyde (1739–1807) II *165*
Parker, H.P. (1795–1873) II *165*
Parker, John (d1765?) II *165*
Parker, Joseph (1830–1902) III *160*
Parker, J.H. (1806–1884) III *160*
Parker, J.W. (1792–1870) II *165*
Parker, L.N. (1852–1944) III *160*
Parker, Matthew (1504–1575) I *105*
Parker, Sir Peter, 1st Bart (1721–1811) II *165*
Parker, Sir Peter, 2nd Bart (1785–1814) II *165*
Parker, Sir Philip (fl 1578–1580) I *105*
Parker, Richard -1767?–1797) II *165*
Parker, Samuel (1681–1730) I *105*
Parker, Sir Thomas (1695?–1784) I *105*
Parker, T.L. (1779–1858) II *165*
Parker, Sir William, 1st Bart (1743–1802) II *165*
Parker, Sir William, 1st Bart (1781–1866) II *165*
Parker of Waddington, Baron (1857–1918) III *160*
Parker of Waddington, Baron (1900–1972) IV *83*
Parkes, David (1763–1833) II *166*
Parkes, E.A. (1819–1876) III *160*
Parkes, Sir Henry (1815–1896) III *160*
Parkes, Sir H.S. (1828–1885) III *160*
Parkes, Samuel (1761–1825) II *166*
Parkhurst, John (1512?–1575) I *105*
Parkhurst, John (1728–1797) II *166*
Parkin, Sir G.R. (1846–1922) III *160*
Parkinson, John (1567–1650) I *105*
Parkyns, Sir Thomas, 2nd Bart (1664–1741) I *105*
Parmoor, 1st Baron (1852–1941) III *160*
Parnell, C.S. (1846–1891) III *160–161*
Parnell, Sir John, 2nd Bart (1744–1801) II *166*
Parnell, Thomas (1679–1718) I *106*
Parr, George (1826–1891) III *161*
Parr, Samuel (1747–1825) II *166*
Parr, Thomas (1483?–1635) I *106*
Parratt, Sir Walter (1841–1924) III *161*
Parris, E.T. (1793–1873) II *166*
Parry, C.H. (1755–1822) II *166*
Parry, Sir C.H.H., Bart (1848–1918) III *161*
Parry, Sir D.H. (1893–1973) IV *83*
Parry, Edward (d1650) I *106*
Parry, Edward (1830–1890) III *161*
Parry, Sir Edward (1893–1972) IV *83*
Parry, John (d1782) II *166*
Parry, John (1776–1851) II *166*
Parry, Joseph (1744–1826) II *166*
Parry, J.H. (1816–1880) III *161*
Parry, J.O. (1810–1879) III *161*
Parry, Sir Thomas (d1560) I *106*
Parry, Sir W.E. (1790–1855) II *166*
Parsons, A.W. (1847–1920) III *161*
Parsons, Sir C.A. (1854–1931) III *161*
Parsons, Edward (1762–1833) II *166*
Parsons, Edward (1797–1844) II *166*
Parsons, Humphrey (1676?–1741) I *106*
Parsons, James (1705–1770) II *166*
Parsons, James (1799–1877) II *166*
Parsons, John (1761–1819) II *166*
Parsons, Sir J.H. (1868–1957) IV *83*
Parsons, Sir L.G. (1879–1950) IV *83*
Parsons, Robert (1546–1610) I *106*
Parsons, R.G. (1882–1948) IV *83*
Parsons, Sir William, 1st Bart (1570?–1650) I *106*
Parsons, William (1658–1725?) I *106*
Parsons, William (1736–1795) II *166*
Parsons, Sir William (1746?–1817) II *166*
Partington, Miles (b1751) II *166*
Partridge, Sir Bernard (1861–1945) IV *83–84*
Partridge, John (1644–1715) I *106*
Partridge, John (1790–1872) II *166*
Partridge, Richard (1805–1873) III *161*
Pasco, John (1774–1853) II *166*
Pasley, Sir C.W. (1780–1861) II *166*
Pasley, Sir Thomas, 1st Bart (1734–1808) II *166*
Pasor, Mathias (1599–1658) I *106*
Passfield, Lady (1858–1943) III *161*
Passfield, Baron (1859–1947) III *161*
Paston, Sir William (1528–1610) I *106*
Patch, Richard (1770?–1806) II *166*
Patch, Thomas (d1782) II *166–167*
Pate, Richard (1516–1588) I *106*
Pater, Walter (1839–1894) III *161*
Paterson, Sir A.H. (1861–1947) IV *84*
Paterson, John (1776–1855) IV *167*
Paterson, William (1658–1719) I *106*
Paterson, William (1874–1956) IV *84*
Paterson, W.P. (1860–1939) IV *84*
Patey, Janet Monach (1842–1894) III *161*
Patmore, Coventry (1823–1896) III *161*
Paton, David (fl 1650–1700) I *106*
Paton, Geroge (1721–1807) II *167*
Paton, J.B. (1830–1911) III *161*
Paton, Sir J.N. (1821–1901) III *161*
Paton, W.H. (1828–1895) III *162*
Patrick, Simon (1626–1707) I *106*

Patterson, Robert (1802–1872) III *162*
Patterson, Sir W.R. (1893–1954) IV *84*
Patteson, Sir John (1790–1861) II *167*
Patteson, J.C. (1827–1871) III *162*
Patti, Adelina (1843–1919) III *162*
Patti, Carlotta (1835–1889) III *162*
Pattison, Dorothy Wyndlow (1832–1878) III *162*
Pattison, Mark (1813–1884) III *162*
Pattison, William (1706–1727) II *167*
Pattrick, George (1746–1800) II *167*
Paul, Sir G.O., 2nd Bart (1746–1820) II *167*
Paul, Hamilton (1773–1854) II *167*
Paul, H.W. (1853–1935) III *162*
Paul, Isabella Howard (1833?–1879) III *162*
Paul, Sir J.D., 2nd Bart (1802–1868) III *162*
Paul, William (1678–1716) I *106*
Paulet, Sir Amias (*d*1538) I *106*
Paulet, Sir Amias (1536?–1588) I *106*
Paulet, Sir Hugh (*d*1572?) I *106*
Paulet, Lord William (1804–1893) III *162*
Paull, James (1770–1808) II *167*
Pauncefote, 1st Baron (1828–1902) III *162*
Pavy, F.W. (1829–1911) III *162*
Paxton, Sir Joseph (1801–1865) III *162*
Paye, R.M. (*d*1821) II *167*
Payn, James (1830–1898) III *162*
Payne, George (1781–1848) II *167*
Payne, George (1803–1878) III *162*
Payne, Joseph (1808–1876) III *162*
Payne, J.F. (1840–1910) III *162*
Payne, J.W. (1752–1803) II *167*
Payne, Roger (1739–1797) II *167*
Payne, W.H.S. (1804–1878) III *162*
Peabody, George (1795–1869) II *167*
Peacock, Sir Barnes (1810–1890) III *162*
Peacock, Sir E.R. (1871–1962) IV *84*
Peacock, George (1791–1858) II *167*
Peacock, Thomas Love (1785–1866) II *167*
Peacocke, J.F. (1835–1916) III *162*
Peake, Sir C.B.P. (1897–1958) IV *84*
Peake, F.G. (1886–1970) IV *84*
Peake, H.J.E. (1867–1946) IV *84*
Peake, Sir Robert (1592?–1667) I *106*
Pearce, E.H. (1865–1930) IV *84*
Pearce, Samuel (1766–1799) II *167*
Pearce, Stephen (1819–1904) III *162*
Pearce, Zachary (1690–1774) I *106*
Peard, J.W. (1811–1880) II *167*
Pearman, William (fl 1810–1824) III *167*
Pears, S.A. (1815–1875) III *162*
Pearsall, Richard (1698–1762) I *106*
Pearsall, Robert Lucas de (1795–1856) II *167*
Pearse, Edward (1633?–1674?) I *106*
Pearson, A.C. (1861–1935) IV *84*
Pearson, Sir C.A., 1st Bart (1866–1921) IV *84*
Pearson, C.H. (1830–1894) III *163*
Pearson, Edward (1756–1811) II *167*
Pearson, George (1751–1828) II *167*
Pearson, Hugh (1817–1882) III *163*
Pearson, John (1613–1686) I *106*
Pearson, J.L. (1817–1897) III *163*
Pearson, Karl (1857–1936) III *163*
Pearson, Sir Richard (1731–1806) II *167*
Pearson, Richard (1765–1836) II *167*
Pearson, Sir R.B. (1871–1952) IV *84*
Pearson, William (1767–1847) II *167*
Pease, Edward (1767–1858) II *167*
Pease, Joseph (1772–1846) II *167*
Pease, Joseph (1799–1872) II *167*
Pease, Sir J.W., 1st Bart (1828–1903) III *163*
Peck, Francis (1692–1743) I *106*
Peckard, Peter (1718?–1797) II *167*
Pecke, Thomas (fl 1655–1664) I *106*
Peckham, John (*d*1292) I *106*
Peckwell, Henry (1747–1787) II *167*
Peddie, James (1758–1845) II *167*
Peecke, Richard (fl 1620–1626) I *106*
Peel, 1st Viscount (1829–1912) III *163*
Peel, 2nd Viscount and 1st Earl (1867–1937) IV *84*
Peel, Sir Frederick (1823–1906) III *163*
Peel, Jonathan (1799–1879) II *167–168*
Peel, Sir Robert, 1st Bart (1750–1830) II *168*
Peel, Sir Robert, 2nd Bart (1788–1850) II *168*
Peel, Sir Robert, 3rd Bart (1822–1895) III *163*
Peel, Sir William (1824–1858) III *163*
Peers, Sir C.R. (1868–1952) IV *84*
Peet, T.E. (1882–1934) IV *84*
Pegge, Sir Christopher (1765–1822) II *168*
Pegge, Samuel (1704–1796) II *168*
Peile, John (1838–1910) III *163*
Peirson, Sir R.E.C. (1892–1970) IV *84*
Peirson, Francis (1757–1781) II *168*
Pelham, George (1766–1827) II *168*
Pelham, Henry (1695?–1754) I *106*
Pelham, H.F. (1846–1907) III *163*
Pelham, J.T. (1811–1894) III *163*
Pell, Sir W.O. (1788–1869) II *168*

Pellatt, Apsley (1791–1863) II *168*
Pellegrini, Carlo (1839–1889) III *163*
Pellett, Thomas (1671?–1744) I *106*
Pelly, Sir J.H., 1st Bart (1777–1852) II *168*
Pelly, Sir Lewis (1825–1892) III *163*
Pember, E.H. (1833–1911) III *163*
Pember, F.W. (1862–1954) IV *84*
Pemberton, C.R. (1765–1822) II *168*
Pemberton, C.R. (1790–1840) II *168*
Pemberton, Sir Francis (1625–1697) I *106–107*
Pemberton, Henry (1694–1771) I *107*
Pemble, William (1592?–1623) I *107*
Pembroke, 1st Earl of (*d*1219) I *107*
Pembroke, 2nd Earl of (*d*1231) I *107*
Pembroke, titular Earl of (*d*1296) I *107*
Pembroke, 2nd Earl of (*d*1324) I *107*
Pembroke, 1st Earl of (1507?–1570?) I *107*
Pembroke, 2nd Earl of (1534?–1601) I *107*
Pembroke, 3rd Earl of (1580–1630) I *107*
Pembroke, 4th Earl of (1584–1650) I *107*
Pembroke, 5th Earl of (1619–1669) I *107*
Pembroke, 8th Earl of (1656–1733?) I *107*
Pembroke, 9th Earl of (1693–1750) I *107*
Pembroke, 10th Earl of (1734–1794) II *168*
Pembroke, 11th Earl of (1759–1827) II *168*
Pembroke, 13th Earl of (1850–1895) III *163*
Pembroke, Countess of (1555?–1621) I *107*
Pembroke and Montgomery, Countess of (1590–1676) I *107*
Pender, Sir John (1815–1896) III *163*
Penderel, Richard (*d*1672) I *107*
Pengelly, Sir Thomas (1675–1730) I *107*
Pengelly, William (1812–1894) III *163*
Penington, Sir John (1568?–1646) I *107*
Penley, A.E. (1807–1870) III *163*
Penley, W.S. (1852–1912) III *163–164*
Penn, Granville (1761–1844) II *168*
Penn, John (1760–1834) II *168*
Penn, Richard (1784–1863) II *168*
Penn, Thomas (1702–1775) II *168*
Penn, Sir William (1621–1670) I *107*
Pennant, Thomas (1726–1798) II *168*
Pennefather, Catherine (1818–1893) III *164*
Pennefather, Edward (1774?–1847) II *168*
Pennefather, Richard (1773–1859) II *168*
Pennington, Sir Isaac (1587?–1661) I *107*
Pennington, Sir Isaac (1745–1817) II *168*
Penny, Edward (1714–1791) II *168*
Penny, Thomas (*d*1589) I *107*
Penny, William (1809–1892) III *164*
Penrhyn, Baron (1737?–1808) II *168–169*
Penrhyn, 1st Baron (1800–1886) III *164*
Penrhyn, 2nd Baron (1836–1907) III *164*
Penrose, Sir C.V. (1759–1830) II *169*
Penrose, Dame Emily (1858–1942) III *164*
Penrose, F.C. (1817–1903) III *164*
Penrose, John (1778–1859) II *169*
Penrose, Thomas (1742–1779) II *169*
Penruddock, John (1619–1655) I *108*
Penshurst, 1st Baron (1780–1855) II *169*
Penzance, Baron (1816–1899) III *164*
Pepler, Sir G.L. (1882–1959) IV *84*
Peploe, Samuel (1668–1752) I *108*
Pepusch, J.C. (1667–1752) I *108*
Pepys, Elizabeth (1640–1669) I *108*
Pepys, Henry (1783–1860) II *169*
Pepys, Sir Lucas, 1st Bart (1742–1830) II *169*
Pepys, Samuel (1633–1703) I *108*
Pepys, W.H. (1775–1856) II *169*
Perceval, Alexander (1787–1858) II *169*
Perceval, Sir Philip (1605–1647) I *108*
Perceval, Sir Richard (1550–1620) I *108*
Perceval, Spencer (1762–1812) II *169*
Percival, A.E. (1887–1966) IV *84*
Percival, John (1834–1918) III *164*
Percy, Alan (*d*1560) I *108*
Percy, Esmé (1887–1957) IV *84*
Percy, George (1580–1632) I *108*
Percy, Hugh (1784–1856) II *169*
Percy, Lord H.H.M. (1817–1877) III *164*
Percy, Thomas (1560–1605) I *108*
Percy, Thomas (1729–1811) II *169*
Percy of Alnwick, Baron (*d*1659) I *108*
Percy of Newcastle, Baron (1887–1958) IV *84*
Pereira, G.E. (1865–1923) IV *84*
Pereira, Jonathan (1804–1853) III *164*
Perigal, Arthur (1816–1884) III *164*
Perkin, A.G. (1861–1937) IV *84*
Perkin, Sir W.H. (1838–1907) III *164*
Perkin, W.H. (1860–1929) IV *84*
Perkins, Joseph (fl 1675–1711) I *108*
Perkins, William (1558–1602) I *108*
Perne, Andrew (1519?–1589) I *108*
Perowne, E.H. (1826–1906) III *164*
Perowne, J.J.S. (1833–1904) III *164*
Perrin, Louis (1782–1864) II *169*

Perring, W.G.A. (1898–1951) IV *84*
Perrins, C.W.D. (1864–1958) IV *84*
Perronet, Vincent (1693–1785) I *108*
Perrot, Sir John (1527?–1592) I *108*
Perrott, Sir Richard, 2nd Bart (*d*1796) II *169*
Perry, Baron (1878–1956) IV *84*
Perry, Charles (1807–1891) III *164*
Perry, George (1793–1862) II *169*
Perry, James (1756–1821) II *169*
Perry, Sampson (1747–1823) II *169*
Perry, Sir T.E. (1806–1882) III *164*
Perryn, Sir Richard (1723–1803) II *169*
Perse, Stephen (1548–1615) I *108*
Perth, 4th Earl and 1st titular Duke of (1648–1716) I *108*
Perth, 5th Earl and 2nd titular Duke of (1675–1720) I *108*
Perth, 6th Earl and 3rd titular Duke of (1713–1746) II *169*
Perth, 7th Earl and 4th titular Duke of (1714–1747) II *169*
Perth, 16th Earl of (1876–1951) IV *84*
Pery, Viscount (1719–1806) II *169*
Peryam, Sir William (1534–1604) I *108*
Petavel, Sir J.E. (1873–1936) IV *84–85*
Peter, 'The Wild Boy' (1712–1785) II *169*
Peterborough, 1st Earl of (*d*1642) I *108*
Peterborough, 3rd Earl of (1658–1735) I *108*
Peterborough, Countess of (*d*1755) I *108*
Peters, Hugh (1598–1660) I *108–109*
Peters, M.W. (1742–1814) II *169*
Peterson, Sir M.D. (1889–1952) IV *85*
Pether, William (1738?–1821) II *169*
Pethick-Lawrence, Baron (1871–1961) IV *85*
Pethick-Lawrence, Lady (1867–1954) IV *85*
Petit, Sir D.M., 1st Bart (1823–1901) III *164*
Petit, J.L. (1736–1780) II *169*
Peto, Sir S.M., 1st Bart (1809–1889) III *164*
Petre, 4th Baron (*c*1626–1684) I *109*
Petre, Edward (1631–1699) I *109*
Petre, Sir G.G. (1822–1905) III *164*
Petrie, Sir Flinders (1853–1942) III *164*
Petrie, George (1789–1866) II *169–170*
Petrucci, Ludovico (fl 1603–1619) I *109*
Pett, Peter (1610–1670) I *109*
Pett, Phineas (1570–1647) I *109*
Pettie, John (1839–1893) III *164*
Pettigrew, J.B. (1834–1908) III *165*
Pettigrew, T.J. (1791–1865) II *170*
Pettus, Sir John (1613–1690) I *109*
Petty, Sir William (1623–1687) I *109*
Petyt, Sylvester (*d*1719) I *109*
Petyt, William (1636–1707) I *109*
Peyton, Sir Henry (*d*1622?) I *109*
Phayre, Sir A.P. (1812–1885) III *165*
Phayre, Sir Robert (1820–1897) III *165*
Phelips, Sir Edward (1560?–1614) I *109*
Phelips, Sir Robert (1586?–1638) I *109*
Phelps, L.R. (1853–1936) III *165*
Phelps, Samuel (1804–1878) III *165*
Philby, H. St. J.B. (1885–1960) IV *85*
Philidor, F.A.D. (1726–1795) II *170*
Philip II of Spain (1527–1598) I *109*
Philip, A.P.W. (1772–1851?) II *170*
Philip, John (1775–1851) II *170*
Philip, J.B. (1824–1875) III *165*
Philip, Robert (1791–1858) II *170*
Philip, Sir R.W. (1857–1939) III *165*
Philiphaugh, Lord (1655–1708) I *109*
Philippa of Hainault (1314?–1369) I *109*
Philipps, Sir Erasmus, 5th Bart (*d*1743) I *109*
Philipps, Fabian (1601–1690) I *109*
Philipps, Sir Ivor (1861–1940) IV *85*
Philipps, Thomas (1774–1841) II *170*
Philips, Ambrose (1675?–1749) I *109*
Philips, F.C. (1849–1921) III *165*
Philips, John (1676–1709) I *109*
Philips, Katherine (1631–1664) I *109*
Philips, Robert (*d*1650?) I *109*
Phillimore, 1st Baron (1845–1929) III *165*
Phillimore, J.S. (1873–1926) IV *85*
Phillimore, Sir R.F. (1864–1940) IV *85*
Phillimore, Sir R.J., 1st Bart (1810–1885) III *165*
Phillip, Arthur (1738–1814) II *170*
Phillip, John (1817–1867) III *165*
Phillips, S.M. (1780–1862) II *170*
Phillips, Sir Thomas, 1st Bart (1792–1872) II *170*
Phillips, Charles (1787?–1859) II *170*
Phillips, Sir Claude (1846–1924) III *165*
Phillips, George (1804–1892) III *165*
Phillips, Henry (1801–1876) III *165*
Phillips, H.W. (1820–1868) III *165*
Phillips, John (1800–1874) III *165*
Phillips, Molesworth (1755–1832) II *170*
Phillips, Sir Richard (1767–1840) II *170*
Phillips, Richard (1778–1851) II *170*
Phillips, Stephen (1864–1915) IV *85*
Phillips, Thomas (1760–1851) II *170*
Phillips, Thomas (1770–1845) II *170*
Phillips, Sir Thomas (1801–1867) III *165*
Phillips, Teresa Constantia (1709–1765) II *170*

Phillips, Sir T.S.V. (1888–1941) IV 85
Phillips, Sir T.W. (1883–1966) IV 85
Phillips, Watts (1825–1874) III 165
Phillips, William (1731?–1781) II 170
Phillpotts, Dame Bertha Surtees (1877–1932) IV 85
Phillpotts, Eden (1862–1960) IV 85
Phillpotts, Henry (1778–1869) II 170
Philpot, Glyn (1884–1937) IV 85
Philpot, John (1516–1555) I 109
Philpott, Henry (1807–1892) III 165
Phipps, Sir Constantine (1656–1723) I 109
Phipps, Sir C.B. (1801–1866) III 165
Phipps, C.J. (1835–1897) III 165
Phipps, Edmund (1760–1837) II 170
Phipps, Edmund (1808–1857) III 165–166
Phipps, Sir E.C.E. (1875–1945) IV 85
Piatti, A.C. (1822–1901) III 166
Pick, Frank (1878–1941) IV 85
Pickard, Benjamin (1842–1904) III 166
Pickard, Sir R.H. (1874–1949) IV 85
Pickering, Sir William (1516–1575) I 109
Pickersgill, F.R. (1820–1900) III 166
Pickersgill, H.W. (1782–1875) II 170
Picton, Sir J.A. (1805–1889) III 166
Picton, Sir Thomas (1758–1815) II 170
Pierce, Edward (d 1698) I 109
Pierce, S.E. (1746–1829) II 170
Piercy, 1st Baron (1886–1966) IV 85
Piers, John (1523?–1594) I 109
Pierson, H.H. (1815–1873) III 166
Pigot, Baron (1719–1777) II 171
Pigot, D.R. (1797–1873) II 170–171
Pigott, Richard (1828?–1889) III 166
Pigou, A.C. (1877–1959) IV 85
Pike, J.D.G. (1784–1854) II 171
Pike, Samuel (1717?–1773) II 171
Pilch, Fuller (1803–1870) III 166
Pilcher, Sir Gonne (1890–1966) IV 85
Pilkington, Laetitia (1712–1750) II 171
Pilkington, Mary (1766–1839) II 171
Pilkington, Sir Thomas (d 1691) I 109
Pillans, James (1778–1864) II 171
Pim, B.C.T. (1826–1886) III 166
Pinchbeck, Christopher (1670?–1732) I 109
Pinchbeck, Christopher (1710?–1783) II 171
Pinckard, George (1768–1835) II 171
Pindar, Sir Paul (1565?–1650) I 109
Pine, John (1690–1756) I 109
Pinero, Sir A.W. (1855–1934) III 166
Pingo, Thomas (1692–1776) I 110
Pinke, Robert (1572?–1647) I 110
Pinkerton, John (1758–1826) II 171
Pinkethman, William (d 1725) I 110
Pinnock, William (1782–1843) II 171
Pinto, G.F. (1787–1806) II 171
Pinto, Thomas (1710?–1773) II 171
Pinwell, G.J. (1842–1875) III 166
Piozzi, Gabriel (1741–1809) II 171
Piozzi, Hester (1741–1821) II 171
Pirbright, 1st Baron (1840–1903) III 166
Pirrie, Viscount (1847–1924) III 166
Pissarro, Camille (1893–1968) IV 85
Pissarro, Lucien (1863–1944) IV 85
Pistrucci, Benedetto (1784–1855) II 171
Pitcairn, David (1749–1809) II 171
Pitcairn, Robert (1793–1855) II 171
Pitcairn, William (1711–1791) II 171
Pitcairne, Archibald (1652–1713) I 110
Pitman, Sir H.A. (1808–1908) III 166
Pitman, Sir Isaac (1813–1897) III 166
Pitt, Ann (1720?–1799) II 171
Pitt, Christopher (1699–1748) I 110
Pitt, William (1759–1806) II 171
Pix, Mary (1666–1720? I 110
Place, Francis (1647–1728) I 110
Place, Francis (1771–1854) II 171
Plampin, Robert (1762–1834) II 171
Planché, J.R. (1796–1880) II 171–172
Planta, Joseph (1744–1827) II 172
Planta, Joseph (1787–1847) II 172
Platnauer, Maurice (1887–1974) IV 85
Playfair, Sir H.L. (1786–1861) II 172
Playfair, John (1748–1819) II 172
Playfair, Sir N.R. (1874–1934) IV 85
Playfair, W.H. (1789–1857) II 172
Playfair, W.S. (1835–1903) III 166
Playfair of St Andrews, Baron (1818–1898) III 166–167
Playford, John (1623–1686?) I 110
Pleasants, Thomas (1728–1818) II 172
Plender, Baron (1861–1946) IV 85
Plimer, Andrew (1763–1837) II 172
Plimer, Nathaniel (1751–1822) II 172
Plimsoll, Samuel (1824–1898) III 167
Plot, Robert (1640–1696) I 110
Plowden, A.C. (1844–1914) III 167
Plowden, Edmund (1518–1585) I 110
Plowden, F.P. (1749–1829) II 172

Plukenet, Leonard (1642–1706) I 110
Plumer, 1st Viscount (1857–1932) III 167
Plumer, Sir Thomas (1753–1824) II 172
Plummer, H.C.K. (1875–1946) IV 85
Plumptre, Anna (1760–1818) II 172
Plumptre, E.H. (1821–1891) III 167
Plumptre, Henry (d 1746) I 110
Plumptre, John (1753–1825) II 172
Plumptre, Robert (1723–1788) II 172
Plumridge, Sir J.H. (1787–1863) II 172
Plunket, 1st Baron, (1764–1854) II 172
Plunket, 4th Baron (1828–1897) III 167
Plunket, Oliver (1629–1681) I 110
Plunkett, Elizabeth (1769–1823) II 172
Plunkett, Sir H.C. (1854–1932) III 167
Plymouth, 1st Earl of (1627?–1687) I 110
Pocahontas (1595–1617) I 110
Pocock, Sir George (1706–1792) II 172
Pocock, Lewis (1808–1882) III 167
Pocock, Nicholas (1741?–1821) II 172
Pococke, Edward (1604–1691) I 110
Poel, William (1814–1900) III 167
Poland, Sir H.B. (1829–1928) III 167
Pole, Sir C.M. (1757–1830) II 172
Pole, Reginald (1500–1558) I 110
Pole, William (1814–1900) III 167
Polidori, J.W. (1795–1821) II 172
Polkemmet, William Baillie, Lord (d 1816) II 172
Pollard, A.F. (1869–1948) IV 85–86
Pollard, A.W. (1859–1944) III 167
Pollard, Robert (1755–1838) II 172
Pollexfen, Sir Henry (1632?–1691) I 110
Pollitt, G.P. (1878–1964) IV 86
Pollitt, Harry (1890–1960) IV 86
Pollock, Bertram (1863–1943) IV 86
Pollock, Sir C.E. (1823–1897) III 167
Pollock, Sir Frederick, 3rd Bart (1845–1937) III 167
Pollock, Sir George, 1st Bart (1786–1872) II 172
Pollock, Sir J.F., 1st Bart (1783–1750) II 172
Pollock, Sir W.F., 2nd Bart (1815–1888) III 167
Pollock, Robert (1798–1827) II 172
Polton, Sir William Calderwood, Lord (1660?–1733) I 110
Polwhele, Richard (1760–1838) II 172–173
Pomfret, 4th Earl of (1770–1833) II 173
Pomfret, Henrietta Louisa Fermor (1703–1761) II 173
Pomfret, Samuel (1650–1722) I 110
Pond, Arthur (1705?–1758) II 173
Ponsonby, 1st Baron (1744–1806) II 173
Ponsonby, Viscount and 2nd Baron (1770?–1855) II 173
Ponsonby, Sir F.C. (1783–1837) II 173
Ponsonby, George (1755–1817) II 173
Ponsonby, Henry (d 1745) I 110
Ponsonby, Sir H.F. (1825–1895) III 167
Ponsonby, John (1713–1787) II 173
Ponsonby, Sarah (1755?–1831) II 173
Ponsonby, Sir William (1772–1815) II 173
Ponsonby of Shulbrede, 1st Baron (1871–1946) IV 86
Ponting, H.G. (1870–1935) IV 86
Ponton, Mungo (1802–1880) III 167
Poole, A.L. (1889–1963) IV 86
Poole, John (1786?–1872) II 173
Poole, Matthew (1624–1679) I 110
Poole, P.F. (1807–1879) III 167
Poole, Robert (1708–1752) II 173
Poole, R.L. (1857–1939) III 167–168
Poole, R.S. (1832–1895) III 168
Pope, Alexander (1688–1744) I 110
Pope, Alexander (1763–1835) II 173
Pope, Clara Maria (d 1838) II 173
Pope, Elizabeth (1740–1797) II 173
Pope, G.U. (1820–1908) III 168
Pope, Jane (1742–1818) II 173
Pope, Maria Ann (1775–1803) II 173
Pope, Samuel (1826–1901) III 168
Pope, Sir Thomas (1507?–1559) I 110
Pope, W.B. (1820–1903) III 168
Pope, Sir W.J. (1870–1939) IV 86
Popham, A.E. (1889–1970) IV 86
Popham, Edward (1610?–1651) I 110
Popham, Sir H.R. (1762–1820) II 173
Popham, Sir John (1531?–1607) I 111
Popham, William (d 1821) II 173
Pordage, John (1607–1681) I 111
Porson, Richard (1759–1808) II 173
Portal, Viscount (1885–1949) IV 86
Portal, Sir G.H. (1858–1894) III 168
Portal, Melville (1819–1904) III 168
Portal of Hungerford, 1st Viscount (1893–1971) IV 86
Porter, Baron (1877–1956) IV 86
Porter, Anna Maria (1780–1832) II 173
Porter, Endymion (1587–1649) I 111
Porter, Sir G.H., 1st Bart (1822–1895) III 168
Porter, Jane (1776–1850) II 173
Porter, Sir R.K. (1777–1842) II 173
Porteus, Beilby (1731–1808) II 173
Portland, 1st Earl of (1577–1635) I 111
Portland, 1st Earl of (1649–1709) I 111

Portland, 3rd Duke of (1738–1809) II 173–174
Portlester, Baron (d 1496) I 111
Portlock, Nathaniel (1747–1817) II 174
Portman, 1st Viscount (1799–1888) III 168
Portman, Sir William, 6th Bart (1641?–1695?) I 111
Portsmouth, 5th Earl of (1825–1891) III 168
Portsmouth, Duchess of (1649–1734) I 111
Post, Jacob (1774–1855) II 174
Postgate, J.P. (1853–1926) III 168
Postgate, R.W. (1896–1971) IV 86
Postlethwaite, Thomas (1731–1798) II 174
Pott, J.H. (1759–1847) II 174
Pott, Percival (1714–1788) II 174
Potter, Barnaby (1577–1642) I 111
Potter, Beatrix (1866–1943) IV 86
Potter, Christopher (1591–1646) I 111
Potter, John (1674?–1747) I 111
Potter, J.P. (1818–1847) III 168
Potter, Richard (1778–1842) II 174
Potter, Robert (1721–1804) II 174
Potter, Stephen (1900–1969) IV 86
Potter, T.B. (1817–1898) III 168
Pottinger, Eldred (1811–1843) III 168
Pottinger, Sir Henry, 1st Bart (1789–1856) II 174
Poulett, 1st Baron (1586–1649) I 111
Poulett, 1st Earl (1663–1743) I 111
Poulton, Sir E.B. (1856–1943) III 168
Pound, Sir Dudley (1877–1943) IV 86
Pounds, John (1766–1839) II 174
Powell, Foster (1734–1793) II 174
Powell, F.Y. (1850–1904) III 168
Powell, Sir John (1633–1696) I 111
Powell, Sir John (1645–1713) I 111
Powell, Richard (1767–1834) II 174
Powell, Sir R.D., 1st Bart (1842–1925) III 168
Powell, William (1735–1769) II 174
Powell, Mrs (d 1831) II 174
Power, Sir A.J. (1889–1960) IV 86
Power, Sir D'Arcy (1855–1941) III 168
Power, Sir J.C., 1st Bart (1870–1950) IV 86
Power, Marguerite A. (1815?–1867) III 168
Power, Tyrone (1797–1841) II 174
Powicke, Sir Maurice (1879–1963) IV 86
Powis, 1st Marquess and titular Duke of (d 1696) I 111
Powis, 2nd Marquess and titular Duke of (d 1745) I 111
Powis, 1st Earl of (1754–1839) II 174
Powis, 2nd Earl of (1785–1848) II 174
Powle, Henry (1630–1692) I 111
Pownall, Sir H.R. (1887–1961) IV 86
Powys, J.C. (1872–1963) IV 86
Powys, Sir Thomas (1649–1719) I 111
Powys, T.F. (1875–1953) IV 86
Poynter, Sir E.J., 1st Bart (1836–1919) III 168
Poynter, William (1762–1827) II 174
Poyntz, Stephen (1685–1750) I 111
Poyntz, Sir Sydenham (fl 1645–1650) I 111
Prad, W.M. (1802–1839) III 168
Prain, Sir David (1857–1944) III 168
Prance, Miles (fl 1680) I 111
Pratt, Hodgson (1824–1907) III 168
Pratt, Sir John (1657–1725) I 111
Pratt, Josiah (1768–1844) II 174
Pratt, J.T. (1797–1870) II 174
Pratt, S.J. (1749–1814) II 174
Pratten, R.S. (1824–1868) III 168
Preece, Sir W.H. (1834–1913) III 168–169
Prendergast, Sir H.N.D. (1834–1913) III 169
Prescott, Robert (1725–1816) II 174
Prestage, Edgar (1869–1951) IV 86
Prestige, Viscount (1648–1695) I 112
Preston, John (1587–1628) I 111–112
Preston, William (1742–1818) II 174
Prestongrange, William Grant, Lord (c 1701–1764) II 174
Prestwich, Sir Joseph (1812–1896) III 169
Previté-Orton, C.W. (1877–1947) IV 86
Prevost, Sir George, 1st Bart (1767–1816) II 175
Price, Arthur (d 1752) I 112
Price, Bartholomew (1818–1898) III 169
Price, Bonamy (1807–1888) III 169
Price, Francis (c 1704–1753) II 175
Price, Hugh (1495?–574) I 112
Price, James (1752–1783) II 175
Price, John (1600–1676?) I 112
Price, John (1734–1813) II 175
Price, Richard (1723–1791) II 175
Price, Robert (1655–1733) I 112
Price, Thomas (1852–1909) III 169
Price, Sir Uvedale, 1st Bart (1747–1829) II 175
Price, W.L. (1810–after 1896) III 169
Price Thomas, Sir Clement (1893–1973) IV 86
Prichard, H.A. (1871–1947) IV 86
Prideaux, Humphrey (1648–1724) I 112
Prideaux, John (1578–1650) I 112
Prideaux, Walter (1806–1889) III 169
Priestley, Joseph (1733–1804) II 175
Priestley, J.B. (b 1894) IV 86–87
Priestley, Sir R.E. (1886–1974) IV 87

Priestley, Timothy (1734–1814) II 175
Priestley, Sir W.O. (1829–1900) III 169
Primrose, Sir H.W. (1846–1923) III 169
Pringle, Sir John, Bart (1707–1782) II 175
Prinsep, James (1799–1840) II 175
Prinsep, V.C. (1838–1904) III 169
Prior, Sir James (1790?–1869) II 175
Prior, Matthew (1664–1721) I 112
Prior, Melton (1845–1910) III 169
Prior, Thomas (1682?–1751) I 112
Prior, T.A. (1809–1886) III 169
Pritchard, Charles (1808–1893) III 169
Pritchard, George (1796–1883) II 175
Pritchard, Hannah (1711–1768) II 175
Pritchard, J.L. (1799–1850) II 175
Pritchard, Sir William (1632?–1705) I 112
Pritchett, Sir Victor (b1900) IV 87
Pritt, D.N. (1887–1972) IV 87
Probert, Lewis (1841–1908) III 169
Probyn, Sir Edmund (1678–1742) I 112
Procter, Adelaide Ann (1825–1864) III 169
Procter, B.W. (1787–1874) II 175
Procter, Francis (1812–1905) III 169
Proctor, R.A. (1837–1888) III 169
Prothero, Sir G.W. (1848–1922) III 169
Proudman, Joseph (1888–1975) IV 87
Prout, Ebenezer (1835–1909) III 169
Prout, J.S. (1806–1876) III 169
Prout, Samuel (1783–1852) II 175
Prout, William (1784–1850) II 175
Prowse, W.J. (1836–1870) III 169
Prujean, Sir Francis (1593–1666) I 112
Pryce, William (1725?–1790) II 175
Pryde, J.F. (1866–1941) IV 87
Prynne, William (1600–1669) I 112
Psalmanazar, George (1679?–1763) I 112
Puckering, Sir Henry, 3rd Bart (1618–1701) I 112
Puckering, Sir John (1544–1596) I 112
Puckle, James (1667?–1724) I 112
Pugh, Sir Arthur (1870–1955) IV 87
Pughe, W.O. (1759–1835) II 175
Pugin, Augustus Charles (1762–1832) II 175
Pugin, Augustus Welby Northmore (1812–1852) III 169
Puleston, Sir J.H. (1830–1908) III 169
Pullen, H.W. (1836–1903) III 169
Pullen, Josiah (1631–1714) I 112
Puller, Sir Christopher (1774–1824) II 175
Pulman, G.P.R. (1819–1880) III 169
Pulteney, Richard (1730–1801) II 175
Pulteney, Sir W.P. (1861–1941) IV 87
Punshon, W.M. (1824–1881) III 169–170
Purbeck, Viscount (1591?–1657) I 112
Purcell, A.A.W. (1872–1935) IV 87
Purcell, Henry (1659–1695) I 112
Purcell, Peter (1788–1846) II 175
Purchas, John (1823–1872) III 170
Purchas, Samuel (1575?–1626) I 112
Purse, B.O. (1874–1950) IV 87
Purser, L.C. (1854–1932) III 170
Pursglove, Robert (1500?–1579) I 112
Pusey, E.B. (1800–1882) III 170
Pusey, Philip (1799–1855) III 170
Pye, Sir D.R. (1886–1960) IV 87
Pye, H.J. (1745–1813) II 175–176
Pye, John (1782–1874) II 176
Pym, John (1584–1643) I 112
Pyne, J.B. (1800–1870) III 170
Pyne, Louisa Fanny (1832–1904) III 170
Pynson, Richard (d1530) I 112

Quain, Sir J.R. (1816–1876) III 171
Quain, Richard (1800–1887) III 171
Quain, Sir Richard, 1st Bart (1816–1898) III 171
Quaritch, Bernard (1819–1899) III 171
Quarles, Francis (1592–1644) I 113
Quarles, John (1624–1665) I 113
Queensberry, 1st Duke of (1637–1695) I 113
Queensberry, 2nd Duke of (1662–1711) I 113
Queensberry, 3rd Duke of (1698–1778) I 113
Queensberry, 4th Duke of (1724–1810) II 177
Queensberry, Duchess of (c1701–1777) II 177
Queensberry, 8th Marquess of (1844–1900) III 171
Quekett, J.T. (1815–1861) III 171
Quekett, William (1802–1888) III 171
Quick, John (1636–1706) I 113
Quick, John (1748–1831) II 177
Quick, Sir John (1852–1932) III 171
Quickswood, Baron (1869–1956) IV 88
Quiller-Couch, Sir Arthur (1863–1944) IV 88
Quilter, R.C. (1877–1953) IV 88
Quilter, Sir W.C., 1st Bart (1841–1911) III 171
Quin, F.H.F. (1799–1878) II 177
Quin, James (1693–1766) I 113

Rackham, Arthur (1867–1939) IV 89
Radcliffe, Charles (1693–1746) I 115
Radcliffe, John (1650?–1714) I 115

Radcliffe, William (1760–1841) II 178
Radley, Sir Gordon (1898–1970) IV 89
Radnor, 1st Earl of (1606–1685) I 115
Radnor, 3rd Earl of (1779–1869) II 178
Radstock, 1st Baron (1753–1825) II 178
Radstock, 2nd Baron (1786–1857) II 178
Rae, Alexander (1782–1820) II 178
Rae, James (1716–1791) II 178
Rae, John (1813–1893) III 172
Raeburn, Sir Henry (1756–1823) II 178
Raffald, Elizabeth (1733–1781) II 178
Raffles, Thomas (1788–1863) II 178
Raffles, Sir T.S.B. (1781–1826) II 178
Raglan, 1st Baron (1788–1855) II 178
Raikes, Henry (1782–1854) II 178
Raikes, H.C. (1838–1891) III 172
Raikes, H.R. (1891–1955) IV 89
Raikes, Robert (1735–1811) II 178
Raikes, Thomas (1777–1848) II 178
Railton, Herbert (1858–1910) III 172
Raimbach, Abraham (1776–1843) II 178
Rainbowe, Edward (1608–1684) I 115
Raine, Matthew (1760–1811) II 178
Rainforth, Elizabeth (1814–1877) III 172
Rainier, Peter (1741?–1808) II 178
Rainolds, John (1549–1607) I 115
Rainsford, Sir Richard (1605–1680) I 115
Rainton, Sir Nicholas (1569–1646) I 115
Rainy, Harry (1792–1876) II 178
Rainy, Robert (1826–1906) III 172
Raistrick, Harold (1890–1971) IV 89
Rait, Sir R.S. (1874–1936) IV 89
Raleigh, Alexander (1817–1880) III 172
Raleigh, Sir Walter (1552?–1618) I 115
Raleigh, Sir W.A. (1861–1922) IV 89
Ram, Sir Granville (1885–1952) IV 89
Ramage, C.T. (1803–1878) III 172
Ramberg, J.H. (1763–1840) II 178
Rambert, Dame Marie (b1888) IV 89
Ramsay, Allan (1686–1758) I 115
Ramsay, Allan (1713–1784) II 178
Ramsay, A.B. (1872–1955) IV 89
Ramsay, Sir A.C. (1814–1891) III 172
Ramsay, Sir A.R.M. (1881–1972) IV 89
Ramsay, Sir B.H. (1883–1945) IV 89
Ramsay, E.B. (1793–1872) III 172
Ramsay, James (1733–1789) II 178–179
Ramsay, Sir James (1589?–1638) I 115
Ramsay, Lady Patricia (1886–1974) IV 89
Ramsay, William (fl 1645–1676) I 115
Ramsay, William (1806–1865) III 172
Ramsay, Sir William (1852–1916) III 172
Ramsay, Sir W.M. (1851–1939) III 172
Ramsden, Jesse (1735–1800) II 179
Rance, Sir Hubert (1898–1946) IV 89
Rand, Isaac (d1743) I 115
Randall, John (1715–1799) II 179
Randall, R.W. (1824–1906) III 172
Randall-MacIver, David (1873–1945) IV 89
Randegger, Alberto (1832–1911) III 172
Randles, Marshall (1826–1904) III 172
Randolph, Francis (1752–1831) II 179
Randolph, John (1749–1813) II 179
Randolph, Thomas (1605–1635) I 115
Randolph, Thomas (1701–1783) II 179
Ranelagh, 1st Earl of (1641?–1712) I 115
Ranelagh, 7th Viscount (1812–1885) III 172
Rank, Baron (1888–1972) IV 89
Rankeillor, Archibald Hope, Lord (1639–1706) I 115
Rankeillour, James Fitzalan Hope, 1st Baron (1870–1949) IV 89
Rankin, Sir G.C. (1877–1946) IV 89
Rankine, A.O. (1881–1956) IV 89
Rankine, W.J.M. (1820–1872) III 172
Ransome, Arthur (1884–1967) IV 89
Ransome, James (1782–1849) II 179
Ransome, J.A. (1806–1875) III 172
Ranson, T.F. (1784–1828) II 179
Raper, R.W. (1842–1915) III 172
Rapin, Paul (1661–1725) I 115
Rapson, E.J. (1861–1937) IV 89
Rasbotham, Dorning (1730–1791) II 179
Rashdall, Hastings (1858–1924) III 172
Rashleigh, Philip (1729–1811) II 179
Raspe, R.E. (1737–1794) II 179
Rassam, Hormuzd (1826–1910) III 172
Rathbone, Basil (1892–1967) IV 89
Rathbone, Eleanor Florence (1872–1946) IV 89
Rathbone, William (1757–1809) II 179
Rathbone, William (1787–1868) III 172
Rathbone, William (1819–1902) III 172
Rauzzini, Venanzio (1747–1810) II 179
Raven, C.E. (1885–1964) IV 89
Raven-Hill, Leonard (1867–1942) IV 89
Ravenet, S.F. (1721?–1774) II 179
Ravensworth, 2nd Baron and 1st Earl of (1797–1878) II 179
Raverat, Gwendolen Mary (1885–1957) IV 89

Ravis, Thomas (1560?–1609) I 115
Ravius, Christian (1613–1677) I 115
Rawdon, Christopher (1780–1858) II 179
Rawdon, Sir George, 1st Bart (1604–1684) I 115
Rawdon, Marmaduke (1610–1669) I 115
Rawlet, John (1642–1686) I 115
Rawlings, Sir Bernard (1889–1962) IV 89
Rawlinson, Baron (1864–1925) IV 89–90
Rawlinson, Christopher (1677–1733) I 115
Rawlinson, George (1812–1902) III 172
Rawlinson, Sir H.C., 1st Bart (1810–1895) III 172–173
Rawlinson, Richard (1690–1755) I 115
Rawlinson, Sir Robert (1810–1898) III 173
Rawlinson, Sir Thomas (1647–1708) I 115
Rawlinson, Sir Thomas (d1769) II 179
Rawson, Sir H.H. (1843–1910) III 173
Ray, John (1627–1705) I 116
Ray, Martha (c1745–1779) II 179
Ray, T.M. (1801–1881) III 173
Rayleigh, 3rd Baron (1842–1919) III 173
Rayleigh, 4th Baron (1875–1947) IV 90
Raymond, 1st Baron (1673–1733) I 116
Raymond, J.G. (1771–1817) II 179
Raymond, Sir Thomas (1627–1683) I 116
Rayner, L.B. (1788?–1855) II 179
Read, Sir C.H. (1857–1929) III 173
Read, Clare Sewell (1826–1905) III 173
Read, D.C. (1790–1851) II 179
Read, Sir Herbert (1893–1968) IV 90
Read, Sir H.J. (1863–1949) IV 90
Read, Samuel (1815?–1883) III 173
Read, Sir William (d1715) I 116
Read, W.W. (1855–1907) III 173
Reade, Charles (1814–1884) III 173
Reading, 1st Marquess of (1860–1935) IV 90
Reading, 2nd Marquess of (1889–1960) IV 90
Reading, Marchioness of (1894–1971) IV 90
Reading, John (1677–1764) I 116
Reay, 11th Baron (1839–1921) III 173
Rebbeck, Sir Frederick (1877–1964) IV 90
Reddish, Samuel (1735–1785) II 179
Redesdale, 1st Baron (1758–1830) II 179
Redesdale, 1st Earl of (1805–1886) III 173
Redesdale, 1st Baron (1837–1916) III 173
Redgrave, Richard (1804–1888) III 173
Redmayne, Sir R.A.S. (1865–1955) IV 90
Redmond, J.E. (1856–1918) III 173
Redmond, W.H.K. (1861–1917) IV 90
Redpath, Anne (1895–1965) IV 90
Reece, Robert (1838–1891) III 173
Reed, Andrew (1787–1862) II 179
Reed, A.L. (1873–1954) IV 90
Reed, Sir Charles (1819–1881) III 173
Reed, Sir E.J. (1830–1906) III 173–174
Reed, Isaac (1742–1807) II 179
Reed, Priscilla (1818–1895) III 174
Reed, Sir Stanley (1872–1969) IV 90
Reed, T.G. (1817–1888) III 174
Reede, Baron (1593–1683) I 116
Rees, Abraham (1743–1825) II 179
Rees, David (1801–1869) III 174
Rees, G.O. (1813–1889) III 174
Rees, Henry (1798–1869) II 179
Rees, Thomas (1815–1885) III 174
Rees, William (1802–1883) III 174
Rees, W.J. (1772–1855) II 179
Reeve, Ada (1874–1966) IV 90
Reeve, Clara (1729–1807) II 179
Reeve, Henry (1813–1895) III 174
Reeve, John (1799–1838) II 179
Reeve, L.A. (1814–1865) III 174
Reeve, Sir Thomas (d1737) I 116
Reeve, William (1757–1815) II 179
Reeves, John (1752–1829) II 179–180
Reeves, J.S. (1818–1900) III 174
Regan, C.T. (1878–1943) IV 90
Regondi, Giulio (1822–1872) III 174
Reid, Baron (1890–1975) IV 90
Reid, A.D. (1844–1908) III 174
Reid, D.B. (1805–1863) III 174
Reid, Forrest (1876–1947) IV 90
Reid, Sir George (1841–1913) III 174
Reid, Sir G.H. (1845–1918) III 174
Reid, John (1721–1807) II 180
Reid, John (1809–1849) III 174
Reid, Mayne (1818–1883) III 174
Reid, Thomas (1710–1796) II 180
Reid, Sir T.W. (1842–1905) III 174
Reid, Sir William (1791–1858) II 180
Reilly, Sir C.H. (1874–1948) IV 90
Reinagle, R.R. (1775–1862) II 180
Reinhold, C.F. (1737–1815) II 180
Reisen, C.C. (1680–1725) I 116
Reith, 1st Baron (1889–1971) IV 90
Relly, James (1722?–1778) II 180
Rendall, M.J. (1862–1950) IV 90
Rendel, J.M. (1799–1856) II 180

Rendle, A.B. (1865–1938) IV *91*
Rennell, 1st Baron (1858–1941) III *174*
Rennell, James (1742–1830) II *180*
Rennell, Thomas (1787–1824) II *180*
Rennie, George (1791–1866) II *180*
Rennie, John (1761–1821) II *180*
Rennie, John (1794–1874) II *180*
Repington, Charles à Court (1858–1925) III *175*
Repton, Humphry (1752–1818) II *180*
Reuter, Baron (1816–1899) III *174*
Revett, Nicholas (1720–1804) II *180*
Reynardson, Sir Abraham (1590–1661) I *116*
Reynell, Carew (1636–1690) I *116*
Reynolds, Edward (1599–1676) I *116*
Reynolds, Frances (1729–1807) II *180*
Reynolds, Frederic (1764–1841) II *180*
Reynolds, G.W.M. (1814–1879) III *174*
Reynolds, H.R. (1745–1811) II *180*
Reynolds, H.R. (1825–1896) III *174*
Reynolds, James (1686–1739) I *116*
Reynolds, Sir James (1684–1747) I *116*
Reynolds, John Hamilton (1796–1852) II *180*
Reynolds, Sir Joshua (1723–1792) II *180*
Reynolds, J.E. (1844–1920) III *174*
Reynolds, Sir J.R., 1st Bart (1828–1896) III *174*
Reynolds, Osborne (1842–1912) III *174*
Reynolds, Richard (1735–1816) II *180*
Reynolds, S.H. (1831–1897) III *174*
Reynolds, S.W. (1773–1835) II *180*
Reynolds, Thomas (1667?–1727) I *116*
Rhodes, Cecil (1853–1902) III *174–175*
Rhodes, Ebenezer (1762–1839) II *180*
Rhodes, F.W. (1851–1905) III *175*
Rhondda, Viscount (1856–1918) III *175*
Rhondda, Viscountess (1883–1958) IV *91*
Rhys, E.P. (1859–1946) III *175*
Rhys, Sir John (1840–1915) III *175*
Ricardo, David (1772–1823) II *180*
Ricardo, Sir H.R. (1885–1974) IV *91*
Rice, James (1843–1882) III *175*
Rich, 1st Baron (1496?–1567) I *116*
Rich, A.W. (1856–1922) III *175*
Rich, Jeremiah (d 1660?) I *116*
Rich, John (1682?–1761) I *116*
Richard I (1157–1199) I *116*
Richard II (1367–1400) I *116*
Richard III (1452–1485) I *116*
Richard, Henry (1812–1888) III *175*
Richards, Sir F.W. (1833–1912) III *175*
Richards, George (1767–1837) II *181*
Richards, Sir G.H. (1820–1896) III *175*
Richards, I.A. (b1893) IV *91*
Richards, J.I. (d1810) II *181*
Richards, Michael (1673–1721) I *116*
Richards, Nathaniel (d1652) I *116*
Richards, William (1643–1705) I *116*
Richards, William (1749–1818) II *181*
Richardson, Sir A.E. (1880–1964) IV *91*
Richardson, Ethel (1870–1946) IV *91*
Richardson, John (d1625) I *116*
Richardson, John (1580–1654) I *116*
Richardson, Sir John (1771–1841) II *181*
Richardson, Sir John (1787–1845) II *181*
Richardson, Jonathan (1665–1745) I *116*
Richardson, Jonathan (1694–1771) I *117*
Richardson, Joseph (1755–1803) II *181*
Richardson, L.F. (1881–1953) IV *91*
Richardson, Sir O.W. (1879–1959) IV *91*
Richardson, Richard (1663–1741) I *117*
Richardson, Robert (1779–1847) II *181*
Richardson, Samuel (1689–1761) I *117*
Richardson, Sir Thomas (1569–1635) I *117*
Richardson, Thomas (1771–1853) II *181*
Richardson, William (1698–1775) I *117*
Richardson, William (1743–1814) II *181*
Richmond, 1st Duke of (1519–1536) I *117*
Richmond, 1st Duke of (1574–1624) I *117*
Richmond, 1st Duke of (1612–1655) I *117*
Richmond, 6th Duke of (1818–1903) III *175*
Richmond, Duchess of (d1557) I *117*
Richmond, Sir B.L. (1871–1964) IV *91*
Richmond, George (1809–1896) III *175–176*
Richmond, Sir H.W. (1871–1946) IV *91*
Richmond, Legh (1772–1827) II *181*
Richmond, Sir W.B. (1842–1921) III *176*
Richmond and Derby, Countess of (1443–1509) I *117*
Richmond and Lennox, 1st Duke of (1672–1723) I *117*
Richmond and Lennox, 2nd Duke of (1701–1750) II *181*
Richmond and Lennox, 3rd Duke of (1735–1806) II *181*
Richmond and Lennox, 4th Duke of (1764–1819) II *181*
Richmond and Lennox, 5th Duke of (1791–1860) II *181*
Richmond and Lennox, Duchess of (1647–1702) I *117*
Ricketts, Charles (1866–1931) IV *91*
Rickman, John (1771–1840) II *181*
Rickman, Thomas (1761–1834) II *181*

Ricraft, Josiah (fl 1645–1679) I *117*
Riddell, H.S. (1798–1870) II *181*
Riddell of Walton Heath, Baron (1865–1934) IV *91*
Ridding, George (1828–1904) III *176*
Riddle, Edward (1788–1854) II *181*
Ridgley, Thomas (1667?–1734) I *117*
Ridgeway, Sir J.W. (1844–1930) III *176*
Ridgeway, Sir William (1853–1926) III *176*
Ridley, 1st Viscount (1842–1904) III *176*
Ridley, Glocester (1702–1774) II *181*
Ridley, Mark (1560–1624) I *117*
Ridley, Nicholas (1500?–1555) I *117*
Riel, Louis (1844–1885) III *176*
Rieu, E.V. (1887–1972) IV *91*
Rigaud, S.J. (1816–1859) III *176*
Rigaud, S.P. (1774–1839) II *181*
Rigby, Edward (1747–1821) II *181*
Rigby, Edward (1804–1860) II *181*
Rigby, Sir John (1834–1903) III *176*
Rigby, Richard (1722–1788) II *181*
Rigg, J.H. (1821–1909) III *176*
Riley, John (1646–1691) I *117*
Ring, John (1752–1821) II *181*
Rintoul, R.S. (1787–1858) II *181–182*
Riou, Edward (1758?–1801) II *182*
Ripon, 1st Earl of (1782–1859) II *182*
Ripon, 1st Marquess of (1827–1909) III *176*
Rippingille, E.V. (1798?–1859) II *182*
Rippon, John (1751–1836) II *182*
Rippon, Thomas (1761–1835) II *182*
Ritchie, A.H. (1804–1870) III *176*
Ritchie, D.G. (1853–1903) III *176*
Ritchie, Lady (1837–1919) III *176*
Ritchie of Dundee, 1st Baron (1838–1906) III *176*
Ritson, Jonathan (1776?–1846) II *182*
Ritson, Joseph (1752–1803) II *182*
Rivers, 2nd Earl (1442?–1483) I *117*
Rivers, 1st Baron (1722?–1803) II *182*
Riviere, Briton (1840–1920) III *176*
Riviere, H.P. (1811–1888) III *176*
Rivington, Charles (1688–1742) I *117*
Rivington, James (1724–1803) II *182*
Robb, Sir James (1895–1968) IV *91*
Robert, Duke of Normandy (1054?–1134) I *117*
Roberton, Sir Hugh (1874–1952) IV *91*
Roberts, 1st Earl (1832–1914) III *177*
Roberts, Sir Abraham (1784–1873) II *182*
Roberts, Sir Alfred (1897–1963) IV *91*
Roberts, Arthur (1852–1933) III *177*
Roberts, B.C. (1789–1810) II *182*
Roberts, David (1796–1864) II *182*
Roberts, Francis (1609–1675) I *117*
Roberts, G.H. (1868–1928) IV *91*
Roberts, Sir H.G. (1800–1860) III *177*
Roberts, John (1712?–1772) II *182*
Roberts, Lewis (1596–1640) I *117*
Roberts, Richard (1789–1864) II *182*
Roberts, Samuel (1763–1848) II *182*
Roberts, Sir Sydney (1887–1966) IV *91*
Roberts, Sir William (1830–1899) III *177*
Roberts, William (1895–1980) IV *91*
Roberts, W.P. (1806–1871) II *182*
Robertson, Baron (1845–1909) III *177*
Robertson, Andrew (1777–1845) II *182*
Robertson, Archibald (1853–1931) III *177*
Robertson, Sir C.G. (1869–1948) IV *91*
Robertson, Sir D.H. (1890–1963) IV *91*
Robertson, D.M.C.L.A. (1837–1909) III *177*
Robertson, E.W. (1815–1874) III *177*
Robertson, F.W. (1816–1853) III *177*
Robertson, G.M. (1864–1932) IV *91*
Robertson, Sir Howard (1888–1963) IV *91*
Robertson, James (1714–1795) II *182*
Robertson, James (1803–1860) III *177*
Robertson, J.M. (1856–1933) III *177*
Robertson, Patrick Robertson, Lord (1794–1855) II *182*
Robertson, Robert (1742–1829) II *182*
Robertson, Sir Robert (1869–1949) IV *91*
Robertson, T.W. (1829–1871) III *177*
Robertson, William (1721–1793) II *182*
Robertson, W.G. (1866–1948) IV *91*
Robertson, Sir W.R., 1st Bart (1860–1933) IV *92*
Robertson, Sir W.T. (1825–1889) III *177*
Robertson-Scott, J.W. (1866–1962) IV *92*
Robertson of Oakridge, Baron (1896–1974) IV *92*
Robertson of Struan, 13th Baron (1670?–1749) I *118*
Robey, Sir G.E. (1869–1954) IV *92*
Robins, Arthur (1834–1899) III *177*
Robins, G.H. (1778–1847) II *182*
Robinson, Baron (1883–1952) IV *92*
Robinson, Sir Arthur (1874–1950) IV *92*
Robinson, Benjamin (1666–1724) I *118*
Robinson, Bryan (1680–1754) I *118*
Robinson, Sir Christopher (1766–1833) II *182*
Robinson, F.W. (1830–1901) III *177*
Robinson, Henry (1553?–1616) I *118*
Robinson, Henry Crabb (1775–1867) II *182*

Robinson, H.R. (1889–1955) IV *92*
Robinson, H.W. (1872–1975) IV *92*
Robinson, John (1650–1723) I *118*
Robinson, John (1682–1762) I *118*
Robinson, John (1727–1802) II *182*
Robinson, John (1774–1840) II *182*
Robinson, Sir John (1839–1903) III *177*
Robinson, J.A. (1858–1933) III *177*
Robinson, Sir J.C. (1824–1913) III *177*
Robinson, J.H. (1796–1871) II *182*
Robinson, Sir J.R. (1828–1903) III *177*
Robinson, Lennox (1886–1958) IV *92*
Robinson, Mary (1758–1800) II *182–183*
Robinson, Mary (fl 1802) II *183*
Robinson, Robert (1735–1790) II *183*
Robinson, Sir Robert (1886–1975) IV *92*
Robinson, Sir Thomas, 1st Bart (1700?–1777) II *183*
Robinson, Thomas (1749–1813) II *183*
Robinson, T.R. (1792–1882) II *183*
Robinson, William (1777–1848) II *183*
Robinson, William Heath (1872–1944) IV *92*
Robison, John (1739–1805) II *183*
Robison, Robert (1883–1941) IV *92*
Robson, Baron (1852–1918) III *177*
Robson, G.F. (1788–1833) II *183*
Robson, T.F. (1822?–1864) III *177*
Roby, John (1793–1850) II *183*
Roby, William (1766–1830) II *183*
Roche, Baron (1871–1956) IV *92*
Roche, Eugenius (1786–1829) II *183*
Rochester, 1st Earl of (1612?–1658) I *118*
Rochester, 2nd Earl of (1647–1680) I *118*
Rochester, Earl of (1641–1711) I *118*
Rochford, 1st Earl of (1645?–1709) I *118*
Rochford, 2nd Earl of (1681–1710) I *118*
Rochford, 3rd Earl of (1682?–1738) I *118*
Rochford, 4th Earl of (1717–1781) I *118*
Rockingham, 1st Baron (1584–1653) I *118*
Rockingham, 2nd Marquess of (1730–1782) II *183*
Rodd, Thomas (1763–1822) II *183*
Roddam, Robert (1719–1808) II *183*
Roden, 1st Earl of (1731–1797) II *183*
Roden, 3rd Earl of (1788–1870) II *183*
Roden, 4th Earl of (1846–1880) III *177–178*
Roden, W.T. (1817–1892) III *178*
Rodney, 1st Baron (1719–1792) II *183*
Rodney, 7th Baron (1857–1909) III *178*
Rodwell, G.H.B. (1800–1852) III *178*
Roe, Sir Thomas (1581?–1644) I *118*
Roebuck, J.A. (1801–1879) III *178*
Roestraten, Pieter van (1627–1700) I *118*
Roettiers, Norbert (1665?–1727) I *118*
Roger of Salisbury (d1139) I *118*
Rogers, Annie (1856–1937) III *178*
Rogers, B.B. (1828–1919) III *178*
Rogers, Charles (1711–1784) I *118*
Rogers, Daniel (1573–1652) I *118*
Rogers, Sir Edward (1498?–1567?) I *118*
Rogers, John (1500?–1555) I *118*
Rogers, John (1572?–1636) I *118*
Rogers, John (1627–1665) I *118*
Rogers, J.E.T. (1823–1890) III *178*
Rogers, Sir Leonard (1868–1962) IV *92*
Rogers, L.J. (1862–1933) IV *92*
Rogers, Nehemiah (1593–1660) I *118*
Rogers, Richard (1532?–1597) I *118*
Rogers, Richard (1550?–1618) I *118*
Rogers, Robert (1727–1800) II *183–184*
Rogers, Samuel (1763–1855) II *184*
Rogers, Thomas (d1616) I *118*
Rogers, Timothy (1658–1728) I *118*
Rogers William (1819–1896) III *178*
Rogers, Woodes (1679–1732) I *118*
Rogers, W.G. (1792–1875) III *178*
Rogerson, J.B. (1809–1859) III *178*
Roget, P.M. (1779–1869) II *184*
Rokeby, 1st Baron (1709–1794) II *184*
Rokeby, 2nd Baron (1713–1800) II *184*
Rokeby, 6th Baron (1798–1883) II *184*
Rokeby, Sir Thomas (1631?–1699) I *118*
Rokewode, J.G. (1786–1842) II *184*
Rolle, Henry (1589?–1656) I *118*
Rolle of Stevenstone, Baron (1750–1842) II *184*
Rolleston, George (1829–1881) III *178*
Rolleston, Sir H.D., Bart (1862–1944) IV *92*
Rollit, Sir A.K. (1842–1922) III *178*
Rollock, Robert (1555?–1599) I *118*
Rolls, C.S. (1877–1910) IV *92*
Rolt, Sir John (1804–1871) III *178*
Romaine, William (1714–1795) II *184*
Romaine, W.G. (1815–1893) III *178*
Romanes, G.J. (1848–1894) III *178*
Romer, Baron (1866–1944) IV *92*
Romer, Sir C.R.R. (1897–1969) IV *92*
Romer, Emma (1814–1868) III *178*
Romer, Sir Robert (1840–1918) III *178*
Romilly, 1st Baron (1802–1874) III *178*

Romilly, Joseph (1791–1864) II *184*
Romilly, Sir Samuel (1757–1818) II *184*
Romney, 1st Earl of (1641–1704) I *118*
Romney, George (1734–1802) II *184*
Romney, Peter (1743–1777) II *184*
Ronald, Sir Landon (1873–1938) IV *92*
Ronalds, Sir Francis (1788–1873) II *184*
Ronan, Stephen (1848–1925) III *178*
Rooke, Sir George (1650–1709) I *118*
Rooke, Sir Giles (1743–1808) II *184*
Rooker, Michael Angelo (1743–1801) II *184*
Rookwood, Baron (1826–1902) III *178*
Rookwood, Ambrose (1578?–1606) I *119*
Roose, E.C.R. (1848–1905) III *178*
Rootes, 1st Baron (1894–1964) IV *92*
Roper, Abel (1665–1726) I *119*
Roper, Margaret (1505–1544) I *119*
Roper, William (1493/8–1578) I *119*
Ros, Robert de (*d* 1227) I *119*
Rosa, C.A.N. (1843–1889) III *178*
Roscoe, Sir H.E. (1833–1915) III *178*
Roscoe, William (1753–1831) II *184*
Roscoe, George (1744–1818) II *184*
Rose, George (1817–1882) III *178*
Rose, John Holland (1855–1942) III *179*
Rose-Innes, Sir James (1855–1942) III *179*
Roseberry, 1st Earl of (1661?–1723) I *119*
Roseberry, 4th Earl of (1783–1863) II *184*
Roseberry, 5th Earl of (1847–1929) III *179*
Rosen, Friedrich August (1805–1837) III *179*
Rosenberg, Isaac (1890–1918) IV *92*
Rosenhagen, Philip (1737?–1798) II *185*
Rosenheim, Otto (1871–1955) IV *92*
Rosewell, Samuel (1679–1722) I *119*
Rosmead, 1st Baron (1824–1897) III *179*
Ross, Alexander (1591–1654) I *119*
Ross, David (1728–1790) II *185*
Ross, Sir David (1877–1971) IV *93*
Ross, Sir Denison (1871–1940) IV *92*
Ross, George (1814–1863) II *179*
Ross, Sir Hew Dalrymple (1779–1868) II *185*
Ross, Horatio (1801–1886) III *179*
Ross, John (1719–1792) II *185*
Ross, Sir John (1777–1856) II *185*
Ross, Sir J.C. (1800–1862) III *179*
Ross, Sir J.L. (1721–1790) II *185*
Ross, Sir J.P. (*b* 1895) IV *93*
Ross, Robert (1766–1814) II *185*
Ross, Sir Ronald (1857–1932) III *179*
Ross, Sir W.C. (1794–1860) II *185*
Rosse, 2nd Earl of (1758–1841) II *185*
Rosse, 3rd Earl of (1840–1908) III *179*
Rossetti, Christina Georgina (1830–1894) III *179*
Rossetti, Dante Gabriel (1828–1882) III *179*
Rossetti, Lucy Madox (1843–1894) III *180*
Rossetti, William Michael (1829–1919) III *180*
Rosslyn, 1st Earl of (1733–1805) II *185*
Rosslyn, 2nd Earl of (1762–1837) II *185*
Rothenstein, Sir William (1872–1945) IV *93*
Rothermere, 1st Viscount (1868–1940) IV *93*
Rotherwick, 1st Baron (1881–1958) IV *93*
Rothes, 7th Earl and 1st Duke of (1630–1681) I *119*
Rothes, 8th Earl of (1679–1722) I *119*
Rothes, 10th Earl of (1698?–1767) I *119*
Rothschild, 1st Baron (1840–1915) III *180*
Rothschild, 2nd Baron (1868–1937) IV *93*
Rothschild, Sir Anthony de (1810–1876) III *180*
Rothschild, A.C. de (1842–1918) III *180*
Rothschild, F.J. de (1839–1898) III *180*
Rothschild, L.N. de (1808–1879) III *180*
Rothschild, M.A. de (1818–1874) III *180*
Rothschild, N.M. (1777–1836) II *185*
Rothwell, Richard (1800–1868) III *180*
Roubiliac, L.F. (1705–1762) I *119*
Roupell, G.L. (1797–1854) II *185*
Rous, Francis (1579–1659) I *119*
Rous, H.J. (1795–1877) II *185*
Rousby, C.M.J. (1852?–1879) III *180*
Rouse, W.H.D. (1863–1950) IV *93*
Routh, E.J. (1831–1907) III *180*
Routh, M.J. (1755–1854) II *185*
Routh, Sir R.I. (1785?–1858) II *185*
Routledge, George (1812–1888) III *180*
Rowan, A.H. (1751–1834) II *185*
Rowan, Sir Charles (1782?–1852) II *185*
Rowbottom, T.C.L. (1823–1875) III *180*
Rowe, Elizabeth (1674–1737) I *119*
Rowe, Harry (1726–1800) II *185*
Rowe, J.B. (1837–1908) III *180*
Rowe, N. (1674–1718) I *119*
Rowlands, Daniel (1713–1790) II *185*
Rowlandson, Thomas (1757–1827) II *185*
Rowley, Baron (1893–1968) IV *93*
Rowley, Sir Charles (1770–1845) II *186*
Rowley, Sir Joshua (1734–1790) II *186*
Rowley, Sir Josias (1765–1842) II *186*

Rowley, Sir William (1690?–1768) I *119*
Rowley, William (1742–1806) II *186*
Rowntree, B.S. (1871–1954) IV *93*
Rowton, Baron (1838–1903) III *180*
Roxburgh(e), 1st Earl (1570?–1650) I *119*
Roxburgh(e), 1st Duke (1680?–1741) I *119*
Roxburgh(e), 3rd Duke (1740–1804) II *186*
Roxburgh(e), 5th Duke (1738–1823) II *186*
Roxburgh, J.F. (1888–1954) IV *93*
Roxburgh, William (1751–1815) II *186*
Royce, Sir Henry (1863–1933) IV *93*
Royden, Baron (1871–1950) IV *93*
Royden, Maude (1876–1956) IV *93*
Royle, J.F. (1799–1858) II *186*
Ruck, Berta (1878–1978) IV *93*
Ruddiman, Thomas (1674–1757) I *119*
Ruding, Rogers (1751–1820) II *186*
Rudyerd, Sir Benjamin (1572–1658) I *119*
Ruffside, 1st Viscount (1879–1959) IV *93*
Rugby, 1st Baron (1877–1969) IV *93*
Ruggle, George (1575–1622) I *119*
Ruggles-Brise, Sir E.J. (1857–1935) III *180*
Rumbold, Sir Horace (1829–1913) III *180*
Rumbold, Sir H.G.M. (1869–1941) IV *93*
Rumbold, Sir Thomas (1736–1791) II *186*
Rumford, Count von (1753–1814) II *186*
Runciman, 1st Baron (1847–1937) III *180*
Runciman, 1st Viscount (1870–1949) IV *93*
Runciman, Alexander (1736–1785) II *186*
Runciman, John (1744–1768) II *186*
Rundle, Sir Leslie (1856–1934) III *180*
Rundle, Thomas (1688?–1743) I *119*
Runnington, Charles (1751–1821) II *186*
Rupert, Prince, Count Palatine (1619–1682) I *119*
Rushbrooke, J.H. (1870–1947) IV *93*
Rushbury, Sir Henry (1889–1968) IV *93*
Rushcliffe, Baron (1872–1949) IV *94*
Rushout, Sir John (1684–1775) I *120*
Rushton, Edward (1756–1814) II *186*
Rushton, Edward (1796–1851) II *186*
Rushworth, John (1612?–1690) I *120*
Ruskin, John (1819–1900) III *180*
Russel, Alexander (1814–1876) III *181*
Russel, 1st Earl (1792–1878) II *186*–*187*
Russell, Bernard Russell, 3rd Earl (1872–1970) IV *94*
Russell, Alexander (1715?–1768) II *186*
Russell, Sir Charles, 3rd Bart (1826–1883) III *181*
Russell, Sir Charles, 1st Bart (1863–1928) IV *94*
Russell, C.W. (1812–1880) III *181*
Russell, Lord Edward (*d* 1551) I *120*
Russell, Lord Francis (*d* 1585) I *120*
Russell, Sir George, 4th Bart (1828–1898) III *181*
Russell, Lord G.W. (1790–1846) II *186*
Russell, G.W. (1867–1935) IV *94*
Russell, Sir Henry, Bart (1751–1836) II *186*
Russell, Henry (1812–1900) III *181*
Russell, James (1754–1836) II *186*
Russell, James (1790–1861) II *186*
Russell, John (1745–1806) II *186*
Russell, John (1787–1863) II *186*
Russell, John (1795–1883) II *186*
Russell, Sir John (1872–1965) IV *94*
Russell, Patrick (1727–1805) II *187*
Russell, Lady Rachel (*d* 1723) I *120*
Russell, S.T. (1769?–1845) II *187*
Russell, Thomas (1767–1803) II *187*
Russell, Sir T.W., 1st Bart (1841–1929) III *181*
Russell, Sir T.W. (1879–1954) IV *94*
Russell, Sir William, 1st Bart (*d* 1654) I *120*
Russell, W.C. (1844–1911) III *181*
Russell, Sir W.H. (1820–1907) III *181*
Russell, William Russell, Lord (1639–1683) I *120*
Russell, Sir W.W. (1867–1949) IV *94*
Russell of Killowen, 1st Baron (1832–1900) III *181*
Russell of Killowen, Baron (1867–1946) IV *94*
Russell of Thornhaugh, 1st Baron (1558?–1613) I *120*
Rustat, Tobias (1606?–1694) I *120*
Rutherford, Daniel (1749–1819) II *187*
Rutherford, John (1695–1779) I *120*
Rutherford, Dame Margaret (1892–1972) IV *94*
Rutherford, Samuel (1600–1661) I *120*
Rutherford, W.G. (1853–1907) III *181*
Rutherford of Nelson, Baron (1871–1937) IV *94*
Rutherfurd, Lord (1791–1854) II *187*
Rutherston, A.D. (1881–1953) IV *94*
Rutland, 1st Earl of (*d* 1543) I *120*
Rutland, 2nd Earl of (*d* 1563) I *120*
Rutland, 3rd Earl of (1549–1587) I *120*
Rutland, 5th Earl of (1576–1612) I *120*
Rutland, 6th Earl of (1578–1632) I *120*
Rutland, 8th Earl of (1604–1679) I *120*
Rutland, 9th Earl and 1st Duke of (1638–1711) I *120*
Rutland, 4th Duke of (1754–1787) II *187*
Rutland, 6th Duke of (1815–1888) III *182*
Rutland, 7th Duke of (1818–1906) III *182*
Ryan, Sir Edward (1793–1875) II *187*
Ryan, V.W. (1816–1888) III *182*

Rycaut, Sir Paul (1628–1700) I *120*
Ryder, Sir A.P. (1820–1888) III *182*
Ryder, Sir Dudley (1691–1756) I *120*
Ryder, Henry (1777–1836) II *187*
Ryder, John (1697?–1775) I *120*
Ryder, John (1814–1885) III *182*
Rylands, Peter (1820–1887) III *182*
Ryland, J.C. (1723–1792) II *187*
Ryland, W.W. (1732–1783) II *187*
Ryle, Gilbert (1900–1976) IV *95*
Ryle, H.E. (1856–1925) III *182*
Ryle, J.C. (1816–1900) III *182*
Rymer, Thomas (1641–1713) I *120*
Rysbrack, J.M. (1693?–1770) I *120*
Ryves, Bruno (1596–1677) I *120*
Ryves, Mrs Lavinia Janetta Horton de Serres (1797–1871) II *187*

Sabine, Sir Edward (1788–1883) II *188*
Sabine, Joseph (1662?–1739) I *121*
Sacheverell, Henry (1674?–1724) I *121*
Sackville, 2nd Baron (1827–1908) III *183*
Sackville, 4th Baron (1870–1962) IV *95*
Sackville-West, Vita (1892–1962) IV *95*
Sadleir, Sir Ralph (1507–1587) I *121*
Sadler, James (1751 1828) II *188*
Sadler, Sir M.E. (1861–1943) IV *95*
Sadler, M.T. (1780–1835) II *188*
Sadler, Thomas (1822–1891) III *183*
St Alban, Viscount (1561–1626) I *121*
St Albans, Earl of (*d* 1684) I *121*
St Albans, 1st Duke of (1670–1726) I *121*
St Albans, Duchess of (*d* 1741) 121 *121*
St Albans, Duchess of (1777?–1837) III *182*
St Aldwyn, 1st Earl (1837–1916) III *183*
St Andre, Nathaniel (1680–1776) I *121*
St Aubyn, Sir John, 5th Bart (1758–1839) II *188*
St Davids, 1st Viscount (1860–1938) IV *95*
Saint-Évremond, Charles de Marguetel de (1613?–1703) I *121*
St Germans, 3rd Earl of (1798–1877) II *188*
St Helens, Baron (*c* 1753–1839) II *188*
St Helier, Baron (1843–1905) III *183*
St John, Oliver (1598?–1673) I *121*
St Just, 1st Baron (1870–1941) IV *95*
St Leger, J.H. (1756–1800) II *188*
St Leonards, E.B.S. (1781–1875) II *188*
St Lo, George (*d* 1718) I *121*
Sainton, P.P.C. (1813–1890) III *183*
Sainton-Dolby, Charlotte Helen (1821–1885) III *183*
Saintsbury, G.E.B. (1845–1933) III *183*
St Vincent, 1st Earl of (1735–1823) II *188*
Sala, G.A.H. (1828–1896) III *183*
Salaman, C.K. (1814–1901) III *183*
Salaman, R.N. (1874–1955) IV *95*
Sale, Florentina, Lady (1790?–1853) II *188*
Sale, Sir R.H. (1782–1845) II *188*
Salisbury, Earl of (*d* 1226) I *121*
Salisbury, 1st Earl of (1563?–1612) I *121*
Salisbury, 3rd Earl (*d* 1683) I *121*
Salisbury, 4th Earl of (*d* 1693) I *121*
Salisbury, 7th Earl and 1st Marquess of (1748–1823) II *188*
Salisbury, 3rd Marquess of (1830–1903) III *183*
Salisbury, 4th Marquess of (1861–1947) IV *95*
Salisbury, 5th Marquess of (1893–1972) IV *95*
Salisbury, Countess of (1473–1541) I *121*
Salisbury, 1st Marchioness of (1750–1835) II *189*
Salisbury, E.R.G. (1819–1890) III *183*
Salisbury, Frank O. (1874–1962) IV *95*
Salisbury, R.A. (1761–1829) II *189*
Salmon, Sir E.C.H. (1896–1946) IV *95*
Salmon, George (1819–1904) III *183*–*184*
Salmon, William (1644–1712) I *121*
Salmond, Sir John (1881–1968) IV *95*
Salomons, J.P. (1745–1815) II *189*
Salomons, Sir David, 1st Bart (1797–1873) II *189*
Salt, Henry (1780–1827) II *189*
Salt, Sir Titus (1803–1876) III *184*
Salter, 1st Baron (1881–1975) IV *95*
Salter, Samuel (*d* 1756?) I *121*
Salter, George (1835–1909) III *184*
Salter, William (1804–1875) III *184*
Salting, George (1835–1909) III *184*
Saltonstall, Charles (fl 1642) I *122*
Saltonstall, Richard (1586–1661?) I *122*
Saltoun, 16th Baron (1785–1853) II *189*
Sambourne, E.L. (1844–1910) III *184*
Sammons, Albert (1886–1957) IV *95*
Sams, Joseph (1784–1860) II *189*
Samson, C.R. (1883–1931) IV *95*
Samuda, J. d'A (1813–1885) III *184*
Samuel, 1st Viscount (1870–1963) IV *95*
Samuelson, Sir Bernhard (1820–1905) III *184*
Sancho, Ignatius (1729–1780) II *189*
Sancroft, William (1617–1693) I *121*
Sanday, William (1843–1920) III *184*
Sandby, Paul (1730/1–1809) II *189*

Sandby, Thomas (1723–1798) II 189
Sandeman, Sir R.G. (1835–1892) III 184
Sanders, Sir A.P.M. (1898–1974) IV 95
Sanders, George (1774–1846) II 189
Sanderson, 1st Baron (1841–1923) III 184
Sanderson, 1st Baron (1868–1939) IV 95
Sanderson, F.W. (1857–1922) III 184
Sanderson, Robert (1587–1663) I 122
Sanderson, Sir William (1586?–1676) I 122
Sandford, 1st Baron (1824–1893) III 184
Sandford, Daniel (1766–1830) II 189
Sandford, Sir D.K. (1798–1838) II 189
Sandford, Francis (1630–1694) I 122
Sandford, Sir H.B. (1826–1892) III 184
Sandhurst, 1st Baron (1819–1876) III 184
Sands, Lord (1857–1934) III 184
Sandwich, 1st Earl of (1625–1672) I 122
Sandwich, 4th Earl of (1718–1792) II 189
Sandwich, 9th Earl of (1874–1962) IV 96
Sandwith, Humphry (1822–1881) III 184
Sandys, Edwin (1516?–1588) I 122
Sandys, Sir Edwin (1561–1629) I 122
Sandys, Frederick (1829–1904) III 184
Sandys, George (1578–1644) I 122
Sangster, W.E.R. (1900–1960) IV 96
Sankey, Viscount (1866–1948) IV 96
Sant, James (1820–1916) III 184
Santley, Sir Charles (1834–1922) III 184
Saphir, Adolph (1831–1891) III 184
Sargent, Sir C.H. (1856–1942) III 185
Sargent, John (1857–1922) III 185
Sargent, John Singer (1856–1925) III 185
Sargent, Sir Malcolm (1895–1967) IV 96
Sargent, Sir Orme (1884–1962) IV 96
Sarmento, J. de C. (1692–1762) I 122
Sartoris, Adelaide (1814?–1879) III 185
Sass, Henry (1788–1844) II 189
Sassoon, Sir A.A.D. (1818–1896) III 185
Sassoon, Sir P.A.G.D. (1888–1939) IV 96
Sassoon, Siegfrid (1886–1967) IV 96
Sassoon, Sir Victor (1881–1961) IV 96
Satow, Sir E.M. (1843–1929) III 185
Saumarez, Philip (1710–1747) II 189
Saundby, Sir R.H.M.S. (1896–1971) IV 96
Saunders, Sir Charles (1713?–1775) II 189
Saunders, Sir Edward (d 1576) I 122
Saunders, George (1762–1839) II 189
Saunders, H. St.G. (1898–1951) IV 96
Saunders, J.C. (1773–1810) II 189
Saunders, Laurence (d 1555) I 122
Saunders, Richard (1613–1687?) I 122
Saunders, William (1743–1817) II 189
Saunders, W.W. (1809–1879) III 185
Saunderson, E.J. (1837–1906) III 185
Saunderson, Nicholas (1682–1739) I 122
Savage, Sir Arnold (d 1410) I 122
Savage, Henry (1604?–1672) I 122
Savage, Sir John (d 1492) I 122
Savage, John (1673–1747) I 122
Savage, S.M. (1721–1791) II 189
Savile, 1st Baron (1818–1896) III 185
Savile, 2nd Baron (1853–1931) III 185
Savile, Sir George (1726–1784) II 189
Savile, Sir Henry (1549–1622) I 122
Savile, Sir John (1545–1607) I 122
Savory, Sir W.S. (1826–1895) III 185
Sawbridge, John (1732?–1795) II 189
Sawyer, Sir Robert (1633–1692) I 122
Saxl, Friedrich (1890–1948) IV 96
Saxton, Sir Charles (1732–1808) II 190
Say, Sir John (d 1478?) I 122
Say, Samuel (1676–1743) I 122
Say, William (1768–1834) II 190
Sayce, A.H. (1845–1933) III 185
Saye, 1st Viscount (1582–1662) I 122
Sayers, Dorothy Leigh (1893–1957) IV 96
Sayers, Frank (1763–1817) II 190
Sayers, James (1748–1823) II 190
Sayers, Tom (1826–1865) III 185
Scaleits, Robert (1499?–1594) I 122
Scambler, Edmund (1510?–1594) I 122
Scarborough, 2nd Earl of (1688?–1740) I 122
Scarborough, 11th Earl of (1896–1969) IV 122
Scarborough, Sir Charles (1616–1694) I 122
Schanck, John (1740–1823) II 190
Scharf, Sir George (1820–1895) III 185
Scharlieb, Dame Mary Ann Dacomb (1845–1930) III 185
Scheemakers, Peter (1691–1781) I 123
Schevez, William (d 1497) I 123
Schetky, J.C. (1778–1874) II 190
Schiavonetti, Luigi (1765–1810) II 190
Schiller, F.C.S. (1864–1937) IV 96
Schimmelpenninck, Mrs Mary Anne (1778–1856) II 190
Schlich, Sir William (1840–1925) III 185
Schmitz, Leonhard (1807–1890) III 185
Schnadhorst, Francis (1840–1900) III 185–186
Scholefield, James (1789–1853) II 190

Scholefield, William (1809–1867) III 186
Scholes, P.A. (1877–1958) IV 96
Schomberg, 1st Duke of (1615–1690) I 123
Schomberg, 3rd Duke of (1641–1719) I 123
Schomberg, Sir Alexander (1720–1804) II 190
Schomberg, Isaac (1714–1780) II 190
Schomberg, Isaac (1753–1813) II 190
Schomberg, Ralph (1714–1792) II 190
Schomburgk, Sir R.H. (1804–1865) III 186
Schonland, Sir B.F.J. (1896–1972) IV 96
Schorlemmer, Carl (1834–1892) III 186
Schreiber, Lady Charlotte Elizabeth (1812–1895) III 186
Schreiner, W.P. (1857–1919) III 186
Schuster, Baron (1869–1956) IV 96
Schuster, Sir Arthur (1851–1934) III 186
Schuster, Sir F.O., 1st Bart (1854–1936) III 186
Schwabe, Randolph (1885–1948) IV 96
Schwanfelder, C.H. (1773–1837) II 190
Schweickhardt, H.W. (1746–1797) II 190
Scobell, Henry (d 1660) I 123
Scobie, Sir R.M. (1893–1969) IV 96
Scoones, Sir G.A.P. (1893–1975) IV 96
Scoresby, William (1760–1829) II 190
Scoresby, William (1789–1857) II 190
Scott, Archibald (1837–1909) III 186
Scott, Caroline Lucy, Lady (1784–1857) II 190
Scott, Cyril (1879–1970) IV 96
Scott, C.P. (1846–1932) III 186
Scott, Lord C.T. Montagu-Douglas (1839–1911) III 186
Scott, C.W. (1841–1904) III 186
Scott, David (1806–1849) III 186
Scott, D.H. (1854–1934) III 186
Scott, Sir George Gilbert (1811–1878) III 186
Scott, Sir Giles Gilbert (1880–1960) IV 96
Scott, Sir Harold (1887–1969) IV 96–97
Scott, H.Y.D. (1822–1883) III 186
Scott, John (1639–1695) I 123
Scott, John (1730–1783) II 190
Scott, John (1774–1827) II 190
Scott, John (1783–1821) II 190
Scott, Sir John (1841–1904) III 186
Scott, Sir L.F. (1869–1950) IV 97
Scott, Michael (1789–1835) II 190
Scott, Sir P.M., 1st Bart (1853–1924) III 186
Scott, Robert (1811–1887) III 186
Scott, Robert Falcon (1868–1912) IV 97
Scott, Samuel (1702?–1772) II 190
Scott, Sir Thomas (1535–1594?) I 123
Scott, Thomas (1580?–1626) I 123
Scott, Thomas (d 1660) I 123
Scott, Thomas (1747–1821) II 190
Scott, Sir Walter (1771–1832) II 190–191
Scott, Sir William (1459–1524) I 123
Scott, William (1797–1848) II 191
Scott, William Bell (1811–1890) III 186
Scougall, Henry (1650–1678) I 123
Scougall, John (1645?–1730?) I 123
Scougall, Patrick (1607?–1682) I 123
Scovell, Sir George (1774–1861) II 191
Scratchley, Sir P.H. (1835–1885) III 186
Scriven, Edward (1775–1841) II 191
Scroggs, Sir William (1623–1683) I 123
Scrope, Adrian (1601–1660) I 123
Scrope, G.J.P. (1797–1876) II 191
Scrope, John (1662?–1752) I 123
Scrope, Richard (1350?–1405) I 123
Scrutton, Sir T.E. (1856–1934) III 186
Scudamore, 1st Viscount (1601–1671) I 123
Scudder, Henry (d 1659?) I 123
Scully, Vincent (1810–1871) III 186
Seafield, 1st Earl of (1664–1730) I 123
Seaford, 1st Baron (1771–1745) II 191
Seaforth, 4th Earl of (d 1701) I 123
Seaforth and Mackenzie, Baron (1754–1815) II 191
Seal, Sir Eric (1898–1972) IV 97
Seale-Hayne, C.H. (1833–1903) III 186
Seaman, Sir Owen, Bart (1861–1936) IV 97
Seaton, 1st Baron (1778–1863) II 191
Sebright, Sir J.S., 7th Bart (1767–1846) II 191
Secker, Thomas (1693–1768) I 123
Sedding, J.D. (1838–1891) III 186
Seddon, John (1644–1700) I 123
Seddon, R.J. (1845–1906) III 187
Sedgwick, Adam (1785–1873) II 191
Sedgwick, Adam (1854–1913) III 187
Sedgwick, Amy (1830–1897) III 187
Sedgwick, Obadiah (1600?–1658) I 123
Sedley, Sir Charles (1639?–1701) I 123
Seed, Jeremiah (1700–1747) II 191
Seeley, Sir J.R. (1834–1895) III 187
Seeman, Enoch (1694–1744) I 123
Seemann, B.C. (1825–1871) III 187
Segar, Sir William (d 1633) I 123
Séguier, William (1771–1843) II 191
Selbie, W.B. (1862–1944) IV 97
Selborne, 1st Earl of (1812–1895) III 187
Selborne, 2nd Earl of (1859–1942) III 187

Selborne, 3rd Earl of (1887–1971) IV 97
Selby, 1st Viscount (1835–1909) III 187
Selby, P.J. (1788–1867) II 191
Selby, Sir W.H.M. (1881–1965) IV 97
Selden, John (1584–1654) I 123
Selfridge, H.G. (1858–1947) III 187
Seligman, C.G. (1873–1940) IV 97
Selincourt, Ernest de (1870–1943) IV 97
Sellar, W.Y. (1825–1890) III 187
Selous, F.C. (1851–1917) III 187
Selous, H.C. (1811–1890) III 187
Selwyn, Sir C.J. (1813–1869) III 187
Selwyn, G.A. (1719–1791) II 191
Selwyn, G.A. (1809–1878) III 187
Selwyn, William (1806–1875) III 187
Semon, Sir Felix (1849–1921) III 187
Semple, J.G. (fl 1799) II 191
Sendall, Sir W.J. (1832–1904) III 187–188
Senior, N.W. (1790–1864) II 191
Seppings, Sir Robert (1767–1840) II 191
Sergison, Charles (1654–1732) I 123
Sermon, William (1629?–1679) I 123
Serres, Dominic (1722–1793) II 191
Serres, Olivia (1772–1834) II 191
Seton, 5th Baron (1531–1585) I 123
Seton, George (1822–1908) III 188
Seton-Watson, R.W. (1879–1951) IV 97
Sever, Henry (d 1471) I 124
Severn, Joseph (1793–1879) II 191
Sewall, Samuel (1652–1730) I 124
Seward, Anna (1742–1809) II 191
Seward, Sir A.C. (1863–1941) IV 97
Seward, Thomas (1708–1790) II 191
Seward, William (1747–1799) II 191
Sewell, J.E. (1810–1903) III 188
Seyer, Samuel (1757–1831) II 191
Seyler, Athene (b 1889) IV 97
Seymour, Lady Arabella (1575–1615) I 124
Seymour, Sir Edward, 4th Bart (1633–1708) I 124
Seymour, Sir E.H. (1840–1929) III 188
Seymour, Sir Francis (1813–1890) III 188
Seymour, Sir G.F. (1787–1870) II 191
Seymour, Sir G.H. (1797–1880) II 191
Seymour, Lord Hugh (1759–1801) II 191–192
Seymour, James (1702–1752) II 192
Seymour, Sir Michael, 1st Bart (1768–1834) II 192
Seymour, Sir Michael (1802–1887) III 188
Seymour, W.D. (1822–1895) III 188
Seymour of Sudeley, Baron (1508?–1549) I 124
Seymour of Trowbridge, 1st Baron (1590?–1664) I 124
Shackleton, Sir D.J. (1863–1938) IV 97
Shackleton, Sir E.H. (1874–1922) IV 97
Shadwell, C.L. (1840–1919) III 188
Shadwell, Sir Lancelot (1779–1850) II 192
Shadwell, Thomas (1642?–1692) I 124
Shaftesbury, 1st Earl of (1621–1683) I 124
Shaftesbury, 3rd Earl of (1671–1713) I 124
Shaftesbury, 7th Earl of (1801–1885) III 188
Shairp, J.C. (1819–1885) III 188
Shakespeare, William (1564–1616) I 124
Shand, 1st Baron (1828–1904) III 188
Shandon, Baron (1857–1930) III 188
Shannon, 1st Earl of (1682–1764) I 124
Shannon, Charles Haslewood (1863–1937) IV 97
Shannon, Sir J.J. (1862–1923) IV 97
Sharington, Sir William (1495?–1553) I 124
Sharp, Cecil James (1859–1924) IV 97
Sharp, Evelyn (1869–1955) IV 97–98
Sharp, Granville (1735–1813) II 192
Sharp, James (1613–1679) I 124
Sharp, John (1645–1714) I 124
Sharp, Thomas (1693–1758) I 124
Sharp, Thomas (1770–1841) II 192
Sharp, William (1749–1824) II 192
Sharp, William (1855–1905) III 188
Sharpe, C.K. (c 1781–1851) II 192
Sharpe, Daniel (1806–1856) III 188
Sharpe, Gregory (1713–1771) II 192
Sharpe, Samuel (1799–1881) II 192
Sharpey, William (1802–1880) III 188
Sharpey-Schafer, Sir E.A. (1850–1935) III 188
Shaw, Sir E.M. (1830–1908) III 188
Shaw, Sir Frederick, 2nd Bart (1799–1876) II 192
Shaw, George (1751–1813) II 192
Shaw, George Bernard (1856–1950) III 188–189
Shaw, Sir James (1764–1843) II 192
Shaw, J.J. (1845–1910) III 189
Shaw, Mary (1814–1876) III 189
Shaw, Peter (1695–1763) I 124
Shaw, R.N. (1831–1912) III 189
Shaw, Stebbing (1762–1802) II 192
Shaw, Sir Napier (1854–1945) III 189
Shaw, Thomas (1694–1751) I 124
Shaw, Thomas (1872–1938) IV 98
Shaw, W.A. (1865–1943) IV 98
Shaw-Lefevre, Sir J.G. (1797–1879) II 192
Sheaffe, Sir R.H. (1763–1851) II 192

Shearman, Sir Montague (1857–1930) III *189*
Shebbeare, John (1709–1788) II *192*
Shee, Sir M.A. (1769–1850) II *192*
Shee, Sir William (1804–1868) III *189*
Sheepshanks, John (1787–1863) II *192*
Sheepshanks, Richard (1794–1855) II *192*
Sheepshanks, Sir T.H. (1895–1964) IV *98*
Sheffield, 1st Earl of (1735–1821) II *192*
Sheffield, Countess of (1764–1832) II *192*
Sheffield, 4th Baron (1839–1925) III *189*
Sheil, R.L. (1791–1851) II *192*
Sheldon, Gilbert (1598–1677) I *124*
Sheldon, John (1752–1808) II *192*
Shelley, George (1666?–1736) I *124*
Shelley, Mary Wollstonecraft (1797–1851) II *193*
Shelley, Percy Bysshe (1792–1822) II *193*
Shelley, Sir Richard (1513?–1589?) I *124*
Shelton, Thomas (1601–1650?) I *124*
Shenstone, William (1714–1763) II *193*
Shepard, E.H. (1879–1976) IV *98*
Shepherd, Antony (1721–1796) II *193*
Shepherd, Sir Fleetwood (1634–1698) I *124*
Shepherd, Sir Samuel (1760–1840) II *193*
Shepherd, William (1768–1847) II *193*
Sheppard, H.R.L. (1880–1937) IV *98*
Sheppard, John (1702–1724) II *193*
Sheppard, Sir J.T. (1881–1968) IV *98*
Shepstone, Sir Theophilus (1817–1893) III *189*
Sherborn, C.W. (1831–1912) III *189*
Sherbrooke, 1st Viscount (1811–1892) III *189*
Sheridan, Elizabeth Ann (1754–1792) II *193*
Sheridan, Esther Jane (1776–1817) II *193*
Sheridan, Frances (1724–1766) II *193*
Sheridan, R.B. (1751–1816) II *193*
Sheridan, Thomas (1687–1738) I *124*
Sheridan, Thomas (1719–1788) II *193*
Sheridan, William (1636–1711) I *125*
Sherlock, Richard (1612–1689) I *125*
Sherlock, Thomas (1678–1761) I *125*
Sherlock, William (1641?–1707) I *125*
Sherman, James (1796–1862) II *193*
Sherring, M.A. (1826–1880) III *189*
Sherrington, Sir C.S. (1857–1952) III *189–190*
Sherwin, J.K. (1751?–1790) II *193*
Sherwin, William (1607–1687?) I *125*
Sherwood, Mary Martha (1775–1851) II *193*
Shield, William (1748–1829) II *193*
Shields, F.J. (1833–1911) III *190*
Shiels, Sir Drummond (1881–1953) IV *98*
Shillitoe, Thomas (1754–1836) II *193*
Shinwell, Baron (*b*1884) IV *98*
Shipley, Sir A.E. (1861–1927) IV *98*
Shipley, Sir Charles (1755–1815) II *193*
Shipley, Jonathan (1714–1788) II *193*
Shipley, William (1714–1803) II *193*
Shipley, W.D. (1745–1826) II *193*
Shipp, John (1784–1834) II *193*
Shippen, Robert (1675–1745) I *125*
Shippen, William (1673–1743) I *125*
Shirley, Sir Anthony (1565–1635?) I *125*
Shirley, James (1596–1666) I *125*
Shirley, Sir Robert (1581?–1628) I *125*
Shirley, Sir Robert, Bart (1629–1656) I *125*
Shirley, Walter (1725–1786) II *193*
Shirley, William (1694–1771) I *125*
Shirley, W.A. (1797–1847) II *193–194*
Shirley, W.W. (1828–1866) III *190*
Shirreff, Emily Anne Eliza (1814–1897) III *190*
Shore, Jane (*d*1527?) I *125*
Short, Augustus (1802–1883) III *190*
Short, Sir Francis (1857–1945) III *190*
Short, James (1710–1768) II *194*
Short, Oswald (1883?–1969) IV *98*
Short, T.V. (1790–1872) II *194*
Shorter, C.K. (1857–1926) III *190*
Shortland, John (1769–1810) II *194*
Shorton, Robert (*d*1535) I *125*
Shortt, Edward (1862–1935) IV *98*
Shovell, Sir Clowdisley (1650–1707) I *125*
Shower, Sir Bartholomew (1658–1701) I *125*
Shower, John (1657–1715) I *125*
Shrapnel, Henry (1761–1842) II *194*
Shrewsbury, 1st Earl of (1388?–1453) I *125*
Shrewsbury, 4th Earl of (1468–1538) I *125*
Shrewsbury, 6th Earl of (1528?–1590) I *125*
Shrewsbury, 7th Earl of (1553–1616) I *125*
Shrewsbury, 1st Duke of (1660–1718) I *125*
Shrewsbury, Countess of (1518–1608) I *125*
Shrubsole, William (1729–1797) II *194*
Shuckburgh, E.S. (1843–1906) III *190*
Shuckburgh, Sir J.E. (1877–1953) IV *98*
Shuckburgh, Sir Richard (1596–1656) I *125*
Shuldham, Baron (1717?–1798) II *194*
Shute, Josiah (1588–1643) I *125*
Shuter, Edward (1728?–1776) II *194*
Shuttleworth, P.N. (1782–1842) II *194*
Sibbald, James (1745–1803) II *194*

Sibbald, Sir Robert (1641–1722) I *125*
Sibbes, Richard (1577–1635) I *125*
Sibly, Sir Franklin (1883–1948) IV *98*
Sibly, Manoah (1757–1840) II *194*
Sibthorp, Humphry (1713–1797) II *194*
Sibthorp, John (1758–1796) II *194*
Sibthorpe, R.W. (1792–1879) II *194*
Sickert, W.R. (1860–1942) IV *98*
Siddal, Elizabeth Eleanor (*d*1862) III *190*
Siddons, Mrs Harriet (1783–1844) II *194*
Siddons, Henry (1774–1815) II *194*
Siddons, Sarah (1755–1831) II *194*
Sidgwick, Eleanor Mildred (1845–1936) III *190*
Sidgwick, Henry (1838–1900) III *190*
Sidgwick, N.V. (1873–1952) IV *98*
Sidmouth, 1st Viscount (1757–1844) II *194*
Sidney, Algernon (1622–1683) I *126*
Sidney, Sir Henry (1529–1586) I *126*
Sidney, Sir Philip (1544–1586) I *126*
Sieff, Baron (1889–1972) IV *98*
Siemens, Sir William (1823–1883) III *190*
Siepmann, Otto (1861–1947) IV *98*
Sieveking, Sir E.H. (1816–1904) III *190*
Sikes, Sir C.W. (1818–1889) III *190*
Silkin, 1st Baron (1889–1972) IV *98*
Sillery, C.D. (1807–1837) III *90*
Sillitoe, Sir Percy (1888–1962) IV *98*
Silverman, Sidney (1895–1968) IV *98*
Sim, Alastair (1900–1976) IV *98*
Simcoe, J.G. (1752–1806) II *194*
Simeon, Charles (1759–1836) II *194*
Simmons, Sir J.L.A. (1821–1903) III *190*
Simmons, Samuel (1777?–1819) II *194–195*
Simms, F.W. (1803–1865) III *190*
Simon, 1st Viscount (1873–1954) IV *98–99*
Simon, Abraham (1617–1692) I *126*
Simon, Sir John (1816–1904) III *190–191*
Simon, Sir John (1818–1897) III *191*
Simon, O.J. (1895–1956) IV *99*
Simon, Thomas (1623?–1665) I *126*
Simon of Wythenshawe, 1st Baron (1879–1960) IV *99*
Simonds, Viscount (1881–1971) IV *99*
Simonsen, Sir J.L. (1884–1957) IV *99*
Simpson, B.F. (1883–1971) IV *99*
Simpson, Christopher (1605?–1669) I *126*
Simpson, David (1745–1799) II *195*
Simpson, Edward (1578–1651) I *126*
Simpson, F.A. (1883–1974) IV *99*
Simpson, Sir George (1792–1860) II *195*
Simpson, Sir George (1878–1965) IV *99*
Simpson, Sir James (1792–1868) II *195*
Simpson, Sir J.H. (1868–1961) IV *99*
Simpson, Sir J.W. (1858–1933) III *191*
Simpson, Sir J.Y., 1st Bart (1811–1870) III *191*
Simpson, Percy (1865–1962) IV *99*
Simpson, Sidrach (1600?–1655) I *126*
Simpson, Thomas (1808–1840) III *191*
Simpson, William (1823–1899) III *191*
Simpson, Sir W.J.R. (1855–1931) III *191*
Sims, Charles (1873–1928) IV *99*
Sims, James (1741–1820) II *195*
Sims, John (1749–1831) II *195*
Simson, Robert (1687–1768) I *126*
Simson, William (1800–1847) III *191*
Sinclair, Sir George (1790–1868) II *195*
Sinclair, James (*d*1762) I *126*
Sinclair, Sir John, 1st Bart (*c*1754–1835) II *195*
Sinclair, John (1791–1857) II *195*
Sinclair of Cleeve, 1st Baron (1893–1979) IV *99*
Singer, C.J. (1876–1960) IV *99*
Singleton, Sir J.E. (1885–1957) IV *99*
Sirr, H.C. (1764–1841) II *195*
Sirr, H.C. (1807–1872) III *191*
Sirr, Joseph D'Arcy (1794–1868) II *195*
Sisam, Kenneth (1887–1971) IV *99*
Sitwell, Dame Edith (1887–1964) IV *99*
Sitwell, Sir Osbert, 5th Bart (1892–1969) IV *99*
Sitwell, Sir Sacheverell, 6th Bart (*b*1897) IV *99–100*
Skae, David (1814–1873) III *191*
Skeat, W.W. (1835–1912) III *191*
Skeffington, Sir L. StG., Bart (1771–1850) II *195*
Skelton, Bevil (fl1661–1692) I *126*
Skelton, Sir John (1831–1897) III *191*
Skelton, William (1763–1848) II *195*
Skene, James (1775–1864) II *195*
Skene, W.F. (1809–1892) III *191*
Skinner, James (1778–1841) II *195*
Skinner, John (1721–1807) II *195*
Skinner, John (1744–1816) II *195*
Skinner, Matthew (1689–1749) I *126*
Skinner, William (1700–1780) II*195*
Skippon, Philip (*d*1660) I *126*
Skipsey, Joseph (1832–1903) III *191*
Skirving, Adam (1719–1803) II *195*
Skirving, Archibald (1749–1819) II *195*
Skynner, Sir John (1723–1805) II *195*
Slade, Sir Adolphus (1804–1877) III *191*

Slade, Felix (1790–1868) II *195*
Slade, Sir G.O. (1891–1962) IV *100*
Slade, Sir John, 1st Bart (1762–1859) II *195*
Sladen, Sir Charles (1816–1884) III *191*
Sladen, Sir E.B. (1827–1890) III *191*
Slanning, Sir Nicholas (1606–1643) I *126*
Slater, Samuel (*d*1704) I *126*
Slater, William (1587–1647) I *126*
Slater, Sir William (1893–1970) IV *100*
Slatin, Baron (1857–1932) III *191*
Slatter, Sir L.H. (1894–1961) IV *100*
Sleath, John (1767–1847) II *195*
Sleigh, W.C. (1818–1887) III *191*
Slim, 1st Viscount (1891–1970) IV *100*
Sloane, Sir Hans (1660–1753) I *126*
Smalbroke, Richard (1672–1749) I *126*
Small, John (1726–1796) II *195*
Smalridge, George (1663–1719) I *126*
Smart, Christopher (1722–1771) II *195*
Smart, Sir G.T. (1776–1867) II *195*
Smart, H.H. (1833–1893) III *191*
Smart, H.T. (1813–1879) III *191*
Smart, John (1741–1811) II *195*
Smart, Sir M.W. (1877–1956) IV *100*
Smart, Peter (1569–1652?) I *126*
Smartt, Sir T.W. (1858–1929) III *191*
Smeaton, John (1724–1792) II *195*
Smedley, F.E. (1818–1864) III *191*
Smedley, Jonathan (fl 1689–1729) I *126*
Smee, Alfred (1818–1877) III *191*
Smellie, William (1697–1763) I *126*
Smellie, William (1740–1795) II *195*
Smetham, James (1821–1889) III *191*
Smibert, John (1684–1751) I *126*
Smillie, Robert (1857–1940) III *191*
Smirke, Robert (1752–1845) II *195–196*
Smirke, Sir Robert (1781–1867) II *196*
Smirke, Sydney (1798–1877) III *196*
Smith, Adam (1723–1790) II *196*
Smith, Alexander (1830–1867) III *191*
Smith, Aquilla (1806–1890) III *191*
Smith, Archibald (1813–1872) III *191*
Smith, Sir A.L. (1836–1901) III *191*
Smith, A.L. (1850–1924) III *192*
Smith, A.R. (1816–1860) III *191*
Smith, Benjamin (*d*1833) II *196*
Smith, B.L. (1828–1913) III *192*
Smith, Sir Benjamin (1879–1964) IV *100*
Smith, Bernard (1630?–1708) I *126*
Smith, Charles (1749?–1824) II *196*
Smith, C.H. (1776–1859) II *196*
Smith, C.R. (1807–1890) III *192*
Smith, Charlotte (1749–1806) II *196*
Smith, D.N. (1875–1962) IV *100*
Smith, Elizabeth (1774–1806) II *196*
Smith, Erasmus (1611–1691) I *126*
Smith, Sir E.W. (1884–1960) IV *100*
Smith, Sir Frank (1879–1970) IV *100*
Smith, Sir F.P. (1808–1874) III *192*
Smith, Sir Frederick (1857–1927) III *192*
Smith, George (1713–1776) I *196*
Smith, George (1815–1871) III *192*
Smith, George (1824–1901) III *192*
Smith, George (1831–1895) III *192*
Smith, George (1840–1876) III *192*
Smith, Sir G.A. (1856–1942) III *192*
Smith, G.B. (1841–1909) III *192*
Smith, G.C. (1782–1863) II *196*
Smith, Goldwin (1823–1910) III *192*
Smith, Sir G.E. (1871–1937) IV *100*
Smith, Sir H.G.W., 1st Bart (1787–1860) II *196*
Smith, Henry (1550?–1591) I *127*
Smith, Sir H.B. (1863–1923) IV *100*
Smith, H.J.S. (1826–1883) III *192*
Smith, Herbert (1862–1938) IV *100*
Smith, Horatio (1779–1849) II *196*
Smith, H.L. (1864–1945) IV *100*
Smith, James (1645–1731) I *127*
Smith, James (1775–1839) II *196*
Smith, James (1782–1867) II *196*
Smith, Sir J.E. (1759–1828) II *196*
Smith, J.E. (1801–1857) III *192*
Smith, Sir Jeremiah (1615–1675) I *127*
Smith, John (1580?–1631) I *127*
Smith, John (1652–1742) I *127*
Smith, John (1655–1723) I *127*
Smith, John (1657–1726) I *127*
Smith, John (1717–1764) II *196*
Smith, J.A. (1863–1939) IV *100*
Smith, J.C. (1752–1795) II *196*
Smith, J.P. (1774–1851) II *196*
Smith, J.R. (1752–1812) II *196*
Smith, J.R. (1810–1894) III *192*
Smith, J.S. (1750–1836) II *196*
Smith, J. (1766–1833) II *196*
Smith, Joseph (1670–1756) I *127*
Smith, L.P. (1865–1946) IV *100*

Smith, Sir M.A.B. (1879–1959) IV *100*
Smith, Miles (1552?–1624) I *127*
Smith, Pleasance, Lady (1773–1877) II *196*
Smith, R.J. (1786–1855) II *196*
Smith, Robert (1689–1768) I *127*
Smith, R.P. (1819–1865) III *192*
Smith, Sir R.M. (1892–1922) IV *100*
Smith, Samuel (1836–1906) III *192*
Smith, S.C. (1806–1872) III *192*
Smith, Sydney (1771–1845) II *196–197*
Smith, Sir Thomas (1513–1577) I *127*
Smith, Sir Thomas (1558?–1625) I *127*
Smith, Thomas (1615–1702) I *127*
Smith, Thomas (1706?–1762) I *127*
Smith, Thomas (1817–1906) III *192*
Smith, Sir Thomas, 1st Bart (1833–1909) III *192*
Smith, T.A. (1776–1858) II *197*
Smith, T.S. (1788–1861) II *197*
Smith, W.C. (1824–1908) III *192*
Smith, William (1460?–1514) I *127*
Smith, William (1651–1735) I *127*
Smith, William (1707–1764) II *197*
Smith, William (1730?–1819) II *197*
Smith, William (1756–1835) II *197*
Smith, Sir William, 2nd Bart (1766–1836) II *197*
Smith, William (1769–1839) II *197*
Smith, William (1808–1876) III *192*
Smith, Sir William (1813–1893) III *192*
Smith, W.H. (1825–1891) III *192*
Smith, W.R. (1846–1894) III *193*
Smith, Sir W.S. (1764–1840) II *197*
Smith, W.T. (1815–1873) III *193*
Smith, Wilson (1897–1965) IV *100*
Smith-Dorrien, Sir H.L. (1858–1930) III *193*
Smithells, Arthur (1860–1939) IV *100*
Smithson, Harriet Constance (1800–1854) III *193*
Smollett, T.G. (1721–1771) II *197*
Smyth, Edward (1749–1812) II *197*
Smyth, Dame Ethel Mary (1858–1944) III *193*
Smyth, Sir H.A. (1825–1906) III *193*
Smyth, Sir J.C., 1st Bart (1779–1838) II *197*
Smyth, Sir Leicester (1829–1891) III *193*
Smyth, Richard (1826–1878) III *193*
Smyth, William (1765–1849) II *197*
Smyth, W.H. (1788–1865) II *197*
Smyth, Sir W.W. (1817–1890) III *193*
Smythies, C.A. (1844–1894) III *193*
Snagge, Thomas (1536–1592) I *127*
Snape, Andrew (1675–1742) I *127*
Snell, Baron (1865–1944) IV *100*
Snell, Hannah (1723–1792) II *197*
Snell, Sir J.F.C. (1869–1938) IV *100*
Snelling, Thomas (1712–1773) II *197*
Snowden, Viscount (1864–1937) IV *100*
Soane, George (1790–1860) II *197*
Soane, Sir John (1753–1837) II *197*
Soddy, Frederick (1877–1956) IV *100*
Soest, Gerard (*d* 1681) I *127*
Sokolova, Lydia (1896–1974) IV *101*
Solander, D.C. (1736–1782) II *197*
Solomon, Abraham (1823–1862) III *193*
Solomon, Sir Richard (1850–1913) III *193*
Solomon, Simeon (1840–1905) III *193*
Solomon, Solomon J. (1860–1927) IV *101*
Somers, Baron (1651–1716) I *127*
Somers, 6th Baron (1887–1944) IV *101*
Somerset, 1st Earl of (1373?–1410) I *128*
Somerset, 1st Duke of (1403–1444) I *128*
Somerset, 2nd Duke of (1588–1660) I *128*
Somerset, 1st Duke of (1506?–1552) I *127*
Somerset, 6th Duke of (1662–1748) I *127*
Somerset, 7th Duke of (1684–1750) I *127*
Somerset, Duchess of (1667–1722) I *127*
Somerset, Earl of (*d* 1645) I *128*
Somerset, 11th Duke of (1775–1855) II *197*
Somerset, 12th Duke of (1804–1885) III *193*
Somerset, Lord G.C.H. (1792–1848) II *197–198*
Somerset, Lady Isabella Caroline (1851–1921) III *193*
Somerset, P.G.H. (1822–1875) III *193*
Somerset, Lord R.E.H. (1776–1842) II *198*
Somervell, T.H. (1890–1975) IV *101*
Somervell of Harrow, Baron (1889–1960) IV *101*
Somerville, 15th Baron (1765–1819) II *198*
Somerville, Alexander (1811–1885) III *193*
Somerville, Sir J.F. (1882–1949) IV *101*
Somerville, Mary (1780–1872) II *198*
Somerville, William (1675–1742) I *128*
Somerville, William (1771–1860) II *198*
Somerville, Sir William (1860–1932) IV *101*
Sommers, William (*d* 1560) I *128*
Somner, William (1598–1669) I *128*
Sophia, Princess, Electress of Hanover (1630–1714) I *128*
Sophia Dorothea of Zell(e) (1666–1726) I *128*
Sophia Dorothea of Prussia (1685–1757) I *128*
Sorby, H.C. (1826–1908) III *193*
Sorley, C.H. (1895–1915) IV *101*

Sorley, Sir R.S. (1898–1974) IV *101*
Sotheby, William (1757–1833) II *198*
Sothern, E.A. (1826–1881) III *193*
Soulbury, 1st Viscount (1887–1971) IV *101*
South, J.F. (1797–1882) II *198*
South, Robert (1634–1716) I *128*
Southampton, Earl of (1490–1542) I *128*
Southampton, 1st Earl of (1505–1550) I *128*
Southampton, 2nd Earl of (1545–1581) I *128*
Southampton, 3rd Earl of (1573–1624) I *128*
Southampton, 4th Earl of (1607–1667) I *128*
Southampton, Countess of (1572?–1648?) I *128*
Southampton, 1st Baron (1737–1797) II *198*
Southborough, 1st Baron (1860–1947) IV *101*
Southcote, John (1511–1585) I *128*
Southcott, Joanna (1750–1814) II *198*
Southerne, Thomas (1660–1746) I *128*
Southesk, 9th Earl of (1827–1905) III *193*
Southey, Sir Richard (1808–1901) III *193*
Southey, Robert (1774–1843) II *198*
Southgate, Richard (1729–1795) II *198*
Southouse-Cheyney, R.E.P. (1896–1951) IV *101*
Southwell, Edward (1671–1731?) I *129*
Southwell, Sir Richard (1504–1564) I *129*
Southwell, Robert (1561?–1595) I *129*
Southwell, Sir Robert (1635–1702) I *129*
Southwell, Sir R.V. (1888–1970) IV *101*
Southwood, Viscount (1873–1946) IV *101*
Sowerby, James (1757–1822) II *198*
Soyer, A.B. (1809–1858) III *193*
Soyer, Elizabeth Emma (1813–1842) III *193*
Spare, A.O. (1886–1956) IV *101*
Sparke, Edward (*d* 1692) I *129*
Sparke, Thomas (1548–1616) I *129*
Sparrow, Anthony (1612–1685) I *129*
Sparrow, John (1615–1665?) I *129*
Spedding, James (1808–1881) III *193–194*
Spearman, C.E. (1863–1945) IV *101*
Spears, Sir E.L., 1st Bart (1886–1974) IV *101*
Speed, Harold (1872–1957) IV *101*
Speed, John (1552?–1629) I *129*
Spcke, J.H. (1827–1864) III *194*
Spelman, Sir Henry (1564?–1641) I *129*
Spence, Elizabeth Isabella (1768–1832) II *198*
Spence, George (1787–1850) II *198*
Spence, James (1812–1882) III *194*
Spence, Joseph (1699–1768) I *129*
Spence, William (1783–1860) II *198*
Spencer, 2nd Earl (1758–1834) II *198*
Spencer, 5th Earl (1835–1910) III *194*
Spencer, 7th Earl (1892–1975) IV *101*
Spencer, A.G. (1795–1872) II *198*
Spencer, Lord Charles (1740–1820) II *198*
Spencer, Gilbert (1892–1979) IV *101*
Spencer, Herbert (1820–1903) III *194*
Spencer, Lord H.J. (1770–1795) II *198*
Spencer, John (1630–1693) I *129*
Spencer, L.J. (1870–1959) IV *101*
Spencer, Sir R.C. (1791–1830) II *199*
Spencer, Sir Stanley (1891–1959) IV *101*
Spencer, Thomas (1791–1811) II *199*
Spencer, Sir W.B. (1860–1929) IV *101*
Spencer-Churchill of Chartwell, Baroness (1885–1977) IV *101–102*
Spencer of Wormleighton, 1st Baron (1570–1627) I *129*
Spender, J.A. (1862–1942) IV *102*
Spens, Sir William (1882–1962) IV *102*
Spenser, John (1559–1614) I *129*
Spielmann, M.H. (1858–1948) III *194*
Spinckes, Nathaniel (1653–1727) I *129*
Spode, Josiah (1733–1797) II *199*
Spode, Josiah (1754–1827) II *199*
Spofforth, F.R. (1853–1926) III *194*
Spooner, W.A. (1844–1930) III *194*
Spotswood, Alexander (1676–1740) I *129*
Spottiswood(e), John (1565–1637?) I *129*
Spottiswood(e), Sir Robert (1596–1646) I *129*
Spottiswoode, William (1825–1883) III *194*
Spragge, Sir Edward (*d* 1673) I *129*
Sprat, Thomas (1635–1713) I *129*
Sprigg, Sir J.G. (1830–1913) III *194*
Spry, H.H. (1804–1842) III *194*
Spurgeon, C.H. (1834–1892) III *194*
Spurgin, John (1797–1866) II *199*
Squire, Sir J.C. (1884–1958) IV *102*
Squire, W.B. (1855–1927) III *194*
Stack, Sir L.O.F. (1868–1924) IV *102*
Stackhouse, John (1742–1819) II *199*
Stackhouse, Thomas (1677–1752) I *129*
Stacpoole, Henry de Vere (1863–1951) IV *102*
Stafford, 1st Viscount (1614–1680) I *129*
Stafford, 1st Marquess of (1721–1803) II *199*
Stafford, R.A. (1801–1854) III *194*
Stainer, Sir John (1840–1901) III *194*
Stair, 1st Viscount (1619–1695) I *129*
Stair, 2nd Earl of (1673–1747) I *129*

Stair, 8th Earl of (1771–1853) II *199*
Stalbridge, 1st Baron (1837–1912) III *195*
Stallybrass, W.T.S. (1883–1948) IV *102*
Stamer, Sir L.T., 3rd Bart (1829–1908) III *195*
Stamford, 1st Earl of (1599?–1673) I *129*
Stamfordham, Baron (1849–1931) III *195*
Stamp, 1st Baron (1880–1941) IV *102*
Stamp, Sir Dudley (1898–1966) IV *102*
Stanbridge, John (1463–1510) I *129*
Stanfield, Clarkson (1793–1867) III *199*
Stanfield, J.F. (*d* 1824) II *199*
Stanford, Sir C.V. (1852–1924) III *195*
Stanger, Christopher (1759–1834) II *199*
Stanhope, 1st Earl of (1673–1721) I *130*
Stanhope, 3rd Earl (1753–1816) II *199*
Stanhope, 4th Earl (1781–1855) II *199*
Stanhope, 5th Earl (1805–1875) III *195*
Stanhope, 7th Earl (1880–1967) IV *102*
Stanhope, Edward (1840–1893) III *195*
Stanhope, George (1660–1728) I *130*
Stanhope, Lady Hester Lucy (1776–1839) II *199*
Stanier, Sir W.A. (1876–1965) IV *102*
Stanley, Sir Arthur (1869–1947) IV *102*
Stanley, A.P. (1815–1881) III *195*
Stanley, Edward (1779–1849) II *199*
Stanley, Edward (1893–1862) II *199*
Stanley, Sir H.J. (1872–1955) IV *102*
Stanley, Sir H.M. (1841–1904) III *195*
Stanley, John (1714–1786) II *199*
Stanley, O.F.G. (1896–1950) IV *102*
Stanley, Thomas (1625–1678) I *130*
Stanley, William (1647–1731) I *130*
Stanley of Alderley, 2nd Baron (1802–1869) III *195*
Stanmore, 1st Baron (1829–1912) III *195*
Stannard, Henrietta Eliza Vaughan (1856–1911) III *195*
Stannard, Joseph (1797–1830) II *199*
Stansfeld, Sir James (1820–1898) III *195–196*
Stansfeld, Margaret (1860–1951) IV *102*
Stansgate, 1st Viscount (1877–1960) IV *102*
Stanton, A.H. (1839–1913) III *196*
Stanyan, Abraham (1669?–1732) I *130*
Stapledon, Sir George (1882–1960) IV *102*
Stapleton, Gregory (1748–1802) II *199*
Stapleton, Sir Philip (1603–1647) I *130*
Stapleton, Sir Robert (*d* 1669) I *130*
Stapleton, Thomas (1535–1598) I *130*
Stark, Freya (*b* 1893) IV *102*
Stark, James (1794–1859) II *199*
Starling, E.H. (1866–1927) IV *102*
Staunton, Sir G.L., 1st Bart (1737–1801) II *199*
Staunton, Sir G.T., 2nd Bart (1781–1859) II *199*
Staunton, Howard (1810–1874) III *196*
Staveley, Sir C.W.D. (1817–1896) III *196*
Stavely, Thomas (1626–1684) I *130*
Stawell, Sir John (1599–1662) I *130*
Stayner, Sir Richard (*d* 1662) I *130*
Stead, W.T. (1849–1912) III *196*
Stebbing, Henry (1687–1763) I *130*
Stebbing, Henry (1799–1883) II *199*
Stedman, J.G. (1744–1797) II *199*
Steed, H.W. (1871–1956) IV *102*
Steel-Maitland, Sir A.H. Drummond-Ramsay, 1st Bart (1876–1935) IV *102*
Steele, Joshua (1700–1791) II *199*
Steel(e), Richard (1629–1692) I *130*
Steele, Sir Richard (1672–1729) I *130*
Steele, Sir T.M. (1820–1890) III *196*
Steele, William (*d* 1680) I *130*
Steell, Sir John (1804–1891) III *196*
Steer, P.W. (1860–1942) IV *102*
Steere, Edward (1828–1882) III *196*
Steevens, George (1736–1800) II *200*
Stein, Sir Aurel (1862–1943) IV *102*
Stennett, Joseph (1663–1713) I *130*
Stennett, Joseph (1692–1758) I *130*
Stennett, Samuel (1728–1795) II *200*
Stenton, Sir F.M. (1880–1967) IV *102–103*
Stephen, King (1097?–1154) I *130*
Stephen, Sir Alfred (1802–1894) III *196*
Stephen, Sir A.C. (1850–1908) III *196*
Stephen, James (1758–1832) II *200*
Stephen, Sir James (1789–1859) II *200*
Stephen, Sir J.F., 1st Bart (1829–1894) III *196*
Stephen, J.K. (1859–1892) III *196*
Stephen, Sir Leslie (1832–1904) III *196*
Stephens, E.B. (1815–1882) III *196*
Stephens, F.G. (1828–1907) III *196*
Stephens, George (1813–1895) III *196*
Stephens, James (1880?–1950) IV *103*
Stephens, J.R. (1805–1879) III *196*
Stephens, Sir Philip, 1st Bart (1725–1809) II *200*
Stephenson, Sir F.C.A. (1821–1911) III *196*
Stephenson, George (1781–1848) II *200*
Stephenson, Sir G.O. (1878–1972) IV *103*
Stephenson, G.R. (1819–1905) III *196*
Stephenson, Marjory (1885–1948) IV *103*
Stephenson, Robert (1803–1859) III *196–197*

Stepney, George (1663–1707) I *130*
Sterling, John (1806–1844) III *197*
Stern, Gladys Bertha (1890–1973) IV *103*
Sterndale, Baron (1848–1923) III *197*
Sterne, John (1624–1669) I *130*
Sterne, John (1660–1745) I *130*
Sterne, Laurence (1713–1768) II *200*
Sterne, Richard (1597–1683) I *130*
Steuart of Goodtrees, Sir James (1635–1713) I *130*
Stevens, Alfred (1818–1875) III *197*
Stevens, Marshall (1852–1936) III *197*
Stevenson, Baron (1873–1926) IV *103*
Stevenson, Sir D.M. (1851–1944) III *197*
Stevenson, Joseph (1806–1895) III *197*
Stevenson, Sir J.A. (1760?–1833) II *200*
Stevenson, Matthew (fl 1660–1680) I *130*
Stevenson, Robert (1772–1850) II *200*
Stevenson, R.A.M. (1847–1900) III *197*
Stevenson, R.L. (1850–1894) III *197*
Stevenson, Thomas (1818–1887) III *197*
Stevenson, Sir Thomas (1838–1908) III *197*
Stevenson, William (1749?–1821) II *200*
Steward, Richard (1593?–1651) I *130*
Stewardson, Thomas (1781–1859) II *200*
Stewart, Alexander (1830–1872) III *197*
Stewart, Anthony (1773–1846) II *200*
Stewart, C.J. (1775–1837) II *200*
Stewart, David (of Garth) (1772–1829) II *200*
Stewart, Dugald (1753–1828) II *200*
Stewart, Sir D.M., 1st Bart (1824–1900) III *197*
Stewart, Sir Findlater (1879–1960) IV *103*
Stewart, Helen D'Arcy Cranstoun (1765–1838) II *200*
Stewart, Sir Herbert (1843–1885) III *197*
Stewart, James (1831–1905) III *197*
Stewart, Sir Malcolm, 1st Bart (1872–1951) IV *103*
Stewart, Patrick (1632–1865) III *197*
Stewart, Sir T.G. (1837–1900) III *197*
Stiles, Sir H.J. (1863–1946) IV *103*
Still, Sir Frederic (1868–1941) IV *103*
Still, John (1543?–1608) I *131*
Stillingfleet, Benjamin (1702–1771) II *200*
Stillingfleet, Edward (1635–1699) I *131*
Stirling, 1st Earl of (1567–1640) I *131*
Stirling, Sir James, 1st Bart (1740?–1805) II *200*
Stirling, Sir James (1791–1865) II *200*
Stirling, Sir James (1836–1916) III *197*
Stirling, J.H. (1820–1909) III *197*
Stirling, Mary Ann (1815–1895) III *197–198*
Stirling, Sir Walter (1718–1786) II *200*
Stirling-Maxwell, Caroline, Lady (1808–1877) III *198*
Stirling-Maxwell, Sir William, 9th Bart (1818–1878) III *198*
Stock, Joseph (1741–1813) II *200*
Stock, Richard (1569?–1626) I *131*
Stockdale, Sir F.A. (1883–1949) IV *103*
Stockdale, John (1749?–1814) II *200*
Stockdale, Percival (1736–1811) II *200*
Stocks, Lumb (1812–1892) III *198*
Stocks, Baroness Mary (1891–1975) IV *103*
Stoddart, Charles (1806–1842) III *198*
Stoddart, T.T. (1810–1880) III *198*
Stokes, Sir F.W.S. (1860–1927) IV *103*
Stokes, Sir G.G., 1st Bart (1819–1903) III *198*
Stokes, J.L. (1812–1885) III *198*
Stokes, Margaret M'Nair (1832–1900) III *198*
Stokes, Whitley (1763–1845) II *200*
Stokes, Whitley (1830–1909) III *198*
Stokes, William (1804–1878) III *198*
Stoll, Sir Oswald (1866–1942) IV *103*
Stone, Andrew (1703–1773) II *200*
Stone, Darwell (1859–1941) III *198*
Stone, Frank (1800–1859) III *198*
Stone, George (1708–1764) II *200*
Stone, Henry (d 1653) I *131*
Stone, Sir J.B. (1838–1914) III *198*
Stone, Marcus (1840–1921) III *198*
Stone, Nicholas (1586–1647) I *131*
Stone, Nicholas (d 1647) I *131*
Stone, William (1603?–1958) III *198*
Stoney, G.G. (1863–1942) IV *103*
Stoney, G.J. (1826–1911) III *198*
Stopes, Marie (1880–1958) IV *103*
Stopford, Sir F.W. (1854–1929) III *198*
Stopford, Sir M.G.N. (1892–1971) IV *103*
Stopford, Sir Robert (1768–1847) II *201*
Stopford of Fallowfield, Baron (1888–1961) IV *103*
Storace, Anna Selina (1766–1817) II *20*
Storer, A.M. (1746–1799) II *201*
Storey, G.A. (1834–1919) III *198*
Storks, Sir H.K. (1811–1874) III *198–199*
Storrs, Sir R.H.A. (1881–1955) IV *103*
Story, R.H. (1835–1907) III *199*
Stothard, C.A. (1786–1821) II *201*
Stothard, Thomas (1755–1834) II *201*
Stoughton, John (1807–1897) III *199*
Stout, G.F. (1860–1944) IV *103*
Stout, Sir Robert (1844–1930) III *199*
Stow, David (1793–1864) II *201*

Stow(e), John (1525?–1605) I *131*
Stowell, Baron (1745–1836) II *201*
Stowell, W.H. (1800–1858) III *199*
Strachan, John (1862–1907) IV *103*
Strachan-Davidson, J.L. (1843–1916) III *199*
Strachey, Sir John (1823–1907) III *199*
Strachey, John St Loe (1860–1927) IV *103*
Strachey, Lytton (1880–1932) IV *103*
Strachey, Philippa (1872–1968) IV *103*
Strachey, Sir Richard (1817–1908) III *199*
Strachie, 1st Baron (1858–1936) III *199*
Stradbroke, 2nd Earl of (1794–1886) II *201*
Stradling, Sir Edward, 2nd Bart (1601–1644) I *131*
Stradling, Sir R.E. (1891–1952) IV *103*
Strafford, 1st Earl of (1593–1641) I *131*
Strafford, 3rd Earl of (1672–1739) I *131*
Strafford, 1st Earl of (1772–1860) II *201*
Strafford, 2nd Earl of (1806–1886) III *199*
Strafford, 3rd Earl of (1830–1898) III *199*
Strahan, William (1715–1785) II *201*
Strakosch, Sir Henry (1871–1943) IV *103*
Strang, William (1859–1921) III *199*
Strange, Alexander (1818–1876) III *199*
Strange, Sir John (1696–1754) I *131*
Strange, Sir Robert (1721–1792) II *201*
Strange, Sir T.A.L. (1756–1841) II *201*
Strangford, 7th Viscount (1818–1857) III *199*
Strangford, 8th Viscount (1826–1869) III *199*
Strangways, A.H.F. (1859–1948) III *199*
Stratford, Nicholas (1633–1707) I *131*
Stratford de Redcliffe, Viscount (1786–1880) II *201*
Strathallan, 1st Viscount (1617?–1688) I *131*
Strathcarron, 1st Baron (1880–1937) IV *103*
Strathclyde, Baron (1891–1985) IV *103*
Strathcona and Mount Royal, 1st Baron (1820–1914) III *199*
Strathmore, 1st Earl of (1643?–1695) I *131*
Strathmore and Kinghorne, 14th and 1st Earl of (1855–1944) III *199*
Strathnairn, 1st Baron (1801–1885) III *199*
Stratton, F.J.M. (1881–1960) IV *103–104*
Strauss, G.L.M. (1807?–1887) III *199*
Streater, Robert (1624–1680) I *131*
Streatfield, Thomas (1777–1848) II *201*
Street, Sir A.W. (1892–1951) IV *104*
Street, G.E. (1824–1881) III *199*
Street, Sir Thomas (1626–1696) I *131*
Streeter, B.H. (1874–1937) IV *104*
Strickland, Baron (1861–1940) IV *104*
Strickland, Agnes (1796–1874) II *201*
Strickland, H.E. (1811–1853) III *199*
Strickland, T.J.F. (1679?–1740) I *131*
Strickland, Walter (fl 1642–1657) I *131*
Strode, Sir George (1583–1663) I *131*
Strong, Eugénie (1860–1943) IV *104*
Strong, L.A.G. (1896–1958) IV *104*
Strong, S.A. (1863–1904) IV *104*
Strong, Sir S.H. (1825–1909) III *199*
Strong, T.B. (1861–1944) IV *104*
Struthers, Sir John (1823–1899) III *199*
Struthers, Sir John (1857–1925) III *199–200*
Strutt, Jedediah (1726–1797) II *201*
Strutt, Joseph (1749–1802) II *201*
Strype, John (1643–1737) I *131*
Stuart, Andrew (d 1801) II *201*
Stuart, Sir Campbell (1885–1972) IV *104*
Stuart, Sir Charles (1753–1801) II *201*
Stuart, Lord D.C. (1803–1854) III *200*
Stuart, Gilbert (1742–1786) II *201*
Stuart, Gilbert (1755–1828) II *201–202*
Stuart, H.W.V. (1827–1895) III *200*
Stuart, James (1713–1788) II *202*
Stuart, James (b 1728) II *202*
Stuart, James (c 1735–1793) II *202*
Stuart, James (1741–1815) II *202*
Stuart, James (1775–1849) II *202*
Stuart, Sir John (1759–1815) II *202*
Stuart, J. McDouall (1815–1866) III *200*
Stuart, William (1755–1822) II *202*
Stuart de Rothesay, Baron (1779–1845) II *202*
Stuart-Jones, Sir Henry (1867–1939) IV *104*
Stuart-Wortley, 1st Baron (1851–1926) III *200*
Stuart-Wortley, Lady Emmeline (1806–1855) III *200*
Stuart-Wortley, J.A. (1805–1881) III *200*
Stuart of Findhorn, 1st Viscount (1897–1971) IV *104*
Stubbs, George (1724–1806) II *202*
Stubbs, Henry (1606?–1678) I *131*
Stubbs, Philip (1665–1738) I *131*
Stubbs, Sir R.E. (1876–1947) IV *104*
Stubbs, William (1825–1901) III *200*
Studd, Sir Kynaston, 1st Bart (1858–1944) III *200*
Stukeley, William (1687–1765) I *131*
Stump, S.J. (1778–1863) II *202*
Sturdee, Sir F.C.D., 1st Bart (1859–1925) III *200*
Sturge, Joseph (1793–1859) II *202*
Sturt, Charles (1795–1869) II *202*
Sturt, John (1658–1730) I *132*
Suckling, Sir John (1609–1642) I *132*

Suckling, Maurice (1725–1778) II *202*
Sueter, Sir M.F. (1872–1960) IV *104*
Suett, Richard (1755–1805) II *202*
Suffield, 3rd Baron (1781–1835) II *202*
Suffolk, 2nd Earl of (1361?–1415) I *132*
Suffolk, 2nd Duke of (1442–1491) I *132*
Suffolk, 1st Duke of (d 1545) I *132*
Suffolk, 2nd Duke of (1535–1551) I *132*
Suffolk, 3rd Duke of (1537?–1551) I *132*
Suffolk, 1st Earl of (1561–1620) I *132*
Suffolk, 2nd Earl of (1584–1640) I *132*
Suffolk, 3rd Earl of (1619–1688) I *132*
Suffolk, Countess of (1681–1767) I *132*
Sullivan, A.M. (1830–1884) III *200*
Sullivan, A.M. (1871–1959) IV *104*
Sullivan, Sir A.S. (1842–1900) III *200*
Sullivan, Barry (1821–1891) III *200*
Summers, Charles (1825–1878) III *200*
Sumner, B.H. (1893–1951) IV *104*
Sumner, C.R. (1790–1874) II *202*
Sumner, J.B. (1780–1862) II *202*
Sunderland, 1st Earl of (1620–1643) I *132*
Sunderland, 2nd Earl of (1640–1702) I *132*
Sunderland, 3rd Earl of (1674–1722) I *132*
Sunderland, Countess of (1617–1684) I *132*
Sunderlin, Baron (1738–1816) II *202*
Sundon, Lady (d 1742) I *132*
Surrey, Earl of (1517?–1547) I *132*
Sussex, 3rd Earl of (1526?–1583) I *132*
Sussex, 5th Earl of (1569?–1629) I *132*
Sussex, Augustus Frederick, Duke of (1773–1843) II *202–203*
Sutherland, 16th Earl of (1660?–1733) I *132*
Sutherland, 1st Duke of (1758–1833) I *203*
Sutherland, 2nd Duke of (1786–1861) II *203*
Sutherland, 3rd Duke of (1828–1892) III *200*
Sutherland, 5th Duke of (1888–1963) IV *104*
Sutherland, Duchess of (1806–1868) III *200*
Sutherland, John (1808–1891) III *200*
Sutherland, Sir Thomas (1834–1922) III *200–201*
Sutro, Alfred (1863–1933) IV *104*
Sutton, Sir B.E. (1886–1946) IV *104*
Sutton, Sir Richard (d 1524) I *132*
Sutton, Thomas (1532–1611) I *132–133*
Swain, Charles (1801–1874) III *201*
Swain, Joseph (1761–1796) II *203*
Swain, Joseph (1820–1909) III *201*
Swaine, J.B. (1815?–1838) III *201*
Swainson, C.A. (1820–1887) III *201*
Swainson, William (1789–1855) II *203*
Swan, J.M. (1847–1910) III *201*
Swan, Sir J.W. (1828–1914) III *201*
Swansea, 1st Baron (1821–1894) III *201*
Swaythling, 1st Baron (1832–1911) III *201*
Sweet, Henry (1845–1912) III *201*
Swete, H.B. (1835–1917) III *201*
Swettenham, Sir Frank (1850–1946) III *201*
Swift, Jonathan (1667–1745) I *133*
Swinburne, A.C. (1837–1909) III *201*
Swinburne, Henry (1743?–1803) II *203*
Swinfen, 1st Baron (1851–1919) III *201*
Swinny, Owen Mac (d 1754) I *133*
Swinton, A.A.C. (1863–1930) IV *104*
Swinton, Sir E.D. (1868–1951) IV *104*
Swinton, 1st Earl of (1884–1972) IV *104*
Sydenham, Baron (1799–1841) II *203*
Sydenham, Cuthbert (1622–1654) I *133*
Sydenham, Thomas (1624–1689) I *133*
Sydenham of Combe, G.S.C. (1848–1933) III *201*
Sydney, 1st Viscount (1733–1800) II *203*
Sydney, 2nd Viscount (1764–1831) II *203*
Sydney, 3rd Viscount and 1st Earl (1805–1890) III *201*
Sydney, Viscountess (1810–1893) III *201*
Syfret, Sir Neville (1889–1972) IV *104*
Sykes, Sir F.H. (1877–1954) IV *104*
Sykes, Sir Mark, 6th Bart (1879–1919) IV *104*
Sykes, Sir M.M., 3rd Bart (1771–1823) II *203*
Sykes, Sir P.M. (1867–1945) IV *104*
Sykes, Sir Tatton, 4th Bart (1772–1863) II *203*
Sylvester, Josuah (1563–1618) I *133*
Sylvester, J.J. (1814–1897) III *201*
Sylvester, Matthew (1636?–1708) I *133*
Syme, James (1799–1870) II *203*
Syme, John (1795–1861) II *203*
Symes-Thompson, Edmund (1837–1906) III *201*
Symington, Andrew (1785–1853) II *203*
Symington, William (1763–1831) II *203*
Symington, William (1795–1862) II *203*
Symmons, Charles (1749–1826) II *203*
Symonds, Sir C.J. (1852–1932) III *201*
Symonds, John (1729–1807) II *203*
Symonds, J.A. (1807–1871) II *201*
Symonds, J.A. (1840–1893) II *201*
Symonds, Sir William (1782–1856) II *203*
Symons, A.W. (1865–1945) IV *104*
Symons, B.P. (1785–1878) II *203*
Synge, J.M. (1871–1909) IV *104*

Taffe, 6th Viscount (1677–1769) I *135*
Taglioni, Marie (1809–1884) III *202*
Tagore, Sir Rabindranath (1861–1941) IV *105*
Tait, A.C. (1811–1882) III *202*
Tait, Sir Campbell (1886–1946) IV *105*
Tait, James (1863–1944) IV *105*
Tait, P.G. (1831–1901) III *202*
Tait, R.L. (1845–1899) III *202*
Talbot, Catherine (1721–1770) II *204*
Talbot, C.R.M. (1803–1890) III *202*
Talbot, E.S. (1844–1934) III *202*
Talbot, Sir G.J. (1861–1938) IV *105*
Talbot, Mary Anne (1778–1808) II *204*
Talbot, Peter (1620–1680) I *135*
Talbot, Thomas (1771–1853) II *204*
Talbot, William (1659?–1730) I *135*
Talbot, W.H.F. (1800–1877) III *202*
Talbot of Hensol, 1st Baron (1685–1737) I *135*
Talbot of Hensol, 2nd Earl (1777–1849) II *204*
Talbot de Malahide, 4th Baron (1805–1883) III *202*
Talfourd, Sir T.N. (1795–1854) II *204*
Tallents, Peter (1619–1708) I *135*
Tallents, Sir S.G. (1884–1958) IV *105*
Tallis, Thomas (1510?–1585) I *135*
Tancred, Christopher (1689–1754) I *135*
Tandy, J.N. (1740–1803) II *204*
Tanfield, Sir Lawrence (d 1625) I *135*
Tangye, Sir Richard (1833–1906) III *202*
Tankerville, 1st Earl of (1654–1701) I *135*
Tankerville, 6th Earl of (1810–1899) III *202*
Tannahill, Robert (1774–1810) II *204*
Tanner, Jack (1889–1965) IV *105*
Tanner, Thomas (1674–1735) I *135*
Tansley, Sir A.G. (1871–1955) IV *105*
Tans'ur William (1706–1783) II *204*
Tarleton, Sir Banastre, Bart (1754–1833) II *204*
Tarlton, Richard (1530–1588) I *135*
Tassie, James (1735–1799) II *204*
Tata, J.N. (1839–1904) III *202*
Tate, Sir Henry, 1st Bart (1819–1899) III *202*
Tate, James (1771–1843) II *204*
Tatham, C.H. (1772–1842) II *204*
Tatham, Edward (1749–1834) II *204*
Tatham, John (fl 1632–1664) I *135*
Tatlow, Tissington (1876–1957) IV *105*
Tattersall, Richard (1724–1795) II *204*
Taunton, Baron (1798–1869) II *204*
Taunton, Sir W.E. (1773–1835) II *204*
Tawney, R.H. (1880–1962) IV *105*
Tayler, Frederick (1802–1889) III *202*
Tayler, J.J. (1797–1869) II *204*
Taylor, Ann (1782–1866) II *204*
Taylor, A.E. (1869–1945) IV *105*
Taylor, A.S. (1806–1880) III *202*
Taylor, Brook (1685–1731) I *135*
Taylor, Sir Brook (1776–1846) II *204*
Taylor, Charles (1781–1859) II *204*
Taylor, Charles (1840–1908) III *202*
Taylor, Edgar (1793–1839) II *204*
Taylor, Edward (1784–1863) II *204*
Taylor, Eva (d 1966) IV *105*
Taylor, F.S. (1897–1956) IV *105*
Taylor, Sir Geoffrey (1886–1975) IV *105*
Taylor, G.W. (d 1841) II *204*
Taylor, Harriette Deborah (1807–1874) III *202*
Taylor, Sir Henry (1800–1886) III *202*
Taylor, Sir Herbert (1775–1839) II *204–205*
Taylor, H.M. (1842–1927) III *203*
Taylor, Isaac (1759–1829) II *205*
Taylor, Isaac (1787–1865) II *205*
Taylor, Isaac (1829–1901) III *203*
Taylor, James (1753–1825) II *205*
Taylor, James (1813–1896) III *203*
Taylor, Jane (1783–1824) II *205*
Taylor, Jeremy (1613–1667) I *135*
Taylor, John (1580–1653) I *135*
Taylor, John (1694–1761) I *135*
Taylor, John (1703–1772) II *205*
Taylor, Sir John, Bart (d 1786?) II *205*
Taylor, John (1711–1788) II *205*
Taylor, John (1757–1832) II *205*
Taylor, John (1779–1863) II *205*
Taylor, John (1781–1864) II *205*
Taylor, J.S. (1795–1841) II *205*
Taylor, L.C. (1874–1969) IV *105*
Taylor, Meadows (1808–1876) III *203*
Taylor, Michael Angelo (1757–1834) II *205*
Taylor, P.A. (1819–1891) III *203*
Taylor, Richard (1781–1858) II *205*
Taylor, Sir Robert (1714–1788) II *205*
Taylor, Thomas (1576–1633) I *135*
Taylor, Thomas (1738–1816) II *205*
Taylor, Thomas (1758–1835) II *205*
Taylor, Tom (1817–1880) III *203*
Taylor, T.E. (1811–1883) III *203*
Taylor, Sir T.M. (1897–1962) IV *105*
Taylor, Sir T.W.J. (1895–1953) IV *105*

Taylor, William (1765–1836) II *205*
Taylor, William (1865–1937) IV *105*
Teale, T.P. (1831–1923) III *203*
Teall, Sir J.J.H. (1849–1924) III *203*
Tedder, 1st Baron (1890–1967) IV *105*
Teesdale, Sir C.C. (1833–1893) III *203*
Tegart, Sir C.A. (1881–1946) IV *105*
Teignmouth, 1st Baron (1751–1834) II *205*
Telford, Thomas (1757–1834) II *205*
Temperley, H.W.V. (1879–1939) IV *105*
Tempest, Dame Marie (1864–1942) IV *105*
Tempest, Pierce (1653–1717) I *135*
Temple, 2nd Earl of (1711–1779) II *205*
Temple, Ann Chambers, Countess (1709–1777) II *205*
Temple, Dorothy, Lady (1627–1695) I *135*
Temple, Frederick (1821–1902) III *203*
Temple, Sir John (1600–1677) I *135*
Temple, Sir Richard, 1st Bart (1826–1902) III *203*
Temple, Sir R.C., 2nd Bart (1850–1931) III *203*
Temple, Sir William (1628–1699) I *135*
Temple, William (1881–1944) IV *105*
Templeman, Peter (1711–1769) I *135*
Templer, Sir Gerald (1898–1979) IV *105–106*
Templeton, John (1802–1886) III *203*
Templewood, 1st Viscount (1880–1959) IV *106*
Tenby, 1st Viscount (1894–1967) IV *106*
Tenison, Edward (1673–1735) I *135*
Tenison, Thomas (1636–1715) I *135–136*
Tennant, Charles (1768–1838) II *205*
Tennant, Sir Charles, Bart (1823–1906) III *203*
Tennant, James (1808–1881) III *203*
Tennant, William (1784–1848) II *205*
Tennant, Sir W.G. (1890–1963) IV *106*
Tennent, Sir J.E., 1st Bart (1804–1869) III *203*
Tenniel, Sir John (1820–1914) III *203*
Tennyson, Alfred Tennyson, 1st Baron (1809–1892) III *203–204*
Tennyson, Frederick (1807–1898) III *204*
Tennyson-D'Eyncourt, Sir E.H.W., 1st Bart (1868–1951) IV *106*
Tenterden, 1st Baron (1762–1832) II *205–206*
Tenterden, 3rd Baron (1834–1882) III *204*
Terrick, Richard (1710–1777) I *136*
Terriss, Ellaline, Lady Hicks (1871–1971) IV *106*
Terriss, William (1847–1897) III *204*
Terrot, C.H. (1790–1872) II *206*
Terry, C.S. (1864–1936) IV *106*
Terry, Daniel (1780–1829) II *206*
Terry, Edward (1590–1660) I *136*
Terry, Dame Ellen (1847–1928) III *204*
Terry, Fred (1863–1933) IV *106*
Tertis, Lionel (1876–1975) IV *106*
Tesdale, Thomas (1547–1610) I *136*
Thackeray, F.R. (1775–1860) II *206*
Thackeray, George (1777–1850) II *206*
Thackeray, W.M. (1811–1863) III *204–205*
Thackwell, Sir Joseph (1781–1859) II *206*
Thane, John (1748–1818) II *206*
Thanet, 9th Earl of (1769–1825) II *206*
Thankerton, Baron (1873–1948) IV *106*
Theed, William (1804–1891) III *205*
Thelwall, Sir Eubule (1562–1630) I *136*
Thelwall, John (1764–1834) II *206*
Therry, Sir Roger (1800–1874) III *205*
Thesiger, A.H. (1838–1880) III *205*
Thesiger, Ernest (1879–1961) IV *106*
Thicknesse, Ann (1737–1824) II *206*
Thicknesse, Philip (1719–1792) II *206*
Thirkell, Angela Margaret (1890–1961) IV *106*
Thirlby, Thomas (1506?–1570) I *136*
Thirlwall, Connop (1797–1875) II *206*
Thiselton-Dyer, Sir W.T. (1843–1928) III *205*
Thistlewood, Arthur (1770–1820) II *206*
Thomas, Duke of Clarence (1388?–1421) I *136*
Thomas, A.G. (1850–1892) III *205*
Thomas, Bert (1883–1966) IV *106*
Thomas, B.S. (1892–1950) IV *106*
Thomas, Edward (1878–1917) IV *106*
Thomas, Elizabeth (1677–1731) I *136*
Thomas, F.W. (1867–1956) IV *106*
Thomas, G.H. (1824–1868) III *205*
Thomas, Sir Henry (1878–1952) IV *106*
Thomas, Honoratus Leigh (1769–1846) II *206*
Thomas, H.O. (1834–1891) III *205*
Thomas, Sir Ivor (1893–1972) IV *106*
Thomas, John (1696–1781) I *136*
Thomas, John (1712–1793) II *206*
Thomas, John (1813–1862) III *205*
Thomas, John (1826–1913) III *205*
Thomas, Joshua (1719–1797) II *206*
Thomas, J.H. (1854–1921) III *205*
Thomas, J.H. (1856–1940) IV *106*
Thomas, M.E. (1787/8–1830) II*206*
Thomas, Sir Noah (1720–1792) II *206*
Thomas, Sir P.E. (1883–1969) IV *106*
Thomas, S.G. (1850–1885) III *205*
Thomas, William (1613–1689) I *136*

Thomas, William (1670–1738) I *136*
Thomas, Sir W.B. (1868–1957) IV *106*
Thomas, W.L. (1830–1900) III *205*
Thomas, W.M. (1828–1910) III *205*
Thomason, Sir Edward (1769–1849) II *206*
Thomond, 6th Earl of (d 1657) I *136*
Thompson, A.H. (1873–1952) IV *106*
Thompson, Benjamin (1776?–1816) II *206*
Thompson, Charles (1740?–1799) II *206*
Thompson, Sir D.W. (1860–1948) IV *106*
Thompson, Edward (1738?–1786) I *136*
Thompson, E.J. (1886–1946) IV *106*
Thompson, Sir E.M. (1840–1929) III *205*
Thompson, Sir E.S. (1898–1975) IV *106*
Thompson, Francis (1859–1907) III *205*
Thompson, George (1804–1878) III *205*
Thompson, Sir Henry, 1st Bart (1820–1904) III *205*
Thompson, Sir Herbert, 2nd Bart (1859–1944) III *205*
Thompson, H.L. (1829–1856) III *205*
Thompson, H.Y. (1838–1928) III *205*
Thompson, Jacob (1806–1879) III *205*
Thompson, James (1817–1877) III *205*
Thompson, Sir James (1835–1906) III *205*
Thompson, J.M. (1878–1956) IV *106*
Thompson, Lydia (1836–1908) III *205*
Thompson, R.C. (1876–1941) IV *106*
Thompson, S.P. (1851–1916) III *205*
Thompson, Theophilus (1807–1860) III *205*
Thompson, Sir T.B., 1st Bart (1766?–1828) II *206*
Thompson, T.P. (1783–1869) II *206*
Thompson, Sir William (1678–1739) I *136*
Thompson, William (1712?–1766) II *206*
Thompson, William (1793–1854) II *206*
Thompson, William (1805–1852) III *205*
Thompson, William (1811–1889) III *206*
Thompson, W.H. (1810–1886) III *206*
Thompson, W.M. (1857–1907) III *206*
Thoms, W.J. (1803–1885) III *206*
Thomson, Baron (1875–1930) IV *107*
Thomson, Sir Alexander (1744–1817) II *207*
Thomson, Alexander (1817–1875) III *206*
Thomson, A.M. (1779–1831) II *207*
Thomson, Sir B.H. (1861–1939) IV *106*
Thomson, Sir C.W. (1830–1882) III *206*
Thomson, George (1757–1851) II *207*
Thomson, Sir G.P. (1892–1975) IV *107*
Thomson, Henry (1773–1843) II *207*
Thomson, James (1700–1748) II *207*
Thomson, John (1765–1846) II *207*
Thomson, John (1778–1840) II *207*
Thomson, John (1805–1841) III *206*
Thomson, John (1856–1926) III *206*
Thomson, Joseph (1858–1894) III *206*
Thomson, Sir J.J. (1856–1940) III *206*
Thomson, R.W. (1822–1873) III *206*
Thomson, Thomas (1768–1852) II *207*
Thomson, Thomas (1773–1852) II *207*
Thomson, Thomas (1817–1878) III *206*
Thomson, William (1819–1890) III *206*
Thomson of Fleet, 1st Baron (1894–1976) IV *107*
Thorburn, Grant (1773–1863) II *207*
Thorburn, Robert (1818–1885) III *206*
Thoresby, Ralph (1658–1725) I *136*
Thornborough, John (1551–1641) I *136*
Thornbrough, Sir Edward (1754–1834) II *207*
Thornbury, G.W. (1828–1876) III *206*
Thorndike, Dame Sybil (1882–1976) IV *107*
Thorne, Robert (1492–1532) I *136*
Thorne, W.J. (1857–1946) III *206*
Thornhill, Sir James (1675–1734) I *136*
Thornton, Bonnell (1724–1768) II *207*
Thornton, Sir Edward (1817–1906) III *206*
Thornton, Henry (1760–1815) II *207*
Thornton, John (1720–1790) II *207*
Thornton, R.J. (1768?–1837) II *207*
Thornton, Samuel (1755–1838) II *207*
Thornton, Thomas (1757–1823) II *207*
Thornton, William (1763–1841) II *207*
Thornton, W.T. (1813–1880) III *206*
Thornycroft, Sir J.I. (1843–1928) IV *107*
Thornycroft, Mary (1814–1895) III *206*
Thornycroft, Thomas (1815–1885) III*206*
Thornycroft, Sir (William) Hamo (1850–1925) III *206*
Thorold, A.W. (1825–1895) III *206*
Thoroton, Robert (1623–1678) I *136*
Thorp, Charles (1783–1862) II *207*
Thorpe, John (1682–1750) I *136*
Thorpe, John (1715–1792) II *207*
Thrale, Henry (1728–1781) II *207*
Threlfall, Sir Richard (1861–1932) IV *107*
Thring, Edward (1821–1887) III *206–207*
Thring, 1st Baron (1818–1907) III *207*
Throckmorton, Sir Nicholas (1515–1571) I *136*
Throsby, John (1740–1803) II *207*
Thrupp, Frederick (1812–1895) III *207*
Thurloe, John (1616–1668) I *136*
Thurlow, 1st Baron (1731–1806) II *207*

hurlow, Thomas (1737–1791) II 207
hurso, 1st Viscount (1890–1970) IV 107
hurston, Sir J.B. (1836–1897) III 207
hurtell, John (1794–1824) II 207–208
hyer, Robert (1709–1781) II 208
hynne, Lord H.F. (1832–1904) III 207
hynne, Sir John (d1580) I 136
hynne, Thomas (1648–1682) I 136
ichborne, Sir Henry (1581?–1667) I 136
ichborne, Robert (d1682) I 136
ickell, Mary (1756?–1787) I 136
ickell, Thomas (1686–1740) I 136
dcomb, John (1642–1713) I 136
erney, George (1761–1830) II 208
erney, Sir M.J., 1st Bart (1776–1845) II 208
ghe, Mary (1742–1810) II 208
llemans, Pieter (1684–1734) I 136
llett, Benjamin (1860–1943) IV 107
lley, Vesta, Lady de Frece (1864–1952) IV 107
lloch, Alexander (1759–1825) II 208
llotson, John (1630–1694) I 130
llyard, E.M.W. (1889–1962) IV 107
ilson, Henry (1659–1695) I 137
imbs, John (1801–1875) III 207
indal, Matthew (1653?–1733) I 137
indal, Nicholas (1687–1774) I 137
indal, Sir N.C. (1776–1846) II 208
insley, William (1831–1902) III 207
inworth, George (1843–1913) III 207
itcomb, J.H. (1819–1903) II 208
te, Sir William (1798–1873) II 208
tiens, Teresa Caroline Johanna (1831–1877) III 207
zard, Sir H.T. (1885–1959) IV 107
od, James (1782–1835) I 208
odd, Elliott D'Arcy (1808–1845) III 207
odd, H.J. (1763–1845) II 208
odd, R.B. (1809–1860) III 207
odhunter, Isaac (1820–1884) III 207
ofts, Mary (1701?–1763) II208
olkien, J.R.R. (1892–1973) IV 107
ollemache, Thomas (1651?–1694) I 137
ollet, George (1725–1779) II 208
om, J.N. (1799–1838) II 208
ombs, Sir Henry (1824–1874) III 207
omes, Sir John (1815–1895) III 207
omkins, Thomas (1573–1616) II 208
omline, Sir G.P., Bart (1750–1827) II 208
omlinson, George (1890–1952) III 207
omlinson, H.M. (1873–1958) IV 107
omlinson, Nicholas (1765–1847) II 208
ompion, Thomas (1639–1713) I 137
ompson, Richard (d1693?) I 137
oms, Peter (d1777) II 208
one, T.W. (1763–1798) II 208
ong, William (1662–1727) I 137
onna, Charlotte Elizabeth (1790–1846) II 208
onson, Jacob (1656?–1736) I 137
onson, Jacob (d1735) I 137
ooke, George (1595–1675) I 137
ooke, J.H. (1736–1812) II 208
ooke, Thomas (1774–1858) II 208
ooke, William (1744–1820) II 208
ooke, William (1777–1863) II 208
oole, J.L. (1830–1906) III 207
opham, Edward (1751–1820) II 208–209
opham, F.W. (1808–1877) III 207
opham, Thomas (1710?–1749) II 209
oplady, A.M. (1740–1778) II 209
opley, W.W.C. (1886–1944) IV 107
orphicen, 7th Baron (d1753) I 137
orrens, Sir A.W. (1809–1855) III 207
orrens, Sir Henry (1779–1828) II 209
orrens, W.T.M. (1813–1894) III 207
orrington, Earl of (1647–1716) I 137
osti, Sir F.P. (1847–1916) III 207
otnes, Earl of (1555–1629) I 137
ottenham, A.L. (1838–1887) III 207
ottenham, Charles (1685–1758) I 137
oulmin, Joshua (1740–1815) II 209
out, T.F. (1855–1929) IV 207
ovey, Sir D.F. (1875–1940) IV 107
ovey of Langton Matravers, Baron (1885–1971) IV 107
owers, John (1747?–1804) II 209
owers, Joseph (1737–1799) II 209
owgood, Michaijah (1700–1792) II 209
owne, Charles (d1850?) II 209
owneley, Charles (1737–1805) II 209
ownley, John (1697–1782) I 137
ownley, James (1714–1778) II 209
ownley, James (1774–1833) II 209
ownsend, George (1788–1857) II 209
ownsend, Isaac (d1765) I 137
ownsend, John (1757–1826) II 209
ownsend, John (1739–1816) II 209
ownsend, Richard (1821–1884) III 207
ownshend, 2nd Viscount (1630?–1687) I 137

Townshend, 2nd Viscount (1674–1738) I 137
Townshend, 3rd Viscount (1790–1764) I 137
Townshend, 1st Marquess (1724–1807) II 209
Townshend, 2nd Marquess (1755–1811) II 209
Townshend, 4th Marquess (1798–1863) II 209
Townshend, 5th Marquess (1831–1899) III 207
Townshend, Charles (1725–1767) II 209
Townshend, C.F. (1795–1817) II 209
Townshend, Chauncey Hare (1798–1868) II 209
Townshend, John, Lord (1757–1833) II 209
Townshend, Thomas (1701–1780) II 209
Towry, G.H. (1767–1809) II 209
Towse, Sir Beachcroft (1864–1948) IV 107
Toynbee, Arnold (1852–1883) III 207
Toynbee, Arnold Joseph (1889–1975) IV 107
Toynbee, Joseph (1815–1866) III 207
Toynbee, P.J. (1855–1932) III 207
Tradescant, John (d1638?) I 137
Tradescant, John (1608–1662) I 137
Traill, H.D. (1842–1900) III 207
Traill, T.S. (1781–1862) II 209
Trapp, John (1601–1669) I 137
Trapp, Joseph (1679–1747) I 137
Traquair, 1st Earl of (1600?–1659) I 137
Travers, Ben (b1886) IV 107
Travers, Benjamin (1783–1858) II 210
Travers, Sir E.S. (1782–1858) II 210
Travers, M.W. (1872–1961) IV 107
Treby, Sir George (1644?–1700) I 137
Tredgold, Thomas (1788–1829) II 210
Tree, Ellen (1805–1880) III 207–208
Tree, Sir H.B. (1852–1917) III 208
Trefusis, Violet (1894–1972) IV 107
Tregonwell, Sir John (d1565) I 137
Tregury, Michael (d1471) I 137
Trelawny, Charles (1654–1731) I 137
Trelawny, Edward John (1792–1881) II 210
Trelawny, Sir Jonathan, 3rd Bart (1650–1721) I 137
Treloar, Sir W.P., Bart (1843–1923) II 208
Tremayne, Sir J.T. (1891–1979) IV 108
Trench, F.H. (1865–1923) IV 108
Trench, Sir F.W. (1775–1859) II210
Trench, Melesina (1768–1827) II 210
Trench, Power le Poer (1770–1839) I 210
Trench, R.C. (1807–1886) III 208
Trenchard, 1st Viscount (1873–1916) IV 108
Trenchard, Sir John (1640–1695) I 137
Trent, 1st Baron (1850–1931) III 208
Tresham, Francis (1567?–1605) I 137–138
Tresham, Henry (1749?–1814) II 210
Tresham, Sir Thomas (d1559) I 138
Tresham, Sir Thomas (d1605) I 138
Trevelyan, Sir C.E., 1st Bart (1807–1886) III 208
Trevelyan, Sir C.P., 3rd Bart (1870–1958) IV 108
Trevelyan, G.M. (1876–1962) IV 108
Trevelyan, Sir G.O., 2nd Bart (1838–1928) III 208
Trevelyan, Hilda (1877–1959) IV 108
Trevelyan, Raleigh (1781–1865) II 210
Trevelyan, Sir W.C., 6th Bart (1797–1879) II 210
Treves, Sir Frederick, Bart (1853–1923) III 208
Trevethin, 1st Baron (1843–1936) IV 108
Trevithick, Richard (1771–1833) II 210
Trevor, Sir John (1626–1672) I 138
Trevor, Sir John (1637–1717) I 138
Trevor, Richard (1707–1771) II 210
Trevor, Sir Sackville (1567–1635) I 138
Trevor, Sir Thomas (1573–1656) I 138
Trevor of Bromham, Baron (1658–1730) I 138
Tribe, Sir F.N. (1893–1958) IV 108
Trimmer, Sarah (1741–1810) II 210
Trimnell, Charles (1663–1723) I 138
Tristram, H.B. (1822–1906) III 208
Trollope, Anthony (1815–1882) III 208
Trollope, A.W. (1768–1827) II 210
Trollope, Edward (1817–1893) III 208
Trollope, Frances (1780–1863) II 210
Trollope, Sir Henry (1756–1839) II 210
Trosse, George (1631–1713) I 138
Trotter, Coutts (1837–1887) III 208
Trotter, Thomas (1760–1832) II 210
Trotter, W.B.L. (1872–1939) IV 108
Troubridge, Sir Thomas, 1st Bart (1758?–1807) II 210
Troubridge, Sir T.H. (1895–1949) IV 108
Troubridge, Sir T. St.V. H.C. (1815–1867) III 208
Troughton, Edward (1753–1835) II 210
Troup, R.S. (1874–1939) IV 108
Troy, J.T. (1739–1823) II 210
Trueman, Sir A.E. (1894–1956) IV 108
Truman, Sir Benjamin (1711–1780) II 210
Trumbull, William (d1635) I 138
Trumbull, Sir William (1639?–1716) I 138
Truro, 1st Baron (1782–1855) II 210–211
Truro, 2nd Baron (1816–1891) III 208
Trusler, John (1735–1820) II 211
Tryon, Sir George (1832–1893) III 208
Tryon, Thomas (1634–1703) I 138
Tucker, Abraham (1705–1774) II 211

Tucker, A.R. (1849–1914) III 208
Tucker, Sir Charles (1838–1935) III 208–209
Tucker, Joseph (fl 1820) II 211
Tucker, Josiah (1712–1799) II 211
Tucker, T.T. (1775–1852) II 211
Tuckney, Anthony (1599–1670) I 138
Tudway, Thomas (1645?–1726) I 138
Tufnell, Henry (1805–1854) III 209
Tufnell, T.J. (1819–1885) III 209
Tuke, Sir Bryan (d1545) I 138
Tuke, H.S. (1858–1929) III 209
Tull, Jethro (1674–1741) I 138
Tulloch, Sir A.M. (1803–1864) III 209
Tulloch, John (1823–1886) III 209
Tunstall, Cuthbert (1474–1559) I 138
Tunstall, Marmaduke (1743–1790) II 211
Tupper, Sir Charles, 1st Bart (1821–1915) III 209
Tupper, M.F. (1810–1889) III 209
Turmeau, John (1777–1846) II 211
Turnbull, H.M. (1875–1955) IV 108
Turnbull, W.B.D.D. (1811–1863) III 209
Turner, Anne (1576–1615) I 138
Turner, Sir Ben (1863–1942) IV 108
Turner, Charles (1774–1857) II 211
Turner, Daniel (1667–1741) I 138
Turner, Dawson (1775–1858) II 211
Turner, Sir Edward, Bart (1719–1766) II 211
Turner, Francis (1638?–1700) I 138
Turner, G.G. (1877–1951) IV 108
Turner, Sir G.J. (1798–1867) II 211
Turner, Sir G.W. (1896–1974) IV 108
Turner, H.H. (1861–1930) IV 108
Turner, James (1608?–1664) I 138
Turner, Sir James (1615–1686?) I 138
Turner, J.M.W. (1775–1851) II 211
Turner, J.S. (1832–1904) III 209
Turner, Robert (fl 1640–1664) I 138
Turner, Sir R.L. (b1888) IV 108
Turner, Sharon (1768–1847) II 211
Turner, Thomas (1591–1672) I 138
Turner, Thomas (1645–1714) I 138
Turner, William (1761–1859) II 211
Turner, William (1789–1862) II 211
Turner, William (1792–1867) II 211
Turner, Sir William (1832–1916) III 209
Turner, W.E.S. (1881–1963) IV 108
Turner, W.J.R. (1889–1946) IV 108
Turnerelli, Peter (1774–1839) II 211
Turnor, Sir Christopher (1607–1675) I 138
Turnor, Sir Edward (1617–1676) I 138
Turpin, Richard (1706–1739) II 211
Turton, Thomas (1780–1864) II 211
Tussaud, Marie (1760–1850) II 211
Tutchin, John (1661?–1707) I 138
Tutton, A.E.H. (1864–1938) IV 108
Tweddell, John (1769–1799) II 211
Tweed, John (1869–19133) IV 108
Tweeddale, 2nd Earl and 1st Marquess of (1626–1697) I 138
Tweeddale, 2nd Marquess of (1645–1713) I 138–139
Tweeddale, 4th Marquess of (c1695–1762) I 139
Tweeddale, 8th Marquess of (1787–1876) II 211
Tweedie, Alexander (1794–1884) II 211
Tweedmouth, 2nd Baron (1849–1909) III 209
Tweedsmuir, 1st Baron (1875–1940) IV 108
Twining, Richard (1749–1824) II 211
Twining, Richard (1772–1857) II 211
Twining, Thomas (1735–1804) II 211
Twisden of Bradbourne, Sir Thomas, 1st Bart (1602–1683) I 139
Twiss, Frances (1759–1822) II 211
Twiss, Horace (1787–1849) II 211
Twiss, Richard (1747–1821) II 211
Twisse, William (1578?–1646) I 139
Twyman, Frank (1876–1959) IV 108
Twysden, John (1607–1688) I 139
Twysden of Roydon, Sir Roger, 2nd Bart (1597–1672) I 139
Tyabji, Badruddin (1844–1906) III 209
Tyerman, Daniel (1773–1828) II 211
Tyers, Jonathan (d1767) I 139
Tyers, Thomas (1726–1787) II 211
Tyldesley, Sir Thomas (1596–1651) I 139
Tyler, J.E. (1789–1851) II 211–212
Tyler, William (d1801) II 212
Tylor, Sir E.B. (1832–1917) III 209
Tyndall, John (1820–1893) III 209
Tynte, C.J.K. (1800–1882) III 209
Tyrconnel, Duchess of (1647?–1730) I 139
Tyrconnel, titular Duke of (1630–1691) I 139
Tyrone, 2nd Earl of (1550?–1616) I 139
Tyrrel, Richard (1716/17–1766) II 212
Tyrrell, Baron (1866–1947) IV 108
Tyrrell, R.Y. (1844–1914) III 209
Tyrrell, Sir Thomas (1594–1672) I 139
Tyrwhitt, Richard St John (1827–1895) III 209
Tyrwhitt, Sir R.Y., 1st Bart (1870–1951) IV 108–109
Tyrwhitt, Thomas (1730–1786) II 212

Tyson, Edward (1650–1708) I *139*
Tyson, Richard (1680–1750) I *139*
Tytler, James (1747?–1805) II *212*
Tytler, P.F. (1791–1849) II *212*
Tytler, William (1711–1792) II *212*

Ullswater, 1st Viscount (1855–1949) III *210*
Underhill, Cane (1634–1710?) I *141*
Underhill, E.B. (1813–1901) III *210*
Underwood, Leon (1890–1975) IV *110*
Unton, Sir Henry (1557?–1596) I *141*
Unwin, Mary (1724–1796) II *213*
Unwin, Sir Raymond (1863–1940) IV *110*
Unwin, Sir Stanley (1884–1968) IV *110*
Unwin, W.C. (1743?–1786) II *213*
Unwin, W.C. (1838–1933) III *210*
Upcott, William (1779–1845) II *213*
Upton, John (1707–1760) II *213*
Ure, Andrew (1778–1857) II *213*
Urquhart, Sir Thomas (1611–1660) I *141*
Urry, John (1666–1715) I *141*
Urswick, Christopher (1448–1522) I *141*
Urswick, Sir Thomas (d 1479) I *141*
Urwick, Thomas (1727–1807) II *213*
Urwick, William (1826–1905) III *210*
Ussher, James (1581–1656) I *141*
Ussher, Sir Thomas (1779–1848) II *213*
Uthwatt, Baron (1879–1949) IV *110*
Utterson, E.V. (1776?–1856) II *213*
Uvarov, Sir Boris (1889–1970) IV *110*
Unwins, Thomas (1782–1857) II *213*
Uxbridge, 3rd Earl of (1744–1812) II *213*

Vachell, H.A. (1861–1955) IV *111*
Vallance, W.F. (1827–1904) III *211*
Vallancey, Charles (1721–1812) II *214*
Valpy, Richard (1754–1836) I *214*
Vanbrugh, Dame Irene (1872–1949) IV *111*
Vanbrugh, Sir John (1664–1726) I *143*
Vanbrugh, Violet (1867–1942) IV *111*
Vancouver, George (1758–1798) I *214*
Vandeleur, Sir J.O. (1763–1849) II *214*
Vandenhoff, Charlotte Elizabeth (1818–1860) III *211*
Vandenhoff, John (1790–1861) II *214*
Vanderbank, John (1694?–1739) I *143*
Vanderbank, Peter (1649–1697) I *143*
Van Der Doort, Abraham (d 1640) I *143*
Van Der Gucht, Gerard (1696–1776) I *143*
Van De Velde, Willem (1610–1693) I *143*
Van De Velde, Willem (1633–1707) I *143*
Van Diest, Adriaen (1656–1704) I *143*
Vandyck, Sir Anthony (1599–1641) I *143*
Vane, Viscountess (1713–1788) I *214*
Vane, Anne (1705–1736) II *214*
Vane, Sir Henry (1589–1655) I *143*
Vane, Sir Henry (1613–1662) I *143*
Van Haecken, Joseph (1699?–1749) I *143*
Van Homrigh, Esther (1690–1723) I *143*
Van Huysum, Jacob (1687?–1746) I *143*
Van Mildert, William (1765–1836) II *214*
Vansittart, Baron (1881–1957) IV *111*
Vansittart, Henry (1732–1770) II *214*
Vansittart, Henry (1777–1843) II *214*
Van Somer, Paul (1576–1621) I *143*
Van Son, J.F. (1658–1718?) I *143*
Van Voerst, Robert (1596–1636) I *143*
Varley, Cornelius (1781–1873) II *214*
Varley, John (1778–1842) II *214*
Vashon, James (1742–1827) II *214*
Vassall, S.T. (1764–1807) II *214*
Vaughan, Benjamin (1751–1835) II *214*
Vaughan, B.J. (1847–1922) III *211*
Vaughan, C.J. (1816–1897) III *211*
Vaughan, Sir C.R. (1774–1849) II *214*
Vaughan, D.J. (1825–1905) III *211*
Vaughan, H.A. (1832–1903) III *211*
Vaughan, H.H. (1811–1885) III *211*
Vaughan, Sir John (1603–1674) I *143*
Vaughan, Sir John (1769–1839) II *214*
Vaughan, Kate (1852?–1903) III *211*
Vaughan, Richard (1550?–1607) I *143*
Vaughan, Robert (1795–1868) II *214*
Vaughan, William (1752–1850) II *214*
Vaughan, W.W. (1865–1938) IV *111*
Vaughan, Williams, Ralph (1872–1958) IV *111*
Vaux of Harrowden, 2nd Baron (1510–1556) I *143*
Vaux of Harrowden, 6th Baron (1804–1883) III *211*
Veale, Sir Douglas (1891–1973) IV *111*
Veitch, Sir H.J. (1840–1924) III *211*
Veitch, William (1794–1885) II *214*
Vellacott, P.C. (1891–1954) IV *111*
Venables, G.S. (1810–1888) III *211*
Venn, Henry (1725–1797) II *214*
Venn, Henry (1796–1873) II *214*
Venn, John (1759–1813) II *214*
Venn, John (1834–1923) III *211*
Venn, J.A. (1883–1958) IV *111*

Venner, Tobias (1577–1660) I *143*
Venning, Ralph (1621?–1674) I *143*
Venning, Sir W.K. (1882–1964) IV *111*
Ventris, Sir Peyton (1645–1691) I *143*
Verdon-Roe, Sir A.V. (1877–1958) IV *111*
Vere, Sir C.B. (1779–1843) I *214*
Vere, Sir Francis (1560–1609) I *143*
Vere of Tilbury, Baron (1565–1635) I *143*
Vermigli, P.M. (1500–1562) I *144*
Verney, Sir Edmund (1590–1642) I *144*
Verney, Sir Harry, 2nd Bart (1801–1894) III *211*
Verney, John (1699–1741) I *144*
Verney, Lady Margaret Maria (1844–1930) III *211*
Verney, Sir Ralph, 1st Bart (1613–1696) I *144*
Vernon, 5th Baron (1803–1866) III *211*
Vernon, 6th Baron (1824–1883) III *211*
Vernon, Edward (1684–1757) I *144*
Vernon, Sir Edward (1723–1794) II *214*
Vernon, James (1646–1727) I *144*
Vernon, Joseph (1738?–1782) II *214–215*
Vernon, Sir Richard (d 1451) I *144*
Vernon, Robert (1774–1849) II *215*
Vernon, Thomas (1654–1721) I *144*
Verrall, A.W. (1851–1912) III *211*
Verrio, Antonio (1639?–1707) I *144*
Vertue, George (1683–1756) I *144*
Vesey, Elizabeth (1715?–1791) II *215*
Vesey, John (1465?–1554) I *144*
Vestey, 1st Baron (1859–1940) III *211*
Vestris, G.A.B. (1729–1808) II *215*
Vestris, Marie Auguste (1760–1842) II *215*
Vetch, Samuel (1668–1732) I *144*
Vezin, Hermann (1829–1910) III *211*
Vezin, Jane Elizabeth (1827–1902) III *211*
Vian, Sir Philip (1894–1968) IV *111*
Vicary, Thomas (d 1561) I *144*
Vickers, K.H. (1881–1958) IV *111*
Victoria, Queen (1819–1901) III *211–213*
Victoria, Princess Royal (1840–1901) III *213–214*
Victoria, Princess (1868–1935) IV *111*
Vidler, William (1758–1816) II *215*
Vígfússon, Gúdbrandr (1828–1889) III *214*
Vignoles, C.B. (1793–1875) II *215*
Vigors, N.A. (1785–1840) II *215*
Villettes, W.A. (1754–1808) II *215*
Villiers, Augustus (1810–1847) III *214*
Villiers, C.P. (1802–1898) III *214*
Villiers, Sir George (1544?–1606) I *144*
Villiers, H.M. (1813–1861) III *214*
Vince, Samuel (1749–1821) II *215*
Vincent, George (1796–1836?) II *215*
Vincent, Sir Howard (1849–1908) III *214*
Vincent, Nathaniel (1639?–1697) I *144*
Vincent, R.B. (1770?–1831) II *215*
Vincent, William (1739–1815) II *215*
Viner, Sir Robert (1631–1688) I *144*
Viner, Sir Thomas, Bart (1588–1665) I *144*
Vines, S.H. (1849–1934) III *214*
Vining, G.J. (1824–1875) III *214*
Vinogradoff, Sir P.G. (1854–1925) III *214*
Vint, William (1768–1834) II *215*
Vivares, François (1716–1780) II *215*
Vives, J.L. (1492–1540) I *144*
Vivian, 1st Baron (1775–1842) II *215*
Vivian, 2nd Baron (1808–1886) III *214*
Vivian, 3rd Baron (1834–1893) III *214*
Vivian, Sir R.J.H. (1802–1887) III *214*
Vizetelly, Henry (1820–1894) III *214*
Voelcker, J.C.A. (1822–1884) III *214*
Vogel, Sir Julius (1835–1899) III *214*
Vokes, F.M. (1846–1888) III *214*
Vokes, Jessie (1851–1884) III *214*
Vokes, Rosina (1858–1894) III *214*
Vokes, Victoria (1853–1894) III *214*
Vos, G.J. (1577–1649) I *144*
Voysey, Charles (1828–1912) III *214*
Voysey, C.F.A. (1857–1941) III *214*
Vulliamy, B.L. (1747–1811) II *215*

Waad, Sir William (1546–1623) I *145*
Wace, Henry (1836–1924) III *215*
Wadd, William (1776–1829) II *216*
Waddilove, R.D. (1736–1828) II *216*
Wadding, Luke (1588–1657) I *145*
Waddington, Edward (1670?–1731) I *145*
Waddington, Samuel (1736–1758) II *216*
Wade, George (1673–1748) I *145*
Wade, Sir T.F. (1818–1895) III *215*
Wadham, Nicholas (1532–1609) I *145*
Wadsworth, E.A. (1889–1949) IV *112*
Wadsworth, Thomas (1630–1676) I *145*
Wager, Sir Charles (1666–1743) I *145*
Waghorn, Thomas (1800–1850) III *215*
Waithman, Robert (1764–1833) II *216*
Wake, William (1657–1737) I *145*
Wake-Walker, Sir W.F. (1888–1945) IV *112*
Wakefield, Viscount (1859–1941) III *215*

Wakefield, Daniel (1776–1846) II *216*
Wakefield, E.G. (1796–1862) II *216*
Wakefield, Gilbert (1756–1801) II *216*
Wakefield, Mrs Priscilla (1751–1832) II *216*
Wakley, Thomas (1795–1862) II *216*
Waldby, Robert (d 1398) I *145*
Waldegrave, 1st Earl of (1685–1741) I *145*
Waldegrave, 2nd Earl of (1715–1763) II *216*
Waldegrave, Countess (1821–1879) III *215*
Waldegrave, Samuel (1817–1869) III *215*
Waldron, F.G. (1744–1818) II *216*
Wale, Samuel (1720–1786) II *216*
Waley, Arthur (1889–1966) IV *112*
Walkden, Baron (1873–1951) IV *112*
Walker, Adam (1731?–1821) II *216*
Walker, Sir A.B., 1st Bart (1824–1893) III *215*
Walker, Sir B.E. (1848–1924) III *215*
Walker, Sir B.W., 1st Bart (1802–1876) III *215*
Walker, C.C. (1877–1968) IV *112*
Walker, C.V. (1812–1882) III *215*
Walker, David (1837–1917) III *215*
Walker, Sir Edward (1612–1677) I *145*
Walker, Elizabeth (1800–1876) III *215*
Walker, Sir Emery (1851–1933) III *215*
Walker, Ernest (1870–1949) IV *112*
Walker, Ethel, Dame (1861–1951) IV *112*
Walker, Frederick (1840–1875) III *215*
Walker, F.J. (1896–1944) IV *112*
Walker, F.W. (1830–1910) III *215*
Walker, George (1645?–1690) I *145*
Walker, George (1734?–1807) II *216*
Walker, Sir G.T., Bart (1764–1842) II *216*
Walker, Sir G.T. (1868–1958) IV *112*
Walker, James (1764–1831) II *216*
Walker, Sir James (1863–1935) IV *112*
Walker, John (1731–1803) II *216*
Walker, John (1732–1807) II *216*
Walker, Sir Mark (1827–1902) III *215*
Walker, Sir N.P. (1862–1942) IV *112*
Walker, Richard (1679–1764) I *145*
Walker, Robert (d 1658?) I *145*
Walker, Sayer (1748–1826) II *216*
Walker, Thomas (1698–1744) I *145*
Walker, Thomas (1749–1817) II *216*
Walker, William (1767?–1816) II *216*
Walkley, A.B. (1855–1926) III *215*
Walkinshaw, C.M.S. (1726?–1802) II *216*
Wall, John (1588–1666) I *145*
Wall, Joseph (1737–1802) II *216*
Wall, Martin (1747–1824) II *217*
Wallace, Baron (1768–1844) II *217*
Wallace, A.R. (1823–1913) III *215*
Wallace, Sir C.S., Bart (1867–1944) IV *112*
Wallace, Sir D.M. (1841–1919) III *216*
Wallace, Edgar (1875–1932) IV *112*
Wallace, Sir Richard, 1st Bart (1818–1890) III *216*
Wallace, Robert (1773–1855) II *217*
Wallace, Robert (1831–1899) III *216*
Wallace, William (1768–1843) II *217*
Wallace, W.R. (1813–1865) III *216*
Wallack, J.W. (1791?–1864) II *217*
Wallars, Graham (1858–1932) III *216*
Waller, Edmund (1606–1687) I *145*
Waller, Lewis (1860–1915) IV *112*
Waller, Sir William (1597?–1668) I *145*
Wallich, Nathaniel (1786–1854) II *217*
Wallis, Sir Barnes (1887–1979) IV *112*
Wallis, George (1811–1891) III *216*
Wallis, John (1616–1703) I *145*
Wallis, P.W.P. (1791–1892) II *217*
Wallis, Miss (fl 1789–1814) II *217*
Walmesley, Charles (1722–1797) II *217*
Walmesley, Sir Thomas (1537–1612) I *146*
Walmisley, T.A. (1814–1856) III *216*
Walmsley, Sir Joshua (1794–1871) II *217*
Walpole, Sir H.S. (1884–1941) IV *112*
Walpole, Robert (1650–1700) I *146*
Walpole, Sir Spencer (1839–1907) III *216*
Walpole, S.H. (1806–1898) III *216*
Walpole of Wolterton, 1st Baron (1678–1757) I *146*
Walsh, J.H. (1810–1888) III *216*
Walsh, William (1663–1708) I *146*
Walsh, W.P. (1820–1902) III *216*
Walsingham, 1st Baron (1719–1781) II *217*
Walsingham, 6th Baron (1843–1919) III *216*
Walter, Henry (1785–1859) II *217*
Walter, Hubert (d 1205) I *146*
Walter, Sir John (1566–1630) I *146*
Walter, John (1739–1812) II *217*
Walter, John (1776–1847) II *217*
Walter, John (1818–1894) III *216*
Walter, John (1873–1968) IV *112*
Walton, Brian (1600?–1661) I *146*
Walton, Sir George (1665–1739) I *146*
Walton, Izaak (1593–1683) I *146*
Walton, Sir Joseph (1845–1910) III *216*
Walton, Sir J.L. (1852–1908) III *216*

Wandesford, Christopher (1592–1640) I 146
Wanley, Humfrey (1672–1726) I 146
Wanley, Nathaniel (1634–1680) I 146
Wanostrocht, Nicholas (1804–1876) III 216
Wansey, Henry (1752?–1827) II 217
Wantage, Baron (1832–1901) III 216
Warbeck, Perkin (1474–1499) I 146
Warburton, Henry (1784?–1858) II 217
Warburton, John (1682–1759) I 146
Warburton, William (1698–1779) I 146
Ward, Sir A.W. (1837–1924) III 216
Ward, Sir Edward (1638–1714) I 146
Ward, Edward (1667–1731) I 146
Ward, E.M. (1816–1879) III 216
Ward, Sir E.W.D., 1st Bart (1853–1928) III 216
Ward, Sir H.G. (1797–1860) II 217
Ward, H.M. (1854–1906) III 216
Ward, James (1769–1859) II 217
Ward, James (1800–1885) III 217
Ward, James (1843–1925) III 217
Ward, John (1692?–1758) I 146
Ward, John (1704–1773) II 217
Ward, John (1866–1934) IV 112
Ward, Joshua (1685–1761) I 147
Ward, Sir J.G., 1st Bart (1856–1930) III 217
Ward, Sir Leslie (1851–1922) III 217
Ward, Mary (1585–1645) I 146
Ward, Mary Augusta (1851–1920) III 217
Ward, N.B. (1791–1868) II 217
Ward, Sir Patience (1629–1696) I 146
Ward, R.P. (1765–1846) II 217
Ward, Samuel (d 1643) I 146
Ward, Sarah (d 1786) II 217
Ward, Seth (1617–1689) I 146
Ward, William (1769–1823) II 217
Ward, W.G. (1812–1882) III 217
Warde, Beatrice (1900–1969) IV 112
Warde, J.P. (1792–1840) II 217
Warder, Joseph (fl 1688–1718) I 146
Wardlaw, Ralph (1779–1853) II 217
Wardlaw, William (1892–1958) IV 113
Wardle, G.L. (1762?–1833) II 217
Wardrop, James (1782–1861) II 217
Ware, Sir F.A.G. (1869–1949) IV 113
Ware, Isaac (d 1766) I 146
Ware, Sir James (1594–1666) I 146
Ware, James (1756–1815) II 217
Warham, William (1450?–1532) I 146
Waring, Sir H.J., 1st Bart (1866–1953) IV 113
Waring, J.B. (1823–1882) III 217
Waring, J.S. (1747–1819) II 217
Waring, William (1610–1679) I 147
Warkworth, John (d 1500) I 147
Warman, Guy (1872–1953) IV 113
Warneford, R.A.J. (1891–1915) IV 113
Warneford, S.W. (1763–1855) II 217–218
Warner, Charles (1846–1909) III 217
Warner, Sir Edward (1511–1565) I 147
Warner, Sir G.F. (1845–1936) III 217
Warner, John (1581–1666) I 147
Warner, Joseph (1717–1801) II 218
Warner, Mary Amelia (1804–1854) III 217
Warner, Sir P.F. (1873–1963) IV 113
Warner, Richard (1763–1857) II 218
Warre, Edmond (1837–1920) III 217
Warre-Cornish, F.W. (1839–1916) III 217
Warren, Charles (1767–1823) II 218
Warren, Sir Charles (1840–1927) III 217
Warren, Frederick (1775–1848) II 218
Warren, John (1730–1800) II 218
Warren, Sir J.B. (1753–1822) II 218
Warren, Pelham (1778–1835) II 218
Warren, Sir Peter (1703–1752) II 218
Warren, Richard (1731–1797) II 218
Warren, Samuel (1781–1862) II 218
Warren, Samuel (1807–1877) III 217
Warren, Thomas (1617?–1694) I 147
Warren, Sir T.H. (1853–1930) III 217
Warrington, 1st Earl of (1652–1694) I 147
Warrington, 2nd Earl of (1675–1758) I 147
Warrington of Clyffe, Baron (1851–1937) III 217
Warton, Joseph (1722–1800) II 218
Warton, Thomas (1728–1790) II 218
Warwick, 12th Earl of (d 1401) I 147
Warwick, 13th Earl of (1481/2–1439) I 147
Warwick, Earl of 'the King-maker' (1428–1471) I 147
Warwick, Earl of (1528?–1590) I 147
Warwick, 2nd Earl of (1587–1658) I 147
Warwick, Countess of (1625–1678) I 147
Warwick, Countess of (1861–1938) IV 113
Warwick, Sir Philip (1609–1683) I 147
Wasse, Joseph (1672–1738) I 147
Waterford, Marchioness of (1818–1891) III 217
Waterhouse, Alfred (1830–1905) III 217
Waterhouse, John (1616–1670) I 147
Waterhouse, G.R. (1810–1888) III 217
Waterhouse, Paul (1861–1924) IV 113

Waterland, Daniel (1683–1740) I 147
Waterlow, Sir E.A. (1850–1919) III 217
Waterlow, Sir S.H., 1st Bart (1822–1906) III 217–218
Waterton, Charles (1782–1865) II 218
Wathen, James (1751?–1828) II 218
Watkin, Sir E.W., 1st Bart (1819–1901) III 218
Watkins, C.F. (1793–1873) II 218
Watkins, John (fl 1792–1831) II 218
Watson, Albert (1828–1904) III 218
Watson, Sir Brook, 1st Bart (1735–1807) II 218
Watson, Charles (1714–1757) II 218
Watson, David (1713?–1761) II 218
Watson, D.M.S. (1886–1973) IV 113
Watson, George (1767–1837) II 218
Watson, Henry (1737–1786) II 218
Watson, H.G. (1796–1879) II 218
Watson, H.W. (1827–1903) III 218
Watson, James (1766?–1838) II 218
Watson, John (1725–1783) II 218
Watson, John (1850–1907) III 218
Watson, Joshua (1771–1855) II 218
Watson, Sir J.A.S. (1889–1966) IV 113
Watson, J.D. (1832–1892) III 218
Watson, Sir Malcolm (1873–1955) IV 113
Watson, M.L. (1804–1847) III 218
Watson, Richard (1737–1816) II 218
Watson, Richard (1781–1833) II 218
Watson, Robert (1746–1838) II 218
Watson, R.S. (1837–1911) III 218
Watson, Samuel (1898–1967) IV 113
Watson, Thomas (d 1686) I 147
Watson, Thomas (1637–1717) I 147
Watson, Sir Thomas, 1st Bart (1792–1882) II 218
Watson, Sir William (1715–1787) II 219
Watson, Sir William (1858–1935) III 218
Watson, William Watson, Lord (1827–1899) III 218
Watson-Watt, Sir Robert (1892–1973) IV 113
Watt, George Fiddes (1873–1960) IV 113
Watt, James (1736–1819) II 219
Watt, Margaret Rose (1868–1948) IV 113
Watts, A.A. (1797–1864) II 219
Watts, George Frederic (1817–1904) III 218
Watts, Isaac (1674–1748) I 147
Watts, John (1861–1902) IV 113
Watts, Sir Philip (1846–1926) III 218
Watts, Richard (1529–1579) I 147
Watts-Dunton, Theodore (1832–1914) III 218
Wauchope, Sir A.G. (1874–1947) IV 113
Waugh, Alexander (1754–1827) II 219
Waugh, Benjamin (1839–1908) III 218
Waugh, Edwin (1817–1890) III 218
Wavell, 1st Earl (1883–1950) IV 113
Wavell, A.J.B. (1882–1916) IV 113
Waverley, 1st Viscount (1882–1958) IV 113
Waverley, Viscountess (1896–1974) IV 113
Way, Albert (1805–1874) II 219
Way, Lewis (1772–1840) II 219
Waylett, Mrs Harriett (1798–1851) II 219
Waynflete, William of (1395?–1486) I 147
Weaver, Sir Lawrence (1876–1930) IV 113
Weaver, Robert (1773–1852) II 219
Webb, Sir Aston (1849–1930) III 219
Webb, A.B. (1839–1907) III 219
Webb, Benjamin (1819–1885) III 219
Webb, C.C.J. (1865–1954) IV 113
Webb, Francis (1735–1815) II 219
Webb, F.W. (1836–1906) III 219
Webb, George (1581–1642) I 147
Webb, Sir John (1772–1852) II 219
Webb, J.R. (1667?–1724) I 147
Webb, Mary Gladys (1881–1927) IV 113
Webb, Matthew (1848–1883) III 219
Webb, Philip (1831–1915) III 219
Webb, P.B. (1793–1854) II 219
Webb, Mrs (d 1793) II 219
Webb-Johnson, 1st Baron (1880–1958) IV 113
Webbe, Samuel (1770?–1843) II 219
Webber, John (1750?–1793) II 219
Webster, Alexander (1707–1784) II 219
Webster, Augusta (1837–1894) III 219
Webster, Benjamin (1797–1882) II 219
Webster, B.N. (1797–1882) II 219
Webster, Sir C.K. (1886–1961) IV 113
Webster, Dame Mary Louise (1865–1948) IV 114
Webster, Thomas (1800–1886) III 219
Webster, Tom (1890–1962) IV 113–114
Weckherlin, G.R. (1584–1653) I 147
Wedgwood, 1st Baron (1872–1943) IV 114
Wedgwood, Josiah (1730–1795) II 219
Wedgwood, Josiah (1899–1968) IV 114
Wedgwood, Sir R.L., 1st Bart (1874–1956) IV 114
Wedgwood, Thomas (1771–1805) II 219
Weekes, Henry (1807–1877) III 219
Weeks, Baron (1890–1960) IV 114
Weever, John (1576–1632) I 147
Weir, 1st Viscount (1877–1959) IV 114
Weir, Sir C.M. (1890–1960) IV 114

Weir, H.W. (1824–1906) III 219
Weir, Sir John (1879–1971) IV 114
Weiss, W.H. (1820–1867) III 219
Welby, Baron (1832–1915) III 219
Welby, Henry (1552–1636) I 147
Welch, A.C. (1864–1943) IV 114
Welchman, Harry (1886–1966) IV 114
Weld, Thomas (1773–1837) II 219
Weldon, Sir Anthony (d 1649?) I 147
Weldon, John (1676–1736) I 148
Weldon, J.E.C. (1854–1937) III 219
Weldon, W.F.R. (1860–1906) IV 114
Wellbeloved, Charles (1769–1858) II 219
Welles, 6th Baron (1405?–1461) I 148
Wellesley, 1st Marquess (1760–1842) II 219–220
Wellesley, F.A. (1844–1931) III 219
Wellesley, G.V. (1809–1882) III 219
Wellesley, Henry (1791–1866) II 219
Wellesz, E.J. (1885–1974) IV 114
Wellington, 1st Duke of (1769–1852) II 220
Wellington, 3rd Duke of (1846–1900) III 219
Wellington, 7th Duke of (1885–1972) IV 114
Wellington, Duchess of (1889–1956) IV 114
Wells, H.G. (1866–1946) IV 114
Wells, H.T. (1828–1903) III 219
Wells, Mary (1759?–1826?) II 220
Wells, Sir T.S., 1st Bart (1818–1897) III 219
Welsby, W.N. (1802?–1864) III 219
Welsh, David (1793–1845) II 220
Welton, Richard (1671?–1726) I 148
Wemyss, D.D. (1760–1839) II 220
Wemyss and March, 10th Earl of (1818–1914) III 219–220
Wenlock, 3rd Baron (1849–1912) III 220
Wensleydale, Baron (1782–1868) II 220
Wentworth, Baroness (1657?–1686) I 148
Wentworth, Sir John (1737–1820) II 220
Wentworth, W.C. (1793–1872) II 220
Wentworth of Nettlestead, 1st Baron (1501–1555) I 148
Wentworth of Nettlestead, 2nd Baron (1525–1584) I 148
Wernher, Sir J.C., 1st Bart (1850–1912) III 220
Wesley, Charles (1707–1788) II 220
Wesley, John (1703–1791) II 220
Wesley, Samuel (1662–1735) I 148
Wesley, Samuel (1766–1837) II 220
Wesley, S.S. (1810–1876) III 220
West, Sir A.E. (1832–1921) III 220
West, Benjamin (1738–1820) II 220–221
West, Gilbert (1703–1756) II 221
West, James (1704?–1772) II 221
West, Dame Rebecca (b 1892) IV 114
West, Richard (d 1726) I 148
West, Robert (d 1770) II 221
West, R.L. (1769–1850) II 221
West, R.L. (1774–1849) II 221
West, Mrs (1790–1876) II 221
Westall, Richard (1765–1836) II 221
Westall, William (1781–1850) II 221
Westbury, 1st Baron (1800–1873) III 220
Westcott, B.F. (1825–1901) III 220
Westcott, G.B. (1745?–1798) II 221
Wester Wemyss, Baron (1864–1933) IV 114
Western, Baron (1767–1844) II 221
Westfield, Thomas (1573–1644) I 148
Westlake, John (1828–1913) III 220
Westmacott, Sir Richard (1775–1856) II 221
Westmacott, Richard (1799–1872) II 221
Westminster, 1st Marquess of (1767–1845) II 221
Westminster, 2nd Marquess of (1795–1869) II 221
Westminster, 1st Duke of (1825–1899) III 220
Westmorland, 1st Earl of (1364–1425) I 148
Westmorland, 5th Earl of (1525?–1563?) I 148
Westmorland, 2nd Earl of (1602–1665) I 148
Westmorland, 7th Earl of (1682?–1762) I 148
Westmorland, 10th Earl of (1759–1841) II 221
Westmorland, 11th Earl of (1784–1859) II 221
Westmorland, 12th Earl of (1825–1891) III 220
Westmorland, Countess of (1793–1879) II 221
Weston, Dame Agnes (1840–1918) III 220
Weston, Frank (1871–1924) IV 114
Weston, Sir Robert (1515?–1573) I 148
Weston, Stephen (1665–1742) I 148
Weston, Stephen (1747–1830) II 221
Weston, Thomas (1737–1776) II 221
Westphaling, Herbert (1533?–1602) I 148
Westwood, J.O. (1805–1893) III 220
Wetenhall, Edward (1636–1713) I 148
Wetherell, Sir Charles (1770–1846) II 221–222
Wewitzer, Ralph (1758–1825) II 222
Weyman, S.J. (1855–1928) III 220
Weymouth, 1st Viscount (1640–1714) I 148
Whalley, G.H. (1813–1878) III 220
Whalley, Peter (1722–1791) II 222
Whalley, T.S. (1746–1828) II 222
Wharncliffe, 1st Baron (1776?–1845) II 222
Wharncliffe, 2nd Baron (1801–1855) III 220
Wharncliffe, 1st Earl of (1827–1899) III 220
Wharton, 4th Baron (1613–1696) I 148

Wharton, 1st Marquess (1648–1715) I *148*
Wharton, Duke of (1698–1731) I *148*
Wharton, Anne, Lady (1632?–1685) I *148*
Wharton, E.R. (1844–1896) III *220*
Wharton, Sir George, 1st Bart (1617–1681) I *148*
Wharton, Henry (1664–1695) I *148*
Wharton, Thomas (1614–1673) I *148*
Whateley, William (1583–1639) I *148*
Whately, Richard (1787–1863) II *222*
Wheatley, Dennis (1897–1977) IV *114*
Wheatley, Francis (1747–1801) II *222*
Wheatley, John (1869–1930) III *114*
Wheatstone, Sir Charles (1802–1875) III *220–221*
Wheeler, Sir Charles (1892–1974) IV *114*
Wheeler, Sir Mortimer (1890–1976) IV *114–115*
Wheeler, Thomas (1754–1847) II *222*
Wheler, Sir George (1650–1723?) I *148*
Whetstone, Sir William (d1711) I *149*
Whewell, William (1794–1866) II *222*
Whibley, Charles (1859–1930) III *221*
Whibley, Leonard (1863–1941) IV *115*
Whichcord, John (1823–1885) III *221*
Whichcote, Benjamin (1609–1683) I *149*
Whipple, R.S. (1871–1953) IV *115*
Whistler, Daniel (1619–1684) I *149*
Whistler, J.A.M. (1834–1903) III *221*
Whistler, Sir Lashmer (1898–1963) IV *115*
Whiston, William (1667–1752) I *149*
Whitaker, Sir Arthur (1893–1968) IV *115*
Whitaker, John (1735–1808) II *222*
Whitaker, John (1776–1847) II *222*
Whitaker, Tobias (d1666) I *149*
Whitaker, T.D. (1759–1821) II *222*
Whitaker, William (1548–1595) I *149*
Whitbread, Samuel (1720–1796) II *222*
Whitbread, Samuel (1764–1815) II *222*
Whitby, Daniel (1638–1726) I *149*
Whitby, Sir L.E.H. (1895–1956) IV *115*
White, Adam (1817–1879) III *221*
White, Anthony (1782–1849) II *222*
White, Charles (1728–1813) II *222*
White, Francis (1564?–1638) I *149*
White, Gilbert (1720–1793) II *222*
White, Henry (1836–1890) III *221*
White, H.J. (1859–1934) III *221*
White, Henry Kirke (1785–1806) II *222*
White, Jeremiah (1629–1707) I *149*
White, John (1570–1615) I *149*
White, Joseph (1745–1814) II *222*
White, J.B. (1775–1841) II *222*
White, Richard (1539–1611) I *149*
White, Robert (1645–1703) I *149*
White, Sir Thomas (1492–1567) I *149*
White, Thomas (1550?–1624) I *149*
White, Thomas (1593–1676) I *149*
White, Thomas (1628–1698) I *149*
White, Sir W.A. (1824–1891) III *221*
White, W.H. (1831–1913) III *221*
White, Sir W.H. (1845–1913) III *221*
Whitefield, George (1714–1770) II *222*
Whitefoord, Caleb (1734–1810) II *222*
Whitehead, A.N. (1861–1947) IV *115*
Whitehead, David (1492?–1571) I *149*
Whitehead, Paul (1710–1774) II *222–223*
Whitehead, William (1715–1785) II *223*
Whitehurst, John (1713–1788) II *223*
Whiteing, Richard (1840–1928) III *221*
Whiteley, Sir J.F.M. (1896–1970) IV *115*
Whiteley, William (1881–1955) IV *115*
Whitelocke, Bulstrode (1605–1675) I *149*
Whitelocke, Sir James (1570–1632) I *149*
Whitelocke, John (1757–1833) II *223*
Whiteside, James (1804–1876) III *221*
Whitgift, John (1530?–1604) I *149*
Whithorne, Thomas (fl 1571–1590) I *149*
Whitla, Sir William (1851–1933) III *221*
Whitley, J.H. (1866–1935) IV *115*
Whitlock, Mrs Elizabeth (1761–1836) II *223*
Whitmore, Sir George (d1654) I *149*
Whitshed, Sir J.H., 1st Bart (1762–1849) II *223*
Whitson, John (1557–1629) I *149*
Whittaker, Sir E.T. (1873–1956) IV *115*
Whittingham, Sir Harold (b1887) IV *115*
Whittington, Richard (d1423) I *149*
Whitworth, Baron (1675–1725) I *149*
Whitworth, G.A. (1883–1951) IV *115*
Whitworth, Sir Joseph, 1st Bart (1803–1887) III *221*
Whymper, Edward (1840–1911) III *221*
Whymper, J.W. (1813–1903) III *221*
Whyte, Alexander (1836–1921) III *222*
Whyte, Samuel (1733–1811) II *223*
Whyte-Melville, G.J. (1821–1878) III *222*
Whytt, Robert (1714–1766) II *223*
Wickens, Sir John (1815–1873) III *222*
Wickham, E.C. (1834–1910) III *222*

Widdrington, Sir Thomas (d1664) I *149*
Wiffen, J.H. (1792–1836) II *223*
Wigan, A.S. (1814–1878) III *222*
Wigan, Horace (1818?–1885) III *222*
Wigan, John (1696–1739) I *149*
Wigan, Leonora (1805–1884) III *222*
Wight, Robert (1796–1872) II *223*
Wightman, Sir William (1784–1863) II *223*
Wightwick, George (1802–1872) III *222*
Wigram, Sir James (1793–1866) II *223*
Wilberforce, E.R. (1840–1907) III *222*
Wilberforce, Samuel (1805–1873) III *222*
Wilberforce, William (1759–1833) II *223*
Wilbraham, Sir P.W.B., 6th Bart (1875–1957) IV *115*
Wilcocks, Joseph (1673–1756) I *149*
Wilcocks, Joseph (1724–1791) II *223*
Wild, Francis (1873–1939) IV *115*
Wilde, Oscar (1856–1900) III *222*
Wilde, Sir William, 1st Bart (1611?–1679) I *149*
Wilde, Sir W.R.W. (1815–1876) III *222*
Wilderspin, Samuel (1792?–1866) II *223*
Wildman, Sir John (1621–1693) I *149*
Wilford, Sir James (1516?–1550) I *149*
Wilkes, John (1727–1797) II *223*
Wilkie, Sir David (1785–1841) II *223*
Wilkie, Sir D.P.D. (1882–1938) IV *115*
Wilkins, A.S. (1843–1905) III *222*
Wilkins, David (1685?–1745) I *149*
Wilkins, John (1614–1672) I *150*
Wilkins, William (1778–1839) II *223*
Wilkinson, Ellen Cicely (1891–1947) IV *115*
Wilkinson, G.H. (1833–1907) III *222*
Wilkinson, John (1728–1808) II *223*
Wilkinson, Sir J.G. (1797–1875) II *223*
Wilkinson, L.U. (1881–1966) IV *115*
Wilkinson, Norman (1878–1971) IV *115*
Wilkinson, Sir N.R. (1869–1940) IV *115*
Wilkinson, Tate (1739–1803) II *223*
Wilks, Robert (1665?–1732) I *150*
Wilks, Sir Samuel, 1st Bart (1824–1911) III *222*
Willan, Robert (1757–1812) II *223*
Willcox, Sir W.H. (1870–1941) IV *115*
Willert, Sir Arthur (1882–1973) IV *115*
Willes, Sir G.O. (1823–1901) III *222*
Willes, Sir John (1685–1761) I *150*
Willes, Sir J.S. (1814–1872) III *222–223*
Willett, Andrew (1562–1621) I *150*
Willett, Ralph (1719–1795) II *223*
Willett, William (1856–1915) III *223*
Willey, Basil (1897–1978) IV *115*
William I, (1027–1087) I *150*
William II, (d1100) I *150*
William of Nassau (1626–1650) I *150*
William III (1650–1702) I *150*
William IV (1765–1837) II *223–224*
Williams, Anna (1706–1783) II *224*
Williams, A.T.P. (1888–1968) IV *115*
Williams, Basil (1867–1950) IV *115*
Williams, Sir C.H. (1708–1759) II *224*
Williams, C.J.B. (1805–1889) III *223*
Williams, C.W.S. (1886–1945) IV *115*
Williams, Daniel (1643?–1716) I *150*
Williams, David (1738–1816) II *224*
Williams, Edward (1746–1826) II *224*
Williams, Edward (1750–1813) II *224*
Williams, E.E. (1793–1822) II *224*
Williams, E.G. Harcourt (1880–1957) IV *115*
Williams, Sir E.L. (1828–1910) III *223*
Williams, Sir George (1821–1905) III *223*
Williams, G.J. (1719–1805) II *224*
Williams, H.H. (1872–1961) IV *115*
Williams, Helen Maria (1762–1827) II *224*
Williams, H.W. (1773–1829) II *224*
Williams, Sir Ifor (1881–1965) IV *115*
Williams, Isaac (1802–1865) III *223*
Williams, John (1582–1650) I *150*
Williams, John (1636?–1709) I *150*
Williams, John (1761–1818) II *224*
Williams, Sir John (1777–1846) II *224*
Williams, John (1792–1858) II *224*
Williams, John (1796–1839) II *224*
Williams, J.C. (1821–1907) III *223*
Williams, Margaret Lindsay (1888–1960) IV *116*
Williams, M.S. (1835–1892) III *223*
Williams, O.L.C. (1836–1904) III *223*
Williams, Rowland (1817–1870) III *223*
Williams, Rowland (1823–1905) III *223*
Williams, Sir R.B.V. (1838–1916) III *223*
Williams, Thomas (1513?–1566) I *150*
Williams, Sir William, 1st Bart (1634–1700) I *150*
Williams, William (1781–1840) II *224*
Williams, William (1800–1879?) III *223*
Williams, William (1801–1869) III *223*
Williams, Sir W.F., Bart (1800–1883) III *223*
Williams, W.P. (1664–1736) I *150*
Williams, W.P. (1742–1832) II *224*
Williams Bulkeley, Sir R.B., Bart (1801–1875) III *223*

Williams-Ellis, Sir Clough (1883–1978) IV *116*
Williams-Wynn, Charles (1822–1896) III *223*
Williams-Wynn, Charlotte (1807–1869) III *223*
Williams-Wynn, Sir Watkin, Bart (1820–1885) III *223*
Williams of Banburgh, Baron (1888–1967) IV *116*
Williamson, A.W. (1824–1904) III *223*
Williamson, Henry (1895–1977) IV *116*
Williamson, Sir Joseph (1633–1701) I *150*
Williamson, Peter (1730–1799) II *224*
Willingdon, 1st Marquess of (1866–1941) IV *116*
Willink, Sir H.U. (1894–1973) IV *116*
Willis, Sir A.U. (1889–1976) IV *116*
Willis, Browne (1682–1760) I *150*
Willis, Francis (1718–1807) II *224*
Willis, Sir G.H.S. (1823–1900) III *223*
Willis, Richard (1664–1734) I *150*
Willis, Robert (1799–1878) II *224*
Willis, Thomas (1621–1675) I *150*
Willison, George (1741–1797) II *224*
Willmore, J.T. (1800–1863) III *223*
Willmott, R.A. (1809–1863) III *223*
Willoughby, Francis (1635–1672) I *150*
Willoughby, Sir J.C., 5th Bart (1859–1918) III *223*
Willoughby, Sir N.J. (1777–1849) II *224*
Willoughby de Broke, 19th Baron (1869–1923) IV *116*
Willoughby de Eresby, Lord (1555–1601) I *150*
Willoughby of Parham, 5th Baron (1613?–1666) I *150*
Wills, Sir Charles (1666–1741) I *150*
Wills, Sir G.A., 1st Bart (1854–1928) III *223*
Wills, John (1741–1806) II *224*
Wills, Thomas (1740–1802) II *224*
Wills, W.G. (1828–1891) III *223*
Wills, W.H. (1810–1880) III *223*
Wills, W.J. (1834–1861) III *224*
Willshire, Sir Thomas, Bart (1789–1862) II *224*
Wilmington, 1st Earl of (1673?–1743) I *150*
Wilmot, Sir J.E. (1709–1792) II *224*
Wilmot, J.E. (1750–1815) II *224–225*
Wilmot, Sir J.E. Eardley-, 2nd Bart (1810–1892) III *224*
Wilmot, Sir Sainthill Eardley- (1852–1929) III *224*
Wilmot of Selmeston, Baron (1895–1964) IV *116*
Wilshaw, Sir Edward (1879–1968) IV *116*
Wilson, 1st Baron (1881–1964) IV *116*
Wilson, Alexander (1714–1786) II *225*
Wilson, Alexander (1766–1813) II *225*
Wilson, Anthony (fl 1793) II *225*
Wilson, Sir Archdale, 1st Bart (1803–1874) III *224*
Wilson, Arthur (1836–1909) III *224*
Wilson, Sir A.K., 3rd Bart (1842–1921) III *224*
Wilson, Sir A.T. (1884–1940) IV *116*
Wilson, Benjamin (1721–1788) II *225*
Wilson, Caroline (1787–1846) II *225*
Wilson, Christopher (1714–1792) II *225*
Wilson, Sir C.R. (1831–1916) III *224*
Wilson, C.T.R. (1869–1959) IV *116*
Wilson, Sir C.W. (1836–1905) III *224*
Wilson, Daniel (1778–1858) II *225*
Wilson, Sir Daniel (1816–1892) III *224*
Wilson, Edward (d1694) I *151*
Wilson, E.A. (1872–1912) IV *116*
Wilson, George (b1765) II *225*
Wilson, George (1808–1870) III *224*
Wilson, George (1818–1859) III *224*
Wilson, Harriette (1789–1846) II *225*
Wilson, H.A. (1876–1961) IV *116*
Wilson, H.H. (1786–1860) II *225*
Wilson, Sir H.H., Bart (1864–1922) IV *116*
Wilson, Sir H.J. (1882–1972) IV *116*
Wilson, Sir Jacob (1836–1905) III *224*
Wilson, James (1805–1860) III *224*
Wilson, John (1595–1674) I *151*
Wilson, Sir John (1741–1793) II *225*
Wilson, John (1785–1854) II *225*
Wilson, John (1800–1849) III *224*
Wilson, John (1812–1888) III *224*
Wilson, J.A. (1795–1882) III *224*
Wilson, J.D. (1833–1908) III *224*
Wilson, John Dover (1881–1969) IV *116*
Wilson, J.L. (1897–1970) IV *116*
Wilson, J.M. (1804–1835) III *224*
Wilson, J.M. (1836–1931) III *224*
Wilson, Mary Anne (1802–1867) III *224*
Wilson, Patrick (1743–1811) II *225*
Wilson, Richard (1714–1782) II *225*
Wilson, Richard (fl 1774–1792) II *225*
Wilson, Sir R.T. (1777–1849) II *225*
Wilson, Sir S.H. (1873–1950) IV *116*
Wilson, Thomas (1525?–1581) I *151*
Wilson, Thomas (1563–1622) I *151*
Wilson, Thomas (1663–1755) I *151*
Wilson, Thomas (1703–1784) II *225*
Wilson, Thomas (1747–1813) II *225*
Wilson, Thomas (1764–1843) II *225*
Wilson, Thomas (1767–1852) II *225*
Wilson, Sir W.J.E. (1809–1884) III *224*
Wilson, Mrs (d1786) II *225*
Wilton, Joseph (1722–1803) II *225*

Wiltshire, Earl of (1477–1539) I 151
Wimbledon, Viscount (1572–1638) I 151
Wimborne, 1st Viscount (1873–1939) IV 116
Winch, Sir Humphrey (1555?–1625) I 151
Winchcombe, John (d 1520) I 151
Winchester, 1st Marquess of (1485?–1572) I 151
Winchester, 5th Marquess of (1598–1675) I 151
Winchester, John (d 1460?) I 151
Winchilsea, 7th Earl of (1647–1730) I 151
Winchilsea, 10th Earl of (1791–1858) II 226
Winchilsea, 11th Earl of (1815–1887) III 224
Windebank, Sir Francis (1582–1646) I 151·
Windham, Sir C.A. (1810–1870) III 224
Windham, William (1717–1761) II 226
Windham, William (1750–1810) II 226
Windsor, Edward, Duke of (1894–1972) IV 116–117
Windsor, Wallis Simpson, Duchess of (b 1896) IV 117
Windus, W.L. (1822–1907) III 224
Winfield, Sir P.H. (1878–1953) IV 117
Wing, Tycho (1696–1750) I 151
Wing, Vincent (1619–1668) I 151
Wingate, Sir J.L. (1846–1924) III 224
Wingate, Sir Reginald, 1st Bart (1861–1953) IV 117
Wingfield, Sir Anthony (1485?–1552) I 151
Winmarleigh, 1st Baron (1802–1892) III 224–225
Winnington, Sir Francis (1634–1700) I 151
Winnington, Thomas (1696–1746) I 151
Winnington-Ingram, A.F. (1858–1946) III 225
Winslow, F.B. (1810–1874) III 225
Winsor, F.A. (1763–1830) II 226
Winstanley, D.A. (1877–1947) IV 117
Winstanley, Hamlet (1698–1756) I 151
Winstanley, William (1628?–1698) I 151
Winster, Baron (1885–1961) IV 117
Winter, Sir Edward (1622?–1686) I 151
Winter, Robert (d 1606) I 151
Winter, Thomas (1572–1606) I 151
Winter, Thomas (1795–1851) II 226
Winterbotham, H.S.P. (1837–1873) III 225
Winterbotham, William (1763–1829) II 226
Winterhalter, F.X. (1806–1873) III 225
Winterstoke, Baron (1830–1911) III 225
Winterton, 6th Earl (1883–1962) IV 117
Wintringham, Sir Clifton, Bart (1710–1794) II 226
Winwood, Sir Ralph (1563–1617) I 151
Winthrop, John (1587?–1649) I 151
Winton, 3rd Earl (1584–1650) I 151
Wise, Henry (1653–1738) I 151
Wiseman, N.P.S., Cardinal (1802–1865) III 225
Wiseman, Richard (1622?–1676) I 151
Wishart, George (1513?–1546) I 151
Wishart, Sir James (d 1723) I 151
Wishart, Robert (d 1316) I 151
Wissing, Willem (1656–1687) I 152
Withering, William (1741–1799) II 226
Witherington, W.F. (1785–1865) II 226
Wither(s), Marquess of (1588–1667) I 152
Witherspoon, John (1723–1794) II 226
Witt, Sir R.C. (1872–1952) IV 117
Wittgenstein, L.J.J. (1889–1951) IV 117
Wivell, Abraham (1786–1849) II 226
Wodehouse, Helen Marion (1880–1964) IV 117
Wodehouse, Sir P.E. (1811–1887) III 225
Wodehouse, Sir P.G. (1881–1975) IV 117
Wodhull, Michael (1740–1816) II 226
Woffington, Margaret (1714?–1760) II 226
Wogan, Sir Charles (1698?–1752?) I 152
Woide, C.G. (1725–1790) II 226
Wolcot, John (1738–1819) II 226
Wolf, Josef (1820–1899) III 225
Wolfe, Charles (1791–1823) II 226
Wolfe, Humbert (1886–1940) IV 117
Wolfe, James (1727–1759) II 226
Wolfe-Barry, Sir J.W. (1836–1918) III 225
Wolff, Sir H.D.C. (1830–1908) III 225
Wolff, Joseph (1795–1862) II 226
Wolfson, Sir Isaac, 1st Bart (b 1897) IV 117
Wollaston, William (1660–1724) I 152
Wollaston, W.H. (1766–1828) II 226
Wolmark, Alfred (1877–1961) IV 117
Wolseley, 1st Viscount (1833–1913) III 225
Wolsey, Thomas (1475?–1530) I 152
Wolstenholme, Sir John (1562–1639) I 152
Wolverhampton, 1st Viscount (1830–1911) III 225
Wolverton, 2nd Baron (1824–1887) III 225–226
Womersley, Sir W.J., 1st Bart (1878–1961) IV 117
Wood, Alexander (1725–1807) II 226
Wood, Anthony (1632–1695) I 152
Wood, Ellen (1814–1887) III 226
Wood, Sir Evelyn (1838–1919) III 226
Wood, Francis Derwent (1871–1926) IV 117
Wood, Sir George (1743–1824) II 226
Wood, Sir G.A. (1767–1831) II 226
Wood, Sir H.J. (1869–1944) IV 117
Wood, James (1760–1839) II 226
Wood, John (1825–1891) III 226

Wood, Sir J.A. (1756–1829) II 226
Wood, J.G. (1827–1889) III 226
Wood, Sir Kingsley (1881–1943) IV 117–118
Wood, Mary Ann (1802–1864) III 226
Wood, Sir Matthew, 1st Bart (1768–1843) II 226–227
Wood, Robert (1716–1771) II 227
Wood, Thomas (1661–1722) I 152
Wood, T.M. (1855–1927) III 226
Wood, Sir William (1609–1691) I 152
Woodall, John (1556?–1643) I 152
Woodall, William (1832–1901) III 226
Woodard, Nathaniel (1811–1891) III 226
Woodd, Basil (1760–1831) I 227
Woodfall, William (1746–1803) II 227
Woodford, J.R. (1820–1885) III 226
Woodford, Sir R.J., Bart (1784–1828) II 227
Woodford, Samuel (1636–1700) I 152
Woodhouse, James (1735–1820) II 227
Woodhouselee, Lord (1747–1813) II 227
Woodington, W.F. (1806–1893) III 226
Woodroffe, Benjamin (1638–1711) I 152
Woods, Sir A.W. (1816–1904) III 226
Woods, Edward (1814–1903) III 226
Woods, E.S. (1877–1953) IV 118
Woods, Sir John (1895–1962) IV 118
Woods, Margaret Louisa (1856–1945) III 226
Woodville, William (1752–1805) II 227
Woodward, Sir A.S. (1864–1944) IV 118
Woodward, Benjamin (1815–1861) III 226
Woodward, C.S. (1878–1959) IV 118
Woodward, Francis (1721–1785) I 227
Woodward, Sir E.L. (1890–1971) IV 118
Woodward, G.M. (1760?–1809) I 227
Woodward, Henry (1714–1777) II 227
Woodward, John (1665–1728) I 152
Woodward, Samuel (1790–1838) II 227
Woolavington, 1st Baron (1849–1935) III 226
Wooler, T.J. (1786?–1853) II 227
Woolf, Leonard (1880–1969) IV 118
Woolf, Virginia (1882–1941) IV 118
Wooll, John (1767–1833) II 227
Woollard, F.G. (1883–1957) IV 118
Woollett, William (1735–1785) II 227
Woolley, Sir Leonard (1880–1960) IV 118
Woolner, Thomas (1825–1892) III 226
Woolston, Thomas (1670–1733) I 152
Woolton, 1st Earl (1883–1964) IV 118
Wootton, John (1686?–1765) I 152
Wootton of Abinger, Baroness (b 1897) IV 118
Worboise, Emma Jane (1825–1887) III 226
Worcester, Earl of (1427?–1470) I 152
Worcester, 1st Earl of (1460?–1526) I 152
Worcester, 3rd Earl of (1526–1589) I 152
Worcester, 4th Earl of (1553–1628) I 152
Worcester, 1st Marquess of (1577?–1646) I 152
Worcester, 2nd Marquess of (1601–1667) I 152
Wordsworth, Charles (1806–1892) III 226
Wordsworth, Christopher (1807–1885) III 226
Wordsworth, Dame Elizabeth (1840–1932) III 227
Wordsworth, John (1805–1839) III 227
Wordsworth, John (1843–1911) III 227
Wordsworth, William (1770–1850) II 227
Wornum, G.G. (1888–1957) IV 118
Wornum, R.N. (1812–1877) III 227
Worsdale, James (1692?–1767) I 152
Worsley, Sir Richard, 7th Bart (1751–1805) II 227
Worthington, Hugh (1752–1813) II 227
Worthington-Evans, Sir Laming, 1st Bart (1868–1931) IV 118
Wortley, Sir Francis, 1st Bart (1591–1652) I 152
Wotton, Sir Henry (1568–1639) I 152
Wotton, Nicholas (1497?–1567) I 152
Woulfe, Stephen (1787–1840) II 227
Wrangham, Francis (1769–1842) II 227
Wraxall, Sir N.W., 1st Bart (1751–1831) II 227
Wray, Sir Cecil, 13th Bart (1734–1805) II227
Wray, Sir Christopher (1524–1592) I 152
Wray, Daniel (1701–1783) II 227
Wren, Christopher (1591–1658) I 152
Wren, Sir Christopher (1632–1723) I 152
Wren, Christopher (1675–1747) I 153
Wren, Matthew (1585–1667) I 153
Wrenbury, 1st Baron (1845–1935) III 227
Wrench, Sir Evelyn (1882–1966) IV 118
Wrey, Sir Bourchier (1714–1784) II 227–228
Wright, Baron (1869–1964) IV 118
Wright, Sir A.E. (1861–1947) IV 118
Wright, Sir Charles, 2nd Bart (1876–1950) IV 118
Wright, Christopher (1570?–1605) I 153
Wright, Sir C.T.H. (1862–1940) IV 118
Wright, E.R. (1813–1859) III 227
Wright, I.C. (1795–1871) II 228
Wright, John (1568?–1605) I 153
Wright, Joseph (1734–1797) II 228
Wright, Joseph (1855–1930) III 227
Wright, J.W. (1769–1805) II 228

Wright, Sir Nathan (1654–1721) I 153
Wright, Mrs Patience (1725–1786) II 228
Wright, Peter (1603–1651) I 153
Wright, Robert (15p1643) I 153
Wright, Sir R.S. (1839–1904) III 227
Wright, Samuel (1683–1746) I 153
Wright, Thomas (1711–1786) II 228
Wright, Thomas (1789–1875) II 228
Wright, Thomas (1810–1877) III 227
Wright, Whitaker (1845–1904) III 227
Wright, William (1830–1889) III 227
Wright, W.A. (1831–1914) III 227
Wright, W.R. (d 1826) II 228
Wrixon-Becher, Lady (1791–1872) II 218
Wroth, Lady (fl 1621) I 153
Wrottesley, 1st Baron (1771–1841) II 228
Wrottesley, 3rd Baron (1824–1910) III 227
Wrottesley, Sir F.J. (1880–1948) IV 118
Wroughton, Richard (1748–1822) II 228
Wyat, Sir Henry (d 1537) I 153
Wyatt, B.D. (1775–1850?) II 228
Wyatt, James (1746–1813) II 228
Wyatt, Sir M.D. (1820–1877) III 227
Wyatt, R.J. (1795–1850) II 228
Wyatt, Sir Thomas (1503?–1542) I 153
Wyatt, Sir Thomas (1521?–1554) I 153
Wyatt, T.H. (1807–1880) III 227
Wyatville, Sir Jeffry (1766–1840) II 228
Wyche, Sir Cyril (1632?–1707) I 153
Wycherley, Sir Bruce (1894–1965) IV 118
Wycherley, William (1640–1716) I 153
Wyck, John (1652–1700) I 153
Wyke, Sir C.L. (1815–1897) III 227
Wykeham, William of (1324–1404) I 153
Wyld, H.C.K. (1870–1945) IV 118
Wyld, James (1812–1887) III 227
Wylde, Henry (1822–1890) III 227
Wylie, Sir F.J. (1865–1952) IV 118
Wylie, J.A. (1808–1890) III 227
Wylie, Sir William (1802–1891) III 227
Wylie, W.L. (1851–1931) III 227
Wyndham, Lady (1861–1931) IV 118–119
Wyndham, Sir Charles (1837–1919) III 227
Wyndham, George (1863–1913) IV 118
Wyndham, Sir Hugh (1603?–1684) I 153
Wyndham, P.S. (1835–1911) III 227
Wyndham, R.H. (1814–1894) III 227
Wyndham, Sir Wadham (1610–1688) I 153
Wyndham, Sir William, 3rd Bart (1687–1740) I 153
Wyndham of Finglass, Baron (1681–1745) I 153
Wynfield, D.W. (1837–1887) III 227
Wynford, 1st Baron (1767–1845) II 228
Wynn, C.W.W. (1775–1850) II 228
Wynn, H.E. (1889–1956) IV 119
Wynn of Gwydir, Sir John, 1st Bart (1553–1626) I 153
Wynn of Gwydir, Sir Richard, 2nd Bart (1588–1649) I 153
Wynne, John (1667–1743) I 153
Wynn, Sir W.W., 3rd Bart (1693?–1749) I 153
Wyon, J.S. (1836–1873) III 228
Wyon, William (1795–1851) II 228
Wyse, Sir Thomas (1791–1862) II 228
Wyvill, Christopher (1740–1822) II 228

Yale, Elihu (1648–1721) I 155
Yarmouth, 1st Earl of (1631–1683) I 155
Yarmouth, Countess (1704–1765) II 229
Yarrell, William (1784–1856) II 229
Yarrow, Sir A.F., 1st Bart (1842–1932) III 229
Yarrow, Sir Harold, 2nd Bart (1884–1962) IV 120
Yates, Edmund (1831–1864) III 229
Yates, Elizabeth (1799–1860) II 229
Yates, F.H. (1797–1842) II 229
Yates, Mary Ann (1728–1787) II 229
Yates, Richard (1706?–1796) II 229
Yates, Richard (1769–1834) II 229
Ycames, W.R. (1835–1918) III 229
Yearsley, Ann (1756–1806) II 229
Yeats, John Butler (1839–1922) III 229
Yeats, Jack Butler (1871–1957) IV 120
Yeats, W.B. (1865–1939) IV 120
Yellowlees, William (1796–c 1859) II 229
Yelverton, Sir Christopher (1536–1612) I 155
Yelverton, Sir William (1400?–1472?) I 155
Yeo, Sir J.L. (1782–1818) II 229
Yeo, Richard (d 1779) II 229
Yonge, Charlotte Mary (1823–1901) III 229
Yonge, Sir George, 5th Bart (1731–1812) II 229
Yonge, John (1463–1526) I 155
Yonge, John (1467–1516) I 155
Yonge, Sir William, 4th Bart (d 1755) I 155
York, Duchess of (1637–1671) I 155
York, C.H.B.M.C.S. (1725–1807) II 229
York and Albany, Duke of (1674–1728) I 155
York and Albany, Duke of (1739–1767) II 229
York and Albany, Duke of (1763–1827) II 229
Yorke, Charles (1722–1770) II 229

Yorke, Sir Charles (1790–1880) II *229*
Yorke, H.R. (1772–1813) II *229*
Yorke, James (fl 1640) I *155*
Yorke, Sir J.S. (1768–1831) II *229*
Yorke, Philip (1743–1804) II *230*
Young, Lord (1819–1907) III *229*
Young, Arthur (1741–1820) II *230*
Young, Sir A.W. (1827–1915) III *229*
Young, Sir C.G. (1795–1869) II *230*
Young, C.M. (1777–1856) II *230*
Young, Edward (1683–1765) I *155*
Young, F.B. (1884–1954) IV *120*
Young, Sir George (1732–1810) II *230*
Young, G.M. (1882–1959) IV *120*
Young, Sir H.W. (1885–1950) IV *120*
Young, John (1514–1580) I *155*
Young, Matthew (1750–1800) II *230*
Young, Sir Peter (1544–1628) I *155*
Young, Sydney (1857–1937) III *229*
Young, Thomas (1507–1568) I *155*
Young, Thomas (1773–1829) II *230*
Young, Sir William, 2nd Bart (1749–1815) II *230*
Young, Sir William (1751–1821) II *230*
Young, W.H. (1863–1942) IV *120*
Younger of Leckie, 1st Viscount (1851–1929) III *229*
Younghusband, Sir F.E. (1863–1942) IV *120*
Yoxall, Sir J.H. (1857–1925) III *229*
Ypres, 1st Earl of (1852–1925) III *229*
Yule, G.U. (1871–1951) IV *120*
Yule, Sir Henry (1820–1889) III *229*

Zangwill, Israel (1864–1926) IV *121*
Zetland, 2nd Marquess (1876–1961) IV *121*
Zimmern, Sir A.E. (1879–1957) IV *121*
Zincke, C.F. (1684?–1767) I *157*
Zoffany, Johan (1733–1810) II *231*
Zouche, 11th Baron (1556?–1625) I *157*
Zouche, 14th Baron (1810–1873) III *230*
Zouche, Richard (1590?–1661) I *157*
Zuccarelli, Francesco (1702–1788) II *231*
Zuccaro, Federigo (d 1609) I *157*
Zukertort, J.H. (1842–1888) III *230*
Zulueta, Francis de (1878–1958) IV *121*